Effective Human Relations

Interpersonal and Organizational Applications

THIRTEENTH EDITION

EFFECTIVE HUMAN RELATIONS

Interpersonal and Organizational Applications

BARRY L. REECE, EMERITUS
*Virginia Polytechnic Institute
and State University*

MONIQUE E. REECE
*University of Denver and
Colorado State University*

CENGAGE
Learning·

Australia • Brazil • Japan • Korea • Mexico • Singapore • Spain • United Kingdom • United States

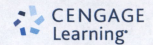

Effective Human Relations: Interpersonal and Organizational Applications, **Thirteenth Edition**
Barry L. Reece and Monique E. Reece

Vice President, General Manager, Social Sciences and Qualitative Business: Erin Joyner

Product Director: Jason Fremder

Product Manager: Mike Roche

Content Developer: Theodore Knight

Product Assistant: Not Yet, Open Position

Marketing Director: Kristen Hurd

Marketing Manager: Emily Horowitz

Marketing Coordinator: Christopher P. Walz

Art and Cover Direction, Production Management, and Composition: Cenveo Publisher Services

Intellectual Property:
   Analyst: Diane Garrity
   Project Manager: Betsy Hathaway

Manufacturing Planner: Ron Montgomery

Cover Image(s): Jose Azel/Getty Images

Printed at CLDPA, USA, 11-20

For product information and technology assistance, contact us at
Cengage Learning Customer & Sales Support, 1-800-354-9706

For permission to use material from this text or product, submit all requests online at **www.cengage.com/permissions**
Further permissions questions can be emailed to
permissionrequest@cengage.com

Library of Congress Control Number: 2015944525

ISBN: 9781305576162

Cengage Learning
20 Channel Center Street
Boston, MA 02210
USA

Cengage Learning is a leading provider of customized learning solutions with office locations around the globe, including Singapore, the United Kingdom, Australia, Mexico, Brazil, and Japan. Locate your local office at: **www.cengage.com/global**

Cengage Learning products are represented in Canada by Nelson Education, Ltd.

To learn more about Cengage Learning Solutions, visit **www.cengage.com**

Purchase any of our products at your local college store or at our preferred online store **www.cengagebrain.com**

To Vera Marie Reece
Our loving wife and mother. Thank you for the support and endless love you give to both of us.

Barry L. Reece and Monique E. Reece

Brief Contents

Contents

About the Authors

BARRY L. REECE is professor emeritus at Virginia Polytechnic Institute and State University. Prior to joining the faculty at Virginia Tech, he held faculty positions at Ellsworth Community College and the University of Northern Iowa. Over the years, he has served as visiting professor at the University of Iowa, University of Missouri, University of Nebraska, University of Northern Colorado, and Wayne State College. He is the author or coauthor of six college textbooks that have been through a total of 41 editions since 1980.

Barry received his Ed.D. from the University of Nebraska. He has been actively involved in teaching, research, consulting, and designing training programs throughout his career. He has conducted more than 500 workshops and seminars devoted to leadership, human relations, communications, sales, customer service, and small business operations. He has received the Excellence in Teaching Award for classroom teaching at Virginia Tech and the Trainer of the Year Award presented by the Valleys of Virginia Chapter of the American Society for Training and Development.

Barry currently divides his time between writing textbooks, writing poetry, and working on various projects for the Veterans for Peace organization. He lives near Chapel Hill, North Carolina, with his wife Vera and a spirited Lakeland terrier named Anna.

MONIQUE E. REECE, is an author, teacher and consultant. She has held the position of Affiliated Executive Faculty at the Institute for Leadership and Organizational Performance at the University of Denver, teaching in both the Executive MBA and Professional MBA programs. She has also served as an executive education faculty member at the Daniels College of Business, University of Denver; online faculty for Colorado State University; and a lecturer at universities. She also designs and facilitates workshops for companies and is a frequent speaker for industry associations and conference events.

Monique has executive management experience working with both Fortune 500 companies and fast-growing entrepreneurial businesses in the United States, Europe, Asia, and South America. She is the founder of MarketSmarter LLC (www.MarketSmarter.com), a consulting and training firm that helps companies improve business performance by linking strategy, company culture, and execution to inspire innovation, employee commitment, and customer loyalty. She formerly served as Executive Vice President at Jones Knowledge, Director of Global Market Development and Corporate Planning at Avaya, and Vice President, Corporate Development at TMVentures.

Monique is the author of four books including *Real-Time Marketing for Business Growth: How to Use Social Media, Measure Marketing and Create a Culture of Execution,* coauthor of *Market Smarter Not Harder,* and the twelfth and thirteenth editions of *Effective Human Relations: Interpersonal and Organizational Applications.* She is a former columnist for the *Denver Business Journal* and she currently serves on the Chief Marketing Officer (CMO) Council Academic Liaison Board. She lives in Denver, Colorado, and Santa Fe, New Mexico.

Preface

The importance of human relations can be summarized in one concise law of personal and organizational success: All work is done through relationships. The quality of our personal and professional relationships, in many ways, determines the quality of our lives.

Those who enter the workforce today encounter a work/life landscape that is more complex and unpredictable than at any other time in history. The mastery of interpersonal relationship skills gives us the self-confidence needed to achieve success in our highly competitive workforce. People who have superb interpersonal skills are more likely to be hired and more likely to receive promotions. Leadership skills become more important the higher you rise in the organization.

Effective Human Relations: Interpersonal and Organizational Applications, thirteenth edition, continues to be one of the most practical and applied textbooks in a wide variety of courses in leading colleges and universities. The revision process involved a review of over 1,200 articles that appeared in *Fast Company, Inc.* magazine, *The Wall Street Journal, Fortune, Harvard Business Review, Health & Spirituality*, and dozens of other resources. The authors have also reviewed many bestselling books and research reports written by scholars who are searching for what is true, right, and lasting in the field of interpersonal relations.

BUILDING ON PREVIOUS STRENGTHS

Effective Human Relations: Interpersonal and Organizational Applications, thirteenth edition, is one of the most widely adopted human relations texts available today. It has been successful because the authors continue to build on strengths that have been enthusiastically praised by instructors and students. The latest workforce developments, global trends, and communication technologies that influence human relations have made this a highly practical text in a wide variety of courses in leading colleges and universities.

- The **"total person" approach** to human relations continues to be a dominant theme of this new edition. We continue to believe that human behavior at work and in our private lives is influenced by many interdependent traits such as emotional balance, self-awareness, integrity, self-esteem, physical fitness, and healthy spirituality. This approach focuses on those interpersonal relationship skills needed to be well-rounded and thoroughly prepared to handle a wide range of human relations problems and issues.
- This edition, like all previous editions, provides the reader with an in-depth presentation of the **seven major themes of effective human relations:** Communication, Self-Awareness, Self-Acceptance, Motivation, Trust, Self-Disclosure, and Conflict Resolution. These broad themes serve as the foundation for contemporary human relations courses and training programs.
- **Self-assessment and self-development opportunities** are strategically placed throughout the entire text. One of the few certainties in today's rapidly changing workplace is the realization that we must assume greater responsibility for developing and upgrading our own skills and competencies. In many cases, self-development begins with self-awareness. A deficit in self-awareness can be damaging to one's personal relationships and career success.

A hallmark of this edition, and of all previous editions, is the use of many **real-world examples** of human relations issues and practices. These examples build the reader's interest and promote understanding of major topics and concepts. Many of the organizations cited in the thirteenth edition have been recognized by the authors of "The 100 Best Companies to Work For," "The 100 Best Corporate Citizens," "100 Best Companies for Working Mothers," and "America's 50 Best Companies for Minorities." The thirteenth edition also includes companies who have received the Top Small Workplace Award given by the *Wall Street Journal*.

STAYING ON THE CUTTING EDGE—NEW TO THIS EDITION

- The thirteenth edition of *Effective Human Relations: Interpersonal and Organizational Applications* is updated to reflect the growing importance of the human element in our service-oriented, information-saturated, global economy. The authors continue to build on topics of emerging importance with expanded coverage of generational differences, the changing issues women and men face in the workplace, and communication technologies that influence human relations.

- This comprehensive edition presents the latest thinking, theories, and data on many of the most important topics of our times: leadership, working virtually, happiness and positive psychology, the importance of "personal branding," social media in the job market, cultural intelligence, emotional intelligence, work-life balance, managing strengths, moral and ethical choices, goal setting, the root causes of negative attitudes, and leading teams. The text also explores the most vital elements organizations need today to create a dynamic and thriving company culture.

- This is a highly practical text designed to help students achieve the insight, knowledge, and relationship skills needed to build a successful career, create enduring relationships in their personal and professional lives, and the mental, physical, and emotional skills needed to adapt and change in a highly connected, global world.

Major Changes and Improvements

These significant changes and improvements can be found in the thirteenth edition:

- Every chapter features new opening vignettes and closing cases.
- Every chapter includes a *Career Insight* that provides practical tips for job hunters and career changers.
- Expanded coverage of workforce diversity and inclusion is presented.
- There are 13 new *Human Relations in Action* featuring fresh new insights from leading companies.
- There are 23 new *Total Person Insights* presented by respected business leaders and authors.
- 20 new chapter cases are updated to reflect current thinking on the most relevant topics to human relations.
- There are 14 *"How To"* examples to guide students in mastering concepts and building skills through practical application.
- Social media and its impact on job search, career management, personal branding, and communication is updated throughout the text.
- New research has been added about positive psychology, and its practical application to organizational and personal communication.
- The significance and essential steps to create a thriving company culture is a prominent theme throughout the text.
- Coverage of generational differences has been updated and expanded, including the complexities of managing four generations in the workforce.
- More than 40 new photographic images and illustrations enhance the learning process.

- Every chapter has been updated to include new real-world and international examples of both large and small companies.
- Expanded coverage of unconscious bias is presented.
- New information is introduced on the practice of mindfulness.

CHAPTER ORGANIZATION

This book is divided into six parts. **Part 1, "Human Relations: The Key to Personal Growth and Career Success,"** provides a strong rationale for the study of human relations and reviews the historical development of this field. One important highlight of Chapter 1 is a detailed discussion of the major developments influencing behavior at work. This material helps students develop a new appreciation for the complex nature of human behavior in a work setting. The communication process—the basis for effective human relations—is explained at both an individual and an organizational level in Chapter 2. Social media and its impact on communication is discussed in this chapter.

Part 2, "Career Success Begins with Knowing Yourself," reflects the basic fact that our effectiveness in dealing with others depends in large measure on our self-awareness and self-acceptance. We believe that by building high self-esteem and by learning to explore inner attitudes, motivations, and values, the reader will learn to be more sensitive to the way others think, feel, and act. Complete chapters are devoted to such topics as communication styles, building high self-esteem, personal values and ethical choices, attitude formation, and motivation.

Part 3, "Personal Strategies for Improving Human Relations," comprises four chapters that feature a variety of practical strategies that can be used to develop and maintain good relationships with coworkers, supervisors, and customers. Chapters on constructive self-disclosure, learning to achieve emotional control, building stronger relationships by applying the fundamentals of positive psychology, and developing a professional presence are featured in this part of the text.

In **Part 4, "If We All Work Together…,"** the concepts of team building and conflict resolution are given detailed coverage. Because employers are increasingly organizing employees into teams, the chapter on team-building leadership strategies (Chapter 12) takes on major importance. The chapter on conflict resolution (Chapter 13) describes several basic conflict resolution strategies, discusses ways to deal with difficult people, and provides an introduction to the role of labor unions in today's workforce.

Part 5, "Special Challenges in Human Relations," is designed to help the reader deal with some unique problem areas—coping with personal and work-related stress, working effectively in a diverse workforce, and understanding the changing roles of men and women. The reader is offered many suggestions on ways to deal effectively with these challenges.

Part 6, "You Can Plan for Success," features the final chapter, which serves as a capstone for the entire text. This chapter offers suggestions on how to develop a life plan for effective human relations. Students will be introduced to a new definition of success and learn how to better cope with life's uncertainties and disappointments. This chapter also describes the nonfinancial resources that truly enrich a person's life.

TOOLS THAT ENHANCE THE TEACHING/LEARNING PROCESS

The extensive supplements package accompanying the thirteenth edition of *Effective Human Relations: Interpersonal and Organizational Applications* includes a variety of new and traditional tools that will aid both teaching and learning. The supplements emphasize learning by doing.

STUDENT SUPPORT

Management CourseMate

This robust website includes interactive games, quizzes, streaming videos, PowerPoint® slides, and more, and is designed for use in conjunction with the text to enhance learning and broaden student understanding.

INSTRUCTOR SUPPORT

Instructor's Resource Manual

The Instructor's Resource Manual, found on the instructor website, includes two parts. Part One contains, for each chapter, a Chapter Preview, Purpose and Perspective, Presentation Outline, Suggested Responses to Critical Thinking and Skill Development Challenges, Answers to Try Your Hand exercises, and additional application exercises. Part Two contains Instructional Games.

Test Bank

The Test Bank contains 20 true/false, 20 multiple choice, 10 completion, 10 short answer/essay, and 5 short case multiple choice questions per chapter.

PowerPoint® Slides

These dynamic slides are available on the instructor companion website. The slides follow the structure of the chapter and facilitate in-class discussion of key concepts. Additional talking points and non-text material are included in the instructor version of the slides. The student versions of the slides are available on the CourseMate website.

DVD

The video package consists of several segments that illustrate chapter concepts using examples from real-world companies. Teaching notes and suggested uses for the segments are included in the DVD Guide found on the instructor website.

Instructor Companion Website

The instructor companion website includes electronic Instructor's Manual files, electronic Test Bank files, PowerPoint® slides, and a DVD Guide.

THE SEARCH FOR WISDOM

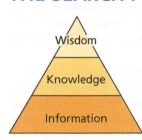

The search for what is true, right, or lasting has become more difficult because we live in the midst of an information explosion. The Internet is an excellent source of mass information, but it is seldom the source of wisdom. Television often reduces complicated ideas to a sound bite. Books continue to be among the best sources of knowledge. Many new books, and several classics, were used as references for the thirteenth edition of *Effective Human Relations: Interpersonal and Organizational Applications. A* sample of the books we used to prepare this edition follows:

How Full Is Your Bucket? by Tom Rath and Donald O. Clifton

A Whole New Mind by Daniel H. Pink

Now Discover Your Strengths by Marcus Buckingham and Donald O. Clifton

The Success Principles by Jack Canfield

The Leadership Challenge by James M. Kouzes and Barry Z. Posner

The Sedona Method by Hale Dwoskin

The Art of Happiness by the Dalai Lama and Howard C. Culter

Mindfulness for Beginners by Ann Demarais and Valarie White

Reinventing You by Dorie Clark

The 4-Hour Workweek by Timothy Ferriss

Be Your Own Brand by David McNally and Karl D. Speak

Civility—Manners, Morals, and the Etiquette of Democracy by Stephen L. Carter

Complete Business Etiquette Handbook by Barbara Pachter and Majorie Brody

Creative Visualization by Shakti Gawain

Do What You Love … The Money will Follow by Marsha Sinetar

Emotional Intelligence by Daniel Goleman

The Speed of Trust by Stephen M. R. Covey

The Four Agreements by Don Miquel Ruiz

Getting to Yes by Roger Fisher and William Ury

How to Win Friends and Influence People by Dale Carnegie

The Human Side of Enterprise by Douglas McGregor

I'm OK—You're OK by Thomas Harris

Minding the Body, Mending the Mind by Joan Borysenko

Multicultural Manners—New Rules of Etiquette for a Changing Society by Norine Dresser

The 100 Absolutely Unbreakable Laws of Business Success by Brian Tracy

1001 Ways to Reward Employees by Bob Nelson

Psycho-Cybernetics by Maxwell Maltz

Self-Matters: Creating Your Life from the Inside Out by Phillip C. McGraw

The 7 Habits of Highly Effective People by Stephen Covey

The 17 Essential Qualities of a Team Player by John C. Maxwell

The Carrot Principle by Adrian Gostick and Chester Elton

The Six Pillars of Self-Esteem by Nathaniel Branden

Spectacular Teamwork by Robert R. Blake, Jane Srygley Mouton, and Robert L. Allen

Working with Emotional Intelligence by Daniel Goleman

The Five Dysfunctions of a Team by Patrick Lencioni

The Happiness Advantage by Shawn Achor

Happier by Talben-Shahar

Real-Time Marketing for Business Growth by Monique Reece

Peak by Chip Conley

Delivering Happiness by Tony Hsieh

Positivity by Barbara Fredrickson

To Sell Is Human by Daniel Pink

Quiet by Susan Cain

StrengthsFinder 2.0 by Tom Rath

Crucial Conversations by Kerry Patterson, Joseph Grenny, Ron McMillian, Al Switzler

Fierce Conversations by Susan Scott

Who Moved My Cheese? by Spencer Johnson

Miss Manners Minds Your Business by Judith Martin and Nicholas Ivor Martin

The Power of Positive Confrontation by Barbara Pachter

ACKNOWLEDGMENTS

Many people have contributed to *Effective Human Relations: Interpersonal and Organizational Applications*. Throughout the years, the text has been strengthened as a result of many helpful comments and recommendations. We extend special appreciation to the following reviewers and advisors who have provided valuable input for this and prior editions:

James Aldrich, North Dakota State School of Science

Thorn Amnotte, Eastern Maine Technical College

Garland Ashbacker, Kirkwood Community College

Sue Avila, South Hills Business School

Linda Babcock, Santa Monica Community College

Shirley Banks, Marshall University

Rhonda Barry, American Institute of Commerce

Kenneth Bell, Ellsworth Community College

James A. Bliven, Haskell Indian Nations University

C. Winston Borgen, Sacramento Community College

Jane Bowerman, University of Oklahoma

Jayne P. Bowers, Central Carolina Technical College

Kathy Broneck, Pima Community College

Charles Capps, Sam Houston State University

Lawrence Carter, Jamestown Community College

Cathy Chew, Orange County Community College

Barbara Ching, Los Angeles City College

John P. Cicero, Shasta College

Anne C. Cowden, California State University Sacramento

Michael Dzik, North Dakota State School of Science

Jim Elias, Muscatine Community College

John Elias, University of Missouri

Patrick G. Ellsberg, Lower Columbia College

Marilee Feldman, Kirkwood Community College

Debra Fells, Mesa Community College

Mike Fernsted, Bryant and Stratton Business Institute

Dave Fewins, Neosho County Community College

Dean Flowers, Waukesha County Technical College

Jill P. Gann, Ann Arundel Community College

M. Camille Garrett, Tarrant County Junior College

Roberta Greene, Central Piedmont Community College

Ralph Hall, Community College of Southern Nevada

Sally Hanna-Jones, Hocking Technical College

Daryl Hansen, Metropolitan Community College

Carolyn K. Hayes, Polk Community College

John J. Heinsius, Modesto Junior College

Stephen Hiatt, Catawba College

Jan Hickman, Westwood College

Larry Hill, San Jacinto College–Central

Bill Hurd, Lowe's Companies, Inc.

Chie Ishihara, Riverside Community College

Lisa R. Jackson, Schoolcraft College

Thomas Jay, Flathead Valley Community College

Dorothy Jeanis, Fresno City College

Marlene Katz, Canada College

Robert Kegel, Jr., Cypress College

Karl N. Kelley, North Central College

Vance A. Kennedy, College of Mateo

Marianne Kozlowski, Evergreen State College

Kristina Leonard, Westwood College

Deborah Lineweaver, New River Community College

Thomas W. Lloyd, Westmoreland County Community College

Jerry Loomis, Fox Valley Technical College

Roger Lynch, Inver Hills Community College

Edward C. Mann, The University of Southern Mississippi

Jerry Manning, Des Moines Community College

Paul Martin, Aims Community College

James K. McReynolds, South Dakota School of Mines and Technology

Herb Meyer, Scott Community College

Russ Moorhead, Des Moines Area Community College

Marilyn Mueller, Simpson College

Erv J. Napier, Kent State University

Barbara Ollhoff, Waukesha County Technical College

Leonard L. Palumbo, Northern Virginia Community College

James Patton, Mississippi State University

C. Richard Paulson, Mankato State University

Naomi W. Peralta, The Institute of Financial Education

William Price, Virginia Polytechnic Institute and State University

Shirley Pritchett, Northeast Texas Community College

Linda Pulliam, Pulliam Associates, Chapel Hill, N.C.

Tom Rankin, University of Denver

Erin Rea, University of Michigan

Lynne Reece, Alternative Services

Jack C. Reed, University of Northern Iowa

Lynn Richards, Johnson County Community College

Khaled Sartawi, Fort Valley State University

Robert Schaden, Schoolcraft College

Mary R. Shannon, Wenatchie Valley College

J. Douglas Shatto, Muskingum Area Technical College

Dan Smith, Ohio Business College

Kaischa Smith, Northwestern Michigan College

Marilee Smith, Kirkwood Community College

Camille Stallings, Pima Community College

Lori Stearns, Minnesota West Community Technical College

Cindy Stewart, Des Moines Area Community College

Rahmat O. Tavallali, Wooster Business College

Jane Tavlin, Delgado Community College

V. S. Thakur, Community College of Rhode Island

Linda Truesdale, Midlands Technical College

Wendy Bletz Turner, New River Community College

David Wang, Gateway Technical College

Greg Watson, Eastern Arizona College

Marc Wayner, Hocking Technical College

Steven Whipple, St. Cloud Technical College

Burl Worley, Allan Hancock College

Tom West, Des Moines Area Community College

Over 200 business organizations, government agencies, and nonprofit institutions provided us with the real-world examples that appear throughout the text. We are grateful to those organizations that allowed us to conduct interviews, observe workplace environments, and use special photographs and materials.

The partnership with Cengage Learning has been very rewarding. Several members of the staff have made important contributions to this project. Sincere appreciation is extended to Acquisitions Editor Michael Roche, Development Editor Ted Knight, Editorial and Production Manager Jennifer Ziegler.

Barry L. Reece

Monique E. Reece

PART 1

Human Relations: The Key to Personal Growth and Career Success

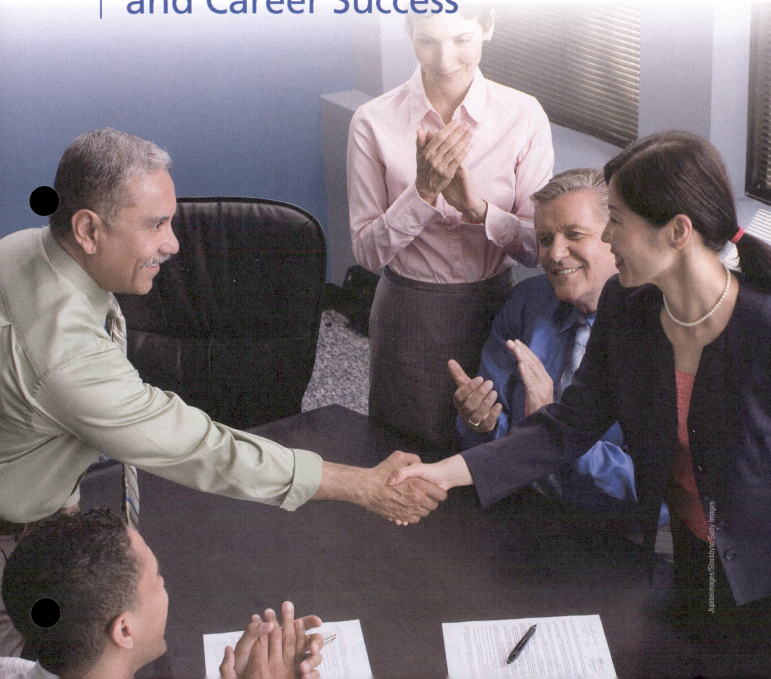

CHAPTER PREVIEW

LEARNING OBJECTIVES

After studying Chapter 1, you will be able to

1-1 Explain the nature, purpose, and importance of human relations.

1-2 Identify major developments in the workplace that have given new importance to human relations.

1-3 Identify major forces influencing human behavior at work.

1-4 Review the historical development of the human relations movement.

1-5 Identify seven major themes that serve as the foundation for effective human relations.

Introduction to Human Relations

TIP OF THE ICEBERG | UNLOCKING HUMAN POTENTIAL

Thanks to the landmark contributions of several contemporary minds, we have learned more about who we are, how we think, and what we do. These eminent writers and thinkers have given us several new principles of psychology. One important example is the research conducted by John Mayer and Peter Salovey that established the theory of *emotional intelligence* (EQ). They discovered that persons with EQ were better liked by others, had better social relations, and attained greater well-being than others.[1]

The best-selling book *Emotional Intelligence* by Daniel Goleman created a great deal of interest in EQ. Goleman stated that academic or technical ability is the threshold requirement to gain entry to a career. Beyond this, the major factors that contribute to career success are such EQ qualities as empathy toward others, adaptability to change, resilience, ability to handle disagreements, and self-awareness. Emotional intelligence can matter more than IQ.

The positive psychology movement, founded by Martin Seligman, represents another landmark development in psychology. Research emerging from positive psychology labs all over the world indicates that we become more successful when we are happier and more positive.[2] The fundamentals of positive psychology have been reported in *Authentic Happiness: Using the New Positive Psychology to Realize Your Potential for Lasting Fulfillment* by Martin Seligman, *The Happiness Advantage* by Shawn Achor, and *Positivity* by Barbara Fredrickson.

How we interact with other people is one of the more complex functions the brain must perform. The study of emotional intelligence, positive psychology and other important topics covered in this text helps us develop the non-technical skills needed in the twenty-first-century workforce.

Consistently ranked as one of the Top 100 Companies to work for by *Fortune magazine*, Whole Foods Market focuses on the satisfaction of both its customers and its employees.

TECHNICAL SKILLS AREN'T ENOUGH

1-1   A lack of technical skills is not the primary reason new hires fail to meet employer expectations and experienced workers falter on the road to career success. Today a growing number of employers seek employees who are skilled in the areas of human interaction. Interpersonal skills, sometimes described as soft or people skills, fall into two categories:[3]

> *Personal qualities:* Treating others with sensitivity, making the right ethical choices, emotional control, ability to work as a team member, etc.
>
> *Thinking skills:* Ability to engage in creative problem solving, make appropriate decisions, apply critical listening skills, etc.

Interpersonal skills are as learnable as software programs or a new electronic messaging system. And, interpersonal skills can enhance a résumé and a job interview.

Total Person Insight

Work requiring extensive human interactions is the fastest-growing category of employment in developed countries. Among these positions are jobs held by a variety of knowledge workers—managers, sales representatives, engineers, medical personnel, lawyers, and other skilled professionals who serve as the engine of the knowledge economy.

Source: Susan Lund, James Manyika, and Sree Ramaswamy, "Preparing for a New Era of Work," *McKinsey Quarterly*, November, 2012; Geoff Colvin, "In the Future, Will There Be Any Work Left for People to Do?" *Fortune*, June 2, 2014, p. 196.

Small Business Career Opportunities

Small business is the biggest driver of job creation in America. Many of the most successful firms seek employees with well-developed interpersonal skills. David Biggar, founder of Vintage Point wine sales, says his philosophy is: "Create a company where relationships mean everything."[4] Ron Conway, cofounder of Altos Computer Systems, wants his employees to form a personal relationship with every customer. The phrase "It's not what you know, but who you know" summarizes his philosophy.[5]

Human Relations Defined

1-2 The term **human relations** in its broadest sense covers all types of interactions among people—their conflicts, cooperative efforts, and group relationships. It is the study of *why* our beliefs, attitudes, and behaviors sometimes cause relationship problems in our personal lives and in work-related situations. The study of human relations emphasizes the analysis of human behavior, prevention strategies, resolution of behavioral problems, and self-development.

Major Developments that Give New Importance to Human Relations

Every organization depends on three essential factors: people, process, and technology. The first success factor is people.[6] Personal and interpersonal effectiveness set the stage for career success. Studies indicate that communication and interpersonal skills are highly rated by nearly all employers who are hiring new employees.

Several important developments in the workplace have given new importance to human relations. Each of the following developments provides support for human relations.

- *The labor market has become a place of churning dislocation caused by the heavy volume of mergers, acquisitions, business closings, bankruptcies, downsizings, and outsourcing of jobs to foreign countries.* Executives often view downsizing as an important step toward profitability. During periods of large-scale employee layoffs, we see the development of an employers' market. Firms take longer to fill jobs, waiting for the perfect employee. They prefer candidates with wide-ranging skill sets who are willing to take on multiple tasks and learn new ones.[7]
- *Changing work patterns create new opportunities and new challenges.* Throughout the past few years, the United States has embraced a flexible labor force. Data reported by the Bureau of Labor Statistics indicates that about 26 percent of working Americans have *nonstandard* jobs. The largest group of people in this category is temporary or part-time workers. Another large segment of the nonstandard workforce are self-employed. When enterprising persons are laid off by corporations, they increasingly become independent consultants, contractors, landscape gardeners, carpenters, and freelancers.[8]
- *Organizations are increasingly oriented toward service to clients, patients, and customers.* We live in a service economy where relationships are often more important than products. Restaurants, hospitals, banks, public utilities, colleges, airlines, and retail stores all must now gain and retain the patronage of their clients and customers. In any service-type firm, there are thousands of "moments of truth"—those critical incidents in which customers come into contact with the organization and form their impressions of its quality and service.

We live in a service economy where relationships are often more important than products.

"Since your job credentials are identical,
we'll play musical chairs."

- *Workplace incivility is increasingly a threat to employee relationships.* In this information-based, high-tech, constantly changing global economy, we are witnessing an increase in workplace incivility. Rude behavior in the form of high-decibel cell phone conversations, use of profanity, or failure to display simple courtesies such as saying "thank you" can damage workplace relationships. A study conducted by Cisco Systems Inc. found that the cost of incivility in its organization topped $8.3 million annually.[9]

- *Many companies are organizing their workers into teams in which each employee plays a part.* Organizations eager to improve quality, improve job satisfaction, increase worker participation in decision making and problem solving, and improve customer service are turning to teams.

Although some organizations have successfully harnessed the power of teams, others have encountered problems. One barrier to productivity is the employee who lacks the skills needed to be a team member. In making the transition to a team environment, team members need skills such as relationship building, group decision making, commitment to team goals and values, conflict resolution, and communications.[10]

- *Diversity has become a prominent characteristic of today's workforce.* A number of trends have contributed to greater workforce diversity. Throughout the past two decades, participation in the labor force by Asian Americans, African Americans, and Hispanics has increased; labor force participation by adult women has risen to a record 60 percent; the employment door for people with physical or mental impairments has opened wider; and larger numbers of young workers are working with members of the expanding 50-plus age group. Within this heterogeneous workforce, we will find a multitude of values, expectations, and work habits. The major aspects of workforce diversity are discussed in Chapters 15 and 16.

Total Person Insight

"The employee skills gaps talked about most are not technical, math or reading problems. Instead, employers' top concern is lack of soft skills needed for success in almost every role."

Source: Bruce Clarke, "Employees Have Hard Time Finding Soft Skills in Workplace," *News & Observer*, January 27, 2013, p. 3E.

The Challenge of Human Relations

To develop and apply the wide range of human relations skills needed in today's workplace can be extremely challenging. You will be working with clients, customers, patients, and other workers who vary greatly in age, work background, communications style, values, cultural background, gender, and work ethic.

Human relations is further complicated by the fact that we must manage three types of relationships (see Figure 1.1). The first relationship is the one with ourselves. Many people carry around a set of ideas and feelings about themselves that are quite negative and in most cases quite inaccurate. People who have negative feelings about their abilities and accomplishments and who engage in constant self-criticism must struggle to maintain a good relationship with themselves. The importance of high self-esteem is addressed in Chapter 4.

human RELATIONS *in Action*

DEFINING TALENT AT PWC

PricewaterhouseCoopers has 175,000 employees working in 154 countries. The company provides a wide range of audit, tax, and advisory services. Dennis Nally, CEO, says having technical skills is important but that's almost a given these days. *Talent* is having the right softer skills in terms of being able to work in a collaborative environment, teaming with people, communicating well, and demonstrating sensitivities to cultural diversity.

Source: Javier Espinoza, "PwC's CEO Switches Tactics to Keep Millennials," *Wall Street Journal*, July 11, 2011, p. B4.

The second type of relationship we must learn to manage is the one-to-one relationships we face in our personal and work lives. People in the health-care field, sales, food service, and a host of other occupations face this challenge many times each day. In some cases, racial, age, or gender bias serves as a barrier to good human relations. Communication style bias, a topic that is discussed in Chapter 3, is another common barrier to effective one-to-one relationships.

The third challenge we face is the management of relationships with members of a group. As already noted, many workers are assigned to a team on either a full-time or a part-time basis. Lack of cooperation among team members can result in quality and productivity problems.

The Influence of the Behavioral Sciences

The field of human relations draws on the behavioral sciences—psychology, sociology, and anthropology. Basically, these sciences focus on the *why* of human behavior. Psychology attempts to find out why *individuals* act as they do, and sociology and anthropology concentrate primarily on *group* dynamics and social interaction. Human relations differs from the behavioral sciences in one important respect. Although also interested in the

Figure 1.1 ■ Major Relationship Management Challenges

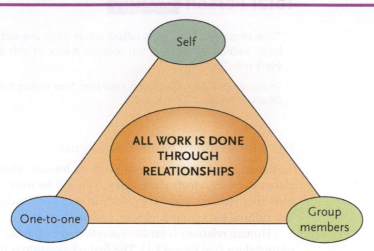

why of human behavior, human relations goes further and looks at what can be done to anticipate problems, resolve them, or even prevent them from happening. In other words, this field emphasizes knowledge that can be *applied* in practical ways to problems of interpersonal relations at work or in our personal lives.

Human Relations and the "Total Person"

The material in this book focuses on human relations as the study of *how people satisfy both personal and work-related needs.* We believe, as do most authors in the field of inter-personal relations, that such human traits as physical fitness, emotional control, self-awareness, self-esteem, and values orientation are interdependent. Although some organizations may occasionally wish they could employ only a person's physical strength or creative powers, all that can be employed is the **total person**. A person's separate characteristics are part of a single system making up that whole person. Work life is not totally separate from home life, and emotional conditions are not separate from physical conditions. The quality of one's work, for example, is often related to one's ability to cope with the stress created by family problems.

Many organizations are beginning to recognize that when the whole person is improved, significant benefits accrue to the firm. These organizations are establishing employee development programs that address the total person, not just the employee skills needed to perform the job. Gregg Appliances, Inc., an appliance and electronics retail chain, offers employees education programs that help them cope with marital stresses.[11] International Business Machines (IBM) has launched a program to combat childhood obesity among employees' children.[12] Some organizations offer lunchtime seminars on financial planning, parenting skills, and other topics.

Total Person Insight

"We know two things for certain: Incivility is expensive, and few organizations recognize or take action to curtail it."

Source: Christine Porath and Christine Pearson, "The Price of Incivility—Lack of Respect Hurts Morale and the Bottom Line," *Harvard Business Review*, January–February 2013, p. 116.

The Need for a Supportive Environment

Some people in leadership positions do not believe that total person development, job enrichment, motivation techniques, or career development strategies help increase productivity or strengthen worker commitment to the job. It is true that when such practices are tried without full commitment or without full management support, there is a good chance they will fail. Such failures often have a demoralizing effect on employees and management alike.

A basic assumption of this book is that human relations, when applied in a positive and supportive environment, can help people achieve greater personal and professional satisfaction from their careers and help increase an organization's productivity and efficiency.

human
RELATIONS
in Action

NUMBER ONE AGAIN

Each year, a list of the 100 best companies to work for is published in *Fortune* magazine. Job seekers need to study the list carefully because these are companies where morale is high and interpersonal relationships are characterized by a high level of trust and camaraderie. Google, the large (34,311 employees) Internet services and retailing company, has been ranked number one five times.

Source: Milton Moskowitz and Robert Levering, "The 100 Best Companies to Work For," *Fortune*, February 3, 2014, p. 108.

THE FORCES INFLUENCING BEHAVIOR AT WORK

1-3 This book will increase your knowledge of factors that influence human behavior in a variety of work settings. An understanding of human behavior at work begins with a review of the six major forces that affect every employee, regardless of the size of the organization. As Figure 1.2 indicates, these are organizational culture, supervisory-management influence, work group influence, job influence, personal characteristics of the worker, and family influence.

Organizational Culture

Every organization, whether a manufacturing plant, retail store, hospital, or government agency, has its own unique culture. The **organizational culture** is the collection of shared values, beliefs, rituals, stories, and myths that foster a feeling of community among organizational members.[13] The culture of an organization is, in most cases, the reflection of the deeply held values and behaviors of a small group of individuals. In a large organization, the chief executive officer (CEO) and a handful of senior executives will shape the culture. In a small company, the culture may flow from the values held by the founder.[14]

It is no exaggeration to say that supervisors and managers are the spokespersons for the organization.

Google, the popular Internet services and retailing company, has developed a culture that emphasizes customer service. One slogan summarizes the Google philosophy: "Focus on the user and all else will follow."[15] Google consistently ranks at or near the top of *Fortune's* Best Companies to Work For list.

In the new economy, almost every source of organizational success—technology, financial structure, and competitive strategy—can be copied in an amazingly short period of time.[16] However, making customers the center of the company culture can take years.

Figure 1.2 ■ Major Forces Influencing Worker Behavior

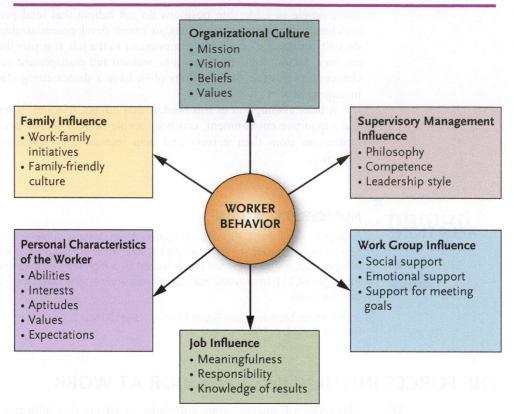

Supervisory-Management Influence

Supervisory-management personnel are in a key position to influence employee behavior. It is no exaggeration to say that supervisors and managers are the spokespersons for the organization. Their philosophy, competence, leadership style, and integrity establish the organization's culture in the eyes of employees. Each employee develops certain perceptions about the organization's concern for his or her welfare. These perceptions, in turn, influence such important factors as productivity, customer relations, safety consciousness, and loyalty to the firm.

Work Group Influence

In recent years, behavioral scientists have devoted considerable research to determining the influence of group affiliation on the individual worker. This research has identified three functions of group membership. First, it can satisfy *social needs*. When employees feel more connected to their colleagues at work, they are generally more productive.[17] Many people find the hours spent at work enjoyable because coworkers provide needed social support. Second, the work group can provide the *emotional support* needed to deal with pressures and problems on or off the job. Finally, the group provides *assistance in solving problems* and *meeting goals*. A cohesive work group lends support and provides the resources we need to be productive workers.

Job Influence

Work in modern societies does more than fulfill economic needs. When we find meaning and fulfillment in our jobs, we become more complete as human beings.[18] As one

Barang/Shutterstock.com

A work group can be a positive influence in employees' lives when group members offer each other job assistance and emotional support.

organizational consultant noted, work has taken center stage in the lives of most people: "We spend most of our waking hours doing our jobs, thinking about work, and getting to and from our workplaces. When we feel good about our work, we tend to feel good about our lives. When we find our work unsatisfying and unrewarding, we don't feel good."[19] Unfortunately, many people hold jobs that do not make them feel good. Many workers perceive their jobs to be meaningless and boring. Some workers experience frustration because they feel powerless to influence their working conditions.

Personal Characteristics of the Worker

Every worker brings to the job a combination of abilities, interests, aptitudes, values, and expectations. Worker behavior on the job is most frequently a reflection of how well the work environment accommodates the unique characteristics of each worker.

Identifying the ideal work environment for today's workforce is difficult. A single parent may greatly value a flexible work schedule and child care. The recipient of a new business degree may seek a position with a new high-tech firm, hoping to make a lot of money in a hurry. Other workers may desire more leisure time, and some workers seek job security.

Coming into the workplace today is a new generation of workers with value systems and expectations about work that often differ from those of the previous generation. Today's better-educated and better-informed workers value identity and achievement. They also have a heightened sense of their rights.

Family Influence

A majority of undergraduates and those currently employed name balancing work and personal life as their top career goal.[20] Most people want time for family, friends, and leisure pursuits. However, finding employers who truly support work/life balance can be difficult, especially during a slowing economy.

The number of dual-income families has doubled since 1950. Both parents have jobs in over 60 percent of married-couple homes. When both partners are working long hours, it may be difficult to balance career and family choices. Some long-standing work and family problems include a lack of quality, affordable child care, inflexible work schedules, and time management problems. These issues will be discussed in Chapter 16.

THE DEVELOPMENT OF THE HUMAN RELATIONS MOVEMENT

 The early attempts to improve productivity in manufacturing focused mainly on trying to improve such things as plant layout and mechanical processes. But, over time, there was more interest in redefining the nature of work and perceiving workers as complex human beings. This change reflected a shift in values from a concern with *things* to a greater concern for *people*. In this section, we briefly examine a few major developments that influenced the human relations movement.

The Impact of the Industrial Revolution

The Industrial Revolution marked a shift from home-based, handcrafted processes to large-scale factory production. Before the Industrial Revolution, most work was performed by individual craft workers or members of craft guilds. Generally, each worker saw a project through from start to finish. Skills such as tailoring, carpentry, and shoemaking took a long time to perfect and were often a source of pride to an individual or a community. Under this system, however, output was limited.

The Industrial Revolution had a profound effect on the nature of work and the role of the worker. Previously, an individual tailor could make only a few items of clothing in a week's time; factories could now make hundreds. However, the early industrial plants were not very efficient because there was very little uniformity in the way tasks were performed. It was this problem that set the stage for research by a man who changed work forever.

Taylor's Scientific Management

In 1874, Frederick W. Taylor obtained a job as an apprentice in a machine shop. He rose to the position of foreman, and, in this role, he became aware of the inefficiency and waste throughout the plant. In most cases, workers were left on their own to determine how to do their jobs. Taylor began to systematically study each job and break it down into its smallest movements. He discovered ways to reduce the number of motions and get rid of time-wasting efforts. Workers willing to follow Taylor's instruction found that their productivity increased.[21]

Frederick W. Taylor started the **scientific management** movement, and his ideas continue to influence the workplace today. Critics of Taylor's approach say that the specialized tasks workers perform often require manual skills but very little or no thinking.

Total Person Insight

"You can only get so much more productivity out of reorganization and automation. Where you really get productivity leaps is in the minds and hearts of people."

Source: James Baughman quote from Frank Rose, "A New Age for Business?" *Fortune*, October 8, 1990, p. 162.

Mayo's Hawthorne Studies

Harvard Business School Professor Elton Mayo and his colleagues accidentally discovered part of the answer to variations in worker performance while conducting research in the mid-1920s at the Hawthorne Western Electric plant, located near Chicago. Their original goal was to study the effect of illumination, ventilation, and fatigue on production workers in the plant. Their research, known as the **Hawthorne studies**, became a sweeping investigation into the role of human relations in group and individual productivity. These studies also gave rise to the profession of industrial psychology by legitimizing the human factor as an element in business operations.[22]

After three years of experimenting with lighting and other physical aspects of work, Mayo made two important discoveries. First, all the attention focused on workers who participated in the research made them feel more important. For the first time, they were getting feedback on their job performance. In addition, test conditions allowed them greater freedom from supervisory control. Under these circumstances, morale and motivation increased and productivity rose.

Second, Mayo found that the interaction of workers on the job created a network of relationships called an **informal organization**. This organization exerted considerable influence on workers' performance.

Although some observers have criticized the Hawthorne studies for flawed research methodology, this research laid the foundation for the field of organizational behavior.[23]

From the Great Depression to Today

During the Great Depression, interest in human relations research waned as other ways of humanizing the workplace gained momentum. During that period, unions increased their militant campaigns to organize workers and force employers to pay attention to such issues as working conditions, higher pay, shorter hours, and protection for child laborers.

After World War II and during the years of postwar economic expansion, interest in the human relations field increased. Countless papers and research studies on worker efficiency, group dynamics, organization, and motivational methods were published. Douglas McGregor, in his classic book *The Human Side of Enterprise*, argued that how well an organization performs is directly proportional to its ability to tap human potential.[24] Abraham Maslow, a noted psychologist, devised a "hierarchy of needs," stating that people satisfied their needs in a particular order. Later, Frederick Herzberg proposed an important theory of employee motivation based on satisfaction. Each theory had considerable influence on the study of motivation and is explored in detail in Chapter 7. Since the 1950s, theories and concepts regarding human behavior have focused more and more on an understanding of human interaction.

Peter Drucker, often described as the greatest management thinker and writer of all time, influenced organizational behavior for a period of 60 years. He originated the view of the corporation as a human community built on trust and respect for the worker. He made clear there is "No business without a customer," a simple concept that created greater support for customer services.[25]

human RELATIONS *in Action*

BIG-BOOK BLOCKBUSTERS

Each year, between 4,000 and 5,000 new books claiming to be about business are published. Here is a list of five heavyweights that have had a major impact on the way we view interpersonal relations:

- *The One Minute Manager* by Kenneth Blanchard and Spencer Johnson. (Published in 1982 and still making best-seller lists.)

- *Reengineering the Corporation* by Michael Hammer and James Champy. (A *BusinessWeek* reviewer said, "May well be the best-written book for the managerial masses since *In Search of Excellence*.")
- *Built to Last* by Jim Collins. (According to *USA Today*, it's "one of the most eye-opening business studies since *In Search of Excellence*.)
- *In Search of Excellence* by Tom Peters and Robert Waterman. (Described by the *Wall Street Journal* as "one of those rare books on management that are both consistently thought provoking and fun to read.")
- *How to Win Friends and Influence People* by Dale Carnegie. (Published in 1936 and still a best seller.) Considered the first managing yourself blockbuster.

Source: Adapted from Ryan Underwood, "A Field Guide to the Gurus," **Fast Company**, November 2004, p. 104; Walter Kiechel, III, "The Management Century," *Harvard Business Review*, November 2012, pp. 63–75.

There is no doubt that management consultants Tom Peters and Robert Waterman also influenced management thinking about the importance of people in organizations. Their best-selling book *In Search of Excellence*, published in 1982, describes eight attributes of excellence found in America's best-run companies. One of these attributes, "productivity through people," emphasizes that excellent companies treat the worker as the root source of quality and productivity. The editors of *Fast Company* magazine say that *In Search of Excellence* "fired the starting gun in the race to the New Economy."[26]

We have provided you with no more than a brief glimpse of selected developments in the human relations movement. Space does not permit a review of the hundreds of theorists and practitioners who have influenced human relations in the workplace. However, in the remaining chapters, we do introduce the views of other influential thinkers and authors.

MAJOR THEMES IN HUMAN RELATIONS

1-5   Seven broad themes emerge from the study of human relations. They are communication, self-awareness, self-acceptance, motivation, trust, self-disclosure, and conflict resolution. These themes reflect the current concern in human relations with the twin goals of (1) personal growth and development and (2) the achievement of organizational objectives. To some degree, these themes are interrelated (see Figure 1.3), and most are discussed in more than one chapter of this book.

Communication

It is not an exaggeration to describe communication as the "heart and soul" of human relations. **Communication** is the means by which we come to an understanding of ourselves and others. To grow and develop as persons, we must develop the awareness and the skills necessary to communicate effectively. Communication is the *human* connection. That is why the subject is covered in more than one section of this book. In Chapter 2, we explore the fundamentals of both personal and organizational communication. It is these fundamentals that provide the foundation for all efforts to improve communication. Chapter 3 provides an introduction to communication styles and outlines several practical tips on how you can cope with communication style bias.

Figure 1.3 ■ Major Themes in Human Relations

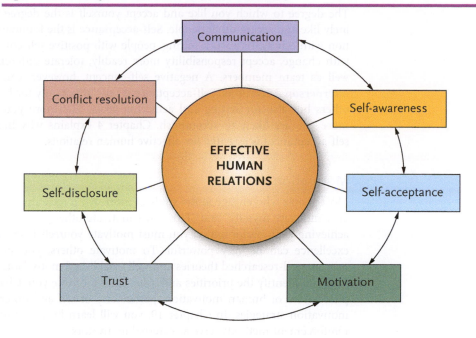

Chapter 8 explains how constructive self-disclosure, an important form of personal communication, can be used to improve human relationships.

Self-Awareness

One of the most important ways to develop improved relationships with others is to develop a better understanding of ourselves. With increased **self-awareness** comes a greater understanding of how our behavior influences others. The late Stephen Covey, author of *The Seven Habits of Highly Effective People*, says that self-awareness enables us to stand apart and examine the way we "see" ourselves, as well as to see other people.[27]

The importance of self-awareness is being recognized by an increasing number of authors, trainers, and educators. Daniel Goleman, introduced at the beginning of this chapter, has given us new insights into the importance of self-awareness. Of all the elements that make up emotional intelligence, Goleman asserts, self-awareness is the most important. He notes that a deficit in self-awareness can be damaging to one's personal relationships and career.[28] Self-awareness is discussed in greater detail in the chapters that are featured in Part 2.

> *The importance of self-awareness is being recognized by an increasing number of authors, trainers, and educators.*

LIFE-CHANGING MEETING

Jim Collins, best-selling author, recalls a life-changing meeting with Peter Drucker. Collins says Drucker altered the direction of his life by focusing the discussion around one simple question: "What do you want to contribute?"

Self-Acceptance

The degree to which you like and accept yourself is the degree to which you can genuinely like and accept other people. **Self-acceptance** is the foundation of successful interaction with others. In a work setting, people with positive self-concepts tend to cope better with change, accept responsibility more readily, tolerate differences, and generally work well as team members. A negative self-concept, however, can create barriers to good **interpersonal relations**. Self-acceptance is crucial not only for building relationships with others but also for setting and achieving goals. The more you believe you can do, the more you are likely to accomplish. Chapter 4 explains why high self-esteem (complete self-acceptance) is essential for effective human relations.

Motivation

Most people who engage in the study of **motivation** seek answers to two questions: "How do I motivate myself?" and "How do I motivate others?" If you are really committed to achieving peak performance, you must motivate yourself from within.[29] Inner drives for excellence can be very powerful. To motivate others, you need to understand time-proven, well-researched theories and well-established motivation strategies. Chapter 5 will help you identify the priorities and values that motivate you. Chapter 7 explores the complex nature of human motivation, particularly of self and others, and examines various motivation strategies. In Chapter 10, you will learn how incentives and various positive reinforcement methods serve as external motivators.

Trust

Trust is the building block of all successful relationships with coworkers, customers, family members, and friends. There is compelling evidence that low levels of trust in a workforce can lead to reduced productivity, stifled innovation, high stress, and slow decision making.[30] When a lack of trust exists in an organization, a decline in the flow of information almost always results. Employees communicate less information to their supervisors, express opinions reluctantly, and avoid discussions. Cooperation, so necessary in a modern work setting, deteriorates. When a climate of trust is present, frank discussion of problems and a free exchange of ideas and information are encouraged. The concept of trust is discussed in Chapters 8 and 12.

Self-Disclosure

Self-disclosure and trust are two halves of a whole. The more open you are with people, the more trust you build. The more trust there is in a relationship, the safer you feel to disclose who you are. Self-disclosure is also part of good communication and helps eliminate unnecessary guessing games. Managers who let their subordinates know what is expected of them help those employees fulfill their responsibilities. Chapter 8 emphasizes the need of individuals to verbalize the thoughts and feelings they carry within them and provides many practical suggestions on how to use constructive self-disclosure.

Conflict Resolution

Conflict in one form or another surfaces almost daily in the lives of many workers. You may experience conflict during a commute to work when a careless driver cuts you

This supervisor is working to resolve conflict between two employees. Conflict resolution skills are critical for every manager to learn.

off at a freeway exit ramp. If your job includes supervisory-management responsibilities, you will spend a great deal of time in **conflict resolution**, attempting to resolve conflicts among members of your staff. As a team member, you may assume the role of mediator when other team members clash. Conflict also surfaces when working parents try to balance the demands of both work and family. Stressful conditions at home often interfere with work performance, and on-the-job pressures create or magnify problems at home.[31] The ability to anticipate or resolve conflict can be an invaluable skill. Although Chapter 13 deals specifically with the topic of conflict resolution, the chapters devoted to communication, achievement of emotional control, and team building provide many valuable suggestions on how conflict can be handled constructively.

HUMAN RELATIONS: BENEFITS TO YOU

As previously noted, the workforce is currently characterized by downsizing, mergers, buyouts, business closings, and other disruptive forces. We are seeing more emphasis on quality products and quality services. In addition, diversity has become a more prominent characteristic of today's workforce. These conditions will very likely continue. One of the best ways to cope with these changes is to develop and apply the interpersonal skills needed for success in today's working world.

Many leaders think that courses in human relations are important because very few workers are responsible to themselves alone. These leaders point out that most jobs today are interdependent. If people in these jobs cannot work effectively as a team, the efficiency of the organization will suffer.

LOOKING BACK: SUMMARY OF LEARNING OBJECTIVES

1. **Explain the nature, purpose, and importance of human relations.**

   The healthy functioning of any organization, large or small, depends on teamwork. Effective human relations are the very foundation of teamwork. Human relations, when applied in a positive and supportive environment, can help increase an organization's productivity and efficiency.

2. **Identify major developments in the workplace that have given new importance to human relations.**

   The restructuring of America from an industrial economy to an information economy has had profound implications for the study of human relations. Several major developments in the workplace have given new importance to this branch of learning. Some of these developments include churning dislocation in the labor market, changing work patterns, the need for higher service standards, increasing workplace incivility, greater reliance on team-based structures, and workforce diversity.

3. **Identify major forces influencing human behavior at work.**

   A key purpose of this text is to increase understanding of major factors that influence human behavior in a variety of work settings. These include organizational culture, supervisory-management influence, work group influence, job influence, personal characteristics of individual workers, and family influence.

4. **Review the historical development of the human relations movement.**

   Early attempts to improve productivity in manufacturing focused on such things as plant layout and mechanical processes. With the passing of time, there was more interest in redefining the nature of work and perceiving workers as complex human beings. Two landmarks in the study of motivation and worker needs are Frederick Taylor's work in scientific management and Elton Mayo's Hawthorne studies. Later research by Douglas McGregor, Frederick Herzberg, Carl Rogers, Peter Drucker, Jim Collins, and others contributed greatly to our understanding of how to achieve productivity through people.

5. **Identify seven major themes that serve as the foundation for effective human relations.**

   Seven major themes emerge from a study of human relations: communication, self-awareness, self-acceptance, motivation, trust, self-disclosure, and conflict resolution. These themes reflect the current concern in human relations with personal growth and satisfaction of organization objectives.

KEY TERMS

human relations, 5	informal organization, 13	motivation, 16
total person, 8	communication, 14	trust, 16
organizational culture, 9	self-awareness, 15	self-disclosure, 16
scientific management, 12	self-acceptance, 16	conflict resolution, 17
Hawthorne studies, 13	interpersonal relations, 16	

CAREER INSIGHT

The daily news sources are constantly reporting on mergers, business closings, downsizing, and changing business trends. With so much uncertainty in the job market, you need to devote time to answering the following questions:

1. What are your career goals? Although you may change careers several times, now is the time to carefully study career options.

2. What transferable skills do you currently possess? What additional skills need to be developed? "Millions of people make a career-change each year without going back to school," says Richard N. Bolles, author of the best-selling book, *What Color is Your Parachute?*[32] They take advantage of various learning pathways.

TRY YOUR HAND

1. In his book, *The Success Principles*, Jack Canfield describes 50 principles that will increase your confidence, help you tackle daily challenges, and teach you how to realize your ambitions. Number one on his list is "Take 100% responsibility for your life." This includes the quality of your relationships, your health and fitness, your income, your career success—everything! He says most of us have been conditioned to blame events outside of our life for those parts of our life we dislike. Reflect on your life up to this point and identify situations in which you blamed someone or something else for your failure to achieve a goal or improve in some area. Do you see any situations in which you felt justified in blaming others or refused to take risks?[33]

2. Human relations and the *total person* concept are interwoven in the 17 chapters of this text. Progressive organizations recognize that most employees are striving to satisfy both personal and work-related needs. They also recognize that employees display a wide range of interrelated human traits such as emotional control, values orientation, and self-awareness.
   a. Analyze the importance of creating an organizational culture that meets the needs of the *total person*.
   b. Many organizations that have been selected for *Fortune* magazine's list of 100 best companies to work for in America provide benefits that meet the needs of the total person. Google, for example, has three wellness centers and a seven-acre sports complex that includes courts for basketball, bocce, and shuffleball. Brainstorm with classmates the benefits you will seek throughout your employment career.

3. Companies featured in *Fortune's* list of the 100 best companies to work for in America are characterized by openness, fairness, camaraderie among employees, job security, opportunities for advancement, and sensitivity to work/family issues. These companies are concerned about the total person, not just the skills that help the company earn a profit. Here are some of the companies that have made the "best companies" list:

Company	Location	Type of Business
NetApp	Sunnyvale, CA	Storage & Data Management
Zappos.com	Henderson, NV	E-Commerce Retailer
Edward Jones	St. Louis, MO	Financial Services
DreamWorks	Glendale, CA	Animation
Marriott International	Bethesda, MD	Hotel Chain
Wegmans Food Markets	Rochester, NY	Grocer

Develop a profile of two of these companies by visiting their websites and reviewing the available information. Also, visit Hoover's Inc. website, a resource that provides access to profiles of thousands of companies. Additional information on each of these companies may be found in *Bloomberg Businessweek*, *Forbes*, *Fortune*, and other business publications.

CRITICAL THINKING CHALLENGE

To achieve a better understanding of the major themes in human relations, complete the following sentences. Work quickly and don't worry too much about the ending. Sentence completion exercises can be powerful vehicles for self-discovery and personal growth.

- To become more self accepting I need to…
- To build a more trusting relationship with others, I need to…
- My greatest strength in the area of communication is…
- To grow in the area of self-awareness, I need to…
- I am motivated to give my best when…

SELF-ASSESSMENT EXERCISE

For each of the following statements, circle the number from 1 to 5 that best represents your response: (1) strongly disagree (never do this); (2) disagree (rarely do this); (3) moderately agree (sometimes do this); (4) agree (frequently do this); (5) strongly agree (almost always do this).

A. I accept the premise that within an organization all work is influenced by relationships.	1	2	3	4	5
B. I accept the view that major developments in the workplace have given new importance to the study of human relations.	1	2	3	4	5
C. I view human relations as the study of how people satisfy both personal and work-related needs.	1	2	3	4	5
D. I understand the major forces influencing worker behavior.	1	2	3	4	5
E. I can explain the major themes that emerge from the study of human relations.	1	2	3	4	5

After identifying your response to each item, select an attitude or skill you would like to improve. Prepare a written goal and then describe the steps you will take to achieve this goal.

YOU PLAY THE ROLE

The college you attend offers career counseling, job placement assistance, and help finding summer internships. You plan to meet with a career counselor and seek help finding a summer internship with a well-established company. You will be meeting with a class member, who will assume the role of career counselor. The purpose of this meeting is to give the counselor some basic information about your career plans and the type of company you would like to work for. Before the meeting, prepare a written outline of information you plan to present during the meeting. Base your notes on your academic studies and your current employment interests. The outline should focus on the following areas:

- Define what type of work would be most meaningful.
- Describe what type of organizational culture would be most appealing to you.
- Identify what you find to be the basic rewards of work.

BELOW THE SURFACE | ACHIEVING PERSONAL GROWTH

Henk Meijer/Alamy

At the beginning of this chapter, we described two groundbreaking concepts that have contributed to our understanding of human behavior. First, we now know that IQ is one of many "intelligences," and it is not a particularly good predictor of workplace success. The authors of *Emotional Intelligence 2.0* indicate that emotional intelligence (EQ) is the foundation for a host of skills needed by employees: empathy, social skills, anger management, trust, and stress tolerance, for example. They note that a little effort spent on increasing your EQ tends to have a wide-ranging, positive impact on your life.[34]

Second, when our brain gets stuck in a pattern that focuses on negativity and failure, we set ourselves up to fail. Once this pattern is well established, we begin scanning our environment looking for annoyances. When this frame of mind is well established, we miss out on the positives in our life.[35] Positivity broadens our minds and expands our range of vision.[36]

QUESTIONS

1. It is possible to increase your EQ. The authors of *Emotional Intelligence 2.0* indicate that people improve their EQ most when the following conditions are present:[37]

   - They have a strong motivation to learn or change.
   - They practice new behaviors consistently.
   - They seek feedback on their own behavior.

   If you are determined to improve your EQ, which of these conditions would be most challenging? Which of these conditions would you like to improve?

2. Over the next few days make a conscious effort to monitor your thinking patterns. If you discover a pattern of negativity, what changes can you make to move in the direction of greater positive thinking?

CLOSING CASE | IN SEARCH OF WORK/LIFE BALANCE

A growing number of workers do not feel there's a healthy balance between work and personal life. Some are tired of working 10- to 12-hour days and weekends. Many want a better balance between work and family. These employees search for companies that offer family-friendly features such as flexible scheduling, telecommuting, and child care. Each year *Working Mother* magazine publishes a list of the 100 best companies for working mothers. Let's look at two of the companies that made the 2011 list.[38]

- *American Express* This financial services company describes its commitment to the health of its employees as a "core business value." Employees who want to lose weight, screen for medical conditions, or reduce stress can consult with nurses, health coaches, dietitians, and physicians at company-sponsored wellness clinics. The company offers seminars on eating well and cafeterias with nutritious meals.
- *Bain & Company* This Boston-based management consulting firm offers all employees flexible schedules and the opportunity to work off-site. Women may reduce their work schedules by 40 percent and still be considered for promotions. The firm offers fully paid maternity leave for up to 12 weeks.

QUESTIONS

1. What are some of the economic benefits that justify the family-friendly services offered by these two companies?

2. Some companies develop work/life programs that focus primarily on employees who have children. What are the advantages and disadvantages of this approach?

CHAPTER 1 ENDNOTES

1. John D. Mayer, ***Personal Intelligence: The Power of Personality and How It Shapes Our Lives*** (New York: Scientific American/Farrar, Straus, and Giroux, 2014), p. 36.
2. Barbara Fredrickson, ***Positivity*** (New York: Crown Publishers, 2009), p. 181. See also Shawn Achor, ***Before Happiness*** (New York: Crown Publishers, 2013) for additional information on positive psychology.
3. Heidi R. Perreault, "What Makes the Soft Skills So Hard," ***The Delta Pi Epsilon Journal***, Fall 2006, pp. 125–127.
4. Steve Heimoff, "2012 Innovator of the Year," ***Wine Enthusiast, Best of Year Edition***, 2012, p. 100.
5. Ron Conway, "The Best Advice I Ever Got," ***Fortune***, November 12, 2012, p. 123.

6. Gerhard Gschwandtner, "The Magic Formula for Sustainable Success," *Selling Power*, June 2006, p. 10.

7. Bridget Carey, "Modern Workers Need the Right Skills and Attitude", *News & Observer*, August 28, 2011, p. 1E.

8. James O'Toole and Edward C. Lawler, III, "A Piece of Work," *Fast Company*, June 2006, p. 88; Peter Cog, Michelle Conlin, and Moira Herbst, "The Disposable Worker," *Bloomberg Businessweek*, January 18, 2010, pp. 33–39. See also Lauren Weber, "Elance Tops Growing Demand for Freelancers," *Wall Street Journal*, February 5, 2014, p. B5.

9. Rachel Feintzeig, "When Co-Workers Don't Play Nice," *Wall Street Journal*, August 28, 2013, p. B6.

10. John C. Maxwell, *The 17 Essential Qualities of a Team Player* (Nashville: Thomas Nelson Publishers, 2002), pp. 10, 13, 46, and 63.

11. Rachel Emma Silverman, "Working on Your Marriage—at Work," *Wall Street Journal*, May 31, 2007, p. 1.

12. William M. Bulkeley, "IBM to Help Pay for Plans to Curb Childhood Obesity," *Wall Street Journal*, October 24, 2007, p. D4.

13. Robert Kreitner, *Management*, 12th ed. (Mason, OH: Cengage Learning, 2011), p. 259.

14. Allan A. Kennedy, interview by, in "The Culture Wars," *Inc.*, 20th Anniversary Issue, 1999, pp. 107–108.

15. David A. Price, "How Google Got Going," *Wall Street Journal*, July 12, 2011, p. A13.

16. Jeffrey Pfeffer, *The Human Equation* (Boston: Harvard Business School Press, 1998), p. 293.

17. Sue Shellenbarger, "Along with Benefits and Pay, Employees Seek Friends on the Job," *Wall Street Journal*, February 20, 2002, p. B1.

18. "Great Expectations," *Fast Company*, November 1999, p. 224.

19. Betsy Jacobson and Beverly Kaye, "Balancing Act," *Training & Development*, February 1993, p. 26.

20. Sue Shellenbarger, "Job Candidates Prepare to Sacrifice Some Frills and Balance—For Now," *Wall Street Journal*, November 21, 2001, p. B1; Stephanie Armour, "Workers Put Family First Despite Slow Economy, Jobless Fears," *USA Today*, June 6, 2002, p. 38; "Work-Life Balance Tops Pay," *USA Today*, March 13, 2008, p. 1B.

21. Alan Farnham, "The Man Who Changed Work Forever," *Fortune*, July 21, 1997, p. 114; Cynthia Crossen, "Early Industry Expert Soon Realized a Staff Has Its Own Efficiency," *Wall Street Journal*, November 6, 2006, p. B1.

22. Bradley J. Rieger, "Lessons in Productivity and People," *Training & Development*, October 19, pp. 56–58.

23. "A Field Is Born," *Harvard Business Review*, July/August 2008, p. 164.

24. Jim Collins, "The Classics," *Inc.*, December 1996, p. 55.

25. John A. Byrne, "The Man Who Invented Management," *BusinessWeek*, November 28, 2005, pp. 97–106.

26. Thomas J. Peters and Robert H. Waterman, Jr., *In Search of Excellence: Lessons from America's Best-Run Companies* (New York: Harper & Row, 1982), p. 14; Tom Peters, "Tom Peters' True Confessions," *Fast Company*, December 2001, p. 80.

27. Stephen R. Covey, *The Seven Habits of Highly Effective People* (New York: Simon & Schuster, 1989), pp. 66–67.

28. Richard Koonce, "Emotional IQ, A New Secret of Success," *Training & Development*, February 1996, p. 19; Cary Cherniss and Daniel Goleman, eds., *The Emotionally Intelligent Workplace* (San Francisco: Jossey-Bass, 2001), pp. 13–26.

29. Denis Waitley, *Empires of the Mind* (New York: Morrow, 1995), p. 133.

30. Michael Crom, "Building Trust in the Workplace," *The Leader*, October 1998, p. 6; Ron Zemke, "Can You Manage Trust?" *Training*, February 2000, pp. 76–83; Steven M.R. Covey, *The Speed of Trust* (New York: Free Press, 2006), pp. 3–6.

31. Harold H. Bloomfield and Robert K. Cooper, *The Power of 5* (Emmaus, PA: Rodale Press, 1995), p. 61.

32. Richard N. Bolles, *What Color is Your Parachute?* (Berkeley, CA: Ten Speed Press, 2004), pp. 8–11.

33. Jack Canfield, *The Success Principles* (New York: Harper Collins, 2005), pp. 3–18.

34. Travis Bradberry and Jean Greaves, *Emotional Intelligence 2.0* (San Diego, CA: *TalentSmart*, 2009), pp. 19–22.

35. Shawn Achor, *Before Happiness* (New York: Crown Business, 2013), pp. 21–27.

36. Barbara Fredrickson, *Positivity* (New York: Crown Publishers, 2009), p. 55.

37. *Emotional Intelligence Appraisal* [cited 19 March 19 2014]. Available from www.talentsmart.com; INTERNET.

38. "The 100 Best Companies for Working Mothers List 2011" [cited 29 December 2011]. Available from workingmother.com; INTERNET.

Henk Meijer/Alamy

CHAPTER PREVIEW

LEARNING OBJECTIVES

After studying Chapter 2, you will be able to

2-1 Explain the communication process.

2-2 Identify and explain the filters that affect communication.

2-3 Identify ways to improve personal communication, including developing listening skills.

2-4 Understand how communications flow throughout an organization.

2-5 Learn how to communicate effectively using social media and other communication technologies.

Improving Personal and Organizational Communications

TIP OF THE ICEBERG | COMMUNICATION BREAKDOWN

Demanding. Impatient. Emotional. Petulant. Intense. Are these the words ever used to describe an effective communication style displayed by a prominent leader? No, not unless you're Steve Jobs. Walter Isaacson, author of the late Steve Jobs' biography, asked Jobs about his inclination to be tough on people. "Look at the results," Jobs replied. "These are all smart people I work with, and any of them could get a top job at another place if they were truly brutalized. But they don't." He then added, "And we got some amazing things done."[1]

And indeed they did. Steve Jobs' vision and drive for innovation led his team at Apple to transform seven different industries and become known as one of the most innovative and valuable companies in the world. Jobs transformed the personal computing industry when he cofounded Apple in his parents' garage in 1976. By the time he died in 2011, the music, phone, tablet, retail stores, animated movies, and digital publishing industries had also transformed under his leadership. For all these reasons, Isaacson says Steve Jobs should be remembered with other great innovators including Henry Ford, Thomas Edison, and Walt Disney.

Steve Jobs was known for being controlling and authoritarian, but he was also known as an effective leader because he was a direct, focused, and charismatic communicator who knew how to motivate and inspire people toward his vision.

For example, after being fired from Apple in 1985, Jobs later returned in 1997, saving the company from bankruptcy. Apple was making a dozen different versions of the Macintosh and after several weeks of review meetings he finally shouted "Stop! This is crazy. Here's what we need." He marched to the front of the room and drew a two-by-two grid on the whiteboard. In the top two columns he wrote "Consumer" and "Pro" and in each row "Desktop" and "Portable." He told his team to focus on making only four great products, one in each quadrant. Focusing on only four products saved Apple, and it also taught his team the power of focus.

Yamada Taro/Photodisc/Getty Images

Steve Jobs tough, emotional, and often abrasive communication style was legendary; however his team was fiercely loyal. Together they transformed six industries and left an indelible mark in history.

A similar situation occurred when Jobs was initially shown complicated navigation screens for the iDVD, which enabled users to burn a video on a disc. He stopped the team and explained, "Here's the new application," drawing a rectangle on the whiteboard. "It's got one window. You drag your video into the window. Then you click the button that says 'Burn.' That's it. That's what we're going to make."[2]

Understanding the complexities and power of effective communication is one of the most important skills you will ever learn, and it is an essential skill to hone throughout your lifetime. Learning how to communicate effectively is different from understanding your leadership style or communication style, which is the topic of the next chapter.

COMMUNICATION IN AN INFORMATION ECONOMY

In this age of information, the problem is not access to information; it is assimilating the massive amount of information we experience daily. Rapid advances in digital technologies, mobile devices, Apps, and social media networks facilitate the ability to communicate in multiple ways, wherever and whenever we want. The stream of information is constant. Its usefulness and effectiveness is not driven so much by ongoing advances in technology, but by each individual's ability to filter, manage, and respond to the steady onslaught of information and communication. Effective communication, both personal and organizational, still depends on the human aspect of interactions. This has made personal and organizational communication skills more important than ever.

The Battle for Our Attention

Maggie Jackson, author of *Distracted: The Erosion of Attention and the Coming Dark Age*, says today's tech-savvy worker is often distracted by the constant flow of information from electronic sources. As the speed and volume of information increase, so do the number of distractions. Many workers say that frequent interruptions and the need to engage in multitasking rob them of time to think. More information does not necessarily make us more knowledgeable. Ms. Jackson says critical thinking, problem solving, reflection, and focused communications are critical to personal and career success.[3]

THE COMMUNICATION PROCESS

2-1 Many people take communication for granted. When they write, speak, or listen to others, they assume that the message given or received is being understood. In reality, messages are often misunderstood because they are incomplete or because different people interpret messages in different ways. The diversity of today's workforce calls for a greater understanding of how to communicate effectively, through technology or face-to-face, with people from different cultures, countries, and lifestyles.

Impersonal Versus Interpersonal Communication

In a typical organization, the types of communication used to exchange information can be placed on a continuum ranging from "impersonal" on one end to "interpersonal" on the other.[4] **Impersonal communication** is a one-way process that transfers basic information such as instructions, policies, and financial data. Generally, organizations use this information-delivery process when sending e-mails or memos as quick, easy ways to "get the word out." Their effectiveness is somewhat limited because there is little, if any, possibility for the person receiving the information to clarify vague or confusing information.

Interpersonal communication is the exchange of information between two or more people. Such words as *share, discuss, argue,* and *interact* refer to this form of two-way communication. Interpersonal communication can take place in meetings, over the phone, in face-to-face interviews, or during classroom discussions between instructors and students. If interpersonal communication is to be effective, some type of **feedback**, or understood response, from the person receiving the information is necessary. When this exchange happens, those involved can determine whether the information has been understood in the way intended. This is one of the reasons many employees prefer person-to-person meetings, telephone calls, video, or web conference meetings.

Sender—Message—Receiver—Feedback

Effective communication is a continuous loop that involves a sender, a receiver, the message, and feedback that clarifies the message.[5] To illustrate, suppose a coworker calls you to ask for clarification of information that your boss gave during a team meeting earlier that morning. You explain the project, providing details about the objective, the deadline, and the various roles and responsibilities of other members on the team. When your coworker asks questions about the project and his role in it, you clarify any misunderstandings, and he understands what he needs to do to fulfill his responsibilities for the project. A simplified diagram of this communication process would look like Figure 2.1.

Figure 2.1 ■ Diagram of a Simple Communication Process

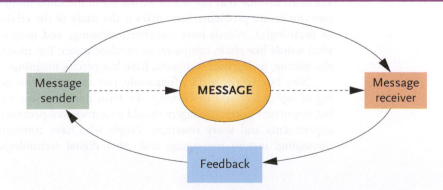

Figure 2.2 ▪ Diagram of More Complex Communication Process

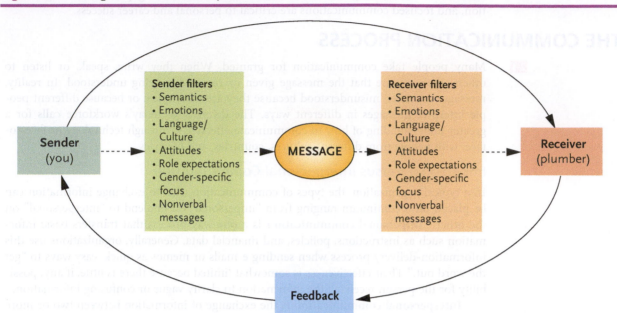

Now suppose you are late for an appointment, and the plumber you had requested three days ago calls you from her cell phone and asks directions to your house. She explains that she has gotten lost in this neighborhood before, and it is obvious that English is her second language. The communication process becomes much more complicated, as shown in Figure 2.2. As your message travels from you to your plumber, it must pass through several "filters," each of which can alter the way your message is understood. Most communications flow through this complex process.

COMMUNICATION FILTERS

2-2   Messages are sent—and feedback is received—through a variety of filters that can distort the intended message (see Figure 2.2.). When people are influenced by one or more of these filters, their perception of the message may be totally different from what the sender was attempting to communicate. Both sender and receiver must be keenly aware of these possible distortions so that they can intercept any miscommunication.

Semantics

We often assume that the words we use mean the same things to others, but this assumption can create problems. **Semantics** is the study of the relationship between a word and its meaning(s). Words have associated meanings and usages. We can easily understand what words like *chair, computer,* or *envelope* mean. But more abstract terms, such as *silo, downsizing,* or *internal customers,* have less precise meanings.

New buzzwords surface frequently. Just about the time people understood the meaning of *rightsizing* and *downsizing,* the term *unsiloing* was introduced to make a simple, but important point: Managers should encourage cooperation and communication across departments and share resources. People who have communicated extensively via text messaging, instant messaging, and other digital technologies often assume that their jargon will be understood by everyone. However, when slang, buzzwords, or acronyms are used in the mainstream of communication within organizations, it can be confusing or can alienate others who do not understand their meaning or don't like the use of certain buzzwords. For example, words and phrases such as "empowerment" (vague and overused), "deck" (PowerPoint or Keynote presentation), and GMTA (great minds think alike) are a turnoff or deemed unprofessional for some people. The impact of generational differences on interpersonal communications will be discussed in future chapters.

Language and Cultural Barriers

The needs of a multicultural workforce are getting more attention today because of globalization and employers' growing support for cultural diversity among their workers. The culture in which we are raised strongly influences our values, beliefs, expressions, and behaviors. **Culture** can be defined as the accumulation of values, rules of behavior, forms of expression, religious beliefs, and the like, for a group of people who share a common language and environment. Culture helps shape just about every aspect of our behavior and our mental processes. Culture is often associated with a particular country, but in fact most countries are multicultural. African Americans, Hispanic Americans, Asian Americans, and American Indians represent a few of the subcultures within the United States.[6]

The ability to interpret human actions, gestures, and speech patterns in a foreign culture is called **cultural intelligence** or CQ. A person with a high CQ quickly analyzes an unfamiliar cultural situation and then responds appropriately.[7] Management professors P. Christopher Earley and Elaine Mosakowski have studied more than 2,000 managers in 60 countries. They have identified three sources of cultural intelligence.[8]

Head. Before visiting a foreign country, learn as much as possible about the host country's customs, religion, politics, morals, social structure, food, table manners, and the roles of men and women.

Body. You can win the respect of foreign hosts, guests, or colleagues by showing you understand their culture. The way you shake hands, order coffee, or accept a gift can demonstrate, to some degree, you have already entered their world.

Heart. Adapting to a new culture is much easier when you have confidence in yourself. In Chapter 4, we introduce *self-efficacy*, the belief that you can achieve what you set out to do. A major source of self-efficacy is the experience of mastery in your area of specialization.

 HOW TO SPEAK IOWAN

One solution to the doctor shortage in rural America is to enlist physicians from Egypt, India, and other countries. At Mercy Medical Center in Mason City, Iowa, about one-third of the physicians are foreign born. The administration was concerned that there might not be a social or emotional connection between patients and international physicians. With help from professors at the University of Northern Iowa, the hospital developed a training course entitled "Topics for Small Talk with Iowans." The foreign-born doctors learned about Iowa's history and traditions, crops, climate, and sporting interests. So, if a patient makes reference to a mixed marriage, the person might be referring to a University of Iowa *Hawkeye* tying the knot with an Iowa State University *Cyclone*.

Source: Miriam Jordan, "Learning to Speak Iowan: Corn, Pigs, Cyclones and Hawkeyes," *Wall Street Journal*, September 9, 2011, pp. A1 and A16.

Emotions

Strong emotions can either prevent people from hearing what a speaker has to say or make them too susceptible to the speaker's point of view. If they become angry or allow themselves to be carried away by the speaker's eloquence, they may "think" with their emotions and make decisions or take action they regret later. Three-time Indianapolis 500 winner Helio Castroneves used a Twitter rant to complain about a penalty imposed during a race. He called IndyCar race director Brian Barnhart a "circus clown." He was fined $30,000 and put on probation.[9]

Detaching yourself from another's feelings and responding to the content of the message is often difficult. It is hard to realize that another person's emotional response is more likely about fear or frustration than it is about you as an individual. Many customer service jobs require that employees remain calm and courteous regardless of a customer's emotional state. Emotional control is discussed extensively in Chapter 9.

Attitudes

Attitudes can be a barrier to communication in much the same way as emotions. The receiver may have a negative attitude toward the sender's voice, accent, gestures, mannerisms, dress, or delivery. These negative attitudes create resistance to the message and can lead to a breakdown in communication. Perhaps the listener has an established attitude about the speaker's topic. For example, a person who is strongly opposed to abortion will most likely find it difficult to listen with objectivity to a prochoice speaker. Keep in mind, however, that an overly positive attitude can also be a barrier to communication. When biased in favor of the message, the listener may not effectively evaluate the speaker's information. More is said about the power of attitudes in Chapter 6.

Role Expectations

Role expectations influence how people expect themselves, and others, to act on the basis of the roles they play, such as boss, customer, or subordinate. These expectations can distort communication in two ways. First, if people identify others too closely with their roles, they may discount what the other person has to say: "It's just the boss again, saying the same old thing." A variation of this distortion occurs when we do not allow others to change their roles and take on new ones. This often happens to employees who are promoted from within the ranks of an organization to management positions. Others may still see "old Chuck" from Accounting rather than the new department head.

Second, role expectations can affect good communication when people use their roles to alter the way they relate to others. This is often referred to as "position power." For example, managers may expect employees to accept what they say simply because of the authority invested in the position. When employees are not allowed to question the manager's decisions or make suggestions, communication becomes one-way information giving.

Gender-Specific Focus

Gender roles learned throughout childhood can influence the way men and women communicate. As adults, women are more likely to view conversation as an opportunity to establish rapport, make connections, and develop relationships. Men are more likely to view conversation as an opportunity to maintain status, exhibit skill and knowledge, or

Say *Ni Hao* (*Hello*) to Home Depot employees who are preparing for work at a store located in Beijing. The world's largest home improvement retailer must embrace lots of cultural adaptation if it is to achieve success in China.

to be competitive. Chapter 16, "The Changing Roles of Men and Women," discusses specific strategies you can use to communicate more effectively with those whose gender differs from your own.

Nonverbal Messages

When we communicate with others, we use both verbal and nonverbal communication. **Nonverbal messages**, commonly referred to as "body language," are the messages we communicate through facial expressions, voice tone, gestures, appearance, posture, and other nonverbal means. Research indicates that when two people communicate, nonverbal messages convey much more than verbal messages. This chapter limits its discussion of nonverbal communication to body language. Physical appearance, another powerful form of nonverbal communication, is discussed in Chapter 11.

Many of us could communicate more clearly, more accurately, and more credibly if we became more conscious of our body language. We can learn to strengthen our communications by making sure our words and our body language are consistent. Research indicates that a stunning 93 percent of all face-to-face communication is nonverbal, yet few people are trained to observe and understand the signs of body language and know what they mean.[10] Research has also shown that those who can effectively read and interpret nonverbal communication, and manage how others perceive it, will enjoy greater success in life than those who lack this skill.[11] For all of these reasons, it's important to learn and practice nonverbal communication skills.

When our verbal and nonverbal messages match, we give the impression that we can be trusted and that what we are saying reflects what we truly believe. If your spoken message and your body language are mismatched, the person receiving the message will respond to the nonverbal message every time.[12] If a manager says to an employee, "I am interested in helping you find a solution to your problem," but then begins to look at her watch and fidget with objects on her desk, the employee will most likely believe the non-verbal rather than the verbal message.

You can improve your communication by monitoring the nonverbal messages you send through your eye contact, facial expressions, gestures, posture, and personal space.

Eye Contact. Eyes transmit more information than any other part of the body. Because eye contact is so revealing, people generally observe some unwritten rules about looking at others. People who hold direct eye contact for only a few seconds, or avoid eye contact altogether, risk communicating indifference. However, a direct, prolonged stare between strangers is usually considered impolite, even potentially aggressive or hostile. Continuous eye contact is especially offensive in Asian and Latin American countries. As a general rule in North America, when you are communicating in a business setting, your eyes should meet the other person's about 60 to 70 percent of the time.

human RELATIONS *in Action*

HOW TO COMMUNICATE WITH AUTHENTICITY AND CHARISMA

Step One: Being Open

When you approach a group meeting or an interview, your manner should be relaxed—no different than if you were talking to a family member or a good friend.

Step Two: Being Connected

Your nonverbal messages should orient you toward the audience; zero in or their issues and problems.

Step Three: Being Passionate

How are you connected with your own feelings and emotions? How do you feel about the content of the material you present?

Step Four: Listening

Authentic and charismatic communication requires that you listen to your audience. Tune in and stay tuned in.

Source: Nick Morgan, *Trust Me—Four Steps to Authenticity and Charisma* (San Francisco, CA: Jossey-Bass, 2009), pp. 30–32.

Facial Expressions. If you want to identify the inner feelings of another person, watch facial expressions closely. A frown or a smile will communicate a great deal. We have all encountered a "look of surprise" or a "look that could kill." Most of our observations are very accurate. However, facial expressions can be intentionally manipulated. When a person is truly happy, the muscles used for smiling are involuntarily controlled by the body's limbic system. When you force a smile, the cerebral cortex (under voluntary control) activates and the person appears to have a "fake" look when he or she smiles. That is why actors often recall a past emotional experience to produce the emotional state they want.[13] If we can accurately assess the facial expressions of others and draw conclusions accordingly, we can be sure that others are doing the same to us.

Gestures. Gestures send messages to people about how you are reacting to them and to the situation in which you find yourself. They often add an element that is perceived as a lively speaking style that keeps the attention of others. In some cultures, if you fail to gesture, you may be perceived as boring and stiff.[14] Some gestures that may be common in one culture may have dramatically different meaning to people from another culture.

Posture. Your posture is important because it can greatly influence the impression you communicate to another person. When interviewing for a job or seeking a favorable decision during salary negotiations, you want to maximize your influence. Your posture can influence a favorable outcome. In fact research has confirmed that the posture a person uses when sitting or standing has a powerful physiological, psychological, and behavioral impact on *both* the sender and the receiver. When people use an open, expansive posture they experience elevations in testosterone, decreases in cortisol (stress hormone), and increased confidence and influence.[15] When standing, stand up straight and avoid slumping shoulders. If you are seated, avoid slouching in your chair, crossing your arms in a closed position, or appearing too relaxed. With a little practice you can increase your confidence and make a good impression each time you are involved in important communication.

Personal Space. Research conducted by Edward Hall provides evidence that people use the space around them to define relationships. It is possible to make others uncomfortable by standing too close to them or too far away from them. A customer may feel uncomfortable if a salesperson stands too close. A job applicant may feel uncomfortable if the interviewer maintains a distance of several feet. Hall identified comfortable distances that help us understand this nonverbal effect on others:[16] For example, *intimate distance* includes touching to approximately 18 inches from another person. *Personal distance* (18 inches to 4 feet) is usually reserved for people we feel close to, such as spouses or close friends. *Social distance* (4 to 12 feet) is used for most business meetings and impersonal social gatherings.

Nonverbal messages such as facial expression, gestures, posture, personal space, and eye contact communicate much more than verbal messages.

Americans should realize that the distances Hall describes may be different when they are attempting to effectively communicate with those from another culture. For example, Asians are accustomed to close contact.

Who Is Responsible for Effective Communication?

The sender and the receiver share *equal* responsibility for effective communication. The communication loop, as shown in Figure 2.2, is not complete if the message the receiver hears, and acts upon, differs from the one the sender intended. When the sender accepts 100 percent of the responsibility for sending a clear, concise message, the communication process begins. But the receiver must also accept 100 percent of the responsibility for receiving the message as the sender intended. Ideally, receivers should provide senders with enough feedback to ensure that an accurate message has passed through all the filters that might alter it.

? HOW TO COMMUNICATE POSITIVE NONVERBAL MESSAGES

- Tune into your body language. Check for deeply ingrained habits (twisting your hair, clasping your hands, or touching your face).
- Exhibit good posture. Stand tall (no slouching) and sit erect.
- Maintain proper eye contact. Look people in the eye, but don't stare them down.
- Avoid negative postures. Don't cross your arms or wring your hands.
- Sound enthusiastic and interested. The tone of your voice has a great effect on the words you speak.

Source: Barbara Pachter, *When the Little Things Count* (Cambridge, MA: DaCapo Press, 2006), pp. 55–57.

HOW TO IMPROVE PERSONAL COMMUNICATION

2-3 Now that you understand the communication process and the various filters messages must pass through, you can begin to take the necessary steps to improve your own personal communication skills.

Send Clear Messages

Send clear, concise messages with as little influence from filters as possible so that you can avoid being misunderstood. Miscommunication can easily be avoided if both parties follow these simple rules:

- *Use clear, concise language.* Avoid slang, jargon, or complex, industry-specific semantics that the receiver might not understand. Tailor your messages to your receivers by using words and concepts they understand.
- *Use repetition.* When possible, use parallel channels of communication. For example, by sending an e-mail and making a phone call, you not only gain the receiver's attention through dialogue but also make sure there is a written record in case specific details need to be recalled.
- *Ask questions.* If you sense the receiver didn't understand your message or may have misinterpreted what you said, stop and ask for clarification using questions and statements such as, "I sense you may not be getting what I'm trying to communicate," "Does that make sense?" or "I'm not sure my message was clear."

- *Use appropriate timing.* An important e-mail or phone call may get no attention simply because it is competing with more pressing problems facing the receiver. When you need someone's cooperation, be acutely aware of his or her schedule so that you can avoid causing any inconvenience or frustration. It's always courteous to ask, "Is this a good time for you? I just have a couple quick questions that will only take a minute or two."

- *Consider the receiver's preferences.* Some people prefer to receive information via e-mail, and others prefer telephone calls or face-to-face contact. Monitor and discover the preferences of those you communicate with on a regular basis, and adjust your communications with them accordingly.

Develop Effective Listening Skills

We may be born with the ability to hear, but we have to *learn how to listen*. We may think we are good listeners, but the truth is that most people don't listen well at all. Too often we are thinking about what we are going to say next, rather than concentrating on what the other person is trying to say. A common obstacle to listening is the tendency to filter and judge what others are saying based on preexisting assumptions and opinions, or listening only long enough to see if the speaker's point of view conforms to our own. Failure to listen well damages relationships and careers and prolongs meetings.[17]

Effective listening skills can greatly enhance your personal and job-related communication. When someone says "You are a good listener," you have received one of the highest forms of praise.

When you become an active listener, you will make fewer mistakes, learn new information, and build stronger relationships.

Total Person Insight

"Success as a new manager will depend on your ability to listen well and communicate clearly, in that order. Nothing else comes close; not likability, empathy, favors, parties, fixing problems, ignoring problems (in hopes they will go away) or even pay increases. Nothing else you offer will affect your success as a manager quite like your willingness and ability to listen to your employees."

Source: Bruce Clarke, "Being a Good Listener Will Make You a Better Manager," *News and Observer*, June 30, 2013, pg. 3E.

Active Listening. **Active listening** is fueled by curiosity and requires your complete concentration on what you are hearing, body language that exhibits your listening attitude, and feedback as to what you think the speaker is trying to tell you. In some cases, a simple statement such as "Please tell me more about that" will help you become an active listener. Susan Scott, author of *Fierce Conversations*, offers this advice: "Dig for full understanding. Use paraphrasing and perception checks; don't be satisfied with what's on the surface."[18] When you become an active listener, you will make fewer mistakes, learn new information, and build stronger relationships.

If you would like to pursue additional resources to help you become a better listener, access the information available through the International Listening Association website. In addition, carefully examine Table 2.1, How to Be an Active Listener, and make every effort to implement its recommendations when you are interacting with others. You may be surprised by the impact you can make.

Critical Listening. To add depth to your active listening skills, consider honing your critical listening skills. **Critical listening** is the attempt to see the topic of discussion from the *speaker's* point of view and to consider how the speaker's perception of the situation may be different from your own. To improve your ability to critically view new information, be sure to listen for evidence that challenges, as well as confirms, your own point of

Table 2.1 ■ How to Be an Active Listener

1. *Develop a listening attitude.* Regard the speaker as worthy of your respect and attention. Maintain good eye contact and lean slightly forward. Don't rush the speaker. Be patient and refrain from planning what to say in response until the speaker has finished talking.

2. *Give the speaker your full attention.* This is not easy because most people can think at twice the rate that people talk. This allows your mind to roam. Your senses are constantly receiving extraneous information that may divert your attention, and many people will need to fight the urge to multitask, such as checking their mobile device.

3. *Clarify by asking questions.* If something is not clear because the speaker has referred to a person or an event that you are not familiar with, ask him or her to back up and explain. If you want the speaker to expand on a particular point, ask open-ended questions such as "How do you feel about that?" or "Can you tell us some ways to improve?"

4. *Acknowledge your understanding of the speaker's message.* Paraphrase, in your own words, your understanding of what the speaker has just said: for example, "Do you mean … ?" "What I hear you saying is … " or "In other words, we … "

view. This is especially important when there is no opportunity for feedback, such as when you are viewing television, listening to podcasts or TV news "sound bites," or reading blogs. Analyze the source of the information and determine its validity and credibility. Critical listening skills will help you avoid perpetuating erroneous information simply because you heard it through gossip, saw it on TV, or read it on a blog.

All of the communications filters identified in Figure 2.2 tend to distort your ability and willingness to listen, so activating your critical thinking/listening skills will take some effort.

To help you in this skill development process, ask yourself the following questions:

- Does the speaker's reasoning make sense?
- What evidence is being offered to support the speaker's views?
- Do I know each point to be valid based on my own experience?
- Is each point based on a source that can be trusted?[19]

Total Person Insight

Plenty of programs teach people to speak—but few train them to listen.

Even before the age of digital distractions, people could remember only about 10 percent of what was said in a face-to-face conversation after a brief distraction, according to a study that gauges conversational recall. Researchers believe listening skills have fallen amid more multitasking and interruptions.

Source: Sue Shellengarger, "Tuning Out: Listening Becomes a Rare Skill," *Wall Street Journal*, July 23, 2014, p. D4.

Empathic Listening. Another dimension to becoming a better listener involves empathy, which means understanding another person's feelings. Many workers today face serious personal or professional problems and feel the need to talk about them with

Empathic listening is an essential skill for business, whether you're a salesperson listening to a customer or a manager listening to an employee.

BlueSkyImage/Shutterstock.com

someone. They do not expect specific advice or guidance; they just want to spend some time with an empathic listener. Stephen Covey, the noted author and consultant, described **empathic listening** as listening with your ears, your eyes, and your heart.[20] If you want to practice empathic listening, adopt the following practices:

- *Avoid being judgmental.* Objectivity is the heart and soul of empathic listening. The person is communicating for emotional release and does not seek a specific response.
- *Acknowledge what is said.* You do not have to agree with what is being said, but you should let the person know you can understand his or her viewpoint.
- *Be patient.* If you are unable or unwilling to take the time to hear what the person has to say, say so immediately. Signs of impatience send a negative message to the person needing to talk.[21]

We live in a culture where empathic listening is quite rare. Interrupting has become all too common as people rush to fill every gap in the conversation. Nevertheless, empathic listening is greatly valued by those with personal or work-related problems—people want to spend time with a good listener.[22]

human RELATIONS in Action

THE POWER OF SILENCE

Each conversation we have with a coworker, a customer, or a significant other can enhance or weaken the relationship. A conversation that has the power to truly transform a relationship requires some silence. Yet, for most Americans, silence in a conversation is almost unendurable. Interrupting the other person or responding too quickly with little or no thought can weaken a relationship. Every important conversation requires moments of silence—time to reflect on what the other person has said and consider our response. During most conversations, do you use silence to improve communication? Analyze your response.

Source: Susan Scott, *Fierce Conversations* (New York, Viking, 2002), pp. 156–157. Chapter 7 is entitled "Let Silence Do the Heavy Lifting."

COMMUNICATIONS IN ORGANIZATIONS

2-4 The healthy functioning of any organization, large or small, depends on effective communication. Organizations use several different types of channels and media to communicate with employees, customers, partners, suppliers, and other stakeholders. This section will discuss trends influencing organizational communication and how organizations are communicating using various types of media. We will also discuss the positive outcomes new media has on both personal and organizational communication, as well as some of the challenges and limitations associated with digital communication.

Communication Channels

Communication flows through vertical hierarchies, horizontally across teams and departments, and cross-functionally in teams and/or across organizational structures. **Horizontal channels** are used to move information among people on the same level of authority, such as all the store managers of a national retail clothing store chain, all department chairpersons within a college, or all the administrative assistants within an organization. **Vertical channels** move information up and down through levels of authority within an organization. A message from the CEO or executive team of the organization will move down to the vice president(s), then to the manager(s), and then to employees.

Cross-functional communication can span across an organization regardless of hierarchy, departments or functions, or among a team comprised of different functional areas within a company such as marketing, sales, operations, customer service, and product development. Cross-functional communication is often used by companies because it increases the speed of communication and it improves decision making, productivity, and efficiency.

When communication channels are working effectively, everyone authorized to initiate and receive companywide communications will receive information in a timely manner. If the level of trust among those sending and receiving the information is fairly high, these messages will usually be understood, believed, accepted, and acted on. If the level of trust is low, however, employees will tend to put more faith in rumors, even if such information conflicts with the formal message.

Improving Upward Communication

Communicating down vertically is fairly routine, but communicating back up can be more difficult because managers sometimes fail to encourage the upward flow of information from employees. Every effort should be made to encourage upward and cross-functional communication. **Upward communication**, the process of encouraging employees to share their feelings and ideas with their managers, is one of the most effective ways to improve organizational communication and culture, and it is common among the best companies to work for in America. Employees with limited power are naturally very cautious about discussing mistakes, complaints, and failings with a more powerful person. However, when managers demonstrate the desire to listen to their subordinates, ideas, suggestions, and complaints begin to flow upward. They recognize that improving communications will inevitably help build trust among all employees, regardless of their position in the organization.

Informal Communication Channels

Messages passed through the horizontal and vertical channels can usually be tracked through linear paths, but the pathway of informal communication may look more like a cobweb interwoven throughout the organizational chart. Informal communication channels, often referred to as **the grapevine**, carry unofficial information and rumors, and they exist in every organization. The grapevine can have either positive or negative effects. Many times, it will clarify information sent through vertical and horizontal channels. At other times, however, messages may be exaggerated, distorted, or completely inaccurate. These rumors develop quickly when at least two conditions exist in an organization: high degrees of anxiety and a great deal of uncertainty. To quell rumors, top management must communicate in a timely and honest way.[23]

Rumors about individuals, or gossip, in the workplace can undermine morale, weaken authority, ruin reputations, and leave even the best teams decimated in its wake. When gossip reaches excessive levels, the most common cause is lack of communication and/or lack of clarity from management on key strategies, objectives, and initiatives. Management needs to work hard to (1) increase communication and (2) anticipate issues that might stimulate rumors and gossip.

COMMUNICATING IN A DIGITAL WORLD

`2-5` ## Enterprise Social Networks

Over the years, what started as intranets, organizations' internal websites and computer networks, evolved to become internal social networks, commonly called **enterprise social**

networks (ESN). Intranets were an interim solution that moved internal communication to an online environment, but it was still largely one-way communication that was fairly static. Enterprise social networks are far more effective because they streamline communication and increase collaboration across an organization. Some ESNs are used only by employees; others include external audiences such as customers and suppliers.

Companies have found enterprise social networks so valuable that adoption has grown quickly, especially in large companies. Deloitte estimated that over 90 percent of Fortune 500 companies had partially or fully implemented an enterprise social network by the end of 2013.[24] Enterprise social networks have a look and feel similar to other social media networks like Facebook and LinkedIn, so employees were quick to embrace them.

In addition to improving the speed of communication and increasing collaboration across work groups, ESNs offer several other benefits, including:

- Increased productivity, transparency, and efficiency as people share information files, resources, and skills.
- Improved collaboration on projects across teams and organizational departments.
- Improved customer service as teams respond more quickly to customers.
- Job satisfaction increases when people post job opportunities or recruit internal candidates to work on projects that match their interests.
- Knowledge transfer and idea generation spark ongoing innovation.
- Improved relationships as people share personal and professional interests across horizontal and vertical channels.

All of these benefits create a company culture that fosters growth, innovation, and improved employee engagement. According to McKinsey, 90 percent of executives in companies that use social technologies report measurable benefits from using them. As a result of accelerating adoption, executives want to increase social media skills with employees.

Working Virtually

The percentage of time people spend communicating through letters, phone calls, and face-to-face conversations has decreased as people use faster, more convenient communication technologies. Text messaging, instant messaging, tweets, e-mail, web and video conferencing, teleconferencing, and livestream events are a few of the technologies that have changed the way workers stay connected in a work setting. There are several factors driving change:

- *Growth of the virtual office.* Thanks to high-speed wireless Internet access and companies becoming more accustomed to a flexible, mobile workforce, millions of people now enjoy the "anytime, anywhere" office.
- *Cost effectiveness.* The low cost of digital communication is unsurpassed. It costs very little to share information with people on a local or global basis. The rising cost of travel has influenced how people choose to communicate.
- *Time effectiveness.* People can communicate with customers and teams across the globe in a fraction of the time it would take to fly to another location. The number of people that can be reached using digital technologies is unsurpassed. A meeting or event can now be streamed live anywhere in the world, reaching tens of millions of people.
- *Globalization.* As more and more organizations serve customers on several continents, or need to communicate with employees working in several different countries, digital communication enables more efficient communication across time zones.

In the frantic speed with which information now flows, many people forget that communication still must be carefully created before it is transmitted. If the message is not handled properly or is poorly written, the sender risks being misunderstood or giving the impression he or she is poorly educated or careless.

Social Media

Social media is comprised of online virtual communities and networks that enable people to share information and communicate with other people. A common thread running through all definitions of social media is a blending of technology and social interaction.[25]

The rapid growth of social media has completely changed communication from a one-way broadcast into a dialogue that enables anyone to interact and influence colleagues, customers, companies, and society with words, videos, photos, and music through the social media networks and media channels they choose to use.

Consumer-generated media created a huge shift in power, and companies are no longer in complete control of their brands. Consumers using sites like TripAdvisor.com and Amazon.com are more likely to trust the words of complete strangers than the companies advertising products and services.

Facebook, Twitter, and LinkedIn are three of the most popular social media networks, but there are dozens of others such as Pinterest, Instagram, and Tumblr that cater to specific niches—and new networks are being developed all the time. Add enterprise social networks to the mix and you can easily see that there is an abundance of communication sharing taking place every day, all day. Social media has increased the demand for employees who can write with clarity, understand the rules of etiquette, and have an awareness of the privacy and security issues that apply to users of various media platforms. Once a comment or photo is posted, it is etched in history forever. No matter how "private" a message is intended to be, it can be forwarded and shared with virtually anyone. If people send messages when they are feeling emotional or not thinking clearly, they may forget the impact their actions can have on their relationships and careers. Think before you hit the "send" button—and when in doubt, wait to send the message! Figure 2.3 summarizes the important social media principles.

Figure 2.3 ■ Social Media Principles

Listen. Social media is all about listening to what people are saying, what is important to them.

Learn. Social media requires an insatiable appetite for learning. It can spark new ideas and give you insight and perspective.

Engage. "Social" means engagement. If your goal is to build a huge following of friends or followers, you must ask: What is the objective?

Transparency. Social media is incredibly transparent. What you do and say is visible to the world.

Live by the golden rule. "Do unto others as you would have them do unto you" is a principle to live by every day.

Give more than you take. Early social media pioneers could have had an attitude of scarcity, but thankfully, they didn't. Share information freely to help others and believe that what goes around comes around.

Brand authenticity. Consistency of brand promise (personal or commercial) is important across all media platforms.

Source: Monique Reece, *Real-Time Marketing for Business Growth* (Upper Saddle River, NJ: Pearson Education, 2010), p. 238.

Mobile Communication

The ability to communicate instantly with anyone in the world, where, when, and how you wish, is influenced by mobile communication devices. Smart phones, cell phones, iPads, tablets, and wearables like watches and headphones are a few of the growing number of mobile devices that function as small computers. Just as most people wouldn't even consider leaving home without their keys and wallet, they won't leave home without at least one of these devices. Throughout the day, they will be used for e-mail, texting, searching the Internet, playing games, watching movies, listening to music, shopping, and dozens of other activities driven by an individual's personal communication preference.

Despite the growing variety and increased functionality of mobile communication devices, the basics of communication etiquette are as important as ever. Messages need to be tailored to the receivers and the situation. Abbreviated messages (OMG, LOL) are okay to use with friends but considered inappropriate in many business environments.

Although texting and e-mails are usually brief when using a small device like an iPhone, take a few seconds to check spelling and reread your message to avoid embarrassing mistakes. And never use your company e-mail or social media accounts to post personal messages on Twitter, Facebook, or other social media networks. Many employees have been fired as a result of a careless comment.

You would think a PR executive would know better than to make a racial tweet. Justine Sacco carelessly made a tweet as she boarded an 11-hour flight from London to Cape Town. By the time she landed in Africa the tweet had gone viral and she faced a raging backlash. Her tweet had become a trending topic on Twitter with the hashtag #HasJustineLandedYet. Although she deleted her offending tweet, and in fact her entire Twitter account soon after the plane landed, it was too late. She was fired from her job as communications director of Internet giant InterActive Corp., and she became infamously known for one of the biggest social media blunders of 2013.[26] As we have stated a few times already, don't be too hasty in clicking the send button. Also be mindful about keeping personal and business communication accounts separate. Many people have been

Source: Justine Sacco/Twitter

A hasty or careless comment posted in social media can lead to dire consequences the sender later regrets.

embarrassed, and even fired, as a result of inappropriate communication posted on a company account instead of a personal account.

Many people choose to bring their own mobile devices to work, and organizations have adopted BYOD (bring your own device) policies to ensure that confidential and classified information remains secure. Some security systems may disable certain apps and programs on company premises, or even between buildings, so it is always important to know and follow security protocols established for the organization you work for.

Voice mail etiquette is also important in a work environment. Be sure your recorded message is professional, includes your full name, and ideally when the caller can expect to have calls returned. If you won't be answering calls for an extended period of time, let callers know this and who they can contact regarding urgent matters during your absence. When you are connected to another person's voice mail, slowly state your full name, *a brief explanation of what information or action you need from that person* (the component most often neglected), your phone number, and the best time to reach you. All four components are necessary to avoid phone tag. Then if the receiver reaches your voice mail when calling back, he or she can simply leave you a voice message with the information you wanted. The communication loop is complete.

E-mail

Members of Generation Y often describe e-mail as "so last millennium." They prefer the instant gratification that comes with the use of instant messaging and text messaging. However, e-mail is still popular, especially for business messages that require persuasion, permanence, or formality. When you use e-mail, follow these guidelines:

Know Your Company's Policies. Most organizations monitor their employees' e-mail. Keep in mind that even deleted messages live on indefinitely in the company's hard drives and may resurface. E-mail that might be sexually offensive could be considered sexual harassment and have serious ramifications. Avoid sending personal e-mail messages on company time.

Use an Appropriate E-mail Address. Carefully design your e-mail address to give the impression you want to convey. Addresses such as Partyboy@___.com may be acceptable for personal e-mail but should never be used in a business setting.

Create a Descriptive Subject Line. This brief introduction to your message will cue the receiver as to the content of your message. Busy readers glance at the subject line and decide when and whether to read the message. Avoid use of a vague one-word subject line such as *important, update,* or *issue.*

Compose Clear, Concise Messages. The authors of *Send,* a combination stylebook and etiquette manual for e-mail users, say their title is intended to be an acronym, guiding us to improved e-mail use. Messages should be **S**imple, **E**ffective, **N**ecessary, and aimed at getting something **D**one. A message written in simple conversational language takes less time to write and is more pleasant to read. Tell readers what action you want them to take.[27]

Recognize E-mail Limitations. The missing element in e-mail and other electronic communication is *rapport,* that bonding state that is easier to establish in person or by phone. Facial expressions, tone of voice, gestures—important social cues—are missing in e-mail.[28] Readers often will not be able to tell if you are serious or being sarcastic, prying or simply curious, angry or merely frustrated. After creating your message, reread it as a stranger might. If words or phrases might be misconstrued, rewrite it to make sure it is clear and *exactly* what you mean to say (see Figure 2.4).

Figure 2.4 ■ E-Mail Best Practices

- Do not send e-mail when you are angry or exhausted.
- When a face-to-face meeting is necessary, do not use e-mail as a substitute.
- When receiving large amounts of e-mail, selectively choose which ones you want to read by scanning the subject lines.
- Make every attempt to create e-mail messages that are concise and error-free.
- Do not use e-mail to share rumors or gossip or to say anything sensitive or critical that touches on someone's job competence.
- Don't use company computers for personal matters.
- Don't send anything you wouldn't want published.

Source: Adapted from Mary Ellen Guffey and Dana Loewy, *Business Communications: Process and Product* (Mason, OH: Cengage Learning, 2011), pp. 196–197.

Blogs

A **blog** is a discussion or information site, usually written by one person, used to communicate perspectives and information about certain topics. Some blogs are integrated into a company website; others are posted separately on a platform like WordPress and reflect views of the CEO. Blogs are often used to keep interested subscribers, customers, and employees informed. Readers often leave feedback, so some blogs serve as a form of communication and market research.

Some companies encourage employees to create their own blogs. At SAS Institute more than 600 employees have their own internal blogs. Leaders at SAS believe that blogs covering a wide range of topics have helped develop a culture of cohesion.[29]

If you work for an organization that allows you to write a blog, make sure you follow established guidelines and protocols to avoid potentially contentious or sensitive issues. Both personal and professional blogging can have a very positive influence on your career and personal brand. Personal branding will be discussed in Chapter 11.

LOOKING BACK: SUMMARY OF LEARNING OBJECTIVES

1. Explain the communication process.

The age of information has given us major advances in technology-based communication. However, successful communication in a work setting requires human involvement. The diversity of today's workforce calls for a greater understanding of how to communicate effectively. Impersonal one-way communication methods can be used effectively to share basic facts, policies, and instructions. If feedback is necessary, rely on interpersonal communication that involves a two-way exchange. As noted in this chapter, two-way communication is often a complex process.

2. Identify and explain the filters that affect communication.

Messages are sent—and feedback is received—through a variety of filters that often distort the messages. Figure 2.2 provides a summary of the most common filters that can challenge both senders and receivers of messages. For example, body language conveys information through eye contact, facial expressions, gestures, and the use of personal space. When you are influenced by one or more of these filters, the message you receive may be totally different from what the sender was attempting to communicate.

3. **Identify ways to improve personal communication, including developing listening skills.**

   The sender and the receiver share equal responsibility for effective communication. Therefore, both sender and receiver should take the necessary steps to improve their personal communication skills. Individuals can make their messages clearer by choosing words carefully, using repetition, timing the message correctly, and considering the receivers' preferences. Personal communication can also be improved by the use of active, critical, and empathic listening skills.

4. **Understand how communications flow throughout an organization.**

   Effective communication in organizations unifies group behavior, builds teamwork, and contributes to improved productivity. Formal communication channels can be vertical or horizontal. The grapevine uses an informal approach to rapidly transmit information, but rumors or gossip may have a negative effect if the information is untrue.

Progressive organizations are constantly searching for ways to improve upward communication. They recognize that frontline employees are often in the best position to recommend ways to improve the organization.

5. **Learn how to communicate effectively using social media and other communication technologies.**

   The use of letters, phone calls, and face-to-face conversations has decreased as the use of digital communication has increased. Virtual offices and networks of workers connected by the latest technology are now mainstream. Digital communication is time efficient and cost-effective for organizations. However, the increase in the use of e-mail, text messaging, social networks, mobile communication, and other communication methods can create human relations problems. The rapid growth of social media has given every person the ability to interact with colleagues, customers, and friends.

KEY TERMS

impersonal communication, 25	active listening, 34	upward communication, 37
interpersonal communication, 25	critical listening, 34	grapevine, 37
feedback, 25	empathic listening, 36	enterprise social networks, 37
semantics, 26	horizontal channels, 36	virtual office, 38
culture, 27	vertical channels, 36	social media, 39
cultural intelligence, 27	cross-functional	blog, 42
nonverbal messages, 29	communication, 36	

CAREER INSIGHT

Business dealings in North America tend to be characterized by informality. Yet, too much informality during the job interview process can create problems. For example, addressing someone by their first name during the interview would be a mistake. And watch the lingo. Tory Johnson, president of New York-based *Women for Hire Inc.*, thought she had found a qualified and enthusiastic intern for her small recruiting firm. Then she received the candidate's thank-you note, which included words such as *hiya* and *thanx*, along with several exclamation points and a smiley-face emoticon. Johnson was put off by the shorthand language and decorative symbols.[30]

TRY YOUR HAND

1. During the next week, study the listening habits of students in another class in which you are enrolled. Keep a journal of your observations by identifying the nonverbal behaviors you witness. Are there barriers to effective communication between the instructor and the student? How do you believe the students' nonverbal behaviors might affect the relationship between the instructor and the students?

2. Print out the most recent e-mails that you have sent or received and bring them to class. Analyze their effectiveness in terms of the e-mail tips in this chapter. Did the messages violate any of the tips? If so, which ones? How could these messages be improved?

3. Begin to notice how you typically sit and stand when you communicate with others. Does your posture tend to project openness and confidence or do you minimize your energy and influence with poor posture? In the coming week, practice using a posture that reflects openness and confidence just prior to a stressful or important situation. What do you notice? Does it increase your confidence? Write down your responses to at least two different situations in which you purposely use posture to influence your outcomes.

4. Many times, we take the conversation away from others and make it our own. This practice not only wastes time, but is a major relationship killer. Here is how it works: At the beginning of the conversation, you tell the other person about a problem you are dealing with and, before you finish the story, the other person says, "I know what you mean," and then describes a personal experience that may or may not have anything to do with your problem. Once the other person takes over the conversation, a valuable exchange of ideas is probably lost. During the next week, monitor your conversations with friends, family members, and coworkers. How often did the other person attempt to take the conversation away from you? How often did you attempt to take over the conversation?[31]

5. Assume that you are currently employed by Toyota International in their Information Technology Department with offices in several countries around the globe. Next week, you will travel to Poland and Greece to check on the installation of new telecommunications equipment. Your manager told you that *most* of the people you will work with speak English. However, you want to be prepared to greet people and say "yes," "no," "thank you," and "goodbye" in the languages of the countries you will visit. Go to www.Babbel.com or to http://www.travlang.com/ and select the foreign language for which you would like to learn basic or advanced words. Begin practicing the basic words you would like to learn.

Now go to *http://www.kwintessential.co.uk/resources/ country-profiles.html* and click on the country that corresponds with the language you learned. Learn more about the country's social customs, such as rules and taboos of doing business, verbal and nonverbal communication techniques, decision-making techniques, and meeting, gift-giving, and dining etiquette.

CRITICAL THINKING CHALLENGE

1. As you build your human relations skills, it is very important to establish an acute sensitivity to the impact communication filters have on your interpersonal relationships at home and at work. Review Figure 2.2, and identify the communication filters that were in place during a recent face-to-face conversation, argument, or confrontation you had with another person. Did any of these filters interfere with your ability to send or receive the information being transmitted during the exchange? Evaluate how, if you were to repeat the interaction with this person, you could reduce the impact of these filters and thereby improve your ability to effectively communicate the messages you were sending and receiving.

2. A close friend and respected financial advisor employed by a brokerage services company sent you the following e-mail message: "It appears that your employer is planning to close one or two distribution centers within the next few months. I will let you know if I receive more specific information." Should you share this information with friends who work at your distribution center? Why or why not?

SELF-ASSESSMENT EXERCISE

Completion of this self-assessment will provide you with information needed to develop goals for self-improvement. Circle the number from 1 to 5 that best represents your response to each statement:

(1) strongly disagree (never do this); (2) disagree (rarely do this); (3) moderately agree (sometimes do this); (4) agree (frequently do this); (5) strongly agree (almost always do this).

A. I am able to send clear, concise verbal messages.	1	2	3	4	5
B. When people talk, I listen attentively and often use active listening skills.	1	2	3	4	5
C. I am conscious of how I express nonverbal messages (facial expression, tone of voice, body language, and so on) when communicating with others.	1	2	3	4	5
D. I understand the flow of communication in organizations and the positive and negative influence of informal communication.	1	2	3	4	5
E. I can describe the role of social media and other forms of digital media in the changing world of personal and professional communication.	1	2	3	4	5

After recording your response to each item, write down a goal for a skill you would like to improve. Describe the steps you will take to achieve this goal.

YOU PLAY THE ROLE

This role-play exercise is designed to enhance your awareness of the filters that can alter or aid a message between a sender and a receiver in the communication process. Review Figure 2.2 before you begin this activity. Select a partner, and be prepared to discuss specific information about your present or past work situation.

Assume the role of sender and share these ideas with the receiver. Did your message match what the receiver understood? What filters led to parallel communication, and what filters led to distortion? After you have discussed the complexity of the communication process, change roles; you are now the receiver and the receiver is the sender.

BELOW THE SURFACE | APPRECIATE COMMUNICATION STYLE DIFFERENCES

Henk Meijer/Alamy

At the beginning of this chapter you learned how Steve Jobs communicated with his team, in a style that was direct and what some may describe as abrasive or insensitive. On the other hand, Jobs was also described as having a deep sense of empathy and intuition for customers. He learned the importance of focus and gained a deep appreciation for intuition while studying Buddhism in India. "Our task is to read things that are not yet on the page."

For example, when a member of the original Macintosh team asked if market research should be done prior to a retreat, Jobs said, "No, because customers don't know what they want until we've shown them." Quoting Henry Ford, he said, "If I'd asked customers what they wanted, they would have told me, 'A faster horse!'"[32]

Biographer Walter Isaacson said people tend to focus on the "rough edges" of Jobs' personality, when in fact his communication style was the essence of his approach to business. His intensity led him to not just create great products, but to transform seven industries. Can you imagine a world with the iPhone, iPad, iMac, iPod, IPod nano, OS X Lion operating sytem, the iTunes Store, or the animation films produced by Pixar? We can't either.[33]

QUESTIONS

1. There is no doubt Steve Jobs was a great visionary. He was also a great entrepreneur who created one of the world's most valuable companies. But how would you describe his communication with others? Would you say

Steve Jobs was an effective communicator? Provide support for your answer, whether yes or no.

2. Imagine you are hired to work at Apple on a team reporting directly to Steve Jobs. How would you respond to working for a boss with his communication style? How would *you* need to change the way you give and receive communication when communicating with Jobs?

3. Imagine you are hired by Steve Jobs to mentor him on how he communicates with his staff and employees. What advice would you give him? How do you think he would respond?

CLOSING CASE

SHOULD EMPLOYERS RESTRICT SOCIAL MEDIA USE?

Just one Tweet, photo, e-mail, video, or post on Facebook can permanently damage a person's reputation and cause significant loss to companies and their investors. At a Domino's pizza store, one employee filmed another doing unappetizing things to food that was intended for a customer, then posted the video on YouTube. Domino's stock quickly plummeted by 10 percent.

Social media is powerful, and it's important to understand the repercussions before making a hasty comment one might later regret. Even a one-sentence post made on Facebook can cause an employee to be fired. Roy Rhone, Jr., a Frito-Lay warehouse employee, was fired after writing on Facebook he was "a hair away from setting it off in that b—."[34] Since facial expressions, gestures, and tone of voice are absent from social media posts, there is a risk that a message could be misunderstood. During the Arab Spring uprising in Egypt in 2011, Kenneth Cole posted, "Millions are in uproar in #Cairo. Rumor is they heard our new spring collection is now available online at [link]-KC." The humor was lost, and the company had to deal with its own uproar against

the brand as angry consumers responded with "#boycottKennethCole."

Companies want to know what their customers and employees are saying about them, so as the popularity of social media has skyrocketed, so has the number of social media monitoring tools. Some search tools like Google Alerts are easy to use, free, and available to anyone. Simply enter a name, company, or topic and you can receive daily alerts about the search term. Other social media monitoring tools like Radian6 and Hearsay are robust, scouring the Internet deep and wide to find what people are saying and report the status of their social reputation score.

Some business leaders who think little is being said about their companies are surprised to learn how much is actually being said. When one big company made this claim, Hearsay CEO Clara Shih said the tool turned up an astonishing 60,000 different social media pages where employees mentioned or discussed company matters (not including the thousands of employee profiles on LinkedIn).[35] Yes, Big Brother is not restricted to government; it has spread to corporate environments, too.

Where should a company draw the line with respect to social media use by its employees?

QUESTIONS

1. Imagine you are the CEO of your own company and answer the following questions:

   ■ What policies, if any, would you put in place for employees using social media? Defend your reasons, pro or con.

   ■ If an employee makes disparaging comments on her Facebook page about the company, should she be fired?

2. Go to http://www.google.com/alerts and sign up for two Google alerts on search terms that are interesting to you, such as a person, company, or sports team. Request daily alerts delivered to your e-mail. Evaluate the number of comments made on your search term, and note how many are positive or negative.

CHAPTER 2 ENDNOTES

1. Isaacson, Walter, "The Real Leadership Lessons of Steve Jobs," *Harvard Business Review*, April 2012, pp. 94–102.
2. Ibid.
3. Maggie Jackson, *Distracted: The Erosion of Attention and the Coming Dark Age* (New York: Prometheus Books, 2008), p. 14; "Maggie Jackson's Call for Focus—Fighting Back in an Age of Distractions," *A Buzzflash Interview*, June 30, 2008 [cited 30 June 2008]. Available from http:// blog.buzzflash.com/interviews/115; INTERNET; David Robinson, "What Were We Talking About?" *Wall Street Journal*, June 12, 2008, p. A15.
4. John Stewart and Gary D'Angelo, *Together—Communicating Interpersonally* (New York: Random House, 1988), p. 5.
5. For more information on the components of communication, see Scot Ober, *Contemporary Business Communication*, 5th ed. (Boston: Houghton Mifflin, 2003), pp. 5–9.
6. Douglas A. Bernstein, Louis A. Penner, Alison Clarke-Stewart, and Edward J. Roy, *Psychology*, 7th ed. (Boston: Houghton Mifflin, 2006), pp. 23–24.
7. P. Christopher Earley and Elaine Mosakowski, "Cultural Intelligence," *Harvard Business Review*, October 2004, p. 139.
8. Earley and Mosakowski, "Cultural Intelligence," pp. 141–142.
9. Reported in *Autoweek*, October 17, 2011, p. 107.
10. Balistreri, Jerry, "Preparing Students for the Workplace Via Body Language," *Techniques*, October 2013, www.acteonline.org/techniques/#.VRTG0vnF91d [registration required].
11. Goleman, Daniel, (1995), *Emotional Intelligence*, New York: Bantam Books, 1995.
12. Nick Morgan, "How to Become an Authentic Speaker," *Harvard Business Review*, November 2008, pp. 62–63.
13. Don Clark, "Communication and Leadership," July 17, 2005, pp. 9, 10 [cited 27 October 2005]. Available from http://www.nwlink.com/donclark/leader/leadcom.html; INTERNET.
14. Ibid., p. 7.
15. Dana R. Carney, Amy J.C. Cuddy, and Andy J. Yap, "Power Posing: Brief Nonverbal Displays Affect Neuroendocrine Levels and Risk Tolerance," *Psychological Science Online First*, September 21, 2010. pp. 1–4.
16. William B. Gudykunst, Stella Ting-Toomey, Sandra Sud-weeks, and Lea Stewart, *Building Bridges: Interpersonal Skills for a Changing World* (Boston: Houghton Mifflin, 1995), pp. 315–316; "Playing Keepaway," *Psychology Today*, June 2007, p. 15.
17. Sue Shellengarger, "Tuning Out: Listening Becomes a Rare Skill," *Wall Street Journal*, July 23, 2014, p. D4.
18. Susan Scott, *Fierce Conversations: Achieving Success at Work and in Life, One Conversation at a Time* (New York: Viking, 2002), pp. 156–157.
19. Michael Toms, "Dialogue—the Art of Thinking Together—Sparks Spirit of 'Aliveness' in Organizations," *The Inner Edge*, August/September 1998.
20. Stephen R. Covey, *The Seven Habits of Highly Effective People* (New York: Simon & Schuster, 1989), pp. 240–241.
21. C. Glenn Pearce, "Learning How to Listen Empathically," *Supervisory Management*, September 1991, p. 11.
22. Robert Epstein, "Waiting," *Psychology Today*, September/October 2001, p. 5.
23. Jared Sandberg, "Ruthless Rumors and the Managers Who Enable Them," *Wall Street Journal*, October 29, 2003, p. B1.
24. Fenn, Jess, "10 Enterprise Networks to Improve Company Communication," Mashable.com, June 14, 2013, http://mashable.com/2013/06/14/enterprise-social-networks/

25. Monique Reece, *Real-Time Marketing for Business Growth*, pp. 235–238; a definition of social media appears in Wikipedia, the free online encyclopedia.

26. Ed Pilkington, "Justine Sacco, PR executive fired over racist tweet, 'ashamed,'" *The Guardian*, December 22, 2013, http://www.theguardian.com/world/2013/dec/22/pr-exec-fired-racist-tweet-aids-africa-apology

27. John Derbyshire, "To: Emailers, Subject: Etiquette," *Wall Street Journal*, March 21, 2007, p. P10; Robert Kreitner, *Management*, 10th ed. (Boston: Houghton Mifflin, 2007), p. 362.

28. Marina Krakovsky, "Caveat Sender—The Pitfalls of E-mail," *Psychology Today*, March/April 2004, pp. 15–16.

29. David A. Kaplan, "The Best Company to Work For," *Fortune*, February 8, 2010, p. 62.

30. Sarah E. Needleman, "Informal Lingo Might Put Off Job Recruiters," *The News & Observer*, August 3, 2008, p. 49.

31. This exercise is based on information taken from Scott, *Fierce Conversations*, pp. 117–118.

32. Isaacson, "The Real Leadership Lessons of Steve Jobs."

33. Barbara Fredrickson, *Positivity* (New York: Crown Publishers, 2009), p. 55.

34. Melanie Trottman, "For Angry Employees, Legal Cover for Rants," *Wall Street Journal*, December 2, 2011, p. B1.

35. David Kirkpatrick, "Social Power and the Coming Corporate Revolution," *Forbes*, September 26, 2011, p. 78.

PART 2

Career Success Begins with Knowing Yourself

Henk Meijer/Alamy

CHAPTER PREVIEW

LEARNING OBJECTIVES

After studying Chapter 3, you will be able to

3-1 Understand the concept of communication style and its effect on interpersonal relations.

3-3 Discuss the major elements of the communication style model.

3-3 Identify your preferred communication style.

3-4 Improve communication with others through style flexing.

Understanding Your Communication Style

TIP OF THE ICEBERG | KNOWING WHO YOU ARE

Denise Russell Fleming, a vice president at BAE Systems Inc., discovered a flaw in her leadership style. She tended to overlook quieter colleagues during meetings and favor input from more talkative personalities. Fleming discovered this **unconscious bias** when she completed a training program offered by her company. She learned that most of us unwittingly favor certain types of people based on upbringing, experience, and values. Unconscious bias can be especially bad when it surfaces during employment interviews and performance reviews.[1]

Career success depends, in large part, on our ability to relate to people who vary a great deal in terms of their thoughts, feelings, and actions. Camille Wright Miller, an experienced trainer, consultant, and author, has worked with many effective leaders over the years. She says many of these leaders have the ability to "mirror" the behaviors of persons they communicate with. Psychologists and sociologists use the term **mirroring** to describe a situation where one person intentionally matches the communication style of the person he or she is meeting with.[2]

In many cases, subtle shifts in how you present yourself can increase the comfort level of the other person. If you participate in a job interview, observe key elements of the person's communication style. If the person speaks slowly and seems to deliberately select each word, consider slowing your own speech pattern. Your goal is not to manipulate or mimic the other person, but to avoid a situation where the other person is distracted by differences.

Photographee.eu/Shutterstock.com

Mirroring, as you see here, is a great way to help the person you're talking to feel more comfortable, which improves communication.

COMMUNICATION STYLES: AN INTRODUCTION

3-1 Have you ever wondered why it seems so difficult to talk with some people and so easy to talk with others? Can you recall a situation where you met someone for the first time and immediately liked that person? Something about the person made you feel comfortable. You may have had this experience when you started a new job or began classes at a new school. A major goal of this chapter is to help you understand the impact your communication style has on the impression others form of you. This chapter also provides you with the information you will need to cope effectively in today's workplace, which is characterized by a growing diversity and an increasing emphasis on teamwork.

human RELATIONS *in Action*

COMPETENT COMMUNICATORS

Competence in communicating starts with an understanding that we all have our own styles of communication—and different styles affect everything we hear and say.

Source: Eric F. Douglas, *Straight Talk* (Palo Alto, CA: Davies-Black Publishing, 1998), p. 1.

Communication Style Defined

The impressions that others form about us are based on what they observe us saying and doing. They have no way of knowing our innermost thoughts and feelings, so they make decisions about us based on what they see and hear.[3] The patterns of behavior that others can observe can be called **communication style**.

Each person has a unique communication style. By getting to know your style, you can achieve greater self-awareness and learn how to develop more effective interpersonal relations. Accurate self-knowledge is truly the starting point for effectiveness at work. It is also essential for managing the three key relationships described in Chapter 1: relationships with self, with another person, and with members of a group. If your career objective is to become a supervisor or manager, you will benefit by being more aware of your employees' communication styles.

Communication-Style Bias

Accurate self-knowledge is truly the starting point for effectiveness at work.

Your communication style is the "you" that is on display every day—the outer pattern of behavior that others see. If your style is very different from the other person's, it may be difficult for the two of you to develop rapport. **Communication-style bias** is a state of mind that exists at the unconscious level. Several training companies offer seminars that provide enrollees with a practical understanding of communication style theory and practice. Wilson Learning (www.wilsonlearning.com) offers a program titled "Building Relationship Versatility: Social Styles at Work." This program helps enrollees develop the interpersonal skills needed to work effectively with persons whose communication style differs from their own.[4]

Personality and Your Communication Style

Psychologists generally view **personality** as a unique pattern of enduring thoughts, feelings, and actions that characterize a person.[5] Scholars and researchers agree that personality is relatively stable, changing in only subtle ways over time. Our style of communicating, on the other hand, is an acquired behavior. Modifying your communication style is a skill that can be learned. Once you learn it, it's a skill you can use all your life.[6]

Fundamental Concepts Supporting Communication Styles

This may be your first introduction to communication styles. Therefore, let's begin by reviewing a few basic concepts that support the study of this dimension of human behavior.

1. *Individual differences exist and are important.* Length of eye contact, use of gestures, speech patterns, facial expressions, and the degree of assertiveness people project to others are some of the characteristics of a personal communication style. We can identify a person's unique communication style by carefully observing these patterns of behavior.[7]

2. *Individual style differences tend to be stable.* The basics of communication style theory were established by Swiss psychiatrist Carl Jung. In his classic book *Psychological Types*, he states that every individual develops a primary communication style that remains quite stable throughout life. Each person has a relatively distinctive way of responding to people and events.[8]

3. *There is a limited number of styles.* Jung observed that people tend to fall into one of several behavior patterns when relating to the world around them. He describes four behavior styles: intuitor, thinker, feeler, and sensor.[9] Those in the same behavior category tend to display similar traits.

4. *A communication style is a way of thinking and behaving.* It is not an ability but instead a preferred way of using the abilities one has. This distinction is very

important. An *ability* refers to how well someone can do something. A *style* refers to how someone likes to do something.[10]

5. *To create the most productive working relationships, it is necessary to get in sync with (mirror) the behavior patterns (communication style) of the people you work with.*[11] The ability to identify another person's communication style, and to know how and when to adapt your own preferred style to it, can give you an important advantage in dealing with people. Learning to adapt your style to fit the needs of another person is called "style flexing," a topic that is discussed later in this chapter.

Total Person | Insight

CLICKING SHAPES OUR LIVES

Whether it's at a party or at work, we all know what it feels like to "click" with another person. New research suggests that clicking plays a significant role in determining our career success.

Source: Ori Brafman and Rom Brafman, "Etc. Social Studies," *Bloomberg Businessweek*, June 20, 2010, pp. 72–73.

THE COMMUNICATION STYLE MODEL

3-2 This section introduces a model that encompasses four basic communication styles. This simple model is based on research studies conducted during the past 70 years and features two important dimensions of human behavior: dominance and sociability. As you study the communication style model, keep in mind that it describes your *preferences*, not your *abilities*.

The Dominance Continuum

In study after study, those "differences that make a difference" in interpersonal relationships point to dominance as an important dimension of style. **Dominance** can be defined as the tendency to display a "take-charge" attitude. Every person falls somewhere on the **dominance continuum**, illustrated in Figure 3.1. David W. Johnson in his book *Reaching Out—Interpersonal Effectiveness and Self-Actualization* states that people tend to fall into one of two dominance categories: low or high.[12]

1. *Low dominance.* These people are characterized by a tendency to be cooperative and eager to assist others. They tend to be low in assertiveness and are more willing to be controlled by others.
2. *High dominance.* These people give advice freely and frequently initiate demands. They are more assertive and tend to seek control over others.

The first step in determining your most preferred communication style is to identify where you fall on the dominance continuum. Do you tend to be low or high on this scale? To answer this question, complete the dominance indicator form in Figure 3.2.

Figure 3.1 ■ Dominance Continuum

Low dominance   High dominance

Source: From Manning, Gerald L., Michael Ahearne, Barry L. Reece, *Selling Today: Partnering to Create Value*, 13th ed., 2015.

Figure 3.2 ■ Dominance Indicator Form

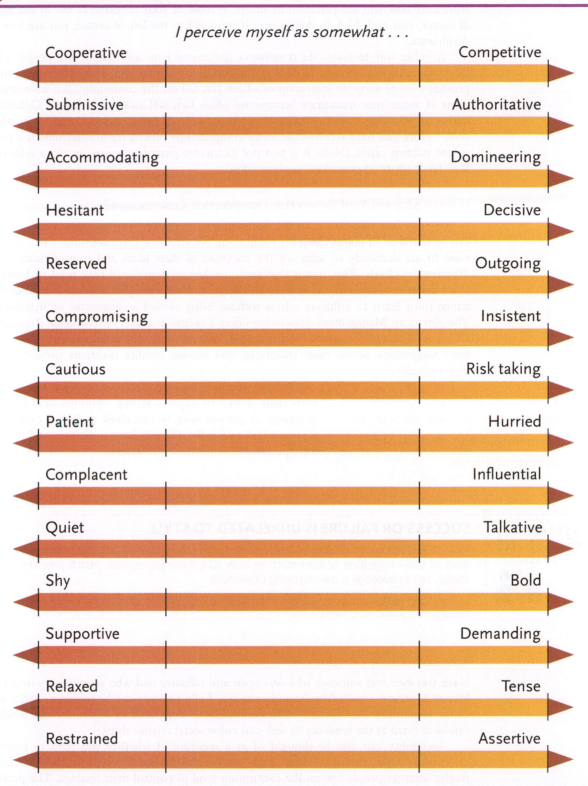

I perceive myself as somewhat . . .

Cooperative	Competitive
Submissive	Authoritative
Accommodating	Domineering
Hesitant	Decisive
Reserved	Outgoing
Compromising	Insistent
Cautious	Risk taking
Patient	Hurried
Complacent	Influential
Quiet	Talkative
Shy	Bold
Supportive	Demanding
Relaxed	Tense
Restrained	Assertive

Source: From Manning, Gerald L., Michael Ahearne, and Barry L. Reece, *Selling Today: Partnering to Create Value*, 13th ed., 2015.

Rate yourself on each scale by placing a checkmark at a point along the continuum that represents how you are perceived by *others*. If most of your checkmarks fall to the right of center, you rank high in dominance. If most fall to the left of center, you are low in dominance.

Another way to assess the dominance dimension is to ask four or five people who know you well to complete the dominance indicator form for you. Their assessment may provide a more accurate indication of where you fall on the continuum. Self-assessment alone is sometimes inaccurate because we often lack self-awareness. Daniel Goleman, author of *Working with Emotional Intelligence*, says self-awareness is a vital foundation skill.[13] Once you have received the forms completed by others, try to determine if a consistent pattern exists. (Note: It is best not to involve parents, spouses, or close relatives. Seek feedback from coworkers or classmates.)

Where Should You Be on the Dominance Continuum?

Is there any best place to be on the dominance continuum? Not really. Successful people can be found at all points along the continuum. Nevertheless, there are times when people need to act decisively to influence the adoption of their ideas and communicate their expectations clearly. This means that someone low in dominance may need to become more assertive temporarily to achieve an objective. New managers who are low in dominance must learn to influence others without being viewed as aggressive or insensitive. The American Management Association offers a course entitled "Assertiveness Training," which is designed for people who want to exercise a greater influence on others, get their suggestions across more effectively, and resolve conflict situations decisively yet diplomatically.[14]

People who are high in dominance must sometimes curb their desire to express strong opinions and initiate demands.

People who are high in dominance must sometimes curb their desire to express strong opinions and initiate demands. A person who is perceived as being extremely strong-willed and inflexible will have difficulty establishing a cooperative relationship with others.

human
RELATIONS
in Action

SUCCESS OR FAILURE IS UNRELATED TO STYLE

Your style is not based on how you see yourself. Your style is based on other people's perceptions of you—regardless of how much or how little those perceptions match your own self-image. Self-knowledge is the beginning of wisdom.

Source: Robert Bolton and Dorothy Grover Bolton, *People Styles at Work* (New York: American Management Association, 1996), p. 13.

The Sociability Continuum

Have you ever met someone who was open and talkative and who seemed easy to get to know? A person who is friendly and expresses feeling openly can be placed near the top of the **sociability continuum**.[15] The continuum is illustrated in Figure 3.3. **Sociability** can be defined as the tendency to seek and enjoy social relationships.

Sociability can also be thought of as a measure of whether you tend to control or express your feelings. Those high in sociability usually express their feelings freely, whereas people low on the continuum tend to control their feelings. The person

Figure 3.3 ■ Sociability Continuum

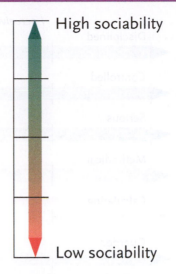

Source: From Manning, Gerald L., Michael Ahearne, and Barry L. Reece, *Selling Today: Partnering to Create Value*, 13th ed., 2015.

who is classified as being high in sociability is open and talkative and likes personal associations. The person who is low in sociability is more reserved and formal in social relationships.

The second step in determining your most preferred communication style is to identify where you fall on the sociability continuum. To answer this question, complete the sociability indicator form shown in Figure 3.4. Rate yourself on each scale by placing a checkmark at a point along the continuum that represents how you are perceived by others. If most of your checkmarks fall to the right of center, you are high in sociability. If most fall to the left of center, you are low in sociability.

The sociability indicator form is not meant to be a precise instrument, but it will provide you with a general indication of where you fall on each of the scales. You may also want to make copies of the form and distribute them to friends or coworkers for completion. (Remember, it is advisable not to involve parents, spouses, or close relatives in this feedback exercise.)

Where Should You Be on the Sociability Continuum?

Where are successful people on the sociability continuum? Everywhere. There is no best place to be. People at all points along the continuum can achieve personal and organizational success. Nevertheless, there are some commonsense guidelines that persons who fall at either end of the continuum are wise to follow.

A person who is low in sociability is more likely to display a serious, no-nonsense attitude when dealing with other people. This person may be seen as impersonal and businesslike. Behavior that is too guarded and too reserved can be a barrier to effective communication. Such persons may be perceived as unconcerned about the feelings of others and interested only in getting the job done. Perceptions are critical in the business world, especially among customers. Even a hint of indifference can create a customer relations problem.

Figure 3.4 ■ Sociability Indicator Form

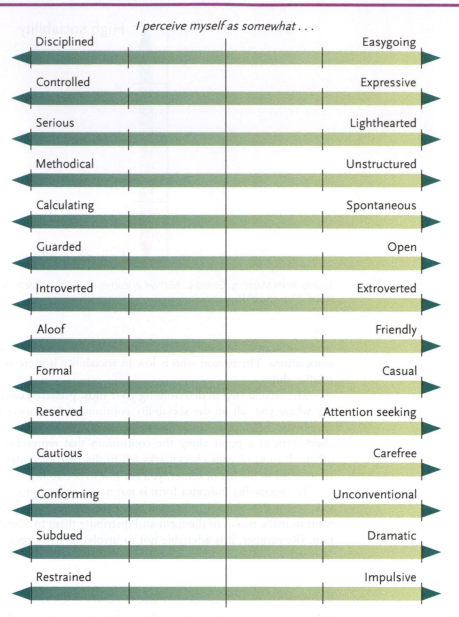

I perceive myself as somewhat . . .

Disciplined				Easygoing
Controlled				Expressive
Serious				Lighthearted
Methodical				Unstructured
Calculating				Spontaneous
Guarded				Open
Introverted				Extroverted
Aloof				Friendly
Formal				Casual
Reserved				Attention seeking
Cautious				Carefree
Conforming				Unconventional
Subdued				Dramatic
Restrained				Impulsive

Source: From Manning, Gerald L., Michael Ahearne, and Barry L. Reece, *Selling Today: Partnering to Create Value*, 13th ed., 2015.

People who are high in sociability openly express their feelings, emotions, and impressions. They are perceived as being concerned with relationships and therefore are easy to get to know. At times, emotionally expressive people need to curb their natural exuberance. Too much informality can be a problem in some work relationships. The importance of adapting your style to accommodate the needs of others is discussed later in this chapter.

Four Communication Styles

The dominance and sociability continua can be combined to form a rather simple model that will tell you more about your communication style (see Figure 3.5).

The **communication style model** will help you identify your most preferred style. Dominance is represented by the horizontal axis and sociability by the vertical axis. The model is divided into quadrants, each representing one of four communication styles: emotive, directive, reflective, or supportive. As you review the descriptions of these styles, you will likely find one that is "most like you" and one or more that are "least like you."

Emotive Style. The upper-right-hand quadrant combines high sociability and high dominance. This is characteristic of the **emotive style** of communication (Figure 3.6).

You can easily form a mental picture of the emotive type by thinking about the phrases used earlier to describe high dominance and high sociability. A good example of the emotive type of person is comedian Jay Leno. Ellen DeGeneres, talk-show host, and Suze Orman, noted authority on money management, also project an outspoken, enthusiastic, and stimulating style. Rachael Ray, host of several Food Network cooking shows, displays the emotive style. She is animated, frequently laughs at herself, and seems to like an informal atmosphere.

Here is a list of verbal and nonverbal clues that identify the emotive person:

1. *Displays spontaneous, uninhibited behavior.* The emotive person is more apt to talk rapidly, express views with enthusiasm, and use vigorous hand gestures. David Letterman,

Figure 3.5 ■ When the dominance and sociability dimensions are combined, the framework for communication style classification is established.

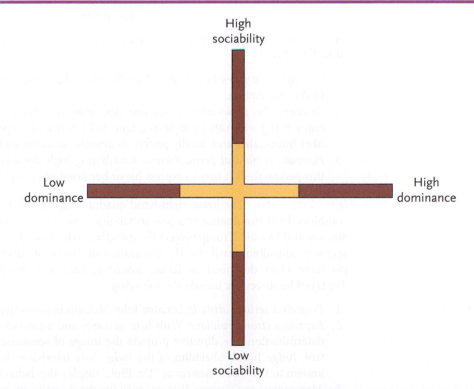

Source: From Manning, Gerald L., Michael Ahearne, and Barry L. Reece, *Selling Today: Partnering to Create Value*, 13th ed., 2015.

Figure 3.6 ■ The emotive style combines high sociability and high dominance.

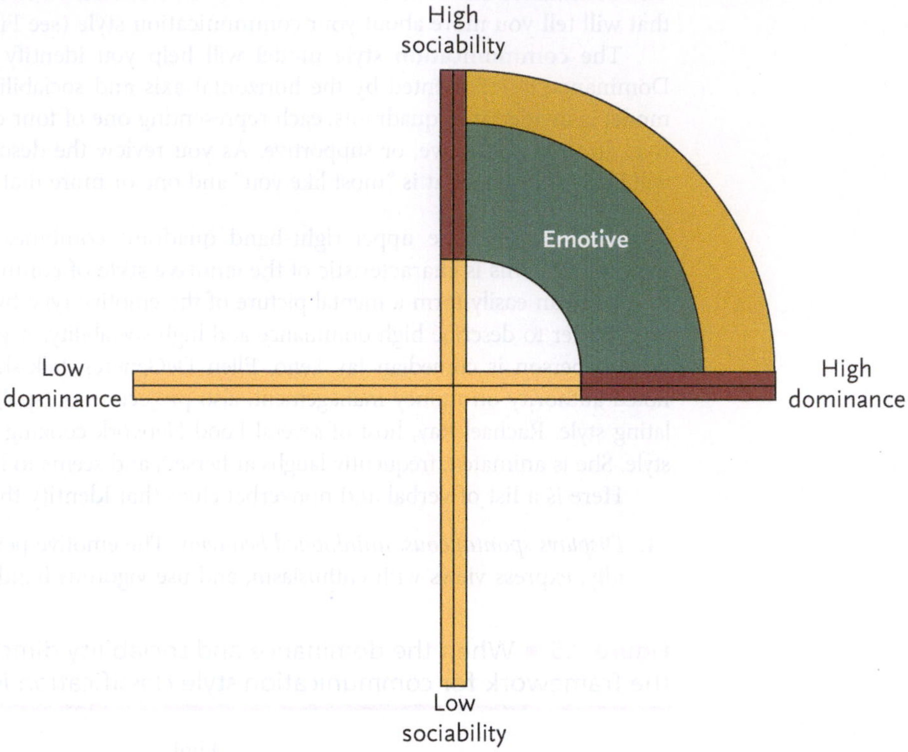

High
sociability

Emotive

Low
dominance

High
dominance

Low
sociability

Source: From Manning, Gerald L., Michael Ahearne, and Barry L. Reece, *Selling Today: Partnering to Create Value*, 13th ed., 2015.

late night talk show host, and Richard Branson, the founder of Virgin Atlantic Airways, fit this description.

2. *Displays the personality dimension described as extroversion.* Extroverts typically enjoy being with other people and tend to be active and upbeat. The emotive person likes informality and usually prefers to operate on a first-name basis.

3. *Possesses a natural persuasiveness.* Combining high dominance and high sociability, this person finds it easy to express his or her point of view dramatically and forcefully.

Directive Style. The lower-right-hand quadrant represents a communication style that combines high dominance and low sociability—the **directive style** (Figure 3.7). Martha Stewart and Donald Trump project the directive style. Tom Peters, the hard-driving management consultant, easily fits the description of this communication style. All these people have been described as frank, assertive, and very determined. Some behaviors displayed by directives include the following:

1. *Projects a serious attitude.* Senator John McCain projects the directive style.

2. *Expresses strong opinions.* With firm gestures and a tone of voice that communicates determination, the directive projects the image of someone who wants to take control. Judge Judith Sheindlin of the *Judge Judy* television show and Phillip McGraw, known to television viewers as "Dr. Phil," display this behavior.

3. *May project indifference.* It is not easy for the directive to communicate a warm, caring attitude. He or she does not find it easy to abandon the formal approach in dealing with people.

Figure 3.7 ■ The directive style combines high dominance and low sociability.

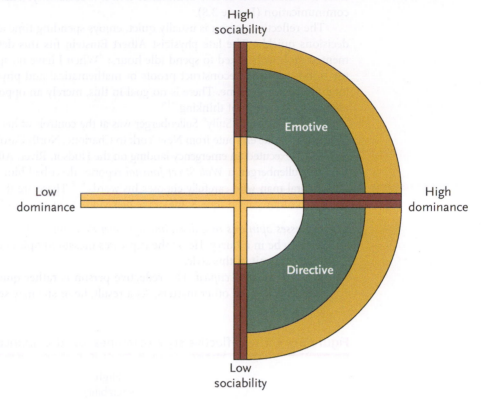

Source: From Manning, Gerald L., Michael Ahearne, and Barry L. Reece, *Selling Today: Partnering to Create Value*, 13th ed., 2015.

Mark Cuban, successful entrepreneur and owner of the NBA Dallas Mavericks basketball team, has been described as frank, demanding, and determined to achieve success.

Reflective Style.   The lower-left-hand quadrant of the communication style model features a combination of low dominance and low sociability. This is the **reflective style** of communication (Figure 3.8).

The reflective person is usually quiet, enjoys spending time alone, and does not make decisions quickly. The late physicist Albert Einstein fits this description. He once commented on how he liked to spend idle hours: "When I have no special problem to occupy my mind, I love to reconstruct proofs of mathematical and physical theorems that have long been known to me. There is no goal in this, merely an opportunity to indulge in the pleasant occupation of thinking."[16]

Captain Chesley "Sully" Sullenberger was at the controls of his Airbus A320 when it suffered a bird strike en route from New York to Charlotte, North Carolina. After the loss of both engines he executed an emergency landing on the Hudson River. After several interviews with Captain Sullenberger, a *Wall Street Journal* reporter described him as "...a precise, methodical, cerebral man who carefully chooses his words."[17] These are the characteristics of the reflective communication style. Some of the behaviors characteristic of this style are as follows:

1. *Expresses opinions in a disciplined, deliberate manner.* The reflective person does not seem to be in a hurry. He or she expresses measured opinions. Emotional control is a common trait of this style.
2. *Seems to be preoccupied.* The reflective person is rather quiet and may often appear preoccupied with other matters. As a result, he or she may seem aloof and difficult to get to know.

Figure 3.8 ■ The reflective style combines low dominance and low sociability.

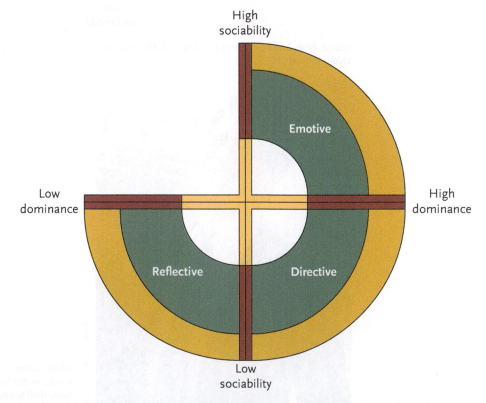

Source: From Manning, Gerald L., Michael Ahearne, and Barry L. Reece, *Selling Today: Partnering to Create Value*, 13th ed., 2015.

3. *Prefers orderliness.* The reflective person prefers an orderly work environment. At a meeting, this person appreciates an agenda. A reflective person enjoys reviewing details and making decisions slowly.

Supportive Style. The upper-left-hand quadrant combines low dominance and high sociability—the **supportive style** of communication (Figure 3.9). People who possess this style tend to be cooperative, patient, and attentive.

The supportive person is reserved and usually avoids attention-seeking behavior. Additional behaviors that commonly characterize the supportive style include the following:

1. *Listens attentively.* Good listeners have a unique advantage in many occupational settings. This is especially true of loan officers, sales personnel, and supervisors. The talent comes more naturally to the supportive person.

2. *Avoids the use of power.* Supportive persons are more likely to rely on friendly persuasion than power when dealing with people. They like to display warmth in their speech and written correspondence. The late Neil Armstrong, Apollo 11 crew member, and Julia Roberts, actress, display these behaviors.

3. *Makes and expresses decisions in a thoughtful, deliberate manner.* Supportive persons appear low-key in a decision-making role. Meryl Streep, Paul Simon, Meg Ryan, Kevin Costner, the late Princess Di, and Mary Tyler Moore all display characteristics of this style.

Figure 3.9 ▪ The supportive style combines low dominance and high sociability.

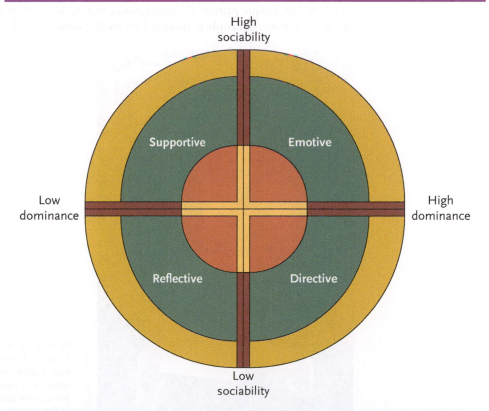

Source: From Manning, Gerald L., Michael Ahearne, and Barry L. Reece, *Selling Today: Partnering to Create Value*, 13th ed., 2015.

human RELATIONS in Action

INTERNATIONAL MARKET FOR FOUR-STYLE TRAINING

Although four-style programs were initially created and marketed in the United States, they have become a global phenomenon. Wilson Learning, a pioneer in four-style training for over 40 years, is doing business in 45 countries. Inscape Publishing, the company that developed the popular DiSC learning instrument over three decades ago, reports that more than 40 million people worldwide have completed DiSC four-dimension workshops.

Source: "A Global Profiling Tool" (Wilson Learning Corporation: Eden Prairie, MN., 1999); Tom Ritchey, *I'm Stuck, You're Stuck* (San Francisco: Berrett-Koehler, 2002), p. 5.

IDENTIFYING YOUR PREFERRED COMMUNICATION STYLE

3-3   A college professor enrolled in a four-style training program offered by Wilson Learning Corporation. After completion of a communication style assessment instrument, he learned that his preferred style was *reflective*. At first, the professor had doubts about the validity of the instrument. Over the years he had made many classroom presentations and viewed himself as an *emotive*. We must avoid stereotyping or pigeonholing persons who work in various occupations. Not all scientists are *reflective* and not all salespeople are *emotive*.

Did you find one communication style that is most like yours? If your first attempt to identify your most preferred style was not successful, do not be discouraged. No one conforms completely to one style. You share some traits with other styles. Also, keep in mind that communication style is just one dimension of personality. As noted previously, your personality is made up of a broad array of psychological and behavioral characteristics. It is this unique pattern of characteristics that makes each person an individual. *Communication style* refers only to those behaviors that others can observe.

Piero Oliosi/Polaris/Newscom

Susan Cain, author of the book *Quiet—The Power of Introverts In A World That Can't Stop Talking*, reminds us that it would be a mistake to view extroversion as the ideal personality trait. She points out that many of the best thinkers and leaders are introverts.

Did you discover a communication style that is least like yours? In many cases, we feel a sense of tension or discomfort when we have contact with persons who speak or act in ways that are at odds with our communication style. Susan Cain, author of the best-selling book *Quiet — The Power of Introverts in a World That Can't Stop Talking*, describes the tension that often surfaces when introverts and extroverts work together. It is often difficult for these two personality types to understand each other's ways of resolving differences.[18]

Online Assessment of Your Communication Style

You can gain additional insight into your communication style by accessing the product support website for this book at www.cengagebrain.com and clicking on the Online Assessment of Your Communication Style link. After completing the assessment, you will be provided with a profile indicating your most preferred communication style.

Variation Within Your Communication Style

Communication styles also vary in intensity. For example, a person may be either moderately or strongly dominant. Note that the communication style model features zones that radiate outward from the center, as illustrated in Figure 3.10. These dimensions might be thought of as **intensity zones**.

Zone 1. People who fall within Zone 1 will display their unique behavioral characteristics with less intensity than people in Zone 2. This means that it may be more difficult to

Figure 3.10 ■ Communication Style Intensity Zones

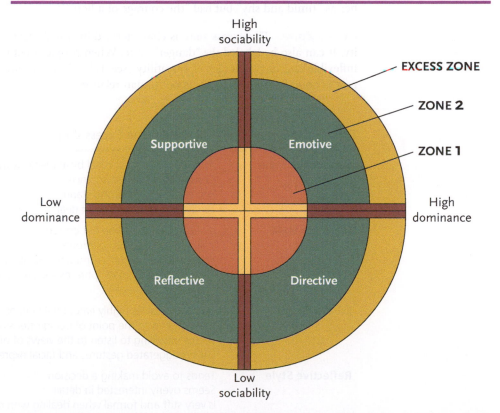

Source: From Manning, Gerald L., Michael Ahearne, and Barry L. Reece, *Selling Today: Partnering to Create Value*, 13th ed., 2015.

identify the preferred communication style of people in Zone 1. They will not be as obvious in their gestures, tone of voice, speech patterns, or emotional expressions. You may have trouble picking up the right clues to identify their communication style.

Zone 2.   People who fall within Zone 2 will display their behavioral characteristics with greater intensity than those in Zone 1. For example, on the following dominance continuum, Sue, Mike, Harold, and Deborah each fall within a different zone.

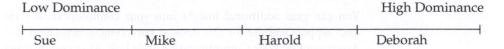

In terms of communication style identification, it is probably easier to distinguish between Sue and Deborah (who are in Zone 2) than between Mike and Harold (who are in Zone 1). Of course, the boundary line that separates Zone 1 from Zone 2 should not be viewed as a permanent barrier. It is important to understand that under certain conditions, people will abandon their preferred style temporarily.

You can sometimes observe this behavior change when a person is upset or angry.

One of the most important civil rights protests of the twentieth century was ignited by a soft-spoken, reserved black woman, Rosa Parks. One day she was returning from work on a crowded bus, seated in the first row of the Colored section. When the driver ordered her to give up her seat to a white passenger, she said, "No." She was arrested and charged with disorderly conduct. At the time of her death a flood of obituaries recalled her as "timid and shy" but had "the courage of a lion."[19]

Excess Zone.   The **excess zone** is characterized by a high degree of intensity and rigidity. It can also be labeled the "danger" zone. When people occupy this zone, they become inflexible and display a lack of versatility (see Table 3.1). Extreme intensity in any quadrant is bound to interfere with good human relations.

Table 3.1 ■ Behaviors Displayed in the Excess Zone

Supportive Style	Attempts to win approval by agreeing with everyone Constantly seeks reassurance Refuses to take a strong stand Tends to apologize a great deal
Directive Style	Is determined to come out on top Will not admit to being wrong Appears cold and unfeeling when dealing with others Tends to use dogmatic phrases such as "always," "never," or "you can't
Emotive Style	Tends to express highly emotional opinions Is outspoken to the point of being offensive Seems unwilling to listen to the views of others Uses exaggerated gestures and facial expressions
Reflective Style	Tends to avoid making a decision Seems overly interested in detail Is very stiff and formal when dealing with others Seeks to achieve perfection

Inflexible and rigid communication styles are likely to lead to a breakdown in human relations.

People often move into the excess zone when they are under stress or not feeling well. A person who feels threatened or insecure may also move into the excess zone. Even a temporary excursion into the excess zone should be avoided if at all possible. Inflexible and rigid communication styles are likely to lead to a breakdown in human relations.

Tips on Style Identification

To identify a person's communication style, focus your full attention on observable behavior. The best clues for identifying styles are nonverbal. Learn to be observant of people's gestures, posture, and facial expressions, and the rapidity and loudness of their speech.[20] Animated facial expressions and high-volume, rapid speech are characteristic of the emotive communication style. Infrequent use of gestures, speaking in a steady monotone, and few facial expressions are characteristic of the reflective style. Of course verbal messages will also be helpful. If a person tends to be blunt and to the point and makes strong statements, you are likely observing a directive.

We have noted that communication style is determined by where a person falls on the sociability continuum and the dominance continuum. Once you have identified as many verbal and nonverbal clues as possible, use this information to place the person on each continuum. Let's assume that the clues indicate that the person is low in dominance. This means you can automatically eliminate the emotive and directive styles because both are characterized by high dominance. The next step is to place the person on the sociability continuum. If the clues indicate that the person is low in sociability, you automatically eliminate the supportive style. By the process of elimination, you conclude that this person is probably reflective. The authors of *People Styles at Work*, however, warn that your initial perception of another person's style should not be carved in stone. You should continue to collect new information and reassess your initial observations (see Table 3.2).[21]

Table 3.2 ■ How to Read Others

Style identification is based on observation of behavior. Behavior is what a person does that can be *seen* and *heard*. Look for specific clues that are useful in discovering a person's style. Consider these examples:

Directive	Emotive
• Decides quickly	• Starts conversations easily
• Gets right to the point	• Makes friends easily
• Takes charge	• Generally outgoing
• Moves quickly	• Persuades others
Supportive	Reflective
• Listens patiently	• Thinks things through
• Relates to others warmly	• Not impulsive
• Avoids arguments	• Plans ahead
• Rarely makes demands of others	• Detailed reports and messages

Source: Robert Bolton and Dorothy Grover Bolton, *People Styles at Work* (New York: American Management Association, 1996), pp. 80–81; Tom Ritchey, *I'm Stuck, You're Stuck* (San Francisco: Berrett-Koehler, 2002), p. 78.

Keep in mind that different situations bring out different behaviors. If you observe someone participating in a classroom discussion, then later observe the same person relaxing with friends at a local restaurant, you may witness two different behavioral patterns. Getting to know someone is hard work, and it's best not to look for shortcuts.[22]

VERSATILITY: THE THIRD DIMENSION

3-4   Earlier in this chapter, we described two important dimensions of the communication style model: dominance and sociability. You will recall that these dimensions of human behavior are independent of each other. Now we are ready to discuss versatility, an important third dimension of human behavior.

Persons who can create and maintain interpersonal relations with others, regardless of their communication styles, are displaying versatility. **Versatility** can be defined as acting in ways that earn a social endorsement. Endorsement means simply other people's approval of our behavior. People give us their endorsement when they feel *comfortable* and *nondefensive* with us.[23]

The dimension of versatility is independent of style. This means that the emotive style is no more or less likely to be versatile than is the reflective style. Communication style remains relatively stable throughout life, whereas versatility is changeable.

Versatility is a trait we exhibit ourselves rather than elicit from others. Versatile people recognize that they can control their half of relationships and that it is easier to modify themselves than it is to modify others. The versatile person asks, "What can I do to make it easier for the other person to relate to me?"[24]

Research on versatility conducted by Wilson Learning Corporation indicates that the ability to adapt to another person's communication style greatly improves interpersonal relationships. People are divided nearly equally across the four communication styles, so we share our own style with only one out of four persons we have contact with. Once we develop and apply versatility skills, a greater number of people will feel comfortable and nondefensive in our presence.[25]

Achieving Versatility Through Style Flexing

Getting classified according to communication style doesn't mean you are typecast for life. You can always learn to strengthen areas of your most preferred communication style in order to get along better with others.[26] One way to broaden your personality is to engage in **style flexing**, which is the deliberate attempt to change your style to meet the needs of another person. It is a temporary effort to act in harmony with the behavior of another person's communication style. Style flexing is communicating in a way that is more agreeable to persons of other styles. As noted earlier in this chapter, you can learn to adapt your style to accommodate others.

human
RELATIONS
in Action

LET ANGRY FLIERS KNOW YOU ARE CONTRITE

Southwest Airlines uses communication style software to prepare letters sent to upset customers. Computers look for key words that show up in letters from angry fliers. The key words place the letter writer into four personality categories: Feelers (supportive); Drivers (directive); Entertainers (emotive); and Thinkers (reflective). The driver wants bullet points and results. The feeler wants to be caressed. A good apology can turn an angry customer into a loyal customer.

Source: Scott McCartney, "Who Is the Sorriest Airline?" *Wall Street Journal*, July 10, 2014, p. D1.

Gary Hershorn/Reuters

Versatility is a trait displayed by journalist Diane Sawyer, shown here with co-anchor Robin Roberts interviewing a guest. She has the ability to adapt to another person's communication style quite easily. The dimension of versatility is independent of style.

Style Flexing at Work.   To illustrate how style flexing can be used in an organizational setting, let's take a look at a communication problem faced by Jeff Walker, buyer of sporting goods for a small chain of sporting goods stores. Jeff's preferred communication style is *emotive*. His immediate supervisor is Rhonda Greenbaum. Her preferred style is *reflective*, and she tends to approach her work in an orderly, systematic manner. Jeff finds it difficult to curb his stimulating, promotional style and therefore is sometimes viewed as "unstable" by Ms. Greenbaum.

What might Jeff do to improve communication with his supervisor? Jeff is naturally an open, impulsive communicator. During meetings with a reflective person, he should appear less spontaneous, slow his rate of speech, and avoid the use of dramatic gestures. He should try to appear more reserved.

The reflective person admires orderliness, so Jeff should be sure he is well prepared. Before each meeting, he should develop a mental agenda of items that he wants to cover. At the beginning of the meeting he might say, "Ms. Greenbaum, there are three things I want to discuss." He would then describe each item concisely and present information slowly and systematically. This disciplined approach will be appreciated by the reflective supervisor.

Strategies for Adapting Your Style

Once you have identified the dominant style of the other person, begin thinking of ways to flex your style to gain a social endorsement. Remember, you can control your half of the relationship. What can be done to meet the interpersonal needs of the other person? Here are a few general style adaptation strategies:

Flexing to the Emotive Style

- Take time to build a social as well as a business relationship. Leave time for relating and socializing.
- Display interest in the person's ideas, interests, and experiences.
- Do not place too much emphasis on details. Emotive people like fast-moving, inspirational verbal exchanges.
- Maintain a pace that is fast and somewhat spontaneous.

Flexing to the Directive Style

- Be specific, brief, and to the point. Use time efficiently.
- Present the facts logically, and be prepared to provide specific answers to questions.
- Maintain a pace that is fast and decisive; project an image of strength and confidence.
- Messages (written or oral) should be short and to the point.

Flexing to the Reflective Style

- Appeal to the person's orderly, systematic approach to life. Be well organized.
- Approach this person in a straightforward, direct manner. Get down to business quickly.
- Be as accurate and realistic as possible when presenting information.
- Messages (written or oral) should be detailed and precise. The pace of verbal messages should be slow and systematic.

Flexing to the Supportive Style

- Show a sincere interest in the person. Take time to identify areas of common interest.
- Patiently draw out personal views and goals. Listen and be responsive to the person's needs.
- Present your views in a quiet, nonthreatening manner. Do not be pushy.
- Put a priority on relationship building and communication.

In those situations where you are trying to win the support or cooperation of another person, look and listen for clues that identify the individual's preferred communication style. Once you can recognize and adjust to communication styles different from your own, gaining a social endorsement will be much easier.

human RELATIONS *in Action*

DO THEM ANYWAY

Figure out what you are meant to contribute to the world and make sure you contribute it. If this requires public speaking or networking or other activities that make you uncomfortable, do them anyway.

Source: Susan Cain, *Quiet—The Power of Introverts* **in** *a World That Can't Stop Talking* (New York: Broadway Paperbacks, 2013), pp. 264–265.

In an organizational setting, style flexing is especially critical when something important is at stake. Let's assume that you are head of a major department in a large hospital. Tomorrow you will meet with the hospital administrator and propose the purchase of expensive new X-ray equipment. This is a good time to think about the administrator's communication style and consider your style-flexing strategies. Every decision is influenced by both reason and emotion, but the weight given to each of these elements during the decision-making process can vary from one person to another. Often we make the mistake of focusing too much attention on the content of our message and not enough on how to deliver that message.[27]

A WORD OF CAUTION

A discussion of communication styles would not be complete without a few words of caution. It is tempting to put a label on someone and then assume the label tells you everything you need to know about that person. In *The Name of Your Game*, Stuart Atkins says we should be careful not to use labels that make people feel boxed in, typecast, or judged. He says we should not classify *people;* we should classify their *strengths* and *preferences* to act one way or another under certain circumstances.[28] As noted in Chapter 1, the "total person" is made up of such interdependent traits as emotional control, values orientation, self-esteem, and self-awareness. To get acquainted with the whole person takes time and effort. Atkins makes this observation: "It requires much more effort to look beyond the label, to experience the person as a dynamic process, to look at the fine print on the box and carefully study the ingredients inside the package. We have been conditioned to trust the label and look no further."[29]

> *It is tempting to put a label on someone and then assume the label tells you everything you need to know about that person.*

You must also be careful not to let the label you place on yourself become the justification for your own inflexible behavior. If you discover that your most preferred communication style is reflective and take the position that "others will simply have to get used to my need for careful analysis of data before making a decision," then you are not displaying the characteristics of a versatile person. Try not to let the label justify or reinforce why you are unable to communicate effectively with others.[30]

Strength/Weakness Paradox

As noted previously in this chapter, there is no best communication style. Each style has its unique strong points. Supportive people are admired for their easygoing, responsive style. Directives are respected for the thoroughness and determination they display. The stimulating, personable style of emotive persons can be very refreshing. And the emotional control and disciplined nature of reflective persons are almost universally admired.

Problems arise when people overextend or rely too much on the strengths of their style. The directive who is too demanding may be viewed by others as "pushy." The supportive person may try too hard to please others and risk being viewed as "wishy-washy." An emotive person may be viewed as too excitable or not serious enough in a business setting. The reflective person who cannot seem to make a decision without mountains of information may be viewed as too cautious and inflexible. Some people rely too heavily on established strengths and fail to develop new skills that will increase their versatility.

LOOKING BACK: SUMMARY OF LEARNING OBJECTIVES

1. Understand the concept of communication style and its effect on interpersonal relations.

Communication styles are our patterns of behaviors that are observable to others. Each of us has a distinctive way of responding to people and events. Communication style bias is likely to surface when you meet someone who displays a style distinctly different from your own.

2. Discuss the major elements of the communication style model.

The communication style model is formed by combining two important dimensions of human behavior: dominance and sociability. Combinations of these two aspects create four communication styles—emotive, directive, reflective, and supportive.

3. Identify your preferred communication style.

With practice you can learn to identify your communication style. The starting point is to rate yourself on each scale (dominance and sociability) by placing a checkmark at a point along the continuum that represents how you perceive yourself. Completion of the dominance and sociability indicator forms will help you achieve greater awareness of your communication style. You may also want to ask others to complete these forms for you.

4. Improve communication with others through style flexing.

A third dimension of human behavior—versatility—is important in dealing with communication styles that are different from your own. You can adjust your own style to meet the needs of others—a process called style flexing.

We must keep an open mind about people and be careful not to use labels that make them feel typecast or judged. Keeping an open mind requires more thought than pigeonholing does.

KEY TERMS

unconscious bias, 51	dominance continuum, 54	reflective style, 62
mirroring, 51	sociability continuum, 56	supportive style, 63
communication style, 53	sociability, 56	intensity zones, 65
communication-style bias, 53	communication style model, 59	excess zone, 66
personality, 53	emotive style, 59	versatility, 68
dominance, 54	directive style, 60	style flexing, 68

CAREER INSIGHT

An organizational consultant noticed something unusual during a visit to a large engineering firm. Most employees wore plastic name tags with large capitalized letters after their names: Sue Banson ENFP or Raymond Bloom INTJ. Every employee in the company had completed the Myers-Briggs personality inventory. Each employees' four-letter personality description was on display so coworkers could quickly understand their personality type. Good idea? This approach will create problems if employees assume the labels of any personality test tells them everything they need to know. The Myers-Briggs personality descriptor is just the tip of the iceberg.

Source: Judith Sills, "When Personalities Clash," *Psychology Today*, November/December 2006, pp. 51–62.

TRY YOUR HAND

1. Jimmy Fallon is a popular late night comedian. Consider the behaviors he displays on his show, and then complete the following exercises:
   a. On the dominance continuum, place a mark where you feel he belongs.
   b. On the sociability continuum, place a mark where you feel he belongs.
   c. On the basis of these two continua, determine Jimmy Fallon's communication style.
   d. In your opinion, does he display style flexibility?

2. Myers-Briggs personality types and Jungian personality types are two very popular descriptions of the concepts in this chapter. Using your search engine, access the Internet sites that refer to these concepts. Type in "Jungian" + personality profiles to access the Jungian personality types. To access the Myers-Briggs types, type in "Myers-Briggs" + personality profiles. To obtain an understanding of your own personality type, complete an actual MBTI test (consisting of yes-or-no questions) available on the Internet. Type awareness can set the stage for better relationships.

3. Self-awareness is very important. As we get to know ourselves, we can identify barriers to acceptance by others. Once you have identified your most preferred communication style, you have taken a big step in the direction of self-awareness. If you have not yet determined your most preferred communication style, take a few minutes to complete the dominance

indicator form (Figure 3.2) and the sociability indicator form (Figure 3.4). Follow the instructions provided.

4. You have been given the opportunity to complete an online assessment of your communication style (see page 65). After completion of this assessment, you were provided with a profile that indicates your most preferred communication style. In some work or social situations, you may find yourself exhibiting a communication style that is different from your preferred style. Reflect on a situation where you engaged in style flexing. What communication style did you display? Did the movement away from your most preferred style improve communication?

5. Visit the websites of Wilson Learning Worldwide and Inscape Publishing and review the popular communication style training programs offered by each company.

CRITICAL THINKING CHALLENGE

1. After you have determined your own place on the dominance scale, think about your closest coworkers and friends. Who is the most dominant in your circle? Who is the least dominant? Can you recall occasions when either low dominance or high dominance created a barrier to effective interpersonal relations?

2. After you have determined your position on the sociability scale, think about your closest coworkers and friends. Who is the highest on the sociability indicator? Who is the lowest? Can you recall an occasion when high sociability or low sociability created a barrier to effective interpersonal relations?

SELF-ASSESSMENT EXERCISE

For each of the following statements, circle the number from 1 to 5 that best represents your response to each statement: (1) strongly disagree (never do this); (2) disagree (rarely do this); (3) moderately agree (sometimes do this); (4) agree (frequently do this); (5) strongly agree (almost always do this).

	1	2	3	4	5
A. I have a clear understanding of the two dimensions of human behavior: dominance and sociability.	1	2	3	4	5
B. I can describe the verbal and nonverbal clues that identify each of the four basic communication styles.	1	2	3	4	5
C. I accept the fact that each communication style has its unique strong points and that there is no "best" communication style.	1	2	3	4	5
D. I make a deliberate attempt to change my communication style (style flexing) in order to meet the needs of other persons.	1	2	3	4	5

After identifying your response to each item, select an attitude or skill you would like to improve. Prepare a written goal and then describe the steps you will take to achieve this goal.

YOU PLAY THE ROLE

For the purpose of this role-play, read the Closing Case: Style Flexing and assume the role of Eric Welch, who is described as a quiet, amiable person who displays the supportive communication style.

You will meet with Susan Hernandez, who has set up an appointment to inspect the property you represent. Prior to the role-play, study the chapter material on style flexing and on how to communicate effectively with persons who display the directive communication style. Prepare for the first five to seven minutes of the meeting. How will you present yourself during the initial contact? What would be the best way to get the meeting off to a good start?

BELOW THE SURFACE | THE CHALLENGE OF UNCONSCIOUS BIAS

The concept of "unconscious bias" was introduced at the beginning of the chapter. Thomas Lynch, a self-described introvert, experienced this bias during his early years at SAP America. As a sales-support executive at this maker of business-applications software, he was very successful. Customers were comfortable with his reflective communication style. He was a good listener and was able to discover client needs with appropriate questions. Despite his excellent sales record, he was passed over for leadership roles because of his quiet personality. He was viewed as someone who lacked drive and ambition. Lynch decided to hire a career and leadership coach who would help him make his strengths clearer to others.[31]

QUESTIONS

1. What steps can Thomas Lynch take to convince others that he can be successful in a senior executive position? What are the best qualities tied to his reflective communication style?

2. What are some risks Lynch will face if he suddenly develops the behavior of a backslapping extrovert?

CLOSING CASE | STYLE FLEXING

Eric Welch has been employed at Grant Real Estate for almost two years. Before receiving his real estate license, he was a property manager with a large real estate agency in another community. During his first year with Grant, he was assigned to the residential property division and sold properties totaling $825,000. He then requested and received a transfer to the commercial division.

Three months ago, Eric obtained a commercial listing that consisted of 26 acres of land near a growing residential neighborhood. The land is zoned commercial and appears to be ideally suited for a medium-size shopping center. Eric prepared a detailed prospectus and sent it to Susan Hernandez, president of Mondale Growth Corporation, a firm specializing in the development of shopping centers. One week later, he received a letter from Ms. Hernandez requesting more information. Shortly after receiving Eric's response, Ms. Hernandez called to set up an appointment to inspect the property. A time and date were finalized, and Eric agreed to meet her plane and conduct a tour of the property.

Eric is a quiet, amiable person who displays the *supportive* communication style. Friends say that they like to spend time with him because he is a good listener.

QUESTIONS

1. If Ms. Hernandez displays the characteristics of the *directive* communication style, how should Eric conduct himself during the meeting? Be specific as you analyze those behaviors that would be admired by Ms. Hernandez.

2. If Ms. Hernandez wants to build rapport with Eric Welch, what behaviors should she display?

3. It is not a good idea to put a label on someone and then assume the label tells us everything about the person. As Eric attempts to build rapport with Ms. Hernandez, what other personal characteristics should he try to identify?

CHAPTER 3 ENDNOTES

1. Joann S. Lublin, "Do You Know Your Hidden Work Biases?" *Wall Street Journal*, January 10, 2014, p. B1.
2. Camille Wright Miller, "Mirroring Others Helps You Connect with Them," *The Roanoke Times*, August 24, 2005.
3. Robert Bolton and Dorothy Grover Bolton, *People Styles at Work* (New York: AMACOM, 1996), p. 10.
4. For a complete description of "Building Relationship Versatility: Social Styles at Work," visit the Wilson Learning website, www.wilsonlearning.com (accessed January 20, 2013).
5. Douglas A. Bernstein, Louis A. Penner, Alison Clarke-Stewart, and Edward J. Roy, *Psychology*, 7th ed. (Boston: Houghton Mifflin, 2006), p. 540.
6. Erik F. Douglas, *Straight Talk* (Palo Alto, CA: Davies-Black Publishing, 1998), pp. 10–11.
7. Tony Alessandra, *Behavioral Profiles: Participant Workbook* (San Diego: Pfeiffer & Company, 1994), p. 12.
8. Bolton and Bolton, *People Styles at Work*, pp. ix–x.
9. Ibid., p. x.
10. Robert J. Sternberg, *Thinking Styles* (New York: Cambridge University Press, 1997), p. 8.
11. Bolton and Bolton, *People Styles at Work*, p. x.
12. David W. Johnson, *Reaching Out—Interpersonal Effectiveness and Self-Actualization* (Boston: Allyn and Bacon, 2003), pp. 82–83. The dominance factor was described in an early book by William M. Marston, *The Emotions of Normal People* (New York: Harcourt, 1928). Research conducted by Rolfe La Forge and Robert F. Suczek resulted in the development of the Interpersonal Check List (ICL), which features a dominant-submissive scale. A person who receives a high score on the ICL tends to lead, persuade, and control others. The Interpersonal Identity Profile, developed by David W. Merrill and James W. Taylor, features a factor called "assertiveness." Persons classified as high in assertiveness tend to have strong opinions, make quick decisions, and be directive when dealing with people. Persons classified as low in assertiveness tend to voice moderate opinions, make thoughtful decisions, and be supportive when dealing with others.
13. Daniel Goleman, *Working with Emotional Intelligence* (New York: Bantam Books, 1998), p. 54.
14. "Assertiveness Training," http://www.amanet.org/ seminars; INTERNET.
15. The research conducted by La Forge and Suczek resulted in identification of the hostile/loving continuum, which is similar to the sociability continuum. Their Interpersonal Check List features this scale. L. L. Thurstone and T. G. Thurstone developed the Thurstone Temperament Schedule, which provides an assessment of a "sociable" factor. Persons with high scores in this area enjoy the company of others and make friends easily. The Interpersonal Identity Profile developed by Merrill and Taylor contains an objectivity continuum. A person with low objectivity is seen as attention seeking, involved with the feelings of others, informal, and casual in social relationships. A person who is high in objectivity tends to be indifferent toward the feelings of others. This person is formal in social relationships.
16. "On the Human Side," *Time*, February 19, 1979, p. 75.
17. Jeffrey Zaslow, "What We Can Learn from Sully's Journey," *Wall Street Journal*, October 14, 2009, p. D1.
18. Susan Cain, *Quiet—The Power of Introverts in a World That Can't Stop Talking* (New York: Broadway Paperbacks, 2013), pp. 224–227.
19. Ibid, pp. 1–2
20. Bolton and Bolton, *People Styles at Work*, p. 87.
21. Ibid.
22. "Ask Dr. E," *Psychology Today*, January/February 2000, p. 28.
23. David W. Merrill and Roger H. Reid, *Personality Styles and Effective Performance* (Radnor, PA: Chilton Book, 1981), p. 88.
24. Wilson Learning Corporation, *Growth Through Versatility* (Eden Prairie, MN.: Wilson Learning Corporation), p. 4.
25. "Versatility: The Key to Sales Performance" (Edina, MN: Wilson Learning Worldwide, 2004), pp. 1–4.
26. Bob Reeves, "It Takes All Types," *Lincoln Star*, May 24, 1994, p. 11.
27. Gary A. Williams and Robert B. Miller, "Changing the Way You Persuade," *Harvard Business Review*, May 2002, pp. 65–67.
28. Stuart Atkins, *The Name of Your Game* (Beverly Hills, CA: Ellis & Stewart, 1981), pp. 49–50.
29. Ibid., p. 51
30. Chris Lee, "What's Your Style?" *Training*, May 1991, p. 28.
31. Sue Shellenbarger, "Career Makeover: Shaking Off a Shy Image," *Wall Street Journal*, January 15, 2014, p. D3.

Henk Meijer/Alamy

Building High Self-Esteem

TIP OF THE ICEBERG | MASTER OF MENTORING

Kevin Ollie, head coach of the University of Connecticut men's basketball team, followed an unusual path to a coaching career. Throughout a 13-year period he played for 11 National Basketball Association franchises. Ollie was not an NBA star who scored a lot of points. General managers kept signing him because of his character. When the Oklahoma City Thunder recruited Ollie, they wanted someone who could reshape the franchise culture. Ollie was viewed as a mentor because of his outstanding human qualities. Rob Hennigan, a member of the front office staff, said:[1]

> There's a certain presence and energy level he has that galvanizes a crowd or a team to want to be a part of whatever it is that he's doing.

Those who are involved in NBA team development say that Keven Ollie has had a positive influence on superstar teammates such as LeBron James and Kevin Durant. Today Ollie is mentoring college athletes, a role he finds very satisfying: "I want to stay invested in the student-athletes' lives on and off the court."[2] After the UConn Huskies won the national college basketball championship in 2014, Ollie was given a five-year contract estimated at $7.5 million. The role of mentoring in increasing self-esteem will be discussed later in this chapter.

Marcy Maloy/Digital Vision/Getty Images

Kevin Ollie has been described as an NBA player in university coach's suit. Prior to being named head coach of the University of Connecticut Men's basketball team, he was a point guard for 11 NBA franchises in his thirteen year professional career.

Jamie Squire/Getty Images

THE IMPORTANCE OF SELF-ESTEEM

4-1   The importance of self-esteem as a guiding force in our lives cannot be overstated. Your self-esteem includes your feelings about your adequacy in the many roles you play in life—friend, brother or sister, daughter or son, employee or employer, a student leader, and so on. In this chapter, we will discuss how self-esteem is developed and identify ways to raise your self-esteem. This information will help you realize your full human potential, both individually and as a group member.

> *The importance of self-esteem as a guiding force in our lives cannot be overstated.*

Self-Esteem = Self-Efficacy + Self-Respect

Nathaniel Branden, author of *The Six Pillars of Self-Esteem* and *Self-Esteem at Work*, has spent the past three decades studying the psychology of self-esteem. He states that the ultimate source of **self-esteem** can only be internal: It is the relationship between a person's self-efficacy and self-respect. **Self-efficacy** is the learned expectation of success. What we do or try to do is controlled by our perceptions or beliefs about our chances of success at a particular task or problem.

human RELATIONS *in Action*

DON'T ACCEPT A DIMINISHED SENSE OF SELF-ESTEEM

Wolfgang Puck, successful chef and restaurateur, started cooking with his mother at age 12. When he was 14, he became a chef's apprentice at a hotel in Austria:

> My stepfather said I was good for nothing. A month into my apprenticeship, the chef fired me. I walked to a bridge—I thought I'd kill myself before I proved my stepfather right. Instead, I asked for my job back. The chef let me stay.

A few years later he was the night chef at a Paris restaurant:

One day the sous chef came over and said, "Who made this sauce?" I said "Me," and he said, "This is the best sauce I've ever had." That's when I knew I was pretty good.

Source: "Wolfgang Puck—How Did I Get Here?" *Bloomberg Businessweek*, January 1, 2014, p. 68.

Self-efficacy can influence which tasks you take on and which ones you avoid. Albert Bandura, a professor at Stanford University and one of the foremost self-efficacy researchers, views this component of self-esteem as a strong belief in your own abilities. For example, an administrative assistant who masters a sophisticated computerized accounting system is more likely to tackle future complicated computer programs than is a person who feels computer illiterate and may not even try to figure out the new program, regardless of how well he or she *could* do it.[3] People with a strong sense of self-efficacy recover quickly from setbacks and disappointments.

Self-respect, the second component of self-esteem, is what you think and feel about yourself. Your judgment of your own value is a primary factor in achieving personal and career success. People who respect themselves tend to act in ways that confirm and reinforce this respect. People who lack self-respect may put up with verbal or physical abuse from others because they feel they are unworthy of praise and deserve the abuse. Nathaniel Branden believes that the healthier our self-esteem, the more inclined we are to treat others with respect, goodwill, and fairness, since we do not tend to perceive them as a threat, and since self-respect is the foundation of respect for others.[4]

To achieve stardom in the competitive world of country music, Alan Jackson had to value and respect himself in spite of years of disappointment. His music was rejected by all of the major Nashville labels before his "star quality" was finally discovered.

Danny E Hooks/Shutterstock.com

Authentic Self-Esteem

The National Association for Self-Esteem (NASE) helps us make the distinction between authentic (healthy) self-esteem and false (unhealthy) self-esteem. *Authentic self-esteem* is not expressed by self-glorification at the expense of others or by the attempt to diminish others so as to elevate oneself.[5] Arrogance, boastfulness, and overestimation of your abilities are more likely to reflect inadequate self-esteem than, as it might appear, too much self-esteem. Aimee Lee Ball, in her groundbreaking article entitled, "The New & Improved Self-Esteem," says: "It's not about pumping yourself up so you feel fabulous 100 percent of the time. It's not about your friends—or your mother— telling you you're the tops, the best in the world, no wait, the entire universe."[6]

HOW SELF-ESTEEM DEVELOPS

4-2   To understand the development of self-esteem, it is helpful to examine how you formed your self-concept. Your **self-concept** is the bundle of facts, opinions, beliefs, and perceptions about yourself that are present in your life every moment of every day.[7] The self-concept you have today reflects information you have received from others and life events that occurred throughout childhood, adolescence, and adulthood. You are *consciously* aware of some of the things you have been conditioned to believe about yourself. But many comments and events that have shaped your self-concept are processed at the *unconscious* level and continue to influence your judgments, feelings, and behaviors whether you are aware of them or not.[8]

Childhood

Researchers in the field of **developmental psychology** are concerned with the course and causes of developmental changes over a person's lifetime. They pay close attention to *genetic* and *environmental* factors (nature versus nurture).[9] Although space does not permit a detailed discussion here of cognitive, social, and emotional development during early childhood, we can state with conviction that developmental experiences during the first few years of life are extremely important. For example, too little attention from nurturing parents and too much television viewing can hinder healthy childhood development.[10] Because childhood events are retained in your brain, poor performance in school, abusive or uncaring parents, or a serious childhood accident can be defining experiences in your life. Messages from siblings, teachers, and various authority figures can have a lasting impact on your self-concept. These childhood experiences can form the foundation for your level of self-esteem that emerges later in life.

Today many parents report that they are struggling to find the right level of self-esteem for their children. Recent research indicates there are risks of overpraising a child. Inflating children's self-esteem too much can backfire, making them feel worse later when they hit setbacks. A better path is to praise children for the *effort* they invest. Parents who provide ample chances for their kids to develop new skills and capabilities allow self-esteem to blossom naturally through experience.[11]

Adolescence

The transition from childhood to adulthood can be a long and difficult period. At about age 11, children begin to describe themselves in terms of social relationships and personality traits. Many of the problems of adolescence are associated with challenges to young people's self-esteem, their sense of being capable, and worthy of respect.[12]

As adolescents attempt to resolve questions about self-worth, sexuality, and independence, they may "try out" alternative identities. Teens often turn to movies, music videos, and magazines for guidance and try to emulate the unrealistic body images and fashions that their peers deem worthwhile. Adolescence can last well into the 20s as each person tries to develop his or her own unique identity.[13]

As adolescents become more self-conscious, they gradually develop a personal identity as unique individuals. That identity may be affected by their *ethnic identity*—the part of a person's identity that is shaped by the racial, religious, or cultural group to which the person belongs. Adolescents who achieve a clear, positive ethnic identity exhibit higher self-esteem, greater optimism, and more social competence.[14]

WHERE HAVE THE GOOD MEN GONE?

Kay Hymowitz, author of *Manning Up: How the Rise of Women Has Turned Men Into Boys*, says today's girls are growing into women and accepting adult responsibilities must faster and more effectively than today's boys. She argues that too many men in their 20s are living in a new kind of extended adolescence. Women now outpace their male peers in getting through college. They are more likely than men to be in graduate school and making strides in the workplace.

Source: Kay S. Hymowitz, "Where Have All the Good Men Gone?" *Wall Street Journal*, February 19–20, 2011 (weekend edition), pp. C1–C2.

Adulthood

When you reach adulthood, you are greatly influenced by a time-reinforced self-concept that has been molded by people and events from all your past experiences. You have been bombarded over the years with positive and negative messages from your family, friends, teachers, supervisors, and the media. You may compare yourself to others, as was so common in adolescence, or you may focus on your own inner sense of self-worth. Emmett Miller, a noted authority on self-esteem, says that as adults we tend to define ourselves in terms of the following items.[15]

The Things We Possess. Miller says this is the most primitive source of self-worth. If we define ourselves in terms of what we have, the result may be an effort to accumulate more and more material things to achieve a greater feeling of self-worth. The idea that we can compensate for self-doubt and insecurity with our checkbook is widely accepted in America.[16] People who define themselves in terms of what they have may have difficulty deciding how much is "enough" and may spend their lives in search of more material possessions.

What We Do for a Living. Miller points out that too often our self-worth and identity depend on something as arbitrary as a job title. Amy Saltzman, author of *Downshifting*, a book on ways to reinvent (or redefine) success, says, "We have allowed our professional identities to define us and control us."[17] She points out that we have looked to outside forces such as the corporation, the university, or the media to provide us with a script for leading a satisfying, worthwhile life.

Our Internal Value System and Emotional Makeup.   Miller says this is the healthiest way for people to identify themselves:

> *If you don't give yourself credit for excellence in other areas of life, besides your job and material possessions, you've got nothing to keep your identity afloat during a job layoff or a troubled family relationship. People who are in touch with their real identity weather the storm better because they have a more varied and richer sense of themselves, owing to the importance they attach to their personal lives and activities.*[18]

As an adult, you will be constantly adjusting the level of your self-esteem as you cope with events at work and in your personal life. Keep in mind that your intelligence isn't fixed. The brain can change and get stronger with practice and hard work.[19]

The Past Programs the Future

Phillip McGraw, better known as "Dr. Phil," has developed a one-sentence guide to understanding the importance of your self-concept: *The past reaches into the present, and programs the future, by your recollections and your internal rhetoric about what you perceived to have happened in your life.*[20] Past experiences and events, which McGraw describes as "defining moments," can influence your thinking for a lifetime and program your future. They get incorporated into your deepest understanding of who you are because they are often the focus of your internal dialogue—a process we call "self-talk." Later in this chapter, we will discuss how to avoid the influence of negative self-talk and build upon positive messages.

Total Person | Insight

Some psychologists and therapists are concerned that self-esteem has morphed into entitlement. A sense of entitlement means that we feel that we have a right to something. Mental health professionals report working with young people who are certain they should be attending a better college or working at a better job, and someone else is to blame. When we put ourselves above others, or expect preferential treatment, then self-esteem has evolved into entitlement.

Source: Anthony B. Robinson, "Articles of Faith: The Unfortunate Age of Entitlement in America," March 23, 2007. (Retrieved from http://seattlepi.com)

SELF-ESTEEM INFLUENCES YOUR BEHAVIOR

4-3   Your level of self-esteem can have a powerful impact on your behavior. Your sense of *competence* and resulting *self-respect*, the two components of self-esteem, stem from the belief that you are generally capable of producing the results in life that you want by making appropriate, constructive choices. This confidence makes you less vulnerable to the negative views of others. People with healthy self-esteem tend to have a sense of personal worth that has been strengthened through various achievements and through accurate self-appraisal.[21]

Characteristics of People with Low Self-Esteem

> *When we rely too heavily on validation from external sources, we can lose control over our lives.*

1. *They tend to maintain an external locus of control.* People who maintain an **external locus of control** believe that their lives are almost totally controlled by outside forces and that they bear little personal responsibility for what happens to them.[22] When something goes wrong, they have a tendency to blame something or someone other than themselves. Even when they succeed, they tend to attribute their success to luck rather than to their own expertise and hard work. They continually rely on other people to make them feel good about themselves, and therefore need an ever-increasing dose of support from others to keep them going. When we rely too heavily on validation from external sources, we can lose control over our lives.[23]

2. *They are more likely to participate in self-destructive behaviors.* If you do not like yourself, there is no apparent reason to take care of yourself. Therefore, people with low self-esteem are more likely to drink too much, smoke too much, and eat too much. Some may develop an eating disorder such as bulimia or anorexia, often with devastating results.

3. *They tend to exhibit poor human relations skills.* People with low self-esteem may have difficulty developing effective interpersonal skills. Workers with low self-esteem may reduce the efficiency and productivity of a group: They tend to exercise less initiative and hesitate to accept responsibility or make independent decisions, and they are less likely to speak up in a group and criticize the group's approach.

Total Person Insight

Because of its momentous influence in many areas of life, self-esteem is one of the most studied of all human traits. Thus assessing your current level of self-esteem should be a top priority.

Source: Sonja Lyubomirsky, *The Myths of Happiness* (New York: The Penguin Press, 2013), p. 75.

Characteristics of People with High Self-Esteem

1. *They tend to maintain an internal locus of control.* People who believe they are largely responsible for what happens to them maintain an **internal locus of control**. They make decisions for their own reasons based on their standards of what is right and wrong. They learn from their mistakes but are not immobilized by them.

2. *They are able to feel all dimensions of emotion without letting those emotions affect their behavior in a negative way.* Although you may not be able to stop feeling the emotions of anger, envy, and jealousy, you can control your thoughts and actions when you are under the influence of these strong emotions. It is okay to have anxious, scared, angry, or depressed feelings—as long as you don't let them stop you from doing what you have to do.[24]

3. *They are less likely to take things personally.* Don Miguel Ruiz, author of the best-selling book *The Four Agreements*, cautions us to avoid taking others' comments personally: "When you make it a strong habit not to take anything personally, you avoid many upsets in your life." He notes that many of these messages come from people who are unable to respect you because they do not respect themselves.[25]

4. *They are able to accept other people as unique, talented individuals.* They learn to accept others for who they are and what they can do. Our multicultural workforce makes this attitude especially important. Individuals who cannot tolerate other people who are "different" are less likely to achieve career success in today's labor market.

5. *They have a productive personality.* They are optimistic in their approach to life and are capable of being creative, imaginative problem solvers. They have the ability to evaluate the dynamics of a relationship and adjust to the demands of the interaction.[26]

HOW TO INCREASE YOUR SELF-ESTEEM

4-4 "The level of our self-esteem is not set once and for all in childhood," says Nathaniel Branden. It can grow throughout our lives or it can deteriorate.[27] Healthy self-esteem comes from realizing what qualities and skills you have that you can rely on and then making a plan to build those qualities and skills that you want in the future. The person you will be tomorrow has yet to be created. Your new, higher level of self-esteem will not happen overnight. Such a change is the result of a slow, steady evolution that begins with the desire to overcome low self-esteem.

Search for the Source of Low Self-Esteem

Many people live with deep personal doubts about themselves but have difficulty determining the source of those feelings. They even have difficulty finding the right words to describe those negative feelings. People with low self-esteem are less likely to see themselves with great clarity. The self-image they possess is like a reflection in a warped funhouse mirror; the image magnifies their weaknesses and minimizes their strengths. Increasing your self-esteem requires achieving a higher level of self-awareness and learning to accurately perceive your particular balance of strengths and weaknesses.[28]

"Can't you keep your parenting to yourselves?"

Barbara Smaller The New Yorker Collection/The Cartoon Bank

To start this process, take time to list and carefully examine the defining moments in your life. Pay special attention to those that were decidedly negative, and try to determine how these moments have shaped your current self-concept. Next, make a list of the labels that others have used to describe you. Study the list carefully, and try to determine which ones you have internalized and accepted. Have these labels had a positive or negative influence on your concept of yourself? Phillip McGraw says, "If you are living to a label, you have molded for yourself a fictional self-concept with artificial boundaries."[29]

Living Consciously

Nathaniel Branden says living consciously is the highest manifestation of life—the basic tool of survival. If we don't bring an appropriate level of consciousness to our life, the penalty is a diminished sense of *self-efficacy* and *self-respect*. One barrier to living consciously is the evasion of facts that make us uncomfortable:

"I know I'm living beyond my means, but—"
"I know my children suffer from having too little time with me, but—"

Branden says that to live consciously means to seek awareness of everything that bears on our actions, purposes, values, and goals. Table 4.1 includes a few examples of how we can live consciously.[30]

Take Responsibility for Your Decisions

Psychologists have found that children who were encouraged to make their own decisions early in their lives have higher self-esteem than those who were kept dependent on their parents for a longer period of time. Making decisions helps you develop confidence in your own judgment and enables you to explore options.

The attitude that you must be right all the time is a barrier to personal growth. With this attitude, you will avoid doing things that might result in mistakes. Much unhappiness comes from the widespread and regrettable belief that it is important to avoid making mistakes at all costs.[31] James Dyson, founder and CEO of Dyson Corporation, says, "I love this side of wrong thinking—of encouraging people who have ideas to go see if they work." Dyson made 5,127 prototypes of the bagless vacuum cleaner before he got it right.[32]

Total Person Insight

"When we are not doing what we're truly good at, we're not living up to our greatest performance capabilities."

Source: Marcus Buckingham, "Bucking the System," *Fast Company*, September 2005, p. 93.

Table 4.1 ■ How to Live Consciously

- Reaching out toward relevant facts rather than ignoring them
- Noticing and confronting my impulses to avoid or deny painful or threatening realities
- Being concerned to know if my actions are in alignment with my purposes
- Searching for feedback from the environment so as to adjust or correct my course when necessary
- Being receptive to new knowledge and willing to reexamine old assumptions

Source: Nathaniel Branden, *The Six Pillars of Self-Esteem* (New York: Bantam, 1994), p. 72.

Engage in Strength Building

Over the past 30 years, the Gallup International Research and Education Center has researched the best way to maximize a person's potential. One of the most important findings can be summarized in a single sentence: Most organizations take their employees' strengths for granted and focus on minimizing their weaknesses. The research findings suggest that the best way to excel in a career is to maximize your strengths.[33]

The Gallup Organization research has been summarized in *Now, Discover Your Strengths* by Marcus Buckingham and Donald Clifton. The first step toward strength building is to discover your greatest talents. A **talent** is any naturally recurring pattern of thought, feeling, or behavior that can be productively applied. A **strength** is a consistent, near perfect performance of an activity; you can see yourself doing it repeatedly, happily and successfully.

Strength building also requires the acquisition of knowledge and skill. As we prepare for a career, we must acquire certain factual knowledge. An accountant must know how to prepare a statement of cash flow. Nurses must know how to administer medications with precision. Skill, the application of knowledge, might be thought of as the "doing" part of strength building.[34]

 ## HOW TO IDENTIFY YOUR TALENTS

When we are not doing what we are truly good at, we are not living up to our greatest performance capabilities. One way to identify your dominant talents is to step back and watch yourself as you try out different activities:

- Complete an elective course.
- Volunteer to chair a committee.
- Accept a part-time job in an area that appeals to you.
- Complete an internship.
- Attend a career fair.

If you flourish in some activities, analyze why this happened.

Source: Marcus Buckingham and Donald O. Clifton, *Now, Discover Your Strengths* (New York: Free Press, 2001), pp. 31–32.

Throughout your lifetime you will be encouraged to embrace the American dream: "You can be anything you want to be, if you just try hard enough." You may love playing golf, but you probably do not have the natural talent to become the next Jordan Spieth. If your goal is to advance to a management position, you must have the talent to develop other people. More than one top salesperson has failed in the role of sales manager.

Tom Rath, author of the best-selling book *StrengthsFinder 2.0*, says society's relentless focus on people's shortcomings is a global obsession. Research conducted by a team of Gallup scientists indicates that people have several times more potential for growth when they invest time and energy developing their strengths instead of correcting their deficiencies.[35] To learn more about the Gallup StrengthsFinder assessment and other Gallup products, visit GallupStrengthsCenter.com.

STRENGTHS LIBRARY

These publications will guide you during the strength-building process:

Now, Discover Your Strengths, by Marcus Buckingham and Donald O. Clifton

Go Put Your Strengths to Work, by Marcus Buckingham

StrengthsFinder 2.0, by Tom Rath

Strengths Based Leadership, by Tom Rath and Barry Conchie

Seek the Support and Guidance of Mentors

A **mentor** is someone who develops another person through tutoring, coaching, and guidance.[36] In most organizations, mentoring is carried out informally, but formal programs that systematically match mentors and protégés are common at large corporations, including consulting firm Deloitte, publisher Time Inc., and investment banks such as Goldman Sachs. Some firms have begun experimenting with more creative forms of mentoring. One approach is a gathering of like-minded individuals who can offer guidance for one another. Facebook COO Sheryl Sandberg describes this approach at Facebook as "lean in circles."[37]

Most people who have had a mentoring experience say it was an effective development tool. However, many surveys indicate that only a small percentage of employees say they have had a mentor. In today's fast-paced work environment, where most people have a heavy workload, you must be willing to take the initiative and build a mentor relationship.[38] The late Warren Bennis, founding chairman of the Leadership Institute at the University of Southern California, states, "Being mentored isn't a passive game. It's nothing less than the ability to spot the handful of people who can make all the difference in your life."[39] Here are some tips to keep in mind:

1. *Search for a mentor who has the qualities of a good coach.* Mentors need to be accomplished in their own right, but success alone does not make someone a good mentor. Look for someone whom you would like to emulate, both in business savvy and in operating style. Be sure it is someone who is absolutely credible, a person you trust enough to talk with about touchy issues.[40]

REVERSE MENTORING

In an effort to help senior executives keep up to date in the areas of technology, social media, and the latest workplace trends, many companies are pairing upper management with younger employees—a practice known as *reverse mentoring*. Cisco Systems has started a Gen Y Reverse Mentoring Program, and the Young Employee Network at Hewlett-Packard is seeking to formalize reverse mentoring throughout the company.

Source: Leslie Kwoh, "Reverse Mentoring Cracks the Workplace," *Wall Street Journal*, November 28, 2011, p. B7.

2. *Market yourself to a prospective mentor.* The best mentor for you may be someone who is very busy. Sell the benefits of a mentoring partnership. For example, point out that mentoring can be a mutually rewarding experience. Describe specific steps you will take to avoid wasting the time of a busy person. You might suggest that meetings be held during lunch or agree to online mentoring.[41]

Many young workers have felt they know more than their bosses. While this may not always be true, they often do possess current knowledge and skills that could be shared with senior managers through reverse mentoring.

In today's complex work environment, one mentor may not meet all of your needs. Kate Mitchell, cofounder of Scale Venture Partners, a California-based investment company, says, "I have never had just one mentor—I've had many. They form an ever-changing composite mentor." A **composite mentor** is a collection of people you draw lessons from. Your challenges are always evolving, so drawing on multiple sources allows you to zero in on the best lessons for different situations.[42]

Set Goals

Research points to a direct link between self-esteem and the achievement of personal and professional goals. People who set goals and successfully achieve them are able to achieve higher self-esteem. Why? Because setting goals enables you to take ownership of the future. Once you realize that just about every behavior is controllable, the possibilities for improving your self-esteem are endless. Self-change may be difficult, but it's not impossible.

The major principles that encompass goal setting are outlined in Table 4.2. Goal setting should be an integral part of your efforts to break old habits or form new ones. Before setting goals, engage in serious reflection. Make a list of the things you want to achieve, and then ask yourself this question: What goals are truly important to me? Are these goals realistic? If you set goals that really excite you, desire will fuel your will to achieve them.[43]

Practice Guided Imagery

Guided imagery is one of the most creative and empowering methods for achieving your goals available today. It provides you with a way to harness the power of the mind and imagination to succeed at something. It can be used to help you relax, set goals (like losing weight), or prepare for a challenging opportunity such as interviewing for a new job. Some heart surgeons use guided imagery to calm their patients, which helps speed recovery.

Table 4.2 ▪ Goal-Setting Principles

Goal setting gives you the power to take control of the present and the future. Goals can help you break old habits or form new ones. You will need an assortment of goals that address the different needs of your life. The following goal-setting principles will be helpful.

1. *Spend time reflecting on the things you want to change in your life.* Take time to clarify your motivation and purpose. Set goals that are specific, measurable, and realistic. Unrealistic goals increase fear, and fear increases the probability of failure. When the "why" behind a goal is big enough, it will motivate you toward achieving it.

2. *Develop a goal-setting plan that includes the steps necessary to achieve the goal.* Put the goal and the steps in writing. Change requires structure. Identify all activities and materials you will need to achieve your goal. Review your plan daily—repetition increases the probability of success.

3. *Modify your environment by changing the stimuli around you.* If your goal is to lose five pounds during a one-month period, make a weight chart so you can monitor your progress. You may need to give up desserts and avoid restaurants that serve huge portions. Gather new information on effective weight-loss techniques, and seek advice from others. This may involve finding a mentor or joining a support group.

4. *Monitor your behavior, and reward your progress.* Focus on small successes, because each little success builds your reservoir of self-esteem. Reinforcement from yourself and/or others is necessary for change. If the passion for change begins to subside, remind yourself why you want to achieve your goal. Be patient—it takes time to change your lifestyle.

Wearing headphones, the patients hear carefully crafted, medically detailed messages that urge them to relax and imagine themselves in a safe, comfortable place: "Feel the new strength flowing through you, through arteries that are wider and more open, more flexible with smoother surfaces than before."[44]

To **visualize** means to form a mental image of something. It refers to what you see in the mind's eye. Once you have formed a clear mental picture of what you want to accomplish, identify the steps needed to get there, and then mentally rehearse them. Rehearsal must be followed by *action* to further your goal. Rami Shapior, award-winning author and teacher says, "It isn't enough to think differently, we must *be* different and *do* differently."[45]

Many athletes choreograph their performances in their imagination before competitions. Studies by the U.S. Olympic Training Center show that 94 percent of the coaches use mental rehearsal for training and competitions.[46] Artists rarely begin a work of art until they have an image of what it is they are going to create. Dancers physically and mentally rehearse their performances hundreds of times before ever stepping on stage. The same techniques can be used in the workplace.

Work-Related Visualization. Let's assume your team members have asked you to present a cost-saving plan to management. The entire team is counting on you. The visualization process should begin with identifying the steps you will take to get approval of the plan. What information will you present? What clothing will you wear? Will you use PowerPoint or some other visual presentation method? Will you use any printed documents? Once you have identified all important contingencies and strategies for success, visualize the actual presentation. See yourself walking into the room with your chin up, your shoulders straight, and your voice strong and confident. Picture yourself making appropriate eye contact with people in the room. The focus of your preparation should be on things within your control.

HOW TO BREAK OUT OF A SLUMP

Major league pitcher John Smoltz, a former star for the Atlanta Braves, recalls starting a season with a dismal record of 2–11. He contacted sports psychologist Jack Llewellyn for help. With guidance from Llewellyn, Mr. Smoltz learned to recover more swiftly from a bad pitch. He repeatedly watched a two-minute tape Dr. Llewellyn had made of a half-dozen of his *perfect* pitches. Then if he made a bad pitch during a game, he did not step back on the mound until he visualized that positive file in his mind. His confidence restored, Mr. Smoltz posted a 12–2 record for the remainder of the season.

Source: Sue Shellenbarger, "Slumping at Work? What Would Jack Do?" *Wall Street Journal*, October 13, 2010, p. D1.

Use Positive Self-Talk

Throughout most of your waking moments, you talk to yourself. **Self-talk** takes place in the privacy of your mind. It can be rational and productive, or it can be irrational and disruptive. Talking to yourself out loud is common. When the focus of this internal conversation is on negative thoughts, you are usually less productive.[47] Some psychologists refer to these negative thoughts as your **inner critic**. The critic keeps a record of your failures but never reminds you of your strengths and accomplishments. A major step toward improving your self-esteem is to understand how to respond to the negative influence of your inner critic.[48]

> *Self-talk takes place in the privacy of your mind.*

When your inner critic talks to you, ask yourself, "Who is this voice that is reminding me of my past failures?" (see Figure 4.1). The chances are it is not your current boss or spouse, but someone in your past such as a teacher, coach, harsh parent, or sibling. Recognize that this critical voice is probably no longer relevant and take the necessary steps to replace those negative messages with positive ones.[49] You can create effective, positive self-talk statements for each of your goals by using the following guidelines:

1. Be *specific* about the behavior you want to change. What do you want to do to increase your effectiveness? You should firmly believe that what you want is truly possible.

Figure 4.1 ■ The Self-Talk Endless Loop

What I tell myself about how I perform

Which helps to determine

Which shapes

The Self-Talk Endless Loop

My internal image of myself

How I act

Which influences

Source: From Jack Canfield, The Success Principle: How to Get from Where You Are to Where You Want to Be.

2. The way you address yourself matters. Research indicates that people who speak to themselves as another person would—using their own name or the pronoun "you"—performed better than people who used the word "I." Before a job interview, build your confidence with positive self-talk such as, "You are well prepared; you have the skills needed for this position."[50] Think of yourself as a life-long best friend who is honest and direct, but most of all supportive.

Jack Canfield, author of *Key to Living the Law of Attraction*, says we should avoid sending mixed signals to ourselves and those around us. When you are against something, you may actually be re-creating it. So, instead of thinking "I don't want to be late," think "I want to be on time." When you create a self-talk statement, always keep in mind your goal.[51]

Positive self-talk that is truly effective consists of thoughts and messages that are realistic and truthful. It is rationally optimistic self-talk, not unfounded rah-rah hype. Tomas Chamorro-Premuzic, author of *Confidence: Overcoming Low Self-Esteem, Insecurity, and Self Doubt*, says people will not value your *confidence* unless it is accompanied by *competence*.[52]

ORGANIZATIONS CAN HELP

4-5 Although each of us ultimately is responsible for increasing or decreasing our own self-esteem, we can make that task easier or more difficult for others. We can either support or damage the self-efficacy and self-respect of the people we work with, just as they have that option in their interactions with us.

When employees do not feel good about themselves, the result will often be poor job performance. This view is shared by many human resource professionals. Many organizations realize that low self-esteem affects their workers' ability to learn new skills, to be effective team members, and to be productive. Research has identified five factors that can enhance the self-esteem of employees in any organization (see Figure 4.2).[53]

- *Workers need to feel valuable.* A major source of worker satisfaction is the feeling that one is valued as a unique person. Self-esteem grows when an organization makes an effort to accommodate individual differences, to recognize individual accomplishments, and to help employees build their strengths.

Figure 4.2 ■ Factors That Enhance the Self-Esteem of Employees

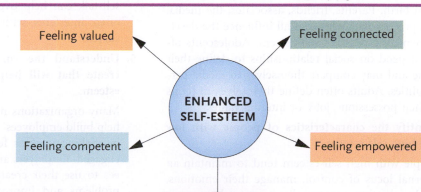

- *Workers need to feel competent.* Earlier in this chapter, we noted that self-efficacy grows when people feel confident in their ability to perform job-related tasks. One of the best ways organizations can build employee confidence is to involve employees in well-designed training programs.
- *Workers need to feel secure.* Employees are more likely to feel secure when they are well informed and know what is expected of them. Managers need to clarify their expectations and provide employees with frequent feedback about their performance.
- *Workers need to feel empowered.* Progressive companies recognize that every employee has something to contribute to the organization. When all employees are treated with respect and given the latitude for individual action within the defined limits of the organization, they are free to use their creativity and ingenuity to solve problems and make customers happy.
- *Workers need to feel connected.* People are likely to achieve high self-esteem when they feel their coworkers accept, appreciate, and respect them. Many companies are fostering these feelings by placing greater emphasis on mentoring and teamwork. Team-building efforts help promote acceptance and cooperation.

LOOKING BACK: SUMMARY OF LEARNING OBJECTIVES

1. Define self-esteem and discuss its impact on your life.

Self-esteem is a combination of self-respect and self-efficacy. If you have high self-esteem, you are more likely to feel competent and worthy. If you have low self-esteem, you are more likely to feel incompetent, unworthy, and insecure. Self-esteem reflects your feelings of adequacy about the roles you play, your personality traits, your physical appearance, your skills, and your abilities. High self-esteem is the powerful foundation for a successful personal and professional life.

2. Discuss how self-esteem is developed.

A person starts acquiring and building self-esteem from birth. Parents, friends, associates, the media, and professional colleagues all influence the development of a person's self-esteem. Adolescents often depend on social relationships to define their value and may compare themselves to media personalities. Adults often define themselves in terms of their possessions, jobs, or internal values.

3. Identify the characteristics of people with low and high self-esteem.

People with high self-esteem tend to maintain an internal locus of control, manage their emotions, rarely take things personally, accept other people as unique and talented, and have productive personalities. People with low self-esteem tend to

maintain an external locus of control, are likely to participate in self-destructive behaviors, and exhibit poor human relations skills. They often rely on the opinions of others to establish their inner self-worth.

4. Identify ways to raise your self-esteem.

To build high self-esteem, people must accept their limitations, take responsibility for their decisions, engage in strength building, identify their talents, and work with a mentor. Taking responsibility for your decisions and living with the consequences, positive or negative, can also help build self-esteem. Goal setting is an integral part of raising one's self-esteem. Guided imagery and positive self-talk can help overcome the inner critic that often interferes with personal and professional success.

5. Understand the conditions organizations can create that will help workers raise their self-esteem.

Many organizations now realize that they need to help build employees' self-esteem and are doing so by making workers feel valuable, competent, and engaged. Employers are empowering their employees to use their creativity and ingenuity to solve problems and improve customer service, which allows workers to develop a sense of personal responsibility.

KEY TERMS

self-esteem, 78
self-efficacy, 78
self-respect, 79
self-concept, 80
developmental psychology, 80
external locus of control, 83

internal locus of control, 83
talent, 86
strength, 86
mentor, 87
composite mentor, 88
guided imagery, 88

visualize, 89
self-talk, 90
inner critic, 90

CAREER INSIGHT

Marcus Buckingham, author of *Go Put Your Strengths to Work*, encourages us to discover our strengths and then engage in activities that will strengthen them. He says "Only 17 percent of people spend most of their work day doing things they really like to do." Take time to compile an inventory of activities you have truly enjoyed as a student, volunteer, or employee.

Think about activities that play to your strengths. Chances are you have talents and strengths that can be enhanced and applied with greater enthusiasm. Set some new goals that focus on strength building.

Source: Marcus Buckingham, *Go Put Your Strengths to Work* (New York: Free Press, 2007), pp. 130–134.

TRY YOUR HAND

1. Review Table 4.2, Goal-Setting Principles. Work through each of the four principles in light of something you would like to change in your world. It could be a physical characteristic, such as weight control or beginning an exercise regimen. It might be a component of your personality, such as becoming more confident or assertive. Perhaps you would like to reexamine your career goals. Whatever your choice, write out your plan for change then follow it through.

2. This chapter identified five characteristics of people with high self-esteem. Read each of the following statements and rate yourself with this scale: U = Usually; S = Sometimes.

	U	S
I maintain an internal locus of control.	☐	☐
I can feel all dimensions of emotions without letting these emotions affect my behavior in a negative way.	☐	☐
I do not take things personally.	☐	☐
I can accept other people as unique, talented individuals.	☐	☐
I feel I have a productive personality.	☐	☐

3. Make a list of four or five people you admire who might be willing to serve as your mentor. Think about the strengths you want to develop, and determine which of these persons can best help you achieve your goals. It's important to learn as much as you can about a prospective mentor before pursuing a mentoring relationship. Make sure the prospective mentor is willing to make time for you and has your interests at heart. Before meeting with a prospective mentor, be prepared to discuss areas where you need help. Also, think about what you can give back during the mentor relationship. A good mentor relationship is seldom a one-way street.

Source: Dorie Clark, *Reinventing You* (Boston: Harvard Business Review Press, 2013), pp. 79–94.

CRITICAL THINKING CHALLENGE

Dale Stephens first dropped out of school in fifth grade because he was bored. He says, "I wanted to spend my time learning and everyone else just wanted to talk about the new Pokemon." After he went to college for six months, he dropped out again. Although Stephens has not earned a college degree, he has received a Thiel Fellowship, which he says helps convince people that "I was a valuable human being." He says the fellowship also provided him with a large number of networking opportunities.[54] In his new book *Hacking Your Education: Ditch the Lectures, Save Tens of Thousands, and*

Learn More than Your Peers Ever Will, Stephens says most young people would do better to train and network on their own:

> Instead of relying on business school to succeed, deliberately practice the skills necessary to become a master in your chosen field. Build a network that supports your professional aspirations. Work on projects that show you can have an impact in the real world, dealing with practical problems.[55]

Do you agree or disagree with the advice provided by Dale Stephens?

SELF-ASSESSMENT EXERCISE

For each statement, circle the number from 1 to 5 that best represents your response: (1) strongly disagree (never do this); (2) disagree (rarely do this); (3) moderately agree (sometimes do this); (4) agree (frequently do this); (5) strongly agree (almost always do this).

A.	I tend to be future oriented and not overly concerned with past mistakes or failures.	1	2	3	4	5
B.	I have developed and maintained high expectations of myself.	1	2	3	4	5
C.	I accept myself as a changing, growing person capable of improvement.	1	2	3	4	5
D.	I have the strength to cope with life's problems and disappointments.	1	2	3	4	5
E.	I can maintain an internal locus of control.	1	2	3	4	5
F.	My goals are clearly defined, attainable, and supported by a plan for achieving each goal.	1	2	3	4	5
G.	I monitor my self-talk in order to maintain high self-esteem.	1	2	3	4	5

After identifying your response to each item, select an attitude or skill you would like to improve. Prepare a written goal and then describe the steps you will take to achieve this goal.

YOU PLAY THE ROLE

You have accepted a summer job with Neiman Marcus. Throughout the summer, you will replace sales staff that are on vacation. In addition to earning money to pay next fall's college tuition, you anticipate that this job will help you develop your customer service skills. To maximize the learning opportunities and explore another area within the company, you want to develop a mentor relationship with the assistant store manager. You have an appointment with her

tomorrow. In this role-play situation, you will meet with a class member who will assume the role of the assistant store manager, who is very busy and has scheduled the meeting to last no more than 15 minutes. During this short period of time, you will explain why you need a mentor and market yourself to this prospective mentor. Prior to the role-play activity, review the information on mentoring in this chapter.

BELOW THE SURFACE | EARNING THE RESPECT OF OTHERS

The chapter-opening vignette describes the career of a very successful athlete. Keven Ollie was a good basketball player, but not outstanding. After his college career he was not drafted by the NBA, and he played in the lower-level Continental Basketball Association. He worked hard to improve himself and was eventually recruited by an NBA team. Over the years he became known as a nomadic point guard, playing for 11 NBA franchises over a period of 13 years. Ollie did not score many points during his long NBA career, but he earned the respect of his teammates. Coaches valued his positive locker-room presence.

QUESTIONS

1. At some point in your career you may be assigned to work with a group of employees who do not work well together as a team. Low morale among these employees is having a negative influence on productivity. What steps can you take to become a "game-changer" and reshape the culture of this group? Reflect on the career of Kevin Ollie as your prepare your answer.

CLOSING CASE | THE MENTORING OF EDWARD

Shoshana Zuboff likes to reflect on some of the special students she taught at the Harvard Business School. Some students, she recalls, "threw themselves at learning as if their lives depended on it." One of those students, Edward, had a troubled past. His parents split up when he was a small boy, and he was on his own much of the time as his mother needed to work. Edward and his mother lived in a neighborhood where drugs and gangs were common. By the sixth grade, he was a drug dealer, and later he ended up in a penitentiary. Then he had the good fortune to meet a judge who offered him two years in a drug rehabilitation program in return for good behavior. After rehab, he got a job, enrolled in a community college, and made the dean's list several times. A counselor encouraged Edward to set his sights high, so he applied and was accepted to an Ivy League school, where he studied business and economics. This success led to his acceptance into the Harvard Business School, where he met Professor Zuboff.

Although Edward had accomplished a great deal since leaving the penitentiary, he felt a growing sense of shame over things he did not know. During one lecture, Professor Zuboff briefly mentioned the name of an author who had written about Auschwitz. After class, Edward asked, "What is Auschwitz?" Because of his disadvantaged childhood, he had missed out on many learning experiences that most students take for granted. To avoid giving away his deep-seated, inner secret, he mastered many defense strategies to protect his image among his peers. Professor Zuboff noted, "he was haunted by the sense of not knowing what he didn't know or how to learn it."

With help from this caring professor and her husband, who agreed to serve as his mentor, Edward began a program of study designed to fill in the gaps in his education. His self-esteem improved greatly as his program of self-improvement unfolded. Today Edward runs a successful consulting firm that focuses on leadership and emotional intelligence.[56]

QUESTIONS

1. Professor Zuboff says Edward was haunted by the sense of not knowing what he didn't know or how to learn it. Is it possible that many employees in today's labor force suffer from that same fear? Explain your answer.

2. Some people can benefit from multiple mentors. What other types of mentors, in addition to Professor Zuboff and her husband, might Edward find helpful?

CHAPTER 4 ENDNOTES

1. Ben Cohen, "This Coach Has Been Around," *Wall Street Journal*, April 3, 2014, p. D6.
2. Andy Katz, "Kevin Ollie Signs New UConn Deal," May 22, 2014. Retrieved from http://ESPN.com. INTERNET
3. Douglas A. Bernstein, Louis A. Penner, Alison Clarke-Stewart, and Edward J. Roy, *Psychology*, 9th ed. (Boston: Cengage Learning, 2012), p. 575.
4. Nathaniel Branden, *The Six Pillars of Self-Esteem* (New York: Bantam, 1994), p. 7.
5. Robert Reasoner, "The True Meaning of Self-Esteem," National Association for Self-Esteem, Normal, IL [cited April 30, 2003]. Available from http://www.self-esteem-nase.org; INTERNET
6. Aimee Lee Ball, "The New & Improved Self-Esteem," *O, The Oprah Magazine*, January 2008, p. 163.
7. Phillip C. McGraw, *Self Matters* (New York: Simon & Schuster, 2001), pp. 69–70.
8. Sharon Begley, "Follow Your Intuition: The Unconscious You May Be the Wiser Half," *Wall Street Journal*, August 30, 2002, p. B1; Sharon Begley, "How Do I Love Thee? Let Me Count the Ways—and Other Bad Ideas," *Wall Street Journal*, September 6, 2002, p. B1; Bernstein et al., *Psychology*, p. 465.
9. Bernstein et al., *Psychology*, p. 465.
10. Marilyn Elias, "Short Attention Span Linked to TV," *USA Today*, April 5, 2004, p. A1; Lyric Wallwork Winik, "The Toll of Video Violence," *Parade*, July 22, 2004, p. 15.
11. Sue Shellenbarger, "Finding the Just-Right Level of Self-Esteem for a Child," *Wall Street Journal*, February 27, 2013, pp. D1 and D2; Sue Shellenbarger, Work & Family Mailbox, *Wall Street Journal*, May 29, 2013, p. D2.
12. Bernstein et al., *Psychology*, p. 502.
13. Ibid., p. 505
14. Ibid.
15. Emmett Miller, *The Healing Power of Happiness* (Emmaus, PA: Rodale Press, 1989), pp. 12–13. To learn more about Emmett Miller's writings, visit http://www.DrMiller.com.
16. Lacey Beckmann, "One More Thing Money Can't Buy," *Psychology Today*, November/December, 2002, p. 16.
17. Amy Saltzman, *Downshifting* (New York: HarperCollins, 1990), pp. 15–16.
18. Miller, *The Healing Power of Happiness*, pp. 12–13.
19. Kendra Cherry, "What Is Self-Efficacy?" May 29, 2014. Retrieved from http://psychology.about.com/self-efficacy; INTERNET
20. Phillip C. McGraw, *Self Matters* (New York: Simon & Schuster, 2001), p. 73.
21. Robert Reasoner, "The True Meaning of Self-Esteem," National Association for Self-Esteem, Normal, IL [cited April 30, 2003]. Available from http://www.self-esteem-nase.org; INTERNET.
22. Arthur H. Goldsmith, Jonathan R. Veum, and William Darity, Jr., "The Impact of Psychological and Human Capital on Wages," *Economic Inquiry*, October 1997, p. 817.
23. Hyrum W. Smith, *The 10 Natural Laws of Successful Time and Life Management* (New York: Warner Books, 1994), p. 178.
24. Annie Gottlieb, "The Radical Road to Self-Esteem," *O, The Oprah Magazine*, March 2001, pp. 101–102.
25. Don Miguel Ruiz, *The Four Agreements* (San Rafael, CA: Amber-Allen Publishing, 1997), pp. 47–61.
26. James J. Messina and Constance M. Messina, *The SEA's Program Model of Self-Esteem* [cited 9 November 2005]. Available from http://www.coping.org/selfesteem/model.htm; INTERNET.
27. Nathaniel Branden, *The Six Pillars of Self-Esteem* (New York: Simon & Schuster, 2001), p. 33.
28. Matthew McKay and Patrick Fanning, *Self-Esteem*, 2d ed. (Oakland, CA: New Harbinger, 1992), p. 42.
29. Phillip C. McGraw, *Self Matters* (New York: Simon & Schuster, 2001), p. 73.
30. Nathaniel Branden, *The Six Pillars of Self-Esteem* (New York: Simon & Schuster, 2001), p. 67–74.
31. Arnold A. Lazarus and Clifford N. Lazarus, *The 60-Second Shrink* (San Luis Obispo, CA: Impact Publishers, 1997), p. 40.
32. David Yellen, "Disrupters," *Fast Company*, December 2011, p. 109.

33. Marcus Buckingham and Donald O. Clifton, ***Now, Discover Your Strengths*** (New York: Free Press, 2001), p. 8.

34. Ibid., pp. 28–31.

35. Tom Rath, ***StrengthsFinder 2.0*** (New York: Gallup Press, 2007), pp. i–iii.

36. Robert Kreitner, ***Management***, 11th ed. (Mason, OH: Houghton Mifflin, 2009), p. 415.

37. Marina Khidekel, "The Misery of Mentoring Millennials," ***Bloomberg Businessweek***, March 24, 2013, pp. 67–68.

38. Carol Hymowitz, "Today's Bosses Find Mentoring Isn't Worth the Time and Risks," ***Wall Street Journal***, March 13, 2006, p. B1.

39. Fiona Haley and Christine Canabou, "The Mentors' Mentors," ***Fast Company***, October 2003, p. 59.

40. Thomas J. DeLong, John J. Gabarro, and Robert J. Lees, ***Harvard Business Review***, January 2008, p. 117.

41. Ginger Adams and Tena B. Crews, "Telementoring: A Viable Tool," ***Journal of Applied Research for Business Education***, Vol. 2, No. 3, 2004, pp. 1–4.

42. Kate Mitchell, "Build Your Own Composite Mentor," ***Wall Street Journal***, May 23, 2013, p. B6.

43. Stan Goldberg, "The 10 Rules of Change," ***Psychology Today***, September/October 2002, pp. 38–44.

44. Andrew Weil, "Images of Healing," ***Dr. Andrew Weil's Self Healing***, November 2003, p. 3; Amy Dockser Marcus, "Heart Surgeons Try Using the Power of Suggestion," ***Wall Street Journal***, February 20, 2004, p. D1.

45. Rami Shapiro, "What Do You Think of 'The Secret'"? ***Spirituality & Health***, May/June 2007, p. 17.

46. James Bauman, "The Gold Medal," ***Psychology Today***, May/June 2000, pp. 62–68.

47. See McGraw, ***Self Matters***, for comprehensive coverage of how internal dialogue influences our self-concept.

48. Matthew McKay and Patrick Fanning, ***Self-Esteem***, 2d ed. (Oakland, CA: New Harbinger, 1992), p. 42.

49. Julie Morgenstern, "Fire Your Inner Critic," ***O, The Oprah Magazine***, August 2004, pp. 75–77.

50. Elizabeth Bernstein, "Self Talk, or a Heart-to-Heart with Your Closest Friend," ***Wall Street Journal***, May 6, 2014, p. D1.

51. Jack Canfield and D.D. Watkins, ***Jack Canfield's Key to Living the Law of Attraction*** (Deerfield Beach, FL: Health Communications, 2007), pp. 31–34.

52. Sarah Green, "The Perils of Self-Promotion," ***Harvard Business Review***, January–February, 2014, pp. 118–119.

53. Roy J. Blitzer, Colleen Petersen, and Linda Rogers, "How to Build Self-Esteem," ***Training & Development***, February 1993, pp. 58–60.

54. Dan Schawbel, "Dale Stephens: Ditch College and Create Your Own Educational Experience," March 5, 2013. Retrieved from http://www.forbes.com/sites/danschawbel; INTERNET

55. Sarah Green, "The Perils of Self-Promotion," ***Harvard Business Review***, January–February, 2014, pp. 118–119.

56. Shoshana Zuboff, "Only the Brave Surrender," ***Fast Company***, October 2004, p. 121.

Henk Meijer/Alamy

CHAPTER PREVIEW

LEARNING OBJECTIVES

After studying Chapter 5, you will be able to

5-1 Explain how moral intelligence contributes to personal and organizational success.

5-2 Understand how personal values are formed.

5-3 Understand values conflicts and how to resolve them.

5-4 Learn how to make the right ethical decisions based on your personal value system.

5-5 Understand the importance of corporate values and ethical choices.

Personal Values Influence Ethical Choices

TIP OF THE ICEBERG | MARY BARRA, FIRST FEMALE CEO OF MAJOR CAR COMPANY

To compile the first-ever global Most Powerful Women ranking, the editors of *Fortune* magazine weighed many of the same factors historically used to measure executive power. Mary Barra, the second most powerful woman on the list, is the first woman to run General Motors.[1] Soon after the MPW list was published, Barra's leadership skills were put to the test. The National Highway Traffic Safety Administration (NHTSA) reported that thousands of GM cars had faulty ignition switches that could disable power steering, power brakes, and air bags. The defect was linked to 31 crashes and 12 deaths in the United States.[2]

Government investigators conducted a criminal probe into the auto maker's mishandling of the faulty ignition switch problem. Documents indicate that GM engineering managers knew about the problem for several years before launching a recall to fix customer cars. This information was not shared with some senior GM executives. Barra quickly announced a safety whistleblower program titled "Speak Up for Safety." The program will reward employees who discover and report safety issues.[3]

The new generation of workers is coming of age at a time when our culture is placing a great deal of emphasis on self-gratification, the crossing of many moral boundaries, and deception reported in daily media stories.[4] This chapter will help you understand how to make the right ethical decisions based on a value system that embraces honor and integrity. It will help you understand how your values are formed, how to clarify which values are important to you, and how to resolve human relations problems that result when your personal values conflict with others' values.

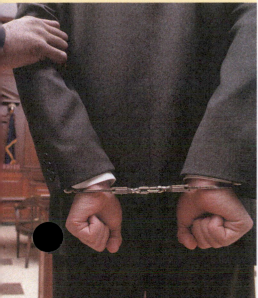

Comstock/Stockbyte/Getty Images

Mary Barra faced major challenges after assuming the duties of Chief Executive Officer of General Motors. The National Highway Safety Administration reported that thousands of GM cars had faulty ignition switches that could disable air bags, power brakes, and power steering

MORAL INTELLIGENCE IN THE WORKPLACE

5-1   Many of America's most successful leaders rank high in the area of moral intelligence. Cognitive intelligence (IQ) is undeniably important, but not sufficient for exceptional performance. **Moral intelligence** is our mental capacity to determine how universal human principles such as responsibility, compassion, forgiveness, and humility should be applied to our personal values, goals, and actions.[5]

Our **character** is composed of personal standards of behavior, including honesty, integrity, and moral strength. It is the main ingredient we seek in our leaders and the quality that earns us respect in the workplace. Former U.S. senator Al Simpson said, "If you have character, that's all that matters; and if you don't have character, that's all that matters, too."[6]

In recent years, we have seen many leaders stray from the ethical path. Ethical violations hurt individuals, businesses, stockholders, and society. In the early 2000s, our attention was focused on scandals at Enron, Tyco, and WorldCom. Today, a long list of American corporations have faced criminal charges related to unethical or illegal behavior.[7]

Integrity is the basic ingredient of character that is exhibited when you achieve congruence between what you know, what you say, and what you do.[8] When your behavior is in tune with your professed standards and values—when you practice what you believe in—you have integrity. When you say one thing but do something else, you *lack* integrity.

How important is it to be viewed as a person with integrity and a strong sense of character in the eyes of your friends, family members, fellow workers, and leaders? When you look closely at the factors that contribute to warm friendships, strong marriages, successful careers, and successful organizations, you quickly come to the conclusion that character and integrity are critical.

HOW TO BUILD AND MAINTAIN INTEGRITY

- Recognize that the key mark of integrity in human relations is consistency.
- Resolve to live in truth with yourself and with every person in your life.
- Make promises carefully, then always keep your word.

Source: Brian Tracy, *The 100 Absolutely Unbreakable Laws of Business Success* (San Francisco, CA: Berrett-Koehler, 2002), pp. 121–123.

HOW PERSONAL VALUES ARE FORMED

5-2 Hyrum Smith, author of *The 10 Natural Laws of Successful Time and Life Management*, says that certain natural laws govern personal productivity and fulfillment. One of these laws focuses on personal beliefs: Your behavior is a reflection of what you truly believe.[9] **Values** are the personal beliefs and preferences that influence your behavior. They are deep-seated in your personality. To discover what really motivates you, carefully examine what it is you value.

Once you are aware of your value priorities, you are in a better position to plan and initiate life-changing activities.

Table 5.1 details the values clarification process. These five steps can help you determine whether or not you truly value something. Many times you are not consciously aware of what is really driving your behavior because values exist at different levels of awareness.[10] Unless you clarify your values, life events are likely to unfold in a haphazard manner. Once you are aware of your value priorities, you are in a better position to plan and initiate life-changing activities.

Core Values Drive Behavior

Everything starts with your **core values**, those values that you consistently rank highest and that guide your behavior. When you can identify your core values, you have a definite picture of the kind of person you want to be and the kind of life you want to have. Anne Mulcahy, former CEO of Xerox Corporation and a mother of two sons, says she and her husband make decisions at home and work based on their core values: "Our kids are absolutely the center of our lives—and we never mess with that."[11] Maura FitzGerald, founder of FitzGerald Communications, Inc., a public relations firm, asks all her employees to adhere to the "FitzGerald Family Values" before accepting a job with her company. All her workers carry with them a wallet-size card listing the organization's basic operating principles, one of which is "Never compromise our integrity—this is our hallmark."[12]

Later in this chapter, you will have an opportunity to identify your core values. First, we will discuss some of the major influences that may have shaped your values.

SETTING THE INTENTION

- Observe your thoughts; they become your words.
- Observe your words; they become actions.
- Observe your actions; they become habits.
- Observe your habits; they become your character.
- Observe your character; it becomes your destiny.

Source: *New Dimensions Annual Journal* (Ukiah, CA: New Dimensions Media, 2002), p. 46.

Table 5.1 ■ A Five-Part Valuing Process to Clarify and Develop Values

THINKING
We live in a confusing world where making choices about how to live our lives can be difficult. Of major importance is developing critical thinking skills that help distinguish fact from opinion and supported from unsupported arguments. Learn to think for yourself. Question what you are told. Engage in higher-level thinking that involves analysis, synthesis, and evaluation.

FEELING
This dimension of the valuing process involves being open to your "gut level" feelings. If it doesn't "feel right," it probably isn't. Examine your distressful feelings such as anger, fear, or emotional hurt. Discover what you prize and cherish in life.

COMMUNICATING
Values are clarified through an ongoing process of interaction with others. Be an active listener and hear what others are really saying. Be constantly alert to communication filters such as emotions, body language, and positive and negative attitudes. Learn to send clear messages regarding your own beliefs.

CHOOSING
Your values must be freely selected with no outside pressure. In some situations, telling right from wrong is difficult. Therefore, you need to be well informed about alternatives and the consequences of various courses of action. Each choice you make reflects some aspect of your values system.

ACTING
Act repeatedly and consistently on your beliefs. One way to test whether something is of value to you is to ask yourself, "Do I find that this value is persistent throughout all aspects of my life?"

Source: Howard Kirschenbaum, *Advanced Values Clarification* (La Jolla, CA: University Associates, 1977).

Influences That Shape Your Values

As you engage in the values clarification process, it helps to reflect on those things that have influenced your values, such as people and events of your generation, your family, religious groups, your education, the media, and people you admire.

Generational Influences. Generational influences are among the most powerful forces shaping our values. Generations follow observable historical patterns and thus offer a powerful tool for predicting future workforce attitudes.[13]

Table 5.2 provides a summary of some of the key events and people who have shaped the values of four generations: the Matures, the Baby Boomers, Generation X, and Millennials/Generation Y. Although workers of different ages want basically the same things—meaningful work, respect, and a fair reward for work done well—they can have very different ideas about what these mean. An older Baby Boomer might believe that respect is due when someone spends many years on the job. To a Generation Xer, respect is

Table 5.2 ■ People and events have influenced the formation of values for four groups of Americans: Matures, Baby Boomers, Generation X, and Millennials (sometimes called Generation Y). This means that today's workforce represents the broadest range of ages and values in American history.

MATURES (BORN 1928–1945)	BABY BOOMERS (BORN 1946–1964)	GENERATION X (BORN 1965–1976)	MILLENNIALS (BORN 1977–2002)	GENERATION?
Eisenhower	Television	AIDS	Corporate downsizing	It's too early to label or generalize about this generation.
MacArthur	The Cold War	The wellness movement	Ethics scandals	It will be formed by the way historical events and moods shape its members' lives. *
The A-bomb	The space race	Watergate	Digital technology	
Dr. Spock	The Civil Rights Act	Glasnost	24/7 economy	
John Wayne	The pill	The Oklahoma City bombing	Jeff Bezos and Mark Zuckerberg	
The Great Depression	The drug culture	MTV	9/11 terrorist attacks	
World War II	Gloria Steinem	The World Wide Web	Wars in Iraq and Afghanistan	
The New Deal	The Vietnam War	Information economy	Income gap	
	JFK and MLK assassinations	Work/life balance concerns	Globalization	
			Employment uncertainty	

*Views expressed by Neil Howe and William Strauss, authors of *Generations: The History of America's Future, 1584 to 2089* and *Fourth Turning: An American Prophecy*, Jeremy Quittner, "Bridging the Generation Gap," *Inc.*, November 2012, pp. 93–97.

expected when someone displays competence. Someone born during the early years of the Baby-Boom generation might be satisfied with feedback during annual or semiannual performance reviews. Generation Xers and Millenials have a need to see results almost daily and receive frequent feedback on their performance. Analyzing the traits of any large population can lead to unfair and unrealistic stereotyping, but generational differences shaped by sociological, political, and economic conditions can be traced to differences in values.[14]

Your Family. Parents must assume many roles, none more important than *moral teacher*. In many families in contemporary society, one parent must assume full responsibility for shaping children's values. Some single parents—those overwhelmed with responsibility for career, family, and rebuilding their own personal lives—may lack the stamina needed to give their children the guidance they need. And in two-parent families, both parents may work outside the home and, at the end of the day, may lack the time or energy to intentionally direct the development of their children's values. The same may be true for families experiencing financial pressures or the strains associated with caring for elderly parents.

Religious Groups. Many people learn their value priorities through religious training. This may be achieved through the accepted teachings of a church, through religious literature such as the Koran and the Bible, or through persons in churches, mosques, or synagogues who are positive role models.

Religious groups that want to define, instill, and perpetuate values may find an eager audience. The late Stephen Covey and other social observers say that many people are determinedly seeking spiritual and moral anchors in their lives and in their work. People who live in uncertain times seem to attach more importance to spirituality.[15] Healthy spirituality is discussed in Chapter 17.

THE DIVORCE GENERATION

"Every generation has its life-defining moments. If you want to find out what it was for a member of the Greatest Generation (Matures), you ask: "Where were you on D-Day?" For Baby Boomers, the questions are: "Where were you when Kennedy was shot?" or "What were you doing when Nixon resigned?" For much of my generation—Generation X, born between 1965 and 1980—there is only one question: "When did your parents get divorced?" Our lives have been framed by the answer. Ask us. We remember everything."

Source: Susan Gregory Thomas, "The Divorce Generation," *Wall Street Journal*, July 9–10, 2011, pp. C1–C2.

Education. Many parents, concerned that their children are not learning enough about moral values and ethical behavior, want character education added to the curriculum. They are concerned about the constant barrage of negative messages children are getting about dishonest behavior in government and corporate America. Research conducted by the Josephson Institute Center for Youth Ethics indicates that parents have reason to worry. The 2012 Report Card on the Ethics of American Youth found that 51 percent of students admitted cheating on an exam. The Josephson Institute of Ethics has developed a variety of grassroots training activities involving what it refers to as the six pillars of character: trustworthiness, respect, responsibility, fairness, caring, and citizenship.[16]

The Media. Mainstream television and many of today's movies seen by young viewers continue to feature a great deal of violence and antisocial behavior. In addition, many young people spend time playing violent video games. Learning can occur not only by doing but also by observing what others do and what happens to them. Learning by watching others is called **observational learning**. There is evidence that exposure to media violence can trigger or amplify viewers' aggressive thoughts and feelings. Too often, media violence provides models that viewers imitate. The vast majority of studies have showed that exposure to media violence results in increased aggressive behavior.[17]

Even at a very young age, people start absorbing ideas and developing their own beliefs about qualities such as trust, respect, and fairness.

People You Admire. In addition to being influenced by the media, you have probably also done some **modeling**—you have shaped your behavior to resemble that of people you admire and embraced the qualities those people demonstrate. Most employees look to their leaders for moral guidance. Unfortunately, there is a shortage of leaders who have a positive impact on ethical decision making. A survey found that fewer than half of employees in large organizations think their senior leadership is highly ethical.[18]

Identifying Your Core Values

Effective interpersonal relations requires clarity about your values. Doug Lennick and Fred Kiel, authors of *Moral Intelligence*, have developed a worksheet that will help you identify your core values.[19] Circle the number at the left of each personal value you believe to be one of your core values. If you feel one or more values are missing, add your own at the bottom of the list. After completion of the worksheet, select five you believe to be your most important core values.

1. Achievement
2. Power
3. Affiliation
4. Thriftiness
5. Creativity
6. Wealth
7. Autonomy

8. Status
9. Comfort
10. Safety
11. Wisdom
12. Enjoyment
13. Friendship
14. Health
15. Security
16. Service
17. Community
18. Independence
19. Loyalty
20. Growth
21. Curiosity
22. Spirituality
23. Altruism
24. Perseverance
25. Order
26. Inner Peace
27. Gratitude
28. Open-Mindedness
29. Meaningful Work
30. Competence
31. Influencing Others
32. Stability
33. Challenges
34. Competition
35. Economic Security
36. Cooperation
37. ___
38. ___
39. ___
40. ___

Once you have examined the various influences on your values, and selected five core values you hold most dear, take time to reflect on your behavior. If you often behave in ways that are in conflict with your core values, consider reexamining your values.

Avoiding Values Drift

Values drift, the slow erosion of your core values over time, can steer you off course. When you observe lying, abuse, theft, or other forms of misconduct at work, or feel pressure to make ethical compromises, carefully and intentionally reflect on the values you hold dear and choose the appropriate ethical behavior that maintains your character and integrity. Monitor your commitment to your values and make adjustments when necessary to get your life back on track.

A friend offers to take you to the movies. She says she will save a few dollars by buying senior tickets online. Neither of you is a senior. What do you do?[20] The person you are dating often picks you up in his mother's car, which has a handicap license plate. He usually parks in spaces reserved for handicapped drivers. Do you say anything? The erosion of your core values can begin with decisions that may seem insignificant.

Total Person Insight

"Every time I've done something that doesn't feel right, it's ended up not being right."
Mario Cuomo, former governor of New York

Source: "Sunbeams" *The Sun*, January 2006, p. 48.

VALUES CONFLICTS

5-3 One of the major causes of conflict within an organization is the clash between the personal values of different people. There is no doubt about it; people are different. They have different family backgrounds, religious experiences, educations, role models, and media exposure. These differences can pop out anywhere and anytime people get together. Many observers suggest that organizations look for **values conflicts** when addressing such problems as declining quality, absenteeism, and poor customer service. The trouble may lie not so much in work schedules or production routines as in the mutual distrust and misunderstanding brought about by clashes in workers' and managers' value preferences. The late Peter Drucker, author of *The Practice of Management*, said: "Organizations are no longer built on force but on trust. The existence of trust between people does not mean that they like one another. It means that they understand one another. Taking responsibility for relationships is therefore an absolute necessity. It is a duty."[21]

Internal Values Conflicts

How you resolve internal values conflicts depends on your willingness to rank your core values in the order of their importance to you.

A person who is forced to choose between two or more strongly held values is experiencing an **internal values conflict**. Soon after the World Trade Center was attacked by terrorists, many people began to reexamine their values. Some decided to spend more time with family and friends, thinking that although overtime might be an opportunity to make more income, it was also an obstacle to maintaining a commitment to their family. Some workers also decided that their "work and spend" lifestyle no longer made sense. Before the terrorist attacks, a 28-year-old market research manager described herself as "very driven" and motivated to acquire things. Following September 11 she said, "Maybe I don't need all this stuff."[22]

How you resolve internal values conflicts depends on your willingness to rank your core values in the order of their importance to you. Prioritizing your values will help you make decisions when life gets complicated and you have to make difficult choices. In 2012, Lance Armstrong was officially stripped of all his bicycling racing titles, including his record run of seven Tour de France wins. The International Cycling Union acted after learning that Armstrong was at the center of a massive team doping scheme. During an interview with Oprah Winfrey he was asked if cheating was wrong. His answer was no.

Over the years Armstrong apparently ranked status, economic security, or some other core value higher than integrity.[23]

Values Conflicts with Others

As we have noted, four distinct generations have come together in the workplace. Employees from each generation bring with them different experiences and expectations. Values conflicts are more likely in this environment.

How will you handle a tense situation where it is obvious your values conflict with those of a colleague? You may discover your supervisor is a racist and you strongly support the civil rights of all people. One option is to become indignant and take steps to reduce contact with your supervisor. The problem with being indignant is that it burns your bridges with someone who can influence your growth and development within the organization. The opposite extreme would be to do nothing. But when we ignore unethical or immoral behavior, we compromise our integrity, and the problem is likely to continue and grow.[24] With a little reflection, you may be able to find a response somewhere between these two extremes. If your supervisor tells a joke that is demeaning to members of a minority group, consider meeting with her and explaining how uncomfortable these comments make you feel. When we confront others' lapses in character, we are strengthening our own integrity.

human RELATIONS *in Action*

TOWARD SOMETHING MEANINGFUL

Tony Dungy, the first African-American head coach to win a Super Bowl, and best-selling author of inspirational books, says his favorite verse in the Bible is Matthew 16:26: "What does it profit a man to gain the whole world but forfeit his soul?" Throughout his 30 years in the NFL, he saw a lot of players who earned huge amounts of money and received many accolades but were not happy because they have not directed their lives toward something meaningful.

Source: Matthew Kaminski, "A Coach's Faith," *Wall Street Journal*, September 12, 2009, p. A13.

PERSONAL VALUES AND ETHICAL CHOICES

5-4   **Ethics** refers to principles that define behavior as right, good, and proper. Your ethics, or the code of ethics of your organization, does not always dictate a single moral course of action, but it does provide a means of evaluating and deciding among several options.[25] Ethics determines where you draw the line between right and wrong.

As competition in the global marketplace increases, moral and ethical issues can become cloudy. Although most organizations have adopted the point of view that "good ethics is good business," exceptions do exist. Some organizations encourage, or at least condone, unethical behaviors. Surveys show that many workers feel pressure to violate their ethical standards in order to meet business objectives.[26] Thus, you must develop your own *personal* code of ethics.

Every job you hold will present you with new ethical and moral dilemmas. And many of the ethical issues you encounter will be very difficult. Instead of selecting from two clear-cut options—one right, one wrong—you often face multiple options.[27]

human
RELATIONS
in Action

A HIPPOCRATIC OATH FOR BUSINESS

Lawyers have their oath of attorney and doctors have the Hippocratic Oath. Now masters of business administration graduates have the *MBA Oath*, which you can find online. It is hoped that this oath will lay the foundation for a new generation of ethical business leaders. Those who sign the MBA Oath make eight promises. The first promise reads:

I will act with utmost integrity and pursue my work in an ethical manner. My personal behavior will be an example of integrity, consistent with the values I publicly espouse.

Source: Max Anderson and Peter Escher, *The MBA Oath* (New York: Penguin Group, 2010), pp. 6–13; 99.

How to Make the Right Ethical Choices

Unethical acts by employees cost U.S. businesses billions of dollars each year. Employee theft, fraud, and bribery represent three of the largest loss categories. Preventing these losses can be an uphill struggle.[28] The following guidelines may help you avoid being part of this growing statistic.

Learn to Distinguish Between Right and Wrong. Although selecting the right path can be difficult, a great deal of help is available through books, magazine articles, and a multitude of online resources. Support may be as close as your employer's code of ethics, guidelines published by your professional organization, or advice provided by an experienced and trusted colleague at work. Some ethical violations, on the surface, seem to be minor transgressions, but the consequences can be severe. Yahoo Inc. Chief Executive Scott Thompson was forced to resign when his misstated academic credentials surfaced. His public biography indicated he had a bachelor's degree in computer science and accounting. His degree from Stonehill College was in accounting, not computer science.[29]

Don't Let Your Life Be Driven by the Desire for Immediate Gratification. Progress and prosperity have almost identical meanings to many people. They equate progress with the acquisition of material things. One explanation is that young business leaders entering the corporate world are under a great deal of pressure to show the trappings of success—a large house or an expensive car, for example.

Some people get trapped in a vicious cycle: They work more so that they can buy more consumer goods; then, as they buy more, they must work more. They fail to realize that the road to happiness is not paved with Rolex watches, Brooks Brothers suits, and a Lexus. Chapter 17 offers support for finding satisfaction through nonfinancial resources that make the biggest contribution to a fulfilling life.

Make Certain Your Values Are in Harmony with Those of Your Employer. You may find it easier to make the right ethical choices if your values are compatible with those of your employer. Many organizations have adopted a set of beliefs, customs, values, and practices that attract a certain type of employee. Harmony between personal and organizational values usually leads to success for the individual as well as the organization.

When Tony Hsieh founded Zappos.com, an online shoe retailer, he was determined to create a culture that thrives on unique values and delivers exceptional levels of personalized customer service. Step one was developing a list of core values (see Figure 5.1) that would serve as the foundation for one of the strongest and most unique company cultures in the world. Step two was finding ways to integrate the core values into the employees' everyday behavior.

Since Zappos is "Powered by Customer Service," one of the biggest challenges is finding employees who love working with other people to deliver "Wow!" customer service. New candidates are screened in two interviews. One interview is focused on skills and the other on core values and cultural fit. Once hired, every employee goes through five weeks of training in culture, core values, and customer service. Zappos is now part of Amazon.com, and the fun, productive, and happy culture remains at this successful online retailer.[30]

Figure 5.1 ■ Zappos, one of America's most successful online retailers, is guided by these core values.

Zappos Core Values

1. **Deliver WOW Through Service**
   Go the "extra mile" to make sure that the customer is completely taken care of.
2. **Embrace and Drive Change**
   Realize that we are a growing company and that change is inevitable if we are going to stay relevant.
3. **Create Fun and a Little Weirdness**
   To ensure that our customers catch our enthusiasm, we need to create an environment worth passing on… not to mention the importance of not taking ourselves too seriously.
4. **Be Adventurous, Creative, and Open-Minded**
   In a setting that is going to change, an attitude of open-mindedness is key. Besides… who knows when the next big idea is going to hit; think "outside the box."
5. **Pursue Growth and Learning**
   Pushing yourself to the next level benefits the individual and the company as a whole.
6. **Build Open and Honest Relationships with Communication**
   It has been said, "Teamwork makes the dream work." Communication is the key to strong teams moving in the same direction for the common good of the company.
7. **Build a Positive Team and Family Spirit**
   Since the majority of one's week is spent at work, it seems only fitting to create an atmosphere worth coming to.
8. **Do More with Less**
   Money is not always the key to success. Sometimes solving the task at hand with limited resources brings about a greater sense of accomplishment and satisfaction for a "job well done."
9. **Be Passionate and Determined**
   Go for your dreams and desires and don't let anyone or anything stop you from doing what you want to do within the company.
10. **Be Humble**
    The truth is that it is not about me; keeping this in mind makes all of the other Core Values not only possible but attainable.

Source: © 2010 Zappos.com, Inc.

The corporate culture at Zappos is built on a foundation of outstanding customer service, which is why the company tends to attract outgoing, friendly, sociable employees.

CORPORATE VALUES AND ETHICAL CHOICES

5-5 What do Starbucks Coffee, UPS, and Marriott International have in common? Each of these companies has earned the World's Most Ethical (WME) Companies designation. The list is compiled each year by the Ethisphere Institute, an independent center of research (www.ethisphere.com) based in Scottsdale, Arizona. The WME designation recognizes companies that truly go beyond making statements about doing business "ethically" and translate those words into action.[31] These successful companies maintain an unwavering commitment to customers, business partners, and employees to perform with integrity and lead by example every day.

Corporate Crime

Many companies have gotten into serious trouble by ignoring ethical principles. In recent years, the media have carried headlines concerning organizations involved in corporate crime. Here are a few examples:

Environmental Damage. A few years ago a giant offshore oil drilling rig caught fire and exploded, killing 11 crew members. Over 200 million gallons of oil poured into the Gulf of Mexico, doing serious damage to the ecosystem. BP, the international energy company responsible for the Deepwater Horizon oil rig, says it has spent $43 billion so far in spill-related costs.[32]

Bribery and Corruption. When a company wants to do business in an emerging foreign market, bribery is used to overcome regulatory obstacles. Violations of the Foreign Corrupt Practices Act can result in multimillion-dollar fines.[33]

Product Safety. Several major corporations have been fined large sums of money for business practices that the U.S. government viewed as detrimental to consumer or employee safety. Merck & Company pleaded guilty to illegal promotion of its painkiller Vioxx and was fined $950 million.[34]

Leaders such as Jeffrey Immelt, CEO of General Electric, believe you can fuse high performance with high integrity. He realizes that employees at all levels of the company will be tempted to "make the numbers" by juggling accounts or cutting corners. From day one, he made a stirring call for performance with integrity. General Electric's 220 officers and 600 senior managers were told that failure to create the right culture would result in termination.[35] General Electric has received the World's Most Ethical Companies award for eight consecutive years.

Competitive pressures sometimes lead well-intentioned managers astray. Tom Chappell, author of *The Soul of a Business*, explains why organizations often have difficulty doing what is morally right and socially responsible: "It's harder to manage for ethical pursuits than it is to simply manage for profits."[36]

How to Prevent Corporate Crime

Establish and Support a Strong Code of Ethics.   We have recently seen an increase in ethical initiatives that make ethics a part of core organizational values. **Codes of ethics**, written statements of what an organization expects in the way of ethical behavior, can give employees a clear indication of what behaviors are acceptable or improper.[37] An ethics code can be a powerful force in building a culture of honesty, but only if it is enforced without exception.

human RELATIONS *in Action*

INTEGRITY IS BAKED IN

Bob's Red Mill Natural Foods started almost 40 years ago. Bob Moore and his wife enjoyed baking bread. They discovered the key to delicious bread was using the best whole-grain flour. They purchased an abandoned old mill and soon were selling quality whole grain flour to natural food stores in the Northwest. The owners say the key to success is to treat the customer like your guest, operating by the rule that the customer is always right.

Source: John Brant, "Bob Moore — Bob's Red Mill," *Inc.*, May 2012, pp. 83–84.

Hire with Care.   The hiring process used at Zappos provides a model for other organizations. First, identify a guiding set of core values and then find people who have those values. Success hinges on effective hiring interviews. At Umpqua Bank, where every element of the culture is focused on great customer service, potential candidates are interviewed by at least four associates who represent different areas of the bank. Those who are involved in the interviews have completed the "Hire the Best" training programs.[38]

Some companies use integrity tests (also called honesty or character tests) to screen out dishonest people. One standardized test designed to measure honesty is the Reid Report (http://en.wikipedia.org/wiki/Employment_integrity_testing). These tests are helpful, but they are not a substitute for rigorous interviewing and reference checks. Résumés that include exaggerations or outright fabrications tell you a lot about the integrity of the applicants.[39]

Provide Ethics Training.   Many ethical issues are complex and cannot be considered in black-and-white moral terms. The fact that an action is legal and does not violate a law does not necessarily make the action morally or ethically acceptable.[40] It is for these reasons that ethics training has become quite common. In some cases, the training involves little more than a careful study of the company ethics code and its implications

"Honesty is the best policy, Fernbaugh, but it's not company policy."

Leo Cullum The New Yorker Collection/The Cartoon Bank

for day-to-day decision making. In other cases, employees participate in in-depth discussions of complex ethical decisions.

In the wake of numerous corporate scandals, business schools have been criticized for producing graduates who are obsessed with making money regardless of the ethical consequences. In response to this criticism, business schools are trying a host of new methods, including required ethics courses and honor oaths.

Develop Support for Whistleblowing. When you discover that your employer or a colleague is behaving illegally or unethically, you have three choices. You can keep quiet and keep working. You can decide you can't be party to the situation and leave. Or you can report the situation in the hope of putting a stop to it. When you reveal wrongdoing within an organization to the public or to those in positions of authority, you are a **whistleblower**.

Total Person Insight

The honor code at West Point sends a clear message about what the U.S. Military Academy expects of its cadets:

"A cadet will not lie, cheat, steal, or tolerate those who do."

The last five words are the most difficult for most cadets. They have a responsibility to report misbehavior in their fellow cadets.

Source: William McGurn, "Duty, Honor, Football," *Wall Street Journal*, August 23, 2011, p. A11.

Table 5.3 ▪ Whistleblower Checklist

Experts say that people who are thinking about blowing the whistle on their company should ask themselves four important questions before doing so.

1. **Is this the only way?**
    Do not blow the whistle unless you have tried to correct the problem by reporting up the normal chain of command and gotten no results. Make sure your allegations are not minor complaints.

2. **Do I have the goods?**
    Gather documentary evidence that proves your case, and keep it in a safe place. Keep good notes, perhaps even a daily diary. Make sure you are seeing fraud, not merely incompetence or sloppiness.

3. **Why am I doing this?**
    Examine your motives. Do not act out of frustration or because you feel underappreciated or mistreated. Do not embellish your case, and do not violate any confidentiality agreements you may have.

4. **Am I ready?**
    Think through the impact on your family. Be prepared for unemployment and the possibility of being blacklisted in your profession.
    For additional information, visit www.whistleblower.org for a comprehensive list of rules and checklists.

Source: Paula Dwyer and Dan Carney, with Amy Borrus and Lorraine Woellert in Washington and Christopher Palmeri in Los Angeles, "Year of the Whistleblower," *BusinessWeek,* December 16, 2002, pp. 107–108; www.whistleblowers.org, February 2015.

Disclosing wrongdoing can be a daunting experience. Your colleagues may resent the disruption your revelations cause in their lives. They may be impressed with your integrity, but not everyone will be on your side in your struggle to do what is right and ethical. The National Whistleblower Center in Washington, D.C., has made significant strides in the worldwide fight against corruption. In January 2015 the organization released the report, *Whistleblower Reward Programs: An International Framework for the Detection of Corruption and Illegal Bribery.* The report recommends a framework for international whistleblower rewards programs. The report also outlines how reward programs are "remarkably successful" in detecting fraud and misconduct.[41] Each person must make his or her own decision whether the disturbing unethical offense is worth the personal cost. Table 5.3 lists four questions potential whistleblowers should ask themselves before taking action. A copy of *The Whistleblower's Handbook* by Stephen Kohn is available at www.whistleblowers.org.

VALUES AND ETHICS IN INTERNATIONAL BUSINESS

If the situation is complex on the domestic scene, values and ethical issues become even more complicated at the international level. American business firms are under great pressure to avoid doing business with overseas contractors that permit human rights violations such as child labor, low wages, and long hours in their factories. The 1977 Foreign Corrupt Practices Act and later amendments prohibit U.S. companies from using bribes or kickbacks to influence foreign officials, and many industrial nations have signed a multinational treaty outlawing corporate bribery. But monitoring illegal activities throughout the world is a difficult task. Doing business in the global marketplace continues to be an ethical minefield with illegal demands for bribes, kickbacks, or special fees standing in the way of successful transactions. American businesses acknowledge that it is difficult to compete with organizations from other countries that are not bound by U.S. laws. However, according to the International Business Ethics Institute (http://www.business-ethics.org), there has been significant progress in the last few years.

The federal government has been stepping up its pursuit of cases that involve violations of the Foreign Corrupt Practices Act. IBM recently agreed to pay a $10 million fine for engaging in widespread payment of bribes to vendors in Asia.[42]

LOOKING BACK: SUMMARY OF LEARNING OBJECTIVES

1. **Explain how moral intelligence contributes to personal and organizational success.**

   A strong sense of character grows out of your personal standards of behavior. When you consistently behave in accordance with your values, you maintain your integrity.

2. **Understand how personal values are formed.**

   Your values are the personal importance you give to an object or idea. People's values serve as the foundation for their attitudes, preferences, opinions, and behaviors. Your core values are largely formed early in life and are influenced by people and events in your life, your family, religious groups, your education, the media, and people you admire.

3. **Understand values conflicts and how to resolve them.**

   Internal values conflicts arise when you must choose between strongly held personal values. Value conflicts with others, often based on age, racial, religious, gender, or ethnic differences, require skilled intervention before they can be resolved.

4. **Learn how to make the right ethical decisions based on your personal value system.**

   Once you have clarified your personal values, your ethical decisions will be easier. You must learn to distinguish right from wrong, avoid the pursuit of immediate gratification, and choose an employer whose values you share. Shared values unify employees in an organization by providing guidelines for behavior and decisions.

5. **Understand the importance of corporate values and ethical choices.**

   Corporate values and ethics on both the domestic and the international levels are receiving increasing attention because of the devastating effect and expense of corporate crime. Many organizations are developing ethics codes to help guide employees' behavior, hiring only those people who share their corporate values, offering ethics training opportunities to all employees, and supporting whistleblowing. As multinational organizations increase in number, the people involved will need to consciously examine their values and ethical standards to deal effectively with differing values structures around the world.

KEY TERMS

moral intelligence, 100	observational learning, 104	ethics, 108
character, 100	modeling, 105	codes of ethics, 112
integrity, 100	values drift, 106	whistleblower, 113
values, 101	values conflicts, 107	
core values, 101	internal values conflict, 107	

CAREER INSIGHT

If you are job hunting, honesty is the best policy. George O'Leary was hired to become the next Notre Dame football coach, then was forced to resign five days later when lies about his academic and athletic achievements surfaced. Marilee Jones, an MIT dean, quit when her credentials proved to be inaccurate. When job seekers are struggling to find a job, they find it harder to resist embellishing their resumes or job applications.

A growing number of employers are checking résumé information, and these checks often reveal discrepancies. Résumé fraud is not uncommon, so employers are looking closely at the information you provide. Did you serve as a department head or did you hold a team leader position? Did you major in accounting or complete just two courses in accounting? Was your graduation GPA 3.00 or 2.7? Did you resign from your last position or were you fired? Now is the time to check your résumé and make sure it provides an accurate presentation of your work and education experience.

Source: Anna Prior, "In Job Hunting, Honesty Is Still the Best Policy," *Wall Street Journal Sunday*, April 25, 2010, p. 4E.

TRY YOUR HAND

1. Recent research indicates that it may take only a few minutes to prevent unethical behavior. When workers face a choice between right and wrong, they are about five times more likely to make the unethical choice when the decision is rushed.[43] Think about times in your life when you faced a moral decision and made the wrong choice. Did you feel rushed to make the decision? If you had taken more time to think or consult an ethical colleague, would you have made a different decision?

2. You work for a company where the HR director has been involved in unethical activities. You know that others are also aware of the situation; however, no one is willing to report the director's behavior to upper management. You do not want to be the whistleblower; however, you realize that guilt and loss of self-respect can result when you do or do not do things that conflict with what you believe. Discuss this situation with two or three classmates. Identify pros and cons of becoming a whistleblower.

3. One of the great challenges in life is the clarification of our values. The five-part valuing process described in Table 5.1 can be very helpful as you try to identify your core values. Select one personal or professional value from the following list, and clarify this value by applying the five-step process:
   a. Respect the rights and privileges of people who may be in the minority because of race, gender, ethnicity, age, physical or mental abilities, or sexual orientation.
   b. Conserve the assets of my employer.
   c. Use leisure time to add balance to my life.
   d. Maintain a healthy lifestyle.
   e. Balance the demands of my work and personal life.

CRITICAL THINKING CHALLENGE

Practice making ethical choices based on your value priorities in the following scenarios.

- You are offered a great job, but you have to relocate to a distant city. Your spouse and children agree that the decision is yours to make, but you know they do not want to move. What do you do?
- You have discovered that your boss lied on her résumé about her academic credentials. She is being considered for a new position in your organization, but you believe you are more qualified than she is. Will you tell the hiring panel about your boss's indiscretion?
- You are taking an online college class and have been offered the final exam from a student who printed a copy for you after taking the exam yesterday. The correct answers are not on the test copy. You are in danger of failing the class and losing your financial aid. Do you accept the document or use it to study for your exam?

SELF-ASSESSMENT EXERCISE

For each of the following statements, circle the number from 1 to 5 that best represents your response to each statement: (1) strongly disagree (never do this); (2) dis- agree (rarely do this); (3) moderately agree (sometimes do this); (4) agree (frequently do this); (5) strongly agree (almost always do this).

A.	I base my personal and professional decisions on clearly defined personal values.	1	2	3	4	5
B.	I accept the fact that others' values may differ from mine, and I respect their right to maintain a value system that differs from my own.	1	2	3	4	5
C.	I have a clear sense of what is right and wrong, and my character reflects the fundamental strengths of honesty, fairness, service, humility, and modesty.	1	2	3	4	5
D.	I maintain my integrity by practicing what I believe in and keeping my commitments.	1	2	3	4	5
E.	When I observe unethical practices, I will report them to the appropriate person(s).	1	2	3	4	5

After identifying your response to each item, select an attitude or skill you would like to improve. Prepare a written goal and then describe the steps you will take to achieve this goal.

YOU PLAY THE ROLE

You are currently employed by a pharmaceutical wholesaler that sells prescription drugs to hospitals in a three-county area. Each morning, you help other employees fill orders that arrive via computer or the telephone. Once the orders are completed and loaded into delivery vans, you spend the rest of the day delivering products to hospitals. Although others help fill the orders, you are responsible for the accuracy of each order and for timely delivery. Rob Howard, a fellow employee, performs the same duties, but delivers items to hospitals in a different territory. Over the past two months, you have noticed that he sometimes makes poor ethical choices. For example, the company's reimbursement for lunch is a maximum of $8. Rob packs each day's lunch and never eats at a restaurant. At the end of each week, however, his reimbursement form claims the maximum amount for each meal. Once he bragged about earning an extra $40 each week for meals that were not purchased.

Rob owns a small landscaping business on the side and sometimes uses the company van to transport items to customers. Recently you drove by a Home Depot store and noticed him loading bags of mulch into the company van. At one point you thought about talking with the supervisor about these ethical lapses, but decided to talk with Rob first. Another class member will assume the role of Rob Howard. Try to convince him that some of these on-the-job activities are unethical.

BELOW THE SURFACE | LEADING A CULTURAL TURNAROUND

Henk Meijer/Alamy

At the beginning of this chapter you were introduced to Mary Barra, chief executive officer of General Motors. Soon after her promotion she faced a growing scandal around the ignition-switch crisis. At a congressional hearing she apologized for GM's slow response to the deadly problem in 2.6 million small cars. She portrayed herself as the leader of a customer-focused "new" General Motors, a person ready to implement new values and policies.

Critics say Barra must lead a full-fledged cultural turnaround. Some suggest she study the actions of Alan Mulally, who became chief executive of Ford Motor Company during one of its darkest periods. When he arrived in 2006 the company was facing major financial losses, low morale, and declining vehicle sales. Executives were not sharing critical information about troubled operations with one another, the same problem that existed at GM. Mulally introduced mandatory weekly meetings of senior leaders. At these meetings they were required to share both good and bad news.[44] He introduced a simplified plan named "One Ford" that was summarized on wallet-size cards. The plan was built upon four expected behaviors:

Foster Functional and Technical Excellence
Own Working Together
Role Model Ford Values
Deliver Results[45]

QUESTIONS

1. Mary Barra, a 33-year veteran of the company, has met with family members of crash victims and announced that GM has hired Ken Feinberg to oversee victim payments. He assumed a similar role after the 9/11 terrorist attacks and BP's oil spill in the Gulf of Mexico. How would you rate Barra's approach to victim compensation?

2. Company correspondence and information from legal depositions suggest a GM culture during the past decade where employees worked in "silos," isolated from other departments and critical information. What steps can Barra take to improve internal lines of communication to be certain that customer complaints and evidence of safety problems get acted on more quickly?

3. Barra has announced a safety whistleblower program for employees. She has said that the "Speak Up for Safety" program will recognize employees who discover and report safety issues. What steps can top executives at GM take to be sure the whistleblower program is a success?

CLOSING CASE | PEOPLE AND PURPOSE AT NEW BELGIUM BREWING

New Belgium Brewing Company, based in Fort Collins, Colorado, was founded by a husband and wife team who met over a beer at a friend's house. A year later, they founded their own brewery, which has grown to become America's third-largest craft brewery.

After they toured several European villages famous for beer, the plan for New Belgium Brewing Company started to take shape. (Touring on a bicycle with fat tires, of course.) The new entrepreneurs wanted to create an outstanding beer and minimize the company's footprint on the planet. They prepared a vision statement and a list of core values before they ever sold a bottle of beer. One of the core values reads: "Environmental stewardship: Honoring nature at every turn of the business." This core value reflects their strong belief in sustainability. As early adopters of the movement toward sustainability, employees voted to make New Belgium Brewing the first 100 percent wind-powered brewery in 1998. The company has set goals to reduce its carbon footprint by 25 percent, reduce water usage by 10 percent, offset eight million car miles by riding bikes, and supporting the on-site recycling center.

An employee ownership plan encourages employees to become more engaged. Employees own about 32 percent of New Belgium through a stock-ownership plan. The company has embraced open-book management practices that include monthly meetings where employees review financial statements, business strategies, and branding plans. They worked hard to create a culture of transparency that fosters trust and respect. The result of New Belgium's passion and purpose tied to business practices is an amazing employee retention rate of 92 percent.[46]

QUESTIONS

1. Carefully review the business practices at New Belgium Brewing Company and determine which of these would be most appealing to you.

2. In 1998, employees at New Belgium Brewing voted to make the company 100 percent wind-powered, even if it meant forfeiting their yearly bonus. Would you support this initiative even if it meant a reduction in your earnings?

3. New Belgium Brewing has created a high-involvement employee culture. What are some of the major benefits of a culture of transparency?

CHAPTER 5 ENDNOTES

1. Rupali Arora, Catherine Dunn, Beth Kowitt, Colleen Leahey, Patricia Sellers, and Anne Vandermey, "Most Powerful Women," *Fortune*, p. 66.

2. Jeff Bennett and Charles Levinson, "GM Criminal Probe Set for New Phase," *Wall Street Journal*, April 10, 2014, p. B4.

3. James R. Healey, "GM Suspends Two Engineers, Seeks NASA Safety Help," *USA Today*, April 11, 2014, p. 2B.

4. Charles M. Blow, "The Millennial Minds," *News & Observer*, March 11, 2014, p. 9A; Christopher Bonanos, "The Lies We Tell at Work," *Bloomberg Businessweek*, February 10, 2013, pp. 71–73.

5. Doug Lennick and Fred Kiel, *Moral Intelligence* (Upper Saddle River, NJ: Pearson Education, 2010), p. 7.

6. David Gergen, "Candidates with Character," *U.S. News & World Report*, September 27, 1999, p. 68. The importance of honesty in leadership positions is discussed in James M. Kouzes and Barry Z. Posner, *The Leadership Challenge*, 3d ed. (San Francisco: Jossey-Bass, 2002), pp. 27–28.

7. Ross Tartell, "Can Leadership Ethics Be Learned?" *Training*, May/June 2011, pp. 16–18.

8. Nathaniel Branden, *Self-Esteem at Work* (San Francisco: Jossey-Bass, 1998), p. 35; Brian Tracy, *The 100 Absolutely Unbreakable Laws of Business Success* (San Francisco, CA: Berrett-Koehler, 2002), p. 121.

9. Hyrum W. Smith, *The 10 Natural Laws of Successful Time and Life Management* (New York: Warner Books, 1994), pp. 14–15.

10. J. David McCracken and Ana E. Falcon-Emmanuelli, "A Theoretical Basis for Work Values Research in Vocational Education," *Journal of Vocational and Technical Education*, April 1994, p. 4.

11. Sue Shellenbarger, "Some Top Executives Are Finding a Balance Between Job and Home," *Wall Street Journal*, April 23, 1997, p. B1. Anne Mulcahy was named CEO of the year in 2008 by *Tech Her*.

12. Katharine Mieszkowski, "FitzGerald Family Values," *Fast Company*, April 1998, p. 194.

13. Neil Howe and William Strauss, "The Next 20 Years: How Customers and Workforce Attitudes Will Evolve," *Harvard Business Review*, July/August 2007, pp. 41–52.

14. Jeffrey Zaslow, "The Latest Generation Gap: Boomers Are Often Unfairly Lumped Together," *Wall Street Journal*, July 8, 2004, p. 1; Shirley Holt, "Generation Gaps in the Workplace," *The Roanoke Times*, March 27, 2005, pp. 1, 3; Karen Auby, "A Boomer's Guide to Communicating with Gen X and Gen Y," *BusinessWeek*, August/ September 1, 2008, p. 63; Roy Saunderson, "Learning Across the Generations," *Training*, May/June 2011, pp. 78–79.

15. Chris Lee and Ron Zemke, "The Search for Spirit in the Workplace," *Training*, June 1993, p. 21.

16. "The Ethics of American Youth," Josephson Institute of Ethics [cited 22 February 2015]. Available from www.josephsoninstitute.org; INTERNET.

17. Douglas A. Bernstein, Louis A. Penner, Alison Clarke-Stewart, and Edward J. Roy, *Psychology*, 9th ed. (Boston: Cengage Learning, 2012), pp. 227–231.

18. O. C. Ferrell, John Fraedrich, and Linda Ferrell, *Business Ethics*, 5th ed. (Houghton Mifflin, 2002), pp. 123–135.

19. Doug Lennick and Fred Kiel, *Moral Intelligence* (Upper Saddle River, NJ: Pearson Education, 2008), p. 46.

20. Jancee Dunn, "Now What Do I Do?" *O, The Oprah Magazine*, March 2008, p. 89.

21. John Hollon, "Drucker Knew Best," *Workforce Management*, November 21, 2005, p. 58.

22. Sue Shellenbarger, "In Cataclysmic Times, Workers Need Room to Rethink Priorities," *Wall Street Journal*, September 19, 2001, p. B1.

23. John Revill and Vanessa O'Connell, "Armstrong Is Stripped of Titles in Cycling," *Wall Street Journal*, October 23, 2012, p. A4; Jason Gay, "Would Lance Believe Lance?" *Wall Street Journal*, January 17, 2013, p. D6; Jim Litke, "Armstrong Admits to Doping," *News & Observer*, January 18, 2013, p. 6C.

24. John Beebe, "Conscience, Integrity and Character," *The Inner Edge*, June/July 2000, pp. 9–11.

25. "Making Sense of Ethics." [cited 13 January 2003]. Available from http://www.josephsoninstitute.org/MED/MED-1makingsense.htm; INTERNET.

26. Craig Mindrum, "Business Ethics—Moral Intelligence and *Workforce* Performance," **Workforce Performance Solutions**, March 2006, pp. 28–32.

27. Price Pritchett, **The Ethics of Excellence** (Dallas, TX: Pritchett & Associates, n.d.), p. 28.

28. "CyberSource* Joins with Association of Certified Fraud Examiners to Support 2002 National Fraud Awareness Week," July 29, 2002. [cited 13 January 2003]. Available from http://phx.corporate-ir.net/phoenix.zhtml?c=94844&p=irol-newsArticle&ID=320302&highlight=; INTERNET; Raymund Flandez, "Stop That Thief," **Wall Street Journal**, June 16, 2008, p. R6.

29. Amir Efrati and Joann S. Lublin, "Yahoo CEO's Downfall," **Wall Street Journal**, May 15, 2012, p. B5.

30. Monique Reece, **Real-Time Marketing for Business Growth** (Upper Saddle River: NJ: Pearson Education, 2010), pp. 14–16.

31. "Ethisphere Announces 2014 World's Most Ethical Companies," March 20, 2014, Retrieved from www.ethisphere.com; INTERNET

32. Tom Fowler, "BP Slapped with Record Fine," **Wall Street Journal**, November 16, 2012, pp. A1 and A6; Daniel Gilbert, "For BP Gulf Fine, Judge Weighs Installment Plan," **Wall Street Journal**, January 21, 2015, p. B1; Campbell Robertson and John Schwartz, "BP Shifts Position on Gulf Payouts," **News & Observer**, April 27, 2014, p. A1. Halliburton Company has acknowledged that it played a role in the accident. See Daniel Gilbert, "Halliburton Agrees to Pay $1.1 Billion for U.S. Gulf Spill," **Wall Street Journal**, September 3, 2014, p. B2.

33. Dan Currell and Tracy Davis Bradley, "Greased Palms, Giant Headaches," **Harvard Business Review**, September 12, 2012, pp. 21–23.

34. Peter Loftus and Brent Kendall, "Merck to Pay $950 Million Vioxx Settlement," **Wall Street Journal**, November 23, 2011, p. B3.

35. Ben W. Heineman, Jr., "Avoiding Integrity Land Mines," **Harvard Business Review**, April 2007, pp. 100–108.

36. "Tom Chappell—Minister of Commerce," **Business Ethics**, January/February 1994, p. 17.

37. Ferrell, Fraedrich, and Ferrell, **Business Ethics**, pp. 182–183.

38. Margery Weinstein, "You're Hired," **Training**, July/August 2011, pp. 34–37. For more information on the importance of cultural fit, read Ari Weinzweig, "Ask Ari Weinzweig," **Inc.**, December 2007, p. 84.

39. Anne Fisher, "How Can You Be Sure We're Not Hiring a Bunch of Shady Liars?" **Fortune**, May 26, 2003, p. 180.

40. Michelle Reece, "Business Ethics and the Pharmaceutical Industry," **SPBT Focus**, Fall 2005, p. 24.

41. www.whistleblowers.org [cited February 22, 2015]; INTERNET.

42. Jessica Holzer and Shayndi Raice, "IBM Settles Bribery Charges," **Wall Street Journal**, March 19, 2011, p. B1.

43. Rachel Emma Silverman, "Take a Deep Breath, Make Ethical Choices," **Wall Street Journal**, March 7, 2012, p. B9.

44. Doron Levin, "New GM: Same As It Ever Was?" **Fortune**, April 29, 2014, pp. 64–67.

45. "One Ford" retrieved from http://operations.blog, i.e edu/one-ford.

46. Kelly K. Spors, "Top Small Workplaces," **Wall Street Journal**, October 13, 2008, pp. R1 and R8; "Workplace Awards" [accessed 28 December 2008]. Available from http://www.winningworkplaces.org; INTERNET; "Our Story" [accessed 29 December 2008]. Available from http://www.newbelgium.com; INTERNET.

Attitudes Can Shape Your Life

TIP OF THE ICEBERG | BRAND DEVELOPMENT AT JIFFY LUBE

Each year *Training* magazine conducts a national study to determine the top 125 companies that excel in the area of training and development. The number one spot on the 2014 list was awarded to Jiffy Lube International, Inc. The company has more than 2,000 franchise-owned service centers in North America.[1]

More than 20,000 highly trained and certified technicians and managers work at Jiffy Lube service centers. Every technician is required to complete a series of training programs designed and implemented by Jiffy Lube University.[2]

The JLU training programs place a great deal of emphasis on shaping attitudes. The brand's core promise is: Jiffy Lube believes every driver deserves to be free from the anxiety of keeping his or her vehicle in top shape. All technicians are required to complete a comprehensive training program so they can speak with authority and establish a high level of trust with the customer. Today customer service scores have achieved an overall positive response level of 90.6 percent.

One of the greatest challenges Jiffy Lube franchises face is the need to develop competent leaders at the store manager level. Team leader certification involves 14 e-learning courses, a three-day Leadership Training instructor-led class, and a Leadership Challenge simulation. Leadership training focuses on key factors in developing a winning team.[3]

The beneficial impact of individual and organizational attitudes is not always easy to measure. However, the correlation between positive attitudes and high performance, low employee turnover, and increased productivity exists in most organizations. At Jiffy Lube International, the average length of employee service is 12 years, and 90 percent of job openings are filled by internal candidates.[4]

Bounce/Cultura/Getty Images

Training magazine conducts a national study to determine the top 125 companies that excel in the area of training and development. The number one spot on the 2014 list was awarded to Jiffy Lube International, Inc. A car leaves a Jiffy Lube store. The company excels in the area of employee training and development.

THE IMPORTANCE OF ATTITUDES

6-1 **Attitudes** are thoughts that you have accepted as true and that lead you to think, feel, or act positively or negatively toward a person, idea, or event. Social psychologists have studied attitude development intensely over many years. They view attitudes as having three components:[5]

- **Cognitive** This component is a set of beliefs about the attitude object. Many years ago, tobacco companies spent millions of dollars publicizing the pleasure of smoking certain cigarette brands. The health-threatening aspects of smoking were not mentioned. Today, the number of adults in the United States who smoke has declined steadily because their beliefs have been shaped by accurate information about the dangers of smoking.
- **Emotional** The emotional, or *affective* component includes feelings about the object. Every year many environmental organizations ask us for generous donations. The messages we receive through the year appeal to our emotions.
- **Behavioral** This component is the way people act toward the object. If you read an article on the homeless in your community, and the message appeals to your emotions, you may be inclined to help them in some way. However, in many areas of lives, our positive thoughts and supportive emotions are never translated into actions.

Bruce Clarke, president and CEO of a North Carolina–based human resource management firm, says, "No one has ever been fired for a bad attitude." He explains that attitude may be the reason given, but the real reason was poor behavior. We cannot know with certainty another person's attitude, but we can observe and act on behaviors.[6]

We should keep in mind that the success of organizations is greatly influenced by the attitudes of their leaders. The traditional purpose of business, according to some economists, is to make money. That narrow focus motivates leaders to maximize short-term profits and deliver good returns to shareholders. Rosabeth Moss Kanter, professor of business administration at Harvard Business School, says great companies generate money, but they are also vehicles for accomplishing societal purposes and providing meaningful livelihoods for those who work for them.[7]

Panda Express is a fast-growing and successful restaurant group. It is a privately owned, 1,500-location "fast casual" Asian restaurant chain. Andrew Cherng and his wife Peggy hold the titles of co-chairman and co-CEO. Cherng says business is really about empowering people to act like owners themselves. He says, "what I am most proud of is seeing our people and the business grow."[8]

Hiring for Attitude

Some of the best companies to work for are willing to go the extra mile to hire people with the right attitude. A good example is Basecamp, a Chicago-based software company. Jason Fried, cofounder of Basecamp, says there is one quality that has never let him down: "It's effort. I hire people on the basis of the effort they put into getting the job." If a candidate sends a standard résumé and cover letter that has been sent to many other employers, the person is given no further consideration. A serious job applicant will customize all application materials, emphasizing specific strengths and give detailed examples of previous accomplishments. During the interview, a well-prepared candidate will be ready to provide additional information about personal strengths and achievements.[9]

Total Person Insight

Each year, thousands of people apply for jobs at Southwest Airlines. Those who are hired are willing and able to champion the corporate culture: *warrior spirit, servant's heart, and fun-loving attitude*.

Source: Alison Beard and Richard Hornik, "It's Hard to Be Good," *Harvard Business Review*, November 2011, pp. 91–92.

Healing Career Wounds

During the recent economic slump, the U.S. Chamber of Commerce reported that 23 million Americans were unemployed, underemployed, or had given up looking for jobs.[10] After losing a job, it's easy to fall into a funk and become pessimistic about the future.

Another alarming development in the American workplace is the number of employees who work in a negative work environment. A recent Gallup survey indicates that about 20 million workers are actively disengaged and dislike going to work. These workers are unhappy and unproductive, and they often spread negativity to coworkers.[11] In Chapter 7 we will discuss ways to increase employee engagement and improve morale.

Core Values Revisited

In Chapter 5, we described *core values* as those values that one consistently ranks higher than others. You were introduced to a five-part valuing process that can help you clarify and develop your values (see Table 5.1). Each of us lives our life according to a unique set of core values. They are fundamental building blocks of your personality. Examples may include honesty, financial security, healthy spirituality, generosity, or maintaining good health. They represent the clearest answers you can give to these questions:[12]

- What are the highest priorities in my life?
- Of these priorities, which do I value most?

Clarifying and developing values is a process that is available throughout our lives. We are constantly choosing from alternatives and considering the consequences of these alternatives. Behavior is more likely to be consistent with attitude when people see their attitudes as important and relevant to their lives—that is, when they match their core values.[13] If you are invited, for example, to be active in a campaign to support the rights of gay men and lesbians, you will likely reflect on your core values.

Total Person Insight

"Our thoughts are private; our emotions are not. Others know how we feel—and that is very important for how people get along with each other."

Source: Dalai Lama, *Destructive Emotions: How Can We Overcome Them?* (New York: Bantam Books, 2003), p. 134.

The Age of Information Mandates Attitude Changes

During the early stages of the information age, many of the best jobs were filled by people who were proficient at reasoning, logical thinking, and analysis. However, as the information age unfolded and the global economy heated up, organizations discovered that it often takes more than quick and accurate information communicated through advanced technology to retain their clients and customers. In many cases, two competing firms, such as banks, may offer customers the same products at the same prices and use the same information technology. The competitive advantage is achieved through superior customer service provided by well-trained employees with effective interpersonal skills.

Daniel Pink, author of *A Whole New Mind*, says we are moving from the information age to the conceptual age. He predicts that one of the major players in the conceptual age will be the **empathizer**. Empathizers have the ability to imagine themselves in someone else's position and understand what that person is feeling. They can understand the subtleties of human interaction.[14] For example, several medical schools have come to the conclusion that empathy is a key element of compassionate medical care. Medical school students at Harvard, Columbia, and Dartmouth are learning that an important part of health care diagnosis is contained in the patient's story. They are trained to identify the subtle details of a patient's condition through caring, compassionate attitudes.[15]

Technology in its many forms will continue to make a major contribution to the workplace. However, we must seek a better balance between "high tech" and "high touch." Leadership, for example, is about empathy. It is about having the ability to relate to and to connect with people. Pink states: "Empathy builds self-awareness, bonds parent to child, allows us to work together, and provides the scaffolding for our morality."[16]

Daniel H. Pink, author of A *Whole New Mind*, predicts that one of the major players in the New Conceptual Age will be the empathizer. These workers have the ability to imagine themselves in someone else's position and understand what that person is feeling.

HOW ATTITUDES ARE FORMED

6-2 Throughout life, you are constantly making decisions and judgments that help form your attitudes. These attitude-shaping decisions are often based on behaviors your childhood authority figures told you were right or wrong, behaviors for which you were rewarded or punished. The role models you select and the various environmental and organizational cultures you embrace also shape your attitudes.

Socialization

The process through which people are integrated into a society by exposure to the actions and opinions of others is called **socialization**. As a child, you interacted with your parents, family, teachers, and friends to learn the skills and social norms necessary to be well-functioning members of society.[17] Children often feel that statements made by these authority figures are the "proper" things to believe.

Peer and Reference Groups

Kurt Mortensen, author of *Maximum Influence—The 12 Universal Laws of Power Persuasion*, says we tend to change our perceptions, opinions, and behaviors in ways that are consistent with group norms. He states that people want to be liked by others and feel connected.[18] As children reach adolescence and begin to break away psychologically from their parents, the **peer group** (people their own age) can have a powerful influence on attitude formation. With the passing of years, reference groups replace peer groups as sources of attitude formation in young adults. A **reference group** consists of several people who share a common interest. Sales and Marketing Executives International would serve as a reference group for persons employed in sales and marketing.

Rewards and Punishment

Attitude formation is often related to rewards and punishment. People in authority generally encourage certain attitudes and discourage others. Naturally, individuals tend to develop attitudes that minimize punishments and maximize rewards. A child who is praised for sharing toys with playmates is more likely to develop positive attitudes toward caring about other people's needs. As an adult, you will discover that your employers will continue to try to shape your attitudes through rewards and punishment at work. Many organizations are rewarding employees who take steps to stay healthy, avoid accidents, increase sales, or reduce expenses.

Total Person Insight

"When doing business internationally, understand that you are the one who needs to adapt. You are the visitor; you must be the one who changes his or her behavior. The old adage, 'When in Rome, do as the Romans do,' is absolutely true."

Source: Barbara Pachter, *When the Little Things Count... and They Always Count*, Cambridge, MA: Da Capo Press, 2006, pp. 167–168.

Role Model Identification

Most young people would like to have more influence, status, and popularity. These goals are often achieved through identification with an authority figure or a role model. A **role model** is that person you most admire or are likely to emulate. As you might expect, role models can exert considerable influence—for better or for worse—on developing attitudes.

Role models can exert considerable influence—for better or for worse—on developing attitudes.

In most organizations, supervisory and management personnel can have the greatest impact on employee attitudes. The new dental hygienist and the recently hired auto mechanic want help adjusting to their jobs. They watch their supervisors' attitudes toward safety, cost control, accuracy, grooming, and customer relations. Tory Burch, CEO and designer at Tory Burch, LLC, based in New York City, wants her company to be known as a great place to work. She says when she started the company, "... I wanted to have a place where it was first of all about kindness and treating people with dignity and respect—treating everyone that way regardless of your position."[19]

Cultural Influences

Our attitudes are influenced by the culture that surrounds us. **Culture** is the sum total of knowledge, beliefs, values, objects, and ethnic customs that we use to adapt to our environment. It includes tangible items, such as foods, clothing, and furniture, as well as intangible concepts, such as education and laws. In companies, corporate culture is influenced by all of these factors, and ultimately it is defined by the way people work together to get things done.[20]

Today's organizations are striving to create corporate cultures that attract and retain productive workers in these volatile times. When employees feel comfortable in their work environment, they tend to stay. As noted previously in this chapter, Southwest Airlines has created a company culture that has built an energetic corps of customer-loving employees.

ATTITUDES SHAPE STEW LEONARD'S CULTURE

Stew Leonard's, a highly profitable four-store supermarket in Connecticut and New York, has developed a distinctive culture that emphasizes teamwork and devotion to customer service. Shortly after opening his first store, Stew Leonard adopted two basic store policies that were chiseled into a 6,000-pound rock next to the front door of his store. The simple message reads:

Rule 1—**THE CUSTOMER IS ALWAYS RIGHT!**

Rule 2—**IF THE CUSTOMER IS EVER WRONG, RE-READ RULE 1.**

Source: Philip Kotler and Gary Armstrong, *Principles of Marketing*, 12th ed. (Upper Saddle River, NJ: Prentice Hall, 2008), p. 20.

The company that sweats together stays together. That is the belief held by Greg Wittstock, CEO of Aquascape, a multimillion-dollar pond-supply company based in St. Charles, Illinois. Several years ago, some employees said that they would like the company to build a soccer field. The company was expanding, so Wittstock decided to build a new home for Aquascape. He decreed that about 20 percent of the new headquarters would be dedicated to "fun stuff." He built a racquetball court, an indoor soccer field, a batting cage, a hot tub, and numerous other places of merriment. Greg Wittstock believes that happy workers are productive workers.[21]

ATTITUDES VALUED BY EMPLOYERS

 Many organizations have discovered the link between workers' attitudes and profitability. This discovery has led to major changes in the hiring and training process. Employers today are less likely to assume that applicants' technical abilities are the best indicators of their future performance. They have discovered that the lack of technical skills is not the primary reason why most new hires fail to meet expectations. Too often new employees are not capable enough in terms of interpersonal skills.[22]

Whether you are looking for your first career position, anticipating a career change, or being retrained for new opportunities, you may find the following discussion helpful concerning what attitudes employers want in their employees.

Basic Interpersonal Skills

In this information-based, high-tech, fast-paced economy, we are witnessing an increase in workplace incivility. Rude behavior in the form of high-decibel cell phone conversations, use of profanity, or failure to display simple courtesies such as saying "thank you" can damage workplace relationships. As we note in Chapter 11, incivility is the ultimate career killer.

Self-Motivation

People who are self-motivated are inclined to set their own goals and monitor their own progress toward those goals.

People who are self-motivated are inclined to set their own goals and monitor their own progress toward those goals. Their attitude is "I am responsible for this job." They do not need a supervisor hovering around them making sure they are on task and accomplishing what they are supposed to be doing. Many find ways to administer their own rewards after they achieve their goals. Employers often retain and promote those employees who take the initiative to make their own decisions, find better ways of doing their jobs, and keep up to date in their area of specialization. Self-motivation is a major theme of Chapter 7.

Openness to Change

In the age of information, the biggest challenge for many workers is adjusting to the rapidly accelerating rate of change. Some resistance to change is normal merely because it may alter your daily routine. However, you will get into trouble if you choose the following three attitudes:[23]

1. *Stubbornness.* Some workers refuse to be influenced by someone else's point of view. They also find fault with every new change.
2. *Arrogance.* Employees who reject advice or who give the impression that they do not want retraining or other forms of assistance send the wrong message to their employer.
3. *Inflexibility.* Displaying a closed mind to new ideas and practices can only undermine your career advancement opportunities.

Team Spirit

In sports, the person who is a "team player" receives a great deal of praise and recognition. A team player is someone who is willing to step out of the spotlight, give up a little personal glory, and help the team achieve a victory. Team players are no less important in organizations. Employers are increasingly organizing employees into teams (health teams, sales teams, product development teams) that build products, solve problems, and make decisions. Chapter 12 contains some tips on how to become a respected team member.

Health Consciousness

The ever growing cost of health care is one of the most serious problems facing companies today. Many organizations are promoting wellness programs for all employees as a way to keep costs in line. These programs include tips on healthy eating, physical fitness exercises, and stress management practices, as well as other forms of assistance that contribute to a healthy lifestyle. Employees who actively participate in these programs often take fewer sick days, file fewer medical claims, and bring a higher level of energy to work. Chapters 14 and 17 discuss health and wellness in greater detail.

Appreciation of Coworker Diversity

To value diversity in the work setting means to make full use of the ideas, talents, experiences, and perspectives of all employees at all levels within the organization. People who differ from each other often add richness to the organization.

Development and utilization of a talented, diverse workforce can be a key to success in a period of fierce global competition. Women and people of color make up a large majority of the new multicultural, global workforce. Many people, however, carry prejudiced attitudes against those who differ from them. They tend to "prejudge" others' value based on the color of their skin, gender, age, religious preference, lifestyle, political affiliation, sexual orientation, or economic status. Chapter 15 contains specific guidance on how to develop positive attitudes toward joining a diverse workforce.

Honesty

Honesty and truthfulness are qualities all employers are searching for in their employees. This is because relationships depend on trust. An honest employee's attitude is "I owe my employer and coworkers the truth." If you cannot be honest with your employer, customers, fellow workers, and friends, they cannot trust you, and strong relationships will be impossible.

HOW TO CHANGE ATTITUDES

 6-4 If you are having difficulty working with other team members, if you believe you were overlooked for a promotion you should have had, or if you go home from work depressed and a little angry at the world, you can almost always be sure you need an attitude adjustment. Unfortunately, people do not easily adopt new attitudes or discard old ones. It is difficult to break the attachment to emotionally laden beliefs. Yet attitudes *can* be changed. There may be times when you absolutely hate a job, but you can still develop a positive attitude toward it as a stepping-stone to another job you actually do want.

> *It is often said that life is 10 percent what happens to you and 90 percent how you react to it.*

There will be times, as well, when you will need to help colleagues change their attitudes so that you can work with them more effectively. And, of course, when events, such as a layoff, are beyond your control, you can accept this fact and move on. It is often said that life is 10 percent what happens to you and 90 percent how you react to it. Knowing how to change attitudes in yourself and others can be essential to effective interpersonal relations—and your success—in life.

Changing Your Own Attitude

You are constantly placed in new situations with people from different backgrounds and cultures. Each time you go to a new school, take a new job, get a promotion, or move to a different neighborhood, you may need to alter your attitudes to cope effectively with the change. The following attitudes will help you achieve positive results in today's world.

Choose Happiness. In his best-selling book *The Art of Happiness*, the Dalai Lama presents happiness as the foundation of all other attitudes. He suggests that the pursuit of happiness is the purpose of our existence. Survey after survey has shown that unhappy people tend to be self-focused, socially withdrawn, and even antagonistic. Happy people, in contrast, are generally found to be more sociable, flexible, and creative and are able to tolerate life's daily frustrations more easily than unhappy people.[24] Tal Ben-Shahar, Harvard University professor and author of *Happier*, sees a strong link between happiness and success:[25] "All else being equal, happy people have better relationships, are more likely to thrive at work, and also live better and longer."

human RELATIONS *in Action*

WHO MOVED MY CHEESE?

Many years ago, Spencer Johnson wrote *Who Moved My Cheese?* In this small book, which has been on the bestseller list for more than a decade, Johnson introduces the reader to a fable on how to cope positively with change. He recognizes that change is a basic fact of life, so learning to cope with it is an important life strategy. Johnson's most important message is that instead of seeing change as the end of something, you need to learn to see it as a beginning. Breaking through your fear of change is a very important attitude shift in our fluid, ever-changing working world.

Source: Tom Butler-Bowdon, *50 Success Classics* (London: Nicholas Brealey, 2004), pp. 168–171.

So, if achieving happiness is truly an important goal, what can we do to achieve it? Here are some important tips:

- *What we choose to focus on largely determines our level of happiness.* The potential for happiness may be all around us, but it may go unnoticed.[26] Let's assume that you are earning an adequate income, but you want to earn more money. Chances are that having more money will not bring greater happiness. It may be time to stop and answer the question: What gives me pleasure? What do I enjoy doing? If earning more money means working longer hours, you may be unable to do things (spend time with family, enjoy more leisure time) that you truly enjoy and that bring you happiness.

- *Mentally reframe events or activities that create unhappiness.* Ralph Waldo Emerson once said, "To different minds, the same world is a hell, and a heaven."[27] Beth Zimmerman, a successful entrepreneur, was not comfortable selling strategic planning services. However, without these sales, her business would fail. She viewed selling as *pushing or peddling products.* Then Zimmerman mentally reframed the personal selling process: "Instead of selling, I think of it as listening to the challenges that my customers face and providing them with a way to help solve them."[28] Once she saw herself as a *consultant* and not a *peddler*, she began to enjoy sales.
- *Seek happiness in relationships.* Two leading positive psychologists studied "very happy people" and compared them to those who were less happy. The only external factor that distinguished the two groups was the presence of "rich and satisfying social relationships." We need to share events, thoughts, and feelings in our lives with friends.[29] John C. Maxwell, author of *Winning with People*, says our ability to build and maintain healthy relationships is the single most important factor in how we get along in every area of life. He says it all starts with people: "All of life's successes come from initiating relationships with the right people and then strengthening those relationships by using good people skills."[30]

Embrace Optimism.   The staff at Mayo Clinic define **optimism** as the belief that good things will happen to you and that negative events are temporary setbacks to be overcome.[31] Optimistic thoughts give rise to positive attitudes and effective interpersonal relationships. When you are an optimist, your coworkers, managers, and—perhaps most important—your customers feel your energy and vitality and tend to mirror your behavior.

It does not take long to identify people with an optimistic outlook. Optimists are more likely to bounce back after a demotion, layoff, or some other disappointment. According to Martin Seligman, professor of psychology at the University of Pennsylvania and author of *Learned Optimism*, optimists are more likely to view problems as merely temporary setbacks on their road to achieving their goals. They focus on their potential success rather than on their failures.[32]

Total Person | Insight

"Research shows that when people work with a positive mindset, performance on nearly every level—productivity, creativity, engagement—improves."

Source: Shawn Achor, "Positive Intelligence," *Harvard Business Review*, January/February 2012, pp. 100–102.

Looking for a job? Research conducted at Duke and Yale universities indicates the importance of optimism during the job search. The research shows that people who have an optimistic outlook on life will have better career prospects than those with a pessimistic disposition.[33]

Pessimists give up more easily when faced with a challenge, are less likely to take personal control of their lives, and are more likely to take personal blame for their misfortune.[34]

Often pessimism leads to **cynicism**, which is a mistrusting attitude about the motives of people. When you are cynical, you are constantly on guard against the "misbehavior" of others.[35] If you begin to think that everyone is screwing up, acting inconsiderately, or otherwise behaving inappropriately, cynicism has taken control of your thought process, and it is time to change.

 ## HOW TO DEAL WITH YOUR PESSIMISTIC THOUGHTS

- *Distraction* Some pessimistic thoughts circle through our minds and grab our attention. Habitual pessimistic thoughts are especially serious thought patterns. Find ways to distract yourself from troublesome beliefs.

- *Disputation* In some cases, we need to go on the attack and dispute the beliefs that serve as barriers to an optimistic life. So, after investing a great deal of time and energy, you learn that your class project earned a B. You hoped to earn an A. Reject feelings of despair and reflect on your past accomplishments.

Source: Martin E. P. Seligman, *Learned Optimism* (New York: Alfred A. Knopf, 1990), pp. 217–219.

Think for Yourself. One of the major deterrents to controlling your own attitude is the power of *groupthink*, which surfaces when everyone shares the same opinion. Individuals can lose their desire and ability to think for themselves as they strive to be accepted by team members, committee members, or coworkers in the same department. You are less likely to be drawn into groupthink if you understand that there are two overlapping relationships among coworkers. *Personal relationships* develop as you bond with your coworkers. When you share common interests and feel comfortable talking with someone, the bonds of friendship may grow very strong. You form small, intense groups. But there still exists the larger group—the organization. Within this setting, *professional relationships* exist for just one purpose: to get the job done.[36] Maintaining two kinds of relationships with the same people can be challenging.

Let's assume you are a member of a project team working on a software application. The deadline for completion is rapidly approaching, yet the team still needs to conduct one more reliability test. At a team meeting, one person suggests that the final test is not needed because the new product has passed all previous tests, and it's time to turn the product over to marketing. Another member of the team, a close friend of yours, enthusiastically supports this recommendation. You have serious concerns about taking this shortcut but hesitate to take a position that conflicts with that of your friend. What should you do? In a professional relationship, your commitment to the organization takes precedence—unless, of course, it is asking you to do something morally wrong.[37]

Keep an Open Mind. We often make decisions and then refuse to consider any other point of view that might lead us to question our beliefs. Often our attitudes persist even in the presence of overwhelming evidence to the contrary. If you have been raised in a family or community that supports racist views, it may seem foreign to you when your colleagues at work openly accept and enjoy healthy relationships with people whose ethnicity is different from your own. Exposing yourself to new information and experiences beyond what you have been socialized to believe can be a valuable growth experience.

In his book *The 100 Absolutely Unbreakable Laws of Business Success*, Brian Tracy suggests reflecting on the "Law of Flexibility." He said, "You are only as free in life as the number of well-developed options you have available to you." The more thoroughly you open your mind to the options available to you, the more freedom you have.[38] This flexibility to see beyond what you thought was true and examine others' perspectives could be one of the most powerful tools you have to inspire the rest of your life.

HELPING OTHERS CHANGE THEIR ATTITUDES

 At some point you may want to help another person change his or her attitude about something. If you try to beg, plead, intimidate, or even threaten him or her into thinking differently, you probably will get nowhere. This process is similar to trying to push a piece of yarn across the top of a table. When you *push* the yarn in the direction you want it to go, it gets all bent out of shape. However, when you gently *pull* the yarn with your fingertips, it follows you wherever you want it to go. Two powerful techniques can help you pull people in the direction you want them to go:

1. Change the *conditions* that precede the behavior.
2. Change the *consequences* that follow the behavior.

Change the Conditions

If you want people to change their attitudes, identify the behaviors that represent the poor attitudes and alter the conditions that *precede* the behavior. Consider the following situation:

A new employee in a retail store is having a problem adjusting to her job. The manager needed her on the sales floor as soon as possible, so he rushed through her job training procedures without taking time to answer her questions. Now she finds there are many questions from customers she cannot answer. She wants to quit, and her negative attitudes are affecting her job performance and the way she handles her customers.

The manager could easily have prevented this employee's negative attitudes by answering all her questions *before* she was placed on the sales floor. Perhaps he could have asked an experienced salesperson to stay with her as she helped her first few customers. Above all, he could have displayed a caring, supportive attitude toward her.

Change the Consequences

Another way to help other people change their attitudes is to alter what happens *after* they exhibit the behavior you are trying to change. A simple rule applies: When an experience is followed by positive consequences, the person is likely to repeat the behavior. When an experience is followed by negative consequences, the person is more likely to stop the behavior. For example, if you are a supervisor, and some of your employees are consistently late for work, you might provide some form of negative consequence each time they are tardy, such as a verbal reprimand. Keep in mind, however, that we should not focus attention on the people who exhibit disruptive attitudes and ignore the employees exhibiting the attitudes we want to encourage. Saying "Thank you for being here on time. I really appreciate your commitment" can be an effective reward for those who arrive at work on time. Behaviors rewarded are more likely to be repeated.

An attitude is nothing more than a personal thought process. We cannot control the thinking that takes place in someone else's mind, but we can sometimes influence it. And sometimes we can't do that either, so we have to set certain rules of behavior. Some organizations have concluded that behavior that offends or threatens others must stop. It may be impossible to stop someone from thinking prejudicial thoughts, but you can establish a zero tolerance policy regarding acts that demean or threaten others.[39]

ORGANIZATIONS' EFFORTS TOWARD IMPROVING EMPLOYEES' ATTITUDES

6-6 People who are asked what they most want from their jobs typically cite mutual respect among coworkers, interesting work, recognition for work well done, the chance to develop skills, and so forth. Of course, workers expect the pay to be competitive, but they want so much more. The late Peter Drucker said, "To make a living is not enough. Work also has to make a life."[40] Organizations are finding creative ways to influence worker attitudes. Here are two examples:

- Physician Health Partners, based in Denver, bases 50 percent of its employees' annual reviews on how well they embrace the company's seven core values, including integrity, teamwork, and joyfulness. How does the company measure joyfulness? Ken Nielsen, president and CEO, says, "To us that really means a lively workplace, and somewhere that's stimulating." He says innovation really happens when employees are having fun.[41]

- When Rodger Riney founded Scottrade, a retail investing firm, he wanted every employee to enjoy coming to work. He wanted "to hire nice people who are honest and that I want to see every day." Celebrations including free birthday lunches, ice cream socials, cook-offs, and a carnival for employees and their families are routine. The company, based in St. Louis, has been recognized as one of the 100 best companies to work for.[42]

What do these organizations have in common? Each has given thought to the attitudes that are important for a healthy work environment and has taken steps to shape these attitudes. Many organizations are trying to improve employee attitudes and productivity by enhancing the quality of their employees' work life.

Google employees are challenged daily by a company culture that expects high performance and a demanding work schedule. High expectations are also one of the reasons the company is viewed as one of the best employers in the nation.

A Final Word

Viktor Frankl, a survivor of the Auschwitz concentration camp and author of *Man's Search for Meaning*, said, "The last of the human freedoms is to choose one's attitude in any given set of circumstances." Changing an attitude can be a challenge, but the process can also be an important step toward your continued growth and success.

LOOKING BACK: SUMMARY OF LEARNING OBJECTIVES

1. **Understand the impact of attitudes on the success of individuals as well as organizations.**

   Attitudes represent a powerful force in every organization. Employees' attitudes and performance cannot be separated. When employees display a positive attitude toward their work and coworkers, teamwork and productivity improve. When employees display a caring attitude toward their customers, the business is likely to enjoy a high degree of customer loyalty and repeat business. When employees display a serious attitude toward safety rules and regulations, fewer accidents are likely to occur.

2. **List and explain the ways people acquire attitudes.**

   People acquire attitudes through early childhood socialization, peer and reference groups, rewards and punishment, role model identification, and cultural influences. However, attitudes are not set in stone. You always have the power to choose your attitude toward any situation.

3. **Describe attitudes that employers value.**

   Employers hire and try to retain employees who have basic interpersonal skills, are self-motivated, accept change, are team players, are concerned about their health, value coworker diversity, and are honest.

4. **Learn how to change your attitudes.**

   You can decide to change your attitudes by choosing to be happy, becoming an optimist, thinking for yourself without undue pressure from others, and keeping an open mind.

5. **Learn how to help others change their attitudes.**

   You can help others change their attitudes by altering the conditions that lead to negative behaviors, such as by providing effective training so that the employee's job performance and personal satisfaction improve. You can also alter the consequences following people's behavior by providing positive consequences if you want them to have a positive attitude toward their behavior and repeat it, and negative consequences to deter them from participating in that behavior again.

6. **Understand what adjustments organizations are making to develop positive employee attitudes.**

   Employers realize that money alone will not make employees happy. Organizations are taking steps to improve employee attitudes by enhancing the quality of their work lives.

KEY TERMS

attitudes, 122	peer group, 125	culture, 126
empathizer, 124	reference group, 125	optimism, 130
socialization, 125	role model, 126	cynicism, 131

CAREER INSIGHT

Shawn Achor, author of *The Happiness Advantage*, says training your brain to be positive is no different from training your muscles at the gym. He says engaging in one brief positive exercise every day for as little as three weeks can have a lasting impact. Choose one of the following five activities that correlate with positive change and perform it each day for three weeks:[43]

- Jot down three things you are grateful for.
- Write a positive message to someone.
- Meditate at your desk for two minutes.
- Exercise for 10 minutes.
- At the end of each day write down three positive things that happened that day.

TRY YOUR HAND

1. Describe your attitudes concerning
   a. a teamwork environment
   b. health and wellness
   c. learning new skills
   How do these attitudes affect you on a daily basis? Do you feel you have a positive attitude in most situations? Can you think of someone you have frequent contact with who displays negative attitudes toward these items? How might you change this person's attitudes?

2. Identify an attitude held by a friend, coworker, or spouse that you would like to see changed. Do any conditions that precede this person's behavior fall under your control? If so, how could you change those conditions so the person might change his or her attitude? What positive consequences might you offer when the person behaves the way you want? What negative consequences might you impose when the person participates in the behavior you are trying to stop?

3. For one week, keep a diary or log of positive and negative events. Positive events might include the successful completion of a project, a compliment from a coworker, or just finding time for some leisure activities. Negative events might include forgetting an appointment, criticism from your boss, or simply looking in the mirror and seeing something you don't like. An unpleasant news story might also qualify as a negative event. At the end of one week, review your entries and determine what type of pattern exists. Also, reflect on the impact of these events. Did you quickly bounce back from the negative events, or did you dwell on them all week? Tal Ben-Shahar, a leader in the field of positive psychology, says the potential for happiness is all around us, but may go unnoticed. During the past week, did you fail to recognize any sources of pleasure?

4. An important step in changing your attitudes is understanding them. To practice the skill of monitoring your current thought patterns, add four or five different endings to each of the following incomplete sentences. Work as rapidly as possible, and don't worry about whether the ending is reasonable or significant; the object is to build awareness of your attitudes toward your life.[44]

   - I am very thankful for…
   - I am glad I'm not…
   - When I wake up in the morning, my first thoughts are…
   - My most common reaction to an annoying situation is…
   - Personal happiness to me means…
   - I often compare myself to…

CRITICAL THINKING CHALLENGE

Identify at least one strong attitude you have for or against an event, a person, or a thing. How did you acquire this attitude? Is it shared by any particular group of people? Do you spend time with these people? Now think of an attitude that a friend or coworker holds but that you strongly disagree with. What factors do you believe contributed to the formation of this person's attitude?

SELF-ASSESSMENT EXERCISE

For each of the following statements, circle the number from 1 to 5 that best represents your response to each statement: (1) strongly disagree (never do this); (2) disagree (rarely do this); (3) moderately agree (sometimes do this); (4) agree (frequently do this); (5) strongly agree (almost always do this).

A.	When forming attitudes about important matters, I maintain an open mind, listen to the views of others, but think for myself.	1	2	3	4	5
B.	I make every effort to maintain a positive mental attitude toward other people and the events in my life.	1	2	3	4	5
C.	I seek feedback and clarification on the influence of my attitudes and behaviors on others.	1	2	3	4	5
D.	I am willing to change my attitudes and behaviors in response to constructive feedback from others.	1	2	3	4	5
E.	I consistently monitor the way I shape the attitudes of others through my system of rewards and punishments.	1	2	3	4	5

After identifying your response to each item, select an attitude or skill you would like to improve. Prepare a written goal and then describe the steps you will take to achieve this goal.

YOU PLAY THE ROLE

In this role-play exercise, you will be trying to mentor a coworker who is a chronic underachiever. She has a great deal of potential, but she does things at work that result in self-sabotage. For example, she tends to procrastinate and often misses deadlines. When she does complete a project, her approach is to get by with the least amount of effort. When things don't go well at work, she tends to blame others. You will meet with another member of your class who will assume the role of your coworker. As a mentor, think about things you might say or do that would help your coworker develop the attitudes that employers value today.

BELOW THE SURFACE | ATTITUDES SHAPE JIFFY LUBE SUCCESS

Henk Meijer/Alamy

Jiffy Lube International, Inc. (JLI) has more than 2,000 franchised service centers in North America. Each year these centers serve approximately 22 million customers. Persons who are considering investing in a franchise may find JLI an attractive option. Jiffy Lube is consistently ranked as one of the top franchising opportunities for entrepreneurs.[45]

Every JLI employee needs to be highly skilled in providing a variety of preventive maintenance services. The competition for these services from automobile dealers, independent garages, and auto service centers is intense. Employees must be prepared to give honest and complete answers to customers' questions: How often should I change my oil? How often should I change my transmission fluid? Should I be using synthetic oil? When should the cooling system fluids be changed?

All JLI employees are encouraged to build repeat business and to suggest purchases when appropriate. Preventive maintenance services are offered for fuel systems, electrical systems, drivetrains, cooling systems, air filtration, air conditioning, and transmissions.

QUESTIONS

1. If you owned a Jiffy Lube franchise, hiring and training employees would be a major responsibility. What employee attitudes would be most important in this type of service business?

2. Jiffy Lube requires all service center technicians to undergo training and achieve appropriate certifications. If you managed a Jiffy Lube service center, how would you motivate employees to participate fully in all available training programs? Some employees would rather be working on cars than attending classes.

CLOSING CASE   ARE YOU FEELING SAUCY?

Panda Express is one of the fastest-growing and most successful restaurant chains in the United States. The Panda Restaurant Group (PRG) is a privately owned, 1,500-location "fast casual" Asian restaurant chain. This success story started in the early 1970s when Andrew Cherng and his chef father arrived as Chinese émigrés. After opening his first restaurant, Cherng worked seven days a week to make it a success. Today, Andrew Cherng and his wife Peggy hold the titles of co-chairman and co-CEO.

Cherng is a strong supporter of self-improvement programs that focus on the *total person*. He urges his employees to eat a well-rounded diet and get plenty of exercise. To be a manager at Panda, you have to be committed to being positive about continued learning. He is a devotee of Stephen Covey's *Seven Habits of Highly Effective People* and Don Miguel Ruiz's *Four Agreements*.[46]

Cherng sees the company's growth in personal terms. Reaching his goals means better service, better execution, and better environment. Each area requires a human touch. When Panda Express employees make a commitment to self-improvement, they often voice their plan in front of their colleagues at company-sponsored training classes. At one meeting, 71 Panda Express managers waited in line to make their public statement. All were wearing orange T-shirts that read "I'm feeling saucy."[47]

QUESTIONS

1. Andrew Cherng and his wife Peggy ask every employee to make a commitment to continuous learning. They believe this employee development philosophy improves every aspect of their business and also makes a tremendous contribution to society. Do you agree? Explain your answer.

2. Andrew and Peggy Cherng say details at the store level are a big deal. Vegetables are cut daily. Sidewalks are clean and washrooms are neat and tidy. They know that when the little things get done, customers will notice it.[48] If small details are important, how can the store manager shape employee attitudes that support this aspect of the Panda Express culture?

CHAPTER 6 ENDNOTES

1. Lorri Freifeld, "Jiffy Lube Revs Up to No. 1," *Training*, January/February 2014, pp. 30–31.
2. "Jiffy Lube Today," July 25, 2014. Retrieved from http://www.jiffylube.com/about/history and mission.
3. Lorri Freifeld, "Jiffy Lube Revs Up to No. 1," *Training*, January/February 2014, pp. 31–36.
4. Ibid, p. 32.
5. Douglas A. Bernstein, Louis A. Penner, Alison Clarke-Stewart, and Edward J. Roy, *Psychology*, 9th ed. (Belmont, CA: Cengage Learning, 2012), pp. 708–709.
6. Bruce Clark, "Employee's Bad Attitude Is Actually Bad Behavior," *News & Observer*, January 15, 2012, p. 3E.

7. Rosabeth Moss Kanter, "How Great Companies Think Differently," **Harvard Business Review**, November 2011, pp. 66–78.

8. "Dinah Eng, "Bringing Chinese Food to the Mall," **Fortune**, February 4, 2013, pp. 27–30.

9. Jason Fried, "Nice Résumé. What Else You Got?" **Inc.**, May 2014, p. 80; "Seven Mistakes That Could Cost You the Job," **News & Observer**, September 15, 2013, p. 4E.

10. "It's Time to Get Serious About Jobs!" U.S. Chamber of Commerce Ad, **Wall Street Journal**, January 24, 2012, p. A9.

11. Ricardo Lopez, "Most Workers Hate Their Jobs or Have 'Checked Out,' Gallup Says," **News & Observer**, June 23, 2013, p. 2E.

12. Hyrum W. Smith, **The 10 Natural Laws of Successful Time and Life Management** (New York: Warner Books, 1994), p. 48.

13. Bernstein et al., **Psychology**, p. 708.

14. Daniel H. Pink, **A Whole New Mind** (New York: Riverhead Books, 2005), pp. 48–63.

15. Laura Landro, "Compassion 101: Teaching M.D.s to Be Nicer," **Wall Street Journal**, September 28, 2005, p. D1.

16. Pink, **A Whole New Mind**, p. 154.

17. Bernstein et al., **Psychology**, p. 491.

18. Kurt Mortensen, **Maximum Influence: The 12 Universal Laws of Power Persuasion** (New York: AMACOM, 2004), pp. 62–68.

19. Caitlin Huston, "A Company's Way of Life," **Wall Street Journal**, August 8, 2013, p. B7.

20. William F. Schoell and Joseph P. Guiltinan, **Marketing**, 5th ed. (Boston: Allyn & Bacon, 1992), pp. 166–167; William M. Pride and O. C. Ferrell, **Marketing** (Boston: Houghton Mifflin, 2000), p. 211.

21. Bobbie Gossoge, "And There Was Happiness in Aqualand," **Inc.**, August 2007, pp. 96–101.

22. Kellye Whitney, "New-Hire Failure Linked to Interpersonal Skills," **Chief Learning Officer Magazine** [cited 5 October 2005]. Available from http://www.clomedia.com; INTERNET.

23. Nathaniel Branden, **Self-Esteem at Work** (San Francisco: Jossey-Bass, 1998), pp. 94–97; "Adjusting an Attitude," **San Jose Mercury News**, August 20, 1997, p. G6.

24. His Holiness the Dalai Lama and Howard C. Cutler, **The Art of Happiness** (New York: Riverhead Books, 1998), pp. 16–17.

25. Tal Ben-Shahar, **Happier** (New York: McGraw-Hill, 2007), p. 33. Also see Shawn Achor, "Positive Intelligence," **Harvard Business Review**, January/February 2012, pp. 100–102.

26. Tal Ben-Shahar, **Happier** (New York: McGraw-Hill, 2007), p. 107.

27. Ibid.

28. Alison Stein Wellner, "Are You Sales Phobic? Alas, the Cure Is to Sell More Often," **Inc.**, March 2007, pp. 52–56.

29. Tal Ben-Shahar, **Happier** (New York: McGraw-Hill, 2007), p. 111.

30. John C. Maxwell, **Winning with People** (Nashville: Nelson Books, 2004), pp. xiv–xv.

31. Jane E. Brody, "How to Grow Optimism," **News & Observer**, June 5, 2012, p. 1D.

32. Patricia Sellers, "Now Bounce Back!" **Fortune**, May 1, 1995, p. 57.

33. Mary Cornatzer, "Study: Optimism Pays in Job Search," **News & Observer**, February 1, 2011, p. 5B.

34. Martin Seligman, **Learned Optimism** (New York: Knopf, 2001), p. 4.

35. Redford Williams and Virginia Williams, **Anger Kills** (New York: Harper Perennial, 1993), p. 12.

36. Bob Wall, **Working Relationships** (Palo Alto, CA: Davies-Black, 1999), pp. 11–12.

37. Ibid., p. 17.

38. Brian Tracy, **The 100 Absolutely Unbreakable Laws of Business Success** (San Francisco: Berrett-Koehler, 2000), pp. 67–70.

39. Nathaniel Branden, **Self-Esteem at Work** (San Francisco: Jossey-Bass, 1998), pp. 111–112.

40. Quoted in Nancy W. Collins, Susan K. Gilbert, and Susan Nycum, **Women Leading: Making Tough Choices on the Fast Track** (Lexington, MA: Stephen Greene Press, 1988), p. 1.

41. Lisa Wirthman, "Profiles in Workplace Culture," **Denver Post**, April 14, 2013, p. 8W.

42. Catherine Dunn, "One Big Happy Brokerage," **Fortune**, November 18, 2013, p. 20.

43. Shawn Achor, "Positive Intelligence," **Harvard Business Review**, January/February 2012, pp. 100–101.

44. Harry E. Chambers, **The Bad Attitude Survival Guide** (Reading, MA: Addison-Wesley, 1998), pp. 6–7.

45. "Jiffy Lube Today," June 25, 2014. Retrieved from http://www.jiffylube.com/about/history and mission.

46. Karl Taro Greenfeld, "The Sharin, Huggin, Lovin, Carin, Chinese Food Money Machine," **Bloomberg Businessweek**, November 22, 2010, pp. 98–103.

47. Ibid.

48. Dinah Eng, "Bringing Chinese Food to the Mall," **Fortune**, February 4, 2013, pp. 27–30.

Henk Meijer/Alamy

CHAPTER PREVIEW

LEARNING OBJECTIVES

After studying Chapter 7, you will be able to

7-1 Understand the complex nature of motivation.

7-2 Describe influential theories of motivation.

7-3 List and describe contemporary motivation strategies.

7-4 Identify motivating factors important to individuals from different generations.

7-5 Describe selected self-motivation strategies.

Hill Street Studios/Blend Images/Getty Images

Motivating Yourself and Others

TIP OF THE ICEBERG | RECORD BREAKERS

Mission impossible! That's the message sent to Tommy Caldwell and Kevin Jorgenson by veteran rock climbers. They were trying to conquer a 3,000-foot vertical wall on El Capitan, the granite pedestal in Yosemite National Park. Caldwell and Jorgenson wanted to be the first to free-climb the vertical, smooth surface rock formation, a feat many had considered impossible. They spent weeks on the wall, thousands of feet above the ground. To free climb means to climb with fingers and toes, without aid. Their "camp" consisted of portable ledges, 4-foot-by-4-foot aluminum frames. They used ropes and safety harnesses to catch them in case of a fall. On January 14, 2015, they reached the top. Mission accomplished![1]

At age 16, Laura Dekker became the youngest person to sail solo around the world. After completing her year-long journey, she was met by a jubilant crowd at St. Maarten harbor in the Caribbean. Before embarking on her trip, Dekker had won a court case against Dutch social services who had objected to the record attempt. They thought it would harm her emotionally.[2]

At age 35, Mylene Paquette accomplished an incredible, record-breaking feat. She became the first North American woman to row, alone, across the Atlantic Ocean. The 129-day trip was exhausting both physically and psychologically.[3]

What motivates these adventurers to pursue their dreams with such determination? The answer may be found in *Drive—The Surprising Truth About What Motivates Us*, by Daniel Pink. He described three basic human needs that have a powerful effect on individual performance and attitude. One of these needs is *autonomy*, the innate desire for self-direction. *Mastery* is the second important need. Most of us yearn for activities that stretch the body and mind in a way that makes the effort rewarding. The urge to master something new and engaging is a powerful force in our lives. The third need is *purpose*. Pink says, "Autonomous people working toward mastery perform at very high levels. But those who do so in the service of some greater objective can achieve even more."[4]

Questions about what motivates anyone are not easily answered, but the research conducted by Daniel Pink and others is very helpful. This chapter will help you gain additional insights into how your needs motivate you to take action.

139

According to Daniel Pink's theories, Laura Dekker, the youngest person to sail solo around the world, was probably motivated by both a desire for mastery and a sense of purpose.

THE COMPLEX NATURE OF MOTIVATION

7-1   People are motivated by many different kinds of needs. We have not only basic needs, but the need for acceptance, recognition, and self-esteem. Each person experiences these needs in different ways and to varying degrees. To complicate matters more, people are motivated by different needs at different times in their lives. Adults, like children and adolescents, continue to develop and change in significant ways throughout life.

Motivation Defined

People interact with each other in a variety of ways because they are driven by a variety of forces. **Motivation** can be defined as the influences that account for the initiation, direction, intensity, and persistence of behavior. Although the number of possible motives for human behavior seems endless, psychologists have found it useful to organize them into four somewhat overlapping categories:[5]

- *Physiological factors* These include the need for food, water, and sleep.
- *Emotional factors* Panic, fear, anger, love, and hatred can influence behavior ranging from jealously to physical violence.
- *Cognitive factors* These include people's perceptions of the world, their beliefs about what they can or cannot do, and their expectations about how others will respond to them.
- *Social factors* These are influenced by teachers, family members, friends, media, and other sociocultural forces. Social factors can, for example, influence your views of clothing fashions and organizational memberships.

human RELATIONS *in Action*

WHAT CAN YOU OFFER?

Daniel Pink, in his best-selling book entitled *A Whole New Mind*, says, "To survive in this age, individuals and organizations must examine what they're doing to earn a living and ask themselves three questions:

1. Can someone overseas do it cheaper?
2. Can a computer do it faster?
3. Is what I'm offering in demand in an age of abundance?

If your answer to question 1 or 2 is yes, or if your answer to question 3 is no, you're in deep trouble.

Source: Daniel H. Pink, *A Whole New Mind* (New York: Riverhead Books, 2005), p. 51.

In a work setting, it is motivated employees who get the work done. Without them, most organizations would falter.

The Motivation to Satisfy Basic Desires

Steven Reiss, professor of psychology and psychiatry at Ohio State University, conducted a major study to determine what *really* drives human behavior. He asked 6,000 people from many stations in life which values were most significant in motivating their behavior and in contributing to their sense of happiness.[6]

The results of his research showed that nearly everything we experience as meaningful can be traced to one of 16 basic desires or to some combination of these desires (see Figure 7.1). Each of us has a different combination of the 16 desires, a mix that can

Two climbers, Kevin Jorgeson and Tommy Caldwell, made it to the top of El Capitan Dawn Wall. They were the first ever to "free climb" the 3000-foot sheer-granite wall in Yosemite National Park.

Figure 7.1 ■ The Sixteen Basic Desires in the Reiss Profile (order of presentation not significant)

DESIRE	DEFINITION
CURIOSITY	The desire for knowledge
ACCEPTANCE	The desire for inclusion
ORDER	The desire for organization
PHYSICAL ACTIVITY	The desire for exercise of muscles
HONOR	The desire to be loyal to one's parents and heritage
POWER	The desire to influence others
INDEPENDENCE	The desire for self-reliance
SOCIAL CONTACT	The desire for companionship
FAMILY	The desire to raise one's own children
STATUS	The desire for social standing
IDEALISM	The desire for social justice
VENGEANCE	The desire to get even
ROMANCE	The desire for sex and beauty
EATING	The desire to consume food
SAVING	The desire to collect things
TRANQUILITY	The desire for emotional calm

Source: Steven Reiss, *Who Am I?* (New York: Berkley Books, 2000), pp. 17–18.

change with time and circumstances. The challenge is to determine which ones (the fundamental values) are most important, and then live your life accordingly. You do not need to satisfy all 16 desires, only the five or six that are the most important to you.

Reiss and his research team found that most people cannot find *enduring* happiness by aiming to have more fun or pleasure. People who focus primarily on "feel-good" happiness (partying, drinking, etc.) discover that this source of satisfaction rarely lasts more than a few hours. It is "value-based" happiness that gives life meaning over the long run.[7]

Characteristics of Motives

Motives have been described as the "why" of human behavior. An understanding of the following five characteristics of motives can be helpful as you seek to understand the complex nature of motivation.[8]

Motives Are Individualistic. People have different needs. What satisfies one person's needs, therefore, may not satisfy another's. This variation in individual motives often leads to a breakdown in human relationships unless we take the time to understand the motives of others. We seek the company of those who have values similar to our own.

Total Person Insight

"The most deeply motivated people—not to mention those who are most productive and satisfied—hitch their desires to a cause larger than themselves."

Source: Daniel H. Pink, *Drive—The Surprising Truth About What Motivates Us* (New York: Riverhead Books, 2009), p. 133.

Motives Change. As noted at the beginning of this chapter, motives change throughout our lives. What motivates us early in our careers may not motivate us later on.

Motives May Be Unconscious. In many cases, we are not fully aware of the inner needs and drives that influence our behavior. The desire to win the "Employee of the Month" award may be triggered by unconscious feelings of inadequacy or the desire for increased recognition.

Motives Are Often Inferred. We can observe the behavior of another person, but we can only infer (draw conclusions about) what motives have caused that behavior. The motives underlying our own behavior and others' behavior are often difficult to understand.

Motives Are Hierarchical. Motives for behavior vary in levels of importance. When contradictory motives exist, the more important motive usually guides behavior. Workers often leave jobs that are secure to satisfy the need for work that is more challenging and rewarding.

INFLUENTIAL MOTIVATIONAL THEORIES

 The work of various psychologists and social scientists has added greatly to the knowledge of what motivates people and how motivation works. The basic problem, as many leaders admit, is knowing how to apply that knowledge in the workplace. Although many theories of motivation have emerged over the years, we will discuss five of the most influential.

human RELATIONS *in Action*

THE IDEA THAT SAVED MY COMPANY

Throughout the glory days of the dot-com boom, Chip Conley built Joie de Vivre, a chain of 17 boutique hotels in the San Francisco Bay area. Conley was hailed as one of America's most prominent boutique hoteliers. Then came the dot-com meltdown, the tragedy of 9/11, and a weak worldwide economy. Annual sales fell from $100 million to $75 million. Faced with a desperate situation, Conley began searching for ways to help his business flourish once again. The key to turning his company around was found in the pages of *Toward a Psychology of Being* by Abraham Maslow. This landmark text helped him understand how he could apply Maslow's *Hierarchy of Needs* concept to winning business practices in the workplace.

Source: Chip Conley, *Peak—How Great Companies Get Their Mojo from Maslow* (San Francisco, CA: Jossey-Bass, 2007), pp. 3–7.

Maslow's Hierarchy of Needs

According to Abraham Maslow, a noted psychologist, people tend to satisfy their needs in a particular order—a theory he calls the **hierarchy of needs**. Maslow's theory rests on three assumptions: (1) people have a number of needs that require some measure of satisfaction; (2) only unsatisfied needs motivate behavior; and (3) the needs of people are arranged in a hierarchy of prepotency, which means that as each lower-level need is satisfied, the need at the next level demands attention.[9] Maslow's theory is illustrated in Figure 7.2.

Physiological Needs.   The needs for food, clothing, sleep, and shelter, or physiological needs, were described by Maslow as survival or lower-order needs. When the economy is strong and most people have jobs, these basic needs rarely dominate because they are reasonably well satisfied. But, needless to say, people who cannot ensure their own and their family's survival, or who are homeless, place these basic needs at the top of their priority list.

Safety and Security Needs.   Most people want order, predictability, and freedom from physical harm in their personal and professional lives and will be motivated to achieve these safety needs once their basic physiological needs are satisfied. At this level of the hierarchy, job security is very important.

Social or Belongingness Needs.   Whereas the first two types of needs deal with aspects of physical safety and survival, social or belongingness needs deal with emotional and mental well-being. Research has shown that needs for affection, for a sense of belonging, and for identification with a group are powerful. There are two major aspects of the need to belong: frequent, positive interactions with the same people and a framework of stable, long-term caring and concern.[10]

Esteem Needs.   People need respect and recognition from others as well as an inner sense of achievement and self-worth. Promotions, honors, and awards from outside sources tend to satisfy this need. Several esteem-building initiatives that build self-respect and self-confidence are discussed in Chapters 4 and 10.

Self-Actualization Needs.   Maslow defined *self-actualization* as a need for self-fulfillment, a full tapping of one's potential. It is the need to "be all that you can be," to have

Figure 7.2 ■ Maslow's Hierarchy of Needs

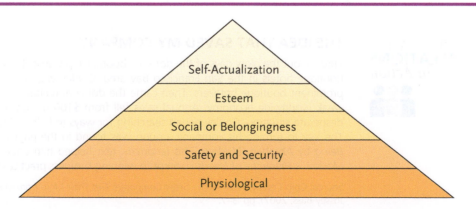

mastery over what you are doing. Self-actualization is people fulfilling their potential or realizing their fullest capacities as human beings (see Table 7.1).

It is worth noting that Maslow's hierarchical arrangement has been questioned and has not always stood up well under actual testing. However, it teaches managers one important lesson: a *fulfilled* need does not motivate a person.[11] If you have food and shelter, you will likely focus on safety and security needs. Maslow's work is considered a classic in the field of management theory, and his original works have been republished in the book *Maslow on Management*.

Herzberg's Motivation-Maintenance (Two-Factor) Theory

Psychologist Frederick Herzberg proposes another motivation theory called the **motivation-maintenance theory**.[12] **Maintenance factors** represent the basic things people consider essential to any job, such as salaries, fringe benefits, working conditions, social relationships, supervision, and organizational policies and administration. We often take such things for granted as part of the job. These basic maintenance factors *do not* act as motivators, according to Herzberg, but if any of them is absent, the organizational climate that results can hurt employee morale and lower worker productivity. Health insurance, for example, generally does not motivate employees to be more productive, but the loss of it can cause workers to look for employment in another organization that provides the desired coverage.

Table 7.1 ■ Ways of Satisfying Individual Needs in the Work Situation

I NEED	ORGANIZATIONAL CONDITIONS
Physiological	Pay
	Breakfast or lunch programs
	Company services
Safety and security	Company benefits plans
	Pensions
	Seniority
	Pay
Social or belongingness	Coffee breaks
	Sports teams
	Company picnics and social events
	Work teams
Esteem	Recognition of work well done
	Mastery
	Responsibility
	Pay (as symbol of status)
	Prestigious office location and furnishings
Self-actualization	Challenge
	Purpose
	Autonomy

Source: Adapted from Judith Gordon, *A Diagnostic Approach to Organizational Behavior*, 3d ed. (Boston: Allyn & Bacon, 1991), p. 144.

Motivational factors are those elements that go above and beyond the basic maintenance factors. They include opportunities for recognition, advancement, or more responsibility. When these are present, they tend to motivate employees to improve their productivity. The workers may seek out new and creative ways to accomplish their organizations' goals as well as their personal goals. Herzberg's list of motivational factors parallels, to some degree, Maslow's hierarchy of needs (see Table 7.2).

Herzberg theorized that if employees' motivational factors are not met, they may begin to ask for more maintenance factors, such as increased salaries and fringe benefits, better working conditions, or more liberal company policies regarding sick leave or vacation time. Critics of Herzberg's theory have pointed out that he assumes that most, if not all, people are motivated only by higher-order needs such as recognition or increased responsibility, and that they seek jobs that are challenging and meaningful. His theory does not acknowledge that some people may prefer more routine, predictable work and may be motivated more by the security of a regular paycheck (a maintenance factor) than by the prospect of advancement. Nonetheless, Herzberg made an important contribution to motivation theory by emphasizing the importance of enriched work.

Expectancy Theory

The **expectancy theory** is based on the assumption that motivational strength is determined by whether or not you *believe* you can be successful at a task. (This theory is an expansion of the self-efficacy concept detailed in Chapter 4.) If you really want something and believe that the probability of your success is high, then your motivation increases. *Perception* is an important element of this theory. Research conducted at the University of Kansas found a link between expectations and achievement in college. Students who wanted to complete college and believed they were capable of doing so earned higher grades and were less likely to drop out. In fact, aspirations combined with expectations predicted achievement better than standardized test scores.[13] This somewhat-mysterious connection between what you expect in life and what you actually achieve is sometimes referred to as the **self-fulfilling prophecy**: If you can conceive it and believe it, you can achieve it.

Table 7.2 ■ Comparison of the Maslow and Herzberg Theories

	MASLOW	HERZBERG
Motivational factors	Self-actualization	Work itself
		Achievement
		Responsibility
	Esteem needs	Recognition
		Advancement
		Status
Maintenance factors	Social or belongingness needs	Social network
		Supervision
	Safety and security needs	Company policy and administration
	Physiological needs	Job security
		Working conditions
		Salary

To increase the desired impact of expectancy theory, managers can attempt the following:[14]

- Determine what rewards (basic desires) each employee values.
- Be clear about what behavior the organization expects of its employees.
- Ensure that desired levels of performance are challenging yet achievable.

McGregor's Theory X/Theory Y

Theory X managers maintain a pessimistic attitude toward their workers' potential.

Douglas McGregor, author of the classic book *The Human Side of Enterprise*, suggests that managers who are placed in charge of motivating their workers are essentially divided into two groups. Theory X managers maintain a pessimistic attitude toward their workers' potential. These managers believe that workers are basically lazy and have to be goaded into doing things with incentives such as pay or with punishment, that they have little or no ambition, that they prefer to avoid responsibility, and that they do only as much work as they have to do to keep their jobs. Theory Y managers, on the other hand, maintain an optimistic view of workers' ambition. These managers believe that their subordinates are serious workers who want to work and do their best, are capable of self-direction, and can learn to both accept and seek responsibility if they are committed to the objectives of the organization. Often the expectancy theory kicks in, and workers perform to their managers' pessimistic or optimistic expectations.

Goal-Setting Theory

Successful people and successful organizations have one thing in common: They share the power of purpose. The more you focus on achieving a desired outcome, the greater your likelihood of success.[15] Your goals play a key role in bringing purpose to your life.

Motivation researchers indicate that goals tend to motivate people in four ways (see Figure 7.3). First, goals provide the power of purpose by directing your attention to a specific target. Second, they encourage you to make the effort to achieve something difficult. Third, reaching a goal requires sustained effort and therefore encourages persistence.

Figure 7.3 ■ A Model of How Goals Can Improve Performance

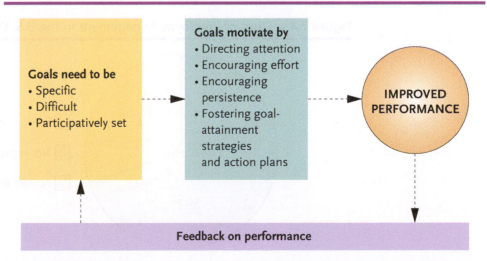

Source: Robert Kreitner and Carlene M. Cassidy, *Management*, 12th ed. (Mason, OH: Cengage Learning, 2011), p. 334.

Fourth, having a goal forces you to bridge the gap between the dream and the reality; it fosters your creating a plan of action filled with strategies that will get you where you want to go.[16]

If your goal is easy to achieve and requires little effort, it may not serve as a motivator. Goals need to be difficult enough to challenge you but not impossible to reach. Goal setting is an excellent self-motivation strategy. Take a moment and review the goal-setting principles listed in Table 4.2 on page 89.

CONTEMPORARY EMPLOYEE MOTIVATION STRATEGIES

7-3 A healthy, mutually supportive relationship based on trust, openness, and respect can create a work climate in which employees want to give more of themselves. However, creating this type of organizational culture may not be easy.

A Gallup survey found that the number of full-time employees who feel involved and truly engaged with their work is quite small. The survey identified three types of workers: actively engaged, not engaged, and actively disengaged (see Figure 7.4). Employees who are actively disengaged are unhappy and unproductive at work and liable to spread negativity to coworkers. It's important to note that about half of the workers are not engaged with their work—they are just going through the motions.[17] Organizations need to consider implementing time-proven motivation strategies that are critical to employee engagement.

Motivation Through Job Design

Today's workers place a high value on jobs that provide rewards such as a sense of achievement, challenge, variety, and personal growth. It is possible to redesign existing jobs so they will have characteristics or outcomes that are intrinsically satisfying to employees. There are several design options.

Job Rotation. **Job rotation** allows workers to move through a variety of jobs in a predefined way over a period of time. For example, a worker might attach a wheel assembly

Figure 7.4 ■ Level of Employee Engagement in the U.S. Working Population

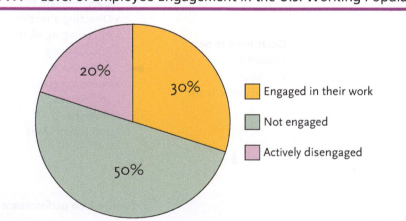

- Engaged in their work — 30%
- Not engaged — 50%
- Actively disengaged — 20%

Source: Ricardo Lopez, "Most Workers Hate Their Jobs or Have Checked Out, Gallup Says," *News & Observer*, June 23, 2013, p. 2E

one week, inspect it the next, organize the parts for assembly during the third week, then return to the original assembly job the fourth week and begin the rotation again.

Job Enlargement. **Job enlargement** means expanding an employee's duties or responsibilities. When a job becomes stale, motivation can often be increased by encouraging employees to learn new skills or take on new responsibilities. In a bank setting, for example, a teller might develop expertise in the area of loan services or opening new accounts.

During the brutal 2008–2009 recession, many U.S. manufacturing companies began searching for ways to reduce production costs. Harley-Davidson decided to embrace a more flexible workforce. Instead of 62 job classifications, the plant now has five, meaning workers have a wider variety of skills.[18]

Job Enrichment. **Job enrichment** is an attempt to make jobs more desirable or satisfying, thereby triggering *internal motivation.* One approach assigns new and more difficult tasks to employees; another grants them additional authority. When American Express decided to give its global customer service division a makeover, it focused on making life better for its 26,000 call center employees. Customer service employees were asked what changes they wanted. The company then provided better pay, flexible schedules, and more career development. To enrich the call center duties, the company switched from a directive to keep calls short and transaction oriented to engaging customers in longer conversations.[19]

Job rotation, job enlargement, and job enrichment appeal to Generation Y workers, who often do not value work for only *external* rewards. These workers are more apt to view work as a valuable learning experience that helps them build a strong résumé.[20]

Motivation Through Incentives

Incentives are often used to improve quality, reduce accidents, increase sales, improve attendance, and speed up production. They often focus on improving behaviors that will cut expenses and improve customer satisfaction. Today a large number of employers are

Thanks to a job enlargement program initiated by Harley-Davidson this employee has developed a wide variety of skills which have application during the assembly of each motorcycle.

offering financial incentives tied to health indicators such as cholesterol levels, body mass index, blood pressure, and tobacco use.[21] We are seeing new incentive plans that erase the idea that everyone is motivated by the same thing—a "one-size-fits-all" approach. Incentives and rewards are discussed in more detail in Chapter 10.

Motivation Through Solicitation of Employees' Ideas and Solutions

One of the best ways to engage workers is to nurture innovation by soliciting their ideas and solutions. Have faith in their experience and insights. Many companies are experimenting with programs that reward the development of new ideas. These programs, known as **intrapreneurships**, encourage employees to pursue an idea, product, or process, with the company providing encouragement and support.

Motivation Through Learning Opportunities

Learning opportunities, both on and off the job, can be a strong motivational force. Education and training are critical to individual growth and opportunity. Capital One Financial Corporation is on Fortune's Best Companies to Work For list. Associates are expected to "own" their careers and take personal ownership for their development. The company provides career counselors who can offer specific advice and training when needed.[22]

Motivation Through Empowerment

Empowerment refers to those policies that share information, authority, and responsibility with the lowest ranks of the organization. When employees are empowered to make decisions for the good of the organization, they experience feelings of pride, self-expression, and ownership.

"I think it's important to note that we really did try hard."

TechTarget, a Needham, Massachusetts, interactive media company, has embraced empowerment to a high degree. All of its 210 employees are free to set their own work schedules. There are no set policies mandating working hours or specifying the number of sick, personal, or vacation days. Managers set quarterly goals and timetables, but employees determine how to achieve them. In exchange for the flexibility, employees are expected to stay in contact with their managers. Greg Strakosch, founder and CEO, says the company's "open-leave" policy is credited with attracting and keeping a very talented and dedicated workforce.[23]

Although empowerment efforts are growing in popularity, this motivational strategy should not be viewed as a quick fix. Empowerment requires a long-term commitment of human and financial resources from top management down. Patrick Lencioni, author of *The Three Signs of a Miserable Job*, says an employee's relationship with his or her direct manager is the most important determinant to employee satisfaction (see Figure 7.5). Yet, many managers are guilty of creating miserable jobs.[24]

Motivation Through Others' Expectations

Earlier in this chapter, you were introduced to the power of your own self-fulfilling prophecy: You will probably get whatever it is you expect. But there is another aspect of the expectancy theory: the power *others'* expectations can have on your motivation.

> *Research has confirmed that people tend to act in ways that are consistent with what others expect of them.*

Research has confirmed that people tend to act in ways that are consistent with what others expect of them. In the classic study *Pygmalion in the Classroom*, Harvard University professors Robert Rosenthal and J. Sterling Livingston described the significant effect of teachers' expectations on students. They discovered that when teachers had high expectations for certain students who they believed had excellent intellectual ability and learning capacity, those students learned at a faster rate than others in the same group— even though the teachers did not consciously treat the higher-achieving students differently. These teachers had unintentionally communicated their high expectations to the students they *thought* possessed strong intellectual abilities.

The source of low expectations in the workplace is often a boss who perceives an employee as a weak performer and then treats the employee differently than high performers. The employee who thinks he or she is a weak performer in the eyes of the boss will often perform down to expectations.[25]

Figure 7.5 ■ Three Signs of a Miserable Job

Patrick Lencioni, author of *The Three Signs of a Miserable Job*, cites research that indicates many people dislike their jobs. These unhappy workers are costing employers billions of dollars in lost productivity. The primary source of job misery resides in the hands of the direct manager. The three signs of a miserable job are:

- **Anonymity.** The feeling that employees get when they realize that their manager has little interest in them as human beings; the manager knows little about their lives, their aspirations, and their interests.
- **Irrelevance.** A condition that takes root when employees cannot see how their job makes a difference in the lives of others.
- **Immeasurement.** The inability of employees to assess for themselves their contribution or success.

Source: "The Three Signs of a Miserable Job–Q&A with Patrick Lencioni," The Table Group Incorporated [cited 7 February 2012]. Available from http://www.tablegroup.com; INTERNET

MOTIVATING THE GENERATIONS

 In Chapter 5, we discussed the variety of historical events that influence the values of various generations (see Table 5.2). It is interesting to discover how those values translate into motivational factors for people in those same generation categories. This information may be helpful in discovering your own motivators, but gaining a greater understanding of these population segments may also be helpful as you learn how to motivate others in your personal and professional life. Figure 7.6 provides a brief summary of motivational factors for each generation.

Learning about the various generations helps you individualize your interactions with them, regardless of your generation. Whether you are a member of one of the older generations or of the younger generations, the majority of the workforce of the future will include Generation X and Y workers. If you are one of them, manage them, or are

Figure 7.6 ■ Motivational Factors for the Generations

MATURES Born between **1928** and **1945**	▶ ■ They are often referred to as *loyalists*. ■ They want to build a legacy, both professionally and personally. ■ They want to be a part of the company's future. ■ Their view of feedback: No news is good news. ■ Rewards that are meaningful to them: the satisfaction of a job well done. ■ Their motivators: money, public recognition, leadership opportunities, organizational loyalty, responsibility, accomplishment, control.
BABY BOOMERS Born between **1946** and **1964**	▶ ■ They are often referred to as the *optimists*. ■ They want to build an outstanding career. ■ They want to move up within the company and gain personal and financial responsibilities. ■ Their view of feedback: performance review once a year, with a lot of documentation. ■ Rewards that are meaningful to them: money, title, recognition, the corner office. ■ Their motivators: more money, public recognition, respect by subordinates, loyalty to self, promotion, peer recognition, control.
GENERATION X Born between **1965** and **1976**	▶ ■ They are often referred to as the *skeptics*. ■ They want to build a portable career. ■ They want to know exactly what they will be doing and whether they are on the right career path. ■ Their view of feedback: they want frequent comments on how they are doing. ■ Rewards that are meaningful to them: freedom. ■ Their motivators: doing good, meeting organizational goals, recognition from the boss, bonuses, and stock options.
MILLENNIALS **(*Generation Y*)** Born between **1977** and **2002**	▶ ■ They are often referred to as the *realists*. ■ They want to build a multifaceted career. ■ They want help seeing the future and the role they will play in it. ■ Their view of feedback: whenever they want it, at the push of a button. ■ Rewards that are meaningful to them: work that has meaning for them. ■ Their motivators: time off, meeting personal goals, recognition from the boss, skills training, stock options, mentoring.

Source: Adapted from Peggy Blake Gleeson, "Managing and Motivating the Generations: Implications for the Student and the Employee" [cited 28 December 2005]. Available from http://www.uwsp.edu/education/facets/links_resource/4413.pdf; INTERNET; "Motivating Generation Y," *Management Issue News* [cited 28 December 2005]. Available from http://www.management-issues.com; INTERNET.

managed by them, it will be critical to your career to adjust your human relations skills accordingly. Some generalizations may be helpful:[26]

- They are more comfortable with diversity.
- They seek opportunities for team collaboration and knowledge sharing.
- They prefer to work with the newest technology.
- They expect rewards based on productivity, not hours at their desk.
- They prefer frequent feedback. Coach them, don't lecture them.
- They are more comfortable with limited bureaucracy. Do not burden them with corporate policies and excessive meetings.

SELF-MOTIVATION STRATEGIES

7-5 The material presented in this chapter explains how, why, when, and where motivation strategies work, and we have identified many organizations that do all they can to motivate their employees to stay on the job and to improve their productivity. However, let's face it—some organizations just don't care if you are motivated or not, as long as you get your job done. If you are satisfied with your life and work, that's great! If you are yearning for a more exciting professional and/or personal life, guess what? It's up to you! The following self-motivation strategies can help you achieve your potential.

Jenny Ice, employed in the Washington office of Ernst & Young LLC, spent 12 weeks in Buenos Aires as a paid volunteer. She provided free accounting services to a small publishing firm. Ms. Ice remained on the company payroll during the time she was gone, and her job as a business advisory services manager was waiting for her when she got back. She describes the experience as among "the best three months of her life."

Superstock/AGE Fotostock

HOW TO KEEP YOUR RESOLUTIONS

The simple act of making a resolution greatly improves your chances of accomplishing a positive change.

- Make a realistic plan in advance.
- Set specific, realistic goals.
- Break each goal into small, measurable steps.
- Alter your surroundings to support your new behavior.
- Plan rewards for yourself as you make progress.

Source: Sue Shellenbarger, "How to Keep a Resolution," *Wall Street Journal*, December 22, 2010, p. D1.

Nurture a Gritty Nature

What factors will contribute most to your future success? A series of recent studies indicate that the quality of **grit**, in the form of hard work and determination, is a major indicator of success. Intelligence accounts for only a fraction of the success formula. Grit has value for people at all levels of ability.[27]

Research conducted by University of Pennsylvania faculty members found that grit is the premier attribute for surviving the grueling first summer of training at West Point. Gritty people tend to be highly self-disciplined and focused on goal achievement. They also bring passion to their tasks.

How do you nurture grit? Self-discipline, an important part of grit, can be achieved by refraining from doing something. M. Scott Peck, author of the best-selling book *The Road Less Traveled*, told his readers that delaying gratification was "the only decent way to live." Early in life, we are encouraged (or required by our parents) to complete our homework before watching television. Later in life, we have to make hard decisions on our own and become self-disciplined. Should I stay with my diet or throw in the towel? Should I stay home and study for an exam or go drinking with friends? Should I add to my credit-card debt or refrain from buying that wide screen television? With a measure of self-discipline, we can learn to schedule the pain first (using Peck's words) and enjoy the pleasure later.[28]

Total Person Insight

> "Genius will get you somewhere, but for the climb to the top you will need grit."
>
> Source: "What's Better than Being Smart? Hanging Tough," *BusinessWeek*, August 17, 2009, p. 6.

Go Outside Your Comfort Zone. Many people do not achieve their full potential because they are afraid to venture outside their "comfort zone." These people often earn less than they deserve, exert little effort to win a promotion to a more challenging position, and refuse assignments that might enhance their careers.

Self-motivation often decreases when we no longer have a sense of balance in our lives.

Strive for Balance. Self-motivation often decreases when we no longer have a sense of balance in our lives. To achieve balance between your work and personal life, take time to reflect on what is most important to you, and then try to make the necessary adjustments.

Take Action. If you are feeling bored or trapped in a dead-end job, you can enhance your self-motivation by taking responsibility for the situation you are in and then taking action to improve it. Taking personal responsibility for your current situation is not easy because change can be threatening. Don't just wait and hope that things get better. Do something!

- Instead of waiting to see what will happen, volunteer for a project or make a request for an assignment.
- Have lunch with the person in your organization who is doing work that you find intriguing.
- Talk to your boss about the things you want to do.
- Follow up on an idea you have had for a long time.
- Read a book, attend a conference, or do something else that will help you grow and learn.[29]

LOOKING BACK: SUMMARY OF LEARNING OBJECTIVES

1. **Understand the complex nature of motivation**.

   Motivation is a major component of human relations because it provides a framework for understanding why people do the things they do. Although the number of possible motives for human behavior seems endless, psychologists have found it useful to organize them into four somewhat overlapping categories: physiological factors, emotional factors, cognitive factors, and social factors.

   Motives are individualistic and can change over the years. In many cases, people are not aware of the factors that motivate their behaviors. We also noted that motives may be unconscious, are often inferred, and are hierarchical.

2. **Describe influential theories of motivation**.

   Maslow's hierarchy of needs theory states that physiological needs will come first, followed by safety and security, social, esteem, and then self-actualization needs. According to Maslow, although any need can be a motivator, only higher-order needs will motivate people over the long run.

   Herzberg's motivation-maintenance theory contends that when motivational factors such as responsibility, recognition, and opportunity for advancement are not present, employees will demand improvement in maintenance factors such as higher salaries, more benefits, and better working conditions.

   Expectancy theory is based on the assumption that personal expectations, as well as the expecta-

tions of others, have a powerful influence on a person's motivation. These expectations can become self-fulfilling prophecies. Managers can motivate employees by expressing belief in their abilities and talents.

   McGregor's Theory X/Theory Y suggests that managers use two distinct motivational strategies when they try to motivate workers to pursue the goals of the organization. Theory X managers believe that people do not really want to work, so they must be pushed, closely supervised, and prodded into doing things. Theory Y managers believe that people want to work and are willing to accept and seek responsibility if they are rewarded for doing so.

   Goal-setting theory suggests that people become more focused and persistent if they establish specific, realistic goals.

3. **List and describe contemporary motivation strategies**.

   Contemporary organizations strive to motivate their employees through positive expectations and job design modifications such as job rotation, job enlargement, and job enrichment. They are also discovering the effects of various incentives, learning opportunities, solicitation of employees' ideas and solutions, and empowerment.

4. **Identify motivating factors important to individuals from different generations**.

   There are specific strategies that can be used to motivate workers from various age brackets such as the Matures, the Baby Boomers, Generation X, and Millennials (Generation Y). Once you understand their motivating factors, you can individualize your interactions with them and enhance your interpersonal relations skills, regardless of your age.

5. Describe selected self-motivation strategies.

People must make their own plans to keep themselves motivated. They can nurture their grit, move beyond their comfort zones, strive for balance between their professional and personal lives, and take action.

KEY TERMS

CAREER INSIGHT

A daily to-do list can be a very important part of your self-motivation plan. It can help you set priorities and save time. Some people like hand written to-do lists, while others think more clearly when they type, sort, and store tasks in computers, tablets, or smart phones. Julie Morgenstern, an expert on time management, says a to-do list is an essential tool for staying grounded, saving your energy, and staying focused on high-priority tasks. Keep in mind that effective to-do lists are limited to specific tasks that can be tackled right away and finished fairly soon. Always assign a priority to each task.[30] As you develop your to-do list, consider which tasks will best advance you toward your most important goals.

TRY YOUR HAND

1. How much grit have you got? On a scale of 1 to 5, rate how well the following statements describe you. In the first section, a 5 is *strongly agree* and a 1 is *strongly disagree*. In the second section, the scoring is reversed: 1 is *strongly agree* and 5 is *strongly disagree*. Total your score and divide the total by 6. If you score over 3.5, consider yourself gritty.[31]

TRY YOUR HAND	STRONGLY AGREE	AGREE	MODERATELY AGREE	DISAGREE	STRONGLY DISAGREE
I'm a hard worker.	5	4	3	2	1
Setbacks don't deter me.	5	4	3	2	1
I am now working on a project that may take years to finish.	5	4	3	2	1
I get interested in new pursuits every few months	1	2	3	4	5
People often tell me that I don't perform to my potential.	1	2	3	4	5
New ideas and new projects sometimes distract me from previous ones.	1	2	3	4	5

2. Prepare a list of all the things you wanted to accomplish during the past year but didn't. Think of activities, responsibilities, and commitments, as well as personal and professional goals. Without making excuses for your behavior, or blaming others, identify self-motivating strategies discussed in this chapter that you can implement to improve your chances of completing those tasks successfully.

3. Are you frustrated with any aspect of your personal or professional life right now? Write down a major frustration on a piece of paper, but do not put your name on it. Form a group of four or five class members who have completed the same task. Pass each other's papers randomly from group member to group member, until your instructor says stop. One at a time, each group member can describe his or her ideas on how to overcome the frustration identified on the paper he or she is holding. At the conclusion of this exercise, describe how this "outsider's" viewpoint of your situation has influenced your thinking.

4. Identify at least one friend or family member from each of the generations discussed in this chapter. Visualize them working for you as you enter a major project with a budget that allows no extra compensation for the additional work you will expect of them. List the ways you would motivate them to put forth their best efforts.

CRITICAL THINKING CHALLENGE

In Chapter 5, you were encouraged to identify and reflect on the values that are important in your life. Return to Table 5.1, and review the five-part values clarification process. Now examine each of the 16 basic desires in Figure 7.1 and identify five or six that seem most important to you. Then apply the five-part valuing process to each of these desires. Do they accurately reflect factors that would motivate you at this point in your life? How might your desires change in the future?

SELF-ASSESSMENT EXERCISE

For each of the following statements, circle the number from 1 to 5 that best represents your response to each statement: (1) strongly disagree (never do this); (2) disagree (rarely do this); (3) moderately agree (sometimes do this); (4) agree (frequently do this); (5) strongly agree (almost always do this).

A.	I understand that people interact with each other in a variety of ways because they are driven by a variety of motivational forces.	1	2	3	4	5
B.	I accept the premise that motives change, may be unconscious, are often inferred, are individualistic, and are hierarchical.	1	2	3	4	5
C.	I am familiar with the most influential motivational theories.	1	2	3	4	5
D.	I am able to provide a brief summary of motivational factors that influence each generation.					
E.	I can apply a variety of self-motivation strategies.	1	2	3	4	5

After identifying your response to each item, select an attitude or skill you would like to improve. Prepare a written goal and then describe the steps you will take to achieve this goal.

YOU PLAY THE ROLE

You just graduated from a prestigious college with your accounting degree and have accepted a job with a large financial institution that has tremendous career potential. You love your work but hate your job because of Marilyn, your immediate supervisor. Marilyn is highly educated, knows everything there is to know about all of the organization's products and services, but seems to know little about how to manage people. Marilyn is about 20 years older than you are and sincerely believes that you can meet your weekly and monthly goals without any feedback as to how well you are doing. Your daily routine is highly restrictive, with two 15-minute breaks and a 30-minute lunch break that must be taken at specific points on the clock. Because you are new to the organization, you feel insecure and need positive reinforcement. You are losing your self-confidence and considering quitting,

but your professional goal is to build a career within this organization. Meet with one of your classmates who will play the role of Marilyn, and discuss your concerns about the lack of feedback. Also, discuss how the organization can make better use of your knowledge, skills, and abilities, which will, in turn, make Marilyn (and you) look good to the executives in charge of promotions and enhance the company's bottom line.

BELOW THE SURFACE | AWAKENING THE DRIVING FORCE WITHIN

Henk Meijer/Alamy

At the beginning of this chapter we described the exceptional accomplishments of Kevin Jorgenson and Tommy Caldwell, who made history by being the first to free-climb the 3,000-foot sheer granite wall in Yosemite National Park. They scaled the wall using only their hands and feet. We also described Mylene Paquette's record-breaking row alone across the Atlantic Ocean and Laura Dekker's solo around-the-world sailing trip. It is also interesting to note that all of these record breakers faced major physical and mental challenges. Dekker also faced a legal challenge. She had to go to court after the Dutch social services objected to the record attempt. Government officials thought the trip would harm her emotionally. Dekker, who was born on a boat, continues to sail and will likely find other records to break. Paquette's journey, lasting 129 days and covering a distance of 2,700 nautical miles, was truly life

threatening. Her boat capsized twice during a storm that generated eight-meter waves. Tommy Caldwell and Kevin Jorgenson spent years preparing to conquer El Capitan. They faced life-threatening challenges every day on the wall.

QUESTIONS

1. Daniel Pink has described three basic human needs: *autonomy, mastery*, and *purpose*. Which of these needs motivated Laura Dekker? Mylene Paquette? Explain your answer.

2. Do you think the power of others' expectations affected these adventurers?

3. Your goals play a key role in bringing purpose and direction to your life. Identify the short-term goals that are currently influencing your behavior. What long-term goals do you hope to achieve in the future?

CLOSING CASE | THE "BOSS FREE" COMPANY

Valve Corporation, a video game maker in Bellevue, Washington, is a unique company. Valve has been "boss free" since its founding in 1996. The company has no managers or assigned projects. Instead, its 300

employees recruit colleagues to work on projects they think are worthwhile. The company prizes mobility, so workers' desks are mounted on wheels, allowing them to move around and form work areas that work best for the project team.

The person who comes up with a new project idea, then recruits other employees to join the team, may become the de facto manager.[32]

Visit the Valve website and you will find a positive statement about the merits of a "no boss" work environment:

> When you give smart, talented people the freedom to create without fear of failure, amazing things happen. We see it every day at Valve. In fact, some of our best insights have come from our biggest mistakes. And we're ok with that! Since 1996, this approach has produced award-winning games, leading-edge technologies, and a groundbreaking social entertainment platform. We're always looking for creative risk-takers who can keep that streak alive.[33]

QUESTIONS

1. We know that a majority of American workers are not engaged or are actively disengaged with their work. Would a boss-free work culture have a positive impact on this problem?

2. One downside of the bossless organization is the delay in identifying bad hiring decisions. How can this problem be corrected?

3. Early in this chapter you were encouraged to identify basic desires that motivate you. Did you discover any basic desires that would make you a good candidate for a boss-free work environment?

CHAPTER 7 ENDNOTES

1. John Branch, "Hanging Out 1,200 Feet Up (Yes, Downtime)," *News & Observer*, January 8, 2015, p. 7B; "2 Free-Climb to Top of El Capitan," *News & Observer*, January 15, 2015, p. 7A.

2. "Dutch Teenager Laura Dekker Breaks Solo Around-the-World Sail Record" [cited 23 January 2012]. Available from http://www.metro.co.uk.com; INTERNET; "Laura Dekker: Stubborn, Self Absorbed and a Devil of a Sailor" [cited 21 January 2012]. Available from http://www.DutchNews.nl.com; INTERNET.

3. "Montreal's Mylene Paquette Completes Solo Row Across Atlantic Ocean," November 12, 2013. Retrieved from http://www.CTVNews.com.

4. Daniel H. Pink, *Drive—The Surprising Truth About What Motivates Us* (New York: Riverhead Books, 2009), pp. 84–91; 109–115; 131–135.

5. Douglas A. Bernstein, Louis A. Penner, Alison Clarke-Stewart, and Edward J. Roy, *Psychology*, 9th ed. (Belmont, CA: Cengage Learning, 2012).

6. Data were collected by use of the Reiss Profile, a standardized psychological test used to measure 16 desires.

7. Steven Reiss, "Secrets of Happiness," *Psychology Today*, January/February 2001, pp. 50–56. To learn more about the Reiss Profile, see *Who Am I: The 16 Basic Desires That Motivate Our Happiness and Define Our Personalities* (New York: Berkley Books, 2000). Also visit "How Motivation Can Be Influenced (And How It Can't)," July 30, 2014. Retrieved from http://www.reissprofile.eu/execution.

8. Cynthia Berryman-Fink, *The Managers' Desk Reference* (New York: AMACOM, 1989), pp. 156–157.

9. Robert Kreitner, *Management*, 10th ed. (Boston: Houghton Mifflin, 2007), pp. 378–380.

10. "Belonging Satisfies Basic Human Need," *The Menninger Letter*, August 1995, p. 6.

11. Robert Kreitner and Carlene M. Cassidy, *Management*, 12th ed. (Mason, OH: Cengage Learning, 2011), p. 331.

12. Frederick Herzberg, Bernard Mausner, and Barbara Black Snyderman, *The Motivation to Work* (New York: Wiley, 1959). For more information on two-factor theory see Ranjay Gulati, Anthony J. Mayo, and Nitin Nohria, *Management* (Mason, OH: Cengage Learning, 2014), p. 467.

13. C. R. Snyder, "Hope Helps," *Psychology Today*, November/December 1999, p. 20. Expectancy theory is discussed in Robert Kreitner, *Management*, 10th ed. (Boston: Houghton Mifflin, 2007), pp. 382–383.

14. Ranjay Gulati, Anthony J. Mayo, and Nitin Nohria, *Management* (Mason, OH: Cengage Learning, 2014), p. 475.

15. Richard Barrett, "The Power of Purpose," *The Inner Edge*, August/September 1999, p. 20.

16. Kreitner and Cassidy, *Management*, 12th ed., pp. 334–335.

17. Toddi Gutner, "Team Building—But Fun," *Wall Street Journal*, April 28, 2014, p. R4; Richard Lopez, "Most Workers Hate Their Jobs or Have 'Checked Out,' Gallup Says," *News & Observer*, June 23, 2013, p. 2E; Steve

Crabtree, "Worldwide, 13% of Employees Are Engaged at Work," October 8, 2013. Retrieved from http://www.gallup.com/poll/165269/worldwide-employees-engaged.

18. James R. Hagerty, "Harley Gets Leaner to Build Its Hogs," *Wall Street Journal*, September 22, 2012, p. B1.

19. Christopher T. Kaczyk, "American Express," *Fortune*, August 16, 2010, p. 14.

20. Karen Auby, "A Boomer's Guide to Communicating with Gen X and Gen Y," *BusinessWeek*, September 1, 2008.

21. Anna Wilde Mathews, "Employers Up the Ante for Getting Healthy," *News & Observer*, December 12, 2012, p. 5E.

22. Lorri Freifeld, "I Want to Work There," *Training*, July/August 2012, p. 18.

23. Patrick J. Sauer, "Open-Door Management," *Inc.*, June 2003, p. 44.

24. "The Three Signs of a Miserable Job—Q&A with Patrick Lencioni," The Table Group Inc. [cited 7 February 2012]. Available from http://www.tablegroup.com; INTERNET.

25. Janice Love, review of *The Set-Up-to-Fail Syndrome*, by Jean-Francois Manzoni and Jean-Louis Barsoux, *Training*, April 2003, p. 49; Sharon Begley, "Expectations May Alter Outcomes Far More Than We Realize," *Wall Street Journal*, November 7, 2003, p. Bl.

26. Ibid.; Ann C. Humphries, "Motivating Generation X" [cited 27 December 2005]. Available from http://www.christianwomentoday.com/workplace/genx; INTERNET. Karen Auby, "A Boomer's Guide to Communicating with Gen X and Gen Y," *BusinessWeek*, September 1, 2008, p. 63.

27. Peter Doskoch, "The Winning Edge," *Psychology Today*, November/December 2005, pp. 42–45.

28. M. Scott Peck, *The Road Less Traveled* (New York: Simon & Schuster, 1978), pp. 18–20; Christine B. Whelan, "The Road Is Heavily Traveled Now," *Wall Street Journal*, October 7, 2005, p. W13.

29. Robin A. Sheerer, *No More Blue Mondays* (Palo Alto, Calif.: Davies-Black Publishing, 1999).

30. Sue Shellenbarger, "Conquering the To-Do List," *Wall Street Journal*, December 28, 2011, pp. D1 and D2; Minda Zetlin, "A Better To-Do List," *Inc.*, February 2013, p. 8.

31. Peter Doskoch, "The Winning Edge," *Psychology Today*, November/December 2005, p. 50.

32. Rachel Emma Silverman, "Who's the Boss? There Isn't One," *Wall Street Journal*, June 20, 2012, pp. B1 and B8.

33. "Welcome to Valve," August 5, 2014. Retrieved from http://www.valvesoftware.com/jobs.

PART 3

Personal Strategies for Improving Human Relations

Henk Meijer/Alamy

JupiterImages/Stockbyte/Getty Images

Henk Meijer/Alamy

CHAPTER PREVIEW

LEARNING OBJECTIVES

After studying Chapter 8, you will be able to

8-1 Explain how constructive self-disclosure contributes to improved interpersonal relationships and teamwork.

8-2 Understand the specific benefits you can gain from self-disclosure.

8-3 Identify and explain the major elements of the Johari Window model.

8-4 Explain the criteria for appropriate self-disclosure.

8-5 Understand the barriers to self-disclosure in an organizational setting.

8-6 Apply your knowledge and practice constructive self-disclosure.

Improving Interpersonal Relations with Constructive Self-Disclosure

TIP OF THE ICEBERG | I NEED TO TELL YOU SOMETHING

Pride that borders on arrogance or conceit can be a major barrier to good interpersonal relations. Jim Teeters learned this lesson the hard way. He accepted a part-time job teaching a beginning-level sociology course at a local community college. In his mind, this teaching assignment was a "step down" from his previous college teaching position. He approached his class with a smug attitude, thinking that these local students were no match for the bright students he was used to teaching.

The class meetings were going well until he started teaching a lesson on the statistical aspects of social research. Suddenly, he felt confused and started rambling. Student expressions turned from interest to confusion. Teeters was not sure how to proceed, so he instructed students to get into their assigned study groups and discuss the material he had just covered. He quickly walked to a nearby restroom and scooped handfuls of water into his dry mouth.

During the weekend, he reflected on the relationship he had established with his students. He was awash with shame and thought about quitting his teaching job. During church services on Sunday, Teeters began crying. The healing process started on that Sunday morning.

At the next meeting with his students he showed a video entitled, *Hello, I Need to Tell You*. As the video ended, he said to his students, "Hello, I need to tell you something." Teeters then told them the whole story. He admitted that he had failed to put his students' learning in front of his own need for recognition. "The class not only forgave me, but they also thanked me for teaching them a wonderful lesson through my self-disclosure. They had never known a professor who was willing to be so 'real' with them."[1]

Self-disclosure, when it comes from the heart, can deepen relationships at home and at work. However, this form of communication can be difficult. Expressing personal thoughts and feelings to a coworker, friend, or family member is often very challenging.

Medioimages/Photodisc/Getty Images

Daniel Acker/Bloomberg/Getty Images

Xerox CEO Ursula Burns is known for her courage to speak openly and candidly, a quality that lies at the heart of self-disclosure.

SELF-DISCLOSURE: AN INTRODUCTION

8-1 As a general rule, relationships grow stronger when people are willing to reveal more about themselves and their work experiences. It is a surprising but true fact of life that two people can work together for many years and never really get to know each other. In many organizations, the culture encourages employees to hide their true feelings. The result is often a weakening of the communication process. Self-disclosure can lead to a more open and supportive environment in the workplace.

In some cases, self-disclosure takes the form of an apology or of granting forgiveness to someone who apologizes to you. If you are a supervisor or manager, self-disclosure may take the form of constructive criticism of an employee whose performance is unsatisfactory. This chapter focuses on constructive self-disclosure and on conditions that encourage appropriate self-disclosure in a work setting.

Self-Disclosure Defined

Self-disclosure is the process of letting another person know what you think, feel, or want. It is one of the important ways you let yourself be known by others. Self-disclosure can improve interpersonal communication, resolve conflict, and strengthen interpersonal relationships.

It is important to note the difference between self-disclosure and self-description. **Self-description** involves disclosure of nonthreatening information, such as your age, your favorite food, or where you went to school. This is information that others could acquire in some way other than by your telling them. Self-disclosure, by contrast, often involves some degree of risk. When you engage in self-disclosure, you reveal private, personal information that cannot be acquired from another source. Examples include your feelings about being a member of a minority group, job satisfaction, and new policies and procedures.

The importance of self-disclosure, in contrast to self-description, is shown by the following situation. You work at a distribution center and are extremely conscious of safety. You take every precaution to avoid work-related accidents. But another employee has a much more casual attitude toward safety rules and often "forgets" to observe the proper procedures, endangering you and other workers. You can choose to disclose your feelings to this person or stay silent. Either way, your decision has consequences.

BENEFITS GAINED FROM SELF-DISCLOSURE

8-2   Before we discuss self-disclosure in more detail, let us examine four basic benefits you gain from openly sharing what you think, feel, or want.

> *Self-disclosure often takes the guesswork out of the communication process.*

1. *Increased accuracy in communication.* Self-disclosure often takes the guesswork out of the communication process. No one is a mind reader; if people conceal how they really feel, it is difficult for others to know how to respond to them appropriately. People who are frustrated by a heavy workload and loss of balance in their lives, but mask their true feelings, may never see the problems resolved. The person who is in a position to solve this problem may be oblivious to what's important to you—unless you spell it out.

Total Person Insight

"Vulnerability is often seen as a weakness; it's actually a sign of strength. People who are genuinely open and transparent prove that they have the confidence and self-esteem to allow others to see them as they really are, warts and all."

Source: Patrick Lencioni, "The Power of Saying We Blew It," *Bloomberg Businessweek*, February 22, 2012, p. 84.

2. *Reduction of stress.* Sidney Jourard, a noted psychologist who wrote extensively about self-disclosure, states that too much emphasis on privacy and concealment of feelings creates stress within a person. Too many people keep their thoughts and feelings bottled up inside, which can result in considerable inner tension. When stress indicators such as blood pressure, perspiration, and breathing increase, our immune function declines. The amount of stress that builds within us depends on what aspects of ourselves we choose to conceal. If you compulsively think about a painful human relations problem but conceal your thoughts and feelings, the consequence will likely be more stress in your life.[2]

3. *Increased self-awareness.* Chapter 1 stated that self-awareness is one of the major components of emotional intelligence at work. Daniel Goleman, author of *Working with Emotional Intelligence*, defines **self-awareness** as the ability to recognize and understand your moods, emotions, and drives, as well as their effect on others.[3] Self-awareness is the foundation on which self-development is built. To plan an effective change in yourself, you must be in touch with how you behave, the factors that influence your behavior, and how your behavior affects others. A young Asian associate at a financial services firm learned from her supervisor that she was perceived as not

Figure 8.1 ■ Self-Disclosure/Feedback/Self-Awareness Cycle

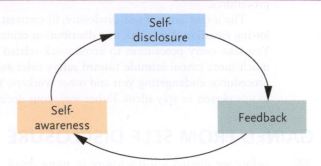

being assertive enough in her dealings with clients. As she reflected on this feedback and listened to views expressed by her female peers, the associate became aware of how her cultural background influenced her communication with clients. This feedback motivated her to modify her communication style.[4]

The quality of feedback from others depends to a large degree on how much you practice self-disclosure. The sharing of thoughts and feelings with others often sets the stage for meaningful feedback (see Figure 8.1).

4. *Stronger relationships.* Another reward from self-disclosure is the strengthening of interpersonal relationships. When two people engage in an open, authentic dialogue, they often develop a high regard for each other's views. Often they discover they share common interests and concerns, and these serve as a foundation for a deeper relationship.

In too many organizations, workers feel they must be careful about what they say and to whom they say it. David Stewart, organizational consultant, says people long for a work environment in which they can say what is on their mind in an honest and straightforward manner. They yearn for an authentic kind of interaction with their boss and coworkers.[5] "People trust you when you are genuine and authentic, not a replica of someone else." These words of wisdom come to us from Bill George, noted author and consultant in the area of authentic leadership.[6]

Authenticity has been defined as the unimpeded operation of one's true or core self in one's daily interactions with others. It requires acting in ways congruent with your own values and needs. Authenticity is necessary for close relationships because intimacy cannot develop without openness and honesty.[7]

THE JOHARI WINDOW: A MODEL FOR SELF-UNDERSTANDING

8-3   The first step in understanding the process of self-disclosure is to look at the **Johari Window**, illustrated in Figure 8.2. The word *Johari* is a combination of the first names of the model's originators: Joseph Luft and Harry Ingham. This communication model takes into consideration that there is some information you know about yourself and other information you are not yet aware of. In addition, there is some information that others know about you and some they are not aware of. Your willingness or unwillingness to engage in self-disclosure, as well as to listen to feedback from others, has a great deal to do with your understanding of yourself and with others' understanding of you.[8]

Figure 8.2 ■ Johari Window

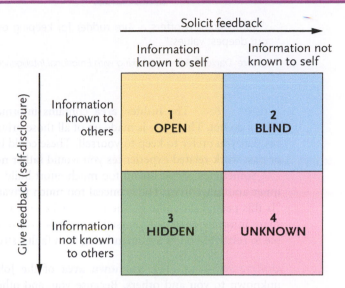

Source: From Joseph Luft, *Group Processes: An Introduction to Group Dynamics.* Copyright © 1984. Reprinted by permission of The McGraw-Hill Companies.

The Four Panes of the Johari Window

The Johari Window identifies four kinds of information about you that affect your communication with others. Think of the entire model as representing your total self as you relate to others. The Johari Window is divided into four panes, or areas, labeled (1) open, (2) blind, (3) hidden, and (4) unknown.[9]

Open Area.   The **open area** of the Johari Window represents your "public" or "awareness" area. This section contains information about you that both you and others know and includes information that you do not mind admitting about yourself. As your relationship with another person matures, the open pane gets bigger, reflecting your desire to be known.

The open pane is generally viewed as the part of the relationship that influences effective interpersonal relations. Therefore, a productive interpersonal relationship is related to the amount of mutually held information. Building a relationship with another person involves working to enlarge the open area. As self-awareness and sharing of information and feelings increase, the open pane becomes larger.

Blind Area.   The **blind area** consists of information about yourself that others know but you are not aware of. Others may see you as aloof and stuffy, whereas you view yourself as open and friendly. Or you may view your performance at work as mediocre, and others see it as above average. You may consider your dress and grooming practices appropriate for work, but others feel your appearance is not suitable for such a setting. Information in the blind area is acquired when you learn about people's perceptions of you.

Building a relationship and improving interpersonal effectiveness often involve working to enlarge the open pane and reduce the size of the blind pane. This can be achieved as you become more self-disclosing and thereby encourage others to disclose more of their thoughts and feelings to you (see Figure 8.1). People are more likely to give feedback to a person who is open and willing to share appropriate personal information with them.

Total Person Insight

"Self-awareness offers a sure rudder for keeping our career decisions in harmony with our deepest values."

Source: Daniel Goleman, *Working with Emotional Intelligence*, New York: Bantam Books, 1998, p. 59.

Hidden Area. The **hidden area** contains information about you that you know but others do not. This pane is made up of all those private feelings, needs, and past experiences that you prefer to keep to yourself. These could be incidents that occurred early in life or past work-related experiences you would rather not share.

Sometimes people spend too much effort building a wall of separation between their inner and outer lives. They conceal too much private information, leading others to ask, "Is this person the same on the inside as he presents himself on the outside?" When you share information about yourself, you allow yourself to be "seen," and it's easier for people to relate to you as a human being with faults, strengths, thoughts, and emotions.[10]

Unknown Area. The **unknown area** of the Johari Window is made up of things unknown to you and others. Because you, and others, can never be known completely, this area never completely disappears. The unknown may represent such factors as unrecognized talents, unconscious motives, or early childhood memories that influence your behavior but are not fully understood. Many people have abilities that remain unexplored throughout their lives. A person capable of rising to the position of department manager may remain a receptionist throughout his or her career because the potential for advancement is unrecognized. You may possess the talent to become an artist or musician but never discover it.

Self-Disclosure/Feedback Styles

Our relationship with others is influenced by two communication processes over which we have control. We can consciously make an effort to disclose our thoughts, ideas, and feelings when such action would improve the relationship. And we can also act to increase the amount of feedback we receive from others. Figure 8.3a represents a

Figure 8.3 ■ Johari Window at the Beginning of a Relationship (a) and After a Closer Relationship Has Developed (b)

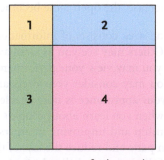
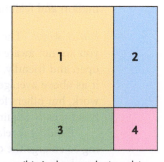

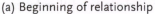
(a) Beginning of relationship   (b) A closer relationship

Source: From Joseph Luft, *Group Processes: An Introduction to Group Dynamics.*

self-disclosure/feedback style that reflects minimum use of self-disclosure and feedback processes. This style represents an impersonal approach to interpersonal relations, one that involves minimal sharing of information. Figure 8.3b represents a self-disclosure/feedback style that reflects considerable use of self-disclosure and feedback. Candor, openness, and mutual respect are characteristics of this style.

You can take positive steps to develop a larger open window (Figure 8.3b) by displaying a receptive attitude when others try to give you feedback. Openness to feedback from supervisors and coworkers, as opposed to defensiveness, is an important key to success in the workplace. If you become defensive, this behavior is likely to cut off the flow of information you need to be more effective in your job.

The Importance of Self-Awareness

As noted in Chapter 1, self-awareness is one of the major themes in human relations. Self-awareness means having a deep understanding of one's emotions, values, motives, strengths, and limitations. Without awareness of these personal qualities, we will be poor at managing them and less able to understand them in others. Self-management flows from self-awareness.[11]

360-Degree Feedback. Many organizations are using an assessment strategy known as **360-degree feedback**. With this approach, employees are rated by persons who have had opportunities to observe their performance. The person who completes the feedback form may be the immediate boss, coworkers, team members, and, in some cases, even customers, clients, or patients. The feedback is generally anonymous and often provides valuable insights into a worker's talents and shortcomings. If problems are identified, they can be addressed through training and development programs.[12]

What can you do if your employer does not use the 360-degree assessment methods? Dorie Clarke, author of *Reinventing You*, recommends you conduct your own 360 interviews to achieve self-awareness. Seek feedback from friends, co-workers, customers, and others who know you well and whom you can trust to give you honest feedback.[13] Table 8.1 provides an example of a 360-degree feedback form.

Increase Self-Awareness Through Journal Writing. One effective way to increase self-awareness is to keep a journal of what you do every day. At the end of the day,

Table 8.1 ■ 360-Degree Feedback Form

One of my current goals is to monitor and shape how I am perceived as a coworker and make adjustments as necessary. Please provide a brief assessment of my performance in each of the following areas:[14]

Gratitude: Expresses thanks and gratitude genuinely.

Listening: Listens well to others before speaking.

Unity: Accepts others and works in harmony with a team.

Attention: Pays careful attention in all situations.

Openness: Is approachable to all.

Imagination: Thinks creatively and likes new ideas.

reflect on thoughts, feelings, worries or plans, and make a short entry (50–100 words). Self-aware people typically find time to reflect quietly, often off by themselves. Jason Womack, a consultant to clients who are seeking greater self-awareness, has prepared a short checklist of questions that can be used to trigger your thinking regarding journal entries.[15]

- What have I learned today?
- What opportunity did I create?
- What questions were answered?

APPROPRIATE SELF-DISCLOSURE

 8-4   At the beginning of this chapter, we stated that the primary goal of self-disclosure should be to build stronger relationships. Self-disclosure is also a requirement for emotional health, according to Sidney Jourard. These goals (strong relationships and good emotional health) can be achieved if you learn how to disclose in constructive ways. Appropriate self-disclosure is a skill that anyone can learn. However, developing this skill often means changing attitudes and behaviors that have taken shape over a lifetime.

In the search for criteria for developing appropriate self-disclosure, many factors must be considered. How much information should be disclosed? How intimate should the information be? Who is the most appropriate person with whom to share information? Under what conditions should the disclosures be made? In this section, we examine several criteria that will help you develop your self-disclosure skills.

Use Self-Disclosure to Repair Damaged Relationships

Many relationships at work and in our personal lives are unnecessarily strained. The strain often exists because people refuse to talk about real or imagined problems. Self-disclosure can be an excellent method of repairing a damaged relationship.

Throughout your career, you will encounter countless workplace problems. Your boss said she would love to give you a salary increase but didn't have the authority to approve raises. Later, you find out that she lied. You miss a team meeting because of an illness. Later, you find out that a team member was highly critical of your work on an important project. Do you confront the foe or suffer in silence?

Most of us revisit the problem numerous times. The process of replaying the incident over and over in our mind is referred to in psychology circles as **rumination**. Some people are inclined to fester in a cycle of anger that results in stress, lost sleep, and loss of concentration.[16]

There will be times when something you say or something you do is highly offensive to someone else. What steps will you take to repair the damaged relationship?

Total Person Insight

"No one can get by in life without being able to issue a sincere apology … [and] without being able to distinguish a sincere apology from something that falls short."

Source: "How not to apologize," *Fort Worth Star-Telegram*, March 7, 2012, page 15-A.

In the heat of the moment, a disagreement can cause harsh words and hurt feelings between friends and coworkers; however, practicing the art of apologizing helps to mend those frayed bonds and restore relationships.

wavebreakmedia/Shutterstock.com

Even in cases where your intention was not to upset or hurt someone, the apology must come from your heart.

The Art of Apologizing. If your actions have caused hurt feelings, anger, or deep-seated ill will, an apology is in order. A sincere apology can have a tremendous amount of healing power for both the receiver and the giver. Beverly Engle, author of *The Art of Apologizing*, says, "Almost like magic, apology has the power to repair harm, mend relationships, soothe wounds, and heal broken hearts."[17]

Of course some apologies do little to improve interpersonal relations, and some make things worse. A *heartfelt apology* demonstrates that you understand and regret the pain you have inflicted. The four apologies described in Table 8.2 are likely to make matters worse.

Do not rely on an e-mail message or a tweet for an important apology. In a private setting, feelings can be exchanged with relative comfort. An effective apology will communicate the three Rs: Regret, Responsibility, and Remedy.[18]

- *Regret*. The regret that you feel must be communicated sincerely. Even in cases where your intention was not to upset or hurt someone, the apology must come from your heart.
- *Responsibility*. Do not make excuses or blame others for what you did. Don't say, "I'm sorry about what happened, but you shouldn't have…" You must accept total responsibility for your actions.
- *Remedy*. A meaningful apology should include a commitment that you will not repeat the behavior. It might also include an offer of restitution.

Table 8.2 ■ Apologies that Make Things Worse

DEFENSIVE APOLOGY	CONTINGENT APOLOGY	TOO-LATE APOLOGY	BULLY APOLOGY
Scenario: "I'm sorry, but…"	**Scenario:** "I'm sorry if I've done something wrong."	**Scenario:** "I realize now that what I did was wrong."	**Scenario:** "Sorry to dump this project on you at 5 p.m."
A self-protective maneuver meant to defend your actions. Never use the word "but" in an apology.	Used to appease a person but don't know what you've done wrong—or don't care.	An expression of regret that comes days, weeks, or months too late.	Entirely insincere, offered only to manipulate the recipient into some action.

Source: Adapted from "I'm Very, Very, Very Sorry … Really?" by Elizabeth Bernstein, *Wall Street Journal*, October 19, 2010, p. D1.

The Art of Forgiveness.   If someone you work with, a friend, or a family member, offers a sincere apology, be quick to forgive. Forgiveness is almost never easy, especially when you feel you have been wronged. But forgiveness is the only way to break the bonds of blame and bitterness. To forgive means to give up resentment and anger. D. Patrick Miller, author of *A Little Book of Forgiveness*, says: "To carry an anger against anyone is to poison your own heart, administering more toxin every time you replay in your mind the injury done to you." He also says forgiveness provides healing and liberates your energy and your creativity.[19]

When you convey an apology to someone or forgive another person, remember that you reveal a great deal through nonverbal messages. The emotion in your voice, as well as your eye contact, gestures, and body posture, will communicate a great deal about your inner thoughts.

Present Constructive Criticism with Care

Constructive criticism is a form of self-disclosure that helps another person look at his or her own behavior without putting that individual on the defensive. Constructive criticism is not the same as blaming. Blaming people for mistakes will seldom improve the situation.

Many people are very sensitive and are easily upset when they receive criticism. However, giving criticism effectively is a skill that can be mastered through learning and practice. Here are two effective methods for giving constructive criticism. First, avoid starting your message with "You," such as "You didn't complete your monthly inventory report" or "You never take our customer service policies seriously." For better results, replace "You-statements" with "I-statements." Say, "I am concerned that you have not completed your monthly inventory report." Another way to avoid defensiveness is to request a specific change in the future instead of pointing out something negative in the past. Instead of saying, "You did not have authorization to order office supplies," try saying, "In the future, please obtain authorization before ordering office supplies."[20]

Responding to Criticism at Work.   No one likes getting criticism at work, but it does provide a chance to show off a rare skill: taking negative feedback well. The ability to learn from criticism fuels the free flow of valuable information that may contribute to greater self-awareness.

"I need something that says, 'I'm sorry about that thing I said that caused you to totally overreact.'"

"Let's offer an apology, but without expression contrition, regret or responsibility."

Douglas Stone, lecturer at Harvard Law School, says people react badly to negative feedback for one of three reasons:[21]

- The criticism may seem wrong or unfair.
- The person receiving the feedback may dislike or lack respect for the person giving it.
- The feedback may rock the listener's sense of identity or security.

When you get negative feedback at work, don't get angry and don't deny it. You want to establish a dialogue, so say something that will help you learn more about the criticism. You might say, "This comes as a surprise. Could you give me some examples?" Don't blame others. Even if you have some justification for blaming someone else, you will likely lose respect. Keep the focus on yourself by seeking more information: "I hadn't considered that point of view. Could you tell me more about how you see that?" All feedback has some truth in it, even if only to reveal how others think.[22]

Discuss Disturbing Situations as They Happen

You should share reactions to a work-related problem or issue as soon after the incident as possible. It is often difficult to recapture a feeling once it has passed, and you may distort the incident if you let too much time go by. Your memory is not infallible. The person who erred is also likely to forget details about the situation.

Total Person Insight

"Receiving feedback well doesn't mean you always have to *take* the feedback. Receiving it well means engaging in the conversation skillfully and making thoughtful choices about whether and how to use the information and what you're learning. It's about managing your emotional triggers so that you can take in what the other person is telling you, and being open to seeing yourself in new ways."

Source: Douglas Stone and Sheila Heen, *Thanks for the Feedback*, Viking Penguin, New York, NY, 2014, p. 8.

If something really bothers you, do not delay expressing your feelings. Clear the air as soon as possible so you can enjoy greater peace of mind. Some people maintain the burden of hurt feelings and resentment for days, weeks, or even years. The avoidance of self-disclosure usually has a negative effect on a person's mental and physical health as well as on-the-job performance.

Accurately Describe Your Feelings and Emotions

It has been said that one of the most important outcomes of self-disclosure is the possibility for others to become acquainted with the "real" you. When you accurately describe your feelings and emotions, others get to know you better. This kind of honesty takes courage because of the risk involved. When you tell another person how you feel, you are putting a great amount of faith in that person. You are trusting the other person not to ridicule or embarrass you for the feelings you express.[23]

People should not be expected to turn off their feelings the moment they arrive at work.

Too often, people consider verbalizing feelings and emotions in a work setting to be inappropriate. However, emotions are an integral part of human behavior. People should not be expected to turn off their feelings the moment they arrive at work. Experiencing feelings and emotions is a part of being human.[24]

What is the best way to state emotions and feelings? Some examples may be helpful. Let's suppose you expected to be chosen to supervise an important project, but the assignment was given to another worker. At a meeting with your boss, you might make the following statement: "For several weeks, I've been looking forward to heading up this project. I guess I didn't realize that anyone else was being considered. Can you tell me why I was not given this assignment?"

As you describe your feelings, be sure the other person realizes that your feelings are temporary and capable of change. You might say, "At this point I feel very frustrated, but I am sure we can solve the problem." Expressing anger can be especially difficult. This special challenge is discussed in Chapter 9.

Select the Right Time and Place

Remarks that otherwise might be offered and accepted in a positive way can be rendered ineffective not because of what we say but because of when and where we say it. When possible, select a time when you feel the other person is not preoccupied and will be able to give you his or her full attention. Also, select a setting free of distractions. Telephone calls or unannounced visitors can ruin an opportunity for **meaningful dialogue**. If there is no suitable place at work to hold the discussion, consider meeting the person for lunch away from work or talking with the person after work at some appropriate location. If necessary, make an appointment with the person to ensure that time is reserved for your meeting.

Total Person Insight

"… the honest sharing of thoughts, feelings, and experiences at work is a double-edged sword: Despite its potential benefits, self-disclosure can backfire if it's hastily conceived, poorly timed, or inconsistent with cultural or organizational norms—hurting your reputation, alienating employees, fostering distrust, and hindering teamwork."

Source: Lisa Rosh and Lynn Offermann, "Be Yourself, But Carefully," *Harvard Business Review*, October 2013, pp. 135–139.

Avoid Overwhelming Others with Your Self-Disclosure

Dr. Joyce Brothers says we must balance the inclination to be open and honest with the need to be protective of each other's feelings.

Although you should be open, do not go too far too fast. Share, but don't overshare. Many strong relationships are built slowly. The abrupt disclosure of highly emotional or intimate information may actually distance you from the other person, who may find your behavior inappropriate. Unrestricted "truth" can create a great deal of anxiety, particularly in an organization where people must work closely together. Dr. Joyce Brothers says we must balance the inclination to be open and honest with the need to be protective of each other's feelings. Disclosure in such areas as mental illness, domestic violence, fertility problems, or drug abuse is usually off limits at work. To be safe, it is also best to avoid expressing strong political or religious beliefs.[25]

Be careful what you disclose in online networking sites, such as Facebook, LinkedIn, and Twitter. When employers are down to a short list of candidates, they may check these sites to see what kind of public image you have created. Posting inappropriate photos, making negative or bizarre statements regarding a company you worked for in the past, or chronicling your behavior at some wild party may create the image of someone who is not very mature.[26]

BARRIERS TO SELF-DISCLOSURE IN AN ORGANIZATIONAL SETTING

 At this point, you might be thinking, "If self-disclosure is such a positive force in building stronger human relationships, why do people avoid it so often? Why do so many people conceal their thoughts and feelings? Why are candor and openness so uncommon in many organizations?" To answer these questions, let's examine some of the barriers that prevent people from self-disclosing.

Lack of Trust

Trust is an element of both character (which includes integrity) and competence. Although trust is intangible, it is at the core of all meaningful relationships. Low-trust relationships can be very frustrating when you are trying to get things done in a timely fashion. It often takes a disproportionate amount of time and energy to reach agreements and execute projects when trust is absent.[27]

Total Person Insight

"We won't be able to rebuild trust in institutions until leaders learn how to communicate honestly—and create organizations where that's the norm."

Source: James O'Toole and Warren Bennis, "A Culture of Candor," *Harvard Business Review*, June 2009, pp. 54–61.

Trust is a complex emotion that combines three components: caring, competency, and commitment. Consider the relationship between a doctor and his or her patient. Trust builds when the patient decides that the doctor is competent (capable of diagnosing the health problem), caring (concerned about the patient's health), and committed (willing to find a solution to the medical problem).[28] Trust between a salesperson and a customer is built upon the same three components. Customers want to do business with a salesperson who can accurately diagnose their needs, prescribe the right product, and provide excellent service after the sale.

Lack of trust is the most common—and the most serious—barrier to self-disclosure. Without trust, people usually fear revealing their thoughts and feelings because the perceived risks of self-disclosure are too high. When trust is present, people no longer feel as vulnerable in the presence of another person, and communication flows more freely.[29]

When trust is present, people function naturally and openly. Without it, they devote their energies to masking their true feelings, hiding thoughts, and avoiding opportunities for personal growth.[30] Within many organizations you will find people who spend time building trust and others who spend time destroying trust. Table 8.3 compares behaviors that build trust with behaviors that destroy it. Essentially, the way to build trust is to be trustworthy all the time.

Trust Index

The **Trust Index**© and Employee Survey is a research tool that measures the level of trust, pride, and camaraderie within the workplace. It consists of 58 statements that address credibility, respect, pride, fairness, and camaraderie, the five dimensions of the *Great Place to Work* model. The Trust Index is the primary survey instrument used to identify organizations that appear on the annual *Fortune* magazine's

The Great Place to Work Institute has selected Four Seasons Hotels as one of the 100 best companies to work for in America. Employees feel a special sense of pride working for this company.

Table 8.3 ■ How Trust Can Be Built and Destroyed

BUILDING TRUST	DESTROYING TRUST
■ Openly share information.	■ Withhold information.
■ Admit your mistakes.	■ Cover up mistakes.
■ Network with coworkers.	■ Keep your distance from coworkers.
■ Display competence.	■ Hide incompetence.
■ Be honest all the time.	■ Be honest only some of the time.
■ Be clear in your convictions.	■ Avoid commitment.
■ Be true to your values.	■ Ignore your values.

100 Best Companies to Work For list. After 25 years of research involving millions of employee surveys, Great Place to Work Institute, Inc. says *trust* is the key to great workplaces.[31]

 ## HOW TO BUILD RELATIONSHIP TRUST

Trust is the foundation of all meaningful relationships. Stephen M. R. Covey, author of *The Speed of Trust*, says that trust is the one thing that changes everything. In his book he outlines four core components of trust:

Core 1: Integrity. Warren Buffett, CEO of Berkshire Hathaway, says he looks for three things in hiring people. The first is personal integrity, the second is intelligence, and the third is a high energy level. He states that if you don't have the first, the other two will kill you.

Core 2: Intent. Covey says the highest form of intent is a desire to find solutions and strategies that benefit everyone.

Core 3: Capability. Your strengths, abilities, and attitude are central to the confidence you create in others.

Core 4: Results. Covey says results matter a great deal. Past results are the best predictor we have of future results.

Source: Stephen M. R. Covey, *The Speed of Trust*, New York: Free Press, 2006. Also see Bruce Clarke, "Trust is a Key Component to a Better-Functioning Workplace," *News & Observer*, May 19, 2013, p. 3E.

PRACTICE SELF-DISCLOSURE

8-6   Many people carry around an assortment of hurt feelings, angry thoughts, and frustrations that drains them of the energy they need to cope with life's daily struggles. Although self-disclosure provides a way to get rid of this burden, some people continue through life imprisoned by negative thoughts and feelings. If you avoid disclosing your thoughts and feelings, you make it harder for others to know the real you. You will recall from the beginning of this chapter that self-disclosure involves revealing personal information that cannot be acquired from other sources, improving the quality of your relationships with others.

Figure 8.4 ▪ Self-Disclosure Indicator

	YES	NO
Instructions: Read each statement and then place a checkmark (✔) in the appropriate space.		
1. In most cases, I avoid sharing personal thoughts and feelings with others.		
2. My relationships with others tend to be quite formal.		
3. I would not be comfortable discussing personal problems at work.		
4. I tend to avoid discussing my concerns even when feelings of frustration build inside me.		
5. I tend to avoid giving praise or criticism to others.		
6. I tend to believe that familiarity breeds contempt.		
7. I find it difficult to apologize.		
8. I find it difficult to forgive the wrongdoer.		

Could you benefit by telling others more about your thoughts, wants, feelings, and beliefs? To answer this question, complete Figure 8.4, which will give you an indication of your self-disclosure style. If you tend to agree with most of these items, consider making a conscientious effort to do more self-disclosing.

> *Becoming a more open person is not difficult if you are willing to practice.*

Becoming a more open person is not difficult if you are willing to practice. If you want to improve in this area, begin by taking small steps. You might want to start with a nonthreatening confrontation with a friend or neighbor. Pick someone with whom you have had a recent minor problem. Tell this person as honestly as possible how you feel about the issue or problem. Keep in mind that your objective is not simply to relate something that is bothering you, but also to develop a stronger relationship with this person.

As you gain confidence, move to more challenging encounters. Maybe you feel your work is not appreciated by your employer. Why not tell this person how you feel? If you are a supervisor and one of the people you supervise seems to be taking advantage of you, why not talk to this person openly about your thoughts? With practice you will begin to feel comfortable with self-disclosure, and you will find it rewarding to get your feelings out in the open. As you become a more open person, the people you contact will be more likely to open up and share more thoughts, ideas, and feelings with you. Everyone wins!

LOOKING BACK: SUMMARY OF LEARNING OBJECTIVES

1. **Explain how constructive self-disclosure contributes to improved interpersonal relationships and teamwork.**

   Open communication is an important key to personal growth and job satisfaction. Self-disclosure—the process of letting another person know what you think, feel, or want—improves communication. Most people want and need opportunities for meaningful dialogue with coworkers and the person who supervises their work.

2. **Understand the specific benefits you can gain from self-disclosure.**

   Constructive self-disclosure can pave the way for increased accuracy in communication, reduction of stress, increased self-awareness, stronger interpersonal relationships, and increased authenticity.

3. **Identify and explain the major elements of the Johari Window model.**

   The Johari Window helps you conceptualize four kinds of information areas involved in communication: The open area, what you and others know about you; the blind area, what others know about you that you do not know about yourself; the hidden area, what you know but others do not; and the unknown area, what neither you nor others know.

4. **Explain the criteria for appropriate self-disclosure.**

   Always approach self-disclosure with the desire to improve your relationship with the other person. Describe your feelings and emotions accurately, and avoid making judgments about the other person. Use self-disclosure to repair damaged relationships. It is helpful to understand the art of apologizing and the art of forgiveness.

5. **Understand the barriers to self-disclosure in an organizational setting.**

   A climate of trust serves as a foundation for self-disclosure. In the absence of trust, people usually avoid revealing their thoughts and feelings to others. Note the four core components of trust presented by Stephen M. R. Covey.

6. **Apply your knowledge and practice constructive self-disclosure.**

   As with learning any new skill, you can improve your ability to disclose your thoughts and feelings by starting with less threatening disclosures and proceeding slowly to more challenging situations.

KEY TERMS

self-disclosure, 164	open area, 167	rumination, 170
self-description, 164	blind area, 167	constructive criticism, 172
self-awareness, 165	hidden area, 168	meaningful dialogue, 174
authenticity, 166	unknown area, 168	trust, 175
Johari Window, 166	360-degree feedback, 169	Trust Index, 176

CAREER INSIGHT

Many nervous job seekers blabber endlessly about irrelevant information. They create a poor impression and cut short the hiring manager's time for further questions.

"Over sharing in an interview is the most dangerous thing you can do," says Anne Stevens, a managing partner at ClearRock, a Boston executive-coaching firm.[32]

TRY YOUR HAND

1. To learn more about your approach to self-disclosure, complete each of the following sentences. Once you have completed them all, reflect on your written responses. Can you identify any changes in your approach to self-disclosure that would improve communications with others? Are there any self-disclosure skills that you need to practice?
   a. "For me, the major barrier to self-disclosure is …"
   b. "To establish a more mutually trusting relationship with others, I need to …"
   c. "In order to receive more feedback from others, I need to …"
   d. "In situations where I should apologize for something or voice forgiveness, I tend to …"

2. On Friday afternoon, a coworker visits your office and requests a favor. She wants you to review a proposal she will give to her boss on Monday morning at 10:00 a.m. You agree to study the proposal sometime over the weekend and give her feedback on Monday before her meeting. You put a photocopy of the proposal in your briefcase and take it home. Over the weekend, you get busy and forget to review the proposal. In fact, you are so busy that you never open your briefcase. On Monday morning you make a call on a customer before reporting to the office. While sitting in the customer's office, you open your briefcase and see the report. It is too late to study the report and give feedback to your coworker. Which of the following actions would you take?
   a. Try to forget the incident and avoid feeling guilty. After all, you did not intentionally avoid your obligation.
   b. Call the person's boss and explain the circumstances. Confess that you simply forgot to read the report.
   c. Meet with your coworker as soon as possible and offer a sincere apology for failing to read the report and provide the feedback.
   Provide a rationale for your choice.

3. What is the best way for a supervisor to get feedback on his or her performance? One approach is to gather your staff in a meeting room and ask, "Who thinks I'm a great boss? Show of hands!" To obtain truly anonymous feedback on your performance, an online 360-degree assessment is a good option. Visit the online clearinghouse HR Guide *(http://www.hr-guide.com)* and review the available resources for 360-degree feedback. Prepare a brief summary of your findings.

CRITICAL THINKING CHALLENGE

Harvard Business Review featured an article titled "Be Yourself, But Carefully" written by Lisa Rosh and Lynn Offermann. The authors note that the honest sharing of thoughts, feelings, and experiences at work can be a double-edged sword. It can backfire if it's hastily conceived, poorly timed, or inconsistent with the organization's culture. Consider these examples:[33]

- Mitch, director of a newly established department at a major U.S. university, was responsible for negotiating agreements and maintaining connections with other educational and research institutions. Attempting to break the ice during the first meeting with the dean of a prominent college, he mentioned that he had wanted to attend it, but had been rejected. The meeting ended without an agreement.

- Helen was asked to introduce herself at the launch meeting of a training program at her home health care agency. The audience wanted to know about her education and industry background. Exhausted after a sleepless night with her sick baby, she shared a detailed description of the night's events, including a graphic description of the baby throwing up.

Can you recall a time in your life when you wanted to build a strong relationship with someone and you shared too much personal information too quickly? When you are preparing for a job interview or some other important meeting, do you engage in self-reflection? Do you think about the type of personal information you will disclose during the conversation?

SELF-ASSESSMENT EXERCISE

For each of the following statements, circle the number from 1 to 5 that best represents your response: (1) strongly disagree (never do this); (2) disagree (rarely do this); (3) moderately agree (sometimes do this); (4) agree (frequently do this); (5) strongly agree (almost always do this).

A.	I engage in appropriate self-disclosure to improve communication and increase my self-awareness.	1	2	3	4	5
B.	I am able to share information about myself in various ways depending on who I am talking with, avoiding the extremes of complete concealment and complete openness.	1	2	3	4	5
C.	I can identify and explain the major elements of the Johari Window model.	1	2	3	4	5
D.	I can explain the criteria for appropriate self-disclosure.	1	2	3	4	5
E.	I understand the barriers to self-disclosure in an organizational setting.	1	2	3	4	5

After identifying your response to each item, select an attitude or skill you would like to improve. Prepare a written goal and then describe the steps you will take to achieve this goal.

YOU PLAY THE ROLE

To prepare for this role-play activity, review the second exercise in this chapter's Try Your Hand. You have decided to take action c, which involves a sincere apology. For the purpose of this role-play, you will assume the role of Taite Edwardson, and the coworker who requested your help is Tyler Johnson. In order to be well prepared for the role-play, read the text material that describes the use of self-disclosure to repair damaged relationships. Keep in mind that when you apologize to someone, you reveal a great deal through nonverbal messages. The emotion in your voice, as well as your eye contact, gestures, and body posture, will communicate a great deal about your inner thoughts.

BELOW THE SURFACE | WINNING STUDENT RESPECT

Henk Meijer/Alamy

At the beginning of the chapter, we described how Jim Teeters struggled to overcome problems related to the powerful influence of pride in his life. He felt superior to students enrolled in one of his classes at a local community college. His smug attitude was quickly altered when he discovered that he was unable to clarify the statistical aspects of social research. After this emotional experience, Teeters was ready to accept the Hebrew proverb, "Pride goes before a fall." His life was changed for the better after meeting with his students and disclosing his thoughts and feelings.

Increased self-awareness is an important key to achieving authenticity. We have defined self-awareness as the ability to recognize and understand your moods, emotions, and drives, as well as their effect on others. Jim Teeters discovered that pride can be a negative emotion, especially when he felt superior to others. In the classroom, he was not acting in ways congruent with his values and needs.

QUESTIONS

1. It has been said that authenticity is correlated with many aspects of psychological well-being such as improving self-esteem and coping skills. How does increased self-awareness help us grow in these important areas?

2. Pride that borders on arrogance can be a major barrier to good interpersonal relations. Can you recall a time in your life when pride had a negative influence on your relationships with others?

CLOSING CASE   XEROX CEO SPEAKS HER MIND

The promotion of Ursula Burns to the top position at Xerox Corporation marked two milestones: the first time an African-American woman was named CEO of a major American corporation and the first time a woman succeeded another woman in the top position at a company of this size. She replaced Anne Mulcahy, who held the job for several years.[34]

After the promotion, Burns had to endure countless interviews from media representatives. They wanted to know if she was ready to cope with the pressures that come with the top job. Her response was, "I'm a black lady from the Lower East Side of New York; not a lot intimidates me."[35]

Burns is known to be tough and someone who has the courage to speak her mind. In the early 1990s, her candor at a meeting of the top Xerox executives set the stage for a major promotion. She and other managers were invited to attend the meeting and instructed to sit off to the side. Paul Allaire, then president of the company, would often declare, "We have to stop hiring." Yet Xerox continued to hire new employees, month after month. At one of the meetings, Burns raised her hand and said, "I'm a little confused. If you keep saying, 'No hiring' and we hire a thousand people every month, who can say 'No hiring' and make it actually happen?" Soon after the meeting, Allaire invited her into his office, thanked her for her candor, and made her his executive assistant.[36]

Burns is working hard to create a culture of candor where leaders communicate honestly. She doles out radical honesty when needed, but has learned to temper her outspokenness. Burns says she is the beneficiary of good coaching and feedback from her business associates.

QUESTIONS

1. Why is a culture of candor especially important when a company is nearing bankruptcy?

2. Does the first African-American woman to lead a major U.S. corporation face special challenges? Explain your answer.

3. The early years offered Ursula Burns many challenges. She was the middle of three children of a single mother who took in ironing and babysat in a Manhattan project. How can these early life challenges help prepare someone for the executive ranks of a major corporation?

CHAPTER 8 ENDNOTES

1. "5 Stories of Quantum Change," *Spirituality & Health*, January/February 2008, pp. 41–43. Note: Within this article is a story titled "When I Surrendered" by Jim Teeters.

2. Martha Beck, "True Confessions," *O, The Oprah Magazine*, June 2002, pp. 183–184.

3. Daniel Goleman, "What Makes a Leader?" *Harvard Business Review*, November/December 1998, p. 95.

4. Cary Cherniss and Daniel Goleman, *The Emotionally Intelligent Workplace* (San Francisco: Jossey-Bass, 2001), p. 258.

5. David Stewart, "Talk at Work: Do You Dialogue?" *Health & Healing*, Vol. 5, No. 6, 2002, p. 2.

6. Bill George, Peter Sims, Andrew N. McLean, and Diana Mayer, "Discovering Your Authentic Leadership," *Harvard Business Review*, February 2007, pp. 129–138.

7. Karen Wright, "In Search of the Real You," *Psychology Today*, May/June 2008, pp. 70–77.

8. Roy M. Berko, Andrew D. Wolvin, and Darlyn R. Wolvin, *Communicating* (Boston: Houghton Mifflin, 1995), p. 46.

9. *Communication Concepts—The Johari Window* (New York: J. C. Penney Company, Consumer Affairs Department, 1979); Roy M. Berks, Andrew D. Wolvin, and Darlyn R. Wolvin, *Communicating—A Social and Career Focus*, 8th ed. (Boston: Houghton Mifflin Company, 2001), pp. 73–75.

10. "Self-Disclosure as a Communication Tool," Communication Resource Center [cited 1 January 2011]. Available from http://work911.com/communication/skillsselfdisclosure.htm. INTERNET.

11. Daniel Goleman, Richard Boyatzis, and Annie McKee, *Primal Leadership* (Boston: Harvard Business School Press, 2002), pp. 29–30.

12. Stephen R. Covey, "360-Degree Alignment," *Training*, May 2009, p. 56.

13. Dorie Clark, *Reinventing You* (Boston: Harvard Business School Press, 2013), pp. 15–18.

14. "The Path of a Heart-Centered Leader," *Spirituality & Health*, May/June 2005, pp. 53–55.

15. Jason Womack, "Journal the Journey," *Training*, July/August 2012, p. 14.

16. Jared Sandberg, "Do You Hear What I Hear? Telling Off a Colleague—Silently," *Wall Street Journal*, October 23, 2007, p. Bl.

17. Beverly Engel, "Making Amends," *Psychology Today*, July/August 2002, pp. 40–42; Elizabeth Bernstein, "Don't Apologize So Fast," *Wall Street Journal*, July 15, 2014, p. D1.

18. Ibid.

19. Sharon Nelton, "The Power of Forgiveness," *Nation's Business*, June 1995, p. 41; Elizabeth Bernstein, "Delicate Art of Fixing a Broken Friendship," *Wall Street Journal*, July 26, 2011, p. D1.

20. Lazarus and Lazarus, *The 60-Second Shrink* (San Luis Obispo, CA: Impact, 1997), pp. 76–79.

21. Sue Shellenbarger, "It's Not My Fault! A Better Response to Criticism at Work," *Wall Street Journal*, June 18, 2014, p. D1.

22. Ibid. Also see Douglas Stone, Bruce Patton, and Sheila Heen, *Difficult Conversations: How to Discuss What Matters Most* (New York: Penguin USA, 2000).

23. Margery Weinstein, "Office Trust Busters," *Training*, July 2006, pp. 10–11.

24. Bob Wall, *Working Relationships* (Palo Alto, CA: Davies-Black, 1999), p. 166.

25. Joyce Brothers, "The Most Important People We Know … Our Friends," *Parade Magazine*, February 16, 1997, pp. 4–6; Sue Shellenbarger, "Ovulating? Depressed? The Latest Rules on What Not to Talk About at Work," *Wall Street Journal*, July 21, 2005, p. Dl. Also see Elizabeth Bernstein, "To Charm and Make Friends Fast: Share, Don't Overshare," *Wall Street Journal*, February 19, 2013, p. D1.

26. John Murawski, "Stray Remarks Can Hurt Your Job Searches, *News & Observer*, April 30, 2006, p. El.

27. Stephen M. R. Covey, *The Speed of Trust* (New York: Free Press, 2006), pp. 5–10.

28. Blaine Hartford, "Trust Your Surgeon? Mate? Friends? Colleagues? What Makes Up a Feeling of Trust?" *Health & Healing*, June 2000, p. 36.

29. Dennis S. Reina and Michelle L. Reina, *Trust and Betrayal in the Workplace* (San Francisco: Berrett-Koehler Publishers, 2006), pp. 34–36.

30. Jack R. Gibb, *Trust: A New View of Personal and Organizational Development* (Los Angeles: Guild of Tutors Press, 1978), p. 29.

31. "Assess Your Organization," [cited 25 February 2012]. Available from http://www.greatplacetowork.com; INTERNET.

32. Joann S. Lublin, "Talking Too Much on a Job Interview May Kill Your Chance," *Wall Street Journal*, October 30, 2007, p. Bl

33. Lisa Rosh and Lynn Offermann, "Be Yourself, But Carefully," *Harvard Business Review*, October 2013, pp. 135–139.

Achieving Emotional Balance in a Chaotic World

TIP OF THE ICEBERG | ACHIEVING A PERSONALITY MAKEOVER

Anger, one of the primary emotions discussed in this chapter, can ruin important relationships and impede your career success. Mike Rice, head coach of the Rutgers University men's basketball program, was fired in 2013 after he was caught on video verbally and physically abusing players. The video, aired on ESPN, showed Rice shoving players, hurling basketballs at their heads, and shouting profanities and sexual epithets.[1]

Rice's inability to handle anger, especially in pressure situations, was common knowledge among school officials. Previously the athletic director had given Rice a three-game suspension and a $50,000 fine for allegations of verbal and physical abuse.[2]

Fallout from the Rutgers abuse scandal did not end with the termination of Coach Mike Rice. Two former Rutgers University basketball players filed suit seeking damages from the school. They sought compensation for physical, mental, and emotional abuse suffered under Coach Rice. The suit claimed Rutgers conspired to cover up the abuse in order to avoid bad public relations.[3]

As noted in Chapter 1, our labor force is increasingly geared toward service to clients, patients, and customers. In a service economy, relationships are usually more important than products. Several national training and development organizations are offering educational programs that help workers achieve emotional balance. Fred Pryor Seminars offers *Managing Emotions Under Pressure* and the American Management Association offers *Managing Emotions in the Workplace.*

Comstock Images/Stockbyte/Getty Images

Michelle O Connor

Michelle O'Connor is president and CEO of CMR Institute, a leading provider of educational programs for health care representatives employed in the pharmaceutical, biotech, and medical device industries. One of the major challenges facing O'Connor is energizing her staff as they manage the stress of staying informed and responsive to the complex issues affecting health care in the United States.

EMOTIONS—AN INTRODUCTION

9-1   An **emotion** is a temporary experience, with positive, negative, or mixed qualities. Emotional experiences tend to alter the thought processes by directing attention toward some things and away from others. Emotions energize our thoughts and behaviors.[4] Emotions can influence our behavior at work and in our personal world. To the extent that we can become more aware of our emotions and assess their influence on our daily lives, we have the opportunity to achieve a new level of self-understanding. Primary emotions include anger, fear, disgust, happiness, sadness, and surprise. Positive emotions will be the major focus of Chapter 10.

Throughout each day, our feelings are activated by a variety of events (see Figure 9.1). You might feel a sense of joy after learning that a coworker has just given birth to a new baby. You might feel overpowering sadness after learning that your supervisor was killed in

Figure 9.1 ■ Behavior Is Influenced By Activating Events

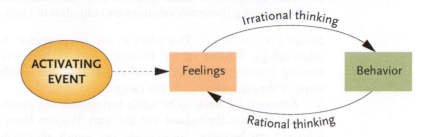

an auto accident. Angry feelings may surface when you discover that someone borrowed a tool without your permission. Once your feelings have been activated, your mind interprets the event. In some cases, the feelings trigger irrational thinking: "No one who works here can be trusted!" In other cases, you may engage in a rational thinking process: "Perhaps the person who borrowed the tool needed it to help a customer with an emergency repair." The important point to remember is that we can choose how we behave. We can gain control over our emotions.

Achieving Emotional Balance—A Daily Challenge

People make choices dictated primarily by either their heads (reason) or their hearts (feelings).

The need to discover ways to achieve emotional balance has never been greater, thanks to the pace of modern life. To be successful in these complex times, we need to be able to think and feel simultaneously. People make choices dictated primarily by either their heads (reason) or their hearts (feelings). The thinking function helps us see issues logically; the feeling function helps us be caring and human.[5] Many organizations are spawning fear, confusion, anger, and sadness because their leaders lack emotional balance.

The basic emotions that drive us have scarcely changed over the years. However, we are now seeing enormous differences in the expression of emotions. Today, people are much more likely to engage in aggressive driving, misbehave at public events, or become abusive when they are unhappy with service. In the workplace, many people experience emotional pain because of disagreeable bosses or uncooperative team members.

Emotional Intelligence

Daniel Goleman, author of several popular books on emotional intelligence (EQ), was briefly introduced in Chapter 1. He challenges the traditional view of the relationship between IQ and success. He says there are widespread exceptions to the rule that IQ predicts success: "At best, IQ contributes about 20 percent to the factors that determine life success, which leaves 80 percent to other forces." **Emotional intelligence** can be described as the ability to monitor and control one's emotions and behavior at work and in social settings. Whereas standard intelligence (IQ) deals with thinking and reasoning, EQ deals more broadly with building social relationships and controlling one's emotions. Several studies indicate that EQ can be increased through a combination of awareness and training.[6] The focus of Goleman's research is the human characteristics that make up what he describes as *emotional competence*. The emotional competence framework is made up of two dimensions.[7]

Personal Competence. This term refers to the competencies that determine how we achieve and maintain emotional balance. The essential component of emotional intelligence is *self-awareness*, the ability to accurately read one's own emotions and hence be better equipped to assess one's level of emotional maturity. Personal competence involves keeping disruptive emotions and impulses in check.

Social Competence. This refers to the competencies that determine how we handle relationships. Sensing others' thoughts, feelings, and intentions; listening openly and sending convincing messages; and negotiating and resolving disagreements represent some of the competencies in this category.

Although IQ tends to be stable throughout life, emotional competence is learnable and can increase throughout our life span. We can learn to manage the thoughts that influence our behavior. For example, our minds are capable of producing outrageously irrational mental images such as dying in a plane crash. We have the option of reacting to those images with rational thinking.

Emotional Expression

We sometimes suffer from a lack of emotional balance because we learn to inhibit the expression of certain emotions and to overemphasize the expression of others. Some families, for example, discourage the expression of love and affection. Some people are taught from an early age to avoid expressing anger. Others learn that a public display of grief (crying, for example) is a sign of weakness. If as a child you were strongly encouraged to avoid the expression of anger, fear, love, or some other emotion, you may repress or block these feelings as an adult.[8]

Emotional imbalance also develops if we become fixated on a single emotion. Jealousy, for example, can be a very painful emotion. It throws the mind into turmoil and may trigger distressing feelings such as fear, sorrow, anger, and betrayal.[9]

human RELATIONS *in Action*

JEALOUSY IS ASTRONAUT'S DOWNFALL

Feelings of jealousy often flare with great intensity. Lisa Nowak experienced this emotion when she learned that a fellow astronaut with whom she had an affair was dating another woman. Nowak drove nonstop from Texas to Orlando, Florida, and attempted to kidnap the new girl-friend. She was dismissed from the astronaut corps and later retired from the U.S. Navy with an "other than honorable" discharge.

Source: Jeff Weiner, "Ex-Astronaut's Discharge to Be 'Other than Honorable'," *News & Observer*, July 30, 2011, p. 11A; Hara Estroff Marano, "Love's Destroyer," *Psychology Today*, July/August 2009, p. 65.

THE EMOTIONAL FACTOR AT WORK

9-2 Emotions play a critical role in the success of every organization, yet many people in key decision-making positions—leaders with outstanding technical skills—fail to understand the important role emotions play in a work setting. In part, the problem can be traced to leadership training that emphasizes that "doing business" is a purely rational or logical process. Some leaders learn to value only those things that can be arranged, analyzed, and defined. One consultant put the problem into proper perspective when he said, "We are still trying to do business as if it requires only a meeting of the minds instead of a meeting of the hearts."[10]

Tim Sanders, former chief solutions officer at Yahoo!, says, "How we are perceived as human beings is becoming increasingly important in the new economy." He notes that compassion is an important key to long-term personal success. This is the human ability to reach out with warmth through eye contact, physical touch, or words. It is a quality machines can never possess.[11]

Relationship Strategy

> *Emotional labor, which taxes the mind, is often more difficult to handle than physical labor, which strains the body.*

Emotional undercurrents are present in almost every area of every organization. Most banks, hospitals, retail firms, hotels, and restaurants realize that they need a relationship strategy—a plan for establishing, building, and maintaining quality relationships with customers. Cisco Systems, for example, measures itself by the quality of its relationships with customers. Salespeople achieve their bonuses based in large part on customer satisfaction instead of on gross sales or profit.[12]

Front-line employees, those persons responsible for delivering quality service and building relationships, engage in **emotional labor**, and those who have frequent contact with the public often find the work very stressful.[13] When a company's competitive advantage is tied to the spontaneous warmth of its employees, the job involves emotional labor. Work that taxes the mind is often more difficult to handle than physical labor, which strains the body. A customer service representative or flight attendant who is told to maintain a smile throughout the day may experience emotional exhaustion and withdrawal.[14]

Toxic Emotions

Peter Frost, author of *Toxic Emotions at Work*, notes that many organizations and their leaders generate emotional pain, which is a form of *toxicity*. Some toxicity can demoralize employees, damage performances, and ultimately contaminate the health of the organization.[15]

People who work as clerks and servers are often a business's "face" to its customers, which is why managers should try to help those employees feel fulfilled, valued, and supported in their work.

Fuse/Jupiter Images

Worker humiliation is a common toxin in the workplace; lack of recognition for work well done is another.

Toxicity often creates the kind of pain that shows up in workers' diminished sense of self-worth. One or more workers who are depressed or angry can poison team or department morale. How people feel can rub off on others. If the boss is feeling optimistic and enthusiastic, these feelings are often transmitted to staff members.[16] Later in this chapter, we will discuss how toxicity creates worker anger.

FACTORS THAT INFLUENCE OUR EMOTIONAL DEVELOPMENT

9-3 The starting point in achieving greater emotional control is to determine the source of emotional difficulties. Why do we sometimes display indifference when the expression of compassion would be more appropriate? Why is it so easy to put down a friend or coworker and so hard to recognize that person's accomplishments? Why do we sometimes worry about events that will never happen? To answer these and other questions, it is necessary to study the factors that influence our emotional development.

Temperament

At the time of birth, we can observe that infants differ from one another in the emotions they express most often. Some infants are happy, active, and vigorous. Others are very quiet. These characteristics make up the infant's **temperament**—the infant's individual style and frequency of expressing needs and emotions. Although temperament mainly reflects nature's contribution to the beginning of one's personality, it can also be affected by environmental factors after birth. For example, the stress experienced by the mother after the baby's birth can affect the baby's temperament. Many events take place between infancy and adulthood that can shift a person's development.[17]

Unconscious Influences

The **unconscious mind** is a vast storehouse of forgotten memories, desires, ideas, and frustrations, according to William Menninger, founder of the famed Menninger Foundation.[18] He noted that the unconscious mind can have a great influence on behavior. It contains memories of past *experiences* as well as memories of *feelings* associated with past experiences. The unconscious is active, continuously influencing conscious decision-making processes.

Although people cannot remember many of the important events of the early years of their lives, these incidents do influence their behavior as adults. Joan Borysenko offers this example

> Inside me there is a seven-year-old who is still hurting from her humiliation at summer camp. Her anguish is reawakened every time I find myself in the presence of an authority figure who acts in a controlling manner. At those moments, my intellect is prone to desert me, and I am liable to break down and cry with the same desolation and helplessness I felt when I was seven.[19]

This example reminds us that childhood wounds can cause us to experience emotions out of proportion to a current situation. Also, we often relive the experience in a context very different from the one we experienced as a child.

HOW TO ACHIEVE A FEARLESS LIFE

Jeff Golliher has written extensively about the power of fear. He says, "Fear can close our hearts, shape our emotional life, and freeze our emotions, but the only power fear has is the power we give it." Here are some tips on how to take that power back:

- Adopt behavioral techniques aimed at replacing upsetting thoughts with alternative thinking patterns. Focus on altering self-defeating thoughts. If you have a fear of flying, remind yourself that flying is much safer than driving. If you fear getting fired, reflect on your recent raise, a positive performance review, or past accomplishments.

- Move through your fear with activities that are relatively stress free. If you have a fear of public speaking, consider attending a "guest" program offered by Toastmaster Club. This organization provides guests with an easy and relatively stress-free forum for persons who want to conquer their fear of public speaking.

Source: Douglas A. Bernstein, Louis A. Penner, Alison Clarke-Stewart, and Edward J. Roy, *Psychology*, 9th ed. (Mason, OH: Cengage Learning); Jeff Golliher, "Five Insights for Fearless Living," *Spirituality & Health*, May–June 2011, p. 80.

Transactional Analysis. A promising breakthrough in understanding the influence of the unconscious came many years ago with the development of the **Transactional Analysis** (TA) theory by Eric Berne.[20] After years of study, Berne concluded that, from the day of birth, the brain acts like a two-track stereo tape recorder. One track records events, and the other records the feelings associated with those events.

To illustrate how feelings associated with early childhood experiences can surface later in life, picture in your mind's eye a three-year-old walking around his mother's sewing room. He picks up a pair of sharp scissors and begins walking toward the staircase. The mother spots the child and cries, "Tommy, drop those scissors! Do you want to kill yourself?" Tommy's tape recorder records both the event (walking with scissors) and the emotions (fear and guilt). Ten years later, Tommy is taking an art class and his teacher says, "Tommy, bring me a pair of scissors." As he begins to walk across the room, his mind is flooded by the feelings of fear and guilt attached to that earlier childhood event.

The practical applications of TA were discussed in such books as *I'm OK—You're OK*, written by Thomas Harris; *Staying OK*, by Amy Bjork Harris and Thomas Harris; and *Born to Win*, by Muriel James and Dorothy Jongeward. TA concepts have been incorporated into many corporate training programs.

Cultural Intelligence

Cultural intelligence (CQ) was introduced in Chapter 2. A person with high CQ has the ability to quickly analyze and interpret human actions, gestures, and speech patterns, and then respond appropriately.[21] The merits of CQ are highlighted in the movie *Outsourced*. A call center based in the United States is outsourced to India. The U.S. manager, Todd Anderson, is sent to Mumbai to train his successor. He received no cross-cultural training prior to his arrival. Serious cultural clashes soon arise as Anderson tries to explain American business practices to befuddled new employees.[22]

Anyone reasonably alert, motivated, and poised can attain an acceptable level of cultural intelligence. Let's assume you are involved in sales and marketing and will soon make calls on prospects in Japan, Germany, and other countries. It would be helpful to know that the Japanese decision-making process is a total group process with all levels involved in the final decision. For Germans, even the most routine decisions are made by top-level management.[23]

Total Person Insight

alexsvirid/Shutterstock.com

USA—Pest
China—Pet
Northern Thailand—Appetizer

– – –

Posters at international airports like Heathrow displayed this message by Global Bank HSBC.

Source: P. Christopher Earley and Elaine Mosakowski, "Cultural Intelligence," *Harvard Business Review*, October 2004, p. 139.

Mindfulness

A growing number of health practitioners are encouraging us to embrace the practice of mindfulness. **Mindfulness** means maintaining awareness of emotions, thoughts, and feelings that occur in the present moment. It is a method of disciplining your mind and controlling your emotions. Mindfulness practice is being employed in psychology to alleviate a variety of mental and physical conditions such as depression, drug addiction, anxiety, and compulsive eating.[24]

The practice of mindfulness has its roots in Eastern meditation practices developed by Buddhist scholars. Years ago, people involved in the development of leadership theories discovered that the fundamentals of mindfulness have application in leadership development. For example, James Scholler, author of *The Three Levels of Leadership*, says personal power—command over one's thoughts, feelings, and unconscious habits—is at the heart of effective leadership.[25]

Of course, mindfulness practices are important to the success of employees at every level, not just leaders. And mindfulness practices have application in our personal lives. Consider the emotions that lead to overeating—the major barrier to weight loss.

Cultural intelligence means taking the time to learn and understand some of the customs and traditions of cultures other than your own, such as the proper way to bow when you greet someone in Japan.

There are psychological reasons why we reach for food for comfort. Mindfulness involves paying attention and being continuously present with the experience. It involves *conscious direction* of our awareness. Jon Kabat-Zinn, author of *Mindfulness for Beginners*, says, "Knowing that you are eating is not the same as eating mindfully."[26]

In Chapter 14 we will introduce mindfulness meditation, a practice that has entered the American mainstream. This form of meditation increases positive emotions while reducing negative emotions and stress.

COPING WITH YOUR ANGER AND THE ANGER OF OTHERS

`9-4` **Anger** may be defined as the thoughts, feelings, physical reactions, and actions that result from unacceptable behavior by others. Anger is almost always a response to *perceived* injustice, and may dissolve with a deeper understanding of the cause. Learning to effectively deal with anger (anger management) is a key component of any healthy lifestyle.[27]

> *Anger is almost always a response to perceived injustice.*

Managing Your Anger

Learning to address your own anger and the anger of other people is one of the most sophisticated and mature skills people are ever required to learn. Intense anger takes control of people and distorts their perceptions, which is why angry people often make poor decisions.[28]

Intense anger often takes the form of rage. Examples include road rage, air rage, and customer rage. Research indicates that 70 percent of customers who have problems with a product or service are in a *rage* by the time they talk with a customer-service worker.[29] We are also witnessing more incidents of "workplace rage." Workplace rage can take the form

Fotosearch/Jupiter Images

of yelling, verbal abuse, and physical violence. It is more likely to occur when workers are stressed by long hours, unrealistic deadlines, cramped quarters, excessive electronic messages, lack of recognition, bullying incidents, or some combination of these factors.

Anger Management

Melissa Hoistion was enjoying dinner with her husband and their three children at a nice restaurant until the waiter disappeared for about 20 minutes. Her husband became increasingly agitated and suddenly screamed, "Excuse me!" at another waiter across the room. He then stormed off to complain to the manager. When the original server finally returned to the table the man yelled, "Where the hell have you been for the last 45 minutes?"[30] Where would you place him on the National Anger Management Association scale? (See Figure 9.2.)

Scream at your boss? Throw your cell phone at your computer monitor? Drive recklessly on a crowded highway? If so, you may find yourself headed to an anger management class. Some organizations are not waiting for anger problems to surface. Several hospitals have programs for "disruptive" physicians, and a few state bar associations now require "civility" training for lawyers renewing their licenses. And some fit-throwing celebrities, road ragers, and delinquent teens are embracing anger management classes as an alternative to jail sentences.[31]

Keeping Cool in Angry Times

These are stressful times, so it is imperative that you develop an anger management program that works for you. Here are some ways to keep your temper in check.[32]

1. Keep an anger diary or journal. Monitor what makes you angry so you can find ways to cope with your triggers. Record not only the source of irritation, but the feelings that surface when you become angry.
2. Reframe the situation that triggered anger. Try not to see every inconvenience or frustration as a personal affront.
3. Be aware of how you talk to yourself. Do you keep telling yourself how "awful this is" and making yourself feel like a victim?
4. If you feel a blow-up coming on, give yourself a time-out before acting on it. For example, wait 15 minutes before you say something, or an hour before you send an e-mail.
5. Pay more attention to the important things in life and recognize that most frustrations, inconveniences, and indignities are trivial and temporary.

Figure 9.2 ■ **National Anger Management Association Scale of Anger**

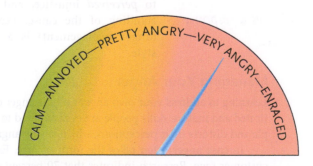

Source: Melinda Beck, "When Anger Is an Illness," *Wall Street Journal*, March 9, 2010. NAMA provides Anger Management Specialist Certification and Domestic Violence Specialist Certification.

Effective Ways to Express Your Anger

Buddha said, "You will not be punished for your anger, you will be punished by your anger." Buddhist teachings tell us that patience is the best antidote to aggression.[33] Intense anger that is suppressed will linger and become a disruptive force in your life unless you can find a positive way to get rid of it. Expressing feelings of anger can be therapeutic, but many people are unsure about the best way to disclose this emotion. To express anger in ways that will improve the chances that the other person will receive and respond to your message, consider these suggestions:

1. *Avoid reacting in a manner that could be seen as emotionally unstable.* If others see you as reacting irrationally, you will lose your ability to influence them.

2. *Do not make accusations or try to fix blame.* It would be acceptable to begin the conversation by saying, "I felt humiliated at the staff meeting this morning." It would not be appropriate to say, "Your comments at the morning staff meeting were mean spirited and made me feel humiliated." The latter statement invites a defensive response.[34]

3. *Express your feelings in a timely manner.* The intensity of anger can actually increase with time. Also, important information needed by you or the person who provoked your anger may be forgotten or distorted with the passing of time.

4. *Be specific as you describe the factors that triggered your anger, and be clear about the resolution you are seeking.* The direct approach, in most cases, works best.

5. *Ban the silent treatment.* The silent treatment is a common but very ineffective way to express your anger. It's important to talk about feelings underlying the conflict before trying to solve the problem that generated the anger.[35]

human RELATIONS *in Action*

ANGER POISONS DECISION MAKING

Recent research has documented the psychological effects of residual anger. Let's assume you have a serious quarrel with your spouse before going to work. This anger-fueled event will likely color your decisions throughout the day, and your work will suffer for it. Angry people tend to rely on cognitive shortcuts rather than engaging in systematic reasoning. They are also quick to blame others rather than studying all aspects of the problem situation.

Source: Jennifer S. Lerner and Katherine Shonk, "Decision Making," *Harvard Business Review*, September 2010, p. 26.

How to Handle Other People's Anger

Dealing with other people's anger may be the most difficult human relations challenge we face. The following skills can be learned and applied to any situation where anger threatens to damage a relationship.

1. *Recognize and accept the other person's anger.* The simple recognition of the intense feelings of someone who is angry does a lot to defuse the situation.

2. *Encourage the angry person to vent his or her feelings.* By asking questions and listening carefully to the response, you can encourage the person to discuss the cause of the anger openly. Zane Bond, team leader at a software company help desk, never takes an angry call personally. He listens intently and tries to start building a relationship. After learning the details of the customer's problem, he tells them confidently, "We are going to fix this."[36]

3. *Do not respond to an angry person with your own anger.* To express your own anger or become defensive will only create another barrier to emotional healing. When you respond to the angry person, keep your voice tone soft. Keep in mind the old biblical injunction, "A soft answer turns away wrath."[37]

4. *Give the angry person feedback.* After venting feelings and discussing specific details, the angry person will expect a response. Briefly paraphrase what seems to be the major concern of the angry person and express a desire to find ways to solve the problem. If you are at fault, accept the blame for your actions and express a sincere apology.

Total Person Insight

"Hate is too great a burden to bear. It injures the hater more than it injures the hated."

Source: Coretta Scott King, University of North Carolina 2012–2013 Academic Monthly, p. 21.

VIOLENCE IN THE WORKPLACE

9-5　　Any discussion of workplace violence is likely to bring to mind a lone employee walking into the office or plant and shooting coworkers or supervisors. These are the images most often presented by the media. The Workplace Violence Research Institute has developed a definition of **workplace violence** that may be more appropriate for today's work environment:

> *Any act against an employee that creates a hostile work environment and negatively affects the employee, either physically or psychologically. These acts include all types of physical or verbal assaults, threats, coercion, intimidation, and all forms of harassment.*[38]

Violence in the workplace is often triggered by loss of a job, conflict between the employee and management, or a personal tragedy, such as divorce or separation. Michele Coleman Mages, senior vice president at Pitney Bowes, a mail- and document-management company, says, "People bring all sorts of demons to work—from problems with spouses and kids to bipolar disease—that they shouldn't think they can solve on their own."[39]

Preventing Workplace Violence

Incidents of workplace violence cost employers and others several billion dollars each year. This figure does not, of course, reflect the human suffering caused by acts of violence. Although violence cannot be eliminated, some steps can help curb violent behavior in the workplace.

1. *Use hiring procedures that screen out unstable persons.* In-depth interviews, drug testing, and background checks can help identify signs of a troubled past.

2. *Develop a strategy for responding to incidents before they actually occur.* Establish policies that make it clear that workplace violence incidents will not be tolerated. Every organization should establish a strong expectation of workplace civility. After an employee at Lockheed Martin's airplane-parts plant shot six coworkers to death, the company formed a task force on workplace violence. One outcome of this action is a zero-tolerance policy (violators can be fired) for hostile or intimidating speech or actions.[40]

> *The simple recognition of the intense feelings of someone who is angry does a lot to defuse the situation.*

3. **When employees are demoted, fired, or laid off, do it in a way that does not demoralize the employee.** When Intel reduced its workforce by 10,500, it used a highly structured process. Intel spokesman Chuck Mulloy says, "The key to making it work is very clear communications, what's going to happen and when."[41]

4. **Provide out-placement services for laid-off or terminated employees.** These services may include development of job-search skills, retraining, or, in cases where the employee is displaying signs of aggression, counseling.

5. **Establish a systematic way to deal with disgruntled employees.** This might involve providing a forum for employees who feel they have been treated unfairly.

6. **Provide supervisors and managers with training that will help them prevent workplace violence and deal effectively with violence if it does occur.** Workplace violence is not the domain of any single department within an organization. Effective programs involve key areas such as human resources, security, employee assistance programs, and legal personnel.[42]

EMOTIONAL STYLES

9-6   A good starting point for achieving emotional control is to examine your current emotional style. How do you deal with emotions? Your style started taking shape before birth and evolved over a period of many years. As an adult, you are likely to favor one of four different emotional styles when confronted with events that trigger your emotions.

Suppressing Your Emotions

Some people have learned to suppress their feelings as much as possible. They have developed intellectual strategies that enable them to avoid dealing directly with emotional reactions to a situation. In response to the loss of a loved one, a person may avoid the experience of grief and mourning by taking on new responsibilities at work. This is not, of course, a healthy way to deal with grief.

Hale Dwoskin, author of *The Sedona Method*, says suppression is "keeping a lid on our emotions, pushing them back down, denying them, repressing them, and pretending they don't exist."[43] He says habitual suppression is unhealthy and unproductive. Dwoskin says an alternative to inappropriate suppression and expression is releasing emotions, an approach he calls the Sedona Method (see Figure 9.3).

To continually suppress feelings, hide fears, swallow annoyances, and avoid displaying anger is not healthy. If suppressing your feelings becomes a habit, you create opportunities for mental and physical health problems to develop.

Capitulating to Your Emotions

People who display this emotional style see themselves as the helpless victims of feelings over which they have no control. By responding to emotion in this manner, one can assign responsibility for the "problem" to external causes, such as other people or unavoidable events. Some people would rather endure feelings of helplessness than find a positive solution to a problem. People who capitulate to their emotions are often overly concerned about the attitudes and opinions of others.[44]

Overexpressing Your Emotions

In a work setting, we need to be seen as responsible and predictable. One of the quickest ways to lose the respect and confidence of the people you work with is to frequently

Figure 9.3 ■ The Sedona Method

Hale Dwoskin, author of *The Sedona Method* and CEO of Sedona Training Associates (*http://www.sedonapress.com*), developed a unique program for making positive changes in your life. He encourages everyone to let go of or release their unwanted emotions. A brief introduction to the process of releasing follows.

Step 1: Focus on an issue you would like to feel better about.
 You may be experiencing guilt or fear. Allow yourself to feel whatever you are feeling at this moment.

Step 2: Ask yourself one of the following questions:

- Could I let this feeling go?
- Could I allow this feeling to be here?
- Could I welcome this feeling?

Each of these questions points you to the experience of letting go.

Step 3: Ask yourself this basic question: Would I? Am I willing to let go?
Step 4: Ask yourself this simpler question: When?

Dwoskin suggests repeating these four steps as often as needed to feel free of a particular feeling.

Source: Hale Dwoskin, *The Sedona Method* (Sedona, AZ: Sedona Press, 2003), pp. 36–44.

display a lack of emotional control. Frequent use of foul and vulgar language, flared tempers, raised voices, and teary eyes are still regarded as unacceptable behavior by most coworkers and supervisors.

One acceptable way to cope with fear, anger, grief, or jealousy is to sit down with pen and paper and write a letter to the person who triggered these emotions. Don't worry about grammar, spelling, or punctuation—just put all your thoughts on paper. Write until you have nothing more to say. Then destroy the letter. Once you let go of your toxic feelings, you will be ready to deal constructively with whatever caused you to become upset.[45] Another approach is to express your feelings through daily journal entries. Studies indicate that a significant emotional uplift and healing effect can result from spending as little as five to ten minutes a day writing about whatever issues or problems are getting you down.[46]

Accommodating Your Emotions

At the beginning of this chapter, we said an emotion can be thought of as a feeling that influences our thinking and behavior. Accommodation means you are willing to recognize, accept, and experience emotions and to try to react in ways appropriate to the situation. This style achieves an integration of one's feelings and the thinking process. People who display the accommodation style have adopted the "think before you act" point of view. It would be normal to feel defensive or angry during a negative performance review by your boss. However, career coaches advise against acting on these emotions. They suggest taking a day or two to digest the feedback and create an appropriate response.[47]

Do we always rely on just one of these four emotional styles? Of course not. Your response to news that a coworker is getting a divorce may be very different from your response to a demeaning comment made by your boss. You may have found appropriate ways to deal with your grief but may not have learned yet to cope with the fear of making a team presentation. Dealing with our emotions is a very complex process.

"Still won't start?"

STRATEGIES FOR ACHIEVING EMOTIONAL CONTROL

9-7 Each day, we wake up with a certain amount of mental, emotional, and physical energy that we can spend throughout the day. If we allow toxic thoughts and unpleasant feelings to deplete our energy, we have less energy to change our life or to give to others.[48] Our emotions do have an impact on our health. The link between emotions and health is quite strong for negative feelings that are associated with anger, anxiety, and depression. Some 30,000 heart attacks each year are triggered by momentary anger, according to research conducted at Harvard University.[49] We can learn to discipline the mind and banish afflicting thoughts that create needless frustration, waste energy, and deplete our immune systems. In this, the final part of the chapter, we share with you some practical suggestions for achieving greater control of the emotions that affect your life.

Identifying Your Emotional Patterns

We could often predict or anticipate our responses to various emotions if we would take the time to study our emotional patterns—to take a running inventory of circumstances that touch off jealousy, fear, anger, or some other emotion. Journal entries can help you discover emotional patterns. Record not only your conscious feelings, such as anxiety or guilt, but feelings in your body, such as a knot in your stomach or muscle tension.

If you don't feel comfortable with journal writing, consider setting aside some quiet time to reflect on your emotional patterns. A period of quiet reflection will help you focus your thoughts and impressions. Becoming a skilled observer of your own emotions is one of the best ways to achieve greater emotional control.

In addition to journal writing and quiet reflection, there is one more way to discover emotional patterns. At the end of the day, construct a chart of your emotional landscape. Make a chart (see Table 9.1) of the range of emotions you experienced and expressed during the day.[50]

> *Becoming a skilled observer of your own emotions is one of the best ways to achieve greater emotional control.*

Michael Crawford/Conde Nast Collection

Table 9.1 ■ Charting Your Emotional Landscape

TIME	CIRCUMSTANCE	EMOTION
6:00 a.m.	Alarm goes off. Mind is flooded by thoughts of all the things that must be done during the day.	Anxiety
7:10 a.m.	Depart for work. Heavy traffic interferes with plan to arrive at work early.	Anger and helplessness
8:00 a.m.	Thirty-minute staff meeting scheduled by the boss lasts fifty minutes. No agenda is provided. Entire meeting seems a waste of time.	Anger and frustration
9:35 a.m.	Finally start work on creative project.	Contentment
10:15 a.m.	Progress on project interrupted when coworker enters office, sits down, and starts sharing gossip about another coworker.	Anger and resentment
11:20 a.m.	Progress is made on creative project.	Contentment
1:45 p.m.	Creative project is complete and ready for review.	Joy and contentment
2:50 p.m.	Give project to boss for review. She says she will not be able to provide any feedback until morning. This delay will cause scheduling problems.	Frustration
4:00 p.m.	Attend health insurance update seminar sponsored by human resources department. No major changes are discussed.	Boredom
5:40 p.m.	Give up on a search for a missing document, turn off computer, and walk to parking lot.	Relief and fatigue

Your first entry might be "I woke up at 6:00 a.m. and immediately felt ___." The final entry might be "I left the office at 5:30 p.m. with a feeling of ___." What emotions surfaced throughout your workday? Resentment? Creative joy? Anxiety? Boredom? Contentment? Anger? Reflect on the completed chart and try to determine which patterns need to be changed. For example, you might discover that having lunch every day with two coworkers who are very negative is a major energy drain. Repeat this process over a period of several days in order to identify your unique emotional patterns.

Fine-Tuning Your Emotional Style

Once you have completed the process of self-examination and have identified some emotional patterns you want to change, it is time to consider ways to fine-tune your emotional style. Bringing about discipline within your mind can help you live a fuller, more satisfying life. Here are four things you can begin doing today.

- *Take responsibility for your emotions.* How you view your emotional difficulties will have a major influence on how you deal with them. If your frustration is triggered by thoughts such as "I can never make my boss happy" or "Things always go wrong in my life," you may never achieve a comfortable emotional state. By shifting the blame to other people and events, you cannot achieve emotional control.

■ *Put your problems into proper perspective.* Why do some people seem to be at peace most of the time, while others seem to be in a perpetual state of anxiety? People who engage in unproductive obsessing (irrational thinking) are unable or unwilling to look at problems realistically and practically, and they view each disappointment as a major catastrophe. To avoid needless misery, anxiety, and emotional upsets, use an "emotional thermometer" with a scale of 0 to 100. Zero means that everything is going well, and 100 denotes something life-threatening or truly catastrophic. Whenever you feel upset, ask yourself to come up with a logical number on the emotional thermometer. If a problem surfaces that is merely troublesome but not terrible, and you give it 60 points, you are no doubt overreacting. This mental exercise will help you avoid seeing every inconvenience or frustration as a "big deal."[51]

■ *Take steps to move beyond toxic emotions such as envy, anger, jealousy, or hatred.* Some people are upset about things that happened many years ago. Some even nurse grudges against people who have been dead for years. The sad thing is that the negative feelings remain long after we can achieve any positive learning from them.[52]

Experts say most people should give themselves two years to recover from a major emotional trauma such as a divorce or loss of a job. Prudence Gourguechon, former president of the American Psychoanalytic Association, says it's important to know roughly how long an emotional disruption will last. It takes time to rethink all the things that may be disrupted by emotional trauma.[53]

■ *Give your feelings some exercise.* Several prominent authors in the field of human relations have emphasized the importance of giving our feelings some exercise. Leo Buscaglia, author of *Loving Each Other*, says, "Exercise feelings. Feelings have meaning only as they are expressed in action."[54] Sam Keen, author of *Fire in the Belly*, said, "Make a habit of identifying your feelings and expressing them in some appropriate way."[55] If you have offended someone, how about sending that person a note expressing regret? If someone you work with has given extra effort, why not praise that person's work? Make a decision to cultivate positive mental states, such as kindness and compassion. A sincere feeling of empathy, for example, will deepen your connection to others.

LOOKING BACK: SUMMARY OF LEARNING OBJECTIVES

1. **Describe how emotions influence our thinking and behavior.**

   We carry inside us a vast array of emotions that can help us cope with our environment. An emotion can be thought of as a feeling that influences our thinking and behavior. Feelings are activated by a variety of events. Angry feelings may surface when another employee borrows something without your permission. Feelings of grief will very likely follow the loss of a close friend. The need to discover ways to achieve emotional balance has never been greater. We sometimes suffer from a lack of emotional balance because we learn to inhibit the expression of certain emotions and to overemphasize the expression of others.

2. **Explain the critical role of emotions in the workplace.**

   Emotions play a critical role in the success of every organization. Emotional undercurrents are present in almost every area of the organization, and they influence employee morale, customer loyalty, and productivity.

3. **Describe the major factors that influence our emotional development.**

   Our emotional development is influenced by temperament (the biological shaper of personality), our unconscious mind, cultural intelligence, and mindfulness. Throughout the long process of emotional development, we learn different ways to express our emotions.

4. **Learn how to cope with your anger and the anger of others**.

   Appropriate expressions of anger contribute to improved interpersonal relations, help us reduce anxiety, and give us an outlet for unhealthy stress. We must also learn how to handle other people's anger. It takes a great deal of effort to learn how to deal with our own anger and the anger of others.

5. **Understand the factors that contribute to workplace violence**.

   Workplace violence encompasses a wide range of activities, including homicides, hostile remarks, physical assaults, and sabotage directed toward the employer or other workers. Although violence cannot be eliminated, steps can be taken to curb violent employee behavior in the workplace.

6. **Identify and explain the most common emotional styles**.

   To achieve emotional balance, we need to start with an examination of our current emotional style. When confronted by strong feelings, we are likely to display one of four different emotional styles: suppressing emotions, capitulating to them, overexpressing them, or accommodating them.

7. **Describe strategies for achieving emotional control**.

   Emotional control is an important dimension of emotional style. The starting point in developing emotional control is to identify your current emotional patterns. One way to do this is to record your anger experiences in a diary or journal. Additional ways to identify emotional patterns include setting aside time for quiet reflection and developing a chart of your emotional landscape.

KEY TERMS

emotion, 186	unconscious mind, 190	anger, 193
emotional intelligence, 187	Transactional Analysis, 191	workplace violence, 196
emotional labor, 189	cultural intelligence, 191	
temperament, 190	mindfulness, 192	

CAREER INSIGHT

Some job interviews are mismanaged by the employer. Poorly trained interviewers often talk too much. They may want to tell you endless details about the job and the company. You may learn only what the interviewer wanted you to hear, and the company learned very little that's useful about you. During the interview you should talk most of the time. Be prepared to assert yourself if the interviewer is talking too much. Here are some points you need to make during the interview:

- Why do you want this job?
- What makes you a good candidate for this job?
- What are your career plans? How does this job fit those goals?

Of course you do not want to talk too much about yourself. After you make your points, invite questions and do your best to create a real dialogue.

Source: Bruce Clark, "Speak Up or You'll Blow the Interview," *News & Observer*, January 9, 2011, p. 3E.

TRY YOUR HAND

1. Recall the last time you were angry at another person or were a victim of a situation that made you angry. For example, someone you trusted divulged some personal information about your family history or accused you of an unethical practice at work. Then answer the following questions:
   a. Did you express your anger verbally? Physically?
   b. Did you suppress any of your anger? Explain.

c. What results did you experience from the way you handled this situation? Describe both positive and negative results.

d. If you could relive the situation, would you do anything differently? Explain.

2. To learn more about the way you handle anger, record your anger responses in a journal for a period of five days. When anger surfaces, record as many details as possible. What triggered your anger? How intense was the anger? How long did your angry feelings last? Did you express them to anyone? At the end of the five days, study your entries and try to determine whether any patterns exist. If you find this activity helpful, consider keeping a journal for a longer period of time.

3. To learn more about how emotions influence your thinking and behavior, complete each of the following sentences. Once you have completed them all, reflect on your written responses. Can you identify any changes you would like to make in your emotional style?

a. "When someone accuses me of wrongdoing, I usually …"

b. "When I feel frustrated, my response is …"

c. "When I am fearful, I …"

d. "My response to a lack of recognition is …"

e. "When I am disappointed, my response is to …"

4. Many people have an anger management problem. Although anger is a natural human emotion, the mismanagement of anger can result in serious interpersonal-relations problems. The National Anger Management Association is an organization dedicated to the advancement of anger management. NAMA recognizes there are varied techniques and methods for treating anger management. The NAMA Anger Management Specialist Certification Program has been popular in recent years. Visit the NAMA website at www.namass.org and become acquainted with this certification program and the other services offered by NAMA.

CRITICAL THINKING CHALLENGE

Anger builds when we perceive an injustice. Take time to remember a few occasions when someone's behavior triggered a torrent of anger in you. With pen and paper (not your computer), start writing about the reasons for your anger. Keep writing until your feelings become more focused and the reasons for your anger more clear. Keep writing until the anger is fully voiced. Then reflect on what you have learned that can be applied to anger management situations in the future.

SELF-ASSESSMENT EXERCISE

For each of the following statements, circle the number from 1 to 5 that best represents your response to each statement: (1) strongly disagree (never do this); (2) disagree (rarely do this); (3) moderately agree (sometimes do this); (4) agree (frequently do this); (5) strongly agree (almost always do this).

A.	I can solve problems and make decisions in a logical manner without allowing my emotions to interfere.	1	2	3	4	5
B.	My relationships with people at home, school, and work do not suffer because of my expressions of anger or impatience.	1	2	3	4	5
C.	I have developed effective ways to cope with my own anger and the anger of others.	1	2	3	4	5
D.	I am familiar with, and can apply, several strategies for achieving emotional control.	1	2	3	4	5

After identifying your response to each item, select an attitude or skill you would like to improve. Prepare a written goal and then describe the steps you will take to achieve this goal.

YOU PLAY THE ROLE

You are currently manager of a bank branch that employs 26 people. About three weeks ago, you learned that one of your employees, Wesla Perez, needed time off to spend with a parent who was very ill. You approved the time off without hesitation. Soon, you learned that the parent (mother) had died. On Monday

morning, Wesla will return to work. You plan to meet with Wesla and express your condolences. In this role-play exercise, a member of your class will play the role of Wesla Perez. The name you will use during the role-play is Evony Hillison.

BELOW THE SURFACE | ANGRY HEAD COACH CREATES PUBLIC RELATIONS SCANDAL

Henk Meijer/Alamy

A major university scandal touches the lives of many people: students, faculty, alumni, and anyone else with ties to the school who feel embarrassed. This chapter opens with a brief report on the coaching scandal at Rutgers University. Head coach Mike Rice was fired after a damning video emerged of him verbally and physically abusing players. The men's basketball program was deeply damaged, and so was the image projected by Rutgers University.

Anger in the workplace can take a toll on employees who are subjected to the discomfort that accompanies rage. A boss who yells at workers, leaving them feeling powerless and constantly on edge, will never be able to build group cohesiveness.

Also, it's exhausting to get angry and yell at others. There's a physiological discomfort that accompanies rage: your pulse picks up, your breathing becomes shallow, and you feel slightly out of control.[56]

QUESTION

1. Months before Coach Rice was fired, the Rutgers athletic director became aware of the coach's lack of emotional control. He decided a three-game suspension and a $50,000 fine would suffice as punishment. Should he have also enrolled the coach in an anger management course?

CLOSING CASE | EMOTIONS TIED TO EATING

There are psychological and physiological reasons we turn to food for comfort. Many emotions such as anger, sadness, loneliness, and happiness can lead to overeating. Emotional eating is a major barrier to weight loss.

As noted in this chapter, knowing that you are eating is not the same as eating mindfully. Mindfulness involves paying attention and being continuously present with the experience. Cathy Leman, a nutritional counselor, says tracking food and identifying your mood while eating is eye-opening: "Many times people have no idea that they turn to food when feeling lonely or frustrated."[57]

QUESTIONS

1. Cathy Leman says one way to increase awareness is tracking food and identifying your mood while eating (an application of mindfulness). She says the type and amount of food may be astonishing once it's in writing. Do you agree? Is keeping a log of your eating habits a practical solution for you?

2. If you are motivated to pull into the next drive-through fast food restaurant or empty the cookie jar, Leman says develop nonfood coping skills. For example, relax with a warm bath and a cup of tea. What are some examples that would work for you?

CHAPTER 9 ENDNOTES

1. Scott Fontana, "Rutgers Waited Too Long," **AM New York**, April 3, 2013, p. 23.

2. Jason Gay, "What Was Lost at Rutgers," **Wall Street Journal**, April 4, 2013, p. D8.

3. David Giambusso, "Two Former Rutgers Basketball Players File Suit Over Mike Rice Abuse Scandal," **Star-Ledger**, March 27, 2014. Retrieved from http://www.nj.com/news/index.ssf/2014/two-more-rutgers-students-file-suit. INTERNET.

4. Bernstein et al., **Psychology**, p. 446.

5. Carol S. Pearson, "The Emotional Side of Workplace Success," **The Inner Edge**, December 1998/ January 1999, p. 3.

6. Daniel Goleman, **Emotional Intelligence** (New York: Bantam Books, 1995), pp. 34 and 43; Stephen R. Covey, "Questions for Covey," **Training**, July/ August 2007, p. 40.

7. Daniel Goleman, **Working with Emotional Intelligence** (New York: Bantam Books, 1998), pp. 24–28; Robert Kreitner, **Management**, 10th ed. (Boston: Houghton Mifflin, 2007), p. 447. To learn more about emotional intelligence, read **Emotional Intelligence 2.0**, by Travis Bradberry and Jean Greaves (San Diego: Talent Smart, 2009).

8. John Selby, **Conscious Healing** (New York: Bantam Books, 1989), p. 32.

9. Hara Estroff Marano, "Love's Destroyer," **Psychology Today**, July/August 2009, p. 65.

10. James Georges, "The Not-So-Stupid Americans," **Training**, July 1994, p. 90.

11. Tim Sanders, **Love Is the Killer App** (New York: Crown Business, 2002), pp. 17–18.

12. Ibid., p. 23.

13. Ron Zemke, "Contact! Training Employees to Meet the Public," **Service Solutions** (Minneapolis: Lakewood Books, 1990), pp. 20–23.

14. Monika Rice, "The Perils of a Fake Smile," **Spirituality & Health**, July/August 2011, p. 27.

15. Peter J. Frost, **Toxic Emotions at Work** (Boston: Harvard Business School Press, 2007), pp. 5–7.

16. Ibid., p. 3.

17. Bernstein et al., **Psychology**, pp. 484–485.

18. William C. Menninger and Harry Levinson, **Human Understanding in Industry** (Chicago: Science Research Associates, 1956), p. 29. To learn more about the unconscious mind, read "Unconscious Mind" from Wikipedia [cited 7 November 2014]. Available from http://en.wikipedia/wiki/Unconscious_mind.

19. Joan Borysenko, **Guilt Is the Teacher, Love Is the Lesson** (New York: Warner Books, 1990), p. 70.

20. Visit the Wikipedia (http://www.wikipediea.org) or Businessballs (http://www.businessballs.com) websites for a comprehensive overview of TA Theory.

21. P. Christopher Earley and Elaine Mosakowski, "Cultural Intelligence," **Harvard Business Review**, October 2004, p. 139. Also see "Cultivating Cultural Intelligence," by Neal Goodman, **Training**, March/April 2011, p. 38.

22. **Outsourced** [accessed 8 December 2008]. Available from http://www.netflix.com; INTERNET.

23. Gerald L. Manning, Michael Ahearne, Barry L. Reece, **Selling Today—Partnering to Create Value**, 13th ed. (New York: Pearson Education, 2015), p. 167.

24. Jon Kabat-Zinn, "What Is Mindfulness?" October 28, 2014. Retrieved from http://greatergood.berkeley.edu/topic/mindfulness.

25. "Three Levels of Leadership Model," November 14, 2014. Retrieved from http://wikipedia.org/wiki/three_levels_of_leadership-model.

26. Jon Kabat-Zinn, **Mindfulness for Beginners** (Boulder, CO: Sounds True, 2012), p. 165.

27. Harold H. Bloomfield and Robert K. Cooper, **The Power of 5** (Emmaus, PA: Rodale Press, 1995), p. 334; Redford

Williams and Virginia Williams, *Anger Kills* (New York: HarperCollins, 1993), p. 3; Redford Williams, "Why Anger Kills," *Duke Medicine Healthline*, Winter 2007, p. 11.

28. Kimes Gustin, *Anger, Rage, and Resentment* (West Caldwell, NJ: St. Ives Press, 1994), p. 1.

29. Sue Shellenbarger, "How to Keep Your Cool in Angry Times," *Wall Street Journal*, September 22, 2010, p. D3.

30. Elizabeth Bernstein, "This Loved One Will Explode in Five, Four…," *Wall Street Journal*, December 14, 2010, p. D1.

31. Melinda Beck, "When Anger Is an Illness," *Wall Street Journal*, March 9, 2010, p. D1.

32. Ibid., p. D6.

33. Pemna Chödrön, "The Answer to Anger and Other Strong Emotions," *Shambhala Sun*, March 2005, p. 32.

34. Rolland S. Parker, *Emotional Common Sense* (New York: Barnes & Noble Books, 1973), pp. 80–81.

35. Elizabeth Bernstein, "Ban the Silent Treatment," *Wall Street Journal*, June 17, 2014, p. D1.

36. Sue Shellenbarger, "How to Keep Your Cool in Angry Times," *Wall Street Journal*, September 22, 2010, p. D3.

37. Les Giblin, *How to Have Confidence and Power in Dealing with People* (Englewood Cliffs, NJ: Prentice-Hall, 1956), p. 37.

38. "Workplace Violence: An Employer's Guide" [accessed 12 December 2008]. Available from http://www.work-violence.com; INTERNET.

39. Carol Hymowitz, "Bosses Have to Learn How to Confront Troubled Employees," *Wall Street Journal*, April 23, 2007, p. Bl.

40. Anne Fisher, "How to Prevent Violence at Work," *Fortune*, February 21, 2005, p. 42; Holman W. Jenkins, Jr., "How Business Tackled Mass Shooters," *Wall Street Journal*, December 19, 2012, p. A17.

41. Pete Carey, "Economic Instability May Lead to Danger," *The Roanoke Times*, November 28, 2008, p. 8.

42. Workplace Violence Research Institute. [cited 19 November 2014]. Available from http://www.workplace.violence.com/services.

43. Hale Dwoskin, *The Sedona Method* (Sedona, AZ: Sedona Press, 2003), p. 30.

44. Walton C. Boshear and Karl G. Albrecht, *Understanding People: Models and Concepts* (San Diego: University Associates, 1977), pp. 41–46.

45. Chris Hill and Toby Hanlon, "Twenty-Six Simple Ways to Change How You Feel," *Prevention*, August 1993, p. 63.

46. Bloomfield and Cooper, *The Power of 5*, p. 368; Jill Neimark, "Open Mind Open Heart," *Spirituality & Health*, May/June 2008, p. 14.

47. Erin White, "Review Went Badly? Stay Cool, Find a Fix or Look to Move On," *Wall Street Journal*, May 23, 2006, p. B7.

48. Don Miguel Ruiz, *The Four Agreements* (San Rafael, CA: Amber-Allen Publishing, 1997), p. 111.

49. Daniel Goleman (ed.), *Healing Emotions* (Boston: Shambhala Publications,1997), p. 33; Melinda Beck, "When Anger Is an Illness," *Wall Street Journal*, March 9, 2010, p. D6.

50. Sam Keen, *Fire in the Belly—On Being a Man* (New York: Bantam Books, 1991), p. 242.

51. Arnold A. Lazarus and Clifford N. Lazarus, *The 60-Second Shrink* (San Luis Obispo, CA: Impact, 1997), pp. 10–11.

52. Borysenko, *Minding the Body, Mending the Mind*, p. 169.

53. Elizabeth Bernstein, "The Good Identity Crisis: It Lasts Two Years, No Shortcuts," *Wall Street Journal*, July 30, 2013, p. D1.

54. Leo F. Buscaglia, *Loving Each Other* (Thorofare, NJ: Slack, 1984), p. 160.

55. Keen, *Fire in the Belly*, p. 242.

56. Melinda Beck, "When Anger Is an Illness," *Wall Street Journal*, March 9, 2010, p. D1; Aisha Sultan, "How I Stopped Getting Angry," *News & Observer*, January 21, 2014, p. 2D.

57. Jill Weisenberger, "Stop Feeding Your Feeling," *Diabetic Living*, Winter 2013, pp. 77 and 80.

Henk Meijer/Alamy

CHAPTER PREVIEW

LEARNING OBJECTIVES

After studying Chapter 10, you will be able to

10-1 Explain how positive energy contributes to improved interpersonal relationships.

10-2 Describe the fundamentals of positive psychology.

10-3 Identify and discuss the positive emotions that contribute to a fulfilling life.

10-4 Describe workplace cultures that generate positive energy.

10-5 Understand how to use positive reinforcement to improve relationships and reward behavior.

10-6 Describe the major barriers to the use of positive reinforcement.

10-7 Explain how to reward individual and team performance.

Building Stronger Relationships with Positive Energy

TIP OF THE ICEBERG | FORMULA FOR SUCCESS: PUT EMPLOYEES BEFORE CUSTOMERS

Many companies pay lip service to the strategy of putting employees first, but The Container Store lives by this value daily. Just ask any of the nearly 6,000 employees.

Defining and communicating a clear sense of purpose is one of the most important activities a company can do. This requires company leaders to clearly and frequently communicate its vision (where the company is going and why), the strategy to get there, and the specific goals it is trying to reach. This type of "breathless communication," as one employee calls it, is woven into the cultural DNA at The Container Store. Employees know exactly where the company is headed and their role in it. "We have no secrets in this company as far as our numbers and our goals. Everybody knows them and understands them," said Sara Jo Smith, an employee who works at a store in Colorado. Employee Beth McGee agrees, saying, "Every part of every store knows the vision of the company." This creates a happy, engaged workforce with an average turnover rate of around 10 percent companywide versus an industry average of more than 100 percent. The Container Store hires only 3 percent of applicants, and many new hires are referred by employees.

At the top of this high-performance culture is a passionate and engaged Chairman and CEO, Kip Tindell. "We really believe that if you put the employee

Anderson Ross/Blend Images/Getty Images

207

containerstore.com

The Container Store has been on Fortune's "100 Best Places to Work For" list 16 times. A constant stream of open communication, training, and generous benefits create a happy, engaged workforce.

first, they really and truly will take better care of the customer than anybody else." "Tindell says employees make their own decisions, adding, "I don't think I'm smart enough to tell any employee how to behave in any given situation." The company's seven Foundation Principles guide employee behavior and decision making. One of the Foundation Principles, "1 Good Person = 3 Good People®," means one great person can easily do the business productivity of three good people".[1] More productivity means the company can pay employees above industry average. The typical full-time store employee makes an average of nearly $50,000 a year and enjoys benefits including a flexible work schedule, health benefits, discounts on pet insurance, 40 percent merchandise discounts, and 266 hours of training for first year full-time employees and 178 hours for first year part-time employees. Both full- and part-time employees earn vacation time. Tindell says, "I think if you're lucky enough to be somebody's employer, you have a moral obligation to make sure they want to get out of bed and come to work in the morning."[2]

Our work should provide a major source of positive energy, but too many people are not fully engaged or satisfied with the type of work they do for a living. This chapter provides groundbreaking information that will help you reenergize your life and achieve a higher level of contentment at work and at home.

We will discuss the impact of positive energy on both individual and group behavior. **Energy** can be defined as the capacity for work, or the force that helps us do things with vitality and intensity. We will examine the field of positive psychology, the power of positive feedback, various types of positive reinforcement, and the reasons why many people have difficulty expressing positive thoughts and feelings. A section of the chapter is devoted to awards and incentive programs that a variety of organizations use.

POSITIVE ENERGY CONTRIBUTES TO IMPROVED INTERPERSONAL RELATIONSHIPS

10-1 It is positive energy that helps us cope with disappointments, uncertainty, and work that is physically and mentally demanding. In the presence of positive energy, people feel uplifted, encouraged, and empowered. Positive energy helps us remain balanced in a work environment that is increasingly characterized by change and uncertainty.[3]

Energy: An Important Force in Our Lives

Judith Orloff, author of *Positive Energy* and pioneer in the field of energy psychiatry, says *energy* is a word with many intriguing dimensions. In basic terms, it is the "get-up-and-go," the stamina that gets you through the day. Envision energy as having one of two qualities: either positive or negative. Positive energy is supportive, loving, and nurturing. Negative energy is fearful, judgmental, and depleting. How you respond to people and places determines, to a large degree, your energy level. Dr. Orloff makes an interesting observation regarding the impact of relationships on our energy level: "Each millisecond of our relationships is governed by a give and take of energy. Some people make us more electric or at ease. Others suck the life right out of us."[4]

POSITIVE PSYCHOLOGY: THEORY AND INITIATIVES

10-2 **Positive psychology** is a fairly recent branch of psychology that focuses on positive human functioning. Marty Seligman, former president of the American Psychological Association, founded positive psychology in 1998. He challenged the field to look at what makes life worth living—what a healthy person acts like, rather than a suffering one. Positive psychologists seek to discover what makes life more fulfilling.[5] Researchers and scientists in this field analyze states of pleasure or flow, values, strengths, virtues, and talents, in addition to how social systems and institutions can support and encourage more of these benefits.

Seligman, in his best-selling book *Authentic Happiness*, states that the field of psychology has been consumed by the study of diagnosing, treating, and curing mental illness, much like traditional medicine. Most scientists in the field focused on negative states such as depression, fear, and anxiety. Seligman wanted to redirect this scientific rigor toward understanding human potential and how to create more happiness and fulfillment.

Positive psychology finds its roots in the research conducted by Abraham Maslow, Carl Rogers, Erich Fromm, and other humanistic psychologists. They developed theories and practices that focus on aspects of the human condition that lead to happiness and fulfillment.[6] Several psychologists now focus exclusively on positive psychology, and they have made important discoveries. The number of positive emotions we feel predicts our overall level of satisfaction with life. Positive thoughts and emotions are available to everyone regardless of age, income, material resources, location, past experiences, and even health. Developing a positive mindset can be learned and applied by anyone who wishes to create a happier, healthier, more fulfilling life.

Forms of Positivity

Psychologist Barbara Fredrickson has spent the past two decades investigating the influence of positive emotions and has written several important books on the topic,

Total Person   Insight

"Everything can be taken from a man but one thing: the last of the human freedoms—to choose one's attitude in any given set of circumstances, to choose one's own way."

Viktor E. Frankl, Holocaust survivor and author, *Man's Search for Meaning*, Boston: Beacon Press, 1959.

including *Positivity* and *Love 2.0*. Positivity is based on two truths. First, positivity broadens and builds. Positive emotions like joy, gratitude, pride, and inspiration touch and open your heart and our minds, making us more receptive and more creative. Second, positivity transforms us for the better. By opening our hearts and our minds, positive emotions allow us to discover and build new skills, new relationships, new knowledge, and new ways of being.

Fredrickson's research and collaboration with Marcial Losada led to a scientific discovery called the "positivity ratio," which says that for every negative emotion we feel, three positive emotions are needed to bring emotions back into balance. Three positive events to one negative event is the tipping point, but some relationships require an even higher positive-to-negative ratio. Research has shown that a 5-to-1 ratio is ideal for married couples. Understanding and practicing the 3-to-1 positivity ratio has important implications for improving relationships and living a richer, more positive life.[7]

The Theory of Flow

In the field of positive psychology, **flow** is the mental state in which a person performing an activity is fully immersed in a feeling of energized focus. In essence, flow is characterized by complete absorption in a task that elicits a deep feeling of enjoyment. This concept was named by Mihaly Csikszentmihalyi, who founded the Quality of Life Research Center at Claremont Graduate University.[8]

Judith Orloff, a pioneer in the field of energy psychiatry, says there are certain intuitive signs you are in the flow:

- You are happy, or at least able to accept what is\ without engaging in an unrelenting internal battle.
- Your energy is high, and you have an ease in relating with people and yourself. If conflicts arise, you breathe deeply and work toward resolution instead of getting rigid or retaliating.
- Hours pass, and you may not even notice. Children get into a flow-consciousness when playing, as do artists when creating.[9]

In order to achieve flow in the workplace, Csikszentmihalyi describes three conditions: (1) goals are clear, (2) feedback is immediate; and (3) balance exists between opportunity and capacity. Flow is less likely to happen when individual workers cannot see where their roles fit into a goal or project. Limited feedback about one's work can reduce motivation and leave employees unaware of their contributions.[10]

The Happiness Advantage

After more than a decade of groundbreaking research in the field of positive psychology, an important principle surfaced: We become more successful *when* we are happier and more positive. Most people think happiness is achieved once they reach a certain goal, thinking that a promotion at work, a raise in pay, or some other accomplishment will result in happiness. The research is finding, however, that happiness and optimism *fuel* performance and achievement. Srikumar Rao, author of "Happiness at Work," says we must get rid of the inaccurate way of "if/then" thinking. "There is nothing you have to get, do, or be in order to be happy."

Tal Ben-Shahar, one of Harvard University's most popular lecturers, defines happiness as the overall experience of pleasure and meaning. This definition does not pertain to a single moment but to a generalized aggregate of one's experiences. Several studies show that happy people are successful across multiple life domains, including friendship, marriage, work performance, income, and health.[11]

Harvard professor Shawn Achor studies happiness and its effect on success in the workplace. He states that 90 percent of long-term happiness is derived from how your brain processes the world and your life experiences. His research has found when people work with a positive mindset, performance on nearly every level—productivity, creativity, engagement—improves.[12]

 ## DEVELOPING THE HAPPINESS ADVANTAGE

Shawn Achor, author of *The Happiness Advantage*, says training your brain to be positive is not so different than training your muscles at the health club. As you develop new habits, you rewire the brain. Achor says there are several simple activities that correlate with positive change:

- Jot down three things you are grateful for. Most of us have many things to be grateful for in our lives.
- Write a positive message to someone who has given you support in some way.
- Meditate at your desk for two minutes.
- Exercise for 10 minutes.
- Take two minutes to record in a journal the most meaningful experience of the past 24 hours.[13]

POSITIVE EMOTIONS: PREREQUISITE FOR A FULFILLING LIFE

10-3   Throughout recent periods of great uncertainty and turbulence, negative energy became a powerful force. Many people went to work every day wondering if they would be the next victim of a merger, buyout, downsizing effort, or business closing. Some wondered if they would be able to cope with rapid technological changes. Stressful working conditions caused by rising productivity demands and long hours can also be the source of negative energy. In a negative, stressful work climate, these pressures often result in physical fatigue, decreased optimism, and less happiness. Positive thoughts and perspective are an inside job.

As you just learned in the preceding pages, happiness and positive emotions do not just happen, they can be created. This is why it is essential to learn how to cultivate them.

Negative emotions, however, are not only inevitable, they are required for flourishing. Negative emotions can stimulate people to reflect more deeply, to create works of art or literature, or to stimulate new relationships and experiences. Refuting negative emotions such as grief, trauma, loss, and humiliation are unhealthy, and no one can avoid these feelings completely.

Learning how to cultivate positive emotions is essential, especially when negative events abound to seize our attention. Psychologists say humans are hardwired with a **negativity bias** causing us to notice negative events more than positive ones. The amygdala section of the brain that triggers fight or flight can be helpful in certain circumstances, such as sensing danger. The good news is that people actually experience far more positive moments in life than negative, which psychologists call the "positivity offset."

We are predisposed to notice negative events, which doesn't always feel like a choice—just think of the daily newscast. Barbara Fredrickson says it takes discipline, willpower, and practice not to focus on negative emotions. Focusing our attention on positive emotions is a choice that requires self-discipline.[14]

Total Person Insight

"Happiness can be a choice. If we link mindset and behavioral change created by small positive habits, we can create long-term, quantifiable positive change at any level and at any age."

Source: Shawn Achor, "Happily Orange After," *Training*, January/February 2014, p. 114.

Research so far has found that positive emotions all appear to have the same positive outcomes; however, some may be easier and faster to implement than others. Review the following emotions and learn how easy it is to trigger them if you do so mindfully.

Gratitude

Gratitude is one of those human qualities that benefits the giver and the receiver. Grateful people experience higher levels of positive emotions such as joy, enthusiasm, happiness, and optimism. The practice of gratitude protects us from destructive impulses such as envy, resentment, and bitterness. One way to develop positive energy is to keep a "gratitude journal." Each day, write down three to five things for which you are grateful.[15] Psychologists agree this is one of the most simple yet effective ways to increase positive emotions. Linda Kaplan, author of *The Power of Nice*, says, "In business, being nice has been underrated."[16] Take time to notice small gestures of goodwill, and thank people for their contributions and assistance. Learn to thank the givers for their time, talent, or thoughtfulness. Write thank-you notes frequently, or if sending an e-mail, consider copying the coworker's boss or CEO if a person contributes to the success of a project.

Total Person Insight

> "Gratitude opens your heart and carries the urge to give back—to do something good in return, either for the person who helped you or someone else."
>
> Source: Barbara Fredrickson, *Positivity* (New York: Crown Publishers, 2009), p. 41.

Pride

Pride is the emotional high that follows performance and success. This definition was developed by Jon Katzenbach, author of *Why Pride Matters More Than Money*. He notes that the power of pride is obvious when you observe the high-performing workforces at Southwest Airlines, Marriott, the U.S. Marine Corps, and Zappos. "Pride is a natural by-product of the successes of those organizations," says Katzenbach.[17]

Katzenbach notes that pride-builders can be found at all levels of the organization. They often get involved in the everyday problems of their employees. Roy Pelaez leads a workforce of 426 people who clean airplanes for Delta Airlines and Southwest Airlines. Many of his staff are recent immigrants, so he brought in an English-language teacher to tutor employees twice a week on their own time. He scheduled Friday citizenship classes to help employees become U.S. citizens. To help single mothers, Pelaez arranged for certified babysitters subsidized by government programs.[18]

Serenity

Our lives are so filled with stimuli it's very difficult to relax and replace tension with feelings of peace. Barbara Fredrickson says **serenity** is a mindful state that carries the urge to savor your current circumstances and find ways to integrate them into your life more fully.[19] It can come with rewarding work in your home, taking a walk, or curling up with a good book. Try to carve out a little quiet time each day for meditation or spending time outside in nature.

Interest

From time to time something new or different draws your attention. These circumstances require effort and increased attention on your part. When you uncover a new set of challenges you may need to build new skills and engage in new learning. Depending on the new interest you may once again feel open and alive.[20] New interests motivate us to use our brains in different ways and are necessary for personal growth.

Social Support

Shawn Achor says one of the most effective ways to train the brain to be positive is to engage positively with people in your social support network (friends and coworkers, for example). A study conducted at Ochsner Health System, a large medical provider serving southeast Louisiana, helps illustrate the effectiveness of social support as a tool for employee happiness. Achor worked with the medical staff to develop an approach called the "10/5 Way":

- When employees walk within 10 feet of another person in the hospital, they must make eye contact and smile.
- When they walk within 5 feet, they must say hello.

The training involved 11,000 employees, leaders, and physicians. Since the introduction of 10/5, Ochsner employees have experienced higher job satisfaction scores and more satisfied patients.[21]

These are just a few examples of the tools available to help you get in touch with your positive emotions. The first step is awareness. Just paying attention to how often you are kind (not necessarily the number of times), or the act of expressing gratitude, increases positive emotions. With a little creative thinking you can discover additional activities.

WORKPLACE CULTURES THAT CREATE POSITIVE ENERGY

10-4 It is positive energy that helps us cope with disappointments, uncertainty, and work that is physically and mentally demanding. In the presence of positive energy, people feel uplifted, encouraged, and empowered.

Several research studies have measured the business benefits companies experience when they create a positive company culture. Some of benefits include higher levels of employee engagement, increased employee retention, creativity, productivity, improved customer satisfaction, and increased sales and profits. Consider these examples:

Clinic Service Corporation. Clinic Service is a Denver-based medical billing company serving physicians for more than 40 years. When Andrew Graham became the president and CEO in 2007 he focused his attention on creating a company culture that would provide staff with learning and personal growth opportunities, and customers with exceptional experiences. Employees receive a minimum of 40 hours of training annually, and up-and-coming, high-performing staff members participate in a leadership development program called "Leaders of the Future."

The Clinic Service culture is described as "team-based, inclusive, fun, results-oriented, and a stimulating learning environment." Quarterly company meetings provide open and honest communication about financial performance, operational results, customer insights, and company goals. Senior management is dedicated to creating a workplace that inspires people to want to excel, continuously improve, and take personal responsibility. Performance is rewarded as people build their capabilities, increase their confidence, and take charge of their future.

The result is a loyal and engaged workforce that is energized and passionate about creating highly satisfied customers. Nearly 30 percent of employees have worked for Clinic Service for over 10 years, and the average employee tenure is eight years. Senior management is known for frequently saying, "How we treat each other is just as important as what we do." This philosophy has earned Clinic Service several "Top Workplace" awards.[22]

Migros Ticaret A.S. This high-end supermarket in Turkey targets the luxury segment of the market. When competitors began to enter the market and potentially cause loyal customers to abandon the well-established brand, the company created two new training programs for employees. One is classroom-based combined with experiential hands-on learning. The second is a cultural development program that gave employees an opportunity to study abroad. The results were impressive. Not only did market share growth more than double in this competitive market, employee loyalty rose by 13 percent and program satisfaction was ranked as high as 4.99 on a 5-point scale.[23]

Salesforce.com. Each year, cloud computing giant Salesforce.com hosts Dreamforce, a four-day mega-event in San Francisco. At the 2014 event, 140,000 employees and customers attended, millions of people watched the event online, and the universities and nonprofits attending turned Dreamforce into the world's largest nonprofit technology conference. The event is the brainchild of CEO Mark Benioff and features a unique mashup of philanthropy, social and environmental causes, new product introductions, education, spiritual and personal transformation programs, and rock concerts. The 2014 lineup of speakers and entertainers included Tony Robbins, Hillary Clinton, Ariana Huffington, Ekert Tolle, former U.S. vice president Al Gore, and several of Silicon Valley's leading CEOs. Entertainers included Bruno Mars, Cake, will.i.am, and MC Hammer.

Not only was Dreamforce an amazing event for customers and employees, many of whom worked side-by-side at several of the fundraising events, it was successful for several charitable causes. More than three million meals were donated, and $9 million was raised for UCSF Benioff Children's Hospitals. Salesforce.com has created a new company event model benefiting all stakeholders in a company and community.[24] Hopefully many other companies will use this model as a way to bridge corporate and philanthropic causes.

Total Person Insight

"Most great ideas for enhancing corporate growth and profits aren't discovered in the lab late at night, or in the isolation of the executive suite. They come from the people who daily fight the company battles, who serve the customers, explore new markets, and fend off the competition."

Source: J. C. Spender and Bruce Strong, "Who Has Innovative Ideas? Employees." *Wall Street Journal*, August 23, 2010, p. R5.

These examples indicate that astute businesses create a positive, caring work environment where employees feel valued. When employees feel valued, they are more productive and engaged, which leads to happy, loyal customers. Higher customer satisfaction leads to increased sales and higher levels of profitability, which ultimately results in higher shareholder value.

This cause-effect chain reaction is known as the **employee-customer profit chain theory**. It is not new, nor is it as easy to implement as it sounds. The theory illustrated in Figure 10.1 was developed by Sears to improve organizational performance following an economic downturn in the 1980s and published in a landmark article by *Harvard Business Review* in 1998. The Sears experiment with the employee-customer profit chain theory provided evidence for the existence of a significant correlation between employee attitude, consumer behaviors, and the bottom line. Research organizations and companies continue to study, experiment, and build on this theory to improve organizational performance.[25]

Figure 10.1 ■ Employee-Service Profit Chain

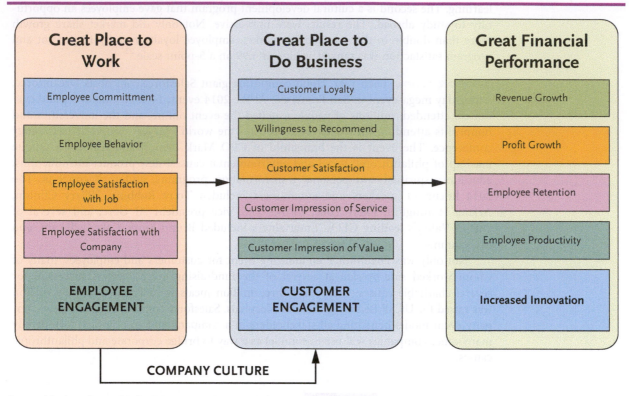

Source: Monique Reece, MarketSmarter, 2015, www.MarketSmarter.com

POSITIVE REINFORCEMENT—CREATING POSITIVE ENERGY

10-5   In recent years, researchers have quantified the cost of negativity in the workplace, and the results are quite shocking. Negative, or "actively disengaged," workers cost the U.S. economy up to $350 billion a year according to the Gallup International Research and Education Center due to lost productivity. "Actively disengaged" employees are defined as "individuals who are unhappy at work and act out their unhappiness."[26] Costs are not only associated with absences, sickness, and turnover, but also with low performance and negativity that has a toxic effect on the people who work with negative people. According to Gallup's 2014 Employee Engagement report, the entire world has a crisis in engagement. The report revealed 87 percent of employees worldwide are not engaged at work.[27]

Engaged employees lead to better business outcomes. In fact, according to Towers Perrin research, companies with engaged workers have 6 percent higher net profit margins, and according to Kenexa Research, engaged companies have five times shareholder returns over five years.

A brief book entitled *How Full Is Your Bucket? (http://www.bucketbook.com)*, written by Gallup Practice Leaders Tom Rath and Donald Clifton, provides a simple yet compelling strategy for dealing with negativity in the workplace. After more than 50 years of comprehensive psychological and workplace research, they were inspired to develop the Theory of the Dipper and the Bucket. According to Rath and Clifton, each of us has an invisible bucket. It is constantly being emptied or filled, depending on what others say or do to us. When our bucket is full, we feel great. A full bucket increases our positive emotions and renews our energy. When it is empty, we feel awful. There are a lot of empty buckets in today's workforce. Survey after survey has found that more than half of the workers in America say they do not feel appreciated in their current jobs.[28] When the cause is a manager, an employee

Expressing positive emotions and behavior improves productivity and engagement.

Konstantin Chagin/Shutterstock.com

may just quit rather than put up with the daily negative energy drain. Surveys have shown that upwards of 65 percent of employees say they would prefer a new boss over a raise.[29]

Total Person Insight

"There are two things people want more than sex and money: recognition and praise."

—Mary Kay Ash, founder of Mary Kay Cosmetics

Source: Robert A. Eckert, "The Two Most Important Words," Harvard Business Review, April 2013, p. 38.

Positive Reinforcement Defined

The goal of positive reinforcement is to encourage productive behaviors. Prior to PAE-TEC being acquired by Windstream Communication, the company was well-known for treating its employees with a high degree of respect. Former CEO Arunas Chesonis, set an example for employees by sharing financial information, acquisition plans, profits, and other information usually discussed only in the boardroom. He answered e-mails from every employee and expects everyone else to do the same. He rewarded information sharing with personal thank-you notes, e-mails, and visits. This pattern was followed in other important areas such as customer service and honoring family life, and resulted in the company being awarded several Best Workplace awards.[30] Positive reinforcement has never been more important than it is today. Large numbers of workers at all levels of organizations encounter energy-draining experiences at work and in their personal lives.

Support from Skinner

The research of B. F. Skinner at Harvard University has contributed to our understanding of reinforcement as a factor influencing the behavior of people in a work setting. Skinner maintained that any living organism will tend to repeat a particular behavior if that behavior is accompanied or followed by a reinforcer. A **reinforcer** is any stimulus that follows a response and increases the probability that the response will occur again. **Positive reinforcers** strengthen a response if they are experienced after that response occurs.[31]

The Power of Recognition

No one should have to wait for an annual performance review for recognition and performance feedback. This is especially true for Generation Y workers (Millennials). Ron Alsop, author of *The Trophy Kids Grow Up: How the Millennial Generation Is Shaking Up the Workplace*, notes that many Millennials grew up receiving a great deal of affirmation and positive reinforcement. Now, they come into the workplace needy for more.[32] For this generation, frequent feedback is vital and often more important than salary or a company's name recognition.

Giving recognition is one of the easiest and most powerful ways to make an employee feel important and needed. When handled correctly, recognition can be an effective reinforcement strategy that ensures repetition of desired behaviors. The authors of *The One Minute Manager*, a book that has sold more than 13 million copies, point out that recognition in the form of praise need not take a great deal of time. The key is to pay attention to what others are doing and try not to miss an opportunity to use praise to generate positive energy. Table 10.1 provides some excellent tips on planning and delivering praise.

Total Person Insight

"A person's true character can be judged by how he treats those who can do nothing for him."

Source: Roy Chitwood, "Still Trying to Slip Past Gatekeepers? Forget It!" *Value-Added Selling 21*, December 26, 2003, p. 1.

Jon Feingersh/Getty Images

Recognizing and appreciating other people creates positive energy and improves employee engagement. Offering praise is fast, simple and free, and it should be used more often in the workplace.

Table 10.1 ■ One-Minute Praisings

ONE-MINUTE PRAISING CAN WORK WELL WHEN YOU:
1. Inform people up front that you'll be giving them feedback.
2. Offer positive reinforcement immediately.
3. Let them know specifically what they did well.
4. Pause for a moment of silence to let them understand how good you feel.
5. Tell them that you feel good about what they did right and that it positively influences the organization and its workers.
6. Offer a handshake or similar physical gesture that lets them know you support them.
7. Ask them to keep up the good work.

Source: "One Minute Praisings" from *The One Minute Manager* by Kenneth Blanchard and Spencer Johnson. 1981, 1982 by Blanchard Family Partnership and Candle Communications Corp., Inc.

Courtesy Can Be Contagious

The poet Alfred Tennyson once said, "The greater the man, the greater the courtesy." Courtesy means being considerate of others in small ways, showing respect for what others revere, and treating everyone, regardless of position, with consideration. In today's fast-paced world, the impact of courtesy can easily be overlooked. Rudeness flourishes in our society, so it is not surprising that common courtesies are sometimes forgotten. Someone arrives late for an important meeting but does not see the need to apologize or even explain why he is late. You schedule an important meeting with your team, and suddenly a member is talking to a friend on her cell phone. These behaviors create negative energy.

Active Listening

As discussed in Chapter 2, everyone feels a sense of personal value when speaking with a good listener. Active listening can be a powerful reinforcer. Active listening is the process of sending back to the speaker what you as a listener think the speaker meant in terms of both content and feelings.

People long for more authentic interactions with coworkers or bosses who are good listeners. This stimulates open and honest communication. Lincoln Financial has created a simple ritual of starting meetings with a "personal and professional check-in" when people share what is going on in their lives for a few minutes before jumping into a meeting agenda. Lisa Buckingham, the chief HR officer, says, "It requires us to be vulnerable, it helps build our relationship as a team—and very often it gives us an opportunity to ask how we can help one another."[33]

Thank You

Two little words can greatly enhance your ability to improve interpersonal relations with friends, coworkers, and complete strangers: *thank you*. Thanking people isn't simply a matter of common courtesy. A major study involving 200,000 managers and employees showed that saying "thank you" correlates with the economic success of an organization. Giving thanks is a great motivational tool.[34]

THE TWO MOST IMPORTANT WORDS: THANK YOU

Whenever I show my thanks, these tips work well for me:

■ Set aside time every week to acknowledge people's good work.

■ Handwrite thank-you notes whenever you can. The personal touch matters in the digital age.

■ Punish in private; praise in public. Make the public praise timely and specific.

■ Remember to cc people's supervisors. "Don't tell me. Tell my boss."

■ Foster a culture of gratitude. It's a game changer for sustainably better performance.

—Robert Eckert, former chairman and CEO of Mattel

Source: Robert A. Eckert, "The Two Most Important Words," *Harvard Business Review*, April 2013, p. 38.

When the former chairman and CEO of Mattel, Robert Eckert, first arrived at Mattel, the company was losing almost a million dollars a day. He held a "town hall" gathering his first day and told workers, "I know how this works. We will turn things around, and because I'm the new outsider CEO, I'll get a lot of the credit. But I know who's really going to deserve the thanks—all of *you*." He was accustomed to saying thank you a lot, and because he could see an immediate effect, he started to say it even more. He created a "Rave Review" program where employees could recognize and thank each other with an e-certificate for a free soft drink or coffee, and gave Chairman's Awards to exceptional senior managers at company meetings. "I believe that habits like those are key to Mattel's having been named, for six years running, one of *Fortune's* Best Companies to Work For."[35]

Peter Post, coauthor of *The Etiquette Advantage in Business*, shares an experience he had while conducting a seminar. A young lady in the audience said, "Have I got a story for you." She applied for a job and was one of three finalists. The other applicants were in-house candidates. She got the job and later her new boss explained why she was hired. He said that after the interview, she was the only candidate who wrote a note to each person on the interview committee. The importance of a thank-you cannot be overstated.[36] A carefully prepared thank-you note provides a great opportunity to gain a competitive edge in today's job market.

A carefully prepared thank-you note (see Figure 10.2) provides a great opportunity to gain a competitive edge in today's job market. If possible, link your skills to solving workplace problems you learned during the interview.

Figure 10.2 ■ Job Interview Note

Dear Ms. Jarrett:

Thank you for taking the time to interview me for your upcoming opening in account development. I enjoyed meeting you and learning more about your successful publication.

As noted during our meeting, I managed the advertising department for the University of North Carolina student newspaper, print and online editions, over a two-year period. In the area of account development, my goal was to build long-term partnerships with our customers.

Please tell your assistant, Tina Jones, I appreciate her help in scheduling the interview. If a second interview is planned, please contact me at 643-292-9230 (cell).

Sincerely,

Paul L. Mason

Paul L. Mason

BARRIERS TO POSITIVE REINFORCEMENT

10-6

If you want attention and appreciation, you must learn to give attention and appreciation.

The material in this chapter is based on two indisputable facts about human nature. First, people want to know how well they are doing. Second, they appreciate recognition for their accomplishments. Performance feedback, encouragement, and positive reinforcement can satisfy these important human needs. People often say they prefer negative feedback to no feedback at all.

Preoccupation with the Self

One of the major obstacles to providing positive reinforcement is preoccupation with the self. The term **narcissism** is often used to describe this human condition. Narcissism is a Freudian term alluding to the mythical youth who wore himself out trying to kiss his own reflection in a pool of water.

Deepak Chopra, author of *The Seven Spiritual Laws of Success*, encourages everyone to practice the "Law of Giving." This law states that you must give in order to receive. If you want attention and appreciation, you must learn to give attention and appreciation. If you want joy in your life, you must give joy to others. He says the easiest way to get what you want is to help others get what they want.[37]

The publication of *Random Acts of Kindness* and many people's acceptance of its central theme may have signaled a movement away from self-preoccupation. Random acts of kindness are those little things that we do for others without receiving payback. They involve giving freely, purely, for no reason.[38]

 ## HOW TO WRITE A THANK-YOU NOTE

Should thank-you notes or notes in general be handwritten and sent via USPS or sent via electronic message? Peter Post, director of the Emily Post Institute, offers these suggestions.

- If you are in doubt, send a short electronic message right away and follow up with a handwritten note.
- An electronic message may be received, read, and then deleted, while a handwritten note may be opened, read, and might stay on the desk—a reminder of you—for hours or even days.
- Make an effort to write and send your note within 24 hours whenever possible.
- If you send a handwritten note, use quality notepaper.
- If your handwriting is not legible, it's OK to type the note and sign it.

Source: Peter Post, "The Note," *Training*, September/October 2010, p. 44.

Misconceptions About Positive Reinforcement

Some people fail to use positive reinforcement because they have misconceptions about this human relations strategy. One misconception is that people will respond to positive feedback by demanding tangible evidence of appreciation. "Tell people they are doing a good job, and they will ask for a raise" seems to be the attitude of some managers. Actually, just the opposite response will surface more often than not. In the absence of intangible rewards (such as praise), workers may demand greater tangible rewards.

A few managers seem to feel they will lose some of their power or control if they praise workers. Yet, if managers rely on power alone to get the job done, any success they achieve will no doubt be short-lived.

The "Too Busy" Syndrome

Ken Blanchard says, "We're often too busy or too stressed to remember that the recognition we crave, others crave as well."[39] When you are under a great deal of pressure to get your work done, and you are struggling to achieve some degree of work/life balance, it is easy to postpone sending a thank-you note or contacting someone simply for the purpose of saying "Thank you."

The key to solving this problem is planning. A consciously planned positive reinforcement program will ensure that recognition for work well done is not overlooked. One approach might be to set aside a few minutes each day to work on performance feedback and positive reinforcement activities (see Table 10.2).

Failing to Identify Commendable Actions

There are many opportunities to recognize the people you work with. By exercising just a little creativity, you can discover many actions that deserve to be commended.

Assume you are the manager of a large auto dealership. One of the key people within your organization is the service manager. This person schedules work to be performed on customers' cars, handles customer complaints, supervises the technicians, and performs a host of other duties. If you want to give your service manager performance feedback and positive recognition, what types of behavior can you praise? Table 10.2 lists some examples.

Table 10.2 ■ Job Performance Behaviors to Be Reinforced

1. Performance Related to Interpersonal Relations
   a. Demonstrates empathy for customer needs and problems
   b. Handles customer complaints in a fast, effective manner
   c. Communicates clearly and effectively with boss and coworkers
   d. Engages with personnel in other departments
   e. Recognizes the accomplishments of others
   f. Exhibits effective leadership
2. Personal Characteristics
   a. Is punctual
   b. Does not violate policies and procedures
   c. Maintains emotional stability
   d. Has a professional appearance
   e. Is alert to new ways to do the job better
   f. Is positive and optimistic
3. Management Skills
   a. Maintains accurate records
   b. Spends time on short- and long-range planning
   c. Takes steps to prevent accidents
   d. Delegates authority and responsibility
   e. Maintains quality standards
   f. Proactively eliminates barriers and obstacles to accomplishing tasks

Figure 10.3 ■ Shared Responsibilities for Positive Reinforcement

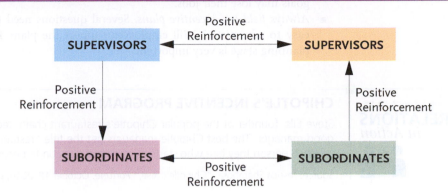

REWARDING INDIVIDUAL AND TEAM PERFORMANCE

10-7   In recent years, we have seen expanded use of positive reinforcement strategies in the workplace. In the past, we viewed positive reinforcement as the responsibility of supervisors and managers. This view was much too narrow. Everyone in the organization has opportunities to recognize the accomplishments of others. Persons in supervisory and management positions can benefit from positive reinforcement initiated by subordinates.

Employees can also be encouraged to recognize the accomplishments of coworkers. In some cases, praise from a respected colleague is more important than praise from the boss. This is especially true when employees work together on a team.

The concept of teamwork and the growing popularity of various types of teams are changing the way companies structure their reward systems. If a workforce is organized into self-directed work teams (discussed in Chapter 12), it makes sense to consider various types of team recognition plans. Such plans often emphasize the recognition of group performance rather than the recognition of individual performance.

Incentive Programs

Every year, organizations spend billions of dollars for incentives and awards given to their employees. An **incentive program** is designed to motivate and reward employees to achieve an organizational objective. Incentive programs are commonly used to award performance in sales teams, but incentives are increasingly being used by organizations to reward employees and teams for increased productivity, improved quality, improved customer service, lower operating costs, or some combination of these factors. These plans include cash and noncash awards that may include vacation trips, plaques, pins, certificates, stock options, merit pay, cash bonuses, and a host of other items.

Although most companies use some type of incentive program, many do not achieve positive results. Programs must be designed to provide benefits to the organization and the individual employee, and care must be taken during the planning stage. Here are a few incentive plan fundamentals:

- *Do not assume that financial rewards provide the most powerful incentive.* Stephen J. Dubner, coauthor of the best-selling book *Freakonomics*, says social and moral incentives are often more powerful.[40] An employee who is working excessive hours may value more time with family, socializing, and recreation. Rewards must satisfy individual needs.
- *Avoid incentives that might foster unethical behavior.* Some retail companies encourage sales personnel to push extended warranties—a high-profit item that many customers don't want or need. In some cases, these sales become the basis for

measuring employee performance. Employees who don't meet established incentive goals may lose their jobs.[41]

■ *Always field-test incentive plans.* Several questions need to be answered: Is the plan easy to administer? Will employees support the plan? Employee input during the planning stage is very important.[42]

CHIPOTLE'S INCENTIVE PROGRAM

Steve Ells, founder of the popular Chipotle's restaurant chain, recognizes the importance of a good manager. The best Chipotle managers get the title "restaurateur" and a $10,000 bonus for each person they hire who starts as crew and goes on to become a manager.

Source: Jessica Shambora, "Chipotle's Rise," *Fortune*, October 18, 2010, p. 72.

Reexamining Our Ideas About Productivity

Developed nations have progressed from a society of farmers, to a society of factory workers, to a society of knowledge workers. And now, according to Daniel Pink, author of *A Whole New Mind*, we are progressing yet again—to a society of creators and empathizers. He says the information age is giving way to a new world in which creative abilities and high-touch abilities mark the fault line between who gets ahead and who falls behind.[43] Organizational culture must be thoughtfully considered and integrated with company values and strategies to bring out the best in employees.

Positive energy flourishes in a supportive environment. Within the organization, there should be respect for each person, regardless of job title, duties performed, or earnings. The prevailing culture within an organization must also be positive. People must feel good about the organization, its leadership, and other employees. Positive energy comes naturally in a positive work environment. But positive energy will almost never flourish in a negative work environment.

LOOKING BACK: SUMMARY OF LEARNING OBJECTIVES

1. Explain how positive energy contributes to improved interpersonal relationships.

Positive energy can have a major influence on employee morale and productivity. Encouragement, positive feedback, and other types of practices that create positive energy are important factors in improving interpersonal relationships.

2. Describe the fundamentals of positive psychology.

Positive psychology is a recent branch of psychology that focuses on positive human functioning. Marty Seligman is considered the founder of the positive psychology movement. It is based on theories and practices that focus on aspects of the human condition that lead to happiness and fulfillment. Research indicates we become more successful when we are happier and more positive.

3. Identify and discuss the positive emotions that contribute to a fulfilling life.

Research in the field of positive psychology has identified lab-tested tools needed to counter the powerful force of negative energy. The tools discussed in this chapter include gratitude, pride, serenity, interest, and social support.

4. Describe workplace cultures that generate positive energy.

In the presence of positive energy, people feel uplifted, encouraged, and empowered. Organizations that foster a high level of employee engagement tend to maintain a higher level of employee satisfaction. This leads to happy, loyal customers. Higher customer satisfaction leads to increased sales and higher levels of profitability, which ultimately results in higher shareholder value.

5. **Understand how to use positive reinforcement to improve relationships and reward behavior**.

   Although many studies indicate that recognition of their accomplishments is important to employees, often more so than monetary rewards and job security, some people seem unable or unwilling to reward a job well done. Praise, pride, courtesy, active listening, written thank-you notes, incentives, and awards can be used to instill positive energy.

6. **Describe the major barriers to the use of positive reinforcement**.

   Preoccupation with self is a major obstacle to providing reinforcement to others. Self-centered persons are likely to overlook the accomplishments of others. Some people say a busy schedule does not allow them time to give recognition to others, and some people have difficulty identifying commendable actions. These and other barriers tend to minimize the use of positive reinforcement.

7. **Explain how to reward individual and team performance**.

   Individual and team performance are often rewarded through the use of incentive programs. Some of the most common incentive programs involve cash payments, profit sharing, production incentives, training and development, and suggestion programs. Employee stock options and bonuses are also popular.

KEY TERMS

energy, 208	pride, 213	reinforcer, 218
positive psychology, 209	serenity, 213	positive reinforcers, 218
flow, 210	employee-customer profit chain	narcissism, 221
negativity bias, 212	theory, 215	incentive program, 223

CAREER INSIGHT

When Tony Schwartz founded his company The Energy Project more than a decade ago, many projects focused on the issue of employee disengagement. Burnout was largely a result of how people managed their energy, not their time, and they needed to learn new ways to expand and renew their personal energy. Schwartz argues that human beings don't run like computers. They can't operate at high speeds continuously and with several programs running at once. He offers the following tips for energy renewal:

- People perform their best when they alternate between periods of intense focus and intermittent renewal.

- Employees can increase their effectiveness by practicing simple rituals that refuel their energy, such as taking a daily walk, or a brief nap or meditation break to get an emotional and mental breather.
- Turning off e-mail for several hours a day helps people feel in control of their time while allowing them time to concentrate on the most important tasks.
- Encourage open and honest communication to build trust.
- Step away from your desk to have lunch, or better yet, leave the office entirely. You will return with renewed energy and focus.

TRY YOUR HAND

1. Organizations are continually searching for ways to reward various employee behaviors. Pretend you are currently working at an upscale retail clothing store and the manager asks you to help her design an incentive plan that would result in improved sales of clothing and accessories.

She asks you to review and comment on the following options:

a. Employee-of-the-month awards for highest sales. (A special plaque would be used to recognize each monthly winner.)

b. Commission on sales. All employees would be given a 5 percent commission on all sales. Each salesperson would receive an hourly wage plus the commission.

c. Time off. Employees who achieve sales goals established by management could earn up to four hours of paid time off each week.

d. Prizes. Employees who achieve weekly sales goals established by management would be eligible for prizes such as sports or theater tickets, dinner at a nice restaurant, gift certificates, or merchandise sold by the store.

Rank these four options by assigning 1 to your first choice, 2 to your second choice, 3 to your third choice, and 4 to your fourth choice. Provide a written rationale for your first choice.

2. There are many small little things we do for others that have big payoffs for both the giver and the receiver. These acts give us an outward focus that helps us move away from self-preoccupation. Plan and initiate at least two acts of kindness, generosity, gratitude, social support, or recognition during the next week, and then reflect on the experience. What impact did the act have on the other person? How did you feel about this experience?

3. Practice various ways to increase positive energy and emotions by practicing the 3-to-1 ratio during the coming week. Consciously pay attention to how often you may say something negative to others. For each time you do say something negative, practice the 3-to-1 positivity principle and respond with positive statements. Experiment with various ratios such as 4 to 1 or 5 to 1 to see if you feel differently when positive comments and actions are taken. What did you learn? How did it make you feel?

CRITICAL THINKING CHALLENGE

Throughout life we form habits that can have a major impact on our ability to develop positive relationships with others. Take a few minutes and reflect on the dipper and bucket metaphor. Do you find it easy or difficult to fill someone else's bucket? Your own bucket? Do you frequently dip from others' buckets?

SELF-ASSESSMENT EXERCISE

For each statement, circle the number from 1 to 5 that best represents your response: (1) strongly disagree (never do this); (2) disagree (rarely do this); (3) moderately agree (sometimes do this); (4) agree (frequently do this); (5) strongly agree (almost always do this).

	1	2	3	4	5
A. I can describe the fundamentals of positive psychology.	1	2	3	4	5
B. I understand how positive emotions contribute to a fulfilling life.	1	2	3	4	5
C. I understand and can apply several forms of positive reinforcement.	1	2	3	4	5
D. I make every effort to recognize the accomplishments of others and celebrate my own successes.	1	2	3	4	5

After identifying your response to each item, select an attitude or skill you would like to improve. Prepare a written goal and then describe the steps you will take to achieve this goal.

YOU PLAY THE ROLE

Peggy Klaus, author of *Brag! The Art of Tooting Your Own Horn Without Blowing It*, says, "You have to let the people above you know what you are doing, what skills you're developing, which goals you're achieving." She says, "Don't make them guess." Self-promotion has become more important today because many careers are being affected by downsizing, mergers, and business closings. For the purpose of this role-play, assume the role of Britten Higgins, a full-time employee in the computer electronics department of Best Buy. You have heard rumors that your department manager may be promoted. You hope to move up within the Best Buy organization, and advancing to department head would be an important first step. You have decided to meet with your manager and discuss two things: (1) your interest in becoming department head and (2) your accomplishments and the steps you have taken to prepare for advancement. Feel free to ad-lib the information you present during the role-play.[44]

BELOW THE SURFACE | DEVELOPING POSITIVE ENERGY

Henk Meijer/Alamy

At the beginning of the chapter we discussed the Containers Store's open and proactive culture of communication. Employee Sara Jo Smith says, "We have no secrets in this company as far as our numbers and our goals. Everybody knows them and understands them." When employees feel there is open, honest communication, it creates trust, positive energy, and the confidence to make decisions. This principle is a hallmark of the company's success. CEO Kip Tindell says, "If you were going to boil down the whole Container Store culture, getting to work with great people and then knowing that everything's communicated to you at all times are the two most important things."[45]

Positive energy and positive emotions don't just happen, they are created. Begin experimenting to see what specific activities recharge your energy and shape your personal outlook. For example, if you own an electric car, you get in the habit of checking your energy reserves. And you learn driving habits that permit you to drive farther between battery recharges. Get in the habit of checking your own personal energy reserves. When it's time to recharge your personal batteries, consider these options:

- *Stop paying attention to bad news*. Reduce TV watching and cut back on time spent on the Internet and social media.

- *Stay connected to others*. Reconnect with those you love and stay in touch with friends. Stop eating alone. Humans are not wired to work solo.[46]
- *Restore your sleep*. Daytime stress can steal hours of deep sleep from you at night. The loss of deep sleep makes tomorrow more stressful. Before you go to bed, relax with a good book and some deep breathing.[47] Resist the urge to binge-watch "just one more" show on Netflix.
- *Give yourself a physical or emotional break*. Walking, biking, swimming, or some other exercise reduces stress and increases "feeling good" brain chemicals.[48]
- *Shake off dark moods*. Practice using proven happiness-inducing techniques such as meditation, expressing gratitude, writing in your journal about things you are thankful for, or reflecting on past events that make you feel good.[49]

QUESTION

1. This case problem describes a few ways to renew your energy at work or at home. Which of these activities would appeal to you?

2. In addition to the preceding activities, have you discovered other ways to renew energy in your life?

CLOSING CASE THE ROLE OF PRIDE IN BUILDING HIGH MORALE

PaeTec Communications wants its employees to engage in exceptional efforts to make customers happy. Arunas Chesonis, former CEO of PaeTec, realized that high morale among his employees was an important key to good customer service. He wanted each employee to feel a sense of pride in the company, so he made every effort to recognize work done well. Rewards ranged from a personal note to a cruise vacation.

Jon R. Katzenbach, author of *Why Pride Matters More Than Money*, says employee pride is what drives high-performing organizations like Southwest Airlines, SAS Institute, the U.S. Marine Corps, and The Container Store. He offers the following toolkit for those who want to become effective pride builders:

- *Personalize the workplace.* This means get involved in the everyday problems of your employees. Managers at some Marriott hotels work with employees from several different countries. These workers often need help learning the English language, preparing to become American citizens, and finding affordable child-care services. Marriott realizes that any problem that affects employees will eventually affect their on-the-job performance.

- *Localize as much as possible.* "Don't wait for your organization or its leaders to instill pride," says Katzenbach. The best pride builders are quick to spot and recognize the small achievements that will instill pride in their people.

- *Make your messages simple and direct.* A pride-building program can be as simple as telling a story that describes how an employee's behavior exemplified a company value, or a story about how an employee solved a customer problem. Not only does this build pride, it demonstrates through example the values and behaviors a company wants to see in its employees.

QUESTIONS

1. Some human resource department employees voice concerns when supervisors or team leaders get involved with the everyday problems of their workers. Discuss your thoughts on this issue.

2. Some leaders in business and industry say that worker pride is the by-product of achievement. What are your thoughts? What factors constitute achievement at your local McDonald's restaurant? Your local community hospital?

CHAPTER 10 ENDNOTES

1. Rachel Feintzeig, "Container Store Bets on $50,000 Retail Worker," *The Wall Street Journal*, October 15, 2014, p. B6.
2. Lisa Wirthman, "Container Store is Right on Course," *The Denver Post*, April 14, 2013, p. 13W.
3. Marshall Goldsmith and Kelly Goldsmith, "How Happiness Happens," *Bloomberg Businessweek*, December 21, 2009, p. 92.
4. Judith Orloff, "Accessing Sacred Energy," *Spirituality & Health*, May/June 2004, pp. 48–51; Judith Orloff, *Positive Energy* (New York: Harmony Books, 2004),
pp. 1–15, 288. More information regarding positive energy can be found in Barbara Frederickson, *Positivity* (New York: Random House, Inc., 2009).
5. Angela Winter, "The Science of Happiness," *The Sun*, May 2009, pp. 5–8.
6. "Positive Psychology," [accessed 24 March 2012]. Available from www.en.wikipedia.org; INTERNET.
7. Barbara Fredrickson, *Positivity* (New York: Random House, 2009), pp. 31–33.
8. Source: http://en.wikipedia.org/wiki/Mihaly_Csikszentmihalyi [Retrieved 23 November 2014].

9. Orloff, *Positive Energy*, pp. 80–81.

10. Retrieved from Flow (psychology), http://en.wikipedia.org/wiki/flow.

11. Tal Ben-Shahar, *Happier* (New York: McGraw-Hill, 2007), pp. 32–33.

12. Shawn Achor, *The Happiness Advantage* (New York: Crown Publishing Group, 2010), pp. 15–16; Shawn Achor, "Positive Intelligence," *Harvard Business Review*, January–February 2012, pp. 100–102.

13. Achor, "Positive Intelligence," pp. 100–101.

14. Winter, "The Science of Happiness," p. 11.

15. Sheldon Lewis, "Another Reason to List What You're Grateful For," *Spirituality & Health*, March/April 2008, p. 27. To learn more about the powerful influence of gratitude, read *Thanks! How the New Science of Gratitude Can Make You Happier*, by Robert Emmons (Boston: Houghton Mifflin, 2007).

16. "Have a Nice Day," *American Way*, January 1, 2007, p. 18.

17. Jon R. Katzenbach, *Why Pride Matters More Than Money* (New York: Crown Business, 2003), pp. 23–24.

18. John A. Byrne, "How to Lead Now," *Fast Company*, August 2003, pp. 62–70.

19. Fredrickson, *Positivity*, p. 42.

20. Ibid., p. 43. Fredrickson also refers to interest as being "beautifully unpredictable" in Winter, "The Science of Happiness," p. 12.

21. Achor, "Positive Intelligence," p. 102.

22. Source: http://www.clinicservice.com/clinic-service-values

23. *Training*, January/February, 2014, p. 99.

24. Monique Reece, "5 Lessons Companies Can Learn From Dreamforce," October 31, 2014. http://www.wobi.com/blog/dreamforce/5-lessons-companies-can-learn-dreamforce

25. Anthony J. Rucci, Steven P. Kirn, and Richard T. Quinn, "The Employee-Customer-Profit Chain at Sears," *Harvard Business Review*, January 1998. https://hbr.org/1998/01/the-employee-customer-profit-chain-at-sears/ar/1

26. Roy Saunderson, "If You're Happy and You Know It…" *Training*, January/February 2014, p. 142.

27. Gallup, "The Culture of an Engaged Workplace," retrieved April 23, 2015, http://www.gallup.com/services/169328/q12-employee-engagement.aspx

28. Holly Dolezalek, "Don't Go," *Training*, July/August 2003, p. 52; Rath and Clifton, *How Full Is Your Bucket?*, pp. 39–40.

29. Verne Harnish, "Five Ways to Keep Employees Excited," *Fortune*, December 3, 2012, p. 40.

30. David Dorsey, "Happiness Pays," *Inc.*, February 2004, pp. 89–94., and http://en.wikipedia.org/wiki/PAETEC_Holding_Corp, retrieved April 23, 2015.

31. Douglas A. Bernstein, Louis A. Penner, Alison Clarke-Stewart, and Edward J. Roy, *Psychology*, 9th ed. (Belmont, CA: Wadsworth, 2012), p. 209.

32. Ron Alsop, "The Trophy Kids Go to Work," *Wall Street Journal*, October 21, 2008, pp. Dl and D4. Profiles of several Generation Y employers can be reviewed in "Cool, Determined, and Under 30," *Inc.*, October 2008, pp. 97–105.

33. Keith Ferrazzi, "Managing Change, One Day at a Time," *Harvard Business Review*, July-August 2014, p. 25.

34. Nancy Lublin, "Two Little Words," *Fast Company*, November 2010, p. 56.

35. Robert A. Eckert, "The Two Most Important Words," *Harvard Business Review*, April 2013, p. 38.

36. Peter Post, "The Note," *Training*, September/October 2010, p. 44.

37. Deepak Chopra, *The Seven Spiritual Laws of Success* (San Rafael, CA: Amber-Allen, 1994), pp. 30–31.

38. *Random Acts of Kindness* (Berkeley, CA: Conari Press, 1993), pp. 1, 54, 68, and 91.

39. Bob Nelson, *1001 Ways to Reward Employees* (New York: Workman, 1994), p. ix.

40. Stephen J. Dunbar, "The Freaky Side of Business," *Training*, February 2006, p. 8.

41. Joel Spolsky, "Employees Will Always Game Incentive Plans—Because the Geniuses Who Design Them Don't Anticipate How Employees Will Respond," *Inc.*, October 2008, p. 85.

42. Dave Murphy, "If You Want Gold, Give Them a Goal," *San Francisco Chronicle*, April 14, p. J1; Jeff Barbian, "Golden Carrots," *Training*, July 2002, p. 18.

43. Daniel H. Pink, *A Whole New Mind* (New York: Riverhead Books, 2005), pp. 48–53.

44. Anne Fisher, "Show Off, Without Being a Blow-Hard," *Fortune*, March 8, 2004, p. 68.

45. Rachel Feintzeig, "Container Store Bets on $50,000 Retail Worker," *Wall Street Journal*, October 15, 2014, p. B6.

46. Michael Roizen and Mehmet Oz, "7 Ways to Recharge Your Personal Batteries," *Roanoke Times*, October 11, 2011, p. 3.

47. Ibid.

48. Ibid.

49. Sue Shellenbarger, "Thinking Happy Thoughts at Work," *Wall Street Journal*, January 27, 2010, p. D2.

CHAPTER PREVIEW

LEARNING OBJECTIVES

After studying Chapter 11, you will be able to

11-1 Explain the importance of professional presence.

11-2 Understand the importance of a favorable first impression.

11-3 Define image, and describe the factors that form the image you project to others.

11-4 Understand how your online presence can help or hinder your personal brand.

11-5 Understand how life and workplace etiquette contributes to improved interpersonal relations.

Developing a Professional Presence

TIP OF THE ICEBERG | PERSONAL BRAND DEVELOPMENT

After graduation from high school, Star Fischer began searching for a career that would not require a great deal of contact with people. She chose accounting because "I thought I could hide in my seat and prepare tax returns. I was shy and timid." Prior to college graduation she joined Moss Adams, a Seattle-based accounting and consulting firm, as a college intern. At the end of the internship she stayed on as a staff accountant at the Everett, Washington, office.

Tom Sanger, Fischer's boss, soon noticed that she was a very smart person with good work habits. She was shy, but had a lot of ambition and wanted to learn and grow. He recruited her to join a new tax-credit consulting group he had founded at the firm. At first consulting was a major challenge. She had to ask questions and think on her feet. Her boss said, "It was a challenge for her to even look them in the eye." Fischer never said no to any task he asked her to do, and soon he encouraged her to recruit new clients. Fischer says at first she was so scared she would spend many hours preparing to meet a client.[1]

Ms. Fischer gradually began to enjoy working with clients. She became a polished speaker and was invited to serve on internal committees where her talents were recognized by senior managers. She was promoted rapidly to senior management, one level below her goal of making partner. Today Star Fischer is a partner at Moss Adams. Senior executives were impressed by her motivation and performance. With the help of a caring mentor and lots of hard work, she successfully reinvented her brand.[2]

Branding can play a crucial role in your success. The authors of *Be Your Own Brand: A Breakthrough Formula for Standing Out from the Crowd* say branding can have a significant impact on your relationships, career, and life. Developing a strong personal brand involves all the small yet significant ways you express what you believe and how you present yourself to others. This chapter presents an abundance of personal brand development information.[3]

Noel Hendrickson/Photographer's Choice RF/Getty Images

231

With encouragement from her boss, Star Fisher accepted more challenging work assignments. Success at each assignment resulted in increased self-confidence and greater motivation to accept new challenges. Today she is a member of the senior management team.

PROFESSIONAL PRESENCE—AN INTRODUCTION

11-1   There are many personal and professional benefits to be gained from a study of the concepts in this chapter. You will acquire new insights into ways to communicate positive impressions during job interviews, business contacts, and social contacts made away from work. You will also learn how to shape an image that will help you achieve your fullest potential in the career of your choice.

This is not a chapter about ways to make positive impressions with superficial behavior and quick-fix techniques. We do not discuss the "power look" or the "power lunch." The material in this chapter will not help you become a more entertaining conversationalist or win new customers by pretending to be interested in their hobbies or families. In his book *The Seven Habits of Highly Effective People*, the late Stephen Covey says that the ability to build effective, long-term relationships is based on character strength and not quick-fix techniques. He notes that outward attitude and behavior changes do little good in the long run *unless* they are based on solid principles governing human effectiveness. These principles include service (making a contribution), integrity and honesty (which serve as a foundation of trust), human dignity (every person has worth), and fairness.[4]

Professional Presence and Personal Branding—A Definition

Professional presence is a dynamic blend of poise, self-confidence, control, and style that empowers us to be able to command respect in any situation.[5] Once acquired, it permits us to project a confidence that others can quickly perceive the first time they meet us. Obviously, to *project* this confidence, you need to *feel* confident.

Minnesota Senator Al Franken was at one point in his life a very successful standup comedian. When he decided to run for public office, he worked hard to rebrand his image.

Your **personal brand** describes the attributes and the image you wish to portray to others when they think of you. For example, words like *dependable*, *passionate*, *loyal*, *creative*, and *professional* are all attributes that portray a positive image. Your personal brand is comprised of many things, including your unique strengths and abilities, the value and service you provide to others, and your personal values.

Your personal brand is manifested through the actions and behaviors you communicate to others. It shines through in everything you do, from face-to-face meetings to your online presence. In situations like a job interview or being considered for a promotion, your personal brand may be the only differentiator that helps you stand out from others with similar skills. Throughout your career, your personal brand is an asset to manage and protect, and the information you learn in this chapter will help you develop your personal brand and reinvent it throughout your career.

THE IMPORTANCE OF MAKING A GOOD FIRST IMPRESSION

11-2 As organizations experience increased competition for clients, patients, or customers, they are giving new attention to the old adage "First impressions are lasting ones." Research indicates that initial impressions do indeed tend to linger. Therefore, a positive first impression can be thought of as the first step in building a long-term relationship.

The development of professional presence begins with a full appreciation of the power of first impressions.

Ann Demarais and Valerie White, authors of *First Impressions*, say the secret to a good first impression is "social generosity"—helping others feel good about themselves. This requires shifting your focus from your own feelings to making others feel good. When you meet someone for the first time, you need to put others' needs and feelings before your own.[6]

The Primacy Effect

The development of professional presence begins with a full appreciation of the power of first impressions. The tendency to form and retain impressions quickly at the time of an initial meeting illustrates what social psychologists call a **primacy effect** in the way people perceive one another. The general principle is that initial information tends to carry more weight than information received later. First impressions establish the mental framework within which a person is viewed, and information acquired later is often ignored or reinterpreted to coincide with this framework.[7]

Demarais and White note that in a first impression, others see only a very small sample of you, a tiny percentage of your life. But to them, that small sample represents 100 percent of what they know of you. And they will weigh initial information much more heavily than later information.[8] Heidi Grant Halvorson, writing in *Harvard Business Review*, says perceiving people accurately is hard: "The way we see one another can be irrational, incomplete, and inflexible."[9]

The First Few Seconds

Malcolm Gladwell, best-selling author of several books including *The Tipping Point* and *Blink*, learned a great deal about the power of first impressions a few years ago when he let his close-cropped hair grow wild. His life changed immediately. He got far more speeding tickets and was routinely pulled out of airport security lines for special attention. People he met knew nothing about him except that he had shaggy hair, but they were ready to think the worst.[10]

Gladwell was inspired to try to understand what happens beneath the surface of rapidly made decisions. His findings later appeared in *Blink: The Power of Thinking Without Thinking*. He says most of us would like to think our decision making is the result of rational deliberation, but in reality, most decisions are made subconsciously in a split second.[11]

Total Person | Insight

"At its heart, branding addresses a hard professional reality: For a successful long-term career, do not look to your company or industry to take care of you. As in every other arena of life, you must take care of yourself. A well-built brand will be your life raft."

Source: Estée Lauder executive Phebe Port; Judith Sills, "Becoming Your Own Brand," *Psychology Today*, January/February, 2008, p. 62.

Understanding Perception

The impression you form of another person during the initial contact is made up of both assumptions and facts. Many people tend to rely heavily on assumptions during the initial meeting. If a job applicant sits slumped in the chair, head bowed, and shoulders slack, you might assume the person is not very interested in the position. Needless to say, the impression you form of another person during the initial contact can be misleading. The briefer the encounter with a new acquaintance, the greater the chance that misinformation will enter into your perception of the other person.

If many of the people you meet for the first time are going to make judgments unconsciously and automatically, how can you prepare to make a good impression? If you are planning to attend a job fair, there are certain basic things you can do to make every second of each face-to-face meeting count:[12]

- *Dress professionally.* Dress for a job fair just as you would for a job interview at a company's office.
- *Prioritize your contacts.* Consider ranking your top five prospective employers and then make sure you learn as much as possible about each company. The worst question you can ask is, "What is it that your company does?"

"*I'm not wasting my life online—I'm building my brand.*"

- *Résumés are important.* Consider preparing a tailored, custom résumé for the employers you have targeted.
- *Be engaged.* Ask questions about the corporate culture and what they are looking for in a job candidate.
- *Accentuate the positive.* Never say anything negative about your prior work experience.

Cultural Influence

Cultural influences, often formed during the early years of our lives, lead us to have impressions of some people even before we meet them. People often develop stereotypes of entire groups. Although differences between cultures are often subtle, they can lead to uncomfortable situations. We need to realize that the Korean shopkeeper is being polite, not hostile, when he puts change on the counter and not in your hand. Some Asian students do not speak up in class out of respect for the teacher, not boredom.[13]

Norine Dresser, author of *Multicultural Manners—Essential Rules of Etiquette for the 21st Century,* notes that it is becoming more difficult for organizations to develop policies that do not offend one ethnic group or another. She argues that it is the collective duty of the mainstream to learn the customs and practices of established minority groups.[14]

THE IMAGE YOU PROJECT

11-3 **Image** is a term used to describe how other people feel about you. In every business or social setting, your behaviors and appearance communicate a mental picture that others observe and remember. This picture determines how they react to you. Think of image as a tool that can reveal your inherent qualities, your competence, your attitude, and your leadership potential. If you wish to communicate your professional capabilities and create your own brand, begin by investing the time and energy needed to refine and enhance your personal image.

Figure 11.1 ■ Major Factors That Form Your Image

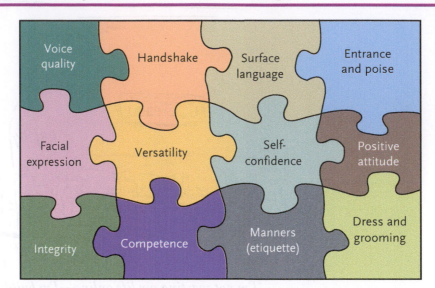

In many respects, the image you project is very much like a picture puzzle, as illustrated in Figure 11.1. It is formed by a variety of factors, including manners, self-confidence, voice quality, versatility (see Chapter 3), integrity (see Chapter 5), entrance and poise, facial expression, competence, positive attitude, handshake, and **surface language**—the pattern of immediate impressions conveyed by appearance. Each of these image-shaping components is under your control, though some are harder to develop than others. As you reflect on the image you want to project, remember that a strong personal brand is built from the inside out.

Rebranding Your Image

Throughout your career you will very likely need to change some aspects of the image you project. Navigating out of your casual college wardrobe and into a workplace setting may be your first challenge. At the MetLife office in Charlotte, North Carolina, workers in sales who interact with customers wear suits and ties (men) or dresses with jackets (women). Workers who don't meet with customers follow a business-casual style.[15]

Aging workers are staying in their jobs longer and making late-career changes more often. Personal style has become a key component of survival for some of these workers. A 49-year-old Apple Valley, Minnesota mom says she wants to appear professional, stylish, and relevant, but worries that what looks good on her younger coworkers might look ridiculous on her.[16]

A good rule to follow is to dress for the job you want, not the job you have.

According to many writers familiar with image formation, clothing is particularly important. Although a more relaxed dress code has evolved in some employment areas, people judge your appearance long before they judge your talents. It would be a mistake not to take your career wardrobe seriously. When making career wardrobe decisions, keep in mind these basic guidelines:[17]

1. *If you want the job, you have to look the part.* Establish personal dress and grooming standards appropriate for the organization where you wish to work.

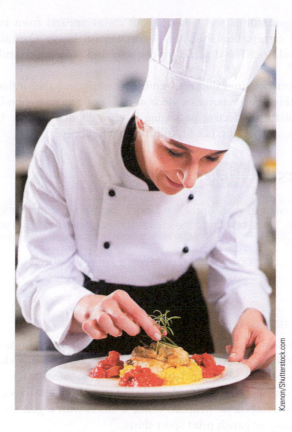

This young chef has given careful attention to the image she conveys to customers at her fine resturant.

2. *If you want the promotion, you have to look promotable.* A good rule to follow is to dress for the job you want, not the job you have.

3. *If you want respect, you have to dress as well as, or better than, your industry standards.* One would expect to find conservative dress standards in banking, insurance, accounting, and law, and more casual dress standards in advertising, sports entertainment, and agriculture.

Selecting Your Career Apparel

Millions of American workers wear a uniform especially designed for a particular job. The judges on the U.S. Supreme Court and the technicians at the local Midas Auto Service Shop have one thing in common—both groups wear a special uniform to work. Companies that have initiated extensive career apparel programs rely on uniforms to project an image of consistent quality, good service, and uniqueness.

In addition to special-design uniforms, there is another type of **career apparel**, somewhat less predictable, worn by a larger number of people in the labor force. Here are two examples:

- A male bank loan officer would be appropriately dressed in a tailored gray or blue suit, white shirt, and tie. This same person dressed in a colorful blazer, sport shirt (without collar), and plaid slacks would be seen as too casual in most bank settings.
- A technician employed by an auto dealership that sells new luxury cars would be appropriately dressed in a matching gray, tan, or blue shirt and pants. The technician would be inappropriately dressed in jeans and a T-shirt.

Many organizations seek advice about career apparel from image consultants who have received certification from the Association of Image Consultants International or Global Protocol, Inc. The demand for etiquette and protocol consultants has increased in recent years.[18]

The information in Table 11.1 outlines three factors that influence choices in career apparel. Use this information as a guide and do not give in to blind conformity. As noted by one consultant, "Effective packaging is an individual matter based on the person's circumstances, age, weight, height, coloring, and objectives."[19]

Total Person Insight

"What you wear to work (including fabrics, fragrances, hairdos, etc.) is the most visible thing you do. It will be part of the impression you leave and it will enhance or harm your business purposes."

Source: Bruce Clarke, "Dress Codes Have a Purpose in the Workplace," *News & Observer*, July 27, 2012, p. 3E.

What Is Business Casual?

The term **business casual** is used to describe the movement toward dress standards that emphasize greater comfort and individuality. Business casual is clothing that allows you to feel comfortable at work but looks neat and professional. For men, it usually means slacks, khaki pants, collared long-sleeved shirts, and shoes with socks. It usually does not include tattered, frayed, or wrinkled jeans; T-shirts with logos; sneakers or sandals; tank tops; sweat pants; or garish print sport shirts.[20]

Many companies have relaxed dress codes, allowing workers to dress casually. The trend for companies to adopt a "casual Friday" day has extended into a seven-days a week policy for several companies, especially those who work in high-tech jobs. Although the late Steve Jobs' "uniform" of a black T-shirt, jeans, and sneakers are the uniform of choice for many Silicon Valley workers, it's hard for most employees to carry off this look in other industries.

Table 11.1 ■ Factors Influencing Your Choice of Clothing for Work

Dress codes are undergoing changes, and this complicates the selection of clothing for work. Use the three factors described here for guidance.

1. *Products and services offered.* In some cases, the organization's products and services more or less dictate a certain type of dress. For example, a receptionist employed by a well-established law firm is likely to wear clothing that is conservative, modest, and in good taste.
2. *Type of person served.* Research indicates that first impressions created by dress and grooming are greatly influenced by unconscious expectations. We form mental images of the apparel common to each of these occupations. When we encounter someone whose appearance does not conform to our past experiences, we often feel uncomfortable.
3. *Desired image projected by the organization.* Some companies establish dress codes that help shape the image they project to the public. Walt Disney Company, for example, maintains a strict dress and grooming code for all its theme-park employees.

Although no precise definition of business casual exists, the following guidelines will help you make wise choices.

1. *Wear dressier business clothing when meeting with customers or clients*. Avoid creating inconsistencies between your message and your appearance.
2. *Respect the boundary between work and leisure clothing*. As a rule, people should avoid wearing anything that shows so much skin that it distracts other people from their work.
3. *Not all trends should be adopted*. Love body piercing and tattoos? If you can't live without it, do it in a discrete place.
4. *Wear clothing that is clean and neat and that fits well*. Casual dress codes tend to emphasize the importance of this guideline.
5. *Be discreet with jewelry, perfume, and cologne*. Nothing is more offensive to people than overbearing perfume and cologne, and many people have allergic reactions from it.

Your Facial Expression

Facial expressions are the cues most people rely on in initial interactions.

After your overall appearance, your face is the most visible part of you. Facial expressions are the cues most people rely on in initial interactions. They provide the clues by which others read your mood and personality and strongly influence people's reactions to each other. The expression on your face can quickly trigger a positive or negative reaction from those you meet. How you rate in the "good looks" department is not nearly as important as your ability to communicate positive impressions with a pleasant smile and eye contact. Facial expressions usually reflect inner emotions more accurately than words. The smile is the most recognizable signal in the world. People everywhere tend to trust a smiling face.[21]

Your Entrance and Poise

The way you enter someone's office or a business meeting can influence the image you project. A nervous or apologetic entrance may ruin your chances of getting a job, closing a sale, or getting the raise you have earned. If you feel apprehensive, try not to let it show in your body language. Hold your head up, avoid slumping forward, and try to project self-assurance. To get off to the right start and make a favorable impression, follow these words of advice from Susan Bixler: "The person who has confidence in himself or herself indicates this by a strong stride, a friendly smile, good posture, and a genuine sense of energy. This is a very effective way to set the stage for a productive meeting. When you ask for respect visually, you get it." Bixler says the key to making a successful entrance is simply believing—and projecting—that you have a reason to be there and have something important to present or discuss. She also says good posture identifies you instantly as someone with something to contribute.[22]

Your Voice Quality and Speech Habits

The tone of your voice, the rate of speed at which you speak (tempo), the volume of your speech, your ability to pronounce words clearly (diction), and your speech habits contribute greatly to the image you project. Consider these real-world examples:

- Kristy Pinand, a youthful-looking 23-year-old, routinely used "teen speak" when talking to colleagues and clients. Words such as "cool" and "like" were frequently part of her speech pattern. With feedback from her supervisor, she was able to correct the problem.[23]

■ A senior project manager at a major financial-service company was surprised when his boss blamed his thick Brooklyn accent for his stalled advancement in the company. Despite his MBA, the project manager was speaking too fast and skipping many consonants. Rapid speech patterns can be very irritating to some people. His frequent use of "deez" and "doze" created the impression that he was poorly educated and inarticulate.[24]

A conscious effort to improve your voice begins with awareness. A tape or video recording of your conversations will help you identify problem areas. If you hear a voice that is too monotone, too nasal, too high-pitched, too weak, too insincere, or too loud, you can target the problem for improvement.

Your Handshake

When two people first meet, a handshake is the most typical physical contact between them. A handshake is a friendly and professional way to greet someone or to take leave, regardless of gender. The handshake can communicate warmth, genuine concern for the other person, and strength. It can also communicate aloofness, indifference, and weakness. Generally speaking, a firm (but not viselike) grip communicates a caring attitude, whereas a weak grip communicates indifference. Maintain eye contact and smile during a handshake to increase the positive impact of your handshake.

Throughout your career, you will likely meet people from many ethnic backgrounds. Each may have a ritual, which might include bowing, kissing, hugging, or giving a "high five." In Jamaica, for example, approval of someone or someone's idea may involve hitting fists.[25]

Total Person Insight

"Young people need to take charge of their career, people's perceptions of them, be self aware, network, and not wait for someone to do it for you."

Source: Estée Lauder executive Phebe Port, quoted in Emily Glazer, "Create a Positive Image," *News & Observer*, October 3, 2010, p. 3.

HOW ONLINE PRESENCE INFLUENCES YOUR PERSONAL BRAND

 In today's competitive job market, it's never too early to begin planning a job search strategy. A major part of your strategy involves building a brand for yourself. Personal branding involves deciding what makes you special in the job market.[26] You will also need to consider how you might use various Internet technologies and tools.

HOW TO MAKE YOUR SOCIAL MEDIA PROFILE CONSISTENT WITH YOUR BRAND

■ Your photo should look professional. It does not need to be taken by a professional photographer and in fact may look better if it is not. It's more important to capture your smile, warmth, and energy in the moment.

■ Do your online profiles reflect the image you wish to portray, both in content and design? What you wear should be consistent with the profession that you are in or hope to join. Include recommendations from other people when appropriate. Save the photos of your dog, friends, siblings, or your boyfriend for your personal site.

- Ask yourself: Is this the image I want my future employer to see when he/she reviews my site? It's likely that an HR department will review your social media profile during a reference check.
- Keep your website and profiles current by posting blogs regularly, commenting on news, and sharing links to informative articles.

Building and Managing Your Personal Brand

Social media networks like LinkedIn, Facebook, and Twitter are very important tools for building your brand image. If you are currently using any of these social networks, you are already (intentionally or unintentionally) establishing your personal brand.

One of the best ways to establish and build your online brand is to write a blog. A blog is like a personal branding portal where you share your knowledge and perspective on topics you find interesting and that you care about. Many students establish blogs during college as a way to promote their brand to future employers. Sometimes it is part of a website where additional types of content such as articles, photos, videos, résumés, and testimonials can be posted. Consider obtaining a website domain through a provider like GoDaddy.com in your own name, such as www.JaneDoe.com, and a Twitter handle in your own name (@JaneDoe) to further establish your brand.

Social media provide many ways to build your personal brand, but they must be used with great care. Everything you say or do online either adds to or detracts from your personal brand. As you learned in previous chapters, what you say in e-mails, social media networks and forums, and anywhere else online is forever etched in digital history. Many people have regretted posting a photo of a night out drinking with friends on Facebook.

Be wary of not only what you post online, but what your friends and complete strangers may post about you. A friend may tag you in an unsavory photo. Or a stranger might record a video of you having a "private" conversation with your girlfriend, or record the regretful insult you hurled at a store clerk—and post them on YouTube. If you saw the movie *Social Network*, you may recall that even Mark Zuckerberg learned a hard lesson about posting remarks in haste. Whatever you say and do can be held against you. Never mind the court of law. It's the court of social media you need to worry about.

human RELATIONS *in Action*

HOW TO RUIN YOUR CAREER IN 10 SECONDS OR LESS

Never, ever make a hasty decision to post a picture, write a Tweet, compose a blog, or respond on Facebook when you are angry or without considering the following:

1. All the potential audiences that will see it now and in the future
2. The long-term implications of your message and how it could be misinterpreted by others
3. How you will be perceived professionally
4. Before you hit the Send or Post button, double-check to see if you are using your personal or your company account.

Social Media Monitoring

You must be just as diligent about monitoring your personal brand as you are creating and building it. The social media monitoring market is growing quickly as firms like Radian6, Reputation.com, and others track and monitor the online **social reputation** of individuals and businesses. There are also free services like Google Alerts to help you track where and how your name is mentioned. Keep an eye on the photos where you are tagged. If they don't reflect the brand persona you wish to portray, un-tag them.

ETIQUETTE FOR A CHANGING WORLD

11-5 Why are so many guides to etiquette crowding bookstore shelves? And why are many organizations hiring consultants to conduct classes on etiquette guidelines? One reason is that we need advice on how to avoid annoying other people, and what to do if they annoy us. In today's fast-paced, often tense, work environment, we have to work a little harder to maintain a climate of fairness, kindness, and mutual respect.[27]

Total Person Insight

"If I had only one piece of advice to offer, it would be to be on time. When you're on time, you start to build the relationship. When you're late, you start by having to recover from a mistake."

Source: Peter Post, director of the Emily Post Institute and coauthor of "The Etiquette Advantage in Business," *Training*, March/April 2011, p. 44.

Etiquette (sometimes called *manners* or *protocol*) is a set of traditions based on kindness, efficiency, and logic.[28] Letitia Baldrige, author and etiquette consultant, says, "It's consideration and kindness and thinking about somebody other than oneself."[29] Sometimes we need new etiquette guidelines to deal with our changing world. Today, smoking at work is usually prohibited or restricted to a certain area. Meetings often begin with the announcement "Please silence your mobile devices." And the nearly universal use of e-mail has spawned hundreds of articles on e-mail etiquette (see Chapter 2). A diverse workforce has created many new challenges in the area of protocol.

Although it is not possible to do a complete review of the rules of etiquette, we will discuss those that are particularly important in an organizational business setting.

Dining Etiquette

Job interviews and business meetings are often conducted at breakfast, lunch, or dinner, so be aware of your table manners. To illustrate decisions you might need to make during a business meal, let's eavesdrop on Tom Reed, a job candidate having a meal with several employees of the company he wants to work for. After introductions, the bread is passed to Tom. He places a roll on the small bread-and-butter plate to the right of his dinner plate. Soon, he picks up the roll, takes a bite, and returns it to the plate. Midway through the meal, Tom rises from his chair, places his napkin on the table, and says, "Excuse me; I need to make a potty run." So far, Tom has made four etiquette blunders: The bread-and-butter plate he used belongs to the person seated on his right; his own is to the left of his dinner plate.

"Fine. Sit there and check your messages. Perhaps it will give you something to contribute to the conversation."

When eating a roll, he should break off one piece at a time and butter the piece as he is ready to eat it. The napkin should have been placed on his chair, indicating his plan to return. (When departing for good, leave it to the left of your plate.) And finally, the words *potty run* are too casual for a business meal. A simple statement such as, "Please excuse me; I'll be back in just a moment," would be adequate.

There are some additional table manners to keep in mind. Do not begin eating until the people around you have their plates. If you have not been served, however, encourage others to go ahead. To prevent awkward moments during the meal, avoid ordering food that is not easily controlled, such as ribs, spaghetti, chicken with bones, or lobster.

Meeting Etiquette

Business meetings should start and end on time, so recognize the importance of punctuality. Anne Marie Sabath, owner of a firm that provides etiquette training for business employees, says, "We teach people that if you're early, you're on time, and if you're on time, in reality, you're late." Showing up late for any meeting will be viewed as rudeness by coworkers, your boss, and your clients. Do not feel obligated to comment on each item on the agenda. Yes, sometimes silence is golden. In most cases, you should not bring up a topic unless it is related to an agenda item. If you are in charge of the meeting, end it by summarizing key points, reviewing the decisions made, and recapping the responsibilities assigned to individuals during the meeting. Always start and end the meeting on a positive note.[30]

Cell phone contempt surfaces in offices, restaurants, houses of worship, and many other places.

Smartphone Etiquette

The smartphones used today enable you to conduct business from virtually anywhere at any time. The phones function much like laptops or tablets. As more people depend on their smartphones, it is important to understand a few basic etiquette guidelines:[31]

1. If you place your phone on the table during an important meeting and check it periodically, you may be sending the message that the person or people you are with don't deserve your full attention.
2. When making or receiving calls, speak in low conversational tones. Microphones on smartphones are quite sensitive, so talking loudly is not necessary. Be courteous to those around you.
3. Don't text during meetings or while conversing with others. Your attention should be on the persons you are meeting with.
4. If a coworker or friend insists on "staying connected" at all times, and this behavior is annoying, confront the person respectfully.

Many workers will confirm that breaches in workplace etiquette that create the most resentment arise from our being more distracted than ever by technology.[32]

Conversational Etiquette

When you establish new relationships, avoid calling people by their first name too soon. Never assume that work-related associates prefer to be addressed informally by their first

Communication technologies can create annoyances. If you are trying to enjoy a meal at your favorite restaurant, you probably do not want to sit next to someone who is talking loudly on their cell phone. If you are making an important presentation at a team meeting, and some members are busy sending out text messages, you will likely feel some frustration. Is anyone listening to me?!

names. Use titles of respect—Ms., Mr., Professor, or Dr.—until the relationship is established. Too much familiarity will irritate some people. When the other person says, "Call me Ruth" or "Call me John," it is all right to begin using the person's first name.

A conversation that includes obscene language can create problems in the workplace. Although the rules about what constitutes profanity have changed over the years, inappropriate use of foul language in front of a customer, a client, or, in many cases, a coworker is a breach of etiquette. An obscenity implies lack of respect for your audience. Also, certain language taboos carry moral and spiritual significance in most cultures. Obscene language is often cited by persons who file sexual harassment charges.[33]

Total Person Insight

"Profanity will always offend someone, but the lack of profanity will never offend anyone."

Source: This quote was attributed to Rand Corporation. See Jared Sandberg, "In the Workplace, Every Bleeping Word Can Show Your Rank," *Wall Street Journal*, March 21, 2006, p. B1.

Networking Etiquette

Networking—making contact with people at meetings, social events, or other venues—is an effective job search method. A large body of research shows that half or more of all jobs come through informal channels—connections to friends, families, and colleagues. Networking is also important to salespeople searching for prospects and to professionals (accountants, lawyers, consultants, etc.) who need to build a client base.[34]

When you meet people at an event, tell them your name and what you do. Avoid speaking negatively about any aspect of your current job or your life. In some cases, you will need to make a date to call or meet with the new contact later. After the event, study your contacts and follow up.

Send a *written* thank-you note if someone has been helpful to you or generous with his or her time. You might also consider sending a newspaper or magazine article that is relevant to the conversation you had with someone, since one goal of networking is providing something of value to another person.

Online Recruiting World

The online recruiting world is trying to replicate word-of-mouth networking. Contact the following social networking and job board sites:

- CareerBuilder
- LinkedIn
- Facebook
- indeed
- Jobvite
- Monster.com

Incivility—The Ultimate Career Killer

Civility in our society is under siege. In recent years, we have witnessed an increase in coarse, rude, and obnoxious behavior. Unfortunately, some of the most outrageous behavior by athletes, coaches, politicians, and business leaders has been rewarded with wealth and influence.

As noted in Chapter 1, civility is the sum of the many sacrifices we are called upon to make for the sake of living together. At work, it may involve refilling the copier paper tray after using the machine or making a new pot of coffee after you take the last cup. It may mean turning down your radio so workers nearby are not disturbed or sending a thank-you note to someone who has helped you complete a difficult project. Small gestures, such as saying "Please" and "Thank you" or opening doors for others, make ourselves and others more content. Learning to discipline your passions so as to avoid obnoxious behavior will also demonstrate your maturity and self-control.

Total Person Insight

"Humility has power. It shows people that you have some give—you get the message, you are capable of self-correcting."

Source: Peggy Noonan, "A Message Sent to a Grudging President," *Wall Street Journal*, November 8, 2014, p. A13.

Professional Presence at the Job Interview

Professional presence has special meaning when you are preparing for a job interview. In most cases, you are competing against several other applicants, so you can't afford to make a mistake. A common mistake among job applicants is failure to acquire background information on the employer. Without this information, it is difficult to prepare questions to ask during the interview, and decisions about what to wear will be more difficult.

Keep in mind that regardless of the dress code of the organization, it is always appropriate to dress conservatively. If you arrive for an interview wearing torn jeans and a T-shirt, the person conducting the interview may think you are not serious about the job. The expectation of most employers is that the job applicant will be well groomed and dressed appropriately.

Joann Lublin, columnist for the *Wall Street Journal*, says interview etiquette begins the minute you walk in the door. Employers are building a picture of you piece by piece. You will always lose credibility if you are late or if you fail to give your full attention during the interview. Don't even think about peeking at your phone.[35]

LOOKING BACK: SUMMARY OF LEARNING OBJECTIVES

1. **Explain the importance of professional presence**.

   Professional presence is a dynamic blend of poise, self-confidence, control, and style. Once acquired, it permits you to be perceived as self-assured and competent. These qualities are quickly perceived the first time someone meets you.

2. **Understand the importance of a favorable first impression**.

   People tend to form impressions of others quickly at the time they first meet them, and these first impressions tend to be preserved. The impression you form of another person during the initial contact is made up of assumptions and facts. Assumptions are often based on perceptions of surface language—the pattern of immediate impressions conveyed by appearance. Verbal messages also influence the impression you make on others.

3. **Define** *image*, **and describe the factors that form the image you project to others**.

   Image is a term used to describe how other people feel about you. In every business or social setting, your behaviors and appearance communicate a picture that others observe and remember. This picture determines how they react to you. Image is formed by a variety of factors, including manners, self-confidence, voice quality, versatility, integrity, entrance and poise, facial expression, surface language, competence, positive attitude, handshake, and the clothing you wear.

4. **Understand how your online presence can help or hinder your personal brand**.

   Everything you do and say online either adds to or detracts from your personal brand. Give careful attention to how you build and maintain your social media profiles and other types of online content. Monitor your social reputation regularly.

5. **Understand how life and workplace etiquette contributes to improved interpersonal relations**.

   Etiquette, sometimes called manners or protocol, is tradition based on kindness, efficiency, and logic. Dining, meeting, smartphone, conversational, and networking etiquette are all important in the workplace.

KEY TERMS

professional presence, 232
personal brand, 233
primacy effect, 234
cultural influences, 235

image, 235
surface language, 236
career apparel, 237
business casual, 238

social reputation, 242
etiquette, 242

CAREER INSIGHT: HANDYMAN ETIQUETTE

Andy Bell, founder of Handyman Matters Franchising Corporation, manages 134 franchises in 37 states and three countries. He has implemented strict initial contact guidelines for all of his technicians. Technicians must take two steps back after ringing a doorbell and wear a clean, neat uniform (collared shirt and slacks) with identifying logo. When the homeowner comes to the door, the technician immediately presents a business card. Handyman technicians receive training in all areas of in-home conduct.[36]

Handyman Matters training is focused on many "small" things because they understand how they ultimately reflect the company's image and create a brand that consumers trust. In an industry such as this, quality is expected, but personal customer care is not, and this is what helps to create the Handyman Matters brand image.

TRY YOUR HAND

1. Many people complain that interrupting has become a major annoyance. You begin speaking and someone finishes your sentence. Marilyn Vos Savant, author of the "Ask Marilyn" column, recommends a technique that can stop interrupters. When someone interrupts you, stop speaking abruptly and say "What?" This will highlight the interruption, and the person who interrupts you will be forced to repeat himself or herself, too, which is an unpleasant experience. Repeat this method, if necessary, until the offender lets you complete your sentences. Marilyn Vos Savant says you should save this method for *chronic* interrupters.[37]

2. The first step toward improving your voice is to hear yourself as others do. Listen to several recordings of your voice on a cell phone message, tape recorder, or digital recording, and then complete the following rating form. Place a checkmark in the appropriate space for each quality.

QUALITY	MAJOR STRENGTH	STRENGTH	WEAKNESS	MAJOR WEAKNESS
Projects confidence	_____	_____	_____	_____
Projects enthusiasm	_____	_____	_____	_____
Speaking rate is not too fast or too slow	_____	_____	_____	_____
Projects optimism	_____	_____	_____	_____
Voice is not too loud or too soft	_____	_____	_____	_____
Projects sincerity	_____	_____	_____	_____

3. You have assumed the duties of sales manager at a new Lexus automobile dealership that is scheduled to open in three weeks. You will hire and train all salespeople. What types of career apparel would you recommend to members of your sales team? What grooming standards would you recommend?

4. Many employers say that Generation Y job applicants arrive at the job interview with an overblown sense of entitlement—an enhanced view of their self-importance. To avoid sending this message, what behaviors should be avoided during the interview?

CRITICAL THINKING CHALLENGE

The authors of *First Impressions* say that making a good first impression means making the person you meet feel positive toward you. When you have contact with someone, do you think about how the other person is feeling during the initial contact, or do you stay focused on yourself? What can you do to make someone feel positively about you?[38]

SELF-ASSESSMENT EXERCISE

For each of the following statements, circle the number from 1 to 5 that best represents your response: (1) strongly disagree (never do this); (2) disagree (rarely do this); (3) moderately agree (sometimes do this); (4) agree (frequently do this); (5) strongly agree (almost always do this).

A.	I project to others an image that matches my talents and aspirations.	1	2	3	4	5
B.	The factors that form my image (career apparel, manners, facial expression, etc.) are appropriate and do not detract from the image I project to others.	1	2	3	4	5
C.	The personal brand I project to others is consistent with my core values.	1	2	3	4	5
D.	When I post content on social media, I consider the long-term impact on my personal brand.	1	2	3	4	5
E.	I understand the importance of creating and managing my personal brand, and do so intentionally.	1	2	3	4	5

After identifying your response to each item, select an attitude or skill you would like to improve. Prepare a written goal and then describe the steps you will take to achieve this goal.

YOU PLAY THE ROLE

After spending a number of years working for a prestigious CPA firm, you established your own company. Cameron, Stanley, and Robert is the area's top accounting firm. You cater to an upscale business clientele who appreciate your outstanding customer service and the quality of your firm's work.

Currently, you employ 10 associates. The newest member of your accounting firm is Annika Johnson, a young CPA who is proud to be a member of Generation Y. Her intelligence, self-confidence, and image impressed you during the hiring process; however, you are now noticing an image change. Although she is well paid, Annika likes to shop at discount clothing stores, always searching for a great bargain. Very often her clothing and accessories communicate a "thrift store" image that clashes with the upscale image of CSR. You have decided to meet with Annika and try to encourage her to agree to a wardrobe that is more appropriate for the clientele she serves. You will meet with another class member who will assume the role of Annika Johnson.

BELOW THE SURFACE | CREATING YOUR PERSONAL BRAND

Henk Meijer/Alamy

Diane Keng shares the same passion for brand building as Star Fischer, the accountant portrayed in the opening story of this chapter. Diane is an 18-year-old freshman at Santa Clara University. Like many other young career-focused adults, Diane understands she must establish her professional brand early in her career and continue to build it throughout her life. She manages two accounts on Facebook; one is personal and the other is professional. Her personal account is strictly for family and friends, and her professional account is regularly updated with information about her tech start-up called MyWeboo.com, where she regularly posts information about women entrepreneurs and engineers. She says that people like to look up others on Facebook before they actually meet them in person, and once first impressions are made, they're really tough to change.[39]

Your personal brand is derived from your core values. Personal brand development begins with self-management practices that help you create and strengthen relationships with other people. Early in his career, Jerry Seinfeld decided he would never use profanity in his comedy routines. This personal decision forced him to use more creativity, and he became a stronger comedian. Jeff Bezos, founder of Amazon.com, recalls an early life experience that changed the way he viewed relationships. He made a comment to his grandmother that hurt her feelings. Later, his grandfather met with him privately and said, "You'll learn, one day, that it's much harder to be kind than clever."[40] This insight has helped Bezos in his professional life.

Developing a distinctive brand that will help you in your interactions with others may require making some changes in your life. To become distinctive, you must stand for something. What you stand for relates to your values. Thus, a strong personal brand is generally built from the inside out. But, to some extent, you can also decide what type of image you want these values to project. This may require changes in your manners, dress, voice quality, facial expression, posture, or behaviors that reflect your integrity.

QUESTIONS

1. Judith Sills, clinical psychologist who writes a column for *Psychology Today*, says your brand is the professional identity you create in the minds of others. What personal qualities will give you greater visibility, recognition, and acceptance in the labor market? These qualities should send the message, "Pick me; I'm special."

2. This chapter described several different ways to use social media to build and grow your personal brand identity. What are some of the ways that you would like to develop your online presence? Summarize a brief action plan that describes the activities and steps you will put in place to build and promote your personal brand.

CLOSING CASE MAKE YOURSELF MEMORABLE

The words *magnetism, charisma, authenticity*, and *class* are used to describe persons who are admired and respected. These special people are also memorable. Some say class and charm are fading fast from the American scene, replaced by bad behavior displayed by professional athletes, movie stars, radio and TV commentators, and politicians. Yet there are some role models worth remembering. The late Paul Newman was a serious actor, a successful racer, and a generous philanthropist. He established Newman's Own brand of food and condiments and then directed more than $250 million to charity. He was dedicated to helping make the world a better place for all.[41]

Arthur Ashe was the first African-American male to win the U.S. Open and Wimbledon tennis tournaments and the first African-American on the U.S. Davis Cup team. He was also the first African-American male ranked number one in the tennis world. He displayed a unique combination of grace and class. His life was marked by personal modesty, civility, and generosity. Ashe led an exemplary family and professional life until his untimely death from AIDS, which he had contracted after heart bypass surgery.

The late Payne Stewart, killed in the bizarre crash of a Learjet, is remembered as a vicious competitor and a classy hero to many golf fans. Cellist Yo-Yo Ma and talk-show host Oprah Winfrey display magnetism and charm.

The authors of *Make Yourself Memorable* say that memorable people have style. They describe the four interlocking elements of style as *look, conduct, speech*, and *presentation*. Ann Landers, the late advice columnist, used to say that if you had class, success would follow. She described some of the elements of class:[42]

- Class never tries to build itself up by tearing others down.
- Class never makes excuses.
- Class knows that good manners are nothing more than a series of small, inconsequential sacrifices.
- Class is comfortable in its own skin. It never puts on airs.
- Class is real. It can't be faked.

QUESTIONS

1. Some social critics say that too many people these days are rude, crude, and inconsiderate of others. Do you agree? Explain.

2. Make a list of prominent people who, in your opinion, have class. Also, make a list of friends or coworkers who have class. List and evaluate the personal qualities displayed by these individuals you most admire.

3. If you want to become a more memorable person—someone with class—what type of self-improvement program would you undertake? Explain. If you decided to develop a strong personal brand, would class be a major component of your brand?

CHAPTER 11 ENDNOTES

1. Sue Shellenbarger, "Image Makeover: From Loyal Sidekick to Partner," **Wall Street Journal**, November 19, 2014, p. D3.
2. Ibid.
3. David McNally and Karl D. Speak, **Be Your Own Brand—A Breakthrough Formula for Standing Out from the Crowd** (San Francisco: Berrett-Koehler Publishers, 2002), p. 112. See also Chapter 2 in **Reinventing You** by Dorie Clark (Boston: Harvard Business Review Press, 2013).
4. Stephen R. Covey, **The Seven Habits of Highly Effective People** (New York: Simon & Schuster, 1989), pp. 22, 34.
5. Susan Bixler, **Professional Presence** (New York: G. P. Putnam's Sons, 1991), p. 16. For more information on professional presence see Judith Sills, "Becoming Your Own Brand," **Psychology Today**, January/February 2008, p. 62.

6. Ann Demarais and Valerie White, *First Impressions* (New York: Bantam Books, 2004), pp. 22–23.

7. Ibid., p. 16. See also Sue Shellenbarger, "Why Likability Matters More Than Ever at Work," *Wall Street Journal*, March 26, 2014, p. D4.

8. Ibid.

9. Heidi Grant Halvorson, "Managing Yourself—A Second Chance to Make the Right Impression," *Harvard Business Review*, January–February 2015, p. 109.

10. Gordon Anders, "Hey, Not So Fast," *Wall Street Journal*, January 11, 2005, p. D9.

11. Danielle Sacks, "The Accidental Guru," *Fast Company*, January 2005, pp. 69–70.

12. David Ranii, "Standing Out in the Job Hunt," *News & Observer*, October 19, 2014, P E1.

13. Clyde Haberman, "No Offense," *New York Times Book Review*, February 18, 1996, p. 11.

14. Norine Dresser, *Multicultural Manners: Essential Rules of Etiquette for the 21st Century* (Hoboken, NJ: John Wiley and Sons, 2005). This book provides comprehensive coverage of multicultural etiquette.

15. Cristina Bolling, "Clothes that Work in the New Job," *News & Observer*, July 10, 2014, p. 8D.

16. Aimee Blanchette, "Sense of Style Matters in the Workplace," *News & Observer*, January 23, 2014, p. 2D.

17. Susan Bixler and Nancy Nix-Rice, *The New Professional Image*, 2nd ed. (Avon, MA: Adams Media Corporation, 2005), p. 311; Susan Bixler and Lisa Scherrer Dugan, *5 Steps to Professional Presence* (Avon, MA: Adams Media Corporation, 2001), pp. 4–8.

18. "The History of Image Consulting," Available from http://www.londonimageinstitute.com/ and [cited April 29, 2015]. "Overview of Image Consulting" [cited January 14, 2009.] Available from http://www.aici.org; INTERNET.

19. Dave Knesel, "Image Consulting—A Well-Dressed Step Up the Corporate Ladder," *Pace*, July/August 1981, p. 74.

20. Cora Daniels, "The Man in the Tan Khaki Pants," *Fortune*, May 1, 2000, p. 338; Susan Bixler and Nancy Nix-Rice, *The New Professional Images*, 2nd ed. (Avon, MA: Adams Media Corporation, 2005), pp. 133–144.

21. Deborah Blum, "Face It!" *Psychology Today*, September/ October 1998, pp. 34, 69.

22. Susan Bixler, *The Professional Image* (New York: Perigee Books, 1984), p. 219; Susan Bixler, *The New Professional Image*, 2nd ed. (Avon, MA: Avon Media, 2005), pp. 188–189.

23. Joann S. Lublin, "To Win Advancement, You Need to Clean Up Any Bad Speech Habits," *Wall Street Journal*, October 5, 2004, p. B1.

24. Ibid.

25. Bixler and Dugan, *5 Steps to Professional Presence*, p. 65.

26. Mary Ellen Guffey and Dana Loewy, *Business Communication*, 8th ed. (Stamford, CT: Cengage Learning 2015, p. 552.

27. Cynthia Crossen, "Etiquette for Americans Today," *Wall Street Journal*, December 28, 2001, p. W13.

28. Barbara Pachter and Mary Brody, *Complete Business Etiquette Handbook* (Englewood Cliffs, NJ: Prentice-Hall, 1995), p. 3. See also Jan Yager, *Business Protocol* (Stamford, CT: Hannacroix Creek Books, 2001); Judith Martin and Nicholas Martin, *Miss Manners Minds Your Business* (New York: W. W. Norton & Company, 2013).

29. Amy Gamerman, "Lunch with Letitia: Our Reporter Minds Her Manners," *Wall Street Journal*, March 3, 1994, p. A14. See also Barbara Pachter, "Greet! Eat! Tweet!" (Cherry Hill, NJ: Pachter & Associates, 2010).

30. Ann Marie Sabath, "Meeting Etiquette: Agendas and More," *DECA Dimensions*, January/February 1994, p. 8; "Is Etiquette a Core Value?" *Inc.*, May 2004, p. 22. See also Roy Saunderson, "Make Your People Matter in Meetings," *Training*, March/April 2013, p. 54.

31. Guffey and Loewy, *Business Communication*, p. 533; Cindy Krischer Goodman, "In Business Manners Still Matter Today," *Wall Street Journal*, December 8, 2013, p. E3.

32. Ibid.

33. Gene Veith, "Curse of the Foul Mouth," *Wall Street Journal*, January 24, 2003, p. D1; Tara Parker-Pope and Kyle Pope, "When #@%&@ Is—and Isn't—Appropriate," *Wall Street Journal Sunday*, featured in *The News & Observer*, January 21, 2001, p. D4.

34. Chris Farrell, "It's Not What Grads Know, It's Who They Know," *Bloomberg Businessweek*, June 18, 2012, p. 9.

35. Joann S. Lublin, "Interview Etiquette Begins the Minute You Walk in the Door," *Wall Street Journal*, August 1, 2006, p. B1.

36. Gwendolyn Bounds, "Handyman Etiquette: Stay Calm, Avert Eyes," *Wall Street Journal*, May 10, 2005, p. B1.

37. Marilyn Vos Savant, "Ask Marilyn," *Parade*, May 30, 2002, p. 19.

38. Demarais and White, *First Impressions*, p. 22.

39. Emily Glazer, Create a Positive Image, *News & Observer*, October 3, 2010, p. 3.

40. "The Right Words at the Right Time," *O, The Oprah Magazine*, May 2002, p. 202.

41. Joe Morgenstern, "Paul Newman: So Much More Than Just a Pretty Face," *Wall Street Journal*, September 30, 2008, p. B17; Mark Vaughn, "Paul Newman 1925–2008," *Autoweek*, October 6, 2008, p. 43.

42. Stephanie G. Sherman, *Make Yourself Memorable* (New York: American Management Association, 1996), pp. 3–4; "People in the News," *U.S. News & World Report*, November 8, 1999, p. 12; Ann Landers, "If You've Got Class, Nothing Else Matters," *The News & Observer*, July 11, 1998, p. E2; Carlin Flora, "The Superpowers," *Psychology Today*, May/June 2005, pp. 40–50.

PART 4

If We All Work Together...

CHAPTER PREVIEW

LEARNING OBJECTIVES

After studying Chapter 12, you will be able to

12-1 Explain the importance of teamwork in an organizational setting.

12-2 Identify and describe common types of work teams.

12-3 Explain the behavioral science principles that support team building.

12-4 Describe the attributes of a high-performing team.

12-5 Describe the team-member skills that employees need.

Team Building: A Leadership Strategy

TIP OF THE ICEBERG | NEW FORMS OF TEAM DEVELOPMENT

Recognition and teamwork are more than management buzzwords at Yum Brands, the world's largest restaurant company with more than 39,000 KFC, Taco Bell, and Pizza Hut locations around the world; they are a strategy for growth. For more than 17 years the company has opened a new restaurant every 14 hours. At the heart of the company's success and rapid growth is a company culture that values recognition and teamwork above all else.

When CEO David Novak was initially charged with leading KFC, the company had not achieved its target profit in several years. As he began to investigate why, he discovered a lot of finger-pointing and blaming taking place between the franchisees and headquarters. So he decided to focus his initial efforts on company culture and improving teamwork. "I think people would much rather work in a fun environment. But people want to win. So I wanted to create a team that was hardworking, very competitive, but we had fun. And I thought the biggest thing I could do was tap into the universal need for recognition."[1] Recognition at Yum Brands does not equate to a plaque or award. Novak believes recognition must be in the moment as well as personal and fun. "You want to give away a piece of yourself," says Novak and hence, the rubber chicken award began. Employees are encouraged to give each other awards whenever they are inspired by the words or actions of another employee. It may be a rubber chicken, a Pizza Hut roof tile with a message written on it, a cheesehead, or something else—as long as it is personal, fun, and in the moment.

Novak developed a leadership development program to teach others how to nurture more collaboration and recognition. *Taking People With You* is a three-day program that is designed to foster teamwork. However, participants

Teamwork is essential in a NASCAR race; every second counts. Each team member is responsible for a task or series of tasks. A small mistake can result in the loss of several positions on the race track. Crew training, with emphasis on teamwork, is essential.

must begin with individual introspection first and foremost. Participants are asked to rate themselves on truthfulness, reliability, openness, and self-centeredness. Novak believes that managers are not ready to lead a team until they have worked hard on themselves first. He asks participants to look inside themselves and evaluate how they treat other people and respond to the mistakes others make.

The results of the programs were significant. Teams began to work together at a much high level than they ever had previously, and open communication nurtured new relationships based on trust. Profits nearly doubled in three years, the company's top leadership tenure grew to an average of 10 years, and the company now attracts top talent from leading organizations who want to work in a thriving culture that values teamwork.

Companies of all sizes have embraced the use of teams to work on many types of projects because it is proven to be an effective strategy. At ICU Medical, Inc., maker of medical devices, any worker can form a team to tackle a project. Team members define the problem, assign tasks, and create deadlines themselves. Over the years, teams have altered production processes, set up 401(k) plans, and solved logistical problems in the movement of parts. George Lopez, a Board Director and the former CEO at ICU, says letting employees form teams has helped him spread out the decision making and encourages input from people closest to the problems.[2]

As competition increases and work-related problems become more complex, organizations understand that employees are their most important asset and are investing in programs to grow and nurture leadership in their organizations, irrespective of the position or rank a person has in the company. Bill George, author of *True North, Authentic Leadership*, and other publications, says too often the wrong

Figure 12.1 ■ Five Practices of Exemplary Leadership

The Leadership Challenge is considered to be the definitive field guide on leadership. There are over a million copies in print, in 15 languages. The authors have devised the following five practices of exemplary leadership:

- **Model the Way**. Leaders must model the behavior they expect from others.
- **Inspire a Shared Vision**. The leader's dream or vision is the force that invents the future. It is the employees' belief in and enthusiasm for the vision that motivates them to give their best.
- **Challenge the Process**. Leaders do not accept the status quo. They search for opportunities to innovate, grow, and improve processes.
- **Enable Others to Act**. Effective leaders make people feel confident, strong, and capable of taking action.
- **Encourage the Heart**. Through good times and bad, leaders encourage the heart of their employees to carry on and do their best.

Source: James M. Kouzes and Barry Z. Posner, *The Leadership Challenge*, 3rd ed. (San Francisco, CA: Jossey-Bass, 2002), pp. 13–20.

people are attaining leadership roles. He states that there are leaders throughout organizations who are waiting for opportunities to lead. Too often these people do not feel empowered to seek leadership roles.[3] Leadership is expected from people in senior roles in a company; however, leadership can be exhibited by anyone in an organization. The saying "Leaders are made, not born" is true. Leadership is a series of skills that can be acquired through study and practice, regardless of whether a person works on the front line with customers, in the back office of a professional services firm, on the factory floor, or as a line cook in a restaurant.

The focus of this chapter is team-building leadership strategies and understanding the characteristics that make a strong team. It is important to understand the difference between leadership and management. **Leadership** is the process of inspiring, influencing, and guiding employees to participate in a common effort.[4] Stephen Covey, in his book *The 8th Habit*, says, "Leadership is communicating people's worth and potential so clearly that they come to see it in themselves only."[5]

Thanks to the efforts of James Kouzes and Barry Posner, we know a great deal about the practices of exemplary leaders. Kouzes and Posner have summarized and reported on many years of research on this topic in *The Leadership Challenge*, a best-selling book.[6] They found that the most effective leaders engage in five practices of exemplary leadership (see Figure 12.1).

Management is the process of coordinating people and other resources to achieve the goals of the organization. Most managers focus on four kinds of resources: material, human, financial, and informational.[7] Leaders achieve their goals by combining effective leadership and management.

LEADERSHIP CHALLENGES IN A CHANGING WORKPLACE

12-1 Today's workplace is characterized by rapid change and demand for increased productivity. As the pace of change quickens and the pressure to work harder increases, the result is greater employee stress and tension. Managers must motivate employees who are expected to do more work with fewer resources and as a result, become tired and frustrated. Some of the most important leadership strategies, such as building trust, empowering employees, and developing the spirit of teamwork take time. How do managers respond to leaders at the top of the organization who want changes implemented quickly?

Diversity and globalization have also become prominent characteristics of today's workforce. Supervising a multicultural and multilingual workforce can be very challenging, especially when workers are scattered across multiple time zones. We are seeing greater use of part-time and temporary workers. Companies today are increasingly looking to attain specific skills as well as operational efficiencies by hiring independent contractors and outsourcing work. Add to this the challenges of managing a multigenerational workforce and you can see that managers have more challenges than they once did.

Team Building: An Introduction

Can the element of teamwork make a difference between the successful and unsuccessful operation of an organization? Yes, research indicates that a leadership style that emphasizes **team building** is positively associated with high productivity and profitability. Problems in interpersonal relations are also less common where teamwork is evident. Teamwork ensures not only that a job gets done but that it gets done efficiently and harmoniously.

There is also evidence that team building can have a positive influence on the physical and psychological well-being of everyone involved. When employees are working together as a team, the leader and members often experience higher levels of job satisfaction and less stress.

Another positive outcome of teamwork is an increase in synergy. **Synergy** is the interaction of two or more parts to produce a greater result than the sum of the parts taken individually.[8] Mathematically speaking, synergy suggests that two plus two equals five. Teamwork synergy is especially important at a time when organizations need creative solutions to complex problems.

Total Person | Insight

HOW THE CREATOR OF *SATURDAY NIGHT LIVE* MOTIVATES HIS TEAM

"You lead by example. If people sense how committed you are, what the standard is, what you believe in, what you expect, they respond to that. And if they care as deeply as you do, it doesn't take a motivational speech."

—Lorne Michaels, creator, *Saturday Night Live*

Source: Alison Beard, "Life's Work," *Harvard Business Review*, September 2013, p. 144.

Characteristics that Influence Team Dynamics

Teamwork and collaboration are required across all parts of an organization. Managing and leveraging the diversity of knowledge in teams enables companies to make decisions, solve complex problems, and quickly respond to continuously changing market and customer needs. However, managing and leading a team is not easy, and it requires work and commitment to continuously improve both technical skills and soft skills.

Understanding the key characteristics that drive teamwork and collaboration will help managers focus on the most important aspects of creating a high-performance team. They include having a shared vision and values, clear goals and objectives, and

The corporate culture at Zappos is so effective that it has developed a training division, Zappos Insights, to teach other companies how to create remarkable company cultures.

establishing team practices in the areas of accountability, communication, and decision making. Leaders must also continuously build trust among team members so they share ideas and knowledge without fear of being criticized. Trust is the result of open, honest communication, and team members following through on their commitments.

Team Core Values

One of the most effective ways to align how a department or business unit team will work together is to create team core values. This creates a sense of ownership, shared vision, and commitment for how people will work together as a team to achieve objectives. The leader facilitates team involvement by developing values that are congruent with the company values, yet are unique to an individual team.

Research has shown that when people work closely as a team with strong feelings of "us," morale and productivity rise. But it's not enough to bring together a group of people who work together and instantly call them a team. They need to understand *why* they are together. The best way to do this is a shared mission. If a leader wants to create a team that will move forward against difficult challenges or work together to complete a significant project, the best way to do this is by instilling a strong sense of mission within the group.[9]

COMMON TYPES OF WORK TEAMS

12-2

Teams are the primary way organizations get things done. There are several types of teams, including cross-functional teams, department teams, management teams, project teams, virtual teams, and special project teams. This section focuses on three of the most common types of teams: self-managed, cross-functional, and virtual teams.

Self-Managed Teams

Self-managed teams, also known as high-performance work teams, assume responsibility for traditional management tasks as part of their regular work routine. Examples include decisions about production quotas, setting quality standards, and interviewing applicants for team positions. A typical self-managed team usually has 5 to 15 members who are responsible for producing a well-defined product (such as a computer) or service (such as processing an insurance claim). Employees who may have only been concerned with their own jobs suddenly become accountable for the work of the total team.[10] It's the end result that matters.

The concept of teaming continues to evolve, and it is an ideal solution for companies that need to assemble a group of people with specialized skills to solve a specific problem or tackle a significant project on a temporary basis. Most teams of this nature work for the same company, but not always. For example, during the Beijing Olympic Games, a global team of architects and engineers from several firms were assembled to develop the 340,000-square-foot Water Cube to host swimming and diving events. Tristram Carfrae, a structural engineer from Australia with the firm Arup, assembled dozens of people from 20 unique disciplines and four countries to develop the structure. Amy Edmondson, professor of leadership and management at Harvard Business School, calls this concept

Andy Gilmore, Hemicube, 2011, digital drawing/HBR.org

The 340,000-square-foot Water Cube was built to host swimming and diving events at the Beijing 2008 Olympic Games. The structure that holds 17,000 people was developed by a team assembled from 20 unique disciples and four countries.

teaming, and she describes it as "teamwork on the fly; a pickup basketball game rather than plays run by a team that has trained as a unit for years."[11]

This concept has been used by medical professionals in emergency rooms for years and is being used by companies in virtually any industry. Despite the inherent challenges of teaming, the benefits are considerable. Companies can quickly respond to opportunities to deliver solutions, and individuals learn new skills, knowledge, and networks. Self-managed teams typically follow three principles:

1. **Hierarchy is based on competence**. Leaders naturally emerge even though there are no job titles, and everyone knows who they are because they have a passion for the work being done and they have clear commitment to the project and to team members, even though there may not be a selection process.
2. **Clear goals**. The memorandum of understanding outlines exactly what must be done, by whom, the expected results, and how they will be measured.
3. **Shared values**. Teams are focused, disciplined, and committed to accomplish specific objectives even though team members may change.[12]

NO BOSSES, NO TITLES, SELF-MANAGING TEAMS

For more than 20 years Morning Star, the world's largest tomato processor, has embraced self-managed teams to make the tough day-to-day decisions—without the help of a boss. Employees write personal mission statements and negotiate "letters of understanding" with colleagues who are affected by their work. Employees define very specific and measurable outcomes in up to 30 activity areas so everyone on a team understands what each person is responsible for achieving.

Source: Geoffrey Colvin, "The Art of the Self-Managing Team," *Fortune*, December 3, 2012, p. 2.

Cross-Functional Teams

Cross-functional teams are task groups staffed with a mix of specialists, focused on a common objective.[13] These teams are often temporary groups with members from different departments and job levels. Team members provide a link among separate functions, such as production, distribution, finance, and customer service. The teams are often involved in developing new work procedures or products, devising work reforms, developing new technology, or finding and developing a solution to a specific company issue. Hypertherm Incorporated, a metal-cutting equipment maker based in Hanover, New Hampshire, developed cross-functional teams for each of its five product lines. Team members represent engineering, marketing, production, and sales. Salespeople and marketers know customers best, so they make an important contribution to new product development. During the hiring process, every effort is made to screen out persons who would not be effective team players.[14]

Virtual Teams

In a competitive global marketplace, **virtual teams** composed of employees physically dispersed throughout the nation or around the world are now common. It is no longer necessary to go to a *place* to get work done. For virtual workers, the workplace is not a building, but the *networks*.[15] Technology makes it possible for employees to collaborate on projects and effectively draw talent with specialized skills and intellectual capital from various departments and locations around the world. The advantages of virtual teams

Figure 12.2 ■ How to Effectively Manage a Virtual Team

- Make sure everyone has a clear concept of the overall goal. If it is not possible to meet in person, host a virtual web conference with webcams for the team to get to know each other and to learn each other's roles.

- Communicate why each team member was selected to be on the team; share strengths and passions. Structure ways for them to get to know each other as both team members and individuals.

- Redefine roles and reassign tasks within the team in order to ensure better outcomes for the project as a whole.

- Require detailed status reports and meeting results, and find structured methods to stay abreast of deadlines and the completion of milestones. This keeps the manager and entire team up-to-date.

- Encourage peer collaboration to continuously improve work structure.

Source: Adapted from GroupONE Solutions/Trina Hoefling's "Practical Tips for Virtual Managers," and Trina Hoefling, *Working Virtually*.

include speed, agility, expanded expertise, improved communication, and real-time collaboration.

Trina Hoefling, an expert on managing virtual work teams and author of *Working Virtually*, says the real purpose of virtual work is to *create synergy* for mission accomplishment *without the limitations* of time or space.[16]

Managing and working with virtual team members in different time zones and different cultures has its challenges, but with the right leadership there is no reason why virtual workers cannot be just as effective as those who meet face-to-face. The guidelines in Figure 12.2 help leaders overcome the challenges of managing virtual teams.

BEHAVIORAL SCIENCE PRINCIPLES SUPPORTING TEAM BUILDING

12-3 One approach to the study of leadership is examining the careers of successful leaders who have demonstrated their ability to develop teamwork. A second approach to the study of leadership is reviewing the findings of scholars who have identified the characteristics of successful leaders. What do successful leaders have in common? See in the sections that follow, how Douglas McGregor, Robert Blake, Jane S. Mouton, and Robert K. Greenleaf have answered this question.

Influential Thought Leaders

In his book *The Human Side of Enterprise*, Douglas McGregor presented convincing arguments that management had been ignoring important facts about how people work effectively in teams. The author said that managers often failed to recognize the potential for growth of most workers and their desire for fulfillment. He identified several characteristics of an effective work team, which included the following: an informal, comfortable work environment where people are engaged and freely express their feelings and ideas; a near-absence of hidden agendas; encouragement of constructive disagreement; and a clear understanding and acceptance of tasks or objectives of the group.[17] McGregor's views on the characteristics of effective work teams have merit today as many authors continue to build on his thinking.

The late Warren Bennis is another influential thought leader. More than 30 years ago he argued that democracy would dominate the workplace. He predicted that the pyramid-shaped organization chart with top management in a position of absolute power and decision making would become obsolete.[18] He envisioned an organization where employee ideas were not only respected but encouraged because this helped the entire organization to improve.

Peter Drucker was widely regarded as the most well-known and respected management expert of our time. His lectures pragmatically linked organizations and society, and predicted changes in our "age of discontinuity," most of which came true. He warned us of the disparity between executive pay and front-line workers. He articulated why leaders should not make decisions based on short-term gain, but the long-term future of the company.

In order to achieve effective results, team members must be willing to openly voice their concerns and collectively hold themselves accountable for the results of their decisions.

Drucker helped leaders think differently. An advocate of innovation, Drucker said, "The best way to predict the future is to create it," meaning companies must be attuned to social changes in order to drive innovation to meet unmet customer needs. He was famous for asking simple, yet powerful questions such as "What should an organization stop doing?" Drucker became the first management guru whose advice was sought by executives trying to figure out how to manage in increasingly turbulent times.[19]

Drucker's contributions to management and leadership were significant. He said leaders must motivate knowledge workers, not simply with money, but by communicating core values and a higher purpose. His ideas of pay for performance and management by objectives have been embraced by companies around the world.

When Peter Drucker died in 1995 at the age of 95, he not only had the satisfaction of seeing so many of his predictions come true, but he witnessed companies transform themselves as a result of his influential thinking.

The Ohio State Model

The wide range of types of leadership positions may cause you to ask: Do people in these positions have much in common? Will team-building strategies work in most situations? The answer to both questions is yes. A great majority of successful leaders share certain behavior characteristics. Two of the most important dimensions of supervisory leadership—*consideration* and *structure*—have been identified in research studies conducted by Edwin Fleishman at Ohio State University[20] and validated by several additional studies. By making a matrix out of these two independent dimensions of leadership, the researchers identified four styles of leadership (see Figure 12.3).

Figure 12.3 ■ Basic Leadership Styles from Ohio State Study

This matrix is similar to the Leadership Grid (formerly called the Managerial Grid) developed by Robert Blake and Jane Mouton. The Leadership Grid is based on two leadership style dimensions: concern for people and concern for production.

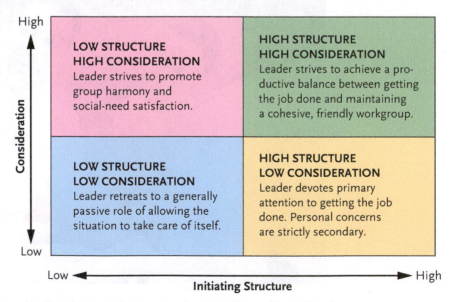

Source: James M. Kouzes and Barry Z. Posner, *The Leadership Challenge*, 3rd ed. (San Francisco, CA: Jossey-Bass, 2002), pp. 13–20.

Consideration

The dimension of **consideration** reflects the extent to which a leader's relationships with subordinates are characterized by mutual trust, respect for the employees, consideration of their feelings, and warmth in interpersonal relationships. When consideration is present, the leader-subordinate relationship is characterized by a climate of good rapport and two-way communication.

Structure

The dimension of **structure** reflects the extent to which a leader is likely to define and direct his or her role and the roles of subordinates toward goal attainment. Leaders who incorporate structure into their leadership style actively direct group activities by planning, setting goals, communicating information, scheduling, and evaluating performance. People who work under the direction of a highly structured leader know what is expected of them.

It is interesting to note that the dimensions of consideration and structure are independent of each other. A leader may be well qualified in one area but lack competence in the other. Anyone who assumes a leadership role can consciously work to develop competence in both areas.

Improving Consideration Skills

Brian Tracy says that effective leaders are guided by the *law of empathy:* "Leaders are sensitive to and aware of the needs, feelings, and motivations of those they lead."[21] This is good advice for anyone who wants to become an outstanding leader. To improve the dimension of consideration, one should adopt the following practices:

Recognize Accomplishments.   When individual achievements are overlooked, leaders miss a valuable opportunity to boost employee self-confidence and build morale. As noted in Chapter 10, people need recognition for good work, regardless of the duties they perform or the positions they hold. Of course, recognition should be contingent on performance.

A supervisor should provide each employee with as many opportunities to succeed as possible.

Provide for Early and Frequent Success.   According to an old saying, "Nothing succeeds like success." A supervisor should provide each employee with as many opportunities to succeed as possible. The foundation for accomplishment begins with a carefully planned orientation and training program. Supervisors and managers should review job duties and responsibilities, organizational policies and procedures, and any other pertinent information with their employees early in the relationship. Successful leaders are successful teachers.

Take a Personal Interest in Each Employee.   Everyone likes to be treated as an individual. Taking a personal interest means learning the names of spouses and children, finding out what employees do during their leisure time, asking about their families, and acknowledging birthdays. The more you learn about the "whole person," the better you will be able to help employees balance their work lives with the rest of their lives.

Therefore, efforts to improve the communication process represent a good use of the supervisor's time and energy.

Establish a Climate of Open Communication.   To establish a climate of open communication, the leader must be available and approachable. Employees should feel comfortable talking about their fears, frustrations, and aspirations. Communication is closely linked to employee morale—morale is directly linked to productivity. Therefore, efforts to improve communication are a good use of a supervisor's time and energy.

Discover Individual Employee Values. Today's lean, flatter organizations offer employees fewer opportunities for promotion, smaller raises, and less job security. As a result, many workers no longer feel secure or identify with the company. Leaders should encourage employees to explore their values and determine whether there is a match between what matters most to them and the work they are doing. If a value conflict turns up, determine whether it is possible to redesign the job or give the employee a new assignment.[22]

Improving Structure Skills

The leader who incorporates structure into his or her leadership style plays an active role in directing group activities. The team builder gives the group direction, establishes performance standards, and maintains individual and group accountability. The following practices can be used to develop the dimension of structure:

Communicate Your Expectations. Members of the group or team must have a clear idea of what needs to be accomplished. The law of expectations, according to Brian Tracy, states, "Whatever you expect, with confidence, becomes your own self-fulfilling prophecy."[23] Leaders must effectively formulate their expectations and then communicate them with conviction.

Bob Hughes, a consultant in the area of team building, suggests establishing baseline performance data so progress can be assessed.[24] In an office that processes lease applications, where accuracy and speed are critically important, the baseline data might include the number of error-free lease applications the team processes in one day. In an ideal situation, team members will be involved in setting goals and will help determine how best to achieve the goals. The goal-setting process is described in Chapter 4.

Provide Specific Feedback Often. Feedback should be relevant to the task performed by the employee and should be given soon after performance. Feedback is especially critical when an employee is just learning a new job. The supervisor should point out improvements in performance, no matter how small, and always reinforce the behavior she or he wants repeated. The most relevant feedback in a self-managed work team usually comes from coworkers, because team members are accountable to one another.

> *A person can make a mistake and still be a valuable employee.*

Deal with Performance Problems Immediately. As a leader, you must deal quickly with the person who does not measure up to your standards of performance. When members of the group are not held accountable for doing their share of the work or for making mistakes, group morale may suffer. Other members of the group will quickly observe the poor performance and wonder why you are not taking corrective action.

To achieve the best results, focus feedback on the situation, issue, or behavior, not on the employee. A person can make a mistake and still be a valuable employee. Correct the person in a way that does not create anger and resentment. Avoid demoralizing the person or impairing his or her self-confidence.[25]

The Center for Creative Leadership (CCL®) creates comprehensive solutions that deliver consistent, proven results in **three key development areas.**

Leadership Strategy

Talent Development

Organizational Leadership

Center for Creative Leadership
www.ccl.org

CCL - Americas
+1 336 545 2810
info@ccl.org

Center for Creative Leadership

Effective leaders never stop learning. Programs offered by the Center for Creative Leadership help managers and executives learn how to work more effectively with people.

Coaching for Peak Performance. **Coaching** and developing people to become effective leaders is a critical competency required by leaders in every organization. In the book *Leading at a Higher Level*, Ken Blanchard defines coaching:[26]

> *Coaching is a deliberate process using focused conversations to create an environment that results in individual growth, purposeful action, and sustained improvement.*

Foreseeing a leadership shortage in coming years, Blanchard says it is important to shift from managing performance to focusing on development. He describes five areas where coaching can be applied:[27]

- *Performance coaching* is used when people need help returning their performance to acceptable standards.
- *Development coaching* is used when high-performing workers are ready to become more fully rounded in their current roles.
- *Career coaching* is employed when people are ready to plan their next career moves.
- *Coaching to support learning* occurs when managers or direct reports need support, encouragement, and accountability to sustain recent training and turn insights into action.
- *Creating an internal coaching culture* is what happens when leaders recognize the value of coaching and use it to develop others.

HOW TO COACH FOR PERFORMANCE IMPROVEMENT

1. Document the performance problem.

2. Talk with and help the employee to recognize that there is a need to improve performance in a specific area. Leaders should not assume employees see problems in the same way they do.

3. Explore options. Let the employee suggest ways to improve performance.

4. Outline a plan that summarizes the specific actions and/or behavioral changes.

5. Get a commitment from the employee to take action.

Follow up to evaluate progress. If the employee is doing well, recognize his or her efforts. If more improvement is needed, communicate this to the employee. Ask questions to understand what is hindering progress.

Situational Leadership

The **Situational Leadership Model**, developed by Paul Hersey and his colleagues at the Center for Leadership Studies *(www.situational.com)*, is a leadership model widely used in several organizations. **Situational leadership** is based on the theory that the most successful leadership occurs when the leader's style matches the situation. Situational leadership theory emphasizes the need for flexibility.[28]

Paul Hersey says that the primary behaviors displayed by effective managers in the Situational Leadership Model can be described as *task behavior* and *relationship behavior*. Task behavior, as Hersey describes it in his book *The Situational Leader*, is very similar to the "concern for production" dimension of the Leadership Grid. And relationship behavior is very similar to the "concern for people" dimension.[29]

Hersey says that, when trying to influence others, you must (1) diagnose the readiness level of the follower for a specific task and (2) provide the appropriate leadership style for that situation. In other words, given the specific situation, you must decide how much task behavior and how much relationship behavior to display. Readiness is defined as the extent to which an employee is able and willing to accomplish a specific task. If an employee has the experience and skill to perform a certain task or activity, this will influence the leader's style. However, the leader must also consider the employee's confidence level, commitment, and motivation to accomplish the task or activity. Hersey reminds us that readiness levels often vary greatly among members of the work group.[30]

SERVANT LEADERSHIP

One of the most important leadership principles is the idea of *servant leadership*, a concept developed by Robert K. Greenleaf. He said, "The servant-leader is servant first. It begins with the natural feeling that one wants to serve, to serve first." Greenleaf believed that true leadership emerges from those whose *primary* motivation is a deep desire to help others. Servant-leadership encourages collaboration, trust, and the ethical use of power and empowerment.

Source: "What Is Servant Leadership?" [cited 11 February 2009]. Available from http://www.greenleaf.org/whatissl/index.html; INTERNET.

Additional Leadership Qualities

In addition to consideration and structure skills, leaders need some additional qualities (see Figure 12.4). One of these is character. As noted in Chapter 5, character is composed

Figure 12.4 ■ Additional Leadership Qualities

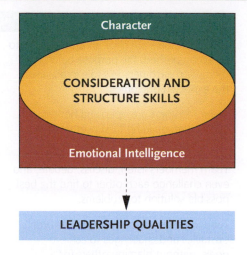

of personal standards of behavior, including honesty, integrity, and moral strength. Effective leadership is characterized by honesty, truthfulness, and straight dealing with every person.[31] Without character it is impossible to build a trusting relationship with the people you lead.

A second important quality is emotional intelligence, a concept that was discussed in Chapter 9. Emotional intelligence is a much more powerful predictor of leadership success than IQ because it gives you the ability to monitor your own and others' emotions and deal with them effectively.[32] A leader with high emotional intelligence is more likely to detect friction and eliminate conflict among team members. This leader is also more flexible, and therefore better able to use situational leadership.

Character and emotional intelligence are leadership qualities that can be developed. Leaders develop themselves—they are not born. One very important key to growth in both of these areas is self-awareness. Without self-awareness we may behave in ways that are potentially ineffective, limiting our potential for growth and opportunity.[33]

TEAMWORK: THE EMPLOYEE'S ROLE

12-4 Each member should assume an active part in helping the team achieve its mission. This means that every member of the work group can and should be a team member and a team builder. These dual roles are achieved when employees assume greater responsibility for the goals and outcomes of the team. Today's most valued employees are those who are willing to assume leadership responsibilities.

Dynamics of Leadership-Team Behavior

Jim Collins, author of bestsellers *Good to Great* and *Built to Last*, was curious why some of the companies profiled in his books had lost their prominence, and a few even failed. Although these companies were at the height of their success during the research study, Collins wanted to learn what caused the companies to go from great to mediocre.[34] One of the areas Collins and his research team studied was the dynamics of team behavior. Figure 12.5 describes the characteristics of high-performing and low-performing teams.

Figure 12.5 ■ Characteristics of High-Performance Teams

HIGH-PERFORMANCE TEAMS	LOW-PERFORMANCE TEAMS
Team members are clear about the goals to be accomplished, the purpose behind them, and each person's role in achieving the expected outcomes.	Goals are not clear, and team members are confused about what must be done. Team members may not ask or care enough to seek clarification.
Team members are open and honest with each other, building trust over time.	Team members withhold information and may seek to undermine others for their own benefit.
Team members listen, discuss, debate, and even challenge each other to find the best possible solution to problems.	Team members interrupt each other, insert their own personal agenda, or may behave in ways that do not build trust.
Team members learn how to overcome obstacles and challenges to achieve goals, without blaming others for setbacks.	When encountering issues and obstacles, team members blame others rather than accept responsibility and find solutions.
Team members like and respect each other and have a friendly competitive spirit that encourages each to perform his or her best.	Team members are uncomfortable with group dynamics. They do not invest the time or effort to support each other or contribute toward a fun, collaborative work environment.
Team members communicate often with each other, collaborate on projects, and foster a culture of learning and continuous improvement.	Team members operate in their own silos with limited collaboration. They do little to help each other learn and grow.
Team members know and operate by a set of defined values that influence their behavior. They are accountable to each other and keep commitments.	Team members do not share common values. They do not always keep commitments and they do not hold each other accountable.

Employees as Leaders

In traditional organizations, there were leaders and followers, and the followers were not expected to develop leadership skills. Today, the most effective leaders are helping their work team members develop leadership skills so that they can develop their capacity to lead, and the team's success will not ride on one person. At a time when most organizations are trying to compete in a complex, ever-changing global market, there is real merit in establishing a diversity of leadership within the work group. If we are willing to expand our definition of leadership, we can see leaders everywhere:[35]

- The quiet "worker bee" often serves as a leader when the issue is how to get the work done during a crisis situation.
- The "corporate counselor," who informally guides coworkers through stressful problems by merely listening, is an emotional leader.
- The rigid "rule follower" keeps our creativity from becoming irresponsible.

BECOMING A VALUED TEAM MEMBER

12-5 Throughout your working life, your success is very likely to depend on your ability to be an effective team member. Here are some tips on how to become a respected team member in any organizational setting.[36]

1. *Avoid becoming part of a clique or subgroup within the team.* As a member of a clique, you are very likely to lose the trust and respect of other team members.
2. *Avoid any action that might sabotage the team.* By engaging in frequent criticism of other team members, gossip, or other unconstructive behaviors, you undermine team efforts.
3. *Keep in mind that effective team participation depends on honest, open communication among team members.* Use the fundamentals of constructive self-disclosure discussed in Chapter 8.
4. As *a team member, do not feel the need to submerge your own strong beliefs, creative solutions, and ideas.* If the team members are about to make a decision that in your opinion is not "right," do not hesitate to speak up and express your views.

Patrick Lencioni, author of *The Five Dysfunctions of a Team*, has spent many years researching factors that contribute to unproductive teams. In his best-selling book, he provides a five-part model that explains how teams typically hurt themselves (see Figure 12.6).

Total Person Insight

"Great challenges require great teamwork, and the quality most needed among teammates amid the pressure of a difficult challenge is collaboration… Each person brings something to the table that adds value to the relationship and synergy to the team."

Source: John C. Maxwell, *The 17 Essential Qualities of a Team Player* (Nashville, TN: Thomas Nelson Publishers, 2002), pp. 13–14.

Teamwork can be a very satisfying experience. It can generate positive energy and contribute to a sense of optimism about the future. As a team member, you have the opportunity to assume a very important leadership role.

Figure 12.6 ■ Five Dysfunctions of a Team

Patrick Lencioni believes that effective teamwork is not common in most organizations. Too often teams fall prey to five interrelated dysfunctions:

Absence of Trust: Trust is the foundation of effective teamwork.

Fear of Conflict: Teams that lack trust are not capable of engaging in open, unfiltered debate.

Lack of Commitment: When team members fail to voice their views openly during passionate debate, they rarely buy in and commit to decisions.

Avoidance of Accountability: Without commitment and buy-in, team members are often hesitant to call their peers on actions and behaviors that seem counterproductive to the good of the team.

Inattention to Results: Failure to hold one another accountable creates an environment where team members put their own needs above the collective goals of the team.

Managing the Relationship with Your Boss

The idea that you should manage the relationship with your boss may sound a little unusual at first. But it makes a lot of sense when you consider the advantages of assuming this responsibility. When the subordinate and the boss are both working to maintain a good relationship, conflict is less likely to surface. The boss-subordinate relationship is not like the one between parent and child—the burden for managing the relationship *should not* and *cannot* fall entirely on the one in authority.

When you take time to manage the relationship with your boss, he or she will become more effective in performing his or her job. In many cases, managers are no more effective than the combined competence of the people they supervise. Some employees do not realize how much their boss needs assistance and support from them. How do you go about managing your boss? Here are some general considerations:

Assess Your Own Strengths. The boss represents only one-half of the relationship. The development of an effective working relationship also requires reflecting on your own strengths. As noted in Chapter 4, the first step toward strength building is to discover your greatest talents.

Develop an Understanding of Your Boss. Become familiar with this person's strengths, weaknesses, work habits, communication style, and needs. Spend time studying your boss. In some cases, the direct approach is best. Ask your boss, "How would you like me to work with you?" Try to determine his or her goals and expectations. What is the

An increased emphasis on social responsibility has prompted companies such as Salesforce.com to promote its model, which represents employees donating 1 percent of their time to volunteer initiatives, the company donating 1 percent of its technology products to nonprofits, and the company donating 1 percent of its equity to social-improvement initiatives. Here, Orlando Magic President Alex Martins is partnering with a Palmetto Elementary School student for a community beautification project during the 2011 Magic Volunteer Program (MVP).

person trying to accomplish? Does your boss enjoy casual meetings to discuss business matters or formal meetings with written agendas?

Flex Your Communication Style.   In terms of communication style, is your boss supportive, emotive, reflective, or directive? Once you have answered this question, begin thinking of how to flex your style in ways that will build rapport and avoid unnecessary stress. Remember, style flexing is a temporary effort to act in harmony with another person's preferred communication style (see Chapter 3).

Be Frank and Candid.   Suppose that to avoid conflict, you almost never disagree with your boss—even when your boss is obviously wrong. Are you making a contribution to his or her growth and development? Obviously not. And don't hesitate to speak up regarding your contributions. Learn how to point out your accomplishments gracefully. You might say, "I know you're busy, so why don't I send you an e-mail explaining what I'm working on and what I've done?"[37]

As organizations become flatter, with fewer layers of management and more projects carried out by teams, collaboration has become more important. Effective team members are those who collaborate actively with their leader and other members of the team.

TIPS FOR YOUNG LEADERS

Wanted: A new breed of boss who can provide strong leadership, handle technology, inspire teamwork, and cope with uncertainty. The person who fits this description may be quite young and inexperienced. Many of today's leaders are no longer molded solely by seniority and experience. Here are some tips for the young manager:

- Keep in mind that watching your own bosses in action is not enough to teach you to be one.
- Never assume that others are motivated by the same things you are.
- Don't ask for suggestions or opinions that you are not seriously prepared to consider.
- Give before you take. Approach relationships (with your employees, your boss, and customers) with what you have to offer, not with what you want.
- Reach out to people with more age and experience.

Source: Dimitry Elias Legger, "Help! I'm the New Boss," *Fortune*, May 29, 2000, p. 281.

LOOKING BACK: SUMMARY OF LEARNING OBJECTIVES

1. Explain the importance of teamwork in an organizational setting.

Teamwork ensures not only that a job gets done but also that it gets done efficiently. Therefore, successful teamwork can often make the difference between the profitable and the unprofitable operation of an organization. The team-building leadership style is effective because it is suited to the needs of most of today's employees.

2. Identify and describe common types of work teams.

Many companies are forming specific types of teams. Three of the most common are self-managed, cross-functional, and virtual teams. Self-managed teams assume responsibility for traditional management tasks as part of their regular work routine. Team members are responsible for producing a well-defined product or service.

They may rotate among the various jobs and acquire the knowledge and skills to perform each one. Cross-functional teams are task groups staffed with a mix of specialists focused on a common objective. These teams are often temporary units with members from different departments. Virtual teams are comprised of employees who work from a variety of locations. The advantages of virtual teams include speed, agility, expanded expertise, improved communication and collaboration.

3. **Explain the behavioral science principles that support team building**.

One way to learn about team building is to study leaders who promote teamwork and scholars who discuss it; examples are McGregor, Blake, Mouton, and Greenleaf. Two important dimensions of supervisory leadership contribute to team building. One of these dimensions, *consideration*, reflects the extent to which a supervisor maintains relationships with employees that are characterized by mutual trust, respect, and rapport. The other dimension, *structure*, reflects the extent to which a supervisor is likely to direct group activities through planning, goal setting, communication, scheduling, and evaluating. The Leadership Grid and the Situational Leadership Model help clarify these two dimensions of leadership. Effective leaders must also develop the qualities of character and emotional intelligence.

4. **Describe the attributes of a high-performing team**.

Managers must learn to leverage the diversity of knowledge, skills, and abilities to enable teams to make decisions and solve complex problems. High-performing teams have a shared vision and values, have clear goals and objectives, keep commitments, and are accountable to each other and the team. Open, honest communication encourages differing ideas, asking tough questions, and learning from mistakes—all factors that build trust and continuous improvement.

5. **Describe the team-member skills that employees need**.

Members of an effective work group should assume effective leadership and membership roles. Each team member helps the group achieve its mission. Everyone assumes the role of team member and team builder. Employees are in a unique position to give guidance and support to their supervisor or manager. Most bosses need this assistance and support to achieve success.

KEY TERMS

CAREER INSIGHT

HARNESS YOUR EMOTIONS

Emotions drive performance, and leaders who do not acknowledge their own or their employee's temperaments can't inspire the best work from their staffs. Employees who work for intimidating or self-absorbed bosses become guarded and are reluctant to share information or new ideas. Daniel Goleman, in his book *Social Intelligence*, says emotional distress can impair the brain's mechanism to learn and think clearly.

Source: Carol Hymowitz, "Business Is Personal, So Managers Need to Harness Emotions," *Wall Street Journal*, November 13, 2006, p. B1.

TRY YOUR HAND

1. Business publications such as the *Wall Street Journal, Fortune, Bloomberg Businessweek,* and *Fast Company* often feature articles describing problem bosses. Managers with STEM backgrounds (science, technology, engineering, and mathematics) may act in an impersonal or reserved manner that can cause frustration in employees who may view their behavior as insensitive or impersonal. These types of managers are often more focused on technology than on people. They have high IQs but rank low in emotional intelligence, and they may lack people skills. The result is often high employee turnover. Let's assume that you are working for a small business and the owner is often described by employees as the "nerd boss from hell." What steps might you take to influence your boss, who seems to spend all his time obsessing about technology and ignoring the needs of his employees? Review the material featured in this chapter and then develop a plan that would help your boss develop a strong team-building leadership style.[38]

2. There is increasing pressure on organizations to allow employees' personal problems to be brought to the attention of the supervisor or manager. Personal problems that can disrupt people's lives include dealing with a teenager on drugs, coping with the needs of a sick parent, losing a babysitter, or getting a divorce. Schedule an interview with two people who hold supervisory-management positions and ask these questions:
   a. Do you assume the role of mentor and counselor when an employee brings a personal problem to your attention?
   b. Should you give the person with a serious problem some special consideration, such as time off, less demanding work, or professional help that is paid for by the company?

3. The skills needed to be an effective leader can be developed by anyone who is willing to invest the time and energy. It is possible to practice important leadership skills before you assume the duties of a supervisor or manager. Review the various ways to improve consideration and structure skills discussed in this chapter, and then begin searching for opportunities to practice these skills. Here are some opportunities for practice:
   a. Volunteer assignments in your community
   b. Group assignments at work, at college, or at your place of worship
   c. Involvement in political, professional, or social activities

4. The authors of *The Leadership Challenge* have identified five practices of exemplary leadership (see Figure 12.1). Review these practices and select the two that you feel present the greatest challenge to someone who has been promoted to a leadership position for the first time. Provide a rationale for your choice.

CRITICAL THINKING CHALLENGE

Reflect on your work experience and experiences in high school or college. Recall situations when you felt like a member of an effective team. What did the supervisor, manager, teacher, or coach do to develop the spirit of teamwork? What were the specific characteristics of individual team members that contributed to team performance? Compare your answers to those in Figure 12.5: Characteristics of High-Performance Teams.

SELF-ASSESSMENT EXERCISE

For each of the following statements, circle the number from 1 to 5 that best represents your response: (1) strongly disagree (never do this); (2) disagree (rarely do this); (3) moderately agree (sometimes do this); (4) agree (frequently do this); (5) strongly agree (almost always do this).

A.	As a team member, I help create an atmosphere of mutual trust and respect.	1	2	3	4	5
B.	In the role of team member, I listen carefully to the views of others and speak frankly about the issues that are on my mind.	1	2	3	4	5
C.	I practice being a servant-leader, meaning my primary desire is to help others.	1	2	3	4	5
D.	As a team member, I get behind a decision once made, and work to make the decision succeed, even if I disagreed with it.	1	2	3	4	5
E.	I enjoy arguing and debating issues with team members, not to improve my personal position, but to find the best possible solution to a problem or challenge.	1	2	3	4	5

After identifying your response to each item, select an attitude or skill you would like to improve. Prepare a written goal and then describe the steps you will take to achieve this goal.

YOU PLAY THE ROLE

You are currently a computer technician employed by Tech Assistance, Inc. The company provides a wide range of services, including computer system setup, PC and server repairs and upgrades, virus and spyware removal, data recovery services, and Internet security. The company was founded by Erin Wilson about five years ago. You are one of five technicians who make service calls and occasionally work in the repair center when needed. You like your work but feel a sense of frustration when fellow employees fail to give their best efforts. The owner is very effective in solving technical problems but often displays poor people skills. She simply does not pay attention to employees, to what they are doing, or to how they are feeling. She knows almost nothing about their hobbies, family status, or personal concerns. There are times when you feel like quitting, but you like solving technical problems and helping customers with their computer needs. You have decided to meet with Erin and provide some suggestions on how to become a more effective leader. Use the name Reagan Simpson during the role-play.

BELOW THE SURFACE | NETFLIX REINVENTS HR

Henk Meijer/Alamy

When Netflix CEO Reed Hastings and HR leader Patty McCord released a 127-slide PowerPoint deck describing the Netflix culture and HR policies, it went viral. In early 2014 the deck had been viewed more than five million times, and it continues to be widely shared. Why the interest in an HR PowerPoint? Because the HR policies were so radically different from those of other companies. They reflect common sense rather than formal policies. Here are a few:

- Hire, Reward, and Tolerate Only Fully Formed Adults
- Tell the Truth About Performance
- Leaders Own the Job of Creating the Company Culture
- Managers Own the Job of Creating Great Teams

Managers at Netflix are continuously reminded that building a great team was their most important responsibility. They weren't measured on coaching, mentoring, or getting paperwork done on time. Teams were evaluated on accomplishments and creating great results. When McCord coached managers on creating great teams, she would tell them to approach team building in the same manner as former defense secretary Donald Rumsfeld, who said,

"You go to war with the army you have, not the army you might want or wish to have at a later time." What she meant was that if a team operates in a fast-changing business environment and the skills of certain team members are no long needed, it's expected that managers will have honest conversations with them so they can find a role better suited to their skills, and they are expected to hire people with the skills they do need.

McCord learned this lesson when she was talking with an engineer who had lost three employees during layoffs following 9/11 and the dotcom bust. When she told him that she knew he was putting in long hours and would hire people soon to help him, he said, "There's no rush—I'm happier now. I've learned that I'd rather work by myself than with sub-par performers." This conversation with the engineer came to describe the most basic element of the Netflix philosophy: "The best thing you can do for employees—a perk better than foosball or free sushi—is hire only "A" players to work alongside them. Excellent colleagues trump everything else."[39]

QUESTIONS

1. If you were a manager at Netflix and rewarded *only* on the results that your team produced and nothing else, would you embrace this policy or be uncomfortable with it?

2. If you are uncomfortable with the policy, what specific actions could you take to feel confident that you and your team could fulfill expectations and deliver results?

Two of the policies under the principle "Hire, Reward, and Tolerate Only Fully Formed Adults" are (1) the expense policy, which states "Act in Netflix's best interests" and (2) There is no set vacation policy for salaried employees. This means employees can take whatever time off they feel is appropriate. Bosses and employees just need to work it out with one another.

3. As a manager, how much time do you think you might take off during a year? Explain your rationale.

4. As a manager, you have an employee who wants to take off 25 days in a row (more than 30 days requires a meeting with HR) and then the same employee says he would like to take another two-week vacation six months later. How would you respond to him? How would you respond to other team members who say they will have issues covering for him during that time?

CLOSING CASE | VIRTUAL TEAMWORK: MAKING IT WORK

Virtual teams are composed of employees who are physically dispersed throughout the nation or around the world. They are linked by various forms of electronic technology. Face-to-face contact is usually minimal or nonexistent. Virtual teams face several challenges: time zone differences, which make quick information exchanges difficult, and cultural miscues, which can cause misunderstandings. When teams don't meet in person, it's less likely they will develop the kind of chemistry common to productive teams that have face-to-face meetings.

Many virtual teams are in continuous danger of becoming dysfunctional.[40]

Recent research has identified certain traits and practices common to most virtual teams. Here are a few important rules for making these teams productive.[41]

- Choose a few team members who already know each other. This will speed up the process of building networks among team members. Invest in online resources that help all team members quickly learn about one another.

- Ensure the task is meaningful to team members and the company. Assign tasks that are challenging and interesting.
- The virtual team should include "boundary spanners," persons who have many connections to useful people outside of the team.
- Develop a team mission statement along with teamwork expectations, project goals, and deadlines.
- Create an online site where team members can collaborate, exchange ideas, and motivate one another. The team should have a shared online workspace that all members can access 24 hours a day.

- Encourage frequent communication and try to reach agreement about preferred communication tools.
- If you are a virtual team leader, find ways to mark team progress toward goals.

QUESTIONS

1. Which of the five dysfunctions of a team (presented in Figure 12.6) would be the greatest barriers to virtual team productivity? Defend your answer.
2. What can be done to avoid information overload when the virtual team is made up of 25 to 30 members?

CHAPTER 12 ENDNOTES

1. Geoff Colvin, "Great Job*Or How Yum Brands Uses Recognition to Build Teams and Get Results," **Fortune**, August 12, 2013, pp. 62–66.
2. Erin White, "How a Company Made Everyone a Team Player," **Wall Street Journal**, August 13, 2007, p. B1.
3. Bill George (with Peter Sims), **True North** (San Francisco: John Wiley & Sons, 2007), p. xxiv.
4. Robert Kreitner, **Management**, 11th ed. (Boston: Houghton Mifflin, 2009), p. 402.
5. "Stephen Covey Talks About the 8th Habit: Effective Is No Longer Enough," **Training**, February 2005, pp. 17–19.
6. James M. Kouzes and Barry Z. Posner, **The Leadership Challenge**, 3rd ed. (San Francisco: Jossey-Bass, 2002), pp. 3–12.
7. William M. Pride, Robert J. Hughes, and Jack R. Kapoor, **Business**, 8th ed. (Boston: Houghton Mifflin, 2005), p. 198.
8. Robert Kreitner, **Management**, 11th ed. (Boston: Houghton Mifflin, 2009), p. 182.
9. George Halvorson, "Getting to Us," **Harvard Business Review**, September 2014, p. 38.
10. Robert Kreitner, **Management**, 11th ed. (Boston: Houghton Mifflin, 2009), pp. 353–354.
11. Amy Edmondson, "Teamwork on the Fly," **Harvard Business Review**, April 2012, pp. 72–80.
12. Geoffrey Colvin, "The Art of the Self-Managing Team," **Fortune**, December 3, 2012, p. 2.
13. Ibid., pp. 482–483.
14. Scott Thurm, "Teamwork Raises Everyone's Game," **Wall Street Journal**, November 7, 2005, p. B8.

15. GroupONE Solutions/Trina Hoefling's "Master Virtual Work Presentation" based on Hoefling's book, **Working Virtually** (Sterling, VA: Stylus Publishing, 2003).
16. Ibid.
17. Adapted from a list in Douglas McGregor, **The Human Side of Enterprise** (New York: McGraw-Hill, 1960), pp. 21, 232–235.
18. Warren Bennis, **An Invented Life—Reflections on Leadership and Change** (Reading, MA: Addison-Wesley, 1993), pp. 37–38.
19. Rosabeth Moss Kanter, "What Would Peter Drucker Say," **Harvard Business Review**, November 2009, pp. 65–70.
20. These two dimensions can be measured by the **Leadership Opinion Questionnaire** developed by Edwin A. Fleishman and available from Pearson Performance Solutions. Available from http://www.pearsonps.com; INTERNET.
21. Brian Tracy, **The 100 Absolutely Unbreakable Laws of Business Success** (San Francisco: Berrett-Koehler, 2000), pp. 138–139.
22. "Making a Nickel Do a Dime's Work," **Training**, April 1994, p. 12.
23. Tracy, **The 100 Absolutely Unbreakable Laws of Business Success**, pp. 19–20.
24. "Tips for Teams," **Training**, February 1994, p. 14.
25. David G. Baldwin, "How to Win the Blame Game," **Harvard Business Review**, July/August 2001, pp. 1–7 (Reprint RO107C).
26. Blanchard, Ken and the Founding Associates and Consulting Partners of The Ken Blanchard Companies,

Leading at a Higher Level: Blanchard on Leadership and Creating High Performing Organizations (Upper Saddle River, NJ: FT Press, 2010), p. 150.

27. Ibid., pp. 150–151.

28. Robert Kreitner, *Management*, 11th ed. (Boston: Houghton Mifflin, 2009), p. 409.

29. Paul Hersey, *The Situational Leader* (Escondido, CA: Center for Leadership Studies, 1984), pp. 29–30. To obtain current information on the Situational Leadership Model, visit http://www.situational.com.

30. Ibid.

31. Tracy, *The 100 Absolutely Unbreakable Laws of Business Success*, p. 121.

32. Cary Cherniss and Daniel Goleman, *The Emotionally Intelligent Workplace* (San Francisco: Jossey-Bass, 2001), pp. 22–23.

33. Will Schutz, *The Human Element* (San Francisco: Jossey-Bass, 1994), pp. 237–238.

34. Collins, Jim, "How the Mighty Fall," *BusinessWeek*, May 25, 2009, pp. 26–33.

35. Margaret Kaeter, "The Leaders Among Us," *Business Ethics*, July/August 1994, p. 46.

36. Peter Koestenbaum, *Leadership—The Inner Side of Greatness* (San Francisco: Jossey-Bass, 1991), pp. 179–183; Stephen Covey, "Why Is It Always About You?" *Training*, May 2006, p. 64.

37. Rachel Leibrock, "Manage Your Manager, Keep Your Job," *News & Observer*, October 12, 2008.

38. Michaele Weissman, "Nerd Alert!" *Wall Street Journal*, May 14, 2001, p. R14.

39. Patty McCord, "How Netflix Reinvented HR," *Harvard Business Review*, January-February 2014, pp. 71–76.

40. Lynda Gratton, "Working Together… When Apart," *Wall Street Journal*, June 16, 2007, p. R4.

41. Ibid.

Henk Meijer/Alamy

CHAPTER PREVIEW

LEARNING OBJECTIVES

After studying Chapter 13, you will be able to

13-1 List and describe some of the major causes of conflict in the workplace.

13-2 Use assertiveness skills in conflict situations.

13-3 Understand when and how to implement effective negotiation skills.

13-4 Identify key elements of the conflict resolution process.

13-5 Discuss the role of labor unions in conflict resolution.

Resolving Conflict and Dealing with Difficult People

TIP OF THE ICEBERG | DON'T SWEAT THE SMALL STUFF

When you hear the word "conflict" it may elicit the idea of big, awful problems, but most people experience conflict in many small ways throughout their day. It's a natural part of life, so if you can begin to view conflict not as bad, but as a challenge to overcome, you will see there are many opportunities for learning and personal growth presented to you each day.

It doesn't take much to set people off with feelings of anger or even a fit of rage. It may be a person who cuts you off to take a parking space you were waiting for, or the person standing in line next to you at Starbucks who is having an obnoxiously loud conversation. Or it could be the person in front of you at the movie theater who is constantly texting on his phone, oblivious to the irritation of everyone around him. We have all experienced moments of anger as the result of inconsiderate behavior from others, even for the smallest of things.

One morning when Mr. Laermer was reading a book while seated in the "quiet" car of a Manhattan commuter train, he couldn't concentrate over the constant click, click, click of the man texting next to him so he kindly asked the man to turn off the clicking sound so they could both be happy. The man responded by jumping out of his seat shouting, "Is this what it's now come to? People want you to type more gently?" After going off in an angry tirade for several minutes he said, "Who do you think you are? Do you really think you can tell me what to do?" The man replied with "Yes, that's exactly right. Please turn the clicks off." People nearby began clapping, and the angry man sat down, red faced and turned his phone off.

Jacob Lindner/Getty Images

Researchers at Duke University call these small injustices "unwritten laws of social behavior rules." The lead author of a new study on this topic is Mark Leary, professor of psychology and neuroscience at Duke. Dr. Leary says these seemingly trivial behaviors make us feel personally violated because people are not "playing by the rules," causing one or both people to feel they are treated unfairly or in a rude, selfish, or inconsiderate manner.[1]

Conflict does not need to escalate into a stressful situation if you know how to deal with it. Managing conflict is a learned skill, and this chapter offers specific guidelines for effectively resolving a wide range of conflicts.

A NEW VIEW OF CONFLICT

Conflict occurs when there is a clash between incompatible people, ideas, or interests. These conflicts are almost always perceived as negative experiences in our society. But when we view conflict as a negative experience, we may be hurting our chances of dealing with it effectively. In reality, conflicts are opportunities for personal growth if we develop and use positive, constructive conflict resolution skills.[2]

> *Much of our growth and social progress comes from the opportunities we have to discover creative solutions to conflicts that surface in our lives.*

Much of our growth and social progress comes from the opportunities we have to discover creative solutions to conflicts that surface in our lives. Dudley Weeks, professor of conflict resolution at American University, says conflict can provide additional ways of thinking about the *source* of conflict and open up possibilities for improving a relationship.[3] When people work together to resolve conflicts, their solutions are often far more creative than they would be if only one person addressed the problem. Creative conflict resolution can shake people out of their mental ruts and give them a new point of view.

Meaningful Conflict

Too much agreement is not always healthy in an organization. Employees who are anxious to be viewed as "team players" may not voice concerns even when they have doubts about a decision being made. Meaningful conflict can be the key to producing healthy, successful organizations because conflict is necessary for effective problem solving and for effective interpersonal relationships.[4] The problem is not with disagreements, but with how they are approached, discussed, and resolved.

FINDING THE ROOT CAUSES OF CONFLICT

13-1 Throughout this text, we have often compared the challenges of interpersonal relations to an iceberg. The tip of the iceberg is in plain view and readily available for consideration. However, most of the iceberg exists below the surface and can create problems if we choose to ignore it. Let's assume that the owner of your company has initiated a new policy on sexual harassment. This behavior has been carefully defined by the company lawyer, and the message seems very clear: Employees who are guilty of sexual harassment will be terminated. The Iceberg of Conflict, Figure 13.1, reveals a wide range of factors that will influence each employee's perception of the new company policy.

When you are in conflict, each level of the iceberg represents something that may influence the conflict resolution process. It is important that we go deep enough to understand the influence of our emotions, self-perceptions, needs, unresolved issues from

Figure 13.1 ■ Iceberg of Conflict

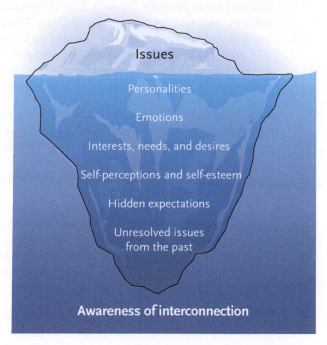

Issues

Personalities

Emotions

Interests, needs, and desires

Self-perceptions and self-esteem

Hidden expectations

Unresolved issues
from the past

Awareness of interconnection

Source: From Kenneth Cloke and Joan Goldsmith, *Resolving Conflicts at Work: A Complete Guide for Everyone on the Job*, pp. 114–116, copyright © 2000 by Jossey-Bass. Reprinted with permission of John Wiley & Sons, Inc.

the past, and other things that exist at each level of the iceberg. The Iceberg of Conflict helps you better understand yourself and how to respond to create a positive outcome.

Conflict Triggers

A **conflict trigger** is a circumstance that increases the chances of intergroup or interpersonal conflict. People encounter many different types of conflicts in any given day or week, so it is wise to learn to handle conflict in a fast, efficient manner. Later in this chapter, you will learn techniques for doing this. First, we will look at some of the most common types of conflicts.

Organizational Change. Organizational change is one of the root causes of conflict. In most organizations, there is tension between opposing forces for stability (maintain the status quo) and change. For example, if management wants to shift more health-care costs onto workers, tension may surface. With too much stability, no change in health-care cost allocation, the organization may lose its competitive position in the marketplace. With too much change, the mission blurs and employee anxiety develops.[5]

Ineffective Communication. A major source of personal conflict is the misunderstanding that results from ineffective communication. In Chapter 2, we discussed the various filters that messages must pass through before effective communication can occur. In the work setting, where many different people work closely together, communication breakdowns are inevitable. Achieving effective two-way communication is always a challenge.

Value and Culture Clashes. In Chapter 5, you read that differences in values can cause conflicts between generations, between men and women, and between people with different value priorities. Today's diverse workforce reflects a kaleidoscope of values and cultures, each with its own unique qualities. The individual bearers of these different values and traditions could easily come into conflict with one another.

As noted in previous chapters, generational influences are among the most powerful forces shaping values in our workforce. Value differences among Matures, Baby Boomers, Generation X, and Generation Y (Millennials) can lead to conflict.

Work Policies and Practices. Interpersonal conflicts can develop when an organization has unreasonable or confusing rules, regulations, and performance standards. The conflicts often surface when managers fail to tune in to employees' perceptions that various policies are unfair. Managers need to address the source of conflict rather than suppress it. Conflict also surfaces when some workers refuse to comply with the rules or neglect their fair share of the workload.

Adversarial Management. Under adversarial management, supervisors may view their employees and even other managers with suspicion and distrust and treat them as "the enemy." Employees usually lack respect for adversarial managers, resenting their authoritarian style and resisting their suggestions for change. This atmosphere makes cooperation and teamwork difficult.

Competition for Scarce Resources. It would be difficult to find an organization, public or private, that is not involved in downsizing or cost-cutting. The result is often destructive competition for scarce resources such as updated computers, administrative support personnel, division and/or department budgets, salary increases, or annual bonuses. When budgets and cost-cutting efforts are not clearly explained, workers may suspect coworkers or supervisors of devious tactics.

"I cooked us a lovely dinner for two—you could at least do the dishes!"

Carolita Johnson/cartoonbank.com

Personality Clashes. There is no doubt about it: Some people just don't like each other. They may have differing communication styles, temperaments, or attitudes. They may not be able to identify exactly what it is they dislike about the other person, but the bottom line is that conflicts will arise when these people have to work together. Even people who get along well with each other in the beginning stages of a work relationship may begin to clash after working together for a few months.

RESOLVING CONFLICT ASSERTIVELY

13-2 Conflict is often uncomfortable whether it is in a personal or professional setting. People sometimes get hurt and become defensive because they feel they are under personal attack. Because we have to work or live with certain people every day, it is best to avoid harming these ongoing relationships. But many people do not know how to approach and manage conflict in a positive way. Many professionals advise going directly to the offending person and calmly discussing his or her irritating behavior rather than complaining to others.[6] Figure 13.2, "Dealing with People You Can't Stand," offers specific strategies you might use. By taking those steps to change *your* behavior, you can facilitate a powerful change in theirs. Keep in mind that some people are unaware of the impact of their behavior, and if you draw their attention to it, they may change it.

Whereas these strategies may be comfortable for some people, such a direct approach may be very uncomfortable for many others. People who try to avoid conflict by simply ignoring things that bother them are exhibiting **nonassertive behavior**. Nonassertive people often give in to the demands of others, and their passive approach makes them less likely to make their needs known. If you fail to take a firm position when such action is appropriate, customers, coworkers, and supervisors may take advantage of you, and management may question your abilities.

Assertive behavior, on the other hand, provides you the opportunity to stand up for your rights and express your thoughts and feelings in a direct, appropriate way that does not violate the rights of others. It is a matter of getting the other person to understand your viewpoint.[7] People who exhibit appropriate assertive behavior skills are able to handle their conflicts with greater ease and assurance while maintaining good interpersonal relations.

Some people do not understand the distinction between being aggressive and being assertive. **Aggressive behavior** in conflict situations involves expressing your thoughts and feelings and defending your rights in a way that *violates* the rights of others. Aggressive people may interrupt, talk fast, ignore others, and use sarcasm or other forms of verbal abuse to maintain control.

How to Become More Assertive

Entire books have been written that describe how to improve your assertiveness skills. The American Management Association is one of many organizations that offer skill-development seminars that focus on assertiveness training, including *Assertiveness Training for Managers* and *Assertiveness Training for Women in Business*.[8] Enrollees can achieve greater credibility by learning how to handle tough situations with composure and confidence. Whether you choose to read books or participate in assertiveness training, know that you can communicate your wants, dislikes, and feelings in a clear, direct manner without threatening or attacking others. Here are three practical guidelines that will help you develop your assertiveness skills.

Figure 13.2 ■ Dealing with People You Can't Stand

THE BULLY	▶ Bullies find ways to manipulate or control others. They are pushy, ruthless, loud, and forceful and tend to intimidate you with in-your-face arguments. They assume that the end justifies the means.	**Strategy:** Keep your cool. Immediately respond calmly and professionally to let the bully know you are not a target: "When you're ready to speak to me with respect, I'll be ready to discuss this matter." Walk away from a ranting bully. Ask the bully to fully explain what he or she is trying to say or do, and then paraphrase your understanding of the bully's real intentions.
THE BACKSTABBER	▶ They present themselves as your friend but do everything in their power to sabotage your relationships with your supervisors, coworkers, and clients. They use tactics such as withholding information from you and then suggesting to others that you are incompetent, witless, and worthy of demotion.	**Strategy:** Once you've discovered your saboteur, tell key people that the person is, in fact, not a friend, which takes power from the backstabber and reveals the smear campaign.
THE WHINER	▶ They wallow in their woe and whine incessantly about the injustices that surround them. A naysayer takes a more premeditated approach to negativity. In meeting they often wait until consensus is nearly reached, then derail progress by talking about all the reasons something can't be done.	**Strategy:** Listen so you can identify and focus on possible solutions. If they remain in "it's hopeless" mode, walk away saying, "Let me know when you want to talk about a solution." Communicate how their behavior brings down others on the team.
THE RAMBLER	▶ Ramblers turn otherwise productive meetings into death by boredom. They get off topic by rambling on and on while people roll their eyes, and look at their watch and start checking e-mail. They suck the life energy of everyone in the room.	**Strategy:** Put a few simple rules and boundaries in place to influence the behavior of these productivity killers. For example, place an object at the center of the meeting table and explain at the beginning of the meeting and request that anyone who thinks the meeting is getting off point, pick up the object. This gives coworkers a way to vent frustration instead of making personal remarks.
THE KNOW-IT-ALL	▶ They will tell you what they know, but they will not bother listening to your "clearly inferior" ideas. Often, they really don't know much, but they don't let that get in the way. They exaggerate, brag, and mislead.	**Strategy:** Acknowledge their expertise, but be prepared with your facts. Use "I" statements, such as "From what I've read and experienced …"
THE COWARD	▶ When faced with a crucial decision, they keep putting it off until it is too late and the decision makes itself, or they say yes to everything but follow through on nothing.	**Strategy:** Help them feel comfortable and safe in their rare decisions to move forward, and stay in touch until the decision is implemented. Arrange deadlines and describe the consequences that will result when they complete the tasks and what will happen if they don't.

(Continued)

Figure 13.2 ■ **Dealing with People You Can't Stand (Continued)**

THE EXPLODERS ▶	They throw tantrums that can escalate quickly. When they blow their tops, they are unable to stop. When the smoke clears and the dust settles, the cycle begins again.	**Strategy:** When an explosion begins, assertively repeat the individual's name to get his or her attention, or repeat a neutral comment such as "Stop!" Calmly address what they said in their first few sentences, which usually reveals the real problem. Give them time to regain self-control. Suggest that they take time out to cool down, and then listen to their problems in private.

Source: Adapted from *Dealing with People You Can't Stand* by Rick Brinkman and Rick Kirshner. Copyright © 1994 by McGraw-Hill, Inc. Reprinted by permission of The McGraw Hill Companies, and "Meet the Meeting Killers" by Sue Shellenbarger, *Wall Street Journal*, D1, May 16, 2012.

Table 13.1 may give you a clearer understanding of how nonassertive, assertive, and aggressive people respond when confronted with conflict situations.

In the Beginning, Take Small Steps. Being assertive may be difficult at first, so start with something that is easy. You might decline the invitation to keep the minutes at the weekly staff meeting if you feel others should assume this duty from time to time. If you are tired of eating lunch at Joe's Diner (the choice of a coworker), suggest a restaurant that you would prefer. If someone insists on keeping the temperature at a cool 67 degrees and you are tired of being cold all the time, approach the person and voice your opinion in a calm manner. *How* you make a request is as important as *what* you say. Discuss a solution that will work for both of you.

Table 13.1 ■ Behaviors Exhibited by Assertive, Aggressive, and Nonassertive Persons During Conflict

	ASSERTIVE PERSON	AGGRESSIVE PERSON	NONASSERTIVE PERSON
In conflict situations	Communicates directly	Dominates	Avoids the conflict
In decision-making situations	Chooses for self	Chooses for self and others	Allows others to choose
In situations expressing feelings	Is open, direct, honest, while allowing others to express their feelings	Expresses feelings in a threatening manner; puts down, inhibits others	Holds true feelings inside
In group meeting situations	Uses direct, clear "I" statements: "I believe that …"	Uses clear but demeaning "you" statements: "You should have known better …"	Uses indirect, unclear statements: "Would you mind if …?"

Use Communication Skills that Enhance Assertiveness. A confident tone of voice, eye contact, firm gestures, and good posture create nonverbal messages that say, "I'm serious about this request." Using "I" messages can be especially helpful in cases where you want to assert yourself in a nonthreatening manner. If you approach the person who wants the thermostat set at 67 degrees and say, "You need to be more considerate of others," the person is likely to become defensive. However, if you say, "I feel uncomfortable when the temperature is so cool," you will start the conversation on a more positive note.

Be Soft on People and Hard on the Problem. The goal of conflict resolution is to solve the problem but avoid doing harm to the relationship. Of course, relationships tend to become entangled with the problem, so there is a tendency to treat the people and the problem as one. Your coworker, Terry, is turning in projects late every week, and you are feeling a great deal of frustration each time it happens. You must communicate to Terry that each missed deadline creates serious problems for you. Practice using tact, diplomacy, and patience as you keep the discussion focused on the problem, not on Terry's personality traits.

LEARN TO NEGOTIATE EFFECTIVELY

13-3

In the past, the responsibility for negotiating an effective resolution to conflicts was often given to supervisors, department heads, team leaders, shop stewards, mediators, and others with established authority and responsibility. Today, many companies have organized workers into teams that are empowered to solve their own problems whenever possible. This means that every employee needs to learn how to effectively negotiate satisfactory resolutions to conflicts. Danny Ertel, author and consultant in the area of negotiations, says, "Every company, today, exists in a complex web of relationships, and the shape of that web is formed, one thread at a time, through negotiations."[9] Team assignments, compensation, promotions, and work assignments are just a few of the areas where you can apply negotiation skills.

After 15 years of marriage, Melodie Reagan and Frank Slavick decided to get divorced. They didn't let this get in the way of the two businesses they own together: i2i Workforce and Crazy Good Marketing. They continue to be business partners, parents, and good friends.

Courtesy of Frank Slavick

Think Win/Win

There are basically three ways to approach negotiations: win/lose, lose/lose, and win/win. When you use the **win/lose approach**, you are trying to reach your goals at the expense of the other party. For example, a manager can say, "Do as I say or find a job somewhere else!" The manager wins; the employee loses. Although this approach may end the conflict on a short-term basis, it does not usually address the underlying cause of the problem. It may simply sow the seeds of another conflict because the "losers" feel frustrated.

When the **lose/lose approach** is used to settle a dispute, each side must give in to the other. If the sacrifices are too great, both parties may feel that too much has been given. This strategy can be applied when there is little time to find a solution through effective negotiation techniques, or when negotiations are at a standstill and no progress is being made. Union–management disputes, for example, often fall into the lose/lose trap when neither side is willing to yield. In these cases, an arbitrator, a neutral third party, may be called in to impose solutions on the disputing parties.

In general, the win/lose and lose/lose approaches to negotiating create an "us versus them" attitude among the people involved in the conflict, rather than a "we versus the problem" approach. "Us versus them" (or "my way versus your way") means that participants focus on whose solution is superior, instead of working together to find a solution that is acceptable to all.

> *The basic purpose of the win/win approach to negotiating is to fix the problem—not the blame!*

The basic purpose of the **win/win approach** to negotiating is to fix the problem—not the blame! Don't think hurt; think help. Negotiating a win/win solution to a conflict is not a debate where you are trying to prove the other side wrong; instead, you are engaging in a dialogue where each side tries to get the other side to understand its concerns, and both sides then work toward a mutually satisfying solution. Your negotiations will go better when you shift your emphasis from a tactical approach of how to counter the other person's every comment to discovering a creative solution that simple haggling obscures.[10]

Perhaps the most vital skill in effective negotiations is listening. When you concentrate on learning common interests, not differences, the nature of the negotiation changes from a battle to win, to a discussion of how to meet the objectives of everyone involved in the dispute.

Beware of Defensive Behaviors

Effective negotiations are often slowed or sidetracked completely by defensive behaviors that surface when people are in conflict with each other. When one person in a conflict situation becomes defensive, others may mirror this behavior. In a short time, progress is slowed because people stop listening and begin thinking about how they can defend themselves against the other person's comments.

We often become defensive when we feel our needs are being ignored. Kurt Salzinger, executive director for science at the American Psychological Association, reminds us that conflicts are often caused by unfulfilled needs for things such as dignity, security, identity, recognition, or justice. He says, "Conflict is often exacerbated as much by the process of the relationship as it is by the issues."[11] Determining the other person's needs requires careful listening and respect for views that differ from your own. If you feel you are trapped in a win/lose negotiation and can hear yourself or the other person becoming defensive, do everything in your power to refocus the discussion toward fixing the problem rather than defending your position.

Figure 13.3 ■ Negotiation Tips

Rob Walker reviewed several of the best-selling books on negotiation, including *Getting to Yes, You Can Negotiate Anything, The Negotiation Tool Kit,* and *The Power of Nice.* He discovered a few basic negotiating tips that recur in these popular advice books:

- Stay rationally focused on the issue being negotiated.
- Exhaustive preparation is more important than aggressive argument.
- Think through your alternatives.
- The more options you feel you have, the better a negotiating position you will be in.
- Spend less time talking and more time listening and asking good questions. Sometimes silence is your best response.
- Let the other side make the first offer. If you are underestimating yourself, you might make a needlessly weak opening move.

Source: Rob Walker, "Take It or Leave It: The Only Guide to Negotiating You Will Ever Need," *Inc.,* August 2003, p. 81.

Total Person Insight

"Any settlement or agreement that leaves one party dissatisfied will come back to hurt you later, sometimes in ways you cannot predict."

Source: Brian Tracy, *The 100 Absolutely Unbreakable Laws of Business Success,* San Francisco: Berrett-Koehler Publishers, 2000, p. 235

NEGOTIATING COMPENSATION

Some of the most challenging negotiations arise when you are preparing to start a new job or seeking a pay raise in your current job. Negotiation is working to reach an agreement that is mutually satisfactory to both parties. Here are some negotiation tips suggested by Victoria Pynchon, a compensation expert.

Do your research. Many salaries are public, especially government jobs or high-profile positions in large public companies. Research compensation plans for jobs at the company you are applying, as well as compensation for similar jobs at other companies using websites such as www.Glassdoor.com. Another option is to call people and ask them for their advice about what the market rate is for a position such as this.

Know what you are worth. Instead of pulling a number out of a hat, use the research you have done and make a case for why you are worth more than what the average person is making. Emphasize the value you can provide and give examples of how you have performed for other companies.

Don't put the first number on the table. It helps to request a salary before an offer is made. Usually the first number on the table influences the negotiation.

Women need to be extra assertive. A Carnegie Mellon University study reported 57 percent of male MBAs negotiated the salary for their job, versus only 7 percent of women. "It's critical to know what men make to avoid unknowingly accepting a low-ball offer. Once you know what you're worth, practice asking for a lot more," Pynchon advises.

Consider the impact on your long-term earning power. The Carnegie Mellon study revealed that the men who negotiated their offer made an average of $4,000 more per year. Keep in mind the salary you negotiate will be the benchmark for future raises and future employers.[12]

Know That Negotiating Styles Vary

Depending on your communication style, assertiveness skills, and past experiences in dealing with conflict in the workplace, individuals naturally develop their own negotiating styles. But negotiating is a skill, and people can learn how and when to adapt their style to deal effectively with conflict situations.

Total Person Insight

WHAT TO DO WHEN YOU ARE THE TARGET OF SOMEONE'S RAGE

"The first thing to do is do nothing. Count to 10 before you respond to these kinds of interactions. Do not send an e-mail. Do not send a text. Do not make a call. Allow yourself to process the feeling of injustice and the feeling of the attack before you do anything. We tend to want to jump directly into reaction, and that's our instinctive impulse—to react to the blow. We just want to pour gasoline on the fire, which starts a cycle of emotional violence: attack, defense, attack, defense. From a spiritual perspective you take the experience into your heart or into meditation … and from that place you will emerge with a wisdom and a clarity and with a peace that you would have not otherwise had, had you not had control of your impulses at that point.

Source: Jennifer Weigel, "Thriving in a Fast-Paced World: To Get More in Life, We Have to Give More, Says Author Marianne Williamson," (Chicago Tribune), *News and Observer*, April 18, 2013, 1D–2D.

Robert Maddux suggests there are five different behavioral styles that can be used during conflict situations. He takes the position that different styles may be appropriate in different situations.

Avoidance Style (Uncooperative/Nonassertive). This style is appropriate when the conflict is too minor or too great to resolve. Any attempt to resolve the conflict might result in damaging a relationship or simply wasting time and energy. Avoidance might take the form of diplomatically sidestepping an issue or postponing your response until a more appropriate time.

Accommodating Style (Cooperative/Nonassertive). This style is appropriate when resolving the conflict is not worth risking damage to the relationship or general disharmony. Individuals who use this approach relinquish their own concerns to satisfy the concerns of someone else. Accommodating might take the form of selfless generosity or blind obedience to another's point of view.

Win/Lose Style (Uncooperative/Aggressive). This style may be appropriate when the conflict involves "survival of the fittest," when you must prove your superior position, or when your opinion is the most ethically or professionally correct. This power-oriented position allows you to use whatever means seem appropriate when it is time to stand up for your rights.

Problem-Solving Style (Assertive/Cooperative). This style is appropriate when all parties openly discuss the issues and a mutually beneficial solution can be found without anyone making a major concession. Problem solvers attempt to uncover underlying issues that may be at the root of the problem, and then focus the discussion toward achieving the most desirable outcome. They seek to replace conflict with collaboration.

Compromising Style (Moderately Aggressive/Moderately Cooperative). This style is appropriate when no one person or idea is perfect, when there is more than one good way to do something, or when you must give to get what you want. Compromise attempts to find mutually acceptable solutions to the conflict that partially satisfy both sides. Never use this style when unethical activities are the cause of the conflict.

How to Have a Crucial Conversation

An important book that describes a process for how to resolve conflict is *Crucial Conversations: Tools for Talking When Stakes Are High*. The authors summarize 25 years of research and evaluations of 25,000 people in high-stakes conversations. Companies that are practicing these methods have experienced significant improvements in innovation, teamwork, and change management.

The authors define a *crucial conversation* as a discussion between two or more people where stakes are high, opinions vary, and emotions run strong. Figure 13.4 illustrates a powerful model anyone can use to create a meaningful dialogue based on mutual understanding.

At the center of the model is a circle called the *Pool of Shared Meaning*, the focus of having an effective dialogue with others. The authors contend that the single most important factor of a crucial conversation boils down to this: People must find a way to get all relevant information (from themselves and others) out into the open. People must be willing and capable of expressing their thoughts, feelings, and emotions openly and honestly, *and they must be willing to do so even when their ideas are controversial.*[13]

Figure 13.4 ■ The Crucial Conversations Model

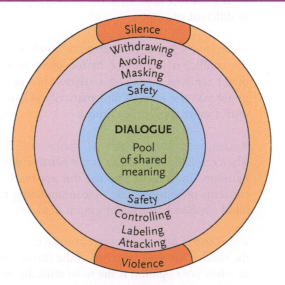

Source: *Crucial Conversations: Tools for Talking When the Stakes Are High*, "The Dialogue Model," Kerry Patterson, Joseph Grenny, Ron McMillan, and Al Switzler, 2002, p. 182.

Unfortunately, the more crucial the conversation, the less likely people are to handle it well. When people move into the realm of *silence* or *violence*, conflict resolution tends to break down. *Silence* occurs when we suppress our thoughts, withhold information, or avoid a topic, limiting the amount of information needed to resolve conflict. *Violence*, which does not imply physical violence, occurs when we begin attacking others' ideas, trying to manipulate them, or hurting their feelings.

To steer the conversation back to a *meaningful dialogue*, the most important area to focus on is creating a safe environment. When we feel safe with others, open communication is possible, and the dialogue stimulates ideas and shared meaning. Lack of safety keeps us from moving into the pool of sharing meaning. As soon as you identify that others may not feel safe, the best way to deal with the conflict is to step out of the content of the issue being discussed and rebuild safety. For example, saying "Can we shift gears for a moment and talk about [the bigger picture of the discussion topic]? It seems we are both trying to force our viewpoints. Can we continue talking to find a solution that will make both of us happy?"

People who are gifted communicators keep a close eye on safety. They learn to step back and ask themselves, "Are we in or out of dialogue?" "Where am I?" "Where are others?" If safety feels weak, they step out of the content of the conversation, focus on increasing safety, then step back into the conversation.

It is also important to understand the interpretations and judgments that people often place on the behavior they observe in others. In a heated discussion, emotions can quickly overrule facts, causing them to "*make up*" a story in their minds to explain what they *see and hear*. This causes them to *feel* a strong emotion and to *act* in a way that is not productive to resolving conflict. Critical thoughts are really stories you have created; they are not necessarily true. For example, let's say Susan works for a boss who constantly cuts her off mid-sentence. The story she "makes up" might be "George always cuts me off during staff meetings—I bet he doesn't think I'm smart enough to lead this team … Or maybe he's thinking that just because I'm a woman, people won't listen to me or respect me." In this case, Susan just made up a negative story in her mind, based on what she saw and heard, that made her feel less safe. She needs to challenge underlying thoughts that may be distorted.[14]

CONFLICT RESOLUTION PROCESS

13-4   The **conflict resolution process** consists of five steps that can be used at work and in your personal life. To apply the five steps requires understanding and acceptance of everything we have discussed up to this point in the chapter: application of assertiveness skills, understanding how to deal with various types of difficult people, support for the win/win approach to conflict resolution, and learning how to negotiate.

> *A misunderstanding is a failure to accurately understand the other person's point. A disagreement, in contrast, is a failure to agree, which would persist despite the most accurate understanding.*

Step One: Decide Whether You Have a Misunderstanding or a True Disagreement

David Stiebel, author of *When Talking Makes Things Worse!*, says a misunderstanding is a failure to accurately understand the other person's point. A disagreement, in contrast, is a failure to agree, which would persist despite the most accurate understanding. In a true disagreement, people want more than your explanation and further details; they want to change your mind.[15] When we fail to realize the distinction between these two possibilities, a great deal of time and energy may be wasted. Consider the following conflict situation.

As Sarah entered the driveway of her home, she could hardly wait to share the news with her husband Paul. Late that afternoon, she had met with her boss and learned she was the number-one candidate for a newly created administrative position. Sarah entered the house and immediately told Paul about the promotion opportunity. In a matter of seconds, it became apparent that he was not happy about the promotion. He said, "We don't need the extra money, and you do not need the headaches that come with an administrative position." Expecting a positive response, Sarah was very disappointed. In the heat of anger, Sarah and Paul both said things they would later regret.

If Sarah and Paul had asked each other a few questions, this conflict might have been avoided. Before arriving home, Sarah had already weighed the pros and cons of the new position and decided it was not a good career move; however, she wanted her husband's input before making the final decision. This conflict was not a true disagreement in which one person tries to change the other person's mind; it was a misunderstanding that was the result of incomplete information. If Sarah and Paul had fully understood each other's position, it would have become clear that a true disagreement did not exist.

Step Two: Define the Problem and Collect the Facts

The saying "A problem well defined is a problem half solved" is not far from the truth. It is surprising how difficult this step can be. Everyone involved needs to focus on the real cause of the conflict, not on what has happened as a result of it.

As you begin collecting information about the conflict, it may be necessary to separate facts from opinions or perceptions. Ask questions that focus on who is involved in the conflict, what happened, when, where, and why. What policies and procedures were involved?

Conflict resolution in the age of information offers us new challenges. As we are faced with information overload, we may be tempted to use the information we already have rather than search for the new information needed to guide a decision.[16]

"Can anyone else feel conflict creeping into the room?"

Step Three: Clarify Perceptions

Your perception is your interpretation of the facts surrounding the situations you encounter. Perceptions can have a tremendous influence on your behavior. In a conflict situation, it is therefore very important that you clarify all parties' perceptions of the problem. You can do this by trying to see the situation as others see it. Take the case of Laura, a sales representative who was repeatedly passed over for a promotion although her sales numbers were among the best in the department.

After a period of time, Laura became convinced that she was the victim of gender discrimination. She filed charges with the Equal Employment Opportunity Commission (EEOC), and a hearing was scheduled. When Laura's boss was given a chance to explain his actions, he described Laura as someone who was very dedicated to her family. He said, "It's my view that she would be unhappy in a sales management position because she would have to work longer hours and travel more." He did not see his actions as being discriminatory. Laura explained that she valued the time she spent with her husband and children, but achieving a management position was an important career goal.

Step Four: Generate Options for Mutual Gain

Once the basic problem has been defined, the facts surrounding it have been brought out, and everyone is operating with the same perceptions, everyone involved in the conflict should focus on generating options that will fix the problem. Some people, however, do not consider generating options to be part of the conflict resolution process. Rather than broadening the options for mutual gain, some people want to quickly build support for a single solution. The authors of the best-selling book *Getting to Yes* say, "In a dispute, people usually believe that they know the right answer—their view should prevail. They become trapped in their own point of view."[17] Group members should be encouraged to generate a wide variety of ideas and possibilities.

Step Five: Implement Options with Integrity

The final step in the conflict resolution process involves finalizing an agreement that offers win/win benefits to those in conflict. Sometimes, as the conflict resolution process comes to a conclusion, one or more parties in the conflict may be tempted to win an advantage that weakens the relationship. This might involve hiding information or using pressure tactics that violate the win/win spirit and weaken the relationship. Even the best conflict solutions can fail unless all conflict partners serve as "caretakers" of the agreement and the relationship.[18]

Establish timetables for implementing the solutions, and provide a plan to evaluate their effectiveness. On a regular basis, make a point to discuss with others how things are going to be sure that old conflict patterns do not resurface.

THE ROLE OF LABOR UNIONS IN CONFLICT RESOLUTION

`13-5` Since the 1930s, labor unions have had the authority to negotiate disputes between union members and management. This arrangement serves as an equalizing factor that allows organized workers the power necessary to challenge managers' decisions. The words *labor union* usually bring blue collar workers to mind, but professionals now make up a majority of the workforce. Lawyers, paralegals, judges, insurance agents, secretaries, and other

When CEO of Market Basket, Arthur T. Demoulas was fired, customers and 25,000 nonunionized workers revolted and went on strike for 40 days to demand reinstatement of the CEO they loved and respected. Two governors finally stepped in to draft an agreement to reinstate the CEO.

white collar workers have started to join unions in some areas. In May 2013, members of New York's UAW Local 2320 voted to go on strike when their employer, Legal Services NYC, pushed to cut benefits during a contract negotiation. Half of the members are lawyers.[19]

Most management–labor union disputes escalate when the employment contracts that establish the workers' wages, benefits, and working conditions expire and need to be renegotiated. The overwhelming majority of employment contracts are settled through **collective bargaining**, a process that defines the rights and privileges of both sides involved in the conflict and establishes the terms of employment and length of the contract (usually from three to five years). However, if labor and management cannot settle their differences, they may submit their disputes to one of the following:

- **Mediation**—A neutral third party listens to both sides and suggests solutions. It carries no binding authority. Both parties are free to reject or accept the mediator's decision.
- **Voluntary arbitration**—Both sides willingly submit their disagreements to a neutral party. The arbitrator's decision must be accepted by both sides.
- **Compulsory arbitration**—When the government decides that the labor–management dispute threatens national health and safety, or will damage an entire industry, it can appoint an arbitrator who dictates a solution that is binding on both sides and can be enforced in a court of law.

When collective bargaining, mediation, and arbitration are not enough to settle disputes, union leaders may recommend, and members may vote, to go on strike against their employers. A strike generally results in a lose/lose situation in which workers lose paychecks, employers lose sales, customers lose products or services, and communities lose economic stability. The Market Basket strike-boycott in 2014 experienced all of these losses, but this particular strike was unprecedented in the history of the United States.

Market Basket is a family-owned 71-store supermarket chain in New England with $4.6 billion in annual revenue. When CEO Arthur T. Demoulas was fired by his cousin and longtime rival, Arthur S. Demoulas and seven top executives, both employees and customers revolted. The 25,000 nonunionized workers went on strike for 40 days, demanding that the company reinstate their beloved CEO. Store shelves were mostly empty as workers refused to stock shelves and most customers elected to boycott the supermarket chain. The main issue fueling the strike was not contracts and higher wages; it was about reinstating a CEO who treated workers like loyal friends. Employees did not want to work for a company that valued profits more than people by cuttings costs and increasing profits. As the two-month strike raged on at a cost of $1 million a day, the governors of Massachusetts and New Hampshire finally stepped in to broker an agreement in the states' best interest, and Arthur T. Demoulas was reinstated as CEO.

This particular case is important because it was a strike without organized labor. Workers rejected offers to be represented by the Teamsters and United Food and Commercial Workers, bringing into question the future of organized labor.[20] Labor scholar Christopher Macklin said it was analogous to the American Revolution. "This is unheard-of in corporate America. It's like 1776—we get to pick who governs us."[21]

The On-Demand, App-Enabled Workforce

The convergence of technology and the decline in full-time employment has created a new category of workers who work on an on-demand freelance basis. Mobile apps have inspired new companies like Uber, Lyft, TaskRabbit, 99designs, and ODesk to provide customers with immediate, on-demand services paid by the hour or by the project, for services such as a driver, a handyman, an errand runner, or graphic design projects. This type of worker is similar, yet different from the way independent contractors have worked in the past. Companies employ workers who want the flexibility to work whenever and wherever they wish by using two simple tools most people already own: a smartphone and an app.

The on-demand, freelance lifestyle appeals to people who want to augment their income with a second job, but it's a stretch to call it full-time employment. A closer look reveals that in many cases, the likely winner of flexible, on-demand employment is the employer. Similar to independent contractor arrangements, employers are not required to pay benefits or even offer minimum wage. Some workers say this arrangement leaves them with all the financial burden and personal risk. Current law recognizes only two types of workers: employees and independent contractors. Employees are protected by minimum wages, workers' compensation, union-organizing rights, antidiscrimination statutes, and other benefits. Independent contractors do not receive any of these benefits and legal protections.[22] So before you jump at the chance to earn $25 an hour as an Uber driver, for example, think about the considerable wear and tear on your vehicle and weigh the true upside to joining the freelance nation.

LOOKING BACK: SUMMARY OF LEARNING OBJECTIVES

1. **List and describe some of the major causes of conflict in the workplace**.

   Conflicts among people at work happen every day and can arise because of changes within the organization, poor communication, value and culture clashes, confusing work policies and practices, competition for scarce resources, or adversarial management. Often, however, conflicts come from coworkers who refuse to carry their fair share of the workload or have a difficult personality. Although unresolved conflicts can have a negative effect on an organization's productivity, a difference of opinion sometimes has a positive effect by forcing team members toward creative and innovative solutions to problems.

2. **Use assertiveness skills in conflict situations**.

   Assertiveness skills are necessary when you want to maintain your rights during a conflict with someone else but want to avoid being overly aggressive, which means interfering with others' rights. Begin building assertiveness skills by tackling relatively minor issues first until you gain the confidence to take on those who try to take away your power. Use "I" statements rather than "you" statements so that the other person does not become defensive. Focus on fixing the problem rather than attacking the other person.

3. **Understand when and how to implement effective negotiation skills**.

   You can vastly improve your human relations skills when dealing with difficult people by learning when and how to intentionally implement Robert Maddux's five negotiating styles: avoidance style, accommodating style, win/lose style, problem-solving style, and compromising style. The Crucial Conversations Model, Figure 13.4, describes a helpful process to create a meaningful dialogue based on mutual understanding when opinions vary and emotions run strong.

4. **Identify key elements of the conflict resolution process**.

   When employees cannot solve their conflicts in an informal manner, many organizations create solutions through a conflict resolution process. The five-step conflict resolution process is described in this chapter.

5. **Discuss the role of labor unions in conflict resolution**.

   Labor leaders and business owners are finding that flexibility and innovation are far more effective than old adversarial styles of negotiating. If labor and management cannot settle their differences, they may submit their disputes to mediation, voluntary arbitration, or compulsory arbitration. When these methods cannot settle disputes, union members may vote to go on strike. This may cause workers to lose paychecks, employers to lose sales, customer to lose products and services, and communities to lose economic stability.

KEY TERMS

conflict, 282
conflict trigger, 283
nonassertive behavior, 285
assertive behavior, 285
aggressive behavior, 285

win/lose approach, 289
lose/lose approach, 289
win/win approach, 289
conflict resolution process, 293
collective bargaining, 296

mediation, 296
voluntary arbitration, 296
compulsory arbitration, 296

CAREER INSIGHT: DEALING WITH WORKPLACE BULLIES

Building a civilized workplace involves getting rid of workplace bullies. Workplace bullying can include sarcastic comments, physical threats, social exclusion, or work sabotage. Unlike sexual or racial harassment, this aggressive behavior is not necessarily illegal. But it does violate company policies that prohibit intimidation. Abusive supervisors and coworkers who cause emotional distress should not be tolerated. One of the most underutilized weapons in the arsenal against bullies is telling them the truth about the way they make you feel.

TRY YOUR HAND

1. Has there been someone in your life (now or in the past) that you just can't (or couldn't) stand? Explain the behaviors this person exhibits that get on your nerves. Carefully examine Figure 13.2, determine which category fits the person best, and then describe what you might do to help this person change his or her behavior. Be specific.

2. Describe a conflict that is disrupting human relations at school, home, or work. It might involve academic requirements at school, distribution of responsibilities at home, or hurt feelings at work.

Identify all the people involved in the conflict, and decide who should be involved in the conflict resolution process. Design a conflict resolution plan by following the steps given in this chapter. Implement your plan using The Crucial Conversations Model, Figure 13.4, and report the results of this conflict resolution process to other class members.

3. To learn more about your level of assertiveness, complete the following short quiz. Simply answer yes or no to each question and then interpret your score.

ARE YOU ASSERTIVE ENOUGH?

Take this short quiz from *The Instant Manager* to find out.

Being assertive is not the same as being aggressive. Assertiveness is confidence translated into action. It is neither bullying nor brow-beating, but simply allowing your convictions to carry a conversation. Honesty combined with a nonconfrontational manner will make assertiveness one of the most valuable tools in your managerial tool kit.

Answer Yes or No to each question. Do you...

Yes ❑	No ❑	1. Apologize when you don't have an instant solution to a problem?
Yes ❑	No ❑	2. Frequently apologize for your decisions?
Yes ❑	No ❑	3. Feel that you do not have the right to change your mind?
Yes ❑	No ❑	4. Feel guilty when you make mistakes, even when they can be fixed?
Yes ❑	No ❑	5. Automatically say yes when someone makes a request?
Yes ❑	No ❑	6. Feel foolish asking questions when you do not understand something?
Yes ❑	No ❑	7. Follow instructions without question?
Yes ❑	No ❑	8. Think your opinion does not count, especially if it differs from the majority?
Yes ❑	No ❑	9. Feel that you do not have the right to ask people to change their behavior toward you?
Yes ❑	No ❑	10. Feel guilty delegating or deferring tasks?
Yes ❑	No ❑	11. Have trouble walking away from an argument?

Total number of Yes [   ]

HOW TO INTERPRET YOUR SCORE

If you answered Yes to:

8 to 11 of the questions: You need serious improvement. Take an acting or public speaking course, review your accomplishments—whatever will boost your self-confidence.

4 to 7 of the questions: You are just squeaking by. Try some speaking and body-language techniques and learn to keep your cool.

0 to 3 of the questions: You are just about right. Keep it up!

Excerpted from *The Instant Manager—More than 100 Quick Tips & Techniques for Great Results,* by Cy Charney (AMACOM 2004).

4. To develop your assertiveness skills, find a partner who will join you for a practice session. The partner should assume the role of a friend, family member, or coworker who is doing something that causes you a great deal of frustration. (The problem can be real or imaginary.) Communicate your dislikes and feelings in a clear, direct manner without threatening or attacking. Then ask your partner to critique your assertiveness skills. Participate in several of these practice sessions until you feel confident that you have improved your assertiveness skills.

CRITICAL THINKING CHALLENGE

Think about and briefly summarize the various conflicts you witnessed among workers within an organization in which you worked as an employee or volunteer. Carefully examine each conflict scenario and determine if the root cause is the same as the generally perceived cause for the disagreements. What did you discover?

SELF-ASSESSMENT EXERCISE

For each of the following statements, circle the number from 1 to 5 that best represents your response: (1) strongly disagree (never do this); (2) disagree (rarely do this); (3) moderately agree (sometimes do this); (4) agree (frequently do this); (5) strongly agree (almost always do this).

A. In my attempts to resolve conflict, I strive for a solution that all parties can accept.	1	2	3	4	5
B. I will put off certain discussions that I know will be difficult longer than I should, rather than get into an argument.	1	2	3	4	5
C. When others don't deliver on a promise, there are times when I judge them more quickly than I should.	1	2	3	4	5
D. In a conflict situation, I make every effort to clarify perceptions.	1	2	3	4	5
E. In a conflict situation, I try to distinguish between a misunderstanding and a true disagreement.	1	2	3	4	5

After identifying your response to each item, select an attitude or skill you would like to improve. Prepare a written goal and then describe the steps you will take to achieve this goal.

YOU PLAY THE ROLE

Assume the role of a business manager for a large hospital. About three weeks ago, you received some incomplete medical records from Ashley Mason, the physician in charge of the emergency room. With a red pen, you marked the areas that were incomplete and sent the forms back to the doctor. You attached a terse note that requested the forms to be returned within 24 hours. Three days passed without a reply, and your anger increased each day. Finally, you sent the doctor an e-mail that basically accused Dr. Mason of incompetence in the area of medical record keeping. The doctor phoned you immediately and said the entire emergency room staff had been extremely busy and did not have a moment to spare. You replied that timely and accurate record keeping is the responsibility of every physician employed by the hospital. Unfortunately, your tone of voice and your selection of words were totally inappropriate. Basically, you treated Dr. Mason like a child who had misbehaved, and the doctor hung up on you. You immediately felt like a fool and regretted your behavior. The next day, the completed forms were returned to you. You have decided to meet with Dr. Mason. Your goal is to repair the damaged relationship and set the stage for effective communications in the future. Before meeting with another class member who will assume the role of Dr. Mason, review the information on the art of apologizing in Chapter 8 and information in this chapter on resolving conflicts.

BELOW THE SURFACE | AVOIDING GRIDLOCK

Henk Meijer/Alamy

The American political scene has been marred in conflict for years. It's not just frustrating, it's embarrassing to watch. Thankfully there are at least two people who know how to get along and play in the sandbox with some manners.

Judd Gregg, a former Republican senator and New Hampshire governor, says the only way to get things accomplished in a bipartisan way with colleagues with completely different views is to just do it. Contrary to media coverage of the U.S. Senate, Gregg says with only a few exceptions, people in the Senate are likable and reasonable. The key to working with people on the other side of the aisle is respect and reasonableness. He says there are almost always areas where progress can be made toward mutual goals, albeit different perspectives. No one expects the other person to give up their core values and beliefs.

Senator Wyden of Oregon, a Democrat, agrees. "You don't have to compromise principles or even like the other side. To get what you want, find a way for the other side to get what they want, too. This means talking 'to' the other side versus 'at' them, listening to their concerns, finding ways to address them through an understanding of what the other side really wants, and looking for ways to achieve it."[23]

Just think what the American government could accomplish if all Republicans and Democrats had good behavior and approached conflict in this manner!

QUESTIONS

ROLE PLAY

Meet in groups of four students per group. Two students will be Democrats and two will be Republicans. You will discuss two controversial and highly "charged" issues. Each side is trying to get the other to see their point of view and adopt their legislation, for or against the topic. Here are your questions.

1. Issue #1: There is a bill proposed to overturn the Roe vs. Wade decision. One team will try to get the other side to overturn this law and the other team will try to persuade the other side that it should remain in place. Each pair can meet separately first for a few moments to determine their strategy.

2. Issue #2: A bill is proposed to raise the minimum wage in every state in the United States by $5.00. One team is in favor of raising the minimum wage, arguing it is required to meet rising health-care costs and inflation. The other team largely favors businesses and is opposed to raising the minimum wage.

   Discuss each issue for 10 to 15 minutes using the Crucial Conversations Model and other material you have learned in this chapter. See if you can find the common ground the two senators describe, resulting in a mutually beneficial resolution.

CLOSING CASE | NOT WHAT THE DOCTOR ORDERED

When a Brazilian man went to the doctor to seek treatment for his hearing problem, he walked out the door with a vasectomy instead. How could this happen? It's easy when the patient doesn't think to question authority. "The strangest thing is that

he asked no questions when the doctor started preparations in the area which had so little to do with his ear," said a spokesperson for the clinic.[24]

When people go to a hospital or clinic, quality health care from qualified medical care professionals is an expectation, right? It is rare when people question the decisions of doctors or the care they receive. But maybe they should. An average of 195,000 Americans die annually from potentially preventable, in-hospital medical errors. The equivalent of 390 jumbo jets full of people are dying each year due to likely preventable, in-hospital medical errors, making this one of the leading killers in the United States, said Dr. Samantha Collier.[25]

In addition to deaths, more than two million infections occur in hospitals each year, many of which could be prevented by people simply washing their hands or by speaking up when they observe incompetence. Studies reveal that a majority of health-care workers regularly see colleagues take dangerous shortcuts, make mistakes, and appear critically incompetent, yet fewer than one in 10 speak up and share their full concerns.

QUESTIONS

1. You are a new nurse in a hospital who is preparing to assist in the operating room. You observe the primary surgeon scrubbing for the surgery, and just before he enters the OR, he stops to sign some papers. How would you approach the surgeon?

2. You work for a tyrant of a doctor who has fired several nurses in your department. You just saw him make an error that might endanger the patient, but you are afraid to speak up. You need the job. What would you do?

3. You are a doctor in a reputable hospital and work with a physician who you regard as incompetent in many areas. Do you speak to the doctor directly or opt to speak to your boss? What are the advantages and disadvantages of each approach?

CHAPTER 13 ENDNOTES

1. Elizabeth Bernstein, "Big Explosions, Small Reasons," *Wall Street Journal*, October 16, 2012, D1, pp. 193–194.
2. Dudley Weeks, *The Eight Essential Steps to Conflict Resolution* (New York: G. P. Putnam's Sons, 1992), p. 7.
3. Ibid., pp. 7–8.
4. Susan M. Heathfield, "Fight for What's Right: Ten Tips to Encourage Meaningful Conflict" [cited 7 February 2006]. Available from http://www.about.com
5. Robert Kreitner and Carlene M. Cassidy, *Management*, 12th ed. (Mason, OH: Cengage Learning, 2011), pp. 418–420.
6. Carol Kleiman, "How to Deal with a Co-worker Who's Getting on Your Nerves, *San Jose Mercury News*, October 3, 1999, p. PCI.
7. "Assertiveness: More Than a Forceful Attitude," *Supervisory Management*, February 1994, p. 3.
8. American Management Association, http://www.amanet.org [retrieved 23 February 2015].
9. Danny Ertel, "Turning Negotiation into a Corporate Capability," *Harvard Business Review*, May/June 1999, p. 3.
10. Rob Walker, "Take It or Leave It: The Only Guide to Negotiating You Will Ever Need," *Inc.*, August 2003, pp. 65–77.
11. Kurt Salzinger, "Psychology on the Front Lines," *Psychology Today*, May/June 2002, p. 34.
12. Claire Suddath, "The Art of Haggling," *Bloomberg Businessweek*, November 26–December 2, 2012.
13. Kerry Patterson, Joseph Grenny, Ron McMillan, and Al Switzler, *Crucial Conversations: Tools for Talking When Stakes Are High*, McGraw-Hill, 2002, p. 20. For more information about the Crucial Conversations Model, visit www.crucialconversations.com
14. Ibid., p. 98.
15. David Stiegel, *When Talking Makes Things Worse!* (Dallas: Whithall & Nolton, 1997), p. 17
16. Roger Fisher and Alan Sharp, *Getting It Done* (New York: Harper Business, 1998), pp. 81–83.
17. Roger Fisher and William Ury, *Getting to Yes* (New York: Penguin Books, 1981), p. 59.
18. Dudley Weeks, *The Eight Essential Steps to Conflict Resolution* (New York: G. P. Putnam's Sons, 1992), p. 228.
19. Alana Semuels, "White-Collar Workers Are Turning to Labor Unions," (*Los Angeles Times*), *News and Observer*, May 28, 2013, p. 3E.
20. Kate Aronoff, "Non-Union Market Basket Workers Bring a Complicated Victory for Labor, Waging Nonviolence, September 1, 2014, http://wagingnonviolence.org/2014/09/non-union-market-basket-workers-bring-complicated-victory-labor/?pf=true.

21. Ibid.

22. Lauren Weber and Rachel Emma Silverman, "On-Demand Workers: We Are Not Robots," *Wall Street Journal*, Jan. 27, 2015, http://www.wsj.com/articles/on-demand-workers-we-are-not-robots-1422406524.

23. Judd Gregg, "Talk to a Democrat" and Ron Wyden, "Talk to a Republican," Businessweek, June 18, 2012, page 88.

24. "Earache Brazilian loses more than hearing," *BBC News*, Wednesday, August 20, 2003. http://news.bbc.co.uk/2/hi/health/3169049.stm.

25. "Study Finds Nearly 200,000 Deaths Annually from Hospital Errors," *Consumer Affairs*, August 12, 2004, retrieved from http://www.consumeraffairs.com/news04/hospital_errors.html

PART 5

Special Challenges in Human Relations

Responding to Personal and Work-Related Stress

TIP OF THE ICEBERG | QUIET THE MIND AND HEIGHTEN AWARENESS

Most successful organizations are searching for ways to help employees cope with stress. The Seattle Seahawks football team is no exception. Michael Gervais, a sports psychologist, is an important member of the coaching staff. He has the freedom to roam the training facility, locker room, and the sidelines of every game to make sure team members feel valued and can communicate effectively in critical situations. He has introduced players to the practice of "mindfulness," the ability to pay precise, nonjudgmental attention to the details of our experience as it arises and subsides, not rejecting anything. Instead of struggling to get away from experiences we find difficult, we practice being able to be with them.[1] The practice of mindfulness, first discussed in Chapter 9, will be discussed in more detail later in this chapter.

Salesforce.com, the cloud-based software giant, is experimenting with a communal workspace where employees can bring their dog to work. The doggy day care program is limited to a small number of employees who can work while supervising their pets. Sara Varni, a vice president of marketing, uses this perk when her dog walker is not available. She says Memphis, her Australian shepherd, seems to elevate everyone's mood on days she brings him to work.[2]

Feeling stressed? Why not take a break and go for a walk? Employees at American Traffic Solutions Inc. in Tempe, Arizona, are encouraged to use the indoor walking track. The track winds around the office, so it's accessible to every walker. Some employees say they can do a lap in about 70 seconds.[3]

Throughout your career, you will encounter many anxiety-provoking and stressful events. We live in a world of continuous change that often creates a heightened sense of urgency. Many organizations are searching for ways to wring more productivity from a smaller number of employees. Tensions build as people work longer hours and live with the possibility that they may be part of the next round of layoffs.

These job applicants are no doubt feeling a great deal of stress. During a period of high unemployment, the competition for fewer jobs is more intense.

THE STRESS FACTORS IN YOUR LIFE

14-1   **Stress** refers to two simultaneous events: an external stimulus, called a stressor, and the physical and emotional responses to that stimulus (anxiety, fear, muscle tension, surging heart rate, and so on). Stress can come from your environment, your body, or your mind.[4] Environmental stress at work may be caused by noise, safety concerns, windowless settings, long hours, or unrealistic deadlines. Some bodily stress can be attributed to poorly designed work areas that produce eye strain, shoulder tension, or lower-back discomfort. However, the stress that comes from our minds is the most common type of stress. Research conducted at McGill University in Montreal describes the negative impact of stress on interpersonal relations:

> It's well established that stress and the hormones secreted when we're stressed alter brain function. They disrupt aspects of learning and memory, impair judgment and impulse control, and increase the risks of anxiety and depression. As it turns out, the hormones also disrupt aspects of empathy.[5]

There can be positive aspects of mental stress. Stress *can* be a powerful stimulus for growth if it motivates you to do your best work. It can build within you the energy and desire needed to perform effectively. It can also promote greater awareness and help you focus on getting tasks completed quickly and efficiently.[6] However, a great deal of the mental stress we encounter every day is caused by our negative thinking and faulty reasoning. For example, someone with large house payments and a great deal of personal debt may begin to worry excessively about the possibility of a layoff; the person who lacks self-confidence may fear each technology change that is introduced at work; or workers in organizations being merged may mentally anguish over who will be laid off next.

However, a great deal of the mental stress we encounter every day is caused by our negative thinking and faulty reasoning.

Responding to Stress

Stress responses consist of three elements: the event or thought (stressor) that triggers stress, your perception of it, and your response to it.[7] In his book *Stress for Success*, James Loehr suggests that as you are exposed to new stressors, you should try to respond in ways that help you establish mental, physical, and emotional balance.[8] Unfortunately, most of us do not take the time to train our minds and bodies so that we build our capacity to handle the stress in our lives.

Total Person Insight

"…most people don't know when they have reached their limits and need to stop saying yes to new activities. Learning to notice and heed early warning signs of overload takes practice and planning."

Source: Sue Shellenbarger, "Driven to Achieve More at Home and Work, Some Find a Sweet Spot; The Signs of Impending Overload," *Wall Street Journal*, May 14, 2014, p. D1.

When people are under stress, surges in the stress hormones adrenaline and cortisol strongly affect their reasoning. When demands become too great for us to handle, soaring cortisol levels and an increase in adrenaline can paralyze our mind's critical abilities. Critical thinking, planning, and creativity are greatly diminished.[9]

As continuous stress builds in a work environment, it may cause a person to respond harshly to a colleague, feel overwhelmed or helpless, and to lose motivation to work on projects, resulting in lost productivity and effectiveness.[10]

Everyone reacts differently to stress, so there is no single best way to manage it. You must train yourself to respond effectively to the stressors in your personal and professional life so that you will not only survive, but thrive. The first step is to understand what might cause or trigger stress.

MAJOR CAUSES OF STRESS

14-2 A study by the American Psychological Association found that 65 percent of the working people in the United States view job stress as a major problem in their lives. Some say the pace at work is so dizzying that it takes them hours to finally relax after the workday ends. Many workers are experiencing *chronic stress*, which often results in an erratic heart rate, tensing of muscles, insomnia, and irritability. David Posen, author of "Is Work Killing You?" says chronic stress reduces all of the things that help productivity—mental clarity, short-term memory, and decision making.[11] Most of us can benefit from learning how to pinpoint the sources of stress in our lives and learn to respond to them in a more effective manner.

> *Some say the pace at work is so dizzying that it takes them hours to finally relax after the workday ends.*

Work/Life Balance

What do workers want most from their jobs? Many surveys indicate that work/life balance is the most important employment benefit.[12] Unfortunately, many workers are unable or unwilling to strike a better work/life balance. In an age of economic uncertainty and constant communication, it has become increasingly more difficult to find balance between our work and the rest of life.[13]

Long Hours/Irregular Schedules. Companies increasingly need employees who can work flexible schedules. Evening shifts, rotating shifts, 12-hour workdays, and weekend work often add stress to workers' lives. Tess Mateo, a director in the CEO's office at PricewaterhouseCoopers, recalls an early morning conference call with eight coworkers who were working in six time zones.[14] When people in U.S. companies schedule important meetings requiring participation, they often don't consider the time zones of employees in other countries.

In recent years, a growing number of workers call workloads excessive and say that they are stressed by increased pressure on the job. Many of the companies that have slashed their payrolls now spread the same amount of work among fewer people. Years of multitasking and workaholism have left workers across the global economic and geographic spectrum feeling exhausted.[15]

Change

Changes in the workplace come in many forms, including the need to do a job faster, to master advanced technology, or to take on a new work assignment. Consider employees who have been accustomed to working alone and now work with a team, or employees who have held jobs that required little contact with the public and now must spend a great deal of time with clients, patients, or customers.

As we look to the future, there are two realities to keep in mind. First, management personnel above you are trying to cope with their own high-pressure responsibilities, so you are not likely to get much emotional handholding from them. Second, the pace of change is not likely to slow down. The authors of *The Stress of Organizational Change* say the secret to coping with high-velocity change is *surrender:* "Surrendering to change does the most to eliminate the stress. It creates the opportunity for *breakthrough* rather than *breakdown.*" They note that much of the pressure we feel these days is self-induced

"What's this I hear about you not having an ulcer?"

stress. Resisting change, or hanging onto old habits and beliefs, requires the investment of a great deal of emotional energy.[16]

Multitasking

It's Monday morning, and you just finished a one-hour meeting with a cross-functional team. You promised the team members you would send them an e-mail that summarizes the decisions made during the meeting. As you walk back to your office, you glance at your tablet and 39 e-mails are waiting for a response. A text message from your boss indicates she wants an updated product shipping report ASAP. Your afternoon includes three meetings, and you must leave the office at 4:30 p.m. to attend your daughter's soccer game.[17] Welcome to the world of multitasking.

While multitasking is common for most people, research finds that it can be counterproductive and can actually lower productivity. Researchers at the University of California found that many workers experience frequent distractions throughout the day, and it often takes up to 25 minutes to return to an abandoned task.

Although multitasking can be stressful, we must find ways to embrace it. We are now living in a complex, fast-response world, and our challenge is to immediately prioritize and address whatever task is most critical. The good news is we can get someone's attention at a moment's notice. In today's environment, not being able to multitask would probably be highly stressful.[18]

Work Environment

The place a person works—open office, cubicle, or remote location—matters less because computers and mobile communication technologies are at the center of our lives. As countless workers spend the majority of their day sitting in front of a computer they may be oblivious to the physical stress this causes on their bodies over time. It may cause back pain, spine and neck problems, aching shoulders, sore elbows, eye fatigue, and carpal tunnel syndrome (a repetitive stress wrist injury). Sitting in a chair that offers little support, hunched over a laptop, or staring at a poorly positioned monitor takes its toll.

Experts in **ergonomics**—techniques for adapting the work environment to the human body—say that anyone who spends hours in front of a computer should become knowledgeable about the basics of ergonomics such as eye level, arm and hand position, and posture to understand how something as simple as sitting can either generate energy or create fatigue and long-term, often irreversible, pain and medical problems.

Work environment stressors can include other factors such as a windowless work area, a small workspace, feeling uncomfortable from working in close proximity to other people, or a cubicle that lacks privacy. If you don't have much control over your work environment, then you need to focus on the things you can change, such as putting pictures of family and friends around your computer, adding flowers or a plant, and taking short breaks to walk outside. All these things help contribute to a positive mood and work performance.

Noise Pollution

Noise is unwanted sound, such as the roar of traffic, your neighbor's loud music, or the loud voice of the person who works nearby. It can increase your stress level without your conscious awareness. It is the uncontrollability of noise, rather than its intensity, that often is the greatest irritant. The noise you can't shut off is likely to have a negative effect on your emotional well-being. Persistent exposure to noise can cause headaches, sleep disturbances, anxiety, and depression. Research indicates that noise affects people more than any other work area pollutant, yet it's not regulated like other forms of pollution.[19]

"QUIET, PLEASE!"

Noise is the enemy of any worker who needs concentration in a space (such as a cubicle) that can't be soundproofed with the closing of a door.

- If you have an exceptionally loud voice, get in the habit of speaking more softly, especially in open spaces.
- Many people tend to unconsciously talk louder when they're on the phone. Place a Post-it reminder next to your phone to lower your voice while talking on the phone.
- If you must listen to music at your desk, keep it low or use headphones if your company allows them.
- When you ask someone to quiet down, do it as politely as possible.

Source: Adapted from *The Etiquette Advantage in Business (2nd ed.) Peggy Post and Peter Post* (New York: William Morrow, 2005), 68–69.

Incompetent Leaders

Organizations often promote people into supervisory positions when they exhibit extraordinary talents in a specific technical field. The most talented electrician becomes maintenance supervisor. The most efficient surgical nurse is promoted to nursing supervisor. The top salesperson is made sales manager. But technical superstars may be poor supervisors. And studies indicate that incompetent supervisors are a major source of stress in the workplace.[20]

Work and Family Transitions

In our fast-moving world, most of us have learned that certain transitions are inevitable. A **transition** can be defined as the experience of being forced to give up something and face a change. It is difficult for anyone to say with any degree of certainty what he or she will face in the future.

Uncertainty about the future is a major trigger of the stress process. Anneli Rufus, writing in *Spirituality & Health* magazine, says, "Chronic worry gets us stuck in ruts—mental, physical, emotional, behavioral—that are literally sickening."[21] Chronic worriers are more likely to engage in dangerous habits such as drinking, smoking, drug use, and overeating. Later in this chapter we will discuss ways to curb worry.

Rumination

Throughout your career, you will face countless disappointments and defeats. Your boss said she would like to give you a salary increase but didn't have the authority to approve raises. Later, you find out that she lied. You miss a team meeting because of an illness. Later you find out that a team member was highly critical of your work on an important project. Do you confront these foes or suffer in silence?

Most of us revisit personal and work-related problems too often. The process of replaying an incident over and over in our minds is referred to in the field of psychology as **rumination**. Ruminative thinking, the recurring intrusion of thoughts about negative events, can result in loss of concentration, loss of sleep, and feelings of depression.[22]

Warning Signals of Too Much Stress

In today's stress-filled world, it makes sense to become familiar with the signals that indicate you are experiencing too much stress in your life. Table 14.1 offers information about physical, emotional, and relational symptoms that may need your attention.

Table 14.1 ■ **Symptoms of Stress**

PHYSICAL	EMOTIONAL	RELATIONAL
■ Sleep disturbances	■ Nervousness, anxiety	■ Increased arguments
■ Tension or migraine headaches	■ Depression, moodiness	■ Isolation from social activities
■ Hair loss	■ Irritability, frustration	■ Conflict with coworkers or employers
■ Sweaty palms or hands	■ Lack of concentration	■ Overreactions
■ Skin problems	■ Substance abuse	■ Road rage
	■ Memory problems	

Source: Adapted from Sheila Hutman, Jaelline Jaffe, Robert Segal, Heather Larson, Lisa F. Dumke, "Stress: Signs and Symptoms, Use and Effects," *Helpguide: Expert, Non-Commercial Information on Mental Health & Lifelong Wellness,* Reprinted with permission from http://www.helpguide.org. © 2006 Helpguide.org. All rights reserved.

When these symptoms persist, you are at risk for serious health problems because stress can exhaust your immune system, making you more vulnerable to colds, flu, fatigue, and infections. Research demonstrates that stress is linked to the six leading causes of death.[23]

STRESS-MANAGEMENT STRATEGIES

14-3   Ideally, we should do everything in our power to eliminate those elements that cause us stress—lack of work/life balance, change, multitasking, noise pollution, long hours/irregular schedules, incompetent leaders, work/family transitions, and rumination—but this is not generally a realistic option. We can try to reduce them, but eliminating them is often not possible. We can, however, learn ways to manage our reactions to the stressors in our daily lives and minimize their negative impact.

There is no one-size-fits-all way to reduce stress. You have to become aware of what works best for you. Do not wait until you are feeling stressed before you employ stress-management techniques; make them part of your daily routine. Once you become aware of what creates a stressful response in you (stress is very individualized), begin looking for stress-management strategies that will help you cope with the stressful situations. Step one is to understand the practice of mindfulness.

Mindfulness

The practice of mindfulness has entered the American mainstream in recent years. Dr. Jon Kabat-Zinn, founder of the Stress Reduction Clinic at the University of Massachusetts Medical Center, is given a great deal of credit for popularizing this important medical advancement. He developed the Mindfulness-Based Stress Reduction (MBSR) program used today in medical centers, hospitals, and clinics around the world.

Mindfulness involves paying attention on purpose, in the present moment, and nonjudgmentally. The idea is to quiet the mind and heighten awareness. It is a discipline all its own that extends into all aspects of life. And while it is simple, it is not easy to maintain mindfulness, even over very short periods of time.[24] U.S. Representative Tim Ryan describes mindfulness this way:[25]

Practicing mindfulness is very much about taking responsibility for your own state of mind and your own condition. It's very much about self-reliance.

In today's high-stress work environment, it's important to set aside uninterrupted time to enjoy the most important aspects of your life, including family, friends, and time for yourself.

To better understand the practice of mindfulness, let's return to the discussion of work and family transitions. We noted that uncertainty about the future is a major trigger of stressful worrying. Keven Gyoerkoe, author of *10 Simple Solutions to Worry*, describes ways to curb worry:[26]

- *First*, focus your attention on the worry and answer this question: Is the worry productive or unproductive? Productive worry is based on threats that are relatively immediate and likely to happen.
- *Second*, if your worry is unproductive, challenge your negative thoughts. Ask yourself, "How many times have I been right about this worry in the past?" "Is there any productive action I can take?"

Keep in mind that the success of mindfulness is to "be in the moment," and maintaining awareness of your thoughts, feelings, and bodily sensations.

Sleep

Perhaps one of the most effective strategies for managing the negative aspects of stress is getting enough quality sleep. Growth hormones and repair enzymes are released and various chemical restoration processes occur during sleep. (This explains why children need considerably more sleep than adults.) To train your body so that you can deepen your capacity to handle stress, follow these guidelines to improve your sleep recovery periods:

- Develop a sleep ritual: Go to bed and get up at the same time as often as possible.
- Mentally wind down before going to bed. Avoid stressful activities.
- Avoid central nervous system stimulants such as caffeine, chocolate, alcohol, or nicotine near bedtime.
- Keep your bedroom cool, well ventilated, and dark.[27]

Many workers get less than the recommended amount of sleep (seven to eight hours) at night and therefore experience daytime drowsiness. This problem is so widespread that many employers encourage employees to take a short nap. Most employees are more productive and less apt to make fatigue-induced errors after waking from a short nap.[28]

Exercise

Study after study has proven that exercise, for most people, is the number one treatment for stress and tension because it releases pleasure-inducing chemicals called endorphins. Exercise designed to reduce stress is not necessarily strenuous and may include aerobic exercise such as walking, swimming, low-impact aerobics, tennis, or jogging. Even gentle exercise such as yoga or tai chi will help you manage your daily stress and improve motivation.

Unfortunately, about 70 percent of Americans do not exercise regularly, and nearly 40 percent are not active at all. Too many people fail to take advantage of the physical and mental benefits of exercise. These benefits include lower cholesterol, weight loss, increased mental alertness, and a stronger heart.

Several companies understand the importance of fun and exercise. They might place foosball or ping pong tables in the lunch room to not only give employees a quick energy boost, but also to improve employees' performance by making them happier. Many companies have on-site exercise facilities or provide reimbursement for joining a neighborhood athletic club. Missy Park, chief executive of Title Nine, a women's athletic-wear company, wants fitness to be part of the company culture. She developed a 2,200-square-foot gym that is located in the middle of its main office. The gym is equipped with treadmills, spinning bikes, a bench press, weights, and other exercise equipment.[29]

Meditation

Mindfulness practice, paying close, nonjudgmental attention to the details of your experiences, prepares you to embrace meditation. **Meditation** is a relaxation technique that

Companies such as Playworks are combining employees' needs for recreation with socially-responsible initiatives, allowing employees to interact with children in team-building activities. Here Mattel and Playworks volunteers are enjoying a Winter Wonderland with LA kids at a Mattel event.

slows your pulse, respiration, and brainwave activity and lowers your blood pressure. It produces feelings of contentment, calmness, and heightened awareness. Meditation is sometimes called the smart person's bubble bath. About 10 million Americans say they practice some form of meditation.[30] Many of the world's most successful business people including Tony Robbins and Arianna Huffington start each day with meditation. Tony Robbins uses a process he calls "priming" that includes deep breathing to put himself into a positive mental state.

Scientific studies show that meditation can have a profound stress-reducing effect because it trains and conditions the mind in the same way exercise trains and conditions the body. Neuroscientists found that monks who spend years meditating actually grow their left prefrontal cortex, the part of the brain most responsible for feeling happy. Practicing meditation regularly can permanently rewire the brain to raise levels of happiness, lower stress, and improve immune function.[31]

Richard Davidson's research at the University of Wisconsin in Madison suggests that through regular meditation, the brain is reoriented from a stressful fight-or-flight mode to one of acceptance, a shift that increases contentment with the realities of life. The process effectively deactivates the frontal areas of the brain, where sensory information is received and processed. Meditation allows people to quietly and intentionally detach from their emotional reactions so that they can respond appropriately. It allows them to peacefully observe their stress-producing thoughts and then choose to release them.[32] Most meditation techniques involve these elements:

1. Sit or lie down in a comfortable, quiet place where you are not likely to be disturbed.
2. Intentionally relax the muscles of your body from your toes to your head. Breathe slowly and deeply, and check every part of your body to make sure you're not holding tension.

3. Breathe in and out gently through your nose; take one breath in and one breath out, over and over again. Allow your mind to settle into your breathing, which activates the body's natural calming signals.

4. Train yourself to think about the calm and peaceful present. If your mind drifts, just slowly bring it back to focusing on your breathing.

human RELATIONS *in Action*

BREATHE BETTER: THE MOST BASIC MEDICINE

Slow, deep breathing can trigger a relaxation response in the body that slows the heart and reduces stress. Taking about five to seven breaths a minute can slow your heart rate compared with a typical 12 to 18 breaths a minute. This is one of the easiest ways to improve mental and physical health.

Source: Sumathi Reddy, "Breathe Better: Doctors Try Using the Most Basic Medicine," *Wall Street Journal*, January 27, 2015, p. D1.

Solitude

Those who are constantly in touch with others can benefit from the therapeutic effect of solitude.

Although some people feel uncomfortable when alone, many others feel "over-connected" because of the need to constantly respond to cell phone, e-mail, Facebook, Twitter, and text messages. Those who are constantly in touch with others can benefit from the therapeutic effect of solitude. Solitude can be viewed as an emotional breather, a restorer of energy, and a form of rest similar to sleep. Ester Buchholz, author of *The Call of Solitude*, says alone-time is a great protector of the self and the human spirit. She also notes that solitude is often required for the unconscious to process thoughts and events.[33] To experience the benefits of solitude, get up 20 minutes earlier in the morning. Use this time for meditation, journal writing, or just sitting in silence. Enjoy this period of solitude free from the current pressures and demands on your life.

Resilience

Resilience means being capable of bouncing back when you are confronted with stressful situations. At 3M's headquarters in Maplewood, Minnesota, more than 7,000 employees have completed a "Resilience at Work" training program that covers such diverse topics as financial planning, time management, and parenting. These topics represent those factors in a person's life that could cause stress if they got out of control. Participants are taught to determine what issues are within their control and how to deal with them when they get out of control.

Resilience is not just a personal characteristic; it applies to teams as well. When people have confidence in themselves, in one another, and in an organization, it motivates people to push the boundaries and strive to achieve more without fear of making a mistake. Rosabeth Moss Kanter says that teams that are immersed in a culture of accountability, collaboration, and initiative are more likely to believe that they can weather any storm.[34]

HOW TO BEAT STRESS IN 10 MINUTES OR LESS

■ **Pet a dog**. Not only will it lower your blood pressure, it will lower the dog's too.

■ **Take a 10-minute walk**. It's the simplest, most effective way to reduce anxiety and improve your mood.

- **Call your mom**. Research proves that calling your mom (or getting a hug) is a powerful way to lower your stress. It floods the system with oxytocin and washes away cortisol caused by stress.

- **Socialize**. There is a good reason you feel so good when you hang out with friends. Your body needs it. Research has shown that the more social connections a person has, the healthier they are. It reduces anxiety, improves concentration and focus, and strengthens your heart and immune system.

Source: Adapted from Monika Rice, "The Mother of All Stress Relief," *Spirituality & Health*, November–December 2010.

USING POSITIVE PSYCHOLOGY TO COMBAT STRESS

14-4   In this section, we will revisit some of the positive psychology concepts covered in Chapter 10. We will describe how you can apply a positive mindset to reduce stress in all areas of your life. Happiness is more than just a mood; it's a way of living and working. Each person has a different "happiness baseline" and fortunately, it's a baseline that can be raised. Over time, by learning how to raise your baseline, you can achieve higher levels of happiness. The highs and lows of emotions can be influenced with positive thoughts and experiences.

Laugh and Have Fun

Laughter is a gentle exercise of the body, a form of "inner jogging." When you laugh, your immune system is given a boost, stress-related hormones such as cortisol are reduced, and your respiratory function is improved.[35] Having fun while you are on the job does not exclude being serious about your work and caring about doing a good job. People can have fun at work without being silly or inappropriate. The goal is to create a positive, fun-loving atmosphere that helps reduce stress levels. Businesses do this in unique ways. Lego Systems holds an annual "Stress Free Day" for its 11,700 employees where they are encouraged to take a break from work to get massages or manicures or play basketball or volleyball. Other companies create a playful and relaxing environment by having open and creative workspaces, or by allowing people to bring their dogs to work.

Many people have lost touch with what is fun for them. Ann McGee-Cooper, author of *You Don't Have to Go Home from Work Exhausted*, recommends making a list of things that are fun for you and then estimating the time they take.[36] This exercise may help you realize that there is plenty of time for fun things in your life. A walk in the park will require only 20 minutes, and reading the comics takes only five minutes out of your day.

Commit Random Acts of Kindness

Many studies have proven that acts of kindness toward friends, family, or even strangers decreases stress levels and improves mental health. In one research study, participants who were told to complete five acts of kindness toward others felt much happier throughout the course of the day, and they continued to feel happier in the days following the experiment.[37] Take a few minutes and write a thank-you note to someone who has helped you in some way.

Regain or Let Go of Control

Another way people experience stress is when they feel they have no control in a situation. They worry and feel stressed by things beyond their control such as the stock

ZUMA/Alamy

Many employers such as Lego encourage their employees to take adequate personal time for themselves, even instituting an annual dedicated "Stress Free Day" when employees are encouraged to take a break from work to have massages or participate in recreational activities.

market, the price of housing, or losing their jobs. Needless worry about things outside of our control is not only a waste of time, it robs people of energy and time that can be put toward other, more productive things they can control.

Try this exercise the next time you feel worried and anxious.

1. On a sheet of paper draw lines to make three columns. In the first column, make a list of all the things that you feel stressed about.
2. When you are done with this, write the words "Control" at the top of the second column and "Can't Control" at the top of the third column.
3. Go through each item on the list and put a check in the column that corresponds to whether you can control it or not.
4. Cross off the things that have a "can't control" check next to them. This should actually give you some relief—and renewed energy.
5. Review the list of items you can control. Develop goals and an action plan for each item that will help you cope or deal more effectively with the stress it causes.

Total Person Insight

"It is impossible to live without failing at something, unless you live so cautiously that you might as well not have lived at all."

Source: J. K. Rowling, *Harvard Business Review*, April 2011, p. 103.

Dogs are best friends and coworkers to employees at Silicon Valley-based Zynga. Zynga is a major provider of social video game services headquartered in San Francisco.

COPING WITH PSYCHOLOGICAL DISORDERS

14-5   In the ideal scenario, when a stressful situation ends, hormonal signals switch off the *fight-or-flight* response, and the body returns to normal. Unfortunately, stress does not always let up. If you are under stress day after day and year after year, your hormonal response never shuts down. This can have a hazardous, even lethal, effect on your body and mental health.[38]

More than one in four American adults has a diagnosable mental-health disorder according to the National Institute of Mental Health. However, in a work setting coworkers and managers may have no idea that a problem exists. Some companies such as Prudential Financial and DuPont are training managers to identify signs of distress in workers.[39] Keep in mind there is no shame in mental illness. There is only shame in not seeking treatment.

Anxiety

Anxiety is a condition in which intense feelings of apprehension are longstanding and usually disruptive. Millions of Americans struggle with unwanted anxiety, and the cost in terms of suffering and lost productivity is very high. For most people, anxious feelings surface from time to time, but they are neither longstanding nor disruptive. If you have ever been tense before taking an exam or making a presentation, you have some idea of what anxiety feels like.[40]

Anxiety becomes a *disorder* only when it persists and prevents you from leading a normal life. Psychiatrists have found that there are several different anxiety disorders. A *phobia*, an irrational fear of a specific object or situation, represents one type of anxiety.

Claustrophobia (fear of confined spaces) and agoraphobia (fear of crowds and public places) are two of the many phobias that can have a disruptive effect on a person's daily life.[41]

What is the best treatment for anxiety? Many anxious states are caused by stress, so consider using the stress-management methods described in this chapter. Various methods of relaxation, for example, can lessen the severity of anxiety symptoms. However, when self-help methods do not bring the desired results, seek professional help (see Figure 14.1).[42]

Depression

Depression is a mood disorder, not a simple sadness. It is a major risk factor for suicide. Nearly 19 million American adults experience it. This psychological disorder costs U.S. businesses nearly $70 billion annually in lost productivity, medical expenditures, and other related expenses. People of all ages can experience depression, but it primarily affects workers in their most productive years: the 20s through 40s.[43]

When depression seriously affects a person's productivity on the job or in interpersonal relationships, psychiatrists consider that person to have a depression. Symptoms such as withdrawal, overwhelming sadness, or hopelessness may persist for weeks or months.

In most cases, depression is a treatable disorder, but it often requires a variety of approaches. An important U.S. study on depression found that two-thirds of patients achieve remission if they stick with therapy. Persisting in treatment is very important.[44] Many employers have found that investing in therapy for depressed employees can reduce absenteeism while improving workers' health.[45] To learn more about therapy options, see Figure 14.1.

Figure 14.1 ■ Getting Professional Help

Anxiety Disorders Association of America http://www.adaa.org	▶ The mission of the ADAA is to promote the prevention, treatment, and cure of anxiety disorders and to improve the lives of all people who suffer from them.
Depression and Bipolar Support Alliance http://www.dbsalliance.org	▶ This organization runs local support groups around the country for people coping with depression and bipolar disorder.
National Alliance on Mental Illness http://www.nami.org	▶ NAMI offers support groups and courses to help people with psychiatric disorders, as well as family members living with and caring for the mentally ill.
The Therapy Directory http://therapists.psychology today.com/rms/prof_search.php	▶ *Psychology Today* magazine maintains a searchable database people can use to find a therapist in their area.
The Mental Health Association http://www.depressionscreening.com	▶ The Mental Health Association offers a free depression screening test, which may help identify depressive symptoms and determine whether a further evaluation by a medical or mental health professional is necessary.
Online Clinics http://www.onlineclinics.com	▶ Online Clinics was created to serve clinics, clinicians, and patients who want to find quality health care services online.

Source: Adapted from Leila Abbound, "Mental Illness Said to Affect One-Quarter of Americans", *Wall Street Journal*, June 6, 2005.

Burnout

Burnout is a gradually intensifying pattern of physical, psychological, and behavioral dysfunction that evolves in response to a continuous flow of stressors.[46] When you experience burnout, you feel that your energy fuel tank is operating on empty. Just as the engine of a car literally stops running without fuel and oil, a complete mental or physical breakdown can result from burnout. The most common symptoms of burnout include the following:

- Increased detachment from coworkers, customers, or clients
- Increased tardiness, absenteeism, cynicism, and moodiness
- Increased disorientation: forgetfulness or low concentration
- Increased personal problems: drug or alcohol abuse, decreased social contacts, or marital discord

Everyone experiences one or two of these symptoms from time to time. But a person experiencing burnout exhibits these behaviors with increasing frequency and intensity. A candidate for burnout is likely to be someone who can't seem to "turn work off," needs to feel in control of their work, puts work before their families and personal lives, and puts in long hours at work.[47]

 HOW TO AVOID BURNOUT

- Avoid the "work martyr complex" by spending time away from work: use your vacation time, take a sabbatical, stop working 60 hours a week, etc.
- Stop allowing communication technologies to rob you of time, energy, and sanity. Some workers spend 10 to 15 hours each week checking e-mail.
- Reduce stress levels by enrolling in yoga, tai chi, or qigong classes.

Source: Rachel Feintzeig, "A Cure for Office Burnout: Mini Sabbaticals," *Wall Street Journal*, October 29, 2014, B7; Caitlin Dewey, "Want to De-Stress? Check Email Less, Study Finds," *News & Observer*, December 14, 2014, p. 3E.

"*No, no, that's not a sin, either. My goodness, you
must have worried yourself to death.*"

Popular Therapy Options

Many organizations offer various **employee-assistance programs (EAPs)** aimed at overcoming anxiety, depression, burnout, alcohol abuse, and drug abuse. These programs are designed to address the negative effects of psychological disorders before employees become dysfunctional.

In addition to EAPs, millions of people choose to participate in one or more relevant **twelve-step programs** for help with drug and alcohol addiction, eating disorders, and gambling addiction. All twelve-step programs rely on the same fundamentals:

- *Working the steps.* This means admitting the problem, recognizing that life has become unmanageable, and turning life over to a higher power.
- *Attending meetings.* Meetings of twelve-step programs are held in convenient locations throughout communities across the country. Members describe their own problems and listen to others who have experienced similar problems. In most cases, members form strong support groups.[48]

Web-based counseling is growing in popularity. Some licensed therapists give their clients a choice of face-to-face counseling or online counseling. In addition, there are thousands of support groups organized around various psychological disorders and moderated by therapists—some are licensed, some are not. Web-based therapy may be risky. There is often no guarantee that the self-proclaimed therapist is legitimate or licensed to practice in your state, and no online therapist can promise confidentiality.[49]

LOOKING BACK: SUMMARY OF LEARNING OBJECTIVES

1. Understand the stress factors in your life.

Stress refers to two simultaneous events: an external stimulus, called a stressor, and the physical and emotional response to that stimulus. Stress at work may be caused by many factors. Our stress response consists of three elements: the event or thought (stressor) that triggers stress, your perception of it, and your response to it.

2. Explain the major personal and work-related causes of stress.

When individuals cannot adequately respond or successfully adapt to change, stress is usually the result. Major causes of stress include failures to achieve work/life balance, long hours and irregular schedules, multitasking, change, poorly designed computer workstations, noise, incompetent leaders, work and family transitions, and rumination.

3. Learn how to identify and implement effective stress-management strategies.

You are more likely to handle the ever-increasing stress of today's demands when you practice mindfulness, maintain a sleep routine and exercise program, practice the relaxing effects of deep breathing and meditation, laugh and have fun, seek out moments of solitude, and learn how to physically and mentally recover once the stress is reduced or ended.

4. Learn how to use positive psychology to combat stress.

Positive psychology can be learned and applied to change and improve your life in countless ways. Small things like taking time to laugh and having fun produce big benefits. Other stress relievers include expressing kindness toward others and training yourself to view situations with optimism. It's also helpful to make a list of the stressors in your life to understand what you can and cannot control, and accept those things you cannot control.

5. Identify stress-related psychological disorders and therapy options.

When stress becomes persistent and overwhelming, it can lead to debilitating psychological disorders such as anxiety, depression, and burnout.

While self-management techniques sometimes help, there may come a time when medication and one-on-one or group therapy with a licensed therapist are needed. Employee-assistance programs at work and community-based twelve-step programs may offer additional support.

KEY TERMS

stress, 308	meditation, 315	employee-assistance programs
ergonomics, 311	resilience, 317	(EAPs), 323
transition, 312	anxiety, 320	twelve-step programs, 323
rumination, 312	depression, 321	
mindfulness, 313	burnout, 322	

CAREER INSIGHT: WANT TO GET MORE DONE? GET MORE SLEEP AND TAKE A BREAK

After breathing, sleep is our most fundamental need and should be our highest priority, says Tony Schwartz, CEO of the Energy Project. Most people need seven to eight hours of sleep, yet sleep is usually the first thing people will give up when they feel like they need to get more done. Sleep deprivation actually makes us much less efficient, so if you want to get more done, give up something other than sleep.

Another way to sustain your energy throughout the day is to take frequent breaks, approximately every 90 minutes throughout your day to keep your body in alignment with its natural rhythms. Just as we cycle through various stages of sleep at night, our body clock cycles every 90 minutes throughout the day, moving between periods of high and low energy. A short nap can also help you sustain your energy.

Source: http://www.theenergyproject.com/tips. Retrieved April 17, 2012.

TRY YOUR HAND

1. Determine what circumstances are causing the most stress in your life. For example, are you trying to work too many hours while going to school? Are you experiencing parental or peer pressure? Do you feel burdened with things you cannot control? Then answer the following questions:
   a. What aspects of the situation are under your control?
   b. Are there any aspects of the situation that are out of your control? Explain.
   c. What steps can you take to help eliminate the stress?
   d. What individual stress-management strategies could you use to counteract the effects of this stress?
2. Consider the following company-sponsored stress-management programs. List them in order from most beneficial to you to least beneficial. Explain your reasoning.

   a. Access to on-site exercise facilities or company-sponsored health club membership
   b. A workshop on stress management sponsored by the company
   c. A cafeteria where healthy, nutritionally balanced foods are served
   d. Access to a soundproof audiovisual room for viewing relaxing videos,, listening to soothing music, or taking a nap
3. Stress often increases as we struggle with time management. How well do you manage your time? Take a few minutes and answer the following questions. Then spend time developing a time-management program that meets your individual needs.
   a. Do you develop a daily to-do list that indicates the activities you hope to work on?
   b. Do you maintain a planning calendar—a single place to record daily appointments, deadlines, and tasks?

c. Do you have a series of personal and professional goals that guide you in setting priorities for the use of your time?

d. Have you learned to say no to proliferating requests for your participation in team activities,

projects, social activities, and so on, that may complicate your life?

4. Try a one-day "news fast." Do not read, watch, or listen to any news for a day and see how you feel.

CRITICAL THINKING CHALLENGE

The best way to cope with stress is to develop a process for coping with it before it disrupts your life. The more systematic you can make this process, the more effective it will be. Try using these steps to create your own personal plan for dealing with stressful events in your life:

1. Assess the sources of stress and the effect they have on you.

2. Identify which stressors you want to address and which ones can be changed.

3. Create a plan to deal with each stressor and the specific steps you will take.

4. Evaluate the outcomes you have as a result of implementing changes to deal with stress, and adjust strategies as needed.

5. Stephen Cope, a pioneer in the practice of yoga, says Americans are practical people, and yoga is a practical way to cultivate well-being. He says, "Yoga induces self-regulation, which is the ability to manage feelings, thoughts, and quiet the mind." Consider enrolling in a yoga class so you can determine if this practice helps you calm your mind.

See Robin Fasano, "Stephen Cope: Twenty-Five Years of Transformation," *Spirituality & Health*, March/April, 2014, p. 29.

SELF-ASSESSMENT EXERCISE

For each of the following statements, circle the number from 1 to 5 that best represents your response: (1) strongly disagree (never do this); (2) disagree (rarely do this); (3) moderately agree (sometimes do this); (4) agree (frequently do this); (5) strongly agree (almost always do this).

A.	I understand what causes or triggers stress in my life.	1	2	3	4	5
B.	I make every effort to screen out negative thoughts and accentuate positive thinking.	1	2	3	4	5
C.	I manage stress and tension so I am not overwhelmed by the negative stressors in my life.	1	2	3	4	5
D.	I have developed good habits of diet, sleep, and exercise in order to cope more effectively with the negative stressors in my life.	1	2	3	4	5
E.	I apply positive psychology strategies and activities to cope with stressful situations.	1	2	3	4	5

After identifying your response to each item, select an attitude or skill you would like to improve. Prepare a written goal and then describe the steps you will take to achieve this goal.

YOU PLAY THE ROLE

Assume you are the spouse of Terry, a call center customer-service representative. Terry routinely comes home from work stressed out and in a surly mood. Each representative at the center handles up to 120 calls per day and faces more frequent personal attacks than workers in most other occupations, with little or no opportunity to respond. The management of the organization is inflexible when it comes to accommodating its customers' needs, so the call center personnel have little power to make the customers happy. Many times they are forced to refuse the customers' requests and respond, "It's corporate policy." Terry has become irritable, impatient, and emotionally unavailable to you and your three elementary-school-aged children. The job pays better than any other opportunities in the area, and your family has become dependent on Terry's income. Upon returning home from work today, Terry walked past you and the kids, went into your bedroom, closed the door, turned on the TV, and began rapidly consuming a cold beer. You've had enough! Rather than escalate the stress by mentioning the divorce option, you have decided to try to talk with Terry about reducing the stress in your lives. Role-play this discussion with one of your classmates, who will play the role of Terry.

BELOW THE SURFACE | IS GOOD STRESS BAD?

Sue Shellenbarger, columnist for the *Wall Street Journal*, says, "Contrary to popular belief, stress doesn't have to be a soul-sucking, health-draining force." However, few people know how to transform their stress into the positive kind that helps them reach their goals. Kate Matheny provides a good example of someone who thought she could have it all, progression to a high-pressure management position, mother of two children, and a daily routine that often started with a 5:00 a.m. marathon-training run. After months of too little sleep and feeling pushed to the brink of losing her mind, she decided to address her stress. Matheny found a less stressful job with more flexibility in her schedule, more support from her boss, and greater work/life balance.[50]

Research conducted by the American Psychological Association found that one-third of employees experience chronic stress related to work. Women report higher levels of work stress than men. Women's stress is rising as families rely more on women's earnings. Women managers in male-dominated fields sometimes find the stress of juggling family responsibilities intolerable.[51] Also, they often discover that men are paid more for the same type of work.

QUESTIONS

1. Kate Matheny was able to make a career change that reduced the amount of bad stress in her life. However, finding a less stressful position is not always an option. Matheny took a pay cut when she moved to a new firm. If she had stayed with her former employer, what steps could she have taken to reduce her stress?

2. Recently a close friend was promoted to human resources manager at a medium-sized law firm that includes 18 lawyers, 10 legal assistants, and 5 support staff. After two months in this position, she called you and described some problems she is facing. Three of the firm's lawyers are battling depression and two others are problem drinkers. These lawyers feel pressure to achieve billable-hour quotas set by senior partners at the firm. What steps would you suggest she take to help these lawyers cope with overwork conditions and mental health problems?

CLOSING CASE | ACHIEVING A MORE BALANCED LIFE

Katherine Garrigan has worked full time at a Chicago museum for almost two years. During that time, the 24-year-old has taken just two short vacations totaling about eight days.[52] Jacqueline Piatt, a 26-year-old account executive at PJ, Inc., a New York–based public relations firm, described her upcoming trip to Barcelona: she plans to spend time at the beach, eat tapas, see the sights, and party until 5:00 a.m. Unfortunately, she has to squeeze it all into one weekend. Her work schedule does not allow for a longer vacation.[53]

Many Americans have adopted a demanding work ethic that leaves little time for a well-rounded life. U.S. workers tend to work long hours and spend less time on vacation than do workers in many other industrialized countries. Long hours at work usually result in loss of leisure time and less time with family and friends. Consider these characteristics of the U.S. workforce:

- A full 35 percent of the employed workers are not taking all of their paid vacation days. During one recent year, Americans failed to take 438 million days of paid vacation.[54]
- McDonalds Corporation offers salaried employees an eight-week paid sabbatical for every 10 years of employment. Sabbaticals, which originated in academia, provide employees time for rest and reflection—a break from 50-hour work weeks. Yet, only 5 percent of American companies offer paid sabbaticals.[55]

- Some companies discourage the use of sick days. Nearly half of the full-time workers in America do not have paid sick days, and those who do have this benefit are often discouraged from using it.[56]

Most workers want to succeed and advance at work, yet they also want to schedule time for family, friends, and leisure activities. Many fail in their attempt to achieve this level of work/life balance.

QUESTIONS

1. Many workers do not use all of the paid vacation time they have earned. Assess which factors may influence workers to make this decision.

2. Some companies feel vacation can have a positive effect on the personal health of their workers. They believe that workers asked to do more with fewer resources may need their vacation time more than ever. Argue whether employers should require workers to take all of their paid vacation days. Why or why not?

3. Several companies, including Accenture, Cisco Systems, and Wells Fargo, offer paid sabbaticals to employees so they can work as volunteers, improve their education, or learn new skills, for example. Evaluate the advantages and disadvantages of this approach to sabbaticals.

CHAPTER 14 ENDNOTES

1. Matthew Futterman, "Where the Seahawks Get Their Mental Edge," *Wall Street Journal*, January 28, 2015, p. D6.

2. Christopher Tkaczyk, "Bring Your Best Friend to Work," *Fortune*, August 11, 2014, p. 26; "Pawsitive Thinking," *UC Berkeley Wellness Letter*, November 2013, p. 1.

3. Lauren Weber, "Companies Slip Workouts Into Work," *Wall Street Journal*, June 19, 2012, p. D4.

4. Bruce Cryer, Rollin McCraty, and Doc Childre, "Pull the Plug on Stress," *Harvard Business Review*, July 2003, pp. 1–2.

5. Robert M. Sapolsky, "If Not for Stress, I Just Might Feel Your Pain," *Wall Street Journal*, January 17, 2015, p. C2.

6. Melinda Beck, "Researchers Prescribe Just Enough Stress to Ace Life's Tests; Too Little is Lazy," *Wall Street Journal*, June 19, 2012, p. D1.

7. Richard Laliberte, "Lighten Up," *New Choices*, June 2001, p. 65.

8. James E. Loehr, *Stress for Success* (New York: Times Books, 1997), p. 4.

9. Daniel Goleman and Richard Boyatzis, "Social Intelligence and the Biology of Leadership," *Harvard Business Review*, September 2008, p. 80.

10. Shawn Achor, *The Happiness Advantage* (New York: Crown Business, 2006), pp. 133–134.

11. Lauren Weber and Sue Shellenbarger, "Chronic Tension Hurts Mental Clarity; For Women, A 'Tend and Befriend' Response," *Wall Street Journal*, March 5, 2013, p. D1.

12. "Work-Life Balance Tops Pay," *USA Today*, March 13, 2008, p. IB.

13. Sue Shellenbarger, "Time-Zoned: Working Around the Round-the-Clock Workday," *Wall Street Journal*, February 15, 2007, p. D1.

14. Ibid.

15. Sonja Steptoe, "Ready, Set, Relax!" *Time*, October 27, 2003, pp. 38–41; Sue Shellenbarger, "Are Saner Workloads the Unexpected Key to More Productivity?" *Wall Street Journal*, March 10, 2000, p. B1.

16. Price Pritchett and Ron Pound, *The Stress of Organizational Change* (Dallas, TX: Pritchett, 2005), pp. 3–8.

17. This hypothetical example was adapted from Mary Donato, "Workplace Stress: A Survival Guide," *Sales & Marketing Management*, November/December 2006, p. 24.

18. David H. Freedman, "Why Interruption, Distraction, and Multitasking Are Not Such Awful Things After All," *Inc.*, February 2007, p. 68.

19. "Sound Bites," *UC Berkeley Wellness Letter*, September 2004, pp. 6–7; Jane Spencer, "Behind the Music: iPods and Hearing Loss," *Wall Street Journal*, January 10, 2006, p. D1; Steve Thompson, "Straight Pipes and Street Civility," *Autoweek*, March 20, 2006, p. 10. Ilima Loomis, "Loud Planet," *Spirituality & Health*, March/April 2014, p. 49.

20. Kenneth Labich, "Psycho Bosses from Hell," *Fortune*, March 18, 1996, p. 123; Vanessa Ho, "Companies Get the Message that Happy Workers Help Bottom Line," *Roanoke Times & World News*, November 13, 1995, p. E6.

21. Anneli Rufus, "Worried Sick," *Spirituality & Health*, March/April, 2013, pp. 34–35.

22. Douglas A. Bernstein, Louis A. Penner, Alison Clarke-Stewart, and Edward J. Roy, *Psychology*, 7th ed. (Boston: Houghton Mifflin, 2006), pp. 515, 605.

23. N. Schneiderman, G. Ironson, and S. D. Siegel, "Stress and Health: Psychological, Behavioral, and Biological Determinants," *Annual Review of Clinical Psychology*, Vol. 1, No. 1 (2005): 607–628; American Psychological Association, "Stress in America: Our Health at Risk," press release, January 2012, www.apa.org/news/press/releases/stress/2011/final-2011.pdf.

24. Jon Kabat-Zinn, *Mindfulness for Beginners* (Boulder, CO: Sounds True, 2012), pp. 51 and 64.

25. Tim Ryan, "Leading the 'Quiet Caucus,'" *Spirituality & Health*, January/February, 2014, pp. 26 and 27.

26. Anneli Rufus, "Worried Sick," *Spirituality & Health*, March/April, 2013, pp. 34–35; Kevin Gyoerkoe and Pamela Wiegartz, *10 Simple Solutions to Worry* (Oakland, CA: New Harbinger Publications, 2006).

27. Loehr, *Stress for Success*, pp. 179, 183; Eilene Zimmerman, "Sleep Less, Feel Better," *Sales & Marketing Management*, June 2004, p. 49.

28. Arlene Weintraub, "Napping Your Way to the Top," *BusinessWeek*, November 27, 2006, pp. 97 and 99.

29. Jen Murphy, "At Work, Fitness Counts As Much As Sales," *Wall Street Journal*, June 26, 2012, p. D4.

30. Joel Stein, "Just Say Om," *Time*, August 4, 2003, p. 50; Katherine Ellison, "Mastering Your Own Mind," *Psychology Today*, September/October, 2006, pp. 70–77.

31. Achor, *The Happiness Advantage*, pp. 51–52.

32. Stein, "Just Say Om," p. 50; Ellison, "Mastering Your Own Mind," pp. 47–56; Richard J. Davidson et al., "Alterations in Brain and Immune Function Produced by Mindfulness Meditation," *Psychosomatic Medicine*, Vol. 65, No. 4, 2003, pp. 564–570 [cited 16 February 2006]. Available from http://www.psychosomaticmedicine.org; INTERNET; "Mindfulness Meditation," *Spirituality & Health*, March/April 2004, p. 74; Michelle Conlin, "Meditation," *BusinessWeek*, August 30, 2004, pp. 136–137.

33. Ester Buchholz, "The Call of Solitude," *Psychology Today*, January–February 1998, pp. 50–54; "Loners May Not Fear Others, They Just Need Some Solitude," *Wall Street Journal*, March 1, 2007, p. B7.

34. Rosabeth Moss Kanter, "Cultivate a Culture of Confidence," *Harvard Business Review*, April 2011, p. 34.

35. Megan Satosus, "No Fun of Any Kind," *CIO Magazine*, May 2, 2005 [cited 16 February 2006]. Available from http://www.cio.com; INTERNET.

36. Ann McGee-Cooper, *You Don't Have to Go Home from Work Exhausted* (New York: Bantam Books, 1992), pp. 52–53.

37. Achor, *The Happiness Advantage*, p. 52.

38. Sheila Hutman, Jaelline Jaffe, Robert Segal, Heather Larson, and Lisa Dumke, "Stress: Signs and Symptoms, Causes and Effects" [cited 11 February 2006]. Available from http://www.helpguide.org/mental/stress_signs.htm; INTERNET.

39. Melissa Korn, "Managing Mental Health on the Job," *Wall Street Journal*, August 29, 2012, p. B6; Leila Abbound, "Mental Illness Said to Affect One-Quarter of Americans," *Wall Street Journal*, June 7, 2005, p. D1.

40. Bernstein et al., *Psychology*, pp. 589–590.

41. Ibid.

42. To learn about specific ways to control your fears, see Jason Zweig, "How to Control Your Fears in a Fearsome Market," *Wall Street Journal*, July 19, 2008, p. B1.

43. Paul Raeburn, "Mental Health: Better Beneftis Won't Break the Bank," *BusinessWeek*, December 17, 2001, p. 100; Andrea Peterson, "Clinic of the Future: Aiming for Faster Depression Relief," *Wall Street Journal*, June 25, 2013, p. D4.

44. Sharon Begley, "New Hope for Battling Depression Relapses," *Wall Street Journal*, January 6, 2004, p. D1; Avery Johnson, "Treatment Works for Two-Thirds of the Depressed," *Wall Street Journal*, November 1, 2006.

45. Lindsey Tanner, "Treating Workers' Depression Pays," *News & Observer*, September 26, 2007, p. 4A.

46. Bernstein et al., *Psychology*, p. 495.

47. Dana Mattioli, "When Devotion to Work Becomes Job Obsession," *Wall Street Journal*, January 23, 2007, p. 88.

48. Tommy Rosen, "Through Yoga, A Path Beyond 12 Steps," *Spirituality & Health*, March/April 2014, p. 38;

Melinda Beck, "Prescription to End Drinking," *Wall Street Journal*, December 16, 2014, p. D1.

49. Rebecca Segall, "Online Shrinks: The Inside Story," *Psychology Today*, May/June 2000, pp. 38–43; Joshua Rosenbaum, "The Typing Cure," *Wall Street Journal*, September 16, 2002, p. R10.

50. Sue Shellenbarger, "Turn Bad Stress Into Good," *Wall Street Journal*, May 8, 2013, p. D1.

51. Lauren Weber and Sue Shellenbarger, "Office Stress: His vs. Hers," *Wall Street Journal*, March 5, 2013, p. D1.

52. Erin White, "For Young Workers, Taking Time Off Can Be Stressful," *Wall Street Journal*, March 27, 2007, p. B10.

53. Anjoli Athavaley, "Vacation Deflation: Breaks Get Shorter," *Wall Street Journal*, August 15, 2007, p. D1.

54. Anjoli Athavaley, "Vacation Deflation: Breaks Get Shorter"; Howard Shapiro, "Vacation Time Going Unused," *News & Observer*, February 17, 2008, p. 8G.

55. Michael Arndt, "Nice Work if You Can Get It," *BusinessWeek*, January 9, 2006, pp. 56–57.

56. Molly Selvin, "Taking Sick Days Often Discouraged," *News & Observer*, May 27, 2007, p. 5E.

CHAPTER PREVIEW

LEARNING OBJECTIVES

After studying Chapter 15, you will be able to

15-1 Define the primary and secondary dimensions of diversity.

15-2 Discuss how prejudiced attitudes are formed.

15-3 Develop an awareness of the various forms of discrimination in the workplace.

15-4 Understand why organizations value diversity and inclusion.

15-5 Identify ways in which organizations can enhance workforce diversity.

15-6 Discuss the current status of affirmative action programs.

Valuing Workforce Diversity and Inclusion

TIP OF THE ICEBERG | DIVERSITY AND INCLUSION— A WORKFORCE IMPERATIVE

A growing number of organizations realize that they need a workforce that reflects the changing demographics of their customers. Diversity is not simply a matter of doing the right thing; it is a business imperative. PepsiCo Incorporated used to have a reputation as a mostly white-male fraternity, but things have changed. In the early 2000s, CEO Steve Reinemund began building up business cases for diversity. He established a scorecard to track diversity performance. Efforts were made to change the company's culture to be inviting and engaging for every employee. Every executive was assigned as a sponsor for a minority group. Recent research conducted at Cornell University recognized PepsiCo as best in class in **managing diversity** and inclusion.[1]

Some segments of our workforce have difficulty recruiting female and other groups of underrepresented technical employees. Today qualified women are leaving the tech industry in record numbers. Research reported in the *Harvard Business Review* found that as many as 50 percent of women working in science, engineering and technology will, over time, leave because of hostile work environments.[2] The topic will be discussed extensively in Chapter 16.

As noted in Chapter 12, teams play a critical role in the way organizations get things done. Diverse team members tend to produce more creative and innovative solutions over the long term than do teams with more homogenous members. An effective team is one in which team members communicate effectively and complete tasks in ways that allow each team member to have a positive team experience.[3]

Disabilities don't stop people from enjoying their favorite activities. Players enjoy a competitive wheelchair rugby match at the Construction Industry Training Board (CITB) Training Center in Norfolk, England, UK.

WORKFORCE DIVERSITY AND INCLUSION

15-1   Diversity can be a source of competitive advantage in the marketplace. It gives organizations an enhanced ability to understand the needs of different market segments. One of the guiding principles at PepsiCo is "Win with diversity and inclusion." The company recognizes that diversity brings new perspectives into the workplace and encourages innovation as well as the ability to identify new market opportunities.

What Are Diversity and Inclusion?

In broad terms, **diversity** is any dimension that can be used to differentiate groups and people from one another. It means respect for and appreciation of differences in ethnicity, gender, age, class, national origin, disability, sexual orientation, religious beliefs and race. But it is much more than this. Anything that makes us unique is part of the definition of diversity.[4]

Inclusion within an organization is a state of being valued, respected, and supported. It's about focusing on the needs of every employee and ensuring the right conditions are in place for each person to achieve his or her full potential. Inclusion should be reflected in an organization's culture, practices, and relationships in order to support a diverse workforce.[5] Later in this chapter we will review some important inclusive practices that should be adopted by every organization.

Dimensions of Diversity

There are primary and secondary dimensions of diversity. The **primary dimensions** are core characteristics of each person that cannot be changed: age, race, gender, physical and mental abilities, ethnic heritage, and sexual orientation (see Figure 15.1). Together they form an individual's self-image and the filters through which each person views the rest of the world. These inborn elements are interdependent; no one dimension stands alone. Each exerts an

Figure 15.1 ■ Primary and Secondary Dimensions of Diversity

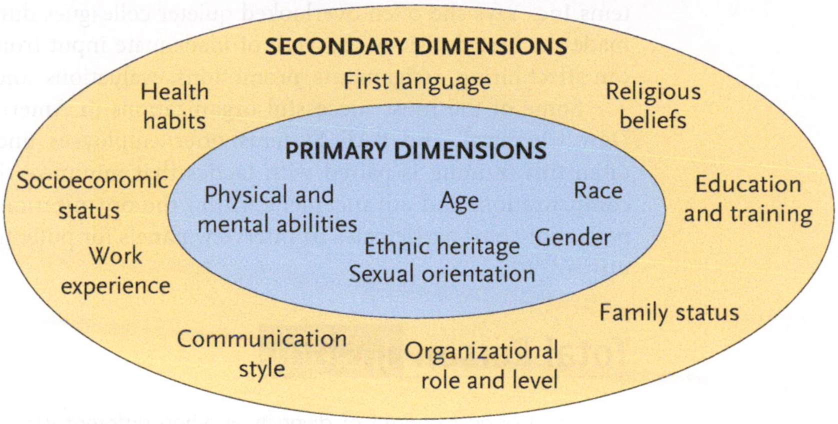

Source: This model is adapted from *Workforce America!* Authored by Marilyn Loden and Judy B. Rosener.

important influence throughout life. Marilyn Loden and Judy Rosener describe individual primary dimensions in their book *Workforce America!* They say, "Like the interlocking segments of a sphere, they represent the core of our individual identities."[6]

The greater the number of primary differences between people, the more difficult it is to establish trust and mutual respect. When we add the secondary dimensions of diversity to the mix, effective human relations become even more difficult. The secondary dimensions of diversity are elements that can be changed, or at least modified. They include a person's work experience, health habits, religious beliefs, education and training, first language, family status, organizational role and level, communication style, and socioeconomic status (see Figure 15.1). These factors all add a layer of complexity to the way we see ourselves and others. The blend of secondary and primary dimensions adds depth to each person and helps shape his or her values, priorities, and perceptions throughout life.[7]

> *The greater the number of primary differences between people, the more difficult it is to establish trust and mutual respect.*

Each of us enters the workforce with a unique perspective, shaped by these dimensions and our own past experiences. Building effective human relationships is possible only when we learn to accept and value the differences in others. Without this acceptance, both primary and secondary dimensions of diversity can become roadblocks to further cooperation and understanding.

PREJUDICED ATTITUDES

15-2   **Prejudice** is a premature judgment or opinion that is formed without examination of the facts. Throughout life, we often prejudge people in light of their primary and secondary dimensions. Rather than treat others as unique individuals, prejudiced people tend to think in terms of **stereotypes**—perceptions, beliefs, and expectations about members of some group. In most cases, a stereotype involves the false assumption that all members of a group share the same characteristics. The most common and powerful stereotypes focus on observable personal attributes such as age, gender, and ethnicity.[8]

Unconscious Bias

Research indicates that we all harbor unconscious or hidden biases. **Unconscious bias** is the result of messages (from a wide array of sources) introduced into our subconscious from an early age. Many of the prejudices that are deeply held in our unconscious mind influence how we act toward one another.[9] Denise Russell, a vice president at BAE Systems Inc., says she often overlooked quieter colleagues during meetings. "I may have not made the best decisions" because of inadequate input from introverts. Unconscious bias can affect hiring, assignments, promotions, evaluations, and dismissals.[10]

Some of the most successful organizations in America such as Google, Microsoft, Dow Chemical, and BAE Systems offer employees unconscious bias training. Very often this training is paired with tactics that minimize the influence of bias in hiring, compensation, and advancement within the organization. For example, a woman or a person of color participates in interview panels for potential middle managers and executives.[11]

Total Person Insight

> "The strongest benefit of diversity is when different ideas and perspectives combine to create new insights."
>
> Source: Tamara J. Erickson, "Diversity Leader As Cruise Director," *Diversity Executive*, July/August 2013, p. 12.

How Prejudicial Attitudes Are Formed and Retained

Several factors contribute to the development of prejudices. Three of the most important influences are childhood experiences, ethnocentrism, and economic conditions.

Childhood Experiences.   Today's views toward others are filtered through the experiences and feelings of childhood. Children watch how their family members, friends, teachers, and other authority figures respond to different racial, ethnic, and religious groups. As a result, they form attitudes that may last a lifetime, unless new information replaces the old perceptions. Prejudicial attitudes are not unalterable. Whatever prejudice is learned during childhood can be unlearned later in life.[12]

human RELATIONS *in Action*

CLASS-BASED BIAS

Paul C. Gorski, professor in the Graduate School of Education at Hamline University, states that many of us need to examine our own class-based prejudices. We sometimes stigmatize victims of income inequality (children, parents, and coworkers), forgetting that they may have experienced savage inequalities in such areas as education, health care, housing, and employment opportunities. Try to avoid letting class-based prejudices color your assumptions about others.

Source: Paul C. Gorski, "The Question of Class," *Teaching Tolerance*, Spring 2007, pp. 26–29.

Ethnocentrism.   The tendency to regard our own culture or nation as better or more "correct" than others is called **ethnocentrism**. The word is derived from *ethnic*, meaning a group united by similar customs, characteristics, race, or other common factors, and *center*. **Ethnic identity** is the part of a person's identity that reflects the racial, religious, or cultural group to which the person belongs.[13] When ethnocentrism is present, the standards and values of our own culture are being used as a yardstick to measure the worth of other cultures.

In their book *Valuing Diversity*, Lewis Brown Griggs and Lente-Louise Louw compare ethnocentrism in an organization to icebergs floating in an ocean. We can see the tips of icebergs above the water level, just as we can see our diverse coworkers' skin color, gender, mannerisms, and job-related talents and hear the words they use and their accents. These are basically "surface" aspects of a person that others can easily learn through observation. However, just as the enormous breadth of an iceberg's base lies beneath the water's surface, so does the childhood conditioning of people from different cultures. As icebergs increase in number and drift too close together, they are likely to clash at their base even though there is no visible contact at the water's surface.[14] As organizations increase the diversity of their workforce, the potential for clashes resulting from deep-seated cultural conditioning and prejudiced attitudes also increases.

Economic Factors. When the economy goes through a recession or depression, and housing, jobs, and other necessities become scarce, people's prejudices against other groups often increase. If enough prejudice is built up against a particular group, members of that group may be barred from competing for jobs. The recent backlash against immigrants can be traced, in part, to a fear that the new arrivals will take jobs that would otherwise be available to American workers. Prejudice based on economic factors has its roots in people's basic survival needs, and, as a result, it is very hard to eliminate.

Increasingly, income and wealth inequality in America is viewed by many as a serious barrier to racial harmony. *Fortune* magazine reports that the average net worth of the top fifth of American households has more than doubled in real terms since 1962; the middle class has seen only a 25 percent rise; and the bottom 20 percent is deeper in debt.[15] America is evolving into a two-caste society.

Total Person Insight

"At Prudential, valuing diversity and inclusion is the way we do business. And we take our business very seriously. Our senior leaders are held accountable for promoting an environment that values inclusion."

Source: Emilio Egea, Chief Diversity Officer, Prudential Financial. [Cited 9 March 2010] Available from www.diversityinc.com.

THE MANY FORMS OF DISCRIMINATION

15-3 **Discrimination** is behavior based on prejudiced attitudes. If, as an employer, you believe that overweight people tend to be lazy, that is a prejudiced attitude. If you refuse to hire someone simply because that person is overweight, you are engaging in discrimination.

Discrimination is behavior based on prejudiced attitudes.

Individuals or groups that are discriminated against are denied equal treatment and opportunities afforded to the dominant group. They may be denied employment, promotion, training, or other job-related privileges on the basis of race, lifestyle, gender, or other characteristics that have little or nothing to do with their qualifications for a job.

Gender

Discrimination based on gender has been, and continues to be, the focus of much attention. The traditional roles women held in society have undergone tremendous changes in the past few decades. Women enter the workforce, not only to supplement family income, but also to pursue careers in previously all-male professions. Men have also been examining the roles assigned them by society and are discovering new options for themselves. Most companies have recognized that discrimination based on gender is a reality and are taking steps to deal with the problem. Chapter 16 is devoted to an in-depth discussion of overcoming gender bias.

Age

People who make up today's workforce are working longer and living longer. Meaningful employment is a source of well-being for many of these workers. In light of our extended life span, it's time to rethink the concept of age. Tom Lowry, author of a *BusinessWeek* article entitled "Extreme Experience" says, "If 60 is the new 40, then 80 is the new 60." He describes 25 persons, who range in age from 75 to 100, who run their companies or wield real influence in the business world.[16] CVS Caremark, a large drugstore chain, is currently recruiting Baby Boomers and other older workers. Stephen Wing, director of CVS workforce initiatives, says, "When you're in your 50s and 60s, you're in your prime."[17]

Of course not every organization has adopted an enlightened view of age. Some companies fail to understand that workers in their 50s and 60s are productive, cost-effective employees—and often the most knowledgeable employees in a company. Since age bias is still pervasive in hiring, older workers should anticipate the most common fears employers have about older workers and defuse them. This means showing plenty of energy, flexibility, reasonable pay expectations, and up-to-date skills.[18]

During the 2007–2009 recession, age-discrimination complaints processed by the Equal Employment Opportunity Commission (EEOC) reached a record high. Some companies replace older workers with younger workers in order to reduce compensation expenses.

human RELATIONS *in Action*

BAD BEHAVIOR DAMAGES GREEK SYSTEM

The Sigma Alpha Epsilon (SAE) chapter at the University of Oklahoma was shut down after a video showed members singing a racist chant. Sigma Phi Epsilon shut its doors last year at the University of Mississippi after three of its members draped a Confederate banner and placed a noose around the statue of the school's first black student. Kappa Sigma suspended its Duke University chapter after students held an international-themed party that mocked Asians.

Source: Nathan Koppel, "Fraternity Chapter Closed Over Video of Racist Chant," *Wall Street Journal*, March 10, 2015, p. A5; Kimberly Hefling and Jesse J. Holland, "Oklahoma Not Alone in Racist Fraternity Incidents," *News & Observer*, March 16, 2015, p. 9A.

Race

Few areas are more sensitive and engender more passion than issues surrounding race. **Race** denotes a category of people who are perceived as distinctive on the basis of certain biologically inherited traits, such as skin color or hair texture.[19] Because people cannot change these inherited traits, they can easily become victims of discrimination.

> *There is as much genetic variability between two people from the same "racial group" as there is between two people from any two different "racial" groups.*

Throughout American history, we have seen attempts to place people in racial categories and judge them as racial symbols rather than as unique individuals. During World War II, many Americans of Japanese ancestry were confined in concentration camps because they were considered a security threat, merely because of their racial heritage. Because of the war on terrorism, today's "racial" targets often include immigrants from Pakistan, Iraq, and other Middle Eastern countries, as well as their American-born children.

The Myth of Race. Critics of racial categories view them as social inventions that intensify and reinforce racist beliefs and actions. They believe that one way to break down racial barriers and promote a race-free consciousness is to get rid of traditional racial categories. A growing number of geneticists and social scientists reject the view that "racial" differences have an objective or scientific foundation.[20] The American Anthropological Association (AAA) has taken the official position that "race" has no scientific justification in human biology. The AAA position is that there is greater variation within "racial" groups than between them and race is about culture, not biology.[21]

It is important to keep in mind that some race categories include people who vary greatly in terms of ethnic identity. The Asian label includes a wide range of groups, such as Vietnamese, Filipino, Chinese, and Korean, with distinct histories and languages. The label "African American" does not take into consideration the enormous linguistic, physical, and cultural diversity of the peoples of Africa.[22]

Multiracial and Multicultural Trends

Marriage across racial and ethnic lines has reached a new high in the United States. About 15 percent of new marriages in 2010 were between individuals of a different race or ethnicity. According to the 2010 Census, they make up one in 10 marriages between opposite-sex couples, a 28-percent increase since 2000. About 9 million people living in the United States identify themselves as multiracial or multicultural.[23] This large group includes Barack Obama, son of a black man and a white woman.

human RELATIONS *in Action*

THE MACACA INCIDENT

George Allen served one term as governor of Virginia and then he was elected to the U.S. Senate. While seeking reelection to the Senate, he used the term "Macaca," an unfamiliar ethnic slur, to describe a dark-skinned man of Indian descent seated in the audience. The use of this sarcastic word triggered an extraordinary fall from political grace. He lost the election.

Source: Frank Bruni, Kim Severson, and Grant Barrett, "Buzzwords are Catchy—and Caustic," *News & Observer*, December 25, 2006, p. 3A.

Race as Social Identity. Although races are not scientifically defensible, they are "real" socially, politically, and psychologically. Race and racism affect our own self-perception and how we are treated by others. Groups that are working to build ethnic pride, such as Native Americans, oppose efforts to get rid of the traditional racial categories, which they consider part of a positive identity.

Chip Somodevilla/Getty Images

The Supreme Court ruled in favor of Samantha Elauf, a Muslim who sued Abercrombie & Fitch claiming discrimination during the hiring process. She insisted on wearing a hijab at work.

Religion

Discrimination based on a person's religious preference has been an issue throughout history. Religion has always had the power to fracture and divide people of faith. The authors of a study at Baylor University say, "American religion is startlingly complex and diverse. Though Americans may agree that God exists, they do not agree on much else.[24]

Charges of religious discrimination in the workplace have increased in recent years, according to Equal Employment Opportunity Commission (EEOC) reports.[25] Muslims face unique challenges as they attempt to balance their prayer schedule with inflexible work schedules. Misunderstandings occur often over relatively minor issues, such as Muslim women's right to wear head scarves and Muslim men's right to maintain facial hair.

Readers of *Spirituality & Health* magazine often voice concerns about lack of tolerance among members of the three major faith groups: Judaism, Christianity, and Islam. Rabbi Rami Shapiro, who writes the "Roadside Assistance for the Spiritual Traveler" column for this publication, offers us this timely advice:[26]

We need to understand all three levels of religion and promote the voices of the ethicists and mystics within each faith, rather than the shrill and fearful screams of fanatics who hew to the tribal vision of their religion.

Total Person Insight

About 56 million people—19 percent of the population—have a disability according to a report released by the U.S. Census Bureau.

Source: U.S. Census Bureau; https://www.census.gov/report released on July 25, 2012. INTERNET

The National Sports Center for the Disabled's mission is to positively impact the lives of people with any physical or mental challenge. Today, the NSCD is one of the largest outdoor therapeutic recreational agencies in the world. Thousands of lessons are provided each year.

Disability

The Americans with Disabilities Act (ADA) bans discrimination against workers and customers with disabilities and requires employers to make "reasonable accommodations" so that disabled people can gain access and work.

The ADA covers a wide range of disabilities, including learning impairments, AIDS, diabetes, alcoholism, visual impairments, and physical impairments that require the use of a wheelchair (visit *http://www.adata.org*). Although legal protection is in place, the unemployment rate for people with disabilities has outpaced that of the general working population. Also, persons with a disability earn much less than those employees without a disability.[27]

Successful implementation of diversity and ADA initiatives may require changes in corporate culture, attitudes, and policies. The starting point should be a review of all job descriptions and qualification standards. Staff training on nondiscrimination practices, disability etiquette, and awareness may be needed. Diversity initiatives should include the active recruitment and retention of people with disabilities.[28]

human RELATIONS *in Action*

MEETING SOMEONE WITH A DISABILITY

Here are a few suggestions for making a good impression. If the person …

… **is in a wheelchair**. Try to chat eye to eye. Don't touch the wheelchair. It is considered within the boundaries of an individual's personal space.

… **has a speech impediment**. Be patient and carefully listen; resist the urge to finish his or her sentences. Don't pretend to understand if you don't.

… is accompanied by a guide dog. Never pet or play with a guide dog; you will distract the animal from its job.

… has a hearing loss. People who are deaf depend on facial expressions and gestures for communication cues. Face the person and speak clearly and slowly. Speak directly to the person, not to an interpreter or assistant if one is present.

Source: Adapted from "When Meeting Someone with a Disability." Adapted from "Communication Solutions." Used by permission of Progressive Business Publications.

Sexual Orientation

Discrimination based on a person's sexual orientation is motivated by *homophobia*, an aversion to homosexuals. Not long ago, gays and lesbians went to great lengths to keep their sexuality a secret. But today many gays, lesbians, bisexual, and transgender people are "coming out of the closet" to demand their rights as members of society. Indeed, many young people entering the workforce who are used to the relative tolerance of college campuses refuse to hide their orientation once they are in the workplace. And some of the nation's most prominent business leaders are no longer hiding their sexual orientation. Apple Inc. Chief Executive Tim Cook recently said he was proud to be gay:[29]

> Being gay has given me a deeper understanding of what it means to be in the minority and provided a window into the challenges that people in other minority groups deal with every day.

Gay rights activists are working hard to create awareness that discrimination based on sexual orientation is no less serious than discrimination based on age, gender, race, or disability. Activist groups, such as the Human Rights Campaign, the Interfaith Alliance, and the Southern Poverty Law Center, are also working to rid the workplace of antigay behaviors, such as offensive jokes, derogatory names, or remarks about gays. An atmosphere in which gays and lesbians are comfortable being themselves is usually more productive than an atmosphere in which they waste their time and energy maintaining alternate, and false, personalities.

In recent years, we have witnessed several workplace trends favorable to gay and lesbian employees. More than 80 percent of *Fortune* 500 companies include sexual orientation in their antidiscrimination policies, and some companies have established lesbian and gay resource groups—known in some companies as affinity groups—that provide a point of contact for previously invisible employees. Also, a majority of the nation's top 500 companies now extend medical benefits to same-sex partners.[30]

On June 26, 2015 the United States legalized same-sex marriage. The U.S. Supreme Court ruled that the denial of marriage licenses and recognition of same-sex couples violates the Due Process and the Equal Protection clauses of the United States constitution.

human RELATIONS *in Action*

THE PAIN OF GROWING UP GAY

At age 14, Mitchell Gold harbored a secret that he felt would forever ruin his chances of happiness and success in life. He was gay and afraid his family would disown him if they knew his secret. Today he is owner of a fast-growing furniture company located in Taylorsville, North Carolina, and he is working hard to make sure no other teenager has to experience what he did. He has launched an educational campaign called Faith in America to combat religion-based prejudices directed toward the gay community. The centerpiece of his campaign is a book entitled *Youth in Crisis: What Everyone Should Know About Growing Up Gay*. These personal stories describe the pain being inflicted on many gay teens.

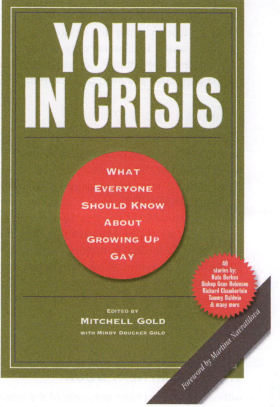

Published by Don Weise/Magnus Books and designed by Linda Kosarin/TheArtDepartment.Biz

Source: Yonat Shimron, "Passion for Justice," *News & Observer*, November 20, 2008, p. D1. For additional information, visit http://www.crisisbook.org.

Subtle Forms of Discrimination

A person who feels he or she has been the victim of discrimination based on gender, age, race, abilities, or sexual orientation can take legal action by filing a complaint with his or her state's office of the Equal Employment Opportunity Commission. However, although many state and federal laws protect people from discrimination based on these issues, they do not specifically protect workers from the more subtle forms of discrimination. For example, those who graduated from an Ivy League college may treat coworkers who graduated from state-funded colleges as inferior. Overweight employees might experience degrading remarks from coworkers. Those who speak with a distinct regional accent may hear snickers behind their backs at work. People who do not value differences often equate a difference with a deficiency.

Total Person Insight

"Talent is a scarce commodity and if you're going to attract the best talent, you better be welcoming to people regardless of gender, regardless of ethnicity, regardless of sexual orientation. If you fail to do any of those, you're artificially constraining the talent pool and you'll be penalized in the long run."

Source: Steve Salbu quote appearing in "Vocal on Gay Issues, Dean Goes Beyond the Classroom," by Melissa Korn. Dr. Salbu is dean of Georgia Institute of Technology's Schiller College of Business. *Wall Street Journal*, March 7, 2013, p. B6.

Discrimination Against the Unemployed. Long-term unemployment has created a new "underclass." Many employers do not want to hire someone who does not have a job. An advocacy group for workers reviewed online job postings and found more than 100 companies that want only applicants who are currently employed. The Equal Employment Opportunity Commission is holding hearings to determine if screening out jobless applicants is a form of discrimination.[31]

What Can You Do?

What should you do if you discover you are the target of some form of subtle, unprotected discrimination because you are different from others at work? If you want to stay in the organization, you will need to determine whether the "difference" is something you can change—your weight, the way you dress, your manner of speaking. If the difference is something you cannot or choose not to change, you may need to address the situation directly. Review the assertiveness skills you studied in Chapter 13. Your assertiveness may help change other people's attitudes and in turn alter their discriminatory behaviors. Another powerful method of eliminating subtle discrimination is to compensate for it by excelling in your work. Become an expert on the job, and work to increase your skills and your value to the organization. As your colleagues gain respect for your talents, they will likely change their attitudes toward you.

human
RELATIONS
in Action

THE MUSLIM NEXT DOOR

Although extremist Islam gets most of the attention in the news media, a very large number of ordinary American Muslims are going about their lives. They are in every blue-collar industry and in white-collar jobs from entry level to the executive suite. However, Muslims face some special challenges. Bias crimes against Muslims, according to FBI reports, remain at high levels. Large numbers of American Muslims have discovered their name is on the federal government's "no-fly" list. And many companies are not being inclusive of Muslims who wish to maintain their religious identity.

Source: Andres T. Tapla, "The Muslim Next Door," *Talent Management Magazine*, January 2015, p. 54; Joel Millman, "Muslims on 'No-Fly' List Claim Harassment," *Wall Street Journal*, May 11, 2012, p. A2.

THE ECONOMICS OF VALUING DIVERSITY AND INCLUSION

15-4

The new millennium has brought greater understanding that diversity and inclusion can be a source of competitive advantage. This occurs when a company makes full use of the ideas, talents, experiences, and perspectives of all employees at all levels of the organization. Joe Watson, a recruiter of minorities, believes that if you want to satisfy clients and customers from diverse backgrounds, you need a diverse mix of employees who are more likely to understand them.[32]

A study conducted by the Society for Human Resource Management revealed diversity initiatives within organizations can affect an organization's bottom line by reducing costs associated with turnover, absenteeism, and low productivity. In addition, efforts to value workers' and customers' diversity reduce complaints and litigation and improve the organization's public image.[33] Organizations that pursue diversity and make it part of their culture usually outperform companies that are less committed to these areas.

"Gays and lesbians getting married—haven't they suffered enough?"

Source: Steven Petrow, *Complete Gay & Lesbian Manners*, New York: Workman Publishing, 2011, p. 188.

> *The price tag for not helping employees learn to respect and value each other is enormous.*

The price tag for *not* helping employees learn to respect and value each other is enormous. Many highly skilled and talented employees will leave an organization that does not value diversity. A comment, gesture, or joke delivered without malice but received as an insult will create tension among workers and customers alike.

MANAGING DIVERSITY AND INCLUSION

15-5 At the beginning of this chapter we noted that many qualified women are leaving the tech industry. Women working in the areas of science, engineering, and technology often report that they don't feel comfortable working for an organization where most of the leadership positions are held by men. Cisco Systems, a large high-tech firm located in San Jose, has worked hard to solve this diversity problem. Currently five out of 13 members of Cisco's operating committee are women, and three of 10 board directors are women. Women working at lower levels can now look up and see opportunities to advance.[34]

What Organizations Can Do

A well-planned and well-executed diversity and inclusion program can promote understanding and defuse tensions between employees who differ in age, race, gender, religious beliefs, and other characteristics. Programs that are poorly developed and poorly executed often backfire, especially in organizations where bias and distrust have festered for years. A comprehensive diversity and inclusion program has three pillars:[35] organizational commitment, employment practices, and training and development (see Figure 15.2).

Organizational Commitment. Diversity and inclusion get a lot of attention in most organizations today, but the upper tiers of management remain stubbornly homogenous.

Figure 15.2 ■ Three Pillars of Diversity

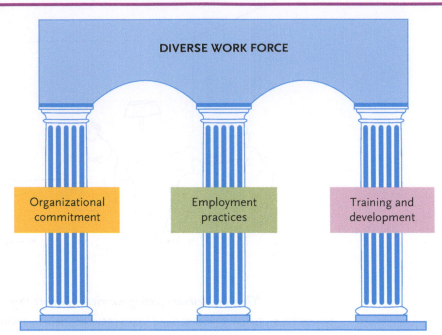

Consider *Fortune* 500 CEOs: only 23 are female, just six are black, and only one is openly gay.[36] If no one person or group is responsible for building a diverse senior management pipeline, then little change may surface at the top of the organization.

When the objective of the diversity initiative is to achieve a stronger competitive position, the commitment is usually quite strong. Ron Glover, vice president of global diversity at IBM, says how we think about diversity and how we deliver it have to be directly connected and deeply embedded in the organization's business objectives.[37]

Companies that see diversity programs as a quick-fix *event*—a one-day workshop that promotes the advantages of a diverse workforce—often create greater, not less, divisiveness among workers. Companies that see diversity programs as a *process* know that the key to a successful diversity program is long-term commitment.

Employment Practices. To achieve workforce diversity and inclusion, organizations need to improve performance and promotion rates in underrepresented groups. Culture change comes more readily from a critical mass of diverse management personnel than from a series of diversity and inclusion seminars. Francine Katsoudas, chief human resources officer at Cisco Systems, says the first challenge is to get young women entering the workforce interested in Cisco. She has emphasized the importance of diverse interview panels and seeking diversity in job candidates.[38]

Organizations must also foster a climate for retention. Newly hired people who are different from the majority must often contend with an atmosphere of tension, instability, and distrust and may soon lose the desire to do their best work. Subtle biases often alienate these employees and create unnecessary stress. Geoff Calvin has looked closely at the *Fortune* 500 best companies to work for and discovered that perks don't make a great workplace.

The real key is interpersonal relationships that thrive in a company culture that focuses on four elements:[39]

Mission: The company is pursuing a larger purpose. For example, Whole Foods seeks to improve customers' health and well-being.

Colleagues The best people want to go where the best people are. Twitter and Container Store, for example, attract more than 100 applicants for every job opening.

Trust: Show people that you consider them trustworthy, and they'll generally prove you right.

Caring: The best companies to work for don't just say "We value employees," they show it.

Training and Development. To develop a culture that values and enhances diversity, organizations need training programs that give managers and employees the tools they need to work more effectively with one another regardless of their backgrounds. Unfortunately, most of the diversity training efforts at American companies are ineffective for these reasons:

- Mandatory programs, often undertaken mainly to avoid liability in discrimination lawsuits, are frequently ineffective and may even be counterproductive. Voluntary diversity training, undertaken to advance the organization's goals, is more effective.[40]
- Middle managers, who play a key role in hiring, development, and promotion decisions, often do not support diversity efforts. To overcome this roadblock, top management must champion diversity and model ideal behaviors to middle management. They should also reward middle managers who take steps to enhance diversity initiatives.[41]

Done well, diversity training programs can promote harmony, reduce conflict, and help give the organization a competitive advantage. Participants should learn which specific behaviors will not be condoned and the basic rules of civil behavior. We may not be able to stop people from bringing their prejudices to work, but they can learn to act as though they have none.

AFFIRMATIVE ACTION: YESTERDAY AND TODAY

15-6 The Civil Rights Act of 1964 marked the beginning of antidiscrimination employment legislation. In an attempt to make up for past discrimination in the areas of employment, education, and business, affirmative action policies were initiated by the federal government. **Affirmative action** involves intentionally seeking and hiring employees from groups that are underrepresented.[42]

Although affirmative action has stirred controversy for many decades, there is no doubt that this initiative has helped minorities gain access to large corporations and top universities. The number of African Americans at the nation's top 50 colleges and universities has doubled in recent decades. Women have also benefited, especially in the 1970s and 1980s, when they began breaking into traditionally male-dominated fields.[43] The flow of controversy over affirmative action sometimes includes references to quotas. Quotas are not legal in the United States.[44]

Affirmative Action Issues. Many people say it is time to rethink affirmative action or even eliminate it. Recent political and legal interpretations of affirmative action have stimulated a nationwide debate over the merits of any program that grants preferential treatment to specific groups. The following are some factors that should guide decisions related to the implementation of affirmative action policies:

- Affirmative action's purpose is not to give unqualified people special rights.[45]
- Affirmative action in the best sense promotes equal consideration, not reverse discrimination.[46]
- One of the most significant changes brought about by affirmative action laws has been the publication of job announcements.[47]
- The definition of employment selection tests has been expanded to include any procedure used as a basis for an employment decision. Informal and formal interviews, performance tests, physical requirements, and other procedures qualify as "tests."[48]

Those who say affirmative action causes companies to hire and promote less qualified people fail to realize that the hiring process usually goes beyond the abilities, knowledge, and skills of the job candidate and includes additional merit-based factors, such as education and experience. When these factors are included in the hiring process, recipients of affirmative action are less likely to feel stigmatized. The way people react to a preferential selection procedure will often depend on how well it is structured and implemented.[49]

LOOKING BACK: SUMMARY OF LEARNING OBJECTIVES

1. **Define the primary and secondary dimensions of diversity**.

   Primary dimensions of diversity include gender, age, race, physical and mental abilities, sexual orientation, and ethnic heritage. Secondary dimensions include religious beliefs, work experience, communication style, organizational role and level, family status, socioeconomic status, first language, education and training, and health habits.

2. **Discuss how prejudiced attitudes are formed**.

   Prejudice is a premature judgment or opinion based partly on observation of others' differences and partly on ignorance, fear, and cultural conditioning. Prejudiced people tend to see others as stereotypes rather than as individuals. Prejudicial attitudes are formed through the effects of childhood experiences, ethnocentrism, and economic factors. Many people have unconscious prejudices, biases they don't know they have.

3. **Develop an awareness of the various forms of discrimination in the workplace**.

   Discrimination is behavior based on prejudicial attitudes. Groups protected by law from discrimination in the workplace include people who share characteristics such as gender, age, race, disability, religion, and sexual orientation. More subtle discrimination can arise when people have different appearances or educational backgrounds. These subtle forms of discrimination may not be illegal, but they are disruptive to a productive workforce.

4. **Understand why organizations value diversity and inclusion**.

   The issue of valuing diversity is an economic one for most organizations. The workforce will soon be made up of a minority of white men and a majority of women, people of color, and immigrants. To remain competitive, organizations must value the contributions of all of their diverse workers and make full use of their ideas and talents. Only then will they be able to understand their equally diverse customers' needs. Valuing diversity is not just a nice idea, but a business imperative.

5. **Identify ways in which organizations can enhance workforce diversity**.

   Individuals can enhance diversity by letting go of their stereotypes and learning to critically and honestly evaluate their prejudiced attitudes as they work and socialize with people who are different. They will need to develop sensitivity to differences and their own personal diversity awareness programs. Organizations must commit to valuing individual differences and implementing effective employment practices that respect and enhance diversity. Their diversity training programs should be an ongoing process rather than a one-time event. They need to seek out, employ, and develop employees from diverse backgrounds.

6. **Discuss the current status of affirmative action programs**.

Affirmative action involves intentionally seeking and hiring employees from groups that are underrepresented in the organization. Affirmative action guidelines have helped bring fairness in hiring and promotion to many organizations. Today, however, some people believe these guidelines are discriminatory because they allow preferential treatment for the people they were designed to protect.

KEY TERMS

managing diversity, 331
diversity, 332
inclusion, 332
primary dimensions, 332
secondary dimensions, 333

prejudice, 333
stereotypes, 333
unconscious bias, 333
ethnocentrism, 334
ethnic identity, 334

discrimination, 335
race, 336
affirmative action, 345
behavioral profiling, 350

CAREER INSIGHT

Discrimination against persons who are unemployed is a modern day problem. If you have been unemployed for a few months or a few years, here are some tips on how to get hired:

- When you are unemployed, keep your skills up to date. Take a class, become active in a professional group, consider becoming a volunteer.
- Redo your résumé. List only the past 10 years of work experience.

- Explore internships, fellowships, or work for a temp agency.
- Network. Tell everyone you are looking for a job.
- Understand that there might be negative perceptions about you because of your work record. Be proactive and bust the stereotype. Be prepared to show they are wrong.

Source: Adapted from Faye Fiore, "Will I Ever Work Again?" *aarp.org/bulletin*, October 2011, pp. 18–19.

TRY YOUR HAND

1. The "managing diversity and inclusion" movement has raised the discussion of equal employment opportunity and affirmative action to a higher level. Consider the following comments by R. Roosevelt Thomas, Jr., which appeared in a *Harvard Business Review* article entitled "From Affirmative Action to Affirming Diversity":

   Managers usually see affirmative action and equal employment opportunity as centering on minorities and women, with very little to offer white males. The diversity I'm talking about includes race, gender, creed, and ethnicity but also age, background, education, function, and personality differences. The objective is not to assimilate minorities and women into a dominant white male culture but to create a dominant heterogeneous culture.[50]

   What does "dominant heterogeneous culture" mean to you? Consider your former or current workplace. Assess how the atmosphere at work would be different if Roosevelt got his wish. Be specific.

2. For one week, keep a journal that records instances in which you see actions or hear comments that reflect prejudicial, negative stereotypes. For example, watch a movie or TV show and observe whether the actors are predominantly of a particular race or ethnic group. Listen to your friends' conversations, and notice any time they make

irrational judgments about others based on stereotypes. Finally, reflect on your own attitudes and perceptions. Do you engage in stereotyping?

Share your experiences with a class member, and propose what steps you can take to help rid the environment of negative stereotyping.

3. Arrange a meeting with someone who is a member of a racial or ethnic group different from your own, and try to build a relationship by discussing the things that are important to each of you. Perhaps it is another student, coworker, or member of your community. As you get to know this person, become aware of his or her beliefs and attitudes. Try not to be diverted by accent, grammar, or personal appearance; rather, really listen to the person's thoughts and ideas. Search for things you and your new acquaintance have in common, and assess how your differences could be opportunities for personal growth.

4. Before, during, and after the terrorist attacks and the war in Iraq, Muslims became victims of discrimination throughout the world, merely because of their religious beliefs and stereotyped physical appearance. To learn more about the Muslim culture, visit the Muslim Public Affairs Council website at www.mpac.org, the Muslim American Society at www.masnet.org, or www.Islam101.net, an introductory guide for non-Muslims. What did you learn that would help you respond to someone who displays a bias against Muslims in your presence?

CRITICAL THINKING CHALLENGE

In an ideal world, everyone would be free of prejudiced attitudes and would avoid thinking in terms of stereotypes. However, childhood experiences can shape attitudes that are difficult to change. Do you carry any prejudices that are obvious carryovers from your childhood or adolescence? Are you doing anything to overcome these prejudices? Explain.

SELF-ASSESSMENT EXERCISE

For each of the following statements, circle the number from 1 to 5 that best represents your response: (1) strongly disagree (never do this); (2) disagree (rarely do this); (3) moderately agree (sometimes do this); (4) agree (frequently do this); (5) strongly agree (almost always do this).

A. I refuse to perpetuate negative stereotypes, and I accept each person as a unique individual worthy of my respect.	1	2	3	4	5
B. I make every effort to identify my own prejudiced attitudes and avoid stereotypical attitudes toward people of color, older people, persons with disabilities, and others who are different from me.	1	2	3	4	5
C. I work hard to combat prejudice because it has a negative impact on my self-esteem and the self-esteem of the victim.	1	2	3	4	5
D. When I witness discriminatory behavior, I speak up and/or take action to defend the victim.	1	2	3	4	5
E. I understand the economics of valuing diversity and inclusion and support my employer's efforts to hire and retain minority employees.	1	2	3	4	5

After identifying your response to each item, select an attitude or skill you would like to improve. Prepare a written goal and then describe the steps you will take to achieve this goal.

YOU PLAY THE ROLE

You are currently supervising 15 employees. Until recently, the work group was working as a productive team and was free of any serious interpersonal relationship problems. Last week, Deaven Erhardt, a relatively new hire, posted an article from the *New York Times* supporting gay marriage on the workroom bulletin board. The article emphasized freedom of marital choice, which some of your senior colleagues find morally offensive. A week later, Erhardt posted another article from the *San Francisco Chronicle* supporting same-sex marriage and a petition to endorse gay marriage in your state. Needless to say, the workroom was becoming a politically contentious environment and was no longer free of interpersonal relationship problems. You explained the situation to your manager, and he suggested that you meet with Erhardt and request that no more articles be displayed in the work area. You will meet with another class member who will assume the role of Deaven Erhardt. Try to convince your role-play partner that these politically sensitive articles are inappropriate in a work setting.

BELOW THE SURFACE | SEX-BIAS TRIAL—QUESTIONS LINGER

Henk Meijer/Alamy

Throughout a three-year period, human resource personnel and others closely monitored the sex-bias suit involving venture capital firm Kleiner Perkins Caulfield & Byers and former executive Ellen Pao. Ms. Pao sued Kleiner, alleging that she was passed over for promotions and then fired after complaining about being sexually harassed by another partner. The trial drew international attention because of the highly charged claim that the venture firm had stymied the career of a promising woman. Also, this trial followed other recent allegations of unfair treatment by Silicon Valley high-tech firms. As the trial unfolded we learned that only about 5 percent of decision makers at venture capital firms are female.[51]

Sam Singer, a consultant in the field of crisis communications, noted that Kleiner Perkins does not have a conventional human resources department. However, the firm does have a policy covering discrimination and retaliation. He said the firm needs to adopt new human resources policies and procedures, and promote women and minorities to repair its image in the venture capital industry. The major thrust of Pao's complaint is that she was not "one of the guys" and her female status undermined any chance she had to rise to the top of the company.[52]

A jury made up of six men and six women ruled that Kleiner Perkins did not discriminate against Ellen Pao and didn't fire her in retaliation for her protesting her treatment. The decision has left a number of uncertainties. Will male-dominated Silicon Valley change its ways? Katia Beauchamp, co-CEO of Birchbox Inc., said the trial got people in the tech community talking, which could propel change. Chris Sacco, an active investor in high-tech companies, said the conversation about technology's "deep gender discrimination problem" shouldn't end with Pao's loss.[53]

QUESTIONS

1. Bernice Ledbetter, a faculty member at Pepperdine University, says "The outcome of the trial sends a message that women simply have to accommodate to such disappointing cultures." She also said, "You'd better work hard and make sure everyone around you knows the quality of your work and make sure that quality is unquestionable."[54] Do you agree with her point of view? Defend your response.

2. What steps should Kleiner Perkins take to make its culture more attractive to talented women and minorities? Explain your answer.

CLOSING CASE | RACIAL VERSUS BEHAVIOR PROFILING

Racial profiling refers to the use of a person's race or ethnicity by law enforcement personnel. It is sometimes a key factor in deciding whether to engage in enforcement. Some traffic stops, for example, are based on racial profiling:[55]

- A Hispanic driver is stopped in a "white" neighborhood because he "looks out of place."
- A group of black teenagers is pulled over because of the kind of car they are driving.

The American Civil Liberties Union (ACLU) has taken the position that racial profiling disproportionately targets people of color. This practice, at the federal level, is challenged by the Fourth Amendment of the U.S. Constitution, which guarantees the right to be safe from unreasonable search and seizure without probable cause.[56]

Behavioral profiling is the process of observing, anticipating, and interpreting a specific behavior. Gestures, body movements, tone of voice, and facial expressions can communicate confidence or fear, trust or mistrust, curiosity or boredom. All U.S. customs agents are required to watch videos teaching them techniques for studying body language in order to identify potential terrorists and drug traffickers.[57]

QUESTIONS

1. Critics of racial profiling argue that the individual rights of a suspect are violated if race is used as a factor in that suspicion. Do you agree or disagree with these critics?

2. Do you believe "behavior profiling" is a viable method of interpreting a person's actions? Why or why not?

3. There is no simple codebook of nonverbal cues that is accepted across all the cultures of the world. How would you enhance the training programs discussed in this case so that they compensate for cultural diversity?

CHAPTER 15 ENDNOTES

1. Pin Zhou and Daniel Dongjin Park, "Which Organizations Are Best in Class in Managing Diversity and Inclusion, and What Does Their Path of Success Look Like?" Cornell University ILR School, Spring 2013 [cited 11 March 2015]. Available from http://digitalcommons.ilr.cornell.edu/student/46/; INTERNET.

2. Tracey Lien, "Why Women Are Leaving the Tech Industry in Droves," *News & Observer*, March 8, 2015, p. 2E.

3. Ranjay Gulati, Anthony Mayo, and Nitin Nohria, *Management* (Mason, OH: Cengage Learning, 2014), pp. 444–445.

4. Royal Bank of Canada website, www.rbc.com/diversity/what is diversity [accessed 15 March 2015] INTERNET; T. Hudson Jordan, *Profiles in Diversity Journal*, November/December 2014, www.diversityjournal.com.

5. Ibid.

6. Marilyn Loden and Judy B. Rosener, *Workforce America!* (Homewood, IL: Business One Irwin, 1991), pp. 114–115. Information on primary and secondary dimensions of diversity can also be found in Marilyn Loden, *Implementing Diversity* (New York: McGraw-Hill, 1996).

7. Ibid., p. 21.

8. Douglas A. Bernstein, Louis A. Penner, Alison Clarke-Stewart, and Edward J. Roy, *Psychology*, 9th ed. (Belmont, CA: Wadsworth, 2012), p. 714.

9. Neal Goodman, "Unconscious Bias," *Training Magazine*, 2014, July/August, p. 62.

10. Joann S. Lubin, "Do You Know Your Hidden Work Biases?" *Wall Street Journal*, January 10, 2014, p. B1.

11. Ibid.

12. D. Stanley Eitzen and Maxine Baca Zinn, *In Conflict and Order* (Boston: Allyn & Bacon, 2001), p. 237.

13. Bernstein et al., *Psychology*, 9th ed., p. 505.

14. Lewis Brown Griggs and Lente-Louise Louw, *Valuing Diversity* (New York: McGraw-Hill, 1995), pp. 3–4, 150–151.

15. Doris Burke, "The Growing Wealth Gap," *Fortune*, November 7, 2011, p. 28.

16. Tom Lowry, "Extreme Experience," *BusinessWeek*, September 8, 2008, p. 46.

17. Joseph Weber, "This Time, Old Hands Keep Their Jobs," *BusinessWeek*, February 9, 2009, p. 50.

18. Sue Shellenbarger, "Work & Family Mailbox," *Wall Street Journal*, April 13, 2006, p. D4; Katie Humphrey, "Older Workers: Don't Be a Tech Fossil," *News & Observer*, December 10, 2013, p. D1.

19. Craig Calhoun, Donald Light, and Suzanne Keller, *Sociology*, 6th ed. (New York: McGraw-Hill, 1994), p. 241.

20. Nicholas D. Kristof, "Is Race Real?" *New York Times*, July 11, 2003; Robert S. Boynton, "Color Us Invisible," *New York Times Book Review*, August 17, 1997, p. 13.

21. Stephen Magagini, "A Race Free Consciousness," *News & Observer*, November 23, 1997, pp. A25–A26. Some science writers state that race does have a biological basis. See Nicholas Wade, "Race Has a Biological Basis. Racism Does Not," *Wall Street Journal*, June 23, 2014, p. A13.

22. Carol Mukhopadhyay and Rosemary C. Henze, "How Real Is Race? Using Anthropology to Make Sense of Human Diversity," *Phi Delta Kappa*, May 2003, p. 675.

23. Hansi LoWang, "Walking Down the Widening Aisle of Interracial marriages, http://www.npr.org/blogs/codeswitch/2014/02/13/276516736/walking-down-the-widening-aisle-of-interracial-marriages, May 7, 2015. Miriam Jordan, "More Marriages Cross Race, Ethnicity Lines," *Wall Street Journal*, February 17, 2012, p. A2; Natalie Morera, "Shades of Gray," *Diversity Executive*, July/August 2011, p. 30.

24. Yonat Shimron, "God as Fearsome Father," *News & Observer*, October 1, 2006, p. 24A.

25. Phred Dvorak, "Religious-Bias Filings Up," *Wall Street Journal*, October 16, 2008, pp. B1–B2.

26. Rabbi Rami Shapiro, "Can We Reconcile Faiths? Did Jesus Walk on Water?" *Spirituality & Health*, November/December 2007, p. 16.

27. Nadine Vogel, "Know the Facts: The EEOC and the ADA," *Diversity Executive*, January/February 2012, pp. 32–35.

28. Ibid.

29. Tim Cook, "Tim Cook Speaks Up," *Bloomberg BusinessWeek*, November 3, 2014, p. 13.

30. Sue Shellenbarger, "Amid Gay Marriage Debate, Companies Offer More Benefits to Same-Sex Couples," *Wall Street Journal*, March 18, 2004, p. D1; Barbara Rose, "Policies to Accommodate Gays Draw Scrutiny," *The News & Observer*, July 3, 2005, p. E12; Rachel Emma Silverman, "Wall Street, a New Push to Recruit Gay Students," *Wall Street Journal*, February 9, 2000, p. B1.

31. John Murawski, "Jobs Scarce, But the Stigma Stays," *News & Observer*, February 12, 2012, p. E1.

32. Chuck Salter, "Diversity Without the Excuses," *Fast Company*, September 2002, p. 44; Tamara J. Erickson,

"Diversity Leader as Cruise Director," *Diversity Executive*, July/August 2013, p. 12.

33. Jessica Marquez, "Survey Says Diversity Contributes to the Bottom Line," *Workforce Management*, November 18, 2005 [cited 23 February 2006]. Available from http://www.workforce.com; INTERNET.

34. Caroline Fairchild, "Solving Tech's Diversity Problem—Starting at the Top," *Fortune*, March 15, 2015, pp. 126–127.

35. Gail Johnson, "Time to Broaden Diversity," *Training*, September 2004, p. 16; Adapted from Leone E. Wynter, "Do Diversity Programs Make a Difference?" *Wall Street Journal*, December 4, 1996, p. B1.

36. Kenji Yoshinto and Christie Smith, "Fear of Being Different Stifles Talent," *Harvard Business Review*, March 2014, p. 28.

37. Sam Ali, "How IBM Holds People Accountable for Diversity Results," *Diversity Inc. Magazine*, December 6, 2010, Available from www.diversityinc.com; INTERNET.

38. Caroline Fairchild, "Solving Tech's Diversity Problem—Starting at the Top," *Fortune*, March 15, 2015, pp. 127.

39. Geoff Calvin, "Personal Bests," *Fortune*, March 15, 2015, pp. 106 to …?

40. Shankar Vedantam, "Forced Diversity Training Fails," *News & Observer*, July 21, 2008, p. 3A.

41. "Diversity Dilemma," *Training*, July/August 2007, p. 10.

42. Ricky W. Griffin, *Principles of Management* (Boston: Houghton Mifflin Company, 2007), p. 195.

43. Jonathon Kaufman, "Fair Enough," *Wall Street Journal*, June 14, 2008, p. A8.

44. "Affirmative Action," [cited 15 April 2012] Available from www.wikipedia.org; INTERNET.

45. Bob Gregg, "Debunking the Affirmative-Action Myth," *Diversity Inc. Magazine*, March 17, 2011. Available from www.diversity.com; INTERNET.

46. Ibid.

47. Ibid.

48. Robert Kreitner and Carlene M. Cassidy, *Management*, 12th ed. (Mason, OH: Cengage Learning, 2011), p. 277.

49. Roger O. Crockett, "How to Narrow the Great Divide," *BusinessWeek*, July 14, 2003, p. 104; Sharon S. Brehm, Saul M. Kassin, and Steven Fein, *Social Psychology*, 5th ed. (Boston: Houghton Mifflin, 2002), pp. 478–480.

50. R. Roosevelt Thomas, Jr., "From Affirmative Action to Affirming Diversity," *Harvard Business Review*, March/April 1990, p. 114.

51. Deborah Gage and Jeff Elder, "Sex-Bias Trial Takes Big Toll on Kleimer," *Wall Street Journal*, March 25, 2015, p. B1.

52. Catherine Ross Dunham, "The Challenges of Gender Bias," *News & Observer*, March 24, 2015, p. 15A; Deborah Gage and Jeff Elder, "Sex-Bias Trial Takes Big

Toll on Kleiner," *Wall Street Journal*, March 25, 2015, p. B7.

53. Jeff Elder, "Silicon Valley Sex-Bias Suit Takes Odd Turn at End," *Wall Street Journal*, March 28, 2015, p. A1; Paresh Dave, "Questions Linger After Loss in Gender-Bias Lawsuit," *News & Observer*, March 29, 2015, p. 4A.

54. Dave, "Questions Linger," p. 4A.

55. "Racial Profiling," [cited 18 April 2012]. Available from http://en.wikipedia.org; INTERNET.

56. "Racial Profiling," [cited 18 April 2012]. Available from www.aclu.org; INTERNET.

57. Ann David, Joseph Pereira, and William M. Bulkeley, "Security Concerns Bring New Focus on Body Language," *Wall Street Journal*, August 15, 2002, pp. A1, A6; "The Power of Body Language," Course Archive [cited 6 January 2003]. Available from www.presentersuniversity.com/courses/show_archive.cfm?RecordID 539; INTERNET.

Henk Meijer/Alamy

The Changing Roles of Men and Women

TIP OF THE ICEBERG | MEN ENLISTED IN FIGHT FOR GENDER EQUALITY

C atalyst is a research and advisory group that has raised awareness of how diversity and inclusion benefit today's global businesses. For over 50 years Catalyst has been a leader in the study of women and men across job levels. The primary goal of this organization is to advance women in business.[1]

Although efforts to level the playing field for women are touted in the media, the gender gap still exists in compensation and other important areas such as the number of women holding senior executive positions and board seats. Women serve in very few top leadership positions, and they are underrepresented in many technical areas such as computer science and engineering. Only 6 percent of the partners in venture capital firms are women.[2] Sheryl Sandberg, COO of Facebook and author of *Lean In*, says "Women are making progress at every level except as leaders. We started accounting for (over) 50% of college degrees 30 years ago, but progress at the top has stalled. For the past decade women in corporate America have held only about 14% of C-suite jobs and 17% of board seats. There aren't enough women sitting at the tables where decisions are made."[3]

In recent years Catalyst has enlisted men in the fight for gender equality. A new Catalyst initiative teaches middle managers and senior executives to understand hurdles facing women and the influence of unconscious bias. About 60 male bosses from Dell, Cardinal Health Inc., and several other companies attended a six-month program organized by Catalyst. A firm called White Men As Full Diversity Partners, coaches men to shift their mind-set and behavior patterns to create a more inclusive work culture, helped design the program. Participants learn that men must be highly involved to change the balance of power in senior management.[4]

Image Source/Vetta/getty images

353

ANDREW GOMBERT/EPA /LANDOV

Sheryl Sandberg, COO of Facebook and author of the book, "Lean In" is a vocal advocate for increasing the number of women in leadership positions, especially those at the highest level who have decision making authority.

TRADITIONAL ROLES ARE CHANGING

16-1 All cultures promote one set of behaviors for boys and a separate set for girls. Children generally learn their socially acceptable roles by the time they are five years old, and these roles are often continually reinforced throughout the life cycle by teachers, parents, authority figures, and the media. These traditional roles can be harmful to both men and women. For instance, the expectation that men should be aggressive and unemotional stifles their sensitivity and creativity. The assumption that women are emotional and weak hinders them in reaching leadership positions. Although men and women will always be different, their career opportunities should not be limited by gender.

Gender bias (also known as sexism) is discrimination on the basis of gender. When employers base employment, promotion, job assignment, and compensation decisions on a person's gender, human relations and productivity suffer. Gender bias is no longer a female-only issue, and many organizations are making the necessary adjustments.

Changes in the Role of Women

In past generations, children were more likely to see their mothers as homemakers and their fathers as breadwinners. Today, a large number of women have assumed the role of primary breadwinner or are part of a dual-earner family. The recent economic downturn and the large number of marriages that end in divorce have accelerated this trend.

The women's movement that began in the 1960s with Betty Friedan's book, *The Feminine Mystique*, has helped women make positive strides toward equality with men in the workplace. Historians often say this book started women down a path that changed family life and American culture. It made American housewives realize they could grow and fulfill their potential as human beings.[5] Katherine Montwieler, an associate professor of women's studies at the University of North Carolina–Wilmington, says when she recently read the reissued book she was stunned by its relevance. "How could a book written for my mother's generation still be applicable or appealing to me, a working mother, in 2013?"[6] One culprit is technology. Constant connectivity creates anxiety. "In spite of living the feminist dream, the women I see are tired, stressed and overworked. With the modern conveniences of Blackberries and smartphones, we're always on—waiting for the text from our bosses, our partners, our children, our children's teachers, our parents, our neighbors. We're hyperattuned, always listening for the beep that warns us of the next emergency (no matter how small)."[7]

Few Women at the Top. Women now make up about half the U.S. workforce and over half of managerial and professional positions. Yet their rise to senior executive positions and corporate boards has stalled. According to Catalyst, women hold only 16.9 percent of board of director seats, 14.6 percent of executive officer positions, and 4.2 percent of CEO positions. They are earning advanced professional degrees in record numbers, and in some areas, surpassing men. The number of women in senior leadership positions is greater in other parts of the world, especially in Europe, but women in some Middle Eastern countries still face major barriers. Catalyst makes the following point: "Doing all the right things" to get ahead works well for men, but does not provide as great an advantage for women.[8] Later in this chapter, we will discuss some initiatives that will help women achieve greater parity with men. Women have made significant gains in a wide range of traditionally male-dominated areas such as law and medicine. Computer science is still a major problem area for women in addition to high-skill, high-paying jobs such as physicians, surgeons, attorneys, CEOs, and most positions in the finance industry. Studies indicate that men continue to dominate manufacturing and construction jobs, whereas women hold only a small percentage of these jobs. The good news is that research shows that men and women are increasingly moving into, and succeeding in, nontraditional careers. If less than 25 percent of the workforce is of one gender, a career is considered nontraditional.[9]

Changes in the Role of Men

As noted in Chapter 4, the transition from childhood to adulthood can be a long and difficult period. This is especially true of young men who are living in a new kind of extended adolescence. Adolescence for males now extends through their 20s and even, for many, into their 30s. Kay Hymowitz, in a *Wall Street Journal* article titled "Where Have All the Good Men Gone," makes the following observation:[10]

> *Not so long ago, the average American man in his 20s had achieved most of the milestones of adulthood: a high-school diploma, financial independence, marriage and children. Today, most men in their 20s hang out in a novel sort of limbo, a hybrid state of semi-hormonal adolescence and responsible self-reliance.*

Hymowitz does not feel that this period of "pre-adulthood" brings out the best in men. John Rosemond, author of the syndicated newspaper column *Parenting*, believes that many underachieving males grew up in homes where the role of father was diminished. The most obvious example is the father-absent home. The high divorce rate has contributed greatly to the diminishment of male influence during the preteen and teen years.[11]

The Burden of Job Loss

The most recent recession in the United States began in December 2007 and ended June 2009. Two male-dominated industries—construction and manufacturing—account for about half of the jobs lost since this period. Men account for 87 percent of the workers in manufacturing and 71 percent in construction. Although the U.S. economy has improved and the unemployment rate is falling, about 17 percent of working-age men are not looking for work. Men without jobs, especially those who have been without a job for one or two years, stand apart in a society that has long celebrated work. Many employers won't hire men out of work too long.[12] For women, the story is different in some industries. Eighty-one percent of health-care workers are women, and this industry has realized a net gain in jobs.[13]

A feature article in *Bloomberg Businessweek* began with this ominous headline: "The Hidden Job Crisis for American Men." The article describes a trend of disengagement for male workers that stretches back six decades. In the early 1970s, only 6 percent of American men ages 25 to 54 were without jobs. By late 2007, it was 13 percent. In 2009, during the worst of the recession, 20 percent were unemployed. Even though the economy is improving and unemployment is dropping, many men in their prime working years are not working, and two-thirds said they were not looking.[14]

Historically, men were more likely to work full time than women. Many of these full-time male workers have assumed the duties of breadwinner, a role accompanied by a great deal of self-imposed as well as societal stress. The sudden loss of a job can be devastating. Many of these men face long periods of unemployment, and when they do return to the labor market, earnings are likely to be much lower.

human RELATIONS *in Action*

SECRET SERVICE SCANDAL SHOWS GENDER GAP

On the morning of April 12, 2012, a U.S. Secret Service officer and a prostitute publicly argued over payment in a hotel hallway. During the investigation of this incident it was learned that a dozen Secret Service employees had hired prostitutes who visited them at their hotel. These agents were part of a large group sent to Colombia ahead of President Barack Obama's visit. Critics of the Secret Service believe that greater diversity would bring more accountability to the agency. Only about 11 percent of agents and uniformed officers are women.

Source: Eric Tucker, "Scandal Shows Gender Gap at Secret Service," *The News & Observer*, April 29, 2012, p. 3A.

PROBLEMS FACING WOMEN IN ORGANIZATIONS

16-2

When women pursue careers, they often face three major challenges: the wage gap, the glass ceiling, and balancing career and family. Many employers are making changes to accommodate women, but more needs to be done.

The Wage Gap

In 1963, John F. Kennedy signed the Equal Pay Act into law. The goal of this law was to end the practice of paying women lower rates for the same job strictly on the basis of their sex. At that time, women with full-time jobs earned on average between 59 and 64 cents for every dollar their male counterparts earned in the same jobs.[15]

Fast forward to National Equal Pay Day held on April 17, 2012. President Barack Obama issued a proclamation that noted women who work full time earn only 77 cents for every dollar their male counterparts earn. He also noted that the pay gap was even greater for Latina and African-American women.[16] In 2013 the wage gap remained virtually unchanged, with women earning 78 percent of what men earn. There has been no real movement in the gender wage gap since 2007, and there is still a long way to go before true pay equity is achieved.[17]

Recent data analysis from the American Association of University Women shows that the gap between men's and women's wages differs greatly depending on the state where you live. Louisiana ranked last, with women earning just 65.9 percent of what their male counterparts do ($31,865 vs. $48,318)).[18] African American women earn 49.1 percent and Latina women 53.4 percent for every dollar a white, non-Hispanic man makes.

The Wage Gap Persists

In many occupations, women still earn less than men doing the same job, working the same number of hours, and bringing to the job the same amount of work experience and education. The Institute for Women's Policy Research says the reasons for discrimination vary, but research indicates that women are less likely to be selected for the best jobs. So they begin their careers at a lower wage and may not catch up. The staff at IWPR says, "Discrimination in who gets hired for the best jobs hits all women but particularly black and Hispanic women."[19]

Today, women are more committed to building a career, but many still take time off to have children. This may work against them because continuous work experience tends to increase both productivity and pay in many employment settings.[20]

The Glass Ceiling

Gender discrimination toward women not only causes a wage gap, it also keeps women from advancing to the most senior-level positions, those with the most power. This is often referred to as the **glass ceiling**. Catalyst has studied women in business and has documented widespread limits on female career advancement to the highest levels of our nation's largest corporations. Although we have seen positive change at the middle-management ranks, women are still being held back by some widely held misconceptions.

The two female students in this photo are less likely to be selected for the best jobs and may face barriers to career advancement. They are more likely to begin their careers at a lower wage and may not catch up.

Hostile Work Cultures in Male-Dominated Industries

You might think that younger workforces in the technology sector would discriminate less, but that is not the case. Google's engineering workforce is only 17 percent female, and it is just 15 percent at Facebook. A *Harvard Business Review* study in 2008, updated in 2014, found that 50 percent of women in science, technology, and engineering will leave over time because of hostile work environments. They say a sense of isolation, lack of a clear career path, and hostile male cultures are the reasons. Most women say the attitudes and behaviors holding them back are subtle, but they happen day after day and often keep women excluded from teams. So despite all the recruiting efforts to fill tech jobs, estimated to double by 2020, it is expected that qualified women will continue to leave the tech industry in droves unless big changes are made.[21]

The picture looks similar in the finance sector. More than one in two workers in Fortune 500 financial services companies is a woman, yet only one in eight is an executive officer.[22]

Building a Better Pipeline.   After many years of aggressive efforts to create opportunities for women who are seeking top management positions, inequality remains entrenched. Companies must come up with better programs to help talented women advance. Here are some suggestions:

- Recognize that first jobs set the stage for all the inequities that follow. Women earn, on average, $4,600 less than their male peers in their first post-MBA job—a gap that widens to more than $31,000 as their careers advance.[23]
- Closing the pay gap involves reducing the influence of the Old Boys' Club. Ilene Lang, president and CEO of Catalyst, says the Club is not necessarily malicious, but "It entails establishing business relationships on high-priced golf courses, at exclusive country clubs, in the executive sky-boxes at sporting events—arenas from which women and minorities are traditionally excluded.[24]
- Smart companies recognize that their high-potential women must be sponsored by top executives, most of whom are men, as pointed out in the opening vignette. These companies hold male executives accountable for the success of female rising stars.[25]

The *Wall Street Journal* compiled a list of 10 female executives whose operational expertise and track record make them likely CEO candidates to head a Fortune 1000 company within five years. Nine members of the group have children, and many have husbands who abandoned the fast track to support their wives' careers.[26]

Women who pursue top-level positions must often cope with jobs structured to accommodate the lives of men with wives who do not have full-time careers. They also must cope with the social pressure to fulfill more traditional, "feminine" roles.[27]

Women on Boards Improves Company Performance

Why should we be concerned about the dominance of men in top leadership positions? A study by Credit Suisse Research Institute found that companies with a market capitalization of more than $10 billion and have women board members outperformed businesses with all-male boards by 26 percent worldwide over a six-year period. Companies with mixed genders perform better in challenging markets than all-male boards by increasing return on equity and curbing risky investments.[28]

Cultures that are totally masculine often lack compassion and give rise to rigid, intolerant practices since they lack the intuitive, empathic qualities more common among women. In some cases, a highly competitive masculine culture encourages greed and corruption. The male-dominated hierarchy at Enron, WorldCom, Bernard L. Madoff Investment Securities LLC, and Tyco, for example, fostered unethical practices on a grand scale.

Total Person Insight

> "Professors at Pepperdine University conducted a massive 19-year survey of 215 *Fortune 500* companies. By every measure of profitability, the study found that companies with the best records for promoting women to executive positions outperform the competition."
>
> Source: Clair Shipman and Katty Kay, *Womenomics: Write Your Own Rules for Success* (New York: HarperCollins, 2009), pp. 2–3.

Macho leadership styles can also alienate women. The idea is not to push men off the stage but to get more women onto the stage with them. In an ideal situation, women and men will share the stage and create a culture where everyone can express the full range of his or her talents.[29]

Balancing Career and Family Choices

Women today know that they will be working for pay for part or all of their adult lives. This expectation is quite a departure from previous generations, when most women assumed the responsibilities of wife and mother. The challenge of performing multiple roles, however, can be stressful and tiring. Most women in two-income families not only contribute significantly to their family's income, but also do most of their family's household chores.

The "Mommy Track" and Maternal Wall Bias. The term **Mommy Track** is used to describe the lifestyle of women who choose a career path that allows a mother flexible or reduced work hours. Unfortunately, this may slow or block advancement.

Contrary to what some hold as popular belief, women are not leaving high-profile jobs because it is a lifestyle choice. Working 10 to 12 hours a day plus the ongoing battle in male-dominated cultures is driving many women to start their own businesses or make career changes. Progressive companies that recognize women want both a career and the flexibility to work remotely, or part-time, or just a 40-hour week (not a job that extends into nights and weekends), are making huge strides in recruiting highly skilled professional women.

human RELATIONS *in Action*

WAYS WOMEN CAN HOLD THEIR OWN IN A MALE WORLD

- *Make sure women are valued.* Check to see whether the company values women and if they are represented on the board and in leadership positions.
- *Identify alpha and beta males.* Separate the two types of men in the office and engage in conversations accordingly. Alpha males have a "get it done" mindset, and beta males are more concerned with "collaboration and partnership."
- *Find a mentor.* Look for a female employee at the company with direct experience in a male-dominated workplace.
- *Speak assertively.* Eliminate the phrase "I'm sorry" from your vocabulary. Apologizing for a situation that you are not responsible for demonstrates weakness. Do not begin a phrase, "*I* think," as it demeans what you are saying.
- *Socialize with the boys.* Make your best effort to socialize with your male coworkers in formal and informal situations.
- *Do not assume stereotypical roles.* Let others "clean up" after your coworkers and bring coffee to meetings.

Source: Dana Mattioli, "Ways Women Can Hold Their Own in a Male World," *The Wall Street Journal,* August 25, 2008, p. D4.

Jeff Gritchen/Long Beach Press-Telegram/ZUMA/ZUMA Press, Inc/Alamy

Anne Sweeney is co-chair of Disney Media Networks and president of Disney ABC Television Group. Her position represents a growing shift in many companies toward diversifying their top-level management.

Women in greater numbers than ever before are combining motherhood and work. Some are willing to trade some career growth and compensation for freedom from the constant pressure to work long hours and weekends. And a growing number of women say, "I want a career and a family." By the time women reach age 40, about 25 percent have both careers and children.[30]

Many women want to expand their life choices but are uncertain about the options available. If you are a woman who wants both career and family, then consider the following:[31]

- Choose a career that will give you the gift of time. Some careers provide more flexibility and are more forgiving of interruptions such as parental leave
- Choose a partner who supports your goal of having a career and a family.
- Choose an employer who has given work/life balance a high priority.
- Be prepared to use your negotiation skills to push for policies and practices that are favorable to employees with children.

According to Judith Warner, who wrote *Perfect Madness—Motherhood in the Age of Anxiety*, mothers who try to achieve work/family balance (I'm a great mom and a great worker) often feel a sense of frustration as they try to "do it all."[32]

PROBLEMS FACING MEN IN ORGANIZATIONS

16-3 Many men are beginning to realize that they have been as rigidly stereotyped in their roles as women have been in theirs. Men encounter resistance from their families, coworkers, and friends when they break out of their stereotypes. The changes a man makes to alter traditional masculine role characteristics can be threatening to others and can cause serious problems in his relationships.

Men Working with Women

Male attitudes toward female ambitions have changed over the years. One reason for this change is the dramatic increase of female college classmates. Men have learned that they will be competing with these smart and ambitious women in the workplace. They are also learning that women can be excellent coworkers, team members, and leaders. Those men who are secure in their talents and abilities welcome the opportunity to work beside equally self-assured women. Those men who are threatened by powerful, talented women need an attitude adjustment.

Balancing Career and Family Choices

Henry David Thoreau observed that "the mass of men lead lives of quiet desperation." Does this dire observation apply to men who are pursuing careers and assuming family roles today? The answer is a qualified yes. Men, like women, now have more choices about marriage and family life and face many barriers to achieving work/life balance.

- The long-term trend toward wage equality gives families more choices about who should assume the roles of breadwinner, child-care provider, and housekeeper. One wife in four now out-earns her husband.
- Men often seek a "package deal" in life that includes four elements: marriage, fatherhood, employment, and homeownership—not necessarily in that order. Yet these goals often conflict. Many men express the desire to be closer to their children than their traditional fathers were to them, but they get caught in the traditional cycle of working long hours to pay for a nice home for their families.[33] Unfortunately, men are often reluctant to talk openly about personal pressures created by these work/family conflicts, and the cycle continues.

Columbia/Everett Collection

The lines between traditional gender roles become blurred as men and women become increasingly integrated within society.

■ Working fathers who want to take paternity leave or time off to help raise their children are reluctant to do so. They fear losing status at work or resentment and teasing from coworkers. About 15 percent of U.S. firms provide some form of paid leave for new fathers, but men are reluctant to take it. Bank of America is one of the most generous, offering 12 weeks of paid leave. Ernst & Young offers six weeks, and Yahoo offers eight weeks off with full pay. In one survey of Fortune 500 companies, 85 percent of new fathers took some time off after the birth of a child, but "the vast majority" takes only a week or two.[34] The concept of paid paternity leave in the rest of the world is quite different. Sweden offers 61 weeks of paid paternity leave, Germany provides 52 weeks, and Canada provides new fathers with 35 weeks.

The United States ranks at the bottom—as one of the only four countries in the world (with Liberia, Suriname, and Papua New Guinea), that do not guarantee paid parental leave.[35] Both men and women feel uneasy about taking parental leave that may unofficially penalize them. Just as women struggle with this issue, men must also step forward and encourage employers to commit to family-friendly workplace policies and practices. Table 16.1 provides some tips for the at-home partner and the breadwinner.

During life's most stressful transitions, such as divorce or loss of a job, men often spend more time reflecting on things they value in life. Those who feel that their male identity is dependent on what is accomplished at work and that success is measured by the size of their paycheck sometimes reestablish their priorities. In a *Wall Street Journal* article entitled "Who's the New Guy at Dinner? It's Dad," one dad explains his transition

Table 16.1 ■ Striking a Balance

If You Are the at-Home Partner

■ Own the choice you've made while recognizing that traditional gender roles don't always correspond with a couple's actual competencies.

■ Inoculate yourself against the loss of identity you may feel, or the isolation you may experience, by forging a strong community of other professionals who have made similar decisions to head home.

■ Understand that your partner's work, while providing time away from child-care duties and household chores, is not vacation.

■ Talk clearly with your partner about what's going to work for a two-year period, not just for the moment. Recognize that your current arrangement is not forever.

If You Are the Breadwinner

■ Some resentments are unavoidable and can convey important information about yourself.

■ Be sensitive to your partner's loss of professional identity. Don't take work inside the home for granted.

■ Give your partner time to adjust to new duties before swooping in to correct their parenting behavior or housekeeping style.

■ Do not assume that because you earn the money, you hold greater decision-making status in your relationship.

Source: Two People, One Breadwinner, sidebar: "Striking a Balance" by Deborah Siegel from *Psychology Today*, July/August 2007. Reprinted with permission from *Psychology Today Magazine* (Copyright © 2007 Sussex Publishers, LLC).

following the loss of his managerial job at AOL. He says he told his young twin daughters, "I'm going to find a new job doing something I love that makes people happy." When he was hired as a fifth-grade teacher, his children were thrilled, and so was he. He can now spend more time with his children.[36]

CHALLENGES AND OPPORTUNITIES FOR WORKING MEN AND WOMEN

`16-4` As men and women struggle with their career and family choices, many progressive organizations are gearing up to meet the needs of their employees in the 21st century. They are recognizing the demands placed on working parents and are trying to address the problems associated with quality child care. At the same time, they realize they should provide flexible work schedules that adjust to the changing roles of men and women.

The Challenge of Child Care

The need for affordable, quality child care has never been greater. Mothers and fathers alike face forced overtime and unpredictable hours as their employers try to cut costs while improving productivity. At the same time, many day-care providers shut their doors at 6:00 p.m. and on weekends. Workers who cannot balance the demands of work with available child care are often disciplined or fired.

Eighty percent of employers report that child-care problems force employees to lose work time.

Some companies provide on-site day-care centers and find this fringe benefit a strong factor in retaining valuable employees who are also parents. Eighty percent of employers report that child-care problems force employees to lose work time.[37]

Many of *Fortune's* 100 Best Companies to Work For have made the list because of their sensitivity to the needs of workers with children; consequently, they have provided programs and activities that meet workers' needs. SAS Institute based in Cary, North Carolina, was number 4 on the list of *100 Best Companies to Work For* in 2015. This company offers employees on-site child care and a modern health and fitness center.

human RELATIONS *in Action*

THE FAMILY AND MEDICAL LEAVE ACT

The Family and Medical Leave Act (FMLA) guarantees continuation of any paid health benefits, plus a return to the same or an equivalent job, for employees (men as well as women) who take up to 12 weeks' unpaid time off—all at once or intermittently—so that they can care for themselves or an ailing family member such as a parent, child, or spouse during a serious health condition, or for childbirth or adoption. (Some states are considering providing financial compensation during part or all of the employee's time off.)

To qualify, you must work for an employer with 50 or more employees and at a location with at least 50 employees within 75 miles. Your employer can deny leave if you have not worked there for at least 12 months and for at least 1,250 hours during the past year. You also may be ineligible for protection if you are among your employer's top 10 percent of employees, based on pay.

According to the Bureau of Labor Statistics, only 11 percent of all private industry workers have access to paid family leave. Low-wage earners fare much worse. Only 5 percent of low-income workers get any paid maternity leave. Although FMLA allows U.S. workers to take some time off, nearly half are unable to do so because they cannot afford to go without income. A few insightful companies realize that offering paid family leave is a competitive advantage that keeps employees from leaving the company. When Google realized it was losing women at twice the rate of men, they changed their policy to offer 18 weeks of paid leave, and attrition dropped by 50 percent. Susan Wojcicki, CEO of YouTube, says paid family leave is good for mothers, "And it's much better for Google's bottom line—to avoid costly turnover, and to retain the valued expertise, skills and perspective of our employees who are mothers."

Source: Lauren Sandler, "How to Love Paid Family Leave," *Bloomberg Business Week*, July 21, 2014; Tara Siegel Bernard, "In Paid Family Leave, U.S. Trails Most of the Globe," *New York Times*, February 23, 2013, pg. B1; Susan Wojcicki, "Paid Maternity Leave Is Good for Business," *Wall Street Journal*, December 17, 2014, p. A17.

Keep in mind, however, the resentment that may build among child-free employees who see employees with children given the opportunity to arrive late or leave early to accommodate the needs of their children. To prevent this potential human relations problem, employers should consider offering flexible schedules to all employees (see Figure 16.1).

Flexible Work Schedule Presents Both Opportunities and Problems

Men and women who are concerned about balancing personal and work lives say that flexible work schedules rank very high on the list of desired benefits. As a result, organizations may allow various scheduling options so that they can recruit and retain the top talent in the labor market. On the other side of this issue is the downside of part-time shifts. The combination of real-time data and workflow optimization software will schedule employees according to what works best for the company. This has created a nightmare for many hourly paid employees who have fluctuating schedules week to week and may not have more than three-days' notice about work schedule. This is especially hard on single-parent families who are left scrambling to arrange child care. For example, Jannette Navarro, a single mother of a four-year-old boy, is a barrista at Starbucks who commutes three hours to work. Sometimes her shift ends at 11:00 p.m. and starts the next day at 4:00 a.m.[38]

Scheduling and workflow may be the only things a manager can do to improve the profitability of a store (and how they are compensated); therefore the burden falls hardest on employees.

Figure 16.1 ■ A Two-Way Street

To make flexible scheduling more fair for working parents and child-free employees alike, some employers are:

- Allowing all employees to apply for flexible schedules
- Requiring proposals that outline how the flexible schedule will impact work that must be completed in a timely manner
- Evaluating flexible setups regularly
- Making scheduling a team responsibility
- Cross-training workers so that they can take over their coworkers' responsibilities when necessary

Source: Figure adapted from Sue Shellenbarger, "A Two-Way Street," *Wall Street Journal*, November 17, 2005, p. D1.

Figure 16.2 ■ Flextime in Action

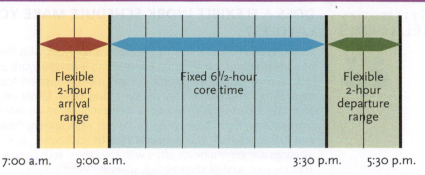

Source: Robert Kreitner and Carlene Cassidy, *Management*, 12th ed. (Mason, OH: Cengage Learning, 2011), p. 348.

Flextime. **Flextime** typically includes a core time when all employees work, usually between 9:00 a.m. and 3:30 p.m. Employees can determine their own arrival and departure times within certain limits, which may mean arriving at 7:00 a.m. or leaving at 5:30 p.m. (see Figure 16.2).[39]

Compressed Workweek. Typically, a **compressed workweek** consists of four 10-hour days—for example, Monday through Thursday or Thursday through Sunday. Employees may be given the opportunity to adjust their work schedules to fit their lifestyles. Another example is the 9/80 schedule. Employees work one extra hour each day for nine days, a total of 80 hours in two weeks, and receive a three-day weekend every other week.[40]

Paid-Time-Off (PTO) Banks. With a **PTO bank**, normal paid-time-off days—vacation allotment, sick days, personal days—are lumped together into a time bank that employees can draw from in hourly increments. Employees can draw from their accounts whenever they need to and for whatever reason. About one-third of the U.S. companies currently have PTO banks.[41]

Job Sharing. With **job sharing**, two employees share the responsibilities of one job. For example, one employee might work the mornings and the other employee might work the afternoons. In some cases, each job sharer works two days alone and one day overlapping with the other person. This means the job is fully covered, and each job sharer knows what the other is doing.[42]

Telecommuting and Virtual Office. The availability of powerful home-office computer and communication technologies have fueled an increase in **telecommuting**—employees working in a virtual office arrangement, usually at home. This not only helps employees balance work and family by eliminating commute time, it also helps employees get more done without the distractions of meetings, social conversation, and other time-consuming activities that can fill up a workday. Employers also benefit from employees who work from their virtual office by saving on real estate and office costs.

DOES A FLEXIBLE WORK SCHEDULE MAKE YOU A TARGET FOR LAYOFFS?

As the economy continues to fluctuate, employees who have chosen flexible work options often fear loss of job security. Maintaining a flexible work schedule requires planning—and luck. In an uncertain workforce climate, many employers focus on those employees who are there 9-to-5 and whom they see on a daily basis. Other employers evaluate costs and view an efficient part-time employee or telecommuter as an asset. In a nontraditional work environment where you have chosen a flexible work option, "you need to be realistic, be flexible, and deliver results." Your schedule may be scrutinized, so it is important to attend important meetings and communicate often with coworkers, your boss, and others in the organization. "To improve your survival chances, ask yourself, 'What's most important to my company right now, and how do I make sure I'm contributing to that, and that my achievement is visible to my boss?'"

Source: Sue Shellenbarger, "Does Avoiding a 9-to-5 Grind Make You a Target for Layoffs?" *Wall Street Journal*, April 22, 2009, p. D1.

HOW TO COPE WITH GENDER-BIASED BEHAVIOR

16-5   Traditional attitudes, beliefs, and practices are not changed easily. If you are a man or a woman breaking into a nontraditional role, you may encounter resistance. Several decades of research has shown that gender biases will perpetuate unless "intentionally interrupted" by introducing a new behavior or action that is designed to change the outcome. For example, researchers Andreas Leibbrant and John List studied the effect of language and salary negotiation with women when certain words are used to advertise administrative positions in male-dominated fields. One version of the job post said nothing about salary and the other said "salary negotiable." By simply including these two words in the job posting, the pay gap between men and women closed by 45 percent. This is an ideal example of a **bias interrupter** because it eliminates the gender issue without even raising the issue of gender.[43]

Unlike random diversity training classes and cultural initiatives, bias interrupters are based on establishing a measurable improvement (target metric) that is tested and measured for improvements in the gender bias. Since every company is unique, it is vitally important to test and measure each action, then test and measure again, so improvements are made in an iterative manner. This process will build change into the business systems so that the new pattern of work style remains integrated into business practices.

Joan Williams, a law professor and founding director of the Center for WorkLife Law at the University of California, suggests specific ways companies can identify, measure, and address gender issues. The first step is to determine if there is a gender issue and specifically define what the gender bias is. An expert trained in gender bias conducts detailed interviews and focus groups to uncover gender bias issues. There are four areas where patterns usually emerge:

1. Hiring practices. For example, the language used in a job posting, how some resumes are selected over others, whether or not women with children are hired less often than those with no children.
2. Work assignments. How is work assigned to people across various organizational levels? Do women tend to be assigned remedial tasks and men given high-profile responsibilities? Do women returning from maternity leave get poor-quality assignments?

3. Performance evaluations. Are men rewarded for being assertive, outspoken, competitive, and direct while women are penalized for the same characteristics and called "bossy" or "too ambitious?" Women walk a fine line between being seen as too feminine to be effective and too masculine to be likeable.[44]

4. Compensation. How is compensation set for women and men in the same roles? In the first three areas described here, research shows women have to provide more evidence of competence than men to be seen as equally capable. Even when promoted they often don't get the title and salary men do.

Women contend with not only the glass ceiling but the "maternal wall" as well if they decide to have children. A classic discrimination study by Shelley Correll, Stephan Bernard, and In Paik found that women with children are 79 percent less likely to be hired than women without children. On the other hand, men with children were seen as the most hirable and called "responsible." The study also found that a mother was 50 percent less likely to be promoted than a childless woman and is offered an average of $11,000 less in salary. If this isn't damaging enough, women were also held to higher performance and punctuality standards—discrimination much larger than what is found in the context of the glass ceiling.[45]

After a company understands what biases exist and how to measure them, the next step is to interrupt the bias with specific actions. The best bias interrupters require no training or even mention of gender bias. When Google learned women were being promoted less often than men, they discovered that seeking a promotion required people to nominate themselves, which women rarely do because they are modest and it goes against their nature. When women were told they were expected to promote themselves to even be considered for a promotion, the gender difference of women nominating themselves disappeared.[46]

Sexual Harassment in the Workplace

One of the most sensitive problems between men and women in organizations is **sexual harassment**, unwelcome verbal or physical behavior that affects a person's job performance or work environment. Employers have a legal and moral responsibility to prevent sexual harassment, which can occur from men harassing women, women harassing men, or same-sex harassment. As men and women work together on teams, more employers are becoming acutely aware of the increased potential for misinterpreted comments and actions between the genders. When sexual harassment is present in the workplace, the cost of increased absenteeism, staff turnover, low morale, and low productivity can be high.

Forms of Sexual Harassment. Under the law, sexual harassment may take one of two forms. The first is **quid pro quo** (something for something), which occurs when a person in a supervisory or managerial position threatens the job security or a potential promotion of a subordinate worker who refuses to submit to sexual advances. These kinds of threats are absolutely prohibited, and employers are liable for damages under the Fair Employment Practices section of the Civil Rights Act. These behaviors can take the form of comments of a personal or sexual nature, unwanted touching and feeling, or demands for sexual favors.

The second form of sexual harassment involves the existence of a **hostile work environment**. Supreme Court decisions have held that sexual harassment exists if a "reasonable person" believes that the behavior is sufficiently severe or pervasive to create

Yahoo CEO Marissa Mayer speaks at the consumer electronics show CES 2014 in Las Vegas, USA, 07 January 2014. The fair runs from 07 January to 10 January 2014.

an abusive working environment, even if the victim does not get fired or held back from a promotion. A hostile work environment exists when supervisors, coworkers, vendors, or customers use sexual innuendo, tell sexually oriented jokes, display sexually explicit photos in the work area, discuss sexual exploits, and so on. Unlike quid pro quo harassment, hostile work environment claims tend to fall in a gray area: What is offensive to one person may not be offensive to another. The bottom line is that most kinds of sexually explicit language, conduct, and behavior are inappropriate in the workplace, regardless of whether such conduct constitutes sexual harassment within the legal meaning of the term.

How to Address Sexual Harassment

Ever since Professor Anita Hill accused Supreme Court justice nominee Clarence Thomas of lewd and overbearing conduct toward her, the country has been trying to determine the difference between innocent comments and sexual harassment.

The key word is *unwelcome*. Victims of sexual harassment need to tell the harasser, in no uncertain terms, that his or her behavior is inappropriate. Meanwhile, victims should record each occurrence in a journal that includes the date and details of the incident. They should also talk with coworkers who can provide emotional support and help verify instances of harassment. Chances are, if one person is being harassed, others are as well. If the harasser continues the behavior, the victim should go to a higher authority such as the harasser's supervisor or the organization's human resources division. Under the law, companies are legally liable if they do not immediately investigate the situation and take action to eliminate the offensive behaviors. These actions can include reprimand, suspension, or dismissal of the harasser.

Clarification of the Law. The U.S. Supreme Court has given employees and employers help in understanding the legal aspects of sexual harassment. The Court handed down two landmark rulings that included the following guidelines:[47]

- Companies can be held liable for a supervisor's sexually harassing behavior, even if the offense was never reported to management.
- An employer can be liable when a supervisor threatens to punish a worker for resisting sexual demands—even if such threats are not carried out.

The court also offered employers advice on how to avoid costly legal fees. A company can deflect sexual harassment charges by developing a *zero-tolerance policy* on harassment, communicating it to employees, and making sure victims can report abuses without fear of retaliation. If the employer can show that an employee failed to use internal procedures for reporting abusive behavior, the company will be protected in a court of law.

Although the courtroom doors are open for workers to protect themselves from unwanted behavior, pressing a sexual harassment charge is a lengthy, expensive, and psychologically draining experience. Before you file charges, be sure you have used all the remedies available to you through your employer.

Indra Nooyi, chairman and CEO of PepsiCo, is a robust, effective leader whose leadership style has helped to maintain Pepsi's strong status within the ever-evolving food and beverage industry.

PREGNANCY DISCRIMINATION

Discrimination against pregnant women in the workforce has increased 23 percent in the past 10 years. It is one of the fastest-growing categories of charges filed with the Equal Employment Opportunity Commission.

The charges are coming from women in entry-level jobs as well as executives. Pregnant women claim they have been unfairly fired, denied promotions, and in some cases urged to terminate pregnancies in order to keep their jobs. Several factors may be behind this trend.

- More pregnant women are staying in the workplace rather than quitting their jobs as in previous generations.
- Pregnancy is expensive for employers. The result is a squeeze on maternity leave pay and time off by employers.
- Stereotypes about pregnant women persist. Mounting research indicates that men and women alike view pregnant women as less competent.
- Employers are making honest mistakes or are confused by conflicting laws. Many states have protections for pregnant women that go beyond the federal law, which allows for 12 weeks of unpaid leave.
- Pregnant workers can sue employers who deny them accommodations afforded to employees with disabilities.

Source: Sue Shellenbarger, "Downsizing Maternity Leave: Employers Cut Pay, Time Off," *Wall Street Journal*, June 11, 2008, p. D1; Shellenbarger, "Government Eases Path for Parents to Sue Employers," *Wall Street Journal*, May 24, 2007, p. D1; Jess Bravin, "Justices Back Worker in Pregnancy Case," *The News & Observer*, March 26, 2015, p. A5.

Learn to Understand and Respect Gender Differences

As mentioned in Chapter 2, gender bias often acts as a filter that interferes with effective communication between men and women. These communication barriers, according to Deborah Tannen, are due to linguistic style. **Linguistic style** refers to a person's speaking pattern and includes such characteristics as directness or indirectness, pacing and pausing, word choice, and the use of such elements as jokes, figures of speech, stories, questions, and apologies. Linguistic style is a series of culturally learned signals that we use to communicate what we mean.[48] Communication experts and psychologists have made the following generalizations concerning gender-specific communication patterns:

- Men tend to be more direct in their conversation, whereas women are more apt to emphasize politeness.
- Men tend to dominate discussions during meetings and are more likely to interrupt.
- Women prefer to work out solutions with another person; men prefer to work out their problems by themselves.
- Men tend to speak in a steady flow, free of pauses, interrupting each other to take turns. Women tend to speak with frequent pauses, which are used for turn taking.
- Male-style humor tends to focus on banter, the exchange of witty, often teasing remarks. A woman's style is often based on anecdotes in which the speaker is more likely to mock herself than she is to make fun of another person.
- Women are likely to downplay their certainty; men are likely to minimize their doubts.[49]

In a comprehensive study comprised of interviews and 360-degree feedback, male executives said they use active words and authoritative statements, avoid hedging, take ownership of their opinions, and build on others' ideas rather than simply agreeing with them. It's not so much *what* women say but *how* they say it. If women wish to be viewed as more authorative and achieve the result they are looking for, they should use active words and authoritative statements.[50]

INSTEAD OF THIS	USE THIS
How about?…	I strongly suggest…
I tend to agree.	That is absolutely right, and here's why…
I think maybe…	My strong advice is…
I agree.	I agree completely because…

Total Person Insight

"The more hours of television a girl watches, the fewer options she thinks she has in life. And the more hours a boy watches, the more sexist his views become."
Geena Davis
Founder, Geena Davis Institute on Gender in Media

Source: Sue Shellenbarger, "What's Holding Women Back?" *Wall Street Journal*, May 7, 2012, p. B11.

A Few Words of Caution

Differences do exist: Most men are somewhat more competitive, assertive, and task-focused, and most women are more sensitive, cooperative, and people-focused than most men. However, our stereotypes about men and women are often too strong and too inflexible.[51] When we place too much emphasis on the ways in which women and men differ, we stop viewing them as individuals. As noted in Chapter 3, it is tempting to put a label on someone and then assume the label tells you everything you need to know about that person.

Once you understand the concept that men and women communicate in different ways, you can begin to flex your style. Refer to Table 16.2 for more specific suggestions on how to communicate better with the opposite gender. Keep in mind, however, that an overextension of a strength *can* become a weakness.

> *When we place too much emphasis on the ways in which women and men differ, we stop viewing them as individuals.*

Men and women have so much to learn from each other. NYU psychologist Carol Gilligan offers this metaphor: "One can think of the oboe and the clarinet as different, yet when they play together, there is a sound that's not either one of them, but it doesn't dissolve the identity of either instrument."[52]

In interviews and written comments, men acknowledged that women often struggle to make themselves heard at meetings, but they didn't always agree with their female peers about the reasons. Table 16.2 explains how language plays a vital role in the ways women and men communicate.

Table 16.2 ■ Gender-Specific Language Barriers

HE SAID...	SHE SAID...
We're afraid of how women will react to criticism.	We don't get feedback, even when we ask for it.
Women need to be concise and remain on point.	We don't like to repackage old ideas or restate the obvious.
Women need a strong point of view.	It's difficult to get a word in.
Women need to speak informally and off-the-cuff.	We like to put together presentations.
Women get defensive when they are challenged.	We obsess about a meeting for days after it's over.
Women are more emotional than men.	It's not emotion—it's passion.
Women are less confident than men.	Yes, but we're outnumbered five to one, and we tend to feel less fully "at the table."

Source: Kathryn Heath, Jill Flynn, and Mary Davis Holt, "Women, Find Your Voice," *Harvard Business Review*, June 2014, pp. 121.

LOOKING BACK: SUMMARY OF LEARNING OBJECTIVES

1. **Describe how the traditional roles of men and women are changing.**

   The traditional roles assigned to both genders limit their opportunities to choose careers and lifestyles best suited to their abilities and true interests. Many men and women are breaking out of these traditional roles. During the past few decades, women have entered the job world in increasing numbers and in professions previously considered all male. Also, a large number of women have assumed the role of breadwinner or are part of a dual-earner family. Women now hold over half of the managerial and professional positions. Today men are more likely to accept women in the role of breadwinner.

2. **Understand problems facing women as a result of gender bias in organizations.**

   Women are still subject to a wage gap, earning less than men receive for similar work, but the gap is narrowing. Moreover, the glass ceiling gives women a view of top-level jobs but blocks their ascent. They are making progress, however, in the mid-management ranks. The real problems seem to be the preconceptions men have of women and the exclusion of women from the informal networks of communication.

3. **Understand problems facing men as a result of gender bias in organizations.**

   Men are working to dispel the myth that men must always be in control, emotionally unexpressive, logical, and achievement oriented. They realize that the rigid male role has had adverse effects on their relationships with their families. Many men are choosing more personally rewarding careers that allow time for family responsibilities even if they must sacrifice some material gain to do so.

4. **Discuss challenges and opportunities for working men and women**.

The need for affordable, quality child care continues to challenge mothers and fathers alike. Progressive companies are more sensitive to the needs of workers with children. Flexible work schedules rank high on the list of most workers. Flextime, compressed workweeks, PTO banks, job sharing, and telecommuting are popular work schedule options.

5. **Explain the forms of sexual harassment and how to cope with gender-biased behavior**.

Sexual harassment may be a problem for men as well as women. It may take on two forms: quid pro quo, a threat to job security or promotion if sexual favors are not granted, or sexually explicit language, photos, or innuendo that create a hostile work environment. Most organizations have developed guidelines to help employees avoid harassment or fight it when it occurs. This chapter also provides information that helps us understand and respect gender differences. Understanding and appreciating linguistic style differences helps men and women communicate more effectively. The introduction of bias interrupters helps companies change old engrained work habits and patterns.

KEY TERMS

gender bias, 354	PTO bank, 365	quid pro quo, 367
glass ceiling, 357	job sharing, 365	hostile work environment, 367
Mommy Track, 359	telecommuting, 365	linguistic style, 370
flextime, 365	bias interrupter, 366	
compressed workweek, 365	sexual harassment, 367	

CAREER INSIGHT

In these uncertain economic times, it's a good idea to explore all of your options. You may want to consider becoming an entrepreneur. There are many tests to help you determine whether you are a good candidate for starting a business. But whether a test can really determine who does or does not make a capable entrepreneur is debatable. There are some personality traits common among successful entrepreneurs, like the tendency to have a higher risk tolerance, drive, and resiliency to overcome failure than the general population, according to experts.

Author Bill Wagner offers an *Entrepreneur IQ* test at his website, http://TheEntrepreneurNextDoor.com, which compares your answers to others. In addition, there are the Strong and MBTI tests used to assess entrepreneurial aptitude.

Many communities have an organization called SCORE (Service Corps of Retired Executives), which includes retired executives who are willing to guide and share their experiences with entrepreneurs and small businesses nationwide.

TRY YOUR HAND

1. The following situations represent either quid pro quo or hostile environment forms of sexual harassment in the workplace. Identify the form represented by each situation, and explain your reasoning. Describe the actions you might take if you were the potential victim in each incident.

a. Julie thinks David is very handsome. She often stares at him when she thinks he is not looking. David is aware of Julie's staring and is very uncomfortable but is too shy and embarrassed to say anything to her.

b. While sitting at her desk, Karen receives the following electronic message from her boss on her computer screen: "Can we discuss your possible promotion over dinner this weekend?"

c. At a convention reception, one of Joan's most important clients invites her out for cocktails and dinner. She politely declines. He announces loudly, "She won't go out to dinner with me, and I'm her best customer!" Under his breath he says, "Honey, if you want my business, you should learn to have an open mind." Joan's boss insists she go to dinner with the client.

2. On a sheet of paper, list and explain the various choices you would make when attempting to balance your career and family responsibilities. For example, will marriage be a part of your future? Will you have children? When? How will you provide care for these children while you and your spouse are at work? Would you prefer home-based work? Which flextime options would you consider valuable? Do you want to work for someone else or own your own business?

3. During a period of one week, analyze your verbal and nonverbal communications with people who are of the opposite gender. Try to determine whether any linguistic style differences are apparent during conversations. If you discover style differences, try to determine if they serve as a barrier or aid effective communication.

4. To examine various flexible work-schedule options, visit *www.workoptions.com*. Write an analysis of how the information available on this site might help people make an educated decision about their personal and professional life choices.

CRITICAL THINKING CHALLENGE

1. Do members of your immediate family hold traditional or nontraditional gender roles? If so, have any of these roles undergone changes during the past decade? Examine why there have been changes.

2. Before marriage, each partner should understand the other partner's expectations with regard to careers, family responsibilities, and priorities. What are your expectations of your spouse (if you are married), or what do you imagine they would be (if you are not)?

SELF-ASSESSMENT EXERCISE

For each of the following statements, circle the number from 1 to 5 that best represents your response: (1) strongly disagree (never do this); (2) disagree (rarely do this); (3) moderately agree (sometimes do this); (4) agree (frequently do this); (5) strongly agree (almost always do this).

A. I refuse to perpetuate negative stereotypes, and I accept each person as a unique individual worthy of my respect.	1	2	3	4	5
B. I make every effort to identify my own prejudiced attitudes and avoid stereotypical attitudes toward people of color, older people, people with disabilities, and others who are different from me.	1	2	3	4	5
C. I work hard to combat prejudice because it has a negative impact on my self-esteem and the self-esteem of the victim.	1	2	3	4	5
D. I encourage my employer to develop flexible work-schedule options.	1	2	3	4	5
E. I understand and respect gender differences.	1	2	3	4	5

After identifying your response to each item, select an attitude or skill you would like to improve. Prepare a written goal and then describe the steps you will take to achieve this goal.

YOU PLAY THE ROLE

If you are looking to use flexible work-schedule options (review the different options listed in this chapter) at your place of work, you need to be prepared when asking for permission. Your supervisor may initially say "no"; however, be prepared with counter arguments. Write a business proposal discussing the benefits of your plan to you and the company. If you select telecommuting, describe the arrangements that you have made for your designated home workspace, the logistics of how often you will check in with your supervisor, and a vehicle for feedback to assess your performance. You must show enthusiasm for this approach. Finally, be a good listener and try to determine the major objections to your proposal. Flexible work-schedule options, specifically telecommuting, may be new to this workplace and require additional education and adjustments. Select a class member to play the role of your supervisor as you present your proposal.

BELOW THE SURFACE | HELPING WOMEN REACH THE TOP

Henk Meijer/Alamy

In the opening vignette, you were presented with facts about the ongoing gap in wages women continue to face today. Despite the overwhelming amount of evidence that women make better leaders and team members, the gap has hardly moved in decades, and it doesn't appear it will any time soon. As a result, women are leaving corporate America in droves. Where are these women going and how are they earning money to support their families? The answer is entrepreneurship. There are more than eight million women-owned firms in the United States. And even though it is widely reported that women receive only a fraction of the capital to fund their businesses (1.9 percent versus 19.4 percent for men), entrepreneurship has a bright future for women.[53]

Take 29-year-old Sophia Amoruso, for example. In 2006 she started selling vintage clothes on eBay and launched her online clothing store, *Nasty Gal*, based on her "idea of what a cool girl looks like." In 2008 her business skyrocketed from $223,000 to $23 million in 2011. Her company ranked number 11 on the Inc. 500 list in 2012.[54]

Another success story is Brandi Temple, a wife and mother with zero corporate job experience, Since starting her online business *Lolly Wolly Doodle* in 2009, revenue has doubled every year, In 2011 her business was valued at $11 million, and in 2013 she received $20 million in funding from AOL cofounder Steve Case. It's estimated the business could grow to $50 million to $100 million. But even more exciting than the large revenue numbers is how Temple managed her business—as a woman. In 2010 when unemployment was 14 percent in Lexington, North Carolina, Temple received a knock at the door. It was a 74-year-old woman with virtually no experience asking her for a job so she could buy her husband's heart medication. Temple hired and trained the woman, and soon word got around that Temple had jobs available and people started showing up to ask for jobs. "Person after person, they'd tell me the same story. "I've lost my house, I've lost my car; what can I do?" Temple says she hired all of them. Giving back to those in need continues to be part of her business model, including the missions she started in Africa and *Moms in a Jam*. She says, "It's not about me creating a business. It was about what we could all do together, the pay-it-forward mentality."[55]

QUESTIONS

1. Sheryl Sanberg said, "There aren't enough women sitting at the tables where decisions are made. Reigniting the revolution means I want us to notice all of this and find ways to

encourage more women to step up and more companies to recognize what women bring to the table." What actions do you believe would ignite action and bring about real change?

2. Madeleine Albright, former U.S. secretary of state, serve on the executive task force that planned the *Wall Street Journal* Women in the Economy conference. She said, "Women are really good at making friends and not good

at networking." Do you agree? Explain your answer.

3. At the end of the Women in the Economy conference, members agreed that progress for women starts at the top: "Hold senior managers accountable by tying promotion and compensation to meeting diversity goals and requiring regular reports to the board of directors." Is this practice realistic? Explain your answer.

CLOSING CASE | A SANER WORKPLACE

Companies everywhere are starting to retool. "The one-size-fits-all workplace doesn't work," says the Alfred P. Sloan Foundation's **Kathleen** Christensen. "The idea that you will work full-time year in and year out, that you will be on a career trajectory that is a straight line, is vanishing. Employees increasingly feel more entitled to say: 'I need and I want to work in a certain way.'"

In their book, *Womenomics: Write Your Own Rules for Success*, broadcasters Claire Shipman and Katty Kay cite studies that show the increasing impact of professional women on companies' bottom lines and give practical advice on how to create "a more sane" work life. Women may be driving the workforce revolution, but men are realizing the benefits, too.

At Capital One Financial, Judy Pahren, director of human resources, realized that *flexibility* was not just a "woman initiative," but rather, a need across an entire employee base. "We had thought that maybe it was gender-based; however, it was true of the men who worked at Capital One Financial also." A few months later, the Flexible Work Arrangements program was implemented for the entire company. The program allows employees to determine their work schedules with their immediate supervisors; options are flextime, telecommuting, a compressed workweek, or part-time employment.

More and more workers of *both* sexes are willing to scale back career goals, according to Families & Work Institute data. In focus groups, employees say things like "I need to make these choices because my family is a priority" or "I need to make these choices to make my life work."

According to Brenda Barnes, CEO of Sara Lee, "Today's business environment provides the opportunity for work-life balance. This doesn't mean employees work less; instead, it means empowering employees to do their work on a schedule that works for them. So if they want to work from their kitchen table at 3:00 a.m., as long as the work gets done, who cares when or where they are doing it? Companies need to recognize that this kind of *flexibility* offers employees the ability to manage and balance their own career and lives, which improves productivity and employee morale."[56]

QUESTIONS

1. On the basis of your personal and professional needs, design a flexible work arrangement that would allow you to have work-life balance in your career.

2. Predict the implications of a flexible work arrangement program for the future. Evaluate the impact on business/industry, management, employees, and consumers. Is the Capital One Financial's Flexible Work Arrangement program

a realistic option for employees who work in retailing? Manufacturing? The hospitality industry? Explain your answer.

3. Capital One thought work *flexibility* was a key issue only for female employees. They realized, with additional inquiry, that it was true for the men employees as well. Analyze why both sexes are willing to scale back career goals and the implications their decisions will have on their career and life choices.

CHAPTER 16 ENDNOTES

1. "Who We Are" http://www.catalyst.org/who-we-are, [cited 10 April 2015]. INTERNET

2. Jeff Elder, "Pao: Gender Issues Won't Go Away," **Wall Street Journal**, March 11, 2015, p. B7.

3. Adi Ignatius, "Now Is Our Time," **Harvard Business Review**, April 2013, pp. 85–86.

4. Joann S. Lubin, "Men Enlist in Fight for Gender Equality," **Wall Street Journal**, March 11, 2015, p. B7.

5. Clyde Frazier, "How Feminine Mystique Shaped Lives in the 1960s," **The News & Observer**, March 27, 2011, p. 6D.

6. Kathleen Montwieler, "Trading Chains for Handcuffs," **The News & Observer**, March 10, 2013, pp. 21A.

7. Ibid.

8. Nancy M. Carter and Christine Silva, "Women in Management: Delusions of Progress," **Harvard Business Review**, March 2010, p. 19; "What's New," [cited 02 April 2015]. Available from www.catalyst.org; INTERNET.

9. "The Pros and Cons of Non-Traditional Careers" [cited 21 April 2009]. Available from http://www.quintcareers.com/pros-cons_non-traditional_careers.html; INTERNET.

10. Kay Hymowitz, "Where Have All the Good Men Gone?" **Wall Street Journal**, February 19–20, 2011, p. C1.

11. John Rosemond, "Today's Males Need Fathers, Not Friends," **The News & Observer**, November 17, 2009, p. 20.

12. Mark Peters and David Wessel, "More Men in Prime Are Out of Work and at Home," **Wall Street Journal**, February 2, 2014, pp. A1.

13. Andrea Coombes, "Men Suffer Brunt of Job Losses in Recession," **Wall Street Journal**, July 7, 2009, p. D6.

14. Peters and Wessel, "More Men in Prime Are Out of Work and at Home," p. A1.

15. Borgna Brunner, "The Wage Gap," [cited 2 May 2012]. Available from www.infoplease.com; INTERNET.

16. Barack Obama, "Presidential Proclamation—National Equal Pay Day, 2012," April 17, 2012. Available from www.whitehouse.gov; INTERNET.

17. By Sarah Jane Glynn, Milia Fisher, and Emily Baxter, "7 Actions that Could Shrink the Gender Wage Gap," September 18, 2014. Available from https://www.americanprogress.org; INTERNET.

18. "Equal Pay Day: AAWW Releases State by State Gender Wage Gap Rankings," [cited 2 April 2015]. Available from http://www.nwlc.org/sites/default/files/pdfs/wage_gap_tables_2013_final.pdf; INTERNET

19. "Women Still Confront Yawning Gender Wage Gap: Study," **Chicago Tribune**, April 18, 2012. Available from http://articles.chicagotribune.com; INTERNET.

20. "A Salary Gap Remains Between Genders, Census Results Indicate," **Wall Street Journal**, March 25, 2003, p. D1; Charles J. Whalen, "Closing the Pay Gap," **BusinessWeek**, August 28, 2000, p. 38.

21. Tracy Lien, "Why Women Are Leaving the Tech Industry in Droves," **The News & Observer**, March 8, 2015, p. 2E.

22. Francesco Guerrera, "Gender Gap Remains for Wall Street Firms," **Wall Street Journal**, December 12, 2013, pp. C1.

23. Ilene H. Lang, "Co-Opt the Old Boys' Club: Make It Work for Women," **Harvard Business Review**, November 2011, p. 44.

24. Ibid.

25. Ibid.

26. Joann Lublin and Kelly Eggers, "More Women are Primed to Land CEO Roles," **Wall Street Journal**, April 30, 2012, pp. B1 and B6.

27. Anna Fels, "Do Women Lack Ambition," **Harvard Business Review**, April 2004, pp. 7–8.

28. Heather Perlberg, "Women on Boards Are Better for Companies," (**Bloomberg News**), **The News & Observer**, August 2012, pp. 5B.

29. "The Emancipated Organization," **Harvard Business Review**, September 2002, pp. 1–3 (Reprint F0209B). (This article features an interview with Kim Campbell, Canada's first female prime minister.)

30. Virginia Postrel, "Mommy Track Without Shame," **Wall Street Journal**, March 26, 2011, p. C12.

31. Sylvia Ann Hewlett, "Executive Women and the Myth of Having It All," **Harvard Business Review**, April 2002, pp. 5–11; Margaret Heffernan, "The Female CEO," **Fast Company**, August 2002, pp. 58–66.

32. Judith S. Nulevitz, "The Mommy Trap," *New York Times Book Review*, February 20, 2005, pp. 1, 12–13.

33. "Today's Dads: Same Old Parenting Trap," *Business-Week*, October 14, 2002, p. 167. (This article summarizes the views of Nicholas Townsend, author of *The Package Deal*, a book about the many life/work conflicts men face.)

34. Lauren Weber, "Why Dads Don't Take Paternity Leave," *Wall Street Journal*, June 13, 2013, p. B1.

35. Lauren Sandler, "How to Love Paid Family Leave," *Bloomberg Business Week*, July 21, 2014.

36. Jeffrey Zaslow, "Who's the New Guy at Dinner? It's Dad; Laid-Off Fathers Face Tough Job at Home," *Wall Street Journal*, October 2, 2002, p. D1.

37. Child Care Connections. Available from http://www.childcareconnections.net/; INTERNET.

38. Jodi Kantor, "As Shifts Vary, Family's Only Constant Is Chaos," (*New York Times*), *The News & Observer*, August 17, 2014, p. 2E.

39. Sue Shellenbarger, "Bob's Mobile Office and Day-Car Center," *Wall Street Journal*, December 26, 2002, p. D1.

40. Kathy Bergen, "Compressed Workweek Pays Off—On 10th Day," *Roanoke Times & World News*, March 30, 1997, p. B2.

41. Robert Kreitner and Carlene Cassidy, *Management*, 12th ed. (Mason, OH: Cengage Learning, 2011), p. 349.

42. Carol Kleiman, "Get Two Workers for the Price of One!" *The News & Observer*, February 26, 2003, p. E14.

43. Joan C. Williams, "Hacking Tech's Diversity Problem," *Harvard Business Review*, October 2014, 96–100.

44. Ibid.

45. Joan C. Williams and Amy J. C. Cuddy, "Will Working Mothers Take Your Company to Court?" *Harvard Business Review*, September 2012, pp. 96

46. Ibid.

47. Susan B. Garland, "Finally, a Corporate Tip Sheet on Sexual Harassment," *BusinessWeek*, July 13, 1998, p. 39.

48. Deborah Tannen, "The Power of Talk: Who Gets Heard and Why," *Harvard Business Review*, September/October 1995, pp. 129–140; Melvin Konner, "A Better World, Ruled By Women," *Wall Street Journal*, March 7, 2015, p. C3.

49. Jayne Tear, "They Just Don't Understand Gender Dynamics," *Wall Street Journal*, November 20, 1995, p. A14; Dianna Booker, "The Gender Gap in Communication," *Training Dimensions* (West Des Moines, IA: American Media Incorporated, Fall 1994), p. 1; Jennifer J. Laabs, "Kinney Narrows the Gender Gap," *Personnel Journal*, August 1994, pp. 83–85; Scot Ober, *Contemporary Business Communication*, 5th ed. (Boston: Houghton Mifflin, 2003), pp. 58–59.

50. Kathryn Heath, Jill Flynn, and Mary Davis Holt, "Women, Find Your Voice," Harvard Business Review, Jun 2014, pp. 120.

51. Sharon S. Brehm, Saul M. Kassin, and Steven Fein, *Social Psychology*, 5th ed. (Boston: Houghton Mifflin, 2002), pp. 154–156.

52. Anastasi Toufexis, "Coming from a Different Place," *Time*, Fall 1990, p. 66.

53. Kauffman Foundation, "How to Close the Startup Gap," *Wall Street Journal*, August 25, 2014, p. R8.

54. D.F., "Innovate," *Inc.*, June 2013, pp. 118.

55. Tom Foster, "Along Came Lolly," *Inc.*, June 2014, pp. 26–36.

56. "A Saner Workplace," *BusinessWeek*, June 1, 2009, pp. 66–69.

PART 6

You Can Plan for Success

CHAPTER PREVIEW

LEARNING OBJECTIVES

After studying Chapter 17, you will be able to

17-1 Learn how to cope with the forces that influence work/life balance.

17-2 Define success by standards that are compatible with your needs and values.

17-3 Discuss the meaning of right livelihood.

17-4 Describe four nonfinancial resources that can enrich your life.

17-5 Provide guidelines for developing a healthy lifestyle.

17-6 Develop a plan for making needed changes in your life.

Jupiterimages/Comstock Imges/Getty Images

A Life Plan for Effective Human Relations

TIP OF THE ICEBERG | THE SEARCH FOR WORK/LIFE BALANCE

Marriott International has been given the 100 Best Companies All-Star award. The company has appeared on the *Fortune* magazine 100 Best Companies to Work For list every year since 1998. It is not only a good company to work for, it is a company that has job openings throughout the world.[1]

The Marriott culture is based on two policies that have guided the company for many years. One follows the mandate to "hire friendly, train technical." In most cases, the company assesses applicants for friendliness first. The company uses an image-based instrument to screen for interpersonal skills, dependability, and disposition. The second policy involves a network of business councils, local and regional teams of general managers who meet regularly to compare notes and prepare reports that are sent to corporate headquarters.[2]

The worldwide chain of Marriott hotels places a great deal of emphasis on customer service. The guiding principle of the company is: "Take care of the associates (employees), the associates take care of the guests, and the guests will come back again and again."[3]

You may have no interest in working for Marriott or any other hotel chain. But keep the Marriott "model" in mind as you seek employment. The ideal company for you may be a small business, or you may decide to start your own business. Look for employers who provide the opportunity for personal growth. Many associates at Marriott say the best perk is the opportunity for career growth. Some of the top executives at Marriott started out cleaning guest rooms or working on the bell stand.

Henk Meijer/Alamy

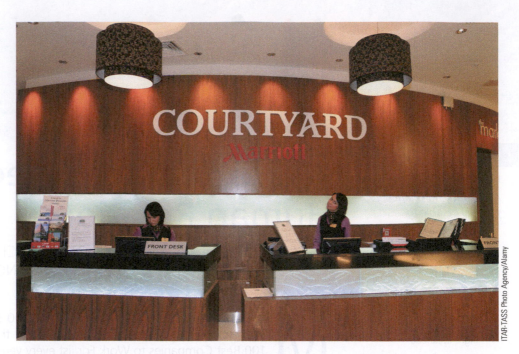

Marriott follows the mandate to hire friendly and train technical. During the hiring process applicants are screened for interpersonal skills, dependability and disposition.

ACHIEVING BALANCE IN A CHAOTIC WORLD

17-1 In this chapter, we help you construct a life plan that will enhance your relationships with people in your personal life and in your work life. This plan will also help you to better manage the mental, physical, emotional, and spiritual aspects of your life. We discuss the meaning of success and suggest ways to cope with major disappointments that will surface in your work life. You will learn how to avoid being trapped by a lifestyle that offers financial rewards but little else. This chapter also helps you define your relationship with money and describes four nonfinancial resources that give meaning to life. Finally, you will learn how to develop the mental and physical fitness needed to keep up in today's frantic, fast-paced world.

Redefining Our Work Lives

In Chapter 1, we noted that the labor market has become a place of churning dislocation caused by the heavy volume of mergers, acquisitions, business closings, bankruptcies, and downsizings. We also noted that changing work patterns have created new opportunities and new challenges. Millions of American workers are self-employed, working as independent consultants, contractors, landscape gardeners, and financial consultants.

In recent years we have seen the evolution of a new class of freelance labor. These on-demand workers are represented by companies like Uber Technologies, Mechanical Turk, and Handbook, better known as Handy. Uber is an international company that develops, markets, and operates mobile app-based transportation networks. If you have a car, Uber uses a scheduling platform to connect you with customers who need transportation. Handy is a company that provides a link between customers and persons seeking on-demand personal assistants and home cleaning services. TaskRabit will connect customers with someone who can perform a specific task such as installing a stereo system. These companies describe their workers as micro-entrepreneurs.[4]

It is important to visualize a future filled with sharp detours and several redefinitions of our work lives. Tom Peters, noted author and consultant, was one of the first observers to recognize that a typical career path is no longer linear and is not always upward. He says, "It's more like a maze, full of hidden turns, zigs, and zags that go in all sorts of directions—even backwards sometimes, when that makes sense."[5] The idea of finding job security and knowing that we have "arrived" is obsolete.

TOWARD A NEW DEFINITION OF SUCCESS

17-2 Most of us have been conditioned to define success in narrow terms. Too often we judge our own success, and the success of others, by work achievements or material possessions. Successful people have been described as those who have a "good job," "make good money," or have "reached the top" in their field. From early childhood on, many people are taught to equate success with pay increases and promotions. Too often, unfortunately, people who try to achieve these career goals are forced to give up everything else that gives purpose and meaning to their lives. Bill George, author of books entitled *True North* and *Authentic Leadership*, suggests we forge an integrated life that blends work with such things as family, friends, community service, exercise, church, and whatever else matters in your life.[6]

> *From early childhood on, many people are taught to equate success with pay increases and promotions.*

Po Bronson, author of *What Should I Do with My Life?* says more people need to search for work they are passionate about. His best-selling book profiles 55 people who struggled to find their calling. One of the persons he interviewed was Ann Miyhares, a Cuban-American who made her family proud by becoming a senior vice president at a bank but lost their respect when she exchanged her banking career for that of a social worker, a career she found much more fulfilling.[7]

Total Person Insight

> "You only have control over three things in your life — the thoughts you think, the images you visualize, and the actions you take (your behavior). How you use these three things determines everything you experience. If you don't like what you are producing and experiencing, you have to change your responses."

Source: Jack Canfield, *The Success Principles* (New York: HarperCollins, 2005), p. 9.

The Need for New Models of Success

In recent years, a growing number of people have become angry, disillusioned, and frustrated because they have had to abruptly change their career and life plans. They gave their best efforts, worked long hours, and then the company eliminated their jobs. A variety of economic, social, and demographic forces have combined to create a high level of career distress among all age groups. Young workers, often burdened with student loans, face the prospect of being unemployed or underemployed. Older workers nearing retirement amid a tech revolution unmatched in scope and speed, find themselves racing to keep their skills updated. They are being told by career counselors to establish a social media presence and to engage in social networks like LinkedIn to look for jobs, network, and manage their personal brand. Older workers must be concerned about how they are perceived. Age discrimination is a major problem for the over-55 group.[8]

Americans are known for burdening themselves with a very demanding work ethic. They spend more time on the job than employees in any other industrialized nation. U.S. workers not only work long hours, but they spend less time on vacation than do workers in most other industrialized countries. As downsizing efforts have left fewer people to do the same amount of work, many people are working even harder.

Total-Person Model

One trend that continues to evolve is that most workers, especially younger workers, yearn for more leisure time. Some of the most successful and progressive organizations in America recognize the need to create a culture that satisfies both personal and work-related needs. They realize the ideal work environment embraces the *total person*, a concept we discussed in Chapter 1.

Some of the top small businesses have created unique cultures and workplaces that embrace the total person concept. Engeo, an environmental engineering firm located in San Ramon, California, helps employees plan personal and professional goals from home buying to careers. Talent Plus, a global human resources consulting firm located in Lincoln, Nebraska, has replaced performance reviews with career investment discussions with managers. Three times a year employees at Daxko, a software maker for nonprofits located in Birmingham, Alabama, take a two-week break to form new teams and develop ideas.[9]

Values-Based Organizational Culture

Companies like Southwest Airlines, Zappos, and Starbucks have created new models of success by developing healthy, thriving company cultures that focus on core values. As a result, these companies have created higher levels of customer service, employee satisfaction, and profitability. Tony Hsieh, founder of Zappos.com, has achieved monetary success, but that is not his goal in life. He wants to unlock the secrets of human happiness, and his company is his research center. His single-minded focus on happiness has resulted in Zappos receiving several "best places to work" awards. His thoughts on achieving happiness are described in his book, *Delivering Happiness*.

Developing Your Own Life Plan

The goal of this chapter is to help you develop a life plan for effective relationships with yourself and others. The information presented thus far has, we hope, stimulated your thinking about the need for a life plan. We have noted that personal life can seldom be separated from work life. The two are very much intertwined. We have also suggested that it is important for you to develop your own definition of success. Too often, people allow others (parents, teachers, friends, a spouse) to define success for them. Finally, as you begin work on your life plan, keep in mind the following advice from Jack Canfield, author of *The Success Principles*:

> *If you want to be successful, you have to take 100% responsibility for everything that you experience in your life. This includes the level of your achievements, the results you produce, the quality of your relationships, the state of your health and physical fitness, your income, your debts, your feelings—everything![10]*

Because work is such an important part of life, we will now move to a discussion of items that will help you in your career planning and the concept of "right livelihood."

TOWARD RIGHT LIVELIHOOD

17-3 Anne Beiler, founder of Auntie Anne's, the largest soft-pretzel franchise in the world, is an unlikely entrepreneur. She grew up in an Amish farm community that did not permit TV or radio in the home. At age 19 she was married and says her only dream was to be a mom. She and her husband had two daughters, and then life turned upside down. One of her daughters was killed in a farm accident. After this tragedy, she and her husband could not connect emotionally. Several years passed before they were able to overcome the marital crisis. They purchased a small Amish-owned store selling pretzels, ice cream, and pizza. She changed the pretzel recipe given to her by the previous owners, and the new product was an immediate success. The little store was named Auntie Anne's Soft Pretzels. With the passing of time, Anne and her husband Jonas opened more stores. Today 1,200 outlets can be found in malls, airports, and boardwalks in 26 countries. The company is now owned by Focus Brands.[11]

Anne Beiler, like many other people, had been searching for "right livelihood." The concept of right livelihood is described in the core teachings of Buddhism.[12] In recent years, the concept has been described by Michael Phillips in his book *The Seven Laws of Money* and by Marsha Sinetar in her book *Do What You Love … The Money Will Follow.* **Right livelihood** is work consciously chosen, done with full awareness and care, and leading to enlightenment. Barbara Sher, author of *Wishcraft* and *I Could Do Anything If I Only Knew What It Was*, says right livelihood means that you wake up in the morning and spend all day working at something you really want to do.[13]

CHUCK KENNEDY/MCT/Landow

Annie Beiler had to overcome loss of a child, a marriage in crisis, and many years of hard work to become a successful entrepreneur. After experimenting with various pretzel recipes she discovered a winning combination of ingredients.

There are three characteristics to right livelihood: choice, emphasis on more than money, and personal growth.

Right Livelihood Is Based on Conscious Choice

Marsha Sinetar says, "When the powerful quality of conscious choice is present in our work, we can be enormously productive."[14] She points out that many people have learned to act on what others say, value, and expect and thus find conscious choice very difficult:

It takes courage to act on what we value and to willingly accept the consequences of our choices. Being able to choose means not allowing fear to inhibit or control us, even though our choices may require us to act against our fears or against the wishes of those we love and admire.[15]

To make the best choices, you must first figure out what you like to do, as well as what you are good at doing—your strengths. What you like doing most is often not obvious. It may take some real effort to discover what genuinely motivates you. Students often get help from career counselors or mentors or explore a career option during a summer internship. If you are employed, consider joining a temporary project team. A team assignment provides an opportunity to work with people who perform different types of duties. You might also consider reassignment within your organization, especially if you have the opportunity to work in another country and experience living in a different culture.

Right Livelihood Places Money in a Secondary Position

People who embrace right livelihood accept that money and security are not the primary rewards in life. Michael Phillips explained that "right livelihood has within itself its own rewards; it deepens the person who practices it."[16] For example, people who work in social services usually do not earn large amounts of money, but many of them receive a great deal of personal satisfaction from their work. You may need to trade some income for self-expression, mental rewards, or some other form of personal satisfaction. People who have made this choice may not make large sums of money, but their work provides enormous personal satisfaction.

Many people who once viewed success in terms of wealth, material possessions, and status are realizing that something is missing from their lives. They once felt pressured to "have it all" but now feel disappointed that their achievements have not brought them real happiness.

Right Livelihood Recognizes That Work Is a Vehicle for Personal Growth

Most of us spend from 40 to 60 hours each week at work. Ideally, we should not have to squelch our real strengths and abilities, ignore our personal goals, and forget our need for stimulation and personal growth during the time we spend at work.[17] Most employees know intuitively that work should fulfill their need for self-expression and personal growth, but this message is not embraced by all leaders. Too few organizations truly empower workers and give them a sense of purpose.

The search for right livelihood should begin with a thoughtful review of your values. The values clarification process (see Table 5.1 in Chapter 5) should be completed *before* you interview for a job. Your values should be reassessed throughout your life as they evolve and your work preferences change. When a job fails to fulfill your expectations, consider changing jobs, changing assignments, or changing careers. If the job is not right for you, your body and your mind will begin sending you messages. When you begin feeling that something is lacking, answer these basic questions:[18]

> *Most employees know intuitively that work should fulfill their need for self-expression and personal growth, but this message is not embraced by all leaders.*

- Do you feel a sense of pride working for your company?
- Are you continuing to grow in your work?
- Do you feel your work is an important part of who you are?
- Do you still have a lot you plan to accomplish in your work?

Your needs will change over time. Self-exploration and continual evaluation of your needs, goals, and job satisfaction are important. Don't wait for a crisis (such as a layoff) to clear your vision.[19]

Defining Your Relationship with Money

Money is a compelling force in the lives of most people. It often influences the choice of a career and the commitment we make to achieve success in that career. Sometimes we struggle to achieve a certain economic goal only to discover that once we get what we want, it does not fulfill us in the way we had hoped. Money does not create or sustain happiness. Happiness comes from social relationships, enjoyable work, fulfillment, a sense that life has meaning, and membership in civic and other groups.[20] As you learned in earlier chapters, research has proven that financial success does not make us happy, but the reverse is true. The happier you are, the more likely it is you will become successful in all areas of your life.

Many people struggle with money management decisions and seem unable to plan for the future. Research conducted by Higher One, a company that markets financial services to colleges and students, indicates that first-year college students feel less prepared to manage their finances than to tackle other aspects of college life.[21] Personal finance decisions represent a major challenge, according to the Pension Research Council

> *The happier you are, the more likely it is you will become successful.*

at the University of Pennsylvania. Americans' lack of financial awareness is becoming a major concern of employers. They worry that anxiety over high debt and poor retirement planning could divert workers' focus on their job and increase stress-related health care costs.[22]

True Prosperity. The way we choose to earn, save, and spend our money determines, in large measure, the quality of our lives. For example, if you think that having more money is going to produce happiness or peace of mind, will you ever earn enough? Shakti Gawain, author of *Creating True Prosperity*, says that more money does not necessarily bring greater freedom, fewer problems, or security. Rather, "prosperity is the experience of having plenty of what we truly need and want in life, material and otherwise." Gawain says, "The key point to understand is that prosperity is an *internal* experience, not an *external* state, and it is an experience that is not tied to having a certain amount of money."[23] Many of us go through life unconscious of our own real needs and desires. We must learn to predict more accurately what will give us lasting pleasure instead of short-term pleasure.[24] How do we do this? Steven Reiss (see Chapter 7) says that nearly everything we experience as meaningful can be traced to one of 16 basic desires or to some combination of those desires (see Figure 7.1). Now would be a good time to revisit this list of basic desires and identify the five or six that seem most important to you.

Mature Money Management. Many people do not have a mature relationship with money. They spend more than they earn, and then have bouts of financial anxiety. People who are deep in debt often experience symptoms of depression. Money issues continue to be the leading cause of marriage problems.[25] Space does not permit a comprehensive examination of money management, but here are two important suggestions from Jonathan Clements, an expert on financial planning:[26]

- *Develop a personal financial plan.* With a financial plan, you are more likely to achieve your financial goals. A key element of your plan is determining where your income is going. With a simple record-keeping system, you can determine how much you spend each month on food, housing, clothing, transportation, and other things. Search for spending patterns you may want to change. Create a budget and stick to it.
- *Understand the economics of credit.* A recent report from TransUnion, the Chicago-based credit bureau, indicates that the average credit-card debt per borrower is $5,234. If you incurred 20 percent in total annual interest cost, that would be about $42,000 in interest over 40 years.

Achieving Wedded Bliss. Many people do not think about financial compatibility before or after marriage. When couples talk about financial issues and problems, the result is usually less conflict and smarter financial decisions. David Bach, author of several books on financial planning, helps couples achieve financial compatibility. He has the partners start by writing down what is most important to each of them—their five top values. They are also instructed to write down what the purpose of money is. He says, "Smart financial planning is more than a matter of numbers; it involves *values* first and *stuff* second."[27]

 HOW TO SAVE MONEY IN PAINLESS WAYS

Let's assume you have decided to develop a three-year savings plan for a major purchase, such as a down payment on a house. The following "incidental expenses" provide some saving options.

	Savings
Take lunch to work three days per week and save $6.50 per day.	$3,000
Rent or stream your movies instead of going to the theater.	$450
Skip the coffee shop and brew your own at home.	$4,000
Buy frozen gourmet pizza instead of ordering delivery.	$1,500
Total Savings	$8,950

Source: Adapted from "Calculate Your Savings Possibilities," SunTrust Banks, Inc. 2009.

DEFINING YOUR NONFINANCIAL RESOURCES

17-4   It is often the **nonfinancial resources** that make the biggest contribution to a happy and fulfilling life. A strong argument can be made that the real wealth in life comes in the form of good health, peace of mind, time spent with family and friends, learning (which develops the mind), and healthy spirituality. Paul Hwoschinsky, author of *True Wealth*, makes this observation about nonfinancial resources: "If you are clear about who you are, and clear about what you want to do, and bring your financial and nonfinancial resources together, it's extraordinary what can happen. I encourage people to really honor their total resources, and magical things happen. New options occur."[28]

If you focus most or all of your attention on work and you suffer a major work-related disappointment, then the result is likely to be feelings of depression and despair.

Thoughts such as "Now I have lost everything" can surface when you fail to get a promotion, find out that you were not selected to be a member of a special project team, or learn that your job has been eliminated. But if you fully understand the power of your nonfinancial resources, then work-related disappointments are easier to cope with. The starting point is to realize that *most* of your resources are nonfinancial. During periods of great uncertainty, it is especially important that you think about all your nonfinancial assets and consider ways to enhance them. We briefly discuss four nonfinancial resources that can enrich your life: physical and mental health, education and training (intellectual growth), leisure time (time for family, socializing, recreation), and healthy spirituality (see Figure 17.1).

Physical and Mental Health

Is the statement "Health means wealth" just a worn-out cliché, or is this slogan a message of inspiration for people who want to get more out of life? If good health is such an important nonfinancial asset, then why are so many people flirting with self-destruction by eating the wrong foods, drinking too much, exercising too little, and generally choosing unhealthy lifestyles? The answer to the second question may be lack of awareness of the benefits of physical fitness. Here are a few benefits of a modest exercise program:[29]

- There is an interrelationship between health and outlook on life. For example, when the physical body is fit, toned, and strong, this condition has a positive effect on the mind. We are more likely to experience higher levels of self-esteem, feel a greater sense of self-confidence, and have a more positive outlook on life.

- Regular exercise and a healthy diet produce greater mental clarity, a higher energy level, and a more youthful appearance. Even low-intensity exercise such as walking can result in weight loss and reduction in the death rate from coronary artery disease and stroke. Recent research indicates that exercise is as effective as drugs at preventing diabetes and averting repeat heart attacks and strokes.

More than 80 percent of the companies with 50 employees have wellness programs. Healthy employees file fewer insurance claims and are less likely to call in sick.[30] Increasingly, incentives are being used to encourage employee participation in various programs.

Figure 17.1 ■ Put Balance in Your Life

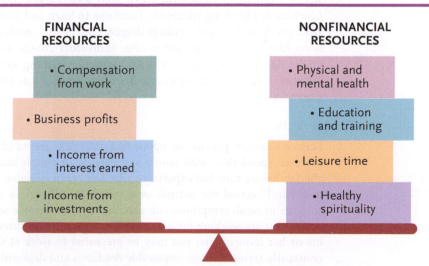

FINANCIAL RESOURCES
- Compensation from work
- Business profits
- Income from interest earned
- Income from investments

NONFINANCIAL RESOURCES
- Physical and mental health
- Education and training
- Leisure time
- Healthy spirituality

Total Person Insight

"Health is more than just the absence of disease; it is the presence of vitality. Health is freedom from obstruction; it's living in a harmonious way that creates both inner and outer peace."

Source: Kris Carr, "Yes, You Can," *Spirituality & Health*, May–June 2012, p. 96.

Education and Training (Intellectual Growth)

The New Economy thrives on a well-educated and well-trained workforce. It rewards workers who take personal responsibility for their learning. The need to continually update, train, and develop yourself must be a high priority in your life.

Develop your Unique Brand. In Chapter 11, we noted that branding can play a crucial role in your career success. Developing a strong personal brand requires knowledge and competence in the areas where you want to become an expert. To do this you must clarify, confirm, and build your strengths (see Chapter 4).

An important first step in building your brand is determining how others view you. Dorie Clark, author of *Reinventing You*, suggests you take a thoughtful look at yourself. How do others perceive your personal brand? Consider using the 360-degree feedback strategy introduced in Chapter 8. Meet with your supervisor and solicit honest feedback about yourself and your performance. Review past performance appraisal reports to identify major strengths and areas needing improvement.[31]

Be Selective in What You Learn. Learning often requires large amounts of time and energy, so consider carefully what knowledge or skill will generate the most improvement.

Take Advantage of Various Learning Pathways. It helps to think of your job as a learning resource. Take full advantage of instructional programs offered by your employer. Volunteer for team assignments that will provide new learning opportunities. Peter Senge, author of *The Fifth Discipline*, says the fundamental learning unit in any organization is a team.[32]

Find a mentor or mentors inside or outside of the company you work for and seek advice from them in several areas. And look outside the company for opportunities. Learning is a life-long adventure. Continue to learn and acquire new skills and knowledge after you have finished a college degree. Universities, community colleges, and organizations like the Learning Annex offer individual classes and programs to expand your knowledge and personal growth. Also consider learning soft skills in programs offered by Toastmasters, Dale Carnegie, or other organizations that offer seminars, conferences, and workshops.

Leisure Time

Leisure time can provide an opportunity to relax, get rid of work-related stress, get some exercise, spend time with family and friends, or simply read a good book. Many people cherish leisure time but experience schedule creep. *Schedule creep* is the tendency of work to expand beyond the normal work schedule and replace available leisure time. It often surfaces in small symptoms—an extra hour or two here, a weekend worked there.[33]

If you are working for a workaholic, someone who may have given up all or most of his or her leisure time, you may be pressured to work at the same pace. If your boss is constantly trying to meet impossible deadlines and deal with last-minute rushes, you may feel the need to give up time for recreation or family. Often a busy, overworked boss may not realize the effect his or her behavior has on others in the organization. If this happens, try to talk to your boss to find a solution that is agreeable to both of you. Identify the consequences of being overworked. Look at the situation from all points of view. If you refuse to work longer hours, what will be the consequences for your relationship with the boss, your relationship with other employees, or your future with the organization?[34]

A few years ago Timothy Ferriss wrote a book entitled *The 4-Hour Workweek*. At the beginning of the book he says, "This book is for anyone who is sick of the deferred-life plan and wants to live life large instead of postpone it." He promises readers a new way to prevent our lives from being all about work. Throughout the book Ferriss displays a sense of humor, He includes some quotes by noted writers such as Robert Frost:

> By working faithfully eight hours a day, you may eventually get to be a boss and work twelve hours a day.

He highly recommends working remotely because many workers will get more work done in less time. Ferriss devotes one entire chapter to mini-retirements, replacing your annual vacation with a trip to one location where you are free from the stresses of a fast-paced culture and you have time to reflect on life.[35]

One of the best ways to feel satisfied about your work is to get away from it when you begin to feel worn out. People who take time off from work often return with new ideas, a stronger focus, and increased energy.

Find some quiet time for yourself each day. You might use it to meditate, take the dog for a walk, or just sit quietly. Use this time to nourish yourself and bring balance to your life.

blue jean images/Getty Images

Even low-intensity exercise such as standing and stretching can help you achieve lifesaving benefits. Prolonged sitting is a barrier to good health.

If you want more leisure time, then you must establish your priorities and set your goals. This may mean saying no to endless requests to work overtime or rejecting a promotion. Sometimes you must pull back from the endless demands of work and "get a life."

Healthy Spirituality

Spirituality is receiving greater attention in education and in the workplace. More business and professional schools are offering courses dealing with spirituality and *personal fulfillment*. Workplace chaplains can be found at more than 1,000 companies in the United States and Canada. These chaplains are a growing segment of corporate America's human-resources group. The goal of these chaplaincy programs is to treat employees holistically. They want people to bring their whole self to work.[36]

human RELATIONS *in Action*

WHAT IS THE DIFFERENCE BETWEEN RELIGION AND SPIRITUALITY?

"Religion is often about who's in and who's out, creating a worldview steeped in 'us *against* them.' Spirituality rejects this dualism and speaks of us *and* them. Religion is often about loyalty to institutions, clergy, and rules. Spirituality is about loyalty to justice and compassion. Religion talks about God. Spirituality helps to make us godly. The two need not be at odds. Religion at its best is spirituality in community."

Source: Rabbi Rami Shapiro, "What Is the Difference Between Religion and Spirituality?" *Spirituality & Health*, May-June 2012, page 17.

Spirituality can be defined as an inner attitude that emphasizes energy, creative choice, and a powerful force for living. It involves opening our hearts and cultivating our capacity to experience reverence and gratitude. It frees us to become positive, caring human beings.[37]

Spirituality encompasses faith, which can be described as what your heart tells you is true when your mind cannot prove it. For some people, faith exists within the framework of a formal religion; for others, it rests on a series of personal beliefs such as "Give others the same consideration, regard, kindness, and gentleness that you would like them to accord you."[38] Many people think of spirituality as a remote, abstract concept. But traditional teachings suggest that spirituality is directly connected to the most ordinary human activities.[39]

> *An understanding of the many aspects of spirituality can give us an expanded vision of what it means to be human.*

An understanding of the many aspects of spirituality can give us an expanded vision of what it means to be human. Although spirituality is often associated with religion, it should be viewed in broader terms. Robert Coles, of Harvard Medical School, likes a definition of spirituality given to him by an 11-year-old girl:

I think you're spiritual if you can escape from yourself a little and think of what's good for everyone, not just you, and if you can reach out and be a good person—I mean live like a good person. You're not spiritual if you just talk spiritual and there's no action. You're a fake if that's what you do.[40]

The words of this young girl remind us that one dimension of spirituality involves showing concern and compassion for others. Thomas Moore, author of the best-selling book *Care of the Soul*, says, "To be spiritual means to mature to a point beyond limited self-interest and anxiety about self."[41] Harvard psychiatrist George Vaillant, author of *Adaptation to Life*, says that defining spirituality is like trying to define Shakespeare's genius. Everyone knows it exists, but no two people would describe it in the same way.

"I think spirituality involves qualities like patience, tolerance, kindness, honesty, and humility—and always, love."

Total Person Insight

"Spirituality I take to be concerned with those qualities of human spirit—such as love and compassion, patience, tolerance, forgiveness, contentment, a sense of responsibility, a sense of harmony—which bring happiness to both self and others."

Source: The Dalai Lama, coauthor, *The Art of Happiness*, "Teaching Tolerance," Spring 2005, p. 28.

Spirituality at Work. In many ways, large and small, work can be made more spiritual. The philosophy of Worthington Industries is expressed in a single sentence: "We treat our employees as we would like to be treated."[42] Herr Foods, Inc. promises, "An atmosphere that enhances the moral and spiritual integrity of each individual."[43]

Research indicates that the new generation of workers, Generation Y, will be looking deep inside companies to see what makes them tick. The person with a passion for environmental issues will be drawn to companies like outdoor apparel maker Patagonia, which contributes 1 percent of sales to environmental causes.[44] Patagonia also appeals to persons who seek an employer who maintains high ethical standards. Patagonia has made the "World's Most Ethical Companies" list six years in a row.

Many activities can be considered spiritual. Visiting an art gallery, listening to a concert, or walking near the ocean can stimulate healthy spirituality. Table 17.1 describes some ways to begin your journey to healthy spirituality.

For many people, a commitment to a specific religion is an important dimension of spirituality. Active membership in a religious group provides an opportunity to clarify spiritual values and achieve spiritual direction. It also provides social connections—an extended family that you can depend on for social support.[45]

Table 17.1 ■ Ways to Achieve Healthy Spirituality

As interest in healthy spirituality grows, people are searching for ways to become more spiritual. The following spiritual practices draw our focus away from ourselves and the anxieties in our lives:

■ *Meditation* Oprah Winfrey described the powerful influence of meditation this way: "There is no greater source of strength and power for me in my life now, than going still, being quiet, and recognizing what real power is." (See Chapter 14 for a step-by-step guide to meditation.)

■ *Prayer* Dr. Larry Dossey, physician and author of many books on the role of spirituality in medicine, says prayer can be a powerful force in our lives. Prayer groups have been established at many organizations.

■ *Spiritual Reading* In addition to sacred readings, consider *Healing and the Mind* by Bill Moyers, *10 Secrets for Success and Inner Peace,* by Dr. Wayne Dyer, and *The Hungry Spirit,* by Charles Handy.

■ *Time with Nature* Spiritual contemplation during a walk in the woods or a visit to a quiet lake can help us balance mind, body, and spirit.

Source: David Elkins and Amanda Druckman, "Four Great Ways to Begin Your Spiritual Journey, *Psychology Today*, September/October 1999, p. 46; Larry Dossey, M.D., "Can We Change the World? *The Inner Edge*, June/July 2000, pp. 22–23.

DEVELOPING A HEALTHY LIFESTYLE

17-5   Earlier in this chapter, we noted that a healthy lifestyle can provide a higher energy level, a greater sense of self-confidence, and, generally, a more positive outlook on life. People who maintain good health usually have more endurance, spend less time feeling tired or ill, and miss less work than people who are not healthy. Good health is receiving greater attention today because many Americans are investing more time and energy in their work. They are being asked to work longer hours and to do more in less time. Good health can help combat stress and tension at work and at home. In this section, we offer guidelines that form the framework for a good diet and a good exercise program.

Guidelines for a Healthy Diet

Eating the right foods is a choice you make every day that directly affects your health and energy level, and, in some cases, extends your life. We will review several important dietary guidelines.

The U.S. Department of Agriculture (USDA) has prepared the *MyPlate* nutritional guide (see Figure 17.2). The dinner plate is divided into four components: vegetables, fruits, grains, and protein—with a small circle off to the side representing dairy foods. It is recommended that you fill half your plate with vegetables and fruit. Grains (preferably whole grains) and protein foods (fish, poultry, meat, eggs, beans, tofu) should each take up about a quarter of the plate.[46]

Half of your daily grain intake should be whole grains. To identify truly whole-grain foods, consider using the 10-to-1 ratio developed at Harvard University. Look for less than a 10-to-1 ratio of total carbohydrates to fiber on the nutrition label of whole-grain products.[47]

Maintain a Healthy Weight

Everyone should monitor their body weight and exercise to determine whether they need to adjust calorie intake.[48] More than 65 percent of Americans are overweight, and these added pounds increase the risk of heart disease, cancer, and diabetes. Inactivity combined

Figure 17.2 ■ U.S. Department of Agriculture's MyPlate

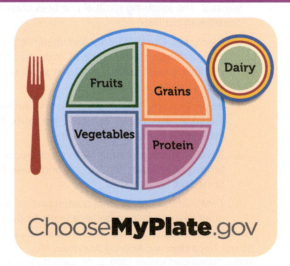

Source: ChooseMyPlate.gov

with diets high in calories, salt, and fats result in serious health problems. Maintaining a healthy weight is all about balance—*calories in versus calories out*. If you consume more calories a day than you burn you will gain weight. To maintain your ideal body weight, the number of calories consumed must equal the calories burned through exercise and physical activity. If you want to lose weight, the number of calories you consume need to be less than the number of calories you burn (see Figure 17.3).

Eating a variety of foods is important because you need more than 40 different nutrients for good health: vitamins and minerals, amino acids (from proteins), essential fatty acids (from fats and oils), and sources of energy (calories from carbohydrates, fats, and proteins). The type of foods you eat is also very important. Whole grains should be substituted for refined grains, and dark leafy greens such as spinach, kale, and Swiss chard are packed with vitamins A, C, and K, folate, potassium, magnesium, calcium, iron, and fiber.

The Hidden Dangers of Eating Out

The foods that are popular with many Americans are high in calories and fat, especially saturated fat, which contributes to high blood cholesterol levels. Many seemingly harmless choices are in disguise. A large tuna melt at Quiznos has 2,090 calories and 175 grams of fat.[49] A Chipotle Chicken Burrito (with tortilla, rice, chicken, pinto beans, cheese, salsa, and sour cream) is 970 calories, 18 grams of saturated fat, and 2,200 mg of sodium. Forget the cheese and sour cream and it drops to 750 calories and only 5.5 grams of saturated fat. A cup of black coffee has zero calories. If you want something fancier, say a Starbucks Venti White Chocolate Mocha, your "coffee" is now 580 calories and 15 grams of saturated fat—worse than a McDonald's Quarter Pounder with Cheese![50]

Exercise Fuels a Healthy Body

There is a connection between health and outlook on life. When we feel our bodies are fit, toned, and strong, this physical condition has a direct correlation to a strong, positive effect on our minds. We are more likely to experience higher levels of self-esteem, feel a greater sense of self-confidence, and have a more positive outlook on life. Regular exercise and a healthy diet produce greater mental clarity, higher energy levels, and a more youthful appearance.

"Sedentary living is so dangerous that it is simply not an option." This is the conclusion of research conducted at Duke University. An inactive lifestyle (sedentary sickness) results in an array of risk factors such as weight gain and increases in bad cholesterol and

Figure 17.3 ■ Balancing Calories In and Calories Out

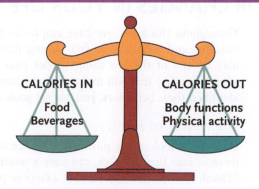

CALORIES IN
Food
Beverages

CALORIES OUT
Body functions
Physical activity

blood sugar levels.[51] For the vast majority of Americans who "travel" from the driver's seat, to their office chair, to the dinner chair, to the couch may be surprised to learn they are literally sitting themselves to death. The popular term "Sitting is the New Smoking" can be credited to Dr. James Levine, director of the Mayo Clinic-Arizona State University Obesity Solutions Initiative. Levine, who is also the inventor of the treadmill desk says, "Sitting is more dangerous than smoking, kills more people than HIV and is more treacherous than parachuting. We are sitting ourselves to death." Other researchers agree and have found evidence that prolonged sitting increases the risk of developing several serious illnesses like various types of cancer, heart disease and type 2 diabetes.[52]

Physical fitness, which involves the performance of the lungs, heart, and muscles, can also have a positive influence on mental alertness and emotional stability. Research indicates that even a moderate level of physical activity can have a surprisingly broad array of health benefits on virtually every major organ system in the body.[53] For most people, a program that involves regular physical activity at least three or four times a week and includes sustained physical exertion for 30 to 35 minutes during each activity period is adequate.[54] This modest investment of time and energy will give you a longer and healthier life. Even low-intensity exercise such as walking 30 minutes a day can result in weight loss and reduction in the death rate from coronary artery disease and stroke.

human RELATIONS *in Action*

DEAN ORNISH'S TIPS FOR HEALTHY LIVING

- **There are no good foods or bad foods**. But some foods are healthier than others. "A plant-based diet low in sugar" is best.

- **A little exercise goes a long way**. "Thirty minutes of walking a day is sustainable, but the little things also add up—taking the stairs instead of the elevator, for instance."

- **How you eat is as important as what you eat**. "If you can eat with awareness, you'll get more pleasure with fewer calories."

- **Meditation makes your fuse longer**. "Just the practice of focusing your awareness on something quiets down your mind and allows you to feel that inner sense of peace. Even a minute of meditation will carry you through the day."

- **Family and friends are critically important**. "Study after study has shown that people who are lonely and depressed are three to 10 times more likely to die than those who have strong connections."

- **Volunteering saves lives**. "Showing compassion for others is healing."

Source: "Dean Ornish's Tips for Healthy Living," *AARP Bulletin/Real Possibilities*, June 2014, p. 28.

PLANNING FOR CHANGES IN YOUR LIFE

17-6 Throughout this book, we have emphasized the concept that you can control your own thoughts and behavior. In fact, during these turbulent times, changes in your behavior may be one of the few things under your control. What are some behaviors you can adopt (or alter) that will make an important positive change in your life? Once you have identified these behaviors, you can set goals and do what is necessary to achieve them.

The Power of Habits

Let's take a look at the powerful influence of habits. Some habits, like taking a long walk three or four times a week, can have a positive influence on our well-being. Simply saying "Thank you" when someone does a favor or pays a compliment can be a habit. Other habits, such as smoking, complaining, feeling jealous, or constantly engaging in self-criticism, are negative forces in our lives. Stephen Covey makes this observation: "Habits are powerful factors in our lives. Because they are consistent, often unconscious patterns, they constantly, daily, express our character and produce our effectiveness … or ineffectiveness."[55]

Breaking deeply embedded habits, such as impatience, procrastination, or criticism of others, can take a tremendous amount of effort. The influences supporting the habit, the actual root causes, are often repressed in the subconscious mind and forgotten.[56] How do you break a negative habit or form a positive habit? The process involves five steps.

Motivation. Once you are aware of the need to change, you must develop the willingness or desire to change. After making a major commitment to change, you must find ways to maintain your motivation. The key to staying motivated is to develop a mindset powerful enough that you feel compelled to act on your desire to change.

Knowledge. Once you clearly understand the benefits of breaking a habit or forming a new one, you must acquire the knowledge you need to change. Seek information, ask for advice, or learn from the experiences of others. This may involve finding a mentor, joining a group, or gathering sufficient material and teaching yourself.

Practice. Information is only as useful as you make it. This means that to change your behavior you must *practice* what you have learned. If you are a shy person, does this mean you need to volunteer to make a speech in front of several hundred people? The answer is no. Although there is always the rare person who makes a major change seemingly overnight, most people find that the best and surest way to develop a new behavior is to do so gradually. It usually takes at least 21 days of consistent behavior change to change a habit.

Feedback. Whenever you can, seek feedback as you try to change a habit. Dieters lose more weight if they attend counseling sessions and weigh-ins. People who want to improve their public speaking skills benefit from practice followed by feedback from a teacher or coach. Everyone has blind spots, particularly when trying something new.

Reinforcement. When you see yourself exhibiting the type of behavior you have been working to develop—or when someone mentions that you have changed—reward yourself! The rewards can be simple, inexpensive ones—treating yourself to a movie, a bouquet of flowers, a favorite meal, or a special event. This type of reinforcement is vital when you are trying to improve old behaviors or develop new ones.

The Choice Is Yours

Are you ready to develop a life plan for effective human relations? We hope the answer is yes. One of the positive aspects of personal planning is that you are making your own choices. You decide what kind of person you want to be and then set your own standards and goals. The results can mean not only career advancement and financial benefits, but also greater happiness and personal fulfillment, and the development of strong, satisfying relationships with others. These relationships may be the key to future opportunities, and you in turn, may be able to help others reach their goals.

In Chapter 1, we talked about the *total person* approach to human relations. By now, we hope you realize that you are someone special! You have a unique combination of talents, attitudes, values, goals, needs, and motivation—all in a state of development. You can decide to tap your potential to become a successful, productive human being however *you* understand those terms. We hope this book helps you to develop your human relations skills and to become what you want to be. You can turn the concepts and guidelines presented here into a plan of action for your own life and career. We'll leave you with this inspiring poem by Dawna Markova, author of *I Will Not Die an Unlived Life*—and we wish you the best!

I Will Not Die an Unlived Life

I will not die an unlived life.
I will not live in fear
of falling or catching fire.
I choose to inhabit my days,
to allow my living to open me,
to make me less afraid,
more accessible;
to loosen my heart
until it becomes a wing,
a torch, a promise.
I choose to risk my significance,
to live so that which came to me as seed
goes to the next as blossom,
and that which came to me as blossom,
goes on as fruit.

Source: Dawna Markova, *I Will Not Die an Unlived Life—Reclaiming Purpose and Passion*, Conari Press, 2000, San Francisco, CA.

LOOKING BACK: SUMMARY OF LEARNING OBJECTIVES

1. Learn how to cope with the forces that influence work/life balance.

The labor market has become a place of great uncertainty due to the heavy volume of mergers, acquisitions, business closings, and downsizing. There is increasing pressure to work harder, work longer hours, and give up more leisure time. Learning how to cope with the forces that influence work/ life balance has never been more challenging.

2. Define success by standards that are compatible with your needs and values.

The traditional definitions of success that most of us know are too confining. They describe success almost entirely in terms of measurable job achievements. These definitions leave out the intangible successes to be had in private and professional life. Many people today are discovering that true success is a combination of achievements.

3. Discuss the meaning of *right livelihood*.

Achieving right livelihood is a very important dimension of success. Right livelihood is work consciously chosen and done with full awareness and care that leads to enlightenment. Right livelihood recognizes that work is a vehicle for self-expression, and it places money in a secondary position.

4. Describe four nonfinancial resources that can enrich your life.

A person's nonfinancial resources often make the biggest contribution to a happy and fulfilling life. Each of us has four nonfinancial resources that can enrich our lives: physical and mental health, education and training (intellectual growth), leisure time (time for friends and family, socializing, recreation), and healthy spirituality.

5. Provide guidelines for developing a healthy lifestyle.

Many Americans are working to achieve healthy lifestyles. Healthy lifestyles can give us a higher energy level, a greater sense of self-confidence, and, generally, a more positive outlook. People who maintain good health usually have more endurance, spend less time feeling tired or ill, and miss less work than those who are not physically fit.

6. **Develop a plan for making needed changes in your life**.

Planning for changes in your life often requires breaking negative habits or forming positive habits. The process of breaking habits and forming new ones involves five steps: motivation, knowledge, practice, feedback, and reinforcement.

KEY TERMS

right livelihood, 385
nonfinancial resources, 388

spirituality, 392
physical fitness, 396

TRY YOUR HAND

1. The concept of *right livelihood* is based on conscious choice, placing money in a secondary position, and work as a vehicle for personal growth. Take time to reflect on the past six months and evaluate if *right livelihood* principles have guided you in your decision-making. If so, discuss the influence of the concept, and if not, evaluate its importance in future decision making.

2. Throughout this chapter, you were encouraged to take control of your life and establish your own definition of success. This chapter has a strong "all development is self-development" theme. Can we really control our own destinies? Can we always make our own choices? Mike Hernacki, author of *The Ultimate Secret of Getting Absolutely Everything You Want*, says yes:

   To get what you want, you must recognize something that at first may be difficult, even painful to look at. You must recognize that you alone are the source of all the conditions and situations in your life. You must recognize that whatever your world looks like right now, you alone have caused it to look that way. The state of your health, your finances, your personal relationships, your professional life—all of it is your doing, yours and no one else's.[57]

   Do you agree with this viewpoint? Take a position in favor of or in opposition to Hernacki's statement. Prepare a short one- or two-paragraph statement that expresses your views.

3. There are many ways to deepen and extend your spirituality. One way is to begin placing a higher value on silence, tranquility, and reflection. If your life is extremely busy, you may not be taking time for thought or reflection. If you are accustomed to living in the presence of noise throughout the day, quiet times may make you feel uncomfortable at first. During a period of one week, set aside a few minutes each day for your own choice of meditation, prayer, contemplation, or reflection. Try to find a quiet place for this activity. At the end of the week, assess the benefits of this activity, and consider the merits of making it part of your daily routine.[58]

CRITICAL THINKING CHALLENGE

For most people, true success is a combination of achievements. These achievements might relate to such things as leisure time, earnings, job status, health, or relationships.

1. On a piece of paper, describe your personal definition of success.

2. If you could design the most ideal way to make a living by doing what you love, what would this be? Would doing this help you achieve your personal definition of success?

SELF-ASSESSMENT EXERCISE

For each of the following statements, circle the number from 1 to 5 that best represents your response: (1) strongly disagree (never do this); (2) disagree (rarely do this); (3) moderately agree (sometimes do this); (4) agree (frequently do this); (5) strongly agree (almost always do this).

A.	I stay connected with family and friends and network with professional and business associates.	1	2	3	4	5
B.	I try to maintain a balance in my life by avoiding an addiction to work and by engaging in leisure-time activities.	1	2	3	4	5
C.	I envision my existence in a larger context and view healthy spirituality as a positive, enlightening force in my life.	1	2	3	4	5
D.	I avoid rigid individualism (self-centered behavior) by investing time and energy in helping others.					
E.	I constantly strive to improve my knowledge, skills, and sense of purpose in my life's work.	1	2	3	4	5
F.	I have established well-thought-out goals for my life, and these goals are tied to my values.	1	2	3	4	5

After identifying your response to each item, select an attitude or skill you would like to improve. Prepare a written goal and then describe the steps you will take to achieve this goal.

YOU PLAY THE ROLE

Ambry Waller, one of your closest friends, used to go fishing quite often, and he loved to hike in the mountains. After getting married, his life changed dramatically. He and his wife purchased a new home, and soon they were raising a family. Once the bills started piling up, he abandoned his leisure-time activities and started working long hours at his job. He eagerly volunteered for overtime in order to increase his earnings. As the years passed, Ambry and his wife adopted many trappings of middle-class life: a big house, two cars, a huge TV in the family room, and a motorboat that sits idle for most of the year. One afternoon, you meet Ambry for a beer at a local bar. The conversation quickly turns serious as Ambry describes his frustration: "I love my wife and children, but I am so tired of working long hours and worrying about my financial obligations. My credit card debt is now over $7,000."

In this role-play activity, you will meet with another class member who will assume the role of Ambry Waller. Your goal is to help Ambry identify some ways he can achieve greater work/life balance. Your name for this role-play will be Corey Cell.

BELOW THE SURFACE | REFLECTING ON THE MEANING OF LIFE

Henk Meijer/Alamy

Google has occupied the top spot on *Fortune* magazine's 100 Best Companies to Work For list six times in recent years. Employees enjoy several perks—a playful work environment, gourmet food, a volleyball court—and they take pride in working for one of America's most successful companies. Google is also known for its punishing fast-paced work culture, with 80-hour workweeks. Employees who struggle to cope with the ongoing stress find help in a Google-sponsored class called "Search Inside Yourself" (SIY). This seven-week class teaches employees how to examine the meaning of success and failure and how their work and relationships are affected by the choices they make.[59]

Like the employees who complete SIY, students at Columbia Business School are learning similar skills in a popular class that "requires thinking about the 'meaning of life,' and not infrequently convinces MBA students that—surprise!—money isn't everything."[60] Srikumar Rao, an ex-marketing executive from Wall Street and Hollywood, is the creator of the class. It has such a long waiting list that Rao had to invent a rigorous application process that requires students to submit a résumé, seven essays, and participate in an interview. As more people struggle to balance demanding jobs and an uncertain economy, it's doubtful that the class will become less popular anytime soon.

While many people are learning how to cope more effectively with the stress of challenging jobs, others have opted out of crazy work schedules to choose work that offers them a lifestyle that makes them much happier.

In 2002, Richard Binder quit his job as a software engineer to become a "pen doctor." He repairs fountain pens sent to him from customers around the world. His gross income is less than what he earned as a software engineer, but he is happier. He says, "Basically, I get my pleasure from making people happy with their pens." For Richard Binder, the search for right livelihood is over.[61]

QUESTIONS

1. Given the changes taking place in our economy, you may need to return to the classroom at age 30, 40, or 50. How would you feel about the prospect of becoming a middle-aged student?

2. Mary Lou Quinlan spent 20 years climbing the ladder in the field of advertising. Finally she became CEO of N.W. Ayer, a successful advertising company. She achieved "success" but she was not happy. She then decided to become an entrepreneur. That decision was made after completing the following steps:

   I got a piece of paper and divided it in half. On the left side, I wrote down what I love to do and what I'm good at, and on the right side, I wrote down what I don't like to do and what I stink at. Unfortunately, what I don't like to do and what I stink at were my job descriptions as CEO.[62]

   Quinlan founded a consulting company named Just Ask a Woman, a firm that helps companies market to women. Evaluate the advantages and disadvantages of the decision-making model used by Quinlan.

3. Many companies are reducing the contribution made to employee retirement programs, and others are eliminating these contributions. Briefly describe the retirement program you would like to establish and maintain during the years ahead. Predict the major barriers to achieving your goal.

CHAPTER 17 ENDNOTES

1. Leigh Gallagher, "Why Employees Love Marriott," *Fortune*, March 15, 2015, pp. 113–118.
2. Ibid, 116–117.
3. Ibid, p. 114.
4. Lauren Weber and Rachel Emma Silverman, "On Demand Workers: 'We Are Not Robots,'" *Wall Street Journal*, January 28, 2015, pp. B1 and B7.
5. Thomas J. Peters and Robert H. Waterman, Jr., *In Search of Excellence: Lessons from America's Best-Run Companies* (New York: Harper & Row, 1982), p. 14; Tom Peters, "Tom Peters' True Confessions," *Fast Company*, December 2001, p. 80.

6. Bill George (with Peter Sims), *True North* (San Francisco: John Wiley & Sons, 2007), p. xxiv; Bill George, Peter Sims, Andrew N. McLean, and Diana Mayer, "Discovering Your Authentic Leadership," *Harvard Business Review*, February 2007, pp. 129–138.
7. Po Bronson, *What Should I Do with My Life?* (New York: Random House, 2002), p. 365; Patricia Kitchen, "Seeking Your Calling," *The Record*, March 9, 2003, p. D1.
8. Katie Humphrey, "Older Workers: Don't Be a Tech Fossil," *News & Observer*, December 10, 2013, p. D1; Chelsey Dulaney, "Older Workers Face Tougher Job," *News & Observer*, August 26, 2012, p. E1.

9. Christopher Tkaczyk, "Small Businesses, Fantastic Employers," *Fortune*, October 7, 2013, pp. 30 and 32.

10. Jack Canfield, *The Success Principles* (New York: HarperCollins, 2005), p. 3.

11. Dinah Eng, "Soft Pretzels Out of Hard Times," *Fortune*, July 22, 2013, pp. 23–26.

12. See His Holiness the Dalai Lama and Howard C. Cutler, *The Art of Happiness at Work* (New York: Riverhead Books, 2003), pp. 157–173.

13. Yvonne V. Chabrier, "Focus on Work," *New Age*, 1998, p. 95.

14. Marsha Sinetar, *Do What You Love … The Money Will Follow* (New York: Dell, 1987), p. 11.

15. Ibid., pp. 11–12.

16. Michael Phillips, *The Seven Laws of Money* (Menlo Park, CA: Word Wheel and Random House, 1997), p. 9.

17. Sinetar, *Do What You Love*, pp. 14–15.

18. Adopted from personal satisfaction survey questions featured in Anne Tergesen, "The Case for Quitting Your Job—Even If You Still Love It," *Wall Street Journal*, October 13, 2014, p. R1.

19. Carole Kanchier, "Dare to Change Your Job and Your Life in 7 Steps," *Psychology Today*, March/April 2000, pp. 64–67.

20. Suze Orman, "The Pursuit of Cold, Hard Happiness," *O, The Oprah Magazine*, March 2004, pp. 54–56; Sharon Begley, "Wealth and Happiness Don't Necessarily Go Hand in Hand," *Wall Street Journal*, August 13, 2004, p. B1.

21. Karen Damato, "College Freshmen Doubt Their Money Skills," *Wall Street Journal*, April 4, 2015, p. B9.

22. Walter Hamilton, "Millions of Americans Lack Financial Literacy, Studies Show," *News & Observer*, January 5, 2014, p. 2E.

23. Shakti Gawain, *Creating True Prosperity* (Novato, CA: New World Library, 1997), p. 7.

24. Carlin Flora, "Happy Hour," *Psychology Today*, January/February 2005, p. 48.

25. "Why Money Matters Are a Leading Cause of Divorce," *Spirituality & Health*, November/December 2006, p. 32; Brett Arends, "Mega-Weddings: Say 'I Don't'," *Wall Street Journal*, October 4, 2014, p. B8.

26. Jonathan Clements, "If You Didn't Save 10% of Your Income This Year, You're Spending Too Much," *Wall Street Journal*, December 22, 2004, p. D1; Jonathan Clements, "Rich, Successful—and Miserable: New Research Probes Midlife Angst," *Wall Street Journal*, October 5, 2005, p. D1; Jonathan Clements, "How to Throw Away a Lot of Money," *News & Observer*, September 14, 2014, p. 4E.

27. Toddi Gutner, "Talk Now, Retire Happily Later," *BusinessWeek*, April 2, 2001, p. 92.

28. "A Field Is Born," *Harvard Business Review*, July/August 2008, p. 164.

29. Shirley S. Wang, "Exercise as Good as Medicine for Several Ills, Study Finds," *Wall Street Journal*, October 2, 2013, p. A6; "Why Do We Love Exercise? Let Us Count the Ways," *UC Berkeley Wellness Letter*, February 2013, p. 6.

30. Dee Gill, "Get Healthy…Or Else," *Inc.*, April 2006, p. 36.

31. Doris Clark, *Reinventing You* (Boston, MA: Harvard Business School Publishing, 2013), pp. 13–14.

32. Ron Zemke, "Why Organizations Still Aren't Learning," *Training*, September 1999, p. 43.

33. Sue Shellenbarger, "Working 9 to 2: Taking Steps to Make Part-Time Job Setups More Palatable," *Wall Street Journal*, February 17, 2005, p. D1.

34. Jay T. Knippen, Thad B. Green, and Kurt Sutton, "Asking Not to Be Overworked," *Supervisory Management*, February 1992, p. 6.

35. Timothy Ferriss, *The 4-Hour Workweek* (New York: Crown Publishers, 2007), pp. 210–216; 233–236.

36. Mark Oppenheimer, "The Rise of the Corporate Chaplain," *BusinessWeek*, August 23, 2012, pp. 58–61.

37. Leo Booth, "When God Becomes a Drug," *Common Boundary*, September/October 1991, p. 30; David N. Elkins, "Spirituality," *Psychology Today*, September/October, 1999, pp. 45–48.

38. Harold H. Bloomfield and Robert K. Cooper, *The Power of 5* (Emmaus, PA: Rodale Press, 1995), p. 484.

39. Thomas Moore, "Sacred Time with Children," *Spirituality & Health*, November/December 2007, p. 12.

40. "Making the Spiritual Connection," *Lears*, December 1989, p. 72.

41. Thomas Moore, "Will We Take the Moral Values Challenge?" *Spirituality & Health*, January/February 2005, pp. 10–11.

42. "Career Opportunities" [cited 1 May 2009]. Available from http://www.worthingtonindustries.com

43. "Our Philosophy" [cited 1 May 2009]. Available from http://www.herrs.com

44. Ann States, "Get Ready for a Pickier Workforce," *BusinessWeek*, September 18, 2006, p. 82.

45. Kevin Helliker, "Body and Spirit: Why Attending Religious Services May Benefit Health," *Wall Street Journal*, May 3, 2005, p. D1.

46. "MyPlate: Goodbye Pyramid," *UC Berkeley Wellness Letter*, Fall Issue, 2014, p. 6.

47. "Whole Grains: The 10-to-1 Rule," *UC Berkeley Wellness Letter*, April 2013, p. 3.

48. Sara Schaefer Munoz, "The Food Pyramid Gets Personalized," *Wall Street Journal*, April 20, 2005, p. D1; "Johanns Reveals USDA's Steps to a Healthier You" [cited 24 February 2006]. Available from http://www.mypyramid.gov; INTERNET.

49. Michael Orey, "A Food Fight Over Calorie Counts," *BusinessWeek*, February 11, 2008, p. 36.

50. Nutrition Action Newsletter, Center for Science in the Public Interest, 2011, www.cspineet.org.

51. "JustMove," *Duke Medicine Health-Line*, Winter 2007, p. 6.

52. Diana Gerstacker, The Active Times, "Sitting Is the New Smoking: Ways a Sedentary Lifestyle Is Killing You," September 29, 2014, The Huffington Post, http://www.huffingtonpost.com/the-active-times/sitting-is-the-new-smokin_b_5890006.html.

53. Robert Langreth, "Every Little Bit Helps," *Wall Street Journal*, May 1, 2000, p. R5; Tara Parker Pope, "Health Matters," *Wall Street Journal*, August 9, 2004, p. R5.

54. John Swartzberg, "Exercise: It's Not Just Physical," *UC Berkeley Wellness Letter*, November 2002, p. 3.

55. Stephen R. Covey, *The Seven Habits of Highly Effective People* (New York: Simon & Schuster, 1989), p. 46.

56. James Fadiman, *Be All That You Are* (Seattle: Westlake Press, 1986), p. 25.

57. Mike Hernacki, *The Ultimate Secret of Getting Absolutely Everything You Want* (New York: Berkley Books, 1988), p. 35.

58. Adapted from Bloomfield and Cooper, *The Power of 5*, pp. 492–493

59. Caitlin Kelly, "Google Class Asks Employees to Take a Deep Breath," (*New York Times*), published in *News & Observer*, Business, May 6, 2012.

60. Anne Fisher, "Catch the New MBA Craze: Raoism," *Fortune*, Vol. 153, No. 3, February 8, 2006.

61. Kate Bonamici, "Fountain Pen Doctor," *Fortune*, January 23, 2006, p. 40.

62. Mary Lou Quinlan, "Just Ask a Woman," *Fast Company*, July 2003, p. 50.

Glossary

A

Active listening   Active listening is fueled by curiosity and requires your complete concentration on what you are hearing, body language that exhibits your listening attitude, and feedback as to what you think the speaker is trying to tell you.

Affirmative action   Involves intentionally seeking and hiring employees from groups that are under-represented.

Aggressive behavior   Behavior that, in conflict situations, involves expressing your thoughts and feelings and defending your rights in a way that *violates* the rights of others.

Anger   The thoughts, feelings, physical reactions, and actions that result from unacceptable behavior by others.

Anxiety   A condition in which intense feelings of apprehension are longstanding and usually disruptive.

Assertive behavior   Behavior that provides you the opportunity to stand up for your rights and express your thoughts and feelings in a direct, appropriate way that does not violate the rights of others.

Attitudes   Thoughts that you have accepted as true and that lead you to think, feel, or act positively or negatively toward a person, idea, or event.

Authenticity   The unimpeded operation of one's true or core self in one's daily interactions with others.

B

Behavioral profiling   The process of observing, anticipating, and interpreting a specific behavior. Gestures, body movements, tone of voice, and facial expressions can communicate confidence or fear, trust or mistrust, curiosity or boredom.

Bias interrupter   Gender biases will perpetuate unless "intentionally interrupted" by introducing a new behavior or action that is designed to change the outcome. Bias interrupters establish a measurable improvement (target metric) that is tested and measured for improvements in the gender bias.

Blind area   The pane of the Johari Window that contains information about yourself that others know but you are not aware of. Others may see you as aloof and stuffy, whereas you view yourself as open and friendly.

Blog   A discussion or information site, usually written by one person, used to communicate perspectives and information about certain topics.

Burnout   A gradually intensifying pattern of physical, psychological, and behavioral dysfunction that evolves in response to a continuous flow of stressors.

Business casual   The movement toward dress standards that emphasize greater comfort and individuality.

C

Career apparel   A type of job-specific uniform worn by a collective group of workers such as UPS drivers or airport security agents.

Character   Personal standards of behavior, including honesty, integrity, and moral strength.

Coaching   Personal tactics for developing people to become effective employees; a critical competency for leaders in every organization.

Codes of ethics   Written statements of what an organization expects in the way of ethical

405

behavior in order to give employees a clear indication of what behaviors are acceptable or improper.

Collective bargaining   A process that defines the rights and privileges of both sides involved in a conflict and establishes the terms of employment and length of the contract (usually from three to five years).

Communication   The means by which we come to an understanding of ourselves and others.

Communication style   The patterns of behavior that others can observe.

Communication-style bias   This bias is most likely to surface when you are talking to a person who has a communication style very different than your own.

Communication style model   A model that helps you identify your most preferred style.

Composite mentor   A collection of people you draw lessons from.

Compressed workweek   A situation where employees may be given the opportunity to adjust their work schedules to fit their lifestyle. One of the newest compressed workweek schedules, often called the 9/80, is growing in popularity. Employees work one extra hour each day for nine days, a total of 80 hours in two weeks, and receive a three-day weekend every other week.

Compulsory arbitration   When the government decides that the labor-management dispute threatens national health and safety, or will damage an entire industry, it can appoint an arbitrator who dictates a solution that is binding on both sides and can be enforced in a court of law.

Conflict   A clash between incompatible people, ideas, or interests.

Conflict resolution   If your job includes supervisory-management responsibilities, you will spend a great deal of time in conflict resolution to resolve conflicts among members of your staff.

Conflict resolution process   A five-step process for resolving conflicts that can be used at work and in your personal life.

Conflict trigger   A circumstance that increases the chances of intergroup or interpersonal conflict.

Consideration   The extent to which a leader's relationships with subordinates are characterized by mutual trust, respect for the employees, consideration of their feelings, and warmth in interpersonal relationships.

Constructive criticism   A form of self-disclosure that helps another person look at his or her own behavior without putting that individual on the defensive.

Core values   Those values that you consistently rank higher than others. When you can identify your core values, you have a definite picture of the kind of person you want to be and the kind of life you want to have.

Critical listening   The attempt to see the topic of discussion from the *speaker's* point of view and to consider how the speaker's perception of the situation may be different from your own.

Cross-functional teams   Task groups staffed with a mix of specialists, focused on a common objective. These teams are often temporary groups with members from different departments and job levels.

Cross-functional communication   Involves people from different departments or business units and different levels in the organization.

Cultural influences   Influences, often formed during the early years of our life, that lead us to have impressions of some people even before we meet them.

Cultural intelligence   The ability to interpret human actions, gestures, and speech patterns in a foreign culture.

Culture   The accumulation of values, rules of behavior, forms of expression, religious beliefs, and the like, for a group of people who share a common language and environment.

Cynicism   A mistrusting attitude regarding the motives of people. When you are cynical, you are constantly on guard against the "misbehavior" of others.

D

Depression   A mood disorder. Symptoms such as withdrawal, overwhelming sadness, or hopelessness may persist for weeks or months.

Developmental psychology   A branch of psychology concerned with the course and causes of developmental changes over a person's lifetime.

Directive style   A communication style that combines high dominance and low sociability.

Discrimination   Behavior based on prejudiced attitudes. If, as an employer, you believe that overweight people tend to be lazy, that is a prejudiced attitude. If you refuse to hire someone simply because that person is overweight, you are engaging in discrimination.

Diversity   Any dimension that can be used to differentiate groups and people from one another.

Dominance   The tendency to display a "take-charge" attitude.

Dominance continuum   Every person falls somewhere on a continuum ranging from low dominance to high dominance.

E

Emotion   A temporary experience, with positive, negative, or mixed qualities.

Emotional intelligence   The ability to monitor and control one's emotions and behavior at work and in social settings.

Emotional labor   Those persons responsible for delivering quality service and building relationships engage in emotional labor.

Emotive style   A style of communication that combines high sociability and high dominance.

Empathic listening   Listening with your ears, your eyes, and your heart.

Empathizers   People who have the ability to imagine themselves in someone else's position and understand what that person is feeling. They can understand the subtleties of human interaction.

Employee-assistance programs (EAPs)   A program aimed at overcoming anxiety, depression, burnout, alcohol abuse, and drug abuse, designed to address the negative effects of psychological disorders before employees become dysfunctional.

Employee-Customer Profit Chain Theory   Based on an experiment first conducted by retail giant Sears that provided evidence for the cause-effect chain reaction and correlation between employee attitudes, consumer behaviors, and bottom-line profitability. When employees feel valued, they are more productive and engaged, which leads to increased customer satisfaction and loyalty, which leads to higher sales and levels of profitability, ultimately resulting in higher shareholder value.

Empowerment   Refers to those policies that share information, authority, and responsibility with the lowest ranks of the organization.

Energy   The capacity for work, or the force that helps us do things with vitality and intensity.

Enterprise social networks   Are similar to social *media* networks like Facebook and LinkedIn, except they are customized to an organization. The purpose of an ESN is to streamline communication, increase collaboration, and share knowledge across an organization.

Ergonomics   Techniques for adapting the work environment to the human body.

Ethics   Principles that define behavior as right, good, and proper.

Ethnic identity   The part of a person's identity that reflects the racial, religious, or cultural group to which the person belongs.

Ethnocentrism   The tendency to regard our own culture or nation as better or more "correct" than others.

Etiquette   A set of traditions based on kindness, efficiency, and logic.

Excess zone   Characterized by a high degree of intensity and rigidity. It can also be labeled the "danger" zone.

Expectancy theory   Based on the assumption that motivational strength is determined by whether or not you *believe* you can be successful at a task.

External locus of control   People who maintain an external locus of control believe that their lives are almost totally controlled by outside forces and that they bear little personal responsibility for what happens to them.

F

Feedback   If interpersonal communication is to be effective, some type of feedback, or understood response, from the person receiving the information is necessary.

Flextime   Typically includes a core time when all employees work, usually between 9:00 a.m. and 3:30 p.m. Employees can determine their own arrival and departure times within certain limits, which may mean arriving at 7:00 a.m. or leaving at 5:30 p.m.

Flow   A mental state in which a person performing an activity is fully immersed in a feeling of energized focus. Flow is characterized by complete absorption in a task that elicits a deep feeling of enjoyment.

G

Gender bias   Discrimination on the basis of gender.

Glass ceiling   A condition in the workplace that gives women a view of top management jobs but blocks their ascent.

Grapevine   An informal communication channel that carries unofficial information.

Grit   A form of hard work and determination that is a major indicator of success.

Guided imagery   Provides you with a way to harness the power of the mind and imagination to succeed at something.

H

Hawthorne studies   Became a sweeping investigation into the role of human relations in group and individual productivity. These studies also gave rise to the profession of industrial psychology by legitimizing the human factor as an element in business operations.

Hidden area   The pane of the Johari Window that contains information about you that you know but others do not. This pane is made up of all those private feelings, needs, and past experiences that you prefer to keep to yourself.

Hierarchy of needs   A theory whereby people tend to satisfy their needs in a particular order.

Horizontal channels   Ways to move information among people on the same level of authority, such as all the store managers of a national retail clothing store chain, all department chairpersons within a college, or all the administrative assistants within an organization.

Hostile work environment   Exists when supervisors, coworkers, vendors, or customers use sexual innuendo, tell sexually oriented jokes, display sexually explicit photos in the work area, discuss sexual exploits, and so on.

Human relations   Covers all types of interactions among people—their conflicts, cooperative efforts, and group relationships.

I

Image   How other people feel about you.

Impersonal communication   A one-way communication process that transfers basic information such as instructions, policies, and financial data.

Incentive program   A planned activity designed to motivate employees to achieve an organizational objective.

Incentive   A type of reward used to improve quality, reduce accidents, increase sales, improve attendance, and speed up production.

Inclusion   A state of being valued, respected, and supported. It's about focusing on the needs of every employee and ensuring the right conditions are in place for each person to achieve his or her full potential. Inclusion should be reflected in an organization's culture, practices, and relationships in order to support a diverse workforce.

Informal organization   A network of relationships that exerts considerable influence on workers' performance.

Inner critic   Negative thoughts that take place in your internal conversation.

Integrity   The basic ingredient of character that is exhibited when you achieve congruence between what you know, what you say, and what you do.

Intensity zones   An indicator of communication style, such as a person who is either moderately or strongly dominant.

Internal locus of control   People who believe they are largely responsible for what happens to them maintain an internal locus of control. They make decisions for their own reasons based on their standards of what is right and wrong.

Internal values conflict   Occurs when a person is forced to choose between two or more strongly held values.

Interpersonal communication   The exchange of information between two or more people.

Interpersonal relationships   The personal dynamics that exist between people, not necessarily defined by the more rigid role relationships.

Intrapreneurships   Programs that encourage employees to pursue an idea, product, or process, with the company providing encouragement and support.

J

Job enlargement   Expanding an employee's duties or responsibilities.

Job enrichment   An attempt to make jobs more desirable or satisfying, thereby triggering internal motivation.

Job rotation   Allows workers to move through a variety of jobs in a predefined way over a period of time.

Job sharing   Two employees share the responsibilities of one job.

Johari Window   The word Johari is a combination of the first names of the model's originators: Joseph Luft and Harry Ingham. This communication model takes into consideration that there is some information you know about yourself and other information you are not yet aware of.

L

Leadership   The process of inspiring, influencing, and guiding employees to participate in a common effort.

Linguistic style   A series of culturally learned signals that we use to communicate what we mean.

Lose/lose approach   When the lose/lose approach is used to settle a dispute, each side must give in to the other.

M

Maintenance factors   Represent the basic things people consider essential to any job, such as salaries, fringe benefits, working conditions, social relationships, supervision, and organizational policies and administration.

Management   The process of coordinating people and other resources to achieve the goals of the organization.

Managing diversity   The process of creating an organizational culture where the primary and secondary dimensions of diversity are respected.

Meaningful dialogue   A type of discussion that stimulates ideas and shared meaning.

Mediation   A neutral third party listens to both sides in a conflict and suggests solutions. It carries no binding authority. Both parties are free to reject or accept the mediator's decision.

Meditation   A relaxation technique that slows your pulse, respiration, and brainwave activity and lowers your blood pressure.

Mentor   Someone who develops another person through tutoring, coaching, and guidance.

Mindfulness   Maintaining an awareness of emotions, thoughts, and feelings that occur in the present moment. It is a method of disciplining your mind and controlling your emotions.

Mirroring   Intentionally matching the communication style of the person you are meeting with.

Modeling   Shaping your behavior to resemble that of people you admire and embracing the qualities those people demonstrate.

Mommy track   The lifestyle of women who choose a career path that offers a mother flexible or reduced work hours.

Moral intelligence   Our mental capacity to determine how universal human principles such as responsibility, compassion, forgiveness, and humility should be applied to our personal values, goals, and actions.

Motivation   The influences that account for the initiation, direction, intensity, and persistence of behavior.

Motivational factors   Those elements that go above and beyond the basic maintenance factors. They include opportunities for recognition, advancement, or more responsibility.

Motivation-maintenance theory   A theory proposed by psychologist Frederick Herzberg whereby employees are not directly motivated by certain maintenance factors (such as health insurance), but the absence of such a benefit would cause the employee to look for a job elsewhere.

N

Narcissism   A Freudian term describing someone obsessed with his or her own self-image, alluding to the mythical youth who wore himself out trying to kiss his own reflection in a pool of water.

Negativity bias   A term used by psychologists that says humans are hardwired to notice negative events more than positive ones. People actually experience far more positive moments in life than negative, which psychologists refer to as the "positivity offset."

Nonassertive behavior   Behavior characterized by people who attempt to avoid conflict by simply ignoring things that bother them.

Nonfinancial resources   Factors that contribute to a happy and fulfilling life, such as good health, peace of mind, time spent with family and friends, learning (which develops the mind), and healthy spirituality.

Nonverbal messages   The messages (other than spoken or written words) we communicate through facial expressions, voice tone, gestures, appearance, posture, and other nonverbal means.

O

Observational learning   Learning by watching others.

Open area   The area of the Johari Window that represents your "public" or "awareness" area. This section contains information about you that both you and others know and includes information that you do not mind admitting about yourself.

Optimism   A positive attitude with a tendency to believe, expect, or hope that things will turn out well.

Organizational culture   The collection of shared values, beliefs, rituals, stories, and myths that foster a feeling of community among organizational members.

P

Peer group   As children reach adolescence and begin to break away psychologically from their parents, the peer group (people their own age) can have a powerful influence on attitude formation.

Personal brand   The attributes and the image you wish to portray to others when they think of you.

Personality   A unique pattern of enduring thoughts, feelings, and actions that characterize a person.

Physical fitness   A set of wellness factors that involves the performance of the lungs, heart, and muscles that can also have a positive influence on mental alertness and emotional stability.

Positive psychology   A relatively new branch of psychology that focuses on positive human functioning.

Positive reinforcers   A type of reward that is given after a response occurs.

Prejudice   A premature judgment or opinion that is formed without examination of the facts.

Pride   The emotional high that follows performance and success.

Primacy effect   The tendency to form and retain impressions quickly at the time of an initial meeting.

Primary dimensions   Core characteristics of each individual that cannot be changed: age, race, gender, physical and mental abilities, ethnic heritage, and sexual orientation.

Professional presence   A dynamic blend of poise, self-confidence, control, and style that empowers us to be able to command respect in any situation.

PTO bank   A bank of paid-time-off days—vacation allotment, sick days, personal days—that employees can draw from in hourly increments.

Q

Quid pro quo   Occurs when a person in a supervisory or managerial position threatens the job security or a potential promotion of a subordinate worker who refuses to submit to sexual advances.

R

Race   Denotes a category of people who are perceived as distinctive on the basis of certain biologically inherited traits, such as skin color or hair texture.

Reference group   Consists of several people who share a common interest. Sales and Marketing Executives International would serve as a reference group for persons employed in sales and marketing.

Reflective style   A type of communication style that features a combination of low dominance and low sociability.

Reinforcer   Any stimulus that follows a response and increases the probability that the response will occur again.

Resilience   Being capable of bouncing back when you are confronted with stressful situations.

Right livelihood   Work consciously chosen, done with full awareness and care, and leading to enlightenment.

Role model   A person you admire or are likely to emulate.

Rumination   The process of replaying an incident over and over in our minds.

S

Scientific management   A movement initiated by Frederick W. Taylor that focused on how jobs, work, and incentive plans can be designed to improve productivity.

Secondary dimensions   Characteristics of a person that can be changed, or at least modified. They include a person's work experience, health habits, religious beliefs, education and training, first language, family status, organizational role and level, communication style, and socioeconomic status.

Self-acceptance   The foundation of successful interaction with others.

Self-awareness   The ability to recognize and understand your moods, emotions, and drives, as well as their effect on others.

Self-concept   The bundle of facts, opinions, beliefs, and perceptions about yourself that are present in your life every moment of every day.

Self-description   Involves disclosure of non-threatening information, such as your age, your favorite food, or where you went to school. This is information that others could acquire in some way other than by your telling them.

Self-disclosure   The process of letting another person know what you think, feel, or want. It is one of the important ways you let yourself be known by others.

Self-efficacy   The learned expectation of success.

Self-esteem   Characterized by the relationship between a person's self-efficacy and self-respect.

Self-fulfilling prophecy   The somewhat mysterious connection between what you expect in life and what you actually achieve: If you can conceive it and believe it, you can achieve it.

Self-managed teams   High-performance work teams that assume responsibility for traditional management tasks as part of their regular work routine.

Self-respect   What you think and feel about yourself.

Self-talk   Takes place in the privacy of your mind. It can be rational and productive, or it can be irrational and disruptive.

Semantics   The study of the relationship between a word and its meaning(s).

Serenity   A mindful state that carries the urge to savor your current circumstances and find ways to integrate them into your life more fully.

Sexual harassment   Unwelcome verbal or physical behavior that affects a person's job performance or work environment.

Situational leadership   Based on the theory that the most successful leadership occurs when the leader's style matches the situation.

Situational Leadership Model   A leadership model developed by Paul Hersey and his colleagues at the Center for Leadership Studies that is widely used in several organizations.

Sociability   The tendency to seek and enjoy social relationships.

Sociability continuum   Characterizes the extent to which a person is friendly and expresses feelings openly.

Social media   Refers to the use of Web-based and mobile technologies to turn communication into an interactive dialogue.

Social reputation   Represents the extent to which a company or individual's online profile reflects a brand.

Socialization   The process through which people are integrated into a society by exposure to the actions and opinions of others.

Spirituality   An inner attitude that emphasizes energy, creative choice, and a powerful force for living.

Stereotypes   Perceptions, beliefs, and expectations about members of some group.

Strength   The ability to consistently, almost perfectly perform an activity; you can see yourself doing it repeatedly, happily, and successfully.

Stress   Refers to two simultaneous events: an external stimulus, called a stressor, and the physical and emotional responses to that stimulus (anxiety, fear, muscle tension, surging heart rate, and so on).

Structure   Reflects the extent to which a leader is likely to define and direct his or her role and the roles of subordinates toward goal attainment.

Style flexing   The deliberate attempt to change or alter your style to meet the needs of another person.

Supportive style   A type of communication that combines low dominance and high sociability.

Surface language   A pattern of immediate impressions conveyed by what we *see*—in other words, by appearance.

Synergy   The interaction of two or more parts to produce a greater result than the sum of the parts taken individually.

T

Talent   Any naturally recurring pattern of thought, feeling, or behavior that can be productively applied.

Team building   A leadership initiative associated with high productivity and profitability. Problems in interpersonal relations are also less common where teamwork is evident. Teamwork ensures not only that a job gets done but also that it gets done efficiently and harmoniously.

Telecommuting   Employees working at home at a personal computer linked to their employer's computer.

Temperament   An infant's individual style and frequency of expressing needs and emotions.

360-degree feedback   With this approach, employees are rated by persons who have had opportunities to observe their performance. The person who completes the feedback form may be the immediate boss, coworkers, team members, and, in some cases, even customers, clients, or patients.

Total person   A person's collective single system that is composed of several separate

characteristics such as emotional control, self-awareness, or physical fitness.

Transactional Analysis   A theory developed by Eric Berne whereby he concluded that, from the day of birth, the brain acts like a two-track stereo tape recorder. One track records events, and the other records the feelings associated with those events.

Transition   The experience of being forced to give up something and face a change.

Trust   The building block of all successful relationships with coworkers, customers, family members, and friends.

Trust Index   A research tool that measures the level of trust, pride, and camaraderie within the workplace.

Twelve-step programs   Initiatives that help with drug and alcohol addiction, eating disorders, and gambling addiction.

U

Unconscious bias   The result of messages (from a wide array of sources) introduced into our subconscious from an early age. Many of the prejudices that are deeply held in our unconscious mind influence how we act toward one another.

Unconscious mind   A vast storehouse of forgotten memories, desires, ideas, and frustrations.

Unknown area   The area of the Johari Window made up of things unknown to you and others. Because you, and others, can never be known completely, this area never completely disappears.

Upward communication   The process of encouraging employees to share their feelings and ideas with their managers.

V

Values   The personal beliefs and preferences that influence your behavior.

Values conflicts   Are the result of a clash between the personal values of different people.

In organizations they may lead to relationship issues or problems such as lack of collaboration, declining work quality, absenteeism, and poor customer service.

Values drift   The slow erosion of your core values over time.

Valuing diversity   Involves appreciating everyone's uniqueness, respecting differences, and encouraging every worker to make his or her full contribution to the organization.

Versatility   Acting in ways that earn other people's approval of our behavior.

Vertical channels   Represent the means whereby information can move up and down through all levels of authority within an organization.

Virtual office   Networks of workers connected by the latest technology.

Virtual teams   Teams composed of employees physically dispersed throughout the nation or around the world.

Visualize   Forming a mental image of something.

Voluntary arbitration   Both sides willingly submitting their disagreements to a neutral party for resolution. The arbitrator's decision must be accepted by both sides.

W

Whistleblower   A person who reveals wrongdoing within an organization to the public or to those in positions of authority.

Win/lose approach   Occurs when someone tries to reach his or her own goals at the expense of the other party's.

Win/win approach   An approach whereby both parties negotiate to fix a problem.

Workplace violence   Any act against an employee that creates a hostile work environment and negatively affects the employee, either physically or psychologically. These acts include all types of physical or verbal assaults, threats, coercion, intimidation, and all forms of harassment.

Name Index

Subject Index